The Natural Heritage of Indiana

The NATURAL HERITAGE of INDIANA

Marion T. Jackson, *Editor*

Published in association with the

Indiana Department of Natural Resources

and the

Indiana Academy of Science

INDIANA UNIVERSITY PRESS

Bloomington and Indianapolis

A WORK OF THIS MAGNITUDE and lavishness would be financially impossible to undertake without substantial subsidy. Indiana University Press wishes to acknowledge and thank the donors who made this volume possible. First and foremost, our gratitude goes to the Martin Foundation of Elkhart, Indiana. The Martins gave their support while the book was in its initial planning phases and remained steadfast despite several postponements. Their confidence and commitment sustained the project throughout its gestation.

Other major donors were the Indiana Academy of Science and Helen and L. K. Caldwell of Bloomington.

Financial support also came from the Wildlife Society and Mary Lee Reith of Goshen, Indiana.

In addition, the authors and the editor gave their time and talent in return for very modest honorariums. The editor, Marion Jackson, spent thousands of hours for wages considerably below the minimum. His institution, Indiana State University, provided office support, supplies, travel, and cartographic work.

The citizens of Indiana owe much to these individuals and institutions. These types of contributions help make the world a more livable and civilized place. The Press is pleased and proud to acknowledge this support. Thank you all.

JOHN GALLMAN
Director

The paper used in this publication meets the minimum requirements of American National Standard for Information Sciences—Permanence of Paper for Printed Library Materials, ANSI Z39.48-1984.

Manufactured in Canada

LIBRARY OF CONGRESS CATALOGING-IN-PUBLICATION DATA

The natural heritage of Indiana / Marion T. Jackson, editor.
  p.   cm.
Includes bibliographical references (p.   ) and index.
ISBN 0-253-33074-2 (cl : alk. paper)
1. Natural history—Indiana. 2. Natural areas—Indiana. 3. Human ecology—Indiana. I. Jackson, Marion T.
QH105.I6N35 1997
508.772—dc21   96-29850

1 2 3 4 5   02 01 00 99 98 97

Preview

O my children! My poor children!
   Listen to the words of wisdom,
   Listen to the words of warning,
   From the lips of the Great Spirit,
   From the Master of Life, who made you!
I have given you lands to hunt in,
I have given you streams to fish in,
I have given you bear and bison,
I have given you roe and reindeer,
I have given you brant and beaver.
   Filled the marshes full of wild-fowl,
   Filled the rivers full of fishes.
Why then are you not contented?
Why then will you hunt each other?

      —HENRY WADSWORTH LONGFELLOW,
      Song of Hiawatha (1855)

For ESTELLA EDITH FOX JACKSON, my Birth Mother, who, by her faith, devotion, gentleness, kindness, and patience, first taught me to love and respect my Earth Mother.

—MARION T. JACKSON
Editor

This book is dedicated with respect and admiration to Drs. Alton Anthony Lindsey and Robert Owen Petty, who taught thousands of their students and colleagues not only to *see* the Indiana landscape and its biota but also to *understand* its rich ecology, varied past, and promising future. Both spent their professional lives as consummate writers and mentors to enlighten, by their words and example, generations of Indiana citizens with the fact that although *sight is a faculty, seeing is truly an art.*

It is further dedicated to Dr. Charles C. Deam, Indiana's first state forester and author of four landmark books on the flora of Indiana. Charlie Deam examined the plant life of our state as no other botanist has, before him or since, traveling to every township of each county in his search for plants, both rare and common.

Additionally, it is dedicated to William B. Barnes, who, first as director of Land Acquisition for the Department of Natural Resources, and later as the first director of the Division of Nature Preserves, was instrumental in acquiring and protecting many tracts of natural land in Indiana at a time when preservation of our natural heritage was the dream of only a few, instead of the concern and activity of so many.

And finally, it is dedicated to the many citizens of Indiana who, privately or as professionals in the field of natural resource protection, have worked tirelessly and endlessly to preserve and protect what remains of Indiana's natural heritage. To name any individual or group who has served selflessly in these endeavors would risk omitting another perhaps equally deserving. Each of you is respected and admired for your contribution, which will be appreciated by generations to come.

We hope that this book, with the contributions of so many writers and photographers, will enable its readers to see Indiana's natural heritage in new dimensions.

—MARION T. JACKSON
Indiana State University

Contents

Preface: Why This Book?

This book is a celebration of Indiana's natural heritage—its natural and human history, its landscape and its life—what it once was, what it is now, and what it promises to be.

If our culture has grown out of the past, and it most assuredly has, then preservation of what is left of that past is certainly our best hope for the future. That we cannot recapture our historical past is obvious, but those who understand what once was cannot help but feel deep inner pangs as we contemplate our loss. More important, understanding our past enables us to achieve a new perspective concerning what we now have; prepares us better to mold Indiana's future; assists us in determining the fate of those places and those species that were here before we came; and also helps us guide our own destiny.

We have attempted to paint, with words, photographs, maps, and diagrams, as accurate a portrait of the state we share as is possible within the confines of a single book. Our aim was not to produce an encyclopedia or an atlas of Indiana, nor a complete compendium of Indiana's natural and human history, although the book is partly each. Instead we tried to meld the various elements into a beautiful, enjoyable volume—one that we hope you will return to again and again for information, and the pleasure in knowing your state somewhat better.

If your favorite place or favorite species has not been included, do not feel slighted; it was not possible to cover everything. Just take the time to enjoy what is presented—the text as well as the photographs—to reflect on the wisdom of the poetry and quoted materials, to study the maps and illustrations. Then if you feel moved to help protect what remains of Indiana's natural heritage, our objective will have been fulfilled.

—MARION T. JACKSON
Indiana State University

Acknowledgments

ONE OF THE FIRST BOOKS that I read after entering college (that was not a course requirement) was Durward L. Allen's classic, *Our Wildlife Legacy*. The most sobering sentence that I read in the entire book was the final one of his preface: "To my wife Dorothy and to Susie, Harley, and Steve, who carried on without me evenings and week-ends, I can only say I had no idea it would take five years." My college-freshman mind could not comprehend *any* writing project encompassing *five years*.

Shortly after this book moved from "an idea" to "in progress," someone casually mentioned that our neighboring state's companion volume, *Natural Ohio,* published in 1982, took *ten* years in preparation, start to finish. Ohioans must be inefficient, I mused to myself; no way will *our* book take that long!

My records indicate that our first organizational meeting to plan this book was held in the State Office Building in Indianapolis on Saturday, January 8, 1986. To the many who kept the faith that *The Natural Heritage of Indiana* would become a reality, I acknowledge and salute you. You have my heartfelt thanks, respect, and admiration. To those whose patience (including mine) was tested again and again by change in editorship, unforeseen delays, fundraising efforts, and illnesses, I can only say I had no idea it would take more than *ten years*.

To my wife, Jaleh, and to Arshia and Grousha, who supported me during this decade-long effort and continued on despite my absence mentally as a result of my being totally immersed in this project, thanks for your steadfast love, encouragement, and faith in its eventual completion.

Now as these introductory passages usually state, the opinions, attitudes, and facts expressed herein are those of the some three dozen authors who wrote this collection of essays. But in a sense, these writings also incorporate much of what has been written about and thought about Indiana and its natural history by literally hundreds or thousands of others during the long span of the last three centuries.

It is impossible to remember and to recognize everyone who contributed to the production of a volume such as this one, and obviously I run the grave risk of slighting the many by naming the few, but there are several whose special contributions must be mentioned.

The idea for this book originated with John Gallman, Director of Indiana University Press. John saw a copy of *Natural Ohio* and, as publishers are wont to do, thought that Indiana should have a similar volume. W. William Weeks, then State Director of The Nature Conservancy's Indiana Chapter, shared the vision and encouraged the Press to proceed. Dr. Delano Z. Arvin of Lafayette was the first editor to accept the challenge and did much to shape the project. He was forced to resign for health reasons and because of time constraints, passing the baton to me. John A. Bacone, Director of Indiana's Division of Nature Preserves, and his colleagues in the DNR were involved with the project from the beginning and made numerous contributions both substantive and psychological. And, of course, all of us are in debt to Dr. Alton A. Lindsey, whose prototype books *Natural Features of Indiana* and *Natural Areas in Indiana and Their Preservation* were the first on their topics for any state.

Special recognition must be given to the Geraldine Martin Foundation of Elkhart, Indiana, whose generosity, through sizable grants, made the publication of this book possible. Similarly, the Indiana Academy of Science granted significant monies to assist with publication costs. Further, it was generous personal contributions from Dr. and Mrs. Lynton K. Caldwell, Mary Jane Reith, and the Indiana Wildlife Society that enabled us to produce the book in its full size.

The services of Jane Lyle and Bobbi Diehl, unusually competent manuscript editors at Indiana University Press, were invaluable in getting the text into final form. Additionally, Maria Wilcox of St. Mary-of-the-Woods, Indiana, offered many helpful editorial comments to several authors as part of her master's degree project in creative writing at Indiana State University.

Without the contributions and support of Indiana State University, this book could never have been completed. Drs. William J. Brett and Charles J. Amlaner, successive Chairpersons of the Department of Life Sciences, were generous beyond any reasonable expectation in providing secretarial services, supplies, vehicles, travel allowances, and released time for me and other faculty and staff to work on editorial and writing assignments. Additionally, they offered their personal assistance, advice, and encouragement throughout the duration of the project. Similarly, Dr. William A. Dando, Chairperson, Department of Geography-Geology, provided released time for Norman Cooprider, Staff Cartographer, to draft many of the maps, line drawings, and other illustrations.

Office staff at Indiana State University that must be mentioned specifically for their contributions toward preparation of final manuscript copy are Laura Bakken, Debbie Church, Barbara Green, Rebecca Johnson, Sharon Long, and Judy Roberts. Without their dedication, expertise, and cheerful assistance, I would have abandoned the project years ago.

Reviewers who read and offered helpful comments regarding selected essays include John Bacone, George Bakken, Susan Berta, Robert Bozarth, William Brett, Phillip Clem, Henry Gray, Michael Homoya, Alton Lindsey, Wilton Melhorn, Jack Munsee, John Oliver, George Parker, Leslie Rissler, Paul Rothrock, Henry Tamar, and John Whitaker.

Some fifty amateur and professional nature photographers submitted their work for consideration. More than ten thousand individual color slides were reviewed before we selected the excellent photographs that support and embellish our story of the natural heritage of Indiana. Recognition is given to the contributing artists in the captions to individual photographs.

Special thanks are extended to my friends and colleagues who wrote these essays which constitute the text. Without your expertise and willingness to share your ideas, the book's total message would be powerless. Collectively, you possess approximately one thousand years—a millennium—of experience in observing, researching, describing, and teaching the incredible natural diversity that is the natural heritage of Indiana. For the careful preparation of your individual contributions, I commend you. Any errors that remain are my responsibility.

Finally, the efforts are recognized of individual citizens, landowners, environmental organizations, and professional natural resource employees who have dedicated much of their time, energy, and finances, plus their personal selves, to preserving and protecting the natural treasures of our beautiful state. Without your efforts over many years, little that is truly natural would have remained, and there would have been little reason to even consider producing this book. What you have maintained in a natural state to this point in time gives us great optimism for an even more promising future for the natural heritage of Indiana.

—MARION T. JACKSON
Indiana State University

Foreword: A Sense of Place

Lynton Keith Caldwell

IN HIS BOOK *Place and Placelessness* (1976), E. C. Relph writes:

> Places are fusions of human and natural order and are significant centres of our immediate experiences of the world. They are defined less by unique locations, landscapes, and communities than by the focusing of experiences and intentions onto particular settings. Places are not abstractions or concepts, but are directly experienced phenomena of the lived-world and hence are full with meanings.

The chapters of this book visit places in Indiana with special meaning for its people, seeing them from the many viewpoints from which these places are appreciated. A sense of place has grown throughout the nation, long dominated by the belief that economic development was the highest and best use of any piece of land. Today, other values are also recognized, and state policy in Indiana has begun to follow this transition.

In 1966, the Indiana Academy of Science published a collection of essays commemorating the sesquicentennial of the state. The volume, *Natural Features of Indiana,* resulted from a symposium held April 22–23 at Wabash College, and was edited by Alton A. Lindsey. Thirty-five essays not only encompassed the physical features of the state, but also included its plant and animal communities and its patterns of agriculture and human settlement. In a concluding "Perspective," Thomas E. Dustin reviewed the changes in the Indiana landscape brought about by European settlement and its transformation of the environment from the pre-settlement condition to its present state. Dustin's retrospective was written on the very eve of the environmental movement, which represented an unprecedented change in American priorities in relation to nature, and the growth of a sense of place.

Natural Areas in Indiana and Their Preservation was published in 1969 by the Indiana Natural Areas Survey of the Department of Biological Sciences of Purdue University. The authors, Alton A. Lindsey, Damian V. Schmelz, and Stanley A. Nichols, described natural areas characterizing the various regions of the state. The present volume complements the foregoing books, giving us a comprehensive picture of the socio-biophysical characteristics of Indiana. The State Department of Historical Preservation and Archaeology provides a corresponding source for information on special sites of human history throughout the state. The "special places" of Indiana are defined by the perceptions of its people—historical, scientific, and sentimental.

The early settlers of America had little sense of place. Their concern with the land was largely confined to prospects for livelihood or profit. The common attitude of the pioneers toward nature, described in the novels of James Fenimore Cooper, was one of indifference bordering on hostility. The mores and morals of the settlers combined Christian fundamentalism, materialism, and rugged individualism. They often saw themselves as latter-day Israelites, populating a promised land with God's blessing. The extirpation of plants and animals and the displacement of native peoples (comparable to Canaanites) was justified in the realization of God's plan. Transformation of the natural environment was undertaken with no thought of preserving any part of it for posterity. Those few natural systems that did survive transformation were regarded as unsuitable for agriculture or economic development. Some places—such as the Lake Michigan Dunes or the Grand Marsh of the Kankakee—temporarily survived transformation because the requisite technology and the economic and political motives were not yet present. Today some parts of these once great places have been set aside as vestiges of Indiana's pre-development past.

The *Natural Features* symposium at Wabash College in 1966 took place on the watershed between the then traditional dominance of economic development in land-use decisions in Indiana and a new sense of value in historic preservation and the natural environment. In the 1960s the effort to save the remaining Indiana dunes was half-lost in the sacrifice of much of the best dune land to a redundant steel mill—on the very eve of the big decline of the basic steel industry in the United States. On the other hand, a well-organized effort to transform the lower Wabash River into the "Ruhr of America" was defeated.

The Save the Dunes Council, formed in 1952, played a major role in protecting as much of the dunes area as could be saved. It continues to be active in defense of this unique place. The Indiana Chapter of The Nature Conservancy, formed in 1959, struggled for a decade to justify its existence. Then with unforeseeable rapidity and external funding, the Indiana Chapter grew to become one of the most active in the nation. In 1960 Acres, Incorporated was formed to acquire and protect places of ecological and esthetic value in northeast Indiana. Other land trusts have been established in the state, preserving and protecting open space and places of community value, with people often discovering a sense of place where none had previously existed. These organizations have been volunteer citizens' efforts to preserve and protect some of Indiana's most distinctive places. People are beginning to see anew places that they had previously taken for granted. They are overcoming the myopia of the familiar. As American communities become more and more alike, with shopping malls, fast-food restaurant chains, and the ubiquitous billboards, every place risks becoming the same place. For this reason, in addition to the others, unique and distinctive places have a growing value. Yet a sense of place is not new in Indiana.

In the 1960s the term *nature lover* was an epithet of scorn in the Indiana State House. But in 1987, on the occasion of the twenty-eighth anniversary of The Nature Conservancy of Indiana, a sympathetic governor addressed a luncheon meeting at the Columbia Club in Indianapolis, which was attended by many of the civic and business leaders of the city and state. This change in overt public attitude may represent the diminution of a paradox in public and political attitudes that has characterized Indiana since the beginning of the twentieth century. This paradox was that Hoosiers seem to attach a sentimental value to a sense of place, while simultaneously endorsing a commitment to material "progress" and economic priorities which would irreversibly alter the qualities of place and environment. Civic club members could sing "On the Banks of the Wabash" at luncheon meetings and then applaud a speaker who urged the river's transformation into an industrial canal.

Impending changes in attitudes and values are often signaled by artists and authors. Indiana painters—notably in the dunes, Brown County, and the Whitewater Valley—expressed a strong sense of place. Writers such as James Whitcomb Riley and Gene Stratton Porter, and cartoonist John T. McCutcheon captured a sense of place implicit in their work, if less site-specific than those of the painters. The development of Indiana's state park system after 1916 was in part an effort toward protection of valued places. A Division of Nature Preserves was established in 1967 in the State Department of Natural Resources. Indiana's Natural Heritage Program (now Data Center), initiated in 1978, has been a more explicit effort to record, preserve, and protect places representative of the unadulterated environment of the area now organized as the state of Indiana.

There is a basic difference between natural features and places, recognized implicitly in this volume and its 1966 predecessor. Natural features are what they are and where they are without regard to human presence, but their significance to humans is determined by how they are understood. To the extent that natural features are altered by humans—as in agriculture or forestry—there is an explicit linkage with human society and values. Place, however, is defined by human perception. Places may be located by reference to other natural features, but even if they are bounded on a topographic map, human reference points are indicated. The qualities and characteristics defining a place express not only its biophysical attributes, but also its aesthetic value and historic significance.

The mobility and materialism of American society tend, for many people, to diminish an identification with place. Many Americans are unable to describe or identify with places where they work or live. Industrial agriculture and standardized architecture tend to homogenize the human environment. Even so, a sense of place—or a desire for distinctiveness of place—seems to be growing in America. This book may be regarded as testimony to changes in public attitudes and values that have occurred in this state since 1966. One may hope that it will help to focus and reinforce this emergence of a sense of place in the natural and cultural environments of Indiana.

Across the Ohio River, the dense hardwood forest seemed illimitable. Nearly half of the state was covered by forest dominated by American beech, sugar maple, and tuliptree.   *Photo by Richard Fields*

Perspective: The Indiana That Was

Marion T. Jackson

I command you this day, that ye may be strong, and go in and possess the land, whither ye go to possess it. And that ye may prolong your days in the land . . . to give unto them and their seed, a land that floweth with milk and honey.

—*Deuteronomy 11:8–9*

THE SETTING

The landscape that became Indiana once was one large natural area with its present boundary unrecognized, uncharted. Within the bounds of present-day Indiana, and stretching from the Ohio River to Lake Michigan, and from the Whitewater River to the Wabash lay more than 36,000 square miles of the finest forests and prairies, swamps and marshes, barrens and savannas, glades and cliffsides, bogs and fens, seeps and springs, and lakes and streams to be found anywhere in the heartland of North America.

During the late eighteenth century, Indiana was part of the great wilderness of deciduous hardwoods that stretched unbroken "beyond the Ohio" to the evergreen forests of the "north country," and to the vast prairies westward, beyond the limit of trees. The familiar map of Indiana today—appearing somewhat like a stylized human foot with truncated toes—was to take shape over nearly a century as the westering surge of settlement and development swept across the land.

According to the best information available on pre-settlement Indiana, the 36,291-square-mile area contained about 20 million acres of forestland, 2 million acres of prairie, 1.5 million acres of water and wetlands, plus glades, barrens, and savanna totaling perhaps another 1 million acres. (These figures total more than the 23,226,240 acres which constitute the state, but all acreages by habitat are only approximate.) Also much of the original forestland occupied floodplains, depressions, or flatwoods, all subject to seasonal inundation by standing water, hence often included as wetlands. Such designation would increase the overall wetland total to as much as 5.6 million acres, according to some estimates.

THE SETTLEMENT

As early as August 1781, Colonel Archibald Lochry, a Pennsylvania officer in the Colonial Army, while in command of about 100 frontier soldiers on their way to link up with General George Rogers Clark in the Western Campaign, encountered and was defeated by a similar-sized band of Indians near the mouth of a creek that now bears the colonel's name (presently Laughery Creek) in far southeastern Indiana. Lochry's defeat was one of the earliest of a number of skirmishes that resulted as the American settlers and their armies wrested ownership of Indiana from the Native Americans.

In the turbulent years following the American Revolution, a young nation turned its eyes and footsteps to the vast, little-known lands beyond the Appalachians for space into which its restless numbers could grow. By the 1790s, "long knife" hunters venturing northward

across the Ohio River from the Kentucky Commonwealth, or westward across the Miami and Whitewater rivers from settlements in the Ohio Territory, returned with glowing tales of towering forests without limit, of fertile valleys so thick with game "you kin smell it."

Though the "frontier mind" was filled with imagination and its humor fueled by exaggeration—"Lord love us, that Indiana soil is so rich that you hafta coat yer corn seed in axle grease or the plants'll burn themselves up shootin' outta th' ground"—many of the stories of the diversity and fecundity of Indiana, the Land of Indians, were true.

They were merely confirming what the French fur traders, with trading posts at Chip-kaw-kay (Vincennes), Kekionga (Fort Wayne), and Ouiatenon (near Lafayette), and their Native American suppliers of furs had long known. These trading posts were selected by the Europeans during the eighteenth century as centers of the finest game regions within the limits of the present state. The peltry from the last-mentioned post alone, in one year in those early times, amounted to about 8,000 pounds sterling.

Only the resident Native Americans, long friendly with the French, stood in the way of full-scale settlement of Indiana by hardy, resourceful, land-hungry immigrants. But the Indian tribes present in pre-settlement Indiana were recent immigrants themselves to this land, having been forced from their homes to the east and north by earlier European settlement and/or shifting tribal boundaries, and were not about to give up their lands in Indiana willingly. Shawanees, Delawares, Miamis, Potawatomis, Weas, Piankishaws, and Wyandots were all resolute in their determination to remain in their newly acquired homeland. Besides, they and their ancestors were well aware of the devastation European settlement had brought to the eastern wilderness in just a few short years.

They had witnessed how the wave of human settlement altered forever the wild fabric of nature, and totally changed the Indian lifestyle in the process. Such an awareness prompted, in part, the half-Indian interpreter William Wells to repeat the following words from the Council of Indian Chiefs to General Anthony Wayne, following the Battle of Fallen Timbers in present-day northwestern Ohio in 1794:

> You are fearful. You cover yourselves with clothing and again with roofs and walls, locking your doors, reading from your black book and quoting distant presidents and kings. You are afraid of hunger and solitude. You want and you want. You are never silent and are never at ease. You are a weak degenerate and fearful people who could not survive without your axes, your guns and your horses. You are destroyers, leveling the forest, hacking roads along the deer trails, driving all game away. You whites are not at war with us; you are at war with the earth.

Thus the advance of settlement into the Indiana wilderness seemed to be as inexorable as it had been back east. Treaty by treaty (most broken wholly or in part by the Americans) opened more and more of Indiana to settlement. Toward the end of the first decade of

Interior of old-growth beech-maple forest known as Hoot Woods in Owen County is reminiscent of the forest the pioneers walked through.
Photo by Marion Jackson

the nineteenth century, Tecumseh, an eloquent chieftain, became convinced that only a major confederacy of tribes throughout the Midwest could break the back of the settlement advance.

> The sun is my father—the earth is my mother and on her bosom I will recline. . . . The great spirit has given all the country as common property to all the tribes; we have been driven from the banks of the Delaware, across the Alleghenies, and our possessions on the Wabash, and the Illinois are now to be taken from us. Like galloping horses, our tribes have been driven towards the setting sun,—as for myself and my warriors we have determined to resist any further aggression of the whites.
>
> —*Chief Tecumseh to General William Henry Harrison at Vincennes (1810)*

But General William Henry Harrison struck the Indian force at present-day Battleground in Tippecanoe County on the morning of November 7, 1811, while Tecumseh was away rallying the tribes, and won a decisive victory over the Native Americans. The uneven conflict with Harrison's army at the Battle of Tippecanoe largely broke the will of the Indian resistance, Tecumseh's dream of a major confederacy was badly shaken, and the way was paved for both Indiana statehood and Harrison's destiny to become president of the United States.

Only now are we beginning to understand fully that the Native Americans were probably right in their view of the relationship of humans to the land; that wilderness is equal to more than the sum of its parts, fragile and vulnerable in the face of hurried, unplanned change. But ecosystem science was still a century and a half into the future in 1800.

To these ebullient, energetic, restless pioneers, recently released from British rule and regimentation, the patterns and processes inherent in wilderness were too esoteric, too random, too unordered, too unpredictable, to appeal to their westering minds. They saw the frontier as an adversary, the wilderness as an enemy to be conquered—a chaotic, undisciplined landscape, largely covered by dense, frightening forests, populated by wild, ferocious beasts, and with savage humans, equally threatening and undisciplined, lurking in the shadows.

To this wild, undisciplined land the settlers came, first as a trickle in the 1790s and early 1800s, then as a freshet following the Battle of Tippecanoe as statehood loomed during the second decade of the nineteenth century; then the floodgates opened to a tidal wave of pioneers about 1820, and the land was inundated with settlers within one human generation. Witness the Indiana population change by decades: 1800—5,600; 1810—24,500; 1820—147,200; 1830—343,000; 1840—686,000; 1850—nearly 1 million.

In 1827 a surveyor named Jonathan Knight surveyed it [the National Road] across Indiana from Richmond to Terre Haute by way of Indianapolis. It was so nearly straight that it is but two miles longer than the state is wide at Indianapolis. . . . A track thirty to forty feet wide in the center was macadamized with ten inches of crushed stone. This at that time and many years after was the finest road in the world. Two six-horse teams could race abreast on it. . . . Hundreds of wagoners hauled freight over it and from 1830 to 1860 a continuous line of homeseekers passed along to the west. So numerous were they that at night their camp fires were almost as thick as street lights. From 1827 to 1836 this flood poured along the National road through Indianapolis at the rate of not less than one family every thirty minutes and often twenty families in a company. It seemed to those living along the "old pike" that no one would be left in the east.

—Logan Esarey, "Old First Roads," in
History of Indiana (1922)

THE WILDLIFE

The wilderness that was Indiana changed apace. The seal of our great state depicts an axeman felling a tree as a bison races away from the rising sun. By December 1816, when Indiana entered statehood, bison were essentially gone from the state except in the far western limits.

For millennia, thousands of these huge, shaggy beasts had periodically moved southeastward from the Illinois and western Indiana prairies, crossed the Wabash River near Vincennes, and stolidly sauntered along the famed Buffalo Trace (now, in part, the route followed by U.S. 150) to the Falls of the Ohio at Louisville, on their journey to Big Bone Lick and the barrens of Kentucky to obtain minerals and salt. According to Butler's History of Kentucky (1834), "Over this wide, well-marked road, evidences of which still remain, countless thousands of Bisons passed annually. From the Ohio River to Big Bone Lick was a wide road which the animals had beaten spacious enough for two waggons [sic] to go abreast."

In densely wooded regions the bison were primarily transients, but in meadows and prairies they abounded. From the summit of a hill near Ouiatenon, a report of 1718 stated, "Nothing is visible to the eye but prairies full of buffaloes."

But as prevalent as they once were, the bison were essentially wiped out in a score of years and were gone from the state by 1830. Elk, panther, black bear, fisher, and beaver disappeared with almost equal rapidity, all nearly gone from Indiana by 1850. Even the tenacious timber wolf, the white-tailed deer, and the bald eagle had been extirpated by the beginning of the twentieth century.

Fortunately, the diaries, journals, and travel logs of many early visitors gave excellent accounts of the Indiana wilderness and its wildlife. John Parsons, a 23-year-old Virginian, captured much of the essence of pristine Indiana's wildness when he recorded his impressions of the Wabash River country in his diary A Tour through Indiana in 1840:

The river rolled its silver current along the edge of the plain, which was besprinkled with wild flowers of every rich and varied tint, intermingled with tall grass that nodded in the passing breeze. . . . The forest rang continually with the songs of the birds and among them I noted particularly, because of their strangeness, the sandhill crane and the Carolina parroquet. The parroquets are beautiful birds, their plumage is green, except the neck, which is yellow, and the head is red. When flying, this bird utters a shrill but cheerful and pleasant note and the flash of its golden and green plumage in the sunlight is indescribably beautiful in its tropical suggestion.

Although white-tailed deer were prevalent in the original forest, they were likely less numerous per square mile than now.   *Photo by Delbert Rust*

Prairie-chickens, the grouse of the treeless expanses, boomed relentlessly during their spring mating rituals. Market hunters killed wagonloads of them in the nineteenth century.   *Photo courtesy of the Indiana Department of Natural Resources*

Waterfowl almost without number cruised the wetland waters. Their flights darkened the sun, and their wings shattered the stillness with their thunderous applause.   *Photo by Richard Fields*

These majestic primeval forests of Indiana were home to almost countless wildlife besides the beautiful Carolina parakeet. Included were the crow-sized ivory-billed woodpecker or "woodscock" in the heaviest timber, and flocks of passenger pigeons so immense that during migration their passage obscured the sun for hours—pigeons whose numbers were so great that

> when darkness settled they descended from the sky and alighted many deep upon the branches of the trees, the weight being sufficient to break off many large limbs. . . . The combined noise of the strokes of millions upon millions of pigeon wings created a wonderful and continuous rumble as of nearby thunder, not unlike the roar of an approaching tornado.
>
> —*Amos W. Butler, Presidential Address, Indiana Academy of Science (1895)*

But the Carolina parakeet and the passenger pigeon have long been globally extinct, and the ivory-bill, if it exists at all, now occurs only in meager numbers on the island of Cuba.

Large predators were well represented in the Indiana wilderness but likely were much fewer in number than the settlers estimated them to be. Pioneers both feared and despised them for depredations on their livestock and for their potential danger to humans, real or imagined. Wolf packs range widely, travel long distances in their daily activities, and actively defend their territories against others of their kind. At an average home range size per wolf of two square miles each, the entire state would have harbored fewer than 20,000 wolves; perhaps 10,000 to 12,000 would be a more likely number. But *any* wolves were far too many to suit the pioneers, especially when their semi-wild livestock were taken by the large canids.

Panthers caterwauled in the deep shades of the forest, but being solitary, unsociable hunters, they were likely never common nor frequently encountered by the settlers. Black bear were important for frontier survival, as both meat and tallow sources, and as hides for barter, cabin rugs, or winter clothing.

Deer, although common in the Indiana wilderness, may have been less numerous then than the present-day herd. A reasonable maximum deer population density in pre-settlement Indiana would likely have been 10 to 12 per square mile on average, for a total of perhaps 400,000 for the entire state. Since venison was an important food source for family use or sale, deer were hunted continually. Deer hides were used for clothing as well as a valued trade commodity—typically bringing about $1.00 for a buckskin, hence our slang expression yet today of "buck" for a dollar.

Initially, small-scale, widely spaced clearings favored deer populations, and their numbers increased temporarily. Unrestricted year-round harvest, plus accelerating clearing by an increasing human population, caused rapid declines in deer numbers after 1850.

With settlement's advance, many wildlife populations declined much faster than did the forests, prairies, wetlands, and soils that supported them. First to go were the large carnivores, then the large herbivores, and finally the natural vegetation. On steeper slopes cropping caused soil fertility declines, followed by a seaward slip of the soils themselves. Ecosystems typically are dismembered from the top down. Indiana was no exception.

It is difficult for those of us living in Indiana today to imagine how abundant many smaller wildlife species were during the early settlement years. A chronicle of gray squirrel abundance and harvest was related by Durward Allen in his excellent book *Our Wildlife Legacy*. A competitive squirrel hunt (called a burgoo by the frontiersmen) was conducted in the fall of 1834 in Bartholomew County in which two teams of 50 hunters each killed squirrels for a three-day period, with the losing team hosting a squirrel barbecue for the winners. Allen concludes, "The winner of the hunt presented *900 squirrels* [italics his] at the end of the three days and the runner-up had 783!"

* * *

This abundance of squirrels and other wildlife was not just a local occurrence. Bounties were routinely paid on squirrel scalps and crow, hawk, or owl feet. Crop damage and livestock losses to wildlife resulted in "fox drives" and other wide-ranging group harvests of "varmints" and "nuisance" wildlife being held throughout the state for many decades.

Wildlife populations respond quickly to changes in available habitat. As noted above, wilderness species, especially large, conspicuous predators and important food animals, declined rapidly as settlement advanced and were gone from the state within decades. As clearings increased in number and size, "farm wildlife" such as fox squirrels, cottontail rabbits, bobwhite quail, along with songbirds typical of field, fencerow, orchard, and lawn, made their homes near human dwellings and thrived in the changed conditions. Finally, those species typical of habitats greatly disturbed by human activities increased (along with alien introductions), becoming successful by replacing usually preferred wildlife species. Now let us look in more detail at how this continuum of landscape alteration occurred.

THE FORESTS

Indiana's original forests were among the finest broadleaved hardwood forests anywhere in the world. Stanley Coulter, in his 1891 publication *The Forest Trees of Indiana,* stated that "forty-two kinds of trees in the Wabash Valley attained a height above 100 feet."

Groves of the finest black walnut trees the world has ever known grew on Indiana's most fertile soils, some individuals of which were 4 to 6 feet in diameter and 100 to 150 feet high. The General Land Office surveyors recognized the close correlation between soil fertility and the presence of black walnut trees when they entered such land descriptions into their field notes as "sugar tree and walnut land, excellent for growing corn." Most were cut and burned to clear the land for crops.

Robert Ridgway, an eminent naturalist who studied and photographed the forests of the Lower Wabash River during the 1870s and 1880s, described the stands of timber of that region as "an exceedingly heavy virgin forest, some of the heaviest hardwood forest I have ever seen—as I have twice visited the Tropics (Central America)—covering almost the entire floodplain on the Indiana side."

Ridgway measured several sycamores at 25 to 30 feet in circumference with overall heights of 160 to almost 200 feet. Several cypress stumps were measured in Knox County at 9 and 10 feet in diameter above their buttressed bases. He also measured a tuliptree, now rarely encountered on floodplains, that taped 25 feet in girth, 91 feet to the first limb, and 190 feet total height. The maximum diameter he recorded for a tuliptree was 11 feet; the average diameter of 18 measured specimens was 6.2 feet. Heights ranged from 110 to 168 feet, averaging 143.5. Ridgway's measurements were of felled trees and cut stumps, so we can be confident of his data.

In contrast, the largest tuliptrees known presently in the state are a pair of "sister trees" standing only about 30 feet apart in Hemmer Woods, Gibson County, which were measured by the author during the late 1960s at nearly 5 feet in diameter and just over 150 feet tall. Presently, they are very old, declining in vigor, and may not live much longer.

One of the most famous trees of the original forest was an enormous Ohio buckeye, which in life grew in the southeast corner

Robert Ridgway (*left*), a noted early naturalist, measured and photographed many huge trees on the Wabash River bottoms, including this enormous sycamore.
Photo by Robert Ridgway

of Rush County and was said to have been, when standing, 27 feet 9 inches in circumference and 90 feet to the first limb. It was felled and crafted into the celebrated buckeye canoe of William Henry Harrison's presidential campaign of 1840. The huge canoe was pulled about the Midwest by six white horses bearing the campaign slogan "Tippecanoe and Tyler Too."

Other magnificent trees (parts of which still survive) from the original forest include two majestic sycamores. A photograph of one served as the frontispiece of Charlie Deam's 1953 volume *Trees of Indiana*. It grew near Worthington in Greene County, and was reported at 42 feet 3 inches in circumference in 1915. Sections of the trunk are preserved in Worthington. A 1936 article featuring Indiana in *National Geographic* magazine contains a photograph of a giant sycamore stump reported to be *56 feet* in circumference which once stood near Kokomo. In life it must have dwarfed even the Worthington specimen, and is larger in girth than any forest-grown temperate hardwood tree that I am aware of. Its stump was moved to a Kokomo city park many years ago for preservation and public viewing, and still exists.

But the most impressive feature of the primeval forests of Indiana was not the size or height of the trees. Rather, it was the dense shade that all but excluded sunlight. In the words of Amos W. Butler in his presidential address to the Indiana Academy of Science in 1895:

Over the greater part of this State were spread dense forests of tall trees—heavy timber—whose limbs met and branches were so interwoven that but occasionally could the sunlight find entrance. There was little or no undergrowth in the heaviest woods, and the gloom of those dense shades and its accompanying silence were terribly oppressive. Mile upon mile, days' journey upon days' journey, stretched these gloomy shades amid giant columns and green arches reared by nature through centuries of time.

Within the penumbra of this dense forest canopy, the first settlers established their homesteads. Those of us accustomed to living in well-lighted homes with expansive views and traveling rapidly across a largely uncanopied Indiana cannot fully appreciate how much their feeling of confinement, and being at the mercy of the wilderness, must have depressed their spirits in that solitary existence. Conrad Richter expressed it well in his book *The Trees* (1940):

All night the wind rose. Now it came and now it went. This was a lull. You could hear the trees dripping. Then far off you could catch the next wave coming for you through the woods. . . . The wind and rain let up about dawn. . . . Then the girl saw that last night's storm had stripped the leaves from half the trees. Her mother looked like a half-blinded human that had lived all

Lowland forests of Indiana were dense with towering trees. Hemmer Woods in Gibson County boasts large sweetgums, elms, oaks, and tuliptrees, among many other species.   *Photo by Marion Jackson*

summer in a cave. She stood there peering up through the branches of an ash at sky so blue it hurt just to look at it. "I never thought I'd live to see this day" she muttered. . . ."

Small wonder the dense forest that is now Shades State Park was called the "Shades of Death" in the early days.

The pioneer's first work was to cut away enough trees to build a cabin, preferably near a spring which purled from the nearby hillside, and remote enough that you "could not see the smoke from any neighbor's chimney." Otherwise there might not be enough wild game to support the large pioneer family until land was cleared and crops raised. To create a wilderness home, they broad-axed cabin timbers, raised a ridgepole, fashioned a roof of froe-split red oak staves, then built a mud-and-stick fireplace chimney so that venison and wild turkeys could be roasted over their hearth. All the while they were itching to begin actual clearing that would "let some daylight into the swamp."

It is difficult for us to imagine in our world of instant comforts what having a home meant to the frontier family, on their own deep within the wilderness. Just a roof, walls, and fire meant survival, the difference between life and death. Again, Richter said it best:

> Sayward watched her mother's eyes take a turn around the cabin. The firelight played sociable fingers on roof and rafters. The logs smelled clean, and the beds of new leaves made you sleepy. Everything was spick and fine as a newborn babe in a log cradle. Piles of knobby hickory nuts and black and white walnuts lay hulled in a corner. . . . They had a roof over their heads and a bag of meal hanging from the rafters. A buckskin door weighted with a short green log shut out the dark and snow.
>
> —*Conrad Richter,* The Trees *(1940)*

As each cabin was built, it foreshadowed a clearing which extended more and more each year. For the most part, the axe and fire performed the work. Great deadenings created during the winter months gave promise of lively logrollings the following spring. Even the giant tuliptrees, red and white oaks, black walnuts, ashes, wild cherries, beeches, and sweet gums were carried on handspikes, or were rolled into heaps in the ravines by the hickory-muscled frontiersmen and their leathery sons, and burned. Across Indiana, fires by the thousands burned day and night for weeks on end, with wood smoke turning the spring skies a sallow yellow. Wood also served every need and demand the human mind could make on the timberlands, used throughout the pioneers' lifetimes from cradle to coffin. Thus were Indiana's forests removed.

But how do you essentially eradicate a wilderness of 36,291 square miles in three score years and ten? Within a single human lifetime or three human generations? In the words of my dear friend the late Dr. Robert O. Petty of Wabash College:

> How do you make a cornfield out of a forest? How do you make a town? How do you clear away trees five feet through and towering one hundred and fifty feet? Forty acres, eighty, a section, a county—how do you "cut the top off" all the flatland between the Cumberlands and the Mississippi? Our minds can only ache to comprehend.

And how do you do it with only axes, grubbing hoes, horses, and oxen? (It may be of interest to the reader that most of Indiana was cleared before even the crosscut saw came into general usage, much less the chain saw.) In the words of my late neighbor John Reynolds, "They worked different then than we do now," when he described how his great-grandparents pit-sawed, by hand, ash logs into rough

boards to floor the stone house they were building in 1845, and which still stands on my Ripley County farm.

John Perlin, a Harvard University professor of forestry, in his thought-provoking book A *Forest Journey,* documented the course of human civilization in terms of available forest resources. He summarized that "every human settlement begins by consumption of the forest surrounding it." Indiana was no exception. We built a state by consuming nature. In the words of Aldo Leopold, "Wilderness is the raw material out of which man has hammered the artifact called civilization." And, I might add, "on an anvil called progress."

If the 20 million acres of forestland believed extant in Indiana in 1790 contained 110 trees above four inches in diameter on an average acre (based on a 108.4 average density for 28 high-quality old-growth stands still occurring in the state), then prior to settlement, Indiana must have contained approximately 2.2 billion trees, or about 400 trees for each Hoosier resident today.

An original forest of 2.2 billion trees, harboring a deer herd of perhaps 400,000, but only 10,000 to 12,000 wolves—this must be an object lesson in food-chain structure and dynamics of wilderness ecosystems!

How do you consume a wilderness resource of 2.2 billion trees, two-thirds of which were cut down before 1870? Assuming that relatively few trees were removed prior to 1800, by either Native Americans or pioneers, it would require the cutting of an average of 20 million trees annually for 70 years—a rate almost equal to that of an average-sized county per year, or more than 7,000 acres per day, on average. Our ancestors did to the Indiana wilderness what is presently occurring in the tropical forests of Brazil, Borneo, Sumatra, New Guinea, Zaire, and elsewhere. But did we as a human species gain much ecological wisdom from what our forebears did to Indiana?

THE PRAIRIES

Those counties, largely located in northwestern Indiana, which were covered by prairies of landscape size for the most part were settled later than those primarily forested. Not only did this reflect the pattern of settlement which occurred generally from southeast to northwest across Indiana, but it was also partly due to the early settlers' belief that "land that would not grow trees" was inferior cropland. What irony. Indiana prairieland is some of the finest agricultural soil in the world.

Here grasses—tall enough to hide a rider on horseback—on the best prairie soils were intermixed with a multitude of forbs, or broadleafed prairie wildflowers. Best typified in Benton and its adjacent counties, the expanse of tall, waving grasses was broken only occasionally by small prairie groves of trees.

> I wanted to walk straight on through the red grass and over the edge of the world, which could not be very far away. The light air about me told me that the world ended here: only the ground and sun and sky were left, and if one went a little farther there would be only sun and sky, and one would float off into them, like the tawny hawks which sailed over our heads making slow shadows on the grass.
>
> —*Willa Cather,* My Antonia *(1918)*

Recurrent fires set by lightning or by Native Americans eliminated invasion of woody species, for the most part. Extensive prairies were excellent habitat for buffalo, prairie chicken, and a host of reptile, small mammal, and songbird species typical of grasslands. Here market gunners of the nineteenth century harvested wagonloads of prairie chickens from the upland prairies, plus additional wagonloads of waterfowl and shorebirds from the wet prairies and marshes.

The pioneers viewed wet prairies, especially, along with swamps, to be unhealthful places to live, believing that the air and water were bad there, and that fevers and agues must be companions of those who settle there. The word *malaria* comes from the Italian *mala aria*, "bad air."

Settlement of the prairies was also impeded by the pioneers' inability to open the prairie soil for growing of crops. Until John Deere developed the chilled steel moldboard for the breaking plow about 1840, would-be homesteaders could not successfully break the tough prairie sod, formed by a centuries-old interlacing of incredible root systems of the myriad prairie plants.

Initially, special professional "breaking teams" of several yoke of oxen pulling huge single-bottom steel plows went from farm to farm, plowing the prairies for the first time on a custom-hire basis. The exceedingly high natural fertility of the deep, virgin, loamy black prairie soils caused such demand for the rich farmland that native prairie was quickly eliminated as a landscape community. Even today we still occasionally hear a product that is selling well being described as "doing a land-office business."

Today, less than 1,000 acres of the original 2 million acres of virgin prairie remain, most of it occurring only as small, often degraded, remnants in pioneer cemeteries or transportation rights-of-way. With the loss of the prairie habitat, the prairie chicken followed suit, extirpated from Indiana during the early 1970s.

When I was a boy in the 1940s, my uncle told me of his experience with breaking the sod of a quarter-section of unplowed prairie just across the Indiana state line in Kankakee County, Illinois. The square 160-acre tract had been used for harvesting prairie hay and pasturing cattle, but never plowed. When my uncle fall-plowed the land in the autumn of 1937, the fat black furrow slice of Brunizeum soil rolled over in one continuous unbroken black ribbon of sod across the entire one-half mile. During the 1938 crop season he planted the field to corn using open-pollinated (non-hybrid) seed, nurtured by only a small application of 3–12–12 starter fertilizer. To witness the productivity of the original prairie, now remembered only vaguely by the oldest farmers, neighbors came from miles around late that summer to marvel at the exceedingly tall corn and its rich black-green color. That fall, 18,000 bushels of corn were harvested from the 160 acres of nitrogen-rich prairie soil, a remarkable yield for the 1930s. Given such agricultural productivity, it is surprising that even the tiny remnants of native prairie remaining in Indiana survived. Over the years, the prairie landscape, like the rest of wild Indiana, became "civilized."

> They drove on, and the trees were spaced wider and wider, pastoral kings, each with his own realm of high meadow to shadow. They lumbered out upon the prairie, praising God for space and earth and wind. Their wagon tracks left bent the astonished grass, left flowers broken. Very slowly the most resilient culms eased up again and faced the breeze. But there were many more wagons to come, and the grass at last learned obedience.

> —*Donald Culross Peattie,* A Prairie Grove *(1938)*

THE WETLANDS

The pioneers hurried the water from the land almost as quickly as they did the trees or the native grasses, because everywhere that the water table stood above or into the soil profile during the growing season, excess water impeded the growth of crops. Sometimes, when the heavy swamp forests were cleared from upland depressions, the water table actually rose temporarily early in the growth season, owing to the removal of the enormous evapotranspirational pull of the trees. Roots of actively growing trees drink thirstily, pumping vast quantities of soil moisture into the atmosphere. With the trees gone, water was even more of a problem until ditches or tile lines were in place.

An observant motorist driving through the swell and swale topography of central or northern Indiana will quickly note that the older farmsteads (those in place a century or more) are almost invariably located on the knolls or low ridges. And for good reason. Those surrounding swales held standing water for periods ranging from two to twelve months annually, depending upon their depth, surface characteristics, and internal drainage. Settlers homesteaded the ridges because only there could they keep their feet dry, and their farm animals comfortable all year long. Also, the water table needed to be below the root zone during summer to grow crops effectively.

Just as the clearing of trees expanded centrifugally and inexorably from the homesteads, so did the battle with the standing water. Early on, ditching was done by hand with shovels, or with slip scoops pulled by oxen or horses, to create open ditches or to open and straighten natural drainage channels. Then mechanical ditchers intensified the efforts, and thousands of miles of subsurface tile lines were soon laid yearly. Everywhere water was being hurried from the land at a rate faster than nature's leisurely pace of runoff and evaporation. The great sponge of the Indiana wetlands was quickly being wrung of most of its life-giving moisture; springs failed, and many stream beds became dry during summer months.

With the now-swifter waters of springtime also went far too much of the topsoil, turning the streams and rivers from gin-clear to the color of well-creamed coffee within one human generation. Downstream, on the larger watercourses especially, the frequency, height, and duration of flooding increased greatly, intensifying the clamor for various flood control measures, each requiring large public expenditure.

> Near by is the graceful loop of an old dry creek bed. The new creek bed is ditched straight as a ruler; it has been uncurled, by the county engineer to hurry the run-off. On the hill in the background are contoured strip-crops; they have been curled, by the erosion engineer to retard the run-off. The water must be confused by so much advice.

> —*Aldo Leopold,* A Sand County Almanac *(1949)*

With the vanishing wetlands went much of the wetland wildlife. No longer did vast flocks of waterfowl darken the skies over the fabled Kankakee Marsh, or raise their wings in thunderous applause when startled into flight. With the disappearing wetlands also went the majority of the beaver, otter, mink, and muskrat, as well as the whistling wings of the crane, heron, rail, plover, sandpiper, snipe, and bittern. So also went the wetland plants of lake and marsh, and swamp, bog, and fen. Indiana was now drier in most places, but a more monotonous landscape with its loss of diversity of wetland habitats and their wild species.

THE CHANGES

The wilderness that was Indiana did not disappear with one giant wave of civilizing frenzy. Instead, it was lost a shot, a trap, a chip, a furrow, a bite, a match, or a ditch at a time, as individual hunters, woodsmen, farmers, grazing animals, fires, developers, or drainage engineers each took their toll.

It was a process that started small, like a snowball rolling down-

Prairie grasses in northwestern Indiana could hide a person on horseback. Indian grass (shown here) grew mixed with big bluestem grass and myriad wildflowers.   *Photo by Marion Jackson*

Wetlands were so interconnected in northern Indiana that during high-water times, canoe travel was possible from South Bend to Illinois. This is Fish Creek Fen in La Porte County.   *Photo by Richard Fields*

hill, accreting size and inertia of motion as it progressed, culminating in an avalanche of change late in the nineteenth century. Mile by mile we bent the wilderness into more productive systems, and we did this with a knowing zeal that we were doing the right thing, almost a religious belief that this was our "manifest destiny." We came into a land "flowing with milk and honey" and converted it into something useful, something civilized.

This process has been going on for two centuries and continues today, only now there are many more of us and our tools have far greater capacity to alter the landscape and the survival potential of its wild inhabitants. In the words of Aldo Leopold, "We are remodeling Alhambra with a steamshovel, and we are proud of our yardage."

No living person will see again the "endless" virgin forests or "limitless" prairies or crystalline waters that greeted our forebears when they entered Indiana nearly two centuries ago. But remnants of various sizes and degrees of naturalness do exist. As the "civilizing" process increased in scope and momentum, the pieces remaining natural became increasingly fragmented and restricted generally to more remote locations.

Nor did the removal of forest affect only the trees. The whole landscape changed, including its geometry, as farm fields, roads, and developments impressed a grid of squares and rectangles upon curvilinear nature. The varied and random patterns of wilderness were replaced with the "dreary commonality," as environmentalist Tom Dustin of the Izaak Walton League once phrased it, of today's landscape.

At first the traces through the wilderness followed animal and Indian trails already in place for centuries. They followed indirect routes along the paths of easiest travel, generally along the contour of the landscape, connecting portages, crossings, or fords of frequented waterways. After the land surveyors had gridded the wilderness along section lines for division into farms and landholdings—square tracts independent of terrain—roads logically were built along property borders. These wide, unshaded roads at mile intervals required much uphill and downhill travel and, in the early years, became floods of dust in summer and seas of mud in winter. Gradually they were "piked" with limestone "metal," sometimes cracked by hand with knapping hammers by local landowners in lieu of paying their property taxes due spring and fall.

Now we cut and fill to fit the landscape to our arrow-straight motorways and real-estate developments. A straight line may be the shortest and most efficient distance between two points, but a curve is certainly a more interesting and pleasant distance.

Roads, more than any single landscape alteration, changed forever the wild fabric of the Indiana wilderness. All remaining fragments of nature are now small and within two or three miles of a road, giving access to all, affording protection to none.

The destruction of the primeval forest cost us much besides the trees that were sacrificed. Most of the lesser plants, vertebrates, lower animals, and even microbes were lost entirely from their altered habitats, unless they were able to survive the change and adapt to the new conditions. Even the soils, the waters, and now the atmosphere itself are drastically modified from what once was. As Professor Alton A. Lindsey aptly put it, "The sky did not fall, we pulled it down."

Change succeeded change. Little by little, but still cumulatively, each cleared field, each drained swamp, each plowed prairie, each polluted natural water body, each one of a thousand variations in cause had its effect upon the number and life histories of our plants and animals. Neither the luxuriant growth of a cornfield nor the greenness of our closely cropped lawn reveals much to the casual passer-by of the natural abundance that formerly occurred there.

Perhaps literary naturalist Gene Stratton-Porter best described the process of fragmentation and destruction of Indiana's vast natural ecosystems by what happened in the wild swampland near the home of Elnora, the young heroine in her book *Girl of the Limberlost*, published early in the twentieth century:

> Men all around were clearing available land. The trees fell wherever corn would grow. Whenever the trees fell the moisture ran low, and at times the bed was dry. With unbroken sweep the winds of the west came, gathering force with every mile . . . blowing the surface from the soil in clouds of fine dust and rapidly changing everything. From coming in with two or three dozen rare moths in a day, in a year's time Elnora had grown to be delighted with finding two or three. Big pursy caterpillars could not be picked from their favorite bushes, when there were no bushes. Dragonflies would not hover over dry places, and butterflies became scarce in proportion to the flowers.

Nature abhors a vacuum in the ecological as well as the physical sense. Sunlit voids created by forest clearing, prairie plowing, and wetland drainage were quickly filled by successional species of plants and animals, each in its own way attempting to heal the wounded landscape, and to staunch the outflow of water, soil, and nutrients—the lifeblood of an ecological community. At first native species that thrive in disturbance conditions—nature's "national guard"—created old-field communities and thickets of saplings while the settlers' backs were turned, as they cleared, plowed, or drained more land. Nature tried desperately to reclaim the lands we

Bison were among the first animals to be extirpated and were gone from Indiana by 1830. *Photo by Marion Jackson*

Early pioneer log cabin for a single family. Note froe-split clapboard roof, wooden guttering, rain barrel, and smokehouse for meat storage. Lincoln Boyhood National Memorial, Spencer County.   *Photo by Richard Fields*

Interior and furnishings of early log cabin.   *Photo by Marion Jackson*

humans temporarily "borrowed from her." But with continued cultivation over longer periods, the seed bank capital and energy reserves of native species were quickly overdrawn and expended, creating opportunities for invasion by alien species of plants and animals.

Known popularly as weeds and pests, most of these exotic species had harried the settlers' ancestors for generations in Britain or Germany, before they arrived, uninvited, in the New World. No doubt pioneer farmers viewed these aggressive competitors for "their" landscape with anathema equal to what Native Americans must have felt toward the invading European settlers who quickly displaced the Indian. Today most of the Indiana landscape is covered by populations of exotic species, either cultivated, domesticated, or weedy. Meanwhile our dedicated state nature preserves devoted to native wild nature cover less total land than do the state's manicured golf courses.

Today the twin processes of development and urbanization likely pose greater threats to the remaining natural diversity of Indiana than do agricultural practices. Development of open land for residential, business, industrial, and transportation purposes became a major enterprise around the turn of the twentieth century and has since escalated. Frederick Simpich, in a 1936 article in *National Geographic* magazine that focused on Indiana, described these processes by explaining how Gary was built in 1906 in the most botanically rich section of the state: "Gary rose instantaneously. It grew so fast that families moved into homes 24 hours after work started on them. To make lawns and gardens on the sand wastes, trainloads of black dirt were hauled in; grown trees were brought and planted."

So we had come full circle in little more than a century—from hacking roads along deer trails to planting large shade trees in the lawns of instant housing projects. In the words of Robert Petty, "What irony, the sons of the world's greatest axemen planting tree seedlings in the shadow of stumps five feet across." Perhaps a city should be defined as a place where they cut down all the trees, then name the streets after them.

THE REMNANTS

Although the state's boundaries are still the same, the nature of its life and landscape has changed drastically in the past two centuries. But vestiges of "the Indiana that was" did, and still do, survive the

Cabin door and latch string, which was "not always out."
Photo by Richard Fields

"civilizing" processes which continue to the present, processes which have converted more than 60 percent of the 36,000 square miles to cropland, another 15 percent to managed forests, and much of the remainder to the "crystallized landscapes" of our cities, towns, and transportation corridors. Curiously, some of our best and most diverse natural remnants escaped the heaviest hand of development and still lie in the very shadows of industrialized Gary and its neighboring towns.

Today much less than 1 percent of the state remains in high-quality natural area. It is indeed sobering to realize that of the 20 million acres of original primeval forest that once occurred in Indiana—nearly enough to encircle the world one and a quarter times as a mile-wide band—today scarcely enough remains of high-quality old-growth forest in private ownership to encompass the Indianapolis Motor Speedway at the same one-mile width.

But a truly surprising diversity of species, habitats, and natural features that are remnants of the original Indiana wilderness still exist. The description of what was, is, and still can be of natural Indiana is the subject of this book. Let the several authors tell you their own absorbing stories of their portion of *The Natural Heritage of Indiana*.

For Genesis County has no surveyed boundaries in time or space . . . it holds within itself both fantasy and truth. Hunt for it in Indiana not to find it, but find instead the delights of the searchers, and if in the search you find yourself, you will solve the riddle of Genesis County.

—*Lynn Doyle, age 18,* The Riddle of Genesis County (1958)

Part 1: The Indiana Landscape

Honeycomb Rock at Pine Hills Nature Preserve in Montgomery County was exposed by rapid downcutting through Pennsylvanian-age sandstone by Indian Creek as it carried glacial meltwater. *Photo by Lee Casebere*

The Terrain and Its Origin

1. Of Time, Rocks, and Ancient Life: Bedrock Geology

Robert C. Howe

Each grain of sand, each minute crystal in the rocks about us is a tiny clock, ticking off the years since it was formed.

—*Patrick M. Hurley,* How Old Is the Earth? *(1959)*

The Earth is very, very old—ancient almost beyond human comprehension. Compare the age of the oldest person you have ever known—barely more than a century—to the antiquity of the oldest rocks on our planet. Even the period since the beginning of civilization some 6,000 years ago is an eyeblink with respect to geologic time, being just slightly more than 1 percent of 1 percent of 1 percent of the age of the Earth.

Indiana's rocks and the fossils of organisms they contain are "textbooks" of Earth's history. What fascinating stories they have to tell. They allow our minds to take us back to ancient times when beautiful corals built limestone reefs in shark-infested seas which covered what is now Indiana; and when lush tropical vegetation that had grown in primeval swamps became compressed into the coal seams of the southwestern part of the state.

INDIANA'S GEOLOGIC SETTING

Have you ever seriously considered what is beneath the cities, farmland, and forests that cover most of our landscape? The answer is soils, sediments, and rocks. Indiana's soils, on which we depend heavily for crop production, rarely exceed a few feet in thickness. Sediments may be more than 400 feet thick, but in most areas they are much less. Bedrock lies below the soils or sediments except where it is exposed at the surface, such as the steep and beautiful sandstone cliffs along Sugar Creek Valley, or at many locations in the hill country of southern Indiana. This bedrock foundation is considerably thicker than the soils or sediments, being measured in thousands of feet or even miles.

Our soils formed in place by the weathering of sediments or bedrock. Sediments were carried to their present locations by the action of wind, water, or glacial ice. Nearly all of Indiana's bedrock which is at or close to the surface is sedimentary rock which was derived by the consolidation of ancient sands, silts, and clays, after deposition by streams or ocean currents 300 to 450 million years ago. In contrast, most places in the world are underlain by much younger rocks. Indiana's rocks are relatively old because our landscape has been above sea level for millions of years, thereby permitting erosion to remove younger rocks that formerly existed.

I saw Eternity the other night
Like a great ring of pure and endless light,
All calm, as it was bright;
And round beneath it, Time in hours, days, years,
Driv'n by the spheres
Like vast shadow mov'd; in which the world
And all her train were hurled.

—*Henry Vaughan,* The World

Planet Earth's approximately 4.6-billion-year-old history can be divided into two vast periods of time—the Precambrian and Phanerozoic eons. Representing about 88 percent of Earth's history, the lengthy Precambrian spans from Earth's beginning to 570 million years ago. During this enormous period of time, life began on Earth, and eventually some types of organisms developed the ability to fix carbon dioxide by photosynthesis. By this process the Earth's carbon dioxide–rich atmosphere was transformed into an oxygen-rich atmosphere that could support more active forms of life. Our record of these early life forms is exceedingly poor because no Precambrian organisms had mineralized shells or skeletons, hence they produced relatively few fossils.

The Phanerozoic eon includes only the last one-eighth of Earth's history, but its story is better known because starting about 570 million years ago (mya) many organisms began secreting mineralized hard parts, which greatly increased their chances of being fossilized. On the basis of differences in fossils, this eon is subdivided into three major time units—the Paleozoic (ancient life), the Mesozoic (middle life), and the Cenozoic (recent life) eras. Major extinctions of life mark the ends of both the Paleozoic and the Mesozoic.

The Paleozoic, which lasted some 325 million years, from 570 to 245 mya, is characterized by a wide variety of invertebrate animals and the development of land plants. Fish also appeared, one type of which gave rise to the amphibians, some groups of which, in turn, evolved into reptiles later in the era.

The Mesozoic era lasted about 180 million years, from 245 to 66 mya. It is often referred to as the Age of Dinosaurs or the Age of Reptiles. During the early Mesozoic, both birds and mammals evolved from reptiles.

The Cenozoic era began about 66 mya and continues to the present. It is widely known as the Age of Mammals, but many other kinds of organisms such as flowering plants have been common

EON	ERA	SELECTED EVENTS	MILLIONS OF YEARS B.P.
PHANEROZOIC	CENOZOIC	MAMMALS BECOME DOMINANT	66
PHANEROZOIC	MESOZOIC	REPTILES ARE DOMINANT BIRDS FIRST APPEAR MAMMALS FIRST APPEAR	245
PHANEROZOIC	PALEOZOIC	VERTEBRATES EVOLVE FROM FISH TO AMPHIBIANS TO REPTILES INVERTEBRATES ARE COMMON	570
PRECAMBRIAN	PROTEROZOIC	MULTICELLULAR ORGANISMS FIRST APPEAR BUT FOSSILS ARE RARE OXIDIZING ATMOSPHERE DEVELOPS	2,500
PRECAMBRIAN	ARCHEOZOIC	OLDEST KNOWN FOSSILS FIRST APPEAR	3,500
PRECAMBRIAN	AZOIC	OLDEST EARTH ROCKS ARE 4,000 MILLION YEARS OLD EARTH FORMS WITHIN SOLAR NEBULA	4,600

Geologic column depicting the total time scale from the origin of the earth to present time. Widths of eons and eras are proportional to the total time period.

Pompey's Pillar, a curious limestone bedrock feature located near Milhousen in Decatur County, was shaped by water erosion plus freezing and thawing of ice. *Photo courtesy of the Indiana Geological Survey*

throughout this era. By comparison, humans are relative latecomers, since fossils of the earliest humans are only about 4 million years old.

All of Indiana's bedrock at the surface or just beneath soil or sediments is Paleozoic in age. Precambrian rocks still exist, but they lie deeply buried beneath the Paleozoic rocks. In contrast, the Mesozoic record has been completely eroded from Indiana's landscape, and what little is left of the Cenozoic record consists entirely of sediments, most of which were deposited during the ice ages. Therefore, it is fruitless to search for fossil dinosaurs in Indiana even though these magnificent beasts roamed throughout the area during the Age of Reptiles. And if the ice ages had not left so much sediment in the state, fossil mammoths and mastodons would be much harder to find.

The Paleozoic era has been divided into seven units of time. These are, from oldest to youngest, the Cambrian, Ordovician, Silurian, Devonian, Mississippian, Pennsylvanian, and Permian periods. The first four are named after tribes or areas in Wales and England where rocks of those ages were first described. The Mississippian is named after the upper Mississippi River Valley, and the Pennsylvanian is named for the state. (In most other parts of the world, the Mississippian and Pennsylvanian are collectively referred to as the Carboniferous period because coal beds of those ages are widespread.) The Permian is named after the province of Perm in Russia.

Like Precambrian rocks, Indiana's Cambrian bedrock lies buried beneath younger rocks and is not exposed at the surface. Rocks of Permian age no longer exist in Indiana, having been removed by erosion. Bedrock units formed during each of the other five Paleozoic periods can be found exposed at the surface somewhere in Indiana; but in most regions they are covered by soil or sediments.

Throughout Paleozoic time, when much of Indiana's bedrock was deposited, what is now the North American continent straddled the equator. Paleomagnetic evidence indicates that where we live now was in the Southern Hemisphere in a latitudinal position similar to that of present-day Recife, Brazil. It was not until the time when dinosaurs reigned that the supercontinent called Gondwanaland broke up and the crustal plate which became North America, including Indiana, slowly drifted into the Northern Hemisphere. This northerly drift has continued into the Cenozoic, bringing the state to its present location. Our position is still changing because the North American crustal plate moves westward a few centimeters each year.

When Indiana lay near the equator during Paleozoic times, it had a climate far different from that of today. Average temperatures were considerably warmer, and much of the time the land that became our state was submerged beneath the ocean. Hurricanes rather than tornadoes affected the state's inhabitants, which were mostly tropical sea creatures. Life teemed in the shallow equatorial seas that alternately advanced and retreated across what is now Indiana. Corals and other creatures formed huge limestone reefs which have been exposed in quarries in various parts of the state.

> We need not be surprised if we learn from geology that the continents and oceans were not always placed where they are now, although the imagination may well be overpowered when it endeavors to contemplate the quantity of time required for such revolutions.
>
> —*Sir Charles Lyell,* The Student's Elements of Geology *(1882)*

Indiana's different geographic positions were the product of plate tectonics—the modern term for continental drift. The outer shell of the Earth is broken up into about 13 large tectonic plates. Indiana has been near the middle part of the North American Plate during all of Phanerozoic time; therefore, its plate tectonic setting has been one of relative quiescence in comparison to those of states (such as California) which are located on a plate margin where major earthquakes are frequent.

However, Indiana has been significantly affected by its proximity to the New Madrid (Missouri) Seismic Zone, which is located along a rift valley similar to a plate margin structure. The most devastating earthquakes in the Midwest in recent history occurred in 1811–12, when four major shocks of magnitude near 8.0 on the Richter Scale struck the New Madrid region. According to eyewitnesses, the extreme force of that temblor caused the Mississippi River to flow upstream temporarily, and opened a rift in the landscape of western Tennessee that is now filled by Reelfoot Lake. New evidence indicates that a 7.5 earthquake occurred near Vincennes about 5,000 years ago. A similar earthquake today would produce considerable damage to buildings in Indiana, especially in the southwestern part. Such a quake will happen eventually, but not necessarily soon.

Other tectonic features have had a more direct effect on Indiana than has the New Madrid Seismic Zone. In Paleozoic time, compressional stress in the Midwest bent the Earth's crust into broad folded structures called arches (or domes) and basins. As a result, Indiana's rocks were tilted a few degrees from their original essentially horizontal orientations. The geologic term for this tilt of bedrock layers

PERIOD	SELECTED EVENTS	MILLIONS OF YEARS B.P.
		245
PERMIAN	NO ROCKS OF THIS AGE HAVE BEEN FOUND IN INDIANA BECAUSE THEY HAVE BEEN ERODED AWAY NUMEROUS MARINE EXTINCTIONS MARK THE END OF THE PERIOD	
		286
PENNSYLVANIAN	REPTILES FIRST APPEAR IN FOSSIL RECORD COAL SWAMPS ARE WIDESPREAD	
		320
MISSISSIPPIAN	CRINOIDS FLOURISH	
		360
DEVONIAN	AMPHIBIANS FIRST APPEAR IN FOSSIL RECORD BRACHIOPODS ARE ESPECIALLY ABUNDANT	
		408
SILURIAN	PLANTS FIRST APPEAR ON LAND NUMEROUS CORAL REEFS IN INDIANA	
		438
ORDOVICIAN	INVERTEBRATES DIVERSIFY FISH FIRST APPEAR IN FOSSIL RECORD	
		505
CAMBRIAN	INDIANA WAS LAND UNTIL LATE IN THE PERIOD WHEN THE SEA INVADED TRILOBITES FLOURISH FOSSILS ARE COMMON FOR THE FIRST TIME	
		570

Geologic column of the geologic periods represented in Indiana with proportional time scale. Conditions and representative organisms are given.

is *dip.* Indiana's bedrock dips gently away from the Cincinnati and Kankakee arches and toward the Illinois and Michigan basins at inclinations of a few degrees or less, about the amount of tilt created by placing a glass marble under one edge of a sheet of plywood.

Erosion of these tilted rocks has resulted in a banded distribution of Indiana's bedrock, with older rocks being near the surface in arched areas and younger rocks nearest the basin centers. Because southeastern Indiana is close to the crest of the Cincinnati Arch and because the Kankakee Arch has not been as deeply eroded, the oldest bedrock exposed in Indiana is found in the southeastern corner of the state.

In contrast, the Evansville area is underlain by the youngest bedrock because it is near the center of the Illinois Basin. Consequently, a trip westward across southern Indiana affords travelers the opportunity to view almost a complete section of Indiana's Paleozoic bedrock from oldest to youngest along roadcuts, stream beds, and hillsides (see also chapter 3, "The View from the Window"). Near the Illinois border, a greater number of Paleozoic rock units are still preserved for geologists to explore; erosion has removed all but the oldest layers in eastern Indiana.

INDIANA'S ROCKS

And some rin up hill and down dale,
knapping the chunky stanes to pieces wi' hammers,
like sae many road makers run daft.
They say it is to see how the world was made.

—*Sir Walter Scott,* St. Ronan's Well *(1824)*

Much of Earth's history has been recorded in rocks. For example, when lava erupted from a volcano cools, the rock into which it solidifies is a record of that eruption. Rock produced in this manner is termed *igneous.* The only igneous bedrock in Indiana of Paleozoic age is some minor compacted volcanic ash, but many Precambrian rocks which underlie Indiana's Paleozoic section have an igneous origin.

As stated earlier, most of Indiana's Paleozoic bedrock is sedimentary. Sediments originate when an earlier landscape is weathered, eroded, and transported to a site of deposition. Most sedimentary rocks form when sediments that have been deposited in layers become compacted by the weight of overlying materials or cemented by groundwater.

Clay-sized sediments are the most common product of weathering and erosion; when compacted, they form shale. Other common sedimentary rocks produced by cementation of silt-sized particles and sand grains, respectively, are siltstone and sandstone. Limestone is formed when calcium-rich materials such as clamshells are cemented together or when calcium carbonate precipitates from water (such as when stalactites and stalagmites form in Indiana caves). Other examples of sedimentary rocks formed by chemical precipitation are evaporites such as salt and gypsum.

During Paleozoic time, streams and, at various times, ocean currents transported considerable clay and silt into what is now Indiana, where it came to rest on the ocean floor or, if the area was above sea level at the time, on an alluvial plain. Consolidation of these sediments produced the shales and siltstones we see today. Sands, which became sandstones, were similarly brought to Indiana but in smaller amounts.

Indiana is especially famous for its limestones, which were formed in the shallow, tropical marine environments. Some limestones were changed to dolomite as a result of having reacted chemically with magnesium-rich water following their deposition on the sea floor.

Close-up of sandstone cliff showing erosional detail. Cliff-dwelling plants and animals frequently colonize such rock crevices.
Photo by Richard Fields.

Metamorphic rocks form when preexisting sedimentary or igneous rocks are exposed to added heat, pressure, or the effects of hot fluids. Within Indiana's Paleozoic section, metamorphic rock is found in minor amounts, and only near Kentland, in Newton County. This unusual isolated occurrence may be the result of a meteoritic impact which caused localized intense fracturing and doming of the rocks. One rock unit was uplifted more than 2,000 feet above its expected position, and the doming created dips as great as 85°, in stark contrast to the almost horizontal dips of surrounding rocks.

INDIANA'S HISTORY AS INTERPRETED FROM ITS ROCKS AND FOSSILS

Except for the anomalous rocks near Kentland, Indiana's bedrock has been tilted only slightly since it was formed. None has been overturned. Therefore, at any location, the rocks are youngest at the surface and become progressively older with depth. A stratigraphic column is a diagram developed by geologists to show the relative ages and sequences of bedrock layers below a given landscape. Such a diagram for Indiana shows the oldest Precambrian rocks at the bottom of the right-hand side, whereas the youngest Pennsylvanian bedrock is shown near the top of the left-hand column. Each unit is younger than those below it and older than those above it. The following geologic history of Indiana begins with the oldest rocks.

Little is known about the Precambrian rocks of Indiana since they have been sampled at only 24 locations where boreholes have penetrated the thick Paleozoic bedrock cover. Most such holes are in northern Indiana along the Kankakee Arch, where the Precambrian rocks are relatively close to the surface (about 3,500 feet deep). To sample Precambrian rocks near Evansville would require a hole nearly 14,000 feet deep.

Igneous rocks, granite and basalt, are most common, but some

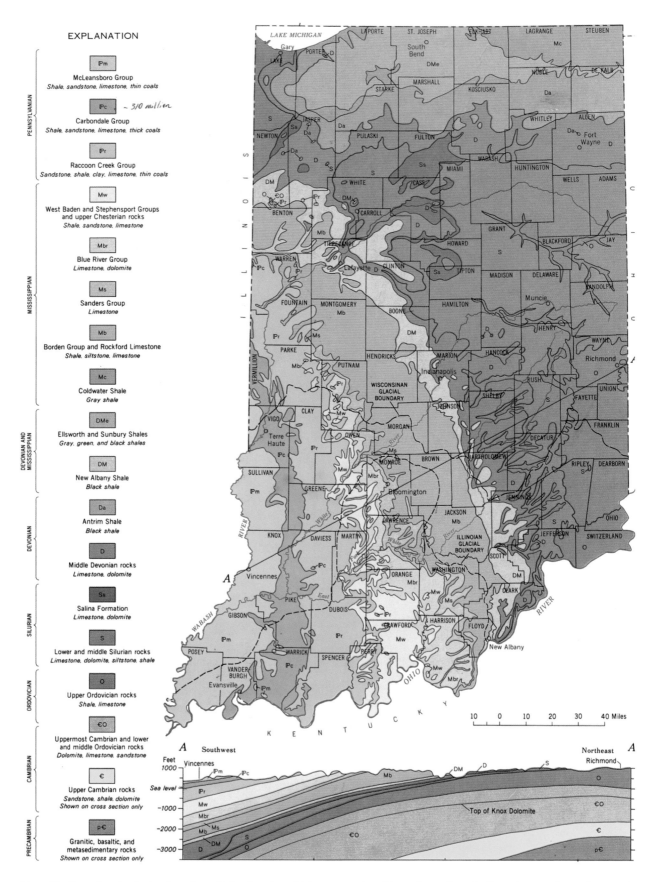

Map of Indiana showing bedrock geology. Bedrock units, which are more in evidence in southern Indiana, increase in age from west to east across the state. The bedrock of northern Indiana is largely obscured by glacial materials and soils.

Map courtesy of the Indiana Geological Survey

The Kentland Structural Anomaly in Newton County represents an isolated occurrence of very old Ordovician-age rocks which are surrounded by much younger strata. An ancient meteoritic impact is one explanation offered for this unusual geologic structure.   *Photo by Richard Fields*

Precambrian rocks are also of sedimentary or metamorphic origin. Our Precambrian granites are about 1.4 billion years old, and the basalts, which apparently formed from lava which flowed into ancient rift valleys, are about 1.1 billion years old. Paleomagnetic evidence suggests that what is now Indiana was located near the South Pole at that time. Indiana's late Precambrian history was obviously very different from that which followed.

> Little drops of water, little grains of sand,
> Make the mighty ocean and the pleasant land.
> So the little moments, humble though they be,
> Make the mighty ages of eternity.
>
> —*Julia A. Fletcher Carney*, Little Things (1845)

The oldest Paleozoic rocks beneath our state are sandstones of late Cambrian age which were derived from land areas in southern Canada. These rocks were laid down along the margin of an advancing sea that entered Indiana from the south and southwest. With time the sea became deeper, and finer sediments were deposited. Before the close of the period, deposition of limestone and dolomite predominated.

Indiana's Cambrian rocks become thicker from the northeast to the southwest, suggesting that either the sea was deepest in the Evansville area or that region was subsiding as deposition took place. Judging from localities in nearby states where rocks of Cambrian age are exposed, most of Indiana's rocks of this age were deposited in warm, shallow, marine water in which tropical organisms thrived. Fish had not yet appeared, but numerous invertebrate organisms lived on the Cambrian seafloor. Most notable were the trilobites (a group of extinct animals related to shrimp and crabs).

The sea continued its presence for several million years into Ordovician time, but waxed and waned in depth. An advance of the sea in the late Ordovician resulted in numerous limestones interbedded with shales being deposited across Indiana in the shallow, tropical marine environment. The shallowest deposition was in southeastern Indiana because of arching in the Cincinnati area.

The late Ordovician sea was loaded with invertebrate organisms (and fish) which left billions of shells and skeletons in Indiana's rocks. Especially common Ordovician fossils in our state are brachiopods and bryozoans. Brachiopods are similar to clams, and bryozoans superficially resemble corals. Trilobites, which are abundant in certain layers, become the prized possessions of avid fossil hunters who search roadcuts in Dearborn and Ripley counties, especially.

The Silurian period in Indiana was a time when reefs flourished. Following a minor regression at the end of Ordovician time, the tropical ocean returned to the shallow marine environment, which fostered the growth of coral animals and other reef-building organisms such as the stromatoporoids (extinct sponge-like organisms). Fossils of this period are generally of poorer quality than those of other periods because many of the Silurian limestone rocks turned to dolomite following their deposition.

In addition to numerous isolated reefs, two extensive carbonate banks developed under Indiana. One bank is well exposed in quarries near Fort Wayne, while the other lies buried beneath Devonian and younger rocks in the Terre Haute area. Regression of the sea from most of Indiana at the end of Silurian time killed these reefs, but coral animals returned to the state in early Devonian time.

A world-famous coral deposit of Devonian age is exposed at the Falls of the Ohio River near Jeffersonville, Indiana. For nearly 200 years, scientists have collected more than 600 fossil species from the rock units at that site, now a national natural landmark and an

Reef-forming marine organisms produced thick limestone beds under what is now Indiana during Silurian time. Such deposits are often quarried for economic use, as at Lapel, Madison County, shown here. *Photo courtesy of the Indiana Geological Survey*

Indiana state park. Especially abundant near the base of the falls is the solitary coral *Siphonophrentis elata*.

> The organized Fossils (which might be called the antiquities of Nature), and their localities also, may be understood by all, even the most illiterate: for they are so fixed in the earth as not to be mistaken.
>
> —*William Smith, Surveyor (1796), in Longwell and Flint,* Physical Geology (1955)

The end of Devonian time and the beginning of the Mississippian are marked by the deposition of New Albany shale. These black marine sediments formed from muds that entered Indiana from the Appalachian area which had been uplifted earlier, then eroded. Relatively deep, stagnant water has been proposed for the environment during deposition of these shales because their fossils apparently swam or floated into the area of deposition, instead of having lived there on the seafloor at the time.

Later in early Mississippian time, after a brief period of erosion, submarine deltas were deposited from northeast to southwest across

Indiana. These deposits were succeeded by the accumulation of almost pure limestones, which in turn were followed by the deposition of carbonates, chert mixed with evaporites, and sandstones. Groundwater from the evaporites is the source of the sulfate in the mineral springs of the French Lick and West Baden areas.

Most of the Mississippian limestones are fossiliferous with crinoids (sea lilies), which are especially common in certain units. A world-famous location for collecting these fossils is an area near Crawfordsville, Indiana, where the Edwardsville Formation has yielded some of the best crinoid fossils ever found.

Prior to deposition of Pennsylvanian strata, the Mississippian and older rocks were uplifted, tilted, and differentially eroded to a maximum relief of about 300 feet by streams that flowed southwesterly across Indiana.

Indiana's Pennsylvanian rocks, like those of late Mississippian age, show evidence of cycles of deposition. However, in contrast to the Mississippian (and older Paleozoic) rocks, which originated in oceans, most Pennsylvanian rock units were deposited in terrestrial environments. Interbedded layers of shale, sandstone, coal, and limestone characterize the sequence. Throughout Pennsylvanian time, sands, silts, and clays were brought to Indiana from the northeast, whereas limestones formed when the ocean entered the state occasionally from the southwest.

The face of places, and their forms decay;
And that is solid earth, that once was sea;
Seas, in their turn, retreating from the shore,
Make solid land, what ocean was before.
　　　　—*Ovid (43* B.C.–A.D. *18)*, Metamorphoses *XV*

Adjacent to the streams, swamps developed in which decaying vegetation accumulated to great thicknesses. The vegetation eventually was compressed and converted to coal. The coal measures of Vigo and Sullivan counties are famous for their Pennsylvanian-age plant fossils embedded in ironstone nodules. These nodules can be found in several huge "gob" piles of Pennsylvanian rocks left by mining activity prior to the passage of reclamation laws, which now require the return of the landscape to nearly its original condition. Since nodules resist weathering, they would accumulate on the surface from the erosion of finer spoil materials if fossil hunters did not annually add them to their collections. A well-aimed strike with a geologist's hammer can split a nodule open, revealing its delicate plant specimen within (see also chapter 33, "The Seed Strategy").

In Parke County, almost complete fossils of sharks have been recovered from the Linton Formation of Pennsylvanian age. Apparently these remains accumulated on the bottom of an ancient lagoon along the margin of the ocean.

Indiana is a rich source of fossils and rock curiosities. *Left:* Devonian solitary coral from the Falls of the Ohio near Jeffersonville. *Top center:* Pennsylvanian plant fossil in ironstone nodule from a surface mine near Terre Haute. *Bottom center:* Half of a Mississippian geode from Harrodsburg Limestone near Bloomington, with beautiful quartz crystal interior displayed. *Right:* Exquisite Mississippian crinoid from the Edwardsville Formation near Crawfordsville.
Photo by Tony Brentlinger, Indiana State University Audio-Visual Center

Of Time, Rocks, and Ancient Life / 11

The Pennsylvanian was the period in which some amphibians gave rise to reptiles, freeing the latter from the necessity of laying their eggs in water; however, to date, only a few amphibian and reptile footprints have been found in Indiana's rocks of this age.

When you were a tadpole and I was a fish,
In the Paleozoic time
And side by side in the sluggish tide
We sprawled in the ooze and slime.

—*Langdon Smith*, Evolution (1895)

Following deposition of the Pennsylvanian rocks, once again Indiana was tilted and eroded, likely the result of plate convergence along the eastern edge of North America, which also folded the Appalachian Mountains. This bending of the crust in Indiana caused the Pennsylvanian rocks to dip toward the Michigan and Illinois basins and away from the Cincinnati and Kankakee arches. Subsequent erosion stripped the Pennsylvanian rocks (and some of the older rocks) from the crests of the arches, creating the pattern of bedrock geology present today. Because erosion exposed rocks of differing resistances to weathering, the surface on which the late Cenozoic Ice Age sediments were deposited was not level, but had a total relief across the state of about 700 feet.

Most other aspects of Indiana's post-Pennsylvanian history are more difficult to determine; but without much doubt, Indiana was above sea level during most of that time. No Permian or Mesozoic rocks have been found in the state except those "recently" brought from Michigan by advancing glaciers. Ice Age materials represent nearly all of Indiana's Cenozoic deposits. Therefore, Permian, Mesozoic, and most of the Cenozoic histories of Indiana are based on conjecture, but we can be fairly sure about some of the post-Pennsylvanian and pre–Ice Age events in Indiana.

In Mesozoic time, dinosaurs and many other reptiles inhabited the state. Mammals were also present but were primitive, small, and largely nocturnal; some may have been similar to today's opossum. Birds and pterosaurs (flying reptiles) invaded the skies. Before the end of the era, flowering plants replaced the gymnosperms (conifers and related species) as the dominant vegetation.

A tremendous catastrophe (probably caused by a huge meteoritic impact) at the end of Mesozoic time greatly affected the entire Earth by causing the extinction of the last of the dinosaurs and many other species of organisms. Because such high mountain ranges as the Rockies, Andes, Alps, and Himalayas had not been uplifted by the time Indiana had drifted almost to its current latitudinal position, its temperatures were considerably warmer than those of today.

During the Cenozoic, Indiana (and the world) experienced an overall steady decline in temperatures which culminated in the ice ages in late Cenozoic time. Following the extinctions that mark the beginning of this era, mammals rapidly expanded in numbers and diversity and became the dominant terrestrial animals. The appearance of grasses in mid-Cenozoic time fostered the development of grazing animals. Humans first appeared on Earth prior to the beginning of the ice ages, but did not invade Indiana until about 12,000 to 15,000 years ago.

Many an Aeon moulded earth before her highest, man was born,
Many an Aeon too may pass when earth is manless and forlorn.

—*Alfred, Lord Tennyson*, Locksley Hall Sixty Years After

THE VALUE OF INDIANA'S ROCKS

Many of Indiana's rocks are or have been of economic value: a number are sources of oil or gas; others serve as building stone or as sources of crushed limestone for construction or agricultural purposes; certain units have yielded coal. An additional few have economic potential.

Because they are practically inaccessible, the Precambrian and Cambrian rocks are of minimal value, although some Cambrian units may eventually yield some petroleum. The first major discovery of petroleum in Indiana came in 1886 from strata just above the Cambrian rocks, when natural gas was recovered from the Ordovician-age Trenton limestone. The ensuing gas boom resulted in the development of the gigantic Trenton Gas Field, located along the crest of the Kankakee Arch in Grant County near Marion and Gas City.

Ordovician rocks exposed at the surface have little commercial value because individual layers tend to be relatively thin and interbedded with other kinds of rocks. In contrast, several of the Silurian and Devonian limestones have been quarried in southeastern Indiana as sources of aggregate or high-purity stone, and the Silurian-age Laurel and Louisville limestones have been used widely as dimension stones—curbs, for example.

The Silurian coral reefs of Indiana have been responsible for the development of compaction structures above them, which has allowed petroleum to collect in younger rocks. Oil and gas production from above the reefs has come mainly from Mississippian rocks, but some Devonian and Pennsylvanian reservoirs also have been tapped along a trend from Vermillion County south-southeast to Spencer County.

The New Albany shale, deposited in late Devonian and early Mississippian time, has the potential to become a significant source of oil. Initially it is most likely to be mined in Jackson, Scott, and Clark counties. However, oil prices will have to rise substantially to make this a reality. Ironically, Jackson, Scott, and Clark counties also have some of the highest radon levels in the state. Radon is released from the New Albany shales as uranium decays. Uranium content in the New Albany shales has been measured as high as 278 ppm, many times higher than normal levels for a marine shale.

Several limestone units of Mississippian age are quarried for crushed stone or cement; but the most famous rock unit in Indiana is the cream-colored Salem limestone, which has been extensively

Salem limestone deposits of Mississippian age yield some of the world's finest building stone from quarries in the Bedford-Bloomington area. Power saws cut huge blocks to shape to facilitate removal and further processing into dimension stone.   *Photo by Marion Jackson*

quarried near Bedford and Bloomington as dimension stone. Fourteen state capitols, including Indiana's, the Empire State Building, the Pentagon, the National Cathedral, and New York's Metropolitan Museum of Art are among the majestic buildings constructed from this valuable resource with its beautiful and unique fine-grained texture.

A magnified view of this stone reveals its delicate mosaic dominated by the spiral shells of a unicellular organism interlaced with stem segments of sea lilies and fragile trellises of bryozoans, among others. The uniformity of its color, texture, and composition throughout most of its 90-foot thickness makes it especially appealing to those in need of 50-ton blocks that could survive the rigors of weathering in the nation's capital.

The Mississippian Harrodsburg limestone is known to rock collectors for its abundance of geodes, whose interiors contain exquisite displays of mineral crystals. The geodes were formed by precipitation of minerals in cavities in the limestone as groundwater seeped through the rock. Gypsum has been mined from the St. Louis limestone near Shoals, Indiana. The Mississippian limestones are also notable for the sinkhole (karst) topography and the caves that have developed on and within them.

The wedge of Pennsylvanian rocks found in the southwest corner of Indiana is host to the state's most important geologic resource. Nearly 40 million tons of coal are produced annually from this erosional remnant, which originally extended across the entire state. More than eight different coal beds have been mined in this area, either at the surface or underground. Most production has come from Vigo, Clay, Sullivan, Greene, Pike, and Warrick counties, where seams are within 50 feet of the surface.

Today surface mines account for most of the coal that is extracted, but in the past numerous mine shafts were dug into Indiana's Pennsylvanian rocks. The effects of this older mining period are still being felt. Occasionally the surface of the ground collapses into one of the old mines. Also, chemical decomposition of iron pyrite (fool's gold) in the gob piles may produce sulfuric acid stream drainage in the vicinity of the mine sites.

Indiana's bedrock is more than just a source of fantastic fossils. Its coal is used to produce nearly all of our electricity, its yield of

Southwestern Indiana is widely underlain by coal-rich Pennsylvanian-age deposits, which are now recovered by surface mining. The large dragline removes the overburden, whereas the small crane recovers the coal seam. *Photo by Marion Jackson*

petroleum helps to power our automobiles, and many of its limestone units have been quarried for construction or agricultural purposes. Its varied resistance to weathering and erosion has contributed to the beauty of the landscape in the southern part of the state. But perhaps the greatest benefit provided by a study of Indiana's bedrock is an increased awareness of some of the many marvelous events that, over enormous periods of time, have happened in this part of the world to bring us to the present.

The earth is not finished, but is now being, and will forevermore be re-made.
—*C. R. Van Hise (1898)*

Matanuska Glacier, Alaska, from near the snout, where meltback approximates advance rate. Lobes of glacial advances into Indiana during the Pleistocene Ice Age may have looked and behaved much like Matanuska Glacier today.   *Photo by Marion Jackson*

2. Indiana on Ice: The Late Tertiary and Ice Age History of Indiana Landscapes

Wilton N. Melhorn

The latest epoch of geologic history has witnessed changes in the physical aspect of the Earth and in the distribution of animals and plants on the Earth's surface such as are not recorded in any earlier span of time of comparable length.

—*Richard Foster Flint,* Glacial and Pleistocene Geology *(1957)*

RELICS OF THE TERTIARY

After the Age of Dinosaurs ended with a bang about 65 million years ago, at the close of the Cretaceous period of geologic time, terrestrial climates began to slowly cool. The downhill climatic spiral that culminated in the Great Ice Age had begun.

Indiana presumably was not high above sea level, during either the Cretaceous or the Tertiary period that followed. Few geological deposits and no fossils of those ages are represented here, so only a nebulous record remains to tell us anything about what happened during that lengthy span of years. The evidence available exists principally as locally restricted, aberrant deposits of sand, silt, and clay, as typified by the Ohio River Formation in Harrison County, southern Indiana.

However, scattered widely elsewhere across the state are the "gravels," a class of rounded, polished, clear quartz or chert pebbles, generally about the size of a small human fingernail. These gravels occur locally in thin layers, only one or two pebbles thick; as hard, iron-cemented clumps (conglomerate); or as isolated pebbles that look like lag deposits left behind by ancient streams that coursed for millions of years across the Indiana landscape. The gravel source is unknown, but the fact that these littered the surface before the glaciers came seems irrefutable, as they are found mixed into glacial deposits in most soybean or corn fields across the state. These gravels today remain one of the great mysteries of midwestern geology, but they seem to represent the best remaining evidence of Tertiary deposits that perhaps once covered Indiana.

Climatic deterioration finally reached a critical threshold, perhaps 2 to 2.5 million years ago, bringing on the geologic time period called the Pleistocene epoch, or Great Ice Age. The most ancient imprint comes from along the Missouri River in western Iowa, where ash fall from a now-extinct volcano in Yellowstone National Park, dated by radiometrics as 2.2 million years old, fell on top of yet older glacial deposits already in place. Unfortunately, this ash fall apparently did not reach as far east as Indiana. Thus, the oldest Pleistocene record we have in Indiana dates back more than 700,000 years.

How do we know this number? Well, it is established that throughout geologic history, Earth's magnetic field has reversed, almost instantaneously, a number of times. Thus, we know that establishment of the present north magnetic pole in the Arctic regions happened during the last major flip of this polarity about 700,000 years ago. However, magnetic minerals, such as iron, in any older deposits will retain the polarity imprint that existed at the time of deposition. Thus, when we find, at the very base of glacial sediments in the Wabash Valley and elsewhere, a strange melange of patchy, usually reddish, silty or clayey sands of reversed polarity, we know that these were laid down more than 700,000 years ago!

CAUSES OF GLACIATION

A glacier is a large mass of ice made up of recrystallized snow and refrozen meltwater that lies primarily on land and that moves or has moved. Glaciers develop wherever snow accumulates faster than it melts.

—*William J. Wayne, "Ice and Land," in* Natural Features of Indiana *(1966)*

Recognition of the climatic threshold that triggered the Pleistocene Ice Age goes back 150 years to the time when the Theory of Continental Glaciation first was proposed in Europe. Although the idea has been almost universally accepted for more than a century, glacialists still lack a singular, unified theory to explain why vast ice sheets, formed on continents by moving oceanic waters onto land in the form of snow, have occurred periodically on Earth's surface in the past. All that is certain is that glaciation, of continental proportions, fundamentally is a result of intermediate to long-term climatic trends within the atmosphere and the oceans.

The proposed causes group broadly into six categories, which range in scale from cosmic down to purely terrestrial, and which likely work in harmony, in some sort of complex conjunction, to produce the observed results:

Variations in rate or amount of solar emissions reaching Earth (sunspot cycles)

Interference, in space, by clouds of dust or gases (cosmic or interplanetary)

Geometric variations, with time, of Earth's orbital motions, axial tilting, etc. (planetary)

Variation in emission-absorption rates of energy at the Earth's surface (atmospheric, biotic)

Changes in heights and/or positions of continents, over time, caused by vertical adjustments of Earth's crust, accompanied perhaps by increased volcanic activity, or by lateral crustal movements (plate tectonics, continental drift)

Changes in oceanic currents and atmospheric circulation patterns, such as storm tracks, probably in response to geologic causes (oceanographic, meteorologic)

Whatever combination is invoked, some effect is felt everywhere, even in Indiana. Elsewhere, at higher latitudes or greater altitudes, the basic requirement for glacial growth is that the balance between precipitation as snow and melting from glacial ice is positive, wherein excess frozen precipitation is available for conversion to glacial ice by physical processes. Formerly we thought that this task took centuries, even millennia, to accomplish. Now, however, we no longer are so sure, as there is some evidence that the entire process, of either glacial buildup or melting, possibly can materialize within a few hundred, perhaps even a few score, years.

Glacial buildup and advances during the recent Pleistocene period were not the only time Planet Earth was exposed to the impact and

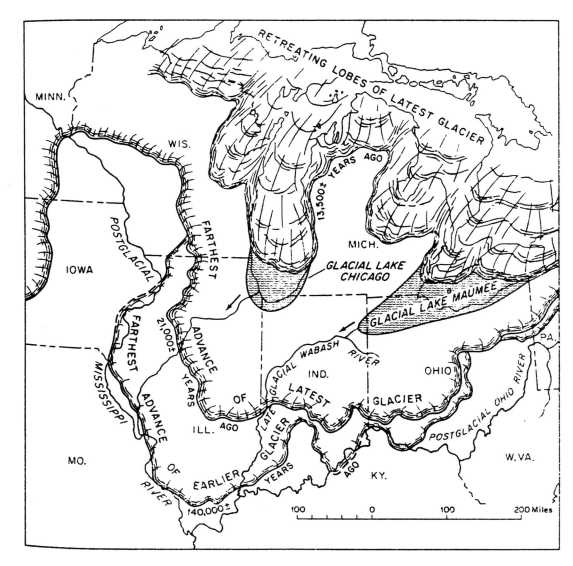

Map of Midwest showing the extent and the impact of glacial advances during successive periods, and including late-glacial lakes which extended beyond their present basins.   *After Shaver 1979*

changes wrought by continental glaciation. Evidence is well established that major glaciation occurred in some parts of the world during the Permian geological period (circa 250 million years ago), and even earlier in the Earth's history. However, Indiana was not subject to these earlier ice invasions because they came prior to continental breakup and subsequent continental shifting, when the state's position was more southerly and therefore not subject to the deteriorating climate conditions that trigger glacial buildup. Furthermore, no Permian-age deposits exist in Indiana, so even if the earlier ice event had occurred here, the corroborating evidence would have been lost.

SOME CLASSIC AND MODERN IDEAS OF GLACIATION

The first public proposal of the glacial theory came in Europe in 1821, when Indiana was still a rough, homespun frontier state. A Swiss civil engineer named Ignatz Venetz-Sitten read a paper before the learned Helvetic Society in Luzerne, proposing that glaciers of the Alps not only had been much larger in the past but had extended

far beyond their present (in 1821) limits. Of course, what was new to science was "old hat" to local farmers and milkmaids, who had known this for hundreds of years!

The word *moraine* for the pile of debris left behind where a former ice front was static (that is, in mass balance) comes, in fact, from the Latin or Roman *moranen* (stone wall), and long had been used by the peasants of the region. Although Venetz-Sitten's paper was the start of one of the fiercest geologic debates of the nineteenth century, argument ended rather abruptly when Louis Agassiz, fisheries biologist and prominent member of the Helvetic Society, declared himself a believer (like Saul on the Damascus Road?) and became a vocal and written champion of the glacial theory in 1836.

> At numerous places in Indiana, vast "flocks and huddles" of these imperishable boulders are lying exposed. . . . It is not uncommon to find these polished fragments shot through with dykes of quartz and feldspar . . . clusters of regular quartz crystals appear in cavities of the stone shining like jewels in a rough but picturesque setting.
>
> —*S. S. Gorby*, 17th Annual Geological Report *(1891)*

At the same time, during the years 1836 and 1837, renowned geologist David Dale Owen of New Harmony became our first state geologist and was busy exploring the rocks of the state. Because news of the glacial theory took a while to reach the American frontier, Owen continued to support the traditional explanation for unexplained cumulations of clay, stones, and boulders far from any reasonable source. This explanation was based on the biblical dogma of the Mosaic flood, or Deluge.

Although the Deluge idea later was modified to include the idea that icebergs in the universal ocean carried or "drifted" huge boulders in flood waters for hundreds of miles to their present site, even this modified theory soon also became untenable. This theory did, however, leave us with that marvelous and commonly used generic term *glacial drift,* which is especially useful as a wastebasket into which all glacial deposits can be tossed, irrespective of origin. The term has maximum utility when the precise process a glacier used to unburden its contained debris load is unknown!

Thus Owen was cautious, though his later writings suggest that he leaned in the direction of glacial theory advocacy. Equally clear is that his brother and colleague Richard Owen supported the glacial theory in the early 1860s. There seems to be absolutely no dissenting opinion about glacial theory after the early 1880s, when the matter was essentially terminated by the publication in 1883 of T. C. Chamberlin's great work on terminal moraines.

HOW GLACIERS ACT

Today, only the eastern Antarctic continent and Greenland have glaciers of true continental scale, big enough and thick enough to tempt a comparison with vanished Ice Age glaciers of the central United States. Realistically, though, any comparison abruptly pales. First, modern ice sheets lie at high latitudes, not the mid-latitude position of Indiana and other states of the Ohio Valley region. Second, present ice caps rest on high ground, plateaus generally ringed by bounding mountains which are partly or totally submerged beneath ice as much as 7,500 feet thick.

A glacier by definition is just a special kind of rock, composed primarily of a single mineral (ice). Scattered throughout the ice in varying abundance may be rock flours (minute particles), grains, pebbles, cobbles, and boulders of varying types, much like raisins scattered in a box of breakfast cereal. How, then, *do* glaciers move or flow?

From the earliest days of glacial study, there was abundant evidence that glaciers, unlike water, could move and had moved uphill, over and around obstacles in the line of flow. This movement, or flow, has two components, *internal deformation* and *basal sliding.* When ice thickness reaches some critical point, internal stress increases, and ice is strained and slowly deforms. At this time, basal creep or sliding begins in the lower part of the mass. Imagine a set of stacked ice cubes, or even something thin, like a deck of playing cards. If no lateral barrier exists, increased pressure from above causes outward movement of the cubes or cards. In glaciers, such movement may be enhanced by the tendency of layers of ice crystals to orient parallel to the direction of flow. The term *extrusion flow* is sometimes used for this "squeezed toothpaste" mode of ice movement.

Two conditions greatly enhance basal sliding. First, also a result of deformation, is the presence of a thin layer of liquid water at the ice sole (base). Second, if existing terrain at any point around a building glacial dome slopes away, or downhill, from the ice mass, then gravity becomes an ally of movement.

Because the ice domes, which seem to have originated some hundreds of miles away in Canada, always were on higher ground

than any point in our state, gravity flow alone made outward movement of ice across Indiana pretty much inevitable. But why did our earlier glaciers stop at about the latitude of the present Ohio River Valley? Well, they simply had come a long way from home, were pooped out, and were rapidly melting. When the mass balance between new ice and the rate of melting became negative because of warming climate, the glacier shrank and eventually disappeared.

> Facing the driven ice
> Of an old storm
> That blows as ever it has blown
> Against imperishable stone.
> —*Mark Van Doren,* The Difference

Later Indiana glaciers did not move so far south; obviously, a null mass balance was reached farther north! Furthermore, this ice seems to have been more effectively stopped by the Knobstone Escarpment, or "Knobs," in central and southern Indiana. If only gravity flow was involved, then earlier ice could not have flowed so easily uphill; probably internal shearing actively promoted a "stacking" effect of ice slabs, so that height disadvantages were overcome and the glacier "ramped up" over obstacles perhaps higher than the original ice surface. In this way, ice probably reached a point only four or five miles north of downtown Bloomington, for there is an abundance of badly weathered, arguably ancient glacial sediments in the area.

When W. J. Wayne wrote on this topic nearly three decades ago, perceptions of how glaciers moved, melted, and left a debris record of their passage differed substantially from what we think today. The original, classic concept of a glacier as a thick, slow-moving ice mass moving ponderously but implacably across the landscape (hence the phrase "with glacial speed") has been replaced by modern interpre-

Other glacial signatures are striations (scratch marks) on rock surfaces. The orientation of such indentations marks the direction of glacial flow.
Photo by Wilton N. Melhorn

tations of field evidence of topography and character of glacial deposits in the lower Great Lakes region. We now think that at least the most recent incursions of ice came as quick-hitting *surges* or *ice streams,* which did not cover the landscape for a long time. These ice streams moved rapidly as relatively thin ice *tongues,* which advanced, stagnated, and quickly melted in place. Some researchers hold that this ice likely was not more than a thousand or so feet thick, at least in west-central Indiana, where an ice tongue moved more than 200 miles westward from the Erie basin in about 600 years, but along a front no more than 50 miles wide!

There is considerable evidence to support this latter interpretation. First, most of glaciated Indiana lacks the long, massive lines, ramparts, or debris zones called moraines, traditionally thought to mark lengthy still-stands of ice in a zone where mass balance equilibrium persisted for many years. Only in far northwestern Indiana (the Valparaiso Moraine), the more or less time-equivalent Fort Wayne Moraine in the northeast, or in a few other places, such as around Culver, is there any textbook-style, massive moraine formed by an ice front in equilibrium.

Second, all across Indiana, especially south of the Wabash Valley, the landscape shows clear signs of such rapid, in-place melting of dead or stagnant ice. The primary indication is the broad expanses of so-called *ground moraine* in the state, gently rolling surfaces of only minor relief, characterized by abundant depressions and organic deposits in small hollows originally formed by melting blocks of ice. This is evidenced in the landscape of Clinton, Boone, Tipton, and Howard counties, for example, and south and east of Lafayette, where there are numerous *crevasse fillings* (meltwater debris deposited in natural cracks or joints in dead ice). Many other evidences of massive meltdown and rapid outflow of meltwaters exist, such as abundant *outwash fans* and *aprons, kames,* remnant *ice-walled lake plains* in Clinton County, and even a few *esker*-like (subterranean ice tunnel) deposits in Delaware County near Muncie, north of New Castle, and in Montgomery County.

Finally, there is finite evidence from radiocarbon dates. A "grounded" yet areally extensive ice sheet, melting irregularly, would be margined by hardy vegetation that rapidly encroaches around each ice block. Thus, dead organic debris from this vegetation, no matter where found in Indiana, should yield similar age dates. That is precisely what one sees; whether from the glacial terminus near Plainfield, south of Indianapolis, from Greencastle, near Lafayette, Marion, or Fort Wayne, most radiocarbon dates fall within a span of about 3,000 years, a mere blip in the glacial time scale described in the next section.

INDIANA ICE AGE CHRONOLOGY:
WHAT, WHEN, WHERE?

During the Pleistocene Epoch, glacial ice extended into Indiana at least three times. Each of the cold periods was followed by a warmer interglacial episode, during which the glaciers melted. The total effect of these several glaciations on the landscape and resources of northern Indiana . . . was vast.

—*William J. Wayne, "Ice and Land," in* Natural Features of Indiana *(1966)*

Within about 30 years after Venetz-Sitten, Agassiz, and others first outlined the theory of glaciation, attention turned to Ice Age history. Extensive field work, especially in eastern and central North America and Europe, focused on recognition and mapping of terrestrial glacial features, particularly landforms, and then putting them, by age, into what we call a *stratigraphic sequence.*

Early midwestern work, such as that of Chamberlin in 1883, concentrated on mapping the distribution of landforms such as moraines, erratic boulders, etc. Later, examination of records from dug wells revealed that glacial drift deposits were commonly separated by interbedded soils, organic zones, even "buried forests." Clearly this was evidence of glacial cyclicity, and gradually the concept of multiple glacial and interglacial stages emerged. Glacialists recognized eventually that Pleistocene glaciers globally had covered, at some time or another, nearly 27 million square kilometers, including more than a third of the North American continent.

Glacialists mapping the distribution of terminal moraines and by correlation (matching deposits between sites) eventually revealed at least four major episodes of Ice Age glaciation in North America. The same number was found independently in Europe. Following each glacial episode, during a time called an interglacial, the ice receded or disappeared as the climate warmed. The four glacial stages—traditionally listed as Nebraskan, Kansan, Illinoian, and Wisconsinan—were named for the states representing the area where those deposits presumably were best exposed; the interglacials were named for localities of well-exposed interglacial soils and other deposits.

It is not definitely known whether the Nebraskan stage ever affected Indiana directly. Presumably, the oldest glacial deposit in the state is in Fayette County, where magnetically reversed clays suggest that the glacial till below them is from a "pre-Kansan" (Nebraskan?) glaciation much older than 700,000 years. Knowledge is also limited about the activity in the state of the Kansan ice sheets, which waxed and waned in an apparently complex manner. Deposits earlier identified as "Kansan," such as clays at the Cagle's Mill spillway in Owen County and at Lake Lemon north of Bloomington, now are known to be magnetically normal, and thus younger than once supposed. At the moment, the oldest event for which definite deposits exist may be the Wilshire ice (named for Wilshire, Ohio), which probably covered at most no more than the northeastern quarter of the state. Somewhat later, glaciers from the northwest deposited tills in Warren and Vermillion counties in west-central Indiana. In succession, there then followed the Hillery Till, whose contained pebbles suggest a northeast source (perhaps from the Michigan Basin). Presumably a concluding "Kansan" event was deposition of the Tilton/Brookston Till, when as much as two-thirds of the state could have been covered by ice.

The classical Kansan stage was followed by the long "mid-Pleistocene summer," the Yarmouth Interglacial. No precise estimate of duration of the Yarmouth is available, though the figure of 200,000 years often is used. Yarmouthian climate was relatively mild, much like that of today. The effects of those conditions are preserved in a few places as well-developed soils formed on the old Kansan tills. W. J. Wayne noted that lime (calcium carbonate) and other solubles have been leached from these soils to a depth of 9 to 12 feet. Clearly this indicates long-duration weathering.

About 220,000 years ago the ice returned, this time as the Illinoian-stage glacier. In the state of Illinois, several substages of this event have been identified. The picture is less clear in Indiana; enigmatic evidence comes from west-central Indiana, where glacial tills of presumed early Illinoian age have been identified in Warren and Carroll counties.

The dominant feature of the Illinoian was the Vandalia event, or substage, when ice covered more than four-fifths of Indiana, with the glacier even advancing in a few places to south of the present Ohio River. Vandalia deposits are at the ground surface across much of the southern part of the state. These deposits normally are brown (from total oxidation of contained iron) and tend to be deeply gullied,

GLACIAL CHRONOLOGY – MIDWESTERN U.S.A.

| HOLOCENE EPOCH | (0–10,000 YEARS AGO) |

PLEISTOCENE EPOCH	WISCONSINAN GLACIAL	POST-TWO CREEKAN ADVANCE (8,000 – 11,000) *TWO CREEKAN RETREAT* (11,800 – 12,500) WOODFORDIAN ADVANCE (12,500 – 22,000) *FARMDALIAN RETREAT* (22,000 – 28,000) ALTONIAN ADVANCE (28,000 – 70,000+)

SANGAMONIAN INTERGLACIAL (70,000 – 110,000)
ILLINOIAN GLACIAL (110,000 – 220,000+)
YARMOUTHIAN INTERGLACIAL
KANSAN GLACIAL (± 700,000 YEARS)
AFTONIAN INTERGLACIAL (APPROXIMATELY 1 M.Y. AGO)
NEBRASKAN GLACIAL

———— 2-3 MILLION YEARS AGO ————

| PLIOCENE EPOCH | |

Glacial history column outlining the glacial stages and their associated deposits.

eroded, and leached. The "break" between characteristic Illinoian and younger Wisconsinan-age deposits to the north is seen better from the air than from the ground.

The Illinoian drift district seems to lack evidence of major glacial landforms. Much of the drift is loose-textured and sandy, and deposits generally lack any internal structure; one has the feeling that although Illinoian ice may have lasted for many years, abundant meltwaters always were available to carry many of the "fines" away from the region, redepositing this material farther downstream, somewhere in the lower Mississippi Valley.

If any glacial event can best fulfill the dreams of glacial geologists, likely it was the Vandalia. In addition to the vast areal coverage, many streams in southern Indiana were dammed by the ice, and valleys became lakes in which silts and clays were deposited. Of all glacial episodes, the Vandalia most closely fits the nineteenth-century image of a single, implacable Ice Age glacier that came down from the north, under severely cold climate that persisted for thousands of years. Yet W. J. Wayne described some thin silts, containing snail shells and vegetation, interbedded within the till of the "Illinoian glacier." If, indeed, these are within what now is called Vandalia, then the enriched silts show that there was life near the ice border, and serve to remind us that no matter how grim a setting, southern Indiana was in a climate where ice melted in the summer months.

We do not know whether the Vandalia ice vanished rather rapidly after persisting for thousands of years, or if the end was marked by relatively brief pulses of colder weather and return of ice to central and northern Indiana. Nor is there an exact fix for inception of the next interglacial stage, the Sangamon, although climatic curves,

obtained from oceanic deposits rather than the continents, suggest that it occurred 110,000 years ago. The Sangamon, like the Yarmouth, was a long, warm period that persisted in Indiana until about 70,000 years ago, and a well-developed soil formed on underlying glacial deposits.

> Within a few millennia our ice may be gone, but if so we shall have paid a fearful price. . . . Ice at its maximum extent is disastrous, but no ice is worse.
>
> —*W. J. Humphreys*

The Wisconsinan stage was not exactly a major event across much of Indiana. Though much of the period between 70,000 and 10,000 years ago likely was cooler, at times perhaps much cooler, than today, most of the state was ice-free. The exception is a few thousand years centering around 20,000 years ago, when galloping ice streams followed each other in quick succession, leaving deposits of till and outwash across half of the state that average 40 to 50 feet in thickness (the range is from several hundred feet in Noble County to near zero over broad areas in western Indiana) and are great for growing the famed Indiana corn and soybeans.

A recent find near Lafayette helps define the limited time of incursion of the various Wisconsinan-age ice streams. The local water company, in drilling a test hole preparatory to expansion of the well field, encountered an assemblage of well-preserved freshwater clams and snails at a depth of 108 feet below the present ground surface. Clearly these critters were not living under a glacier. Perhaps not surprising, radiocarbon dating shows that the clams are

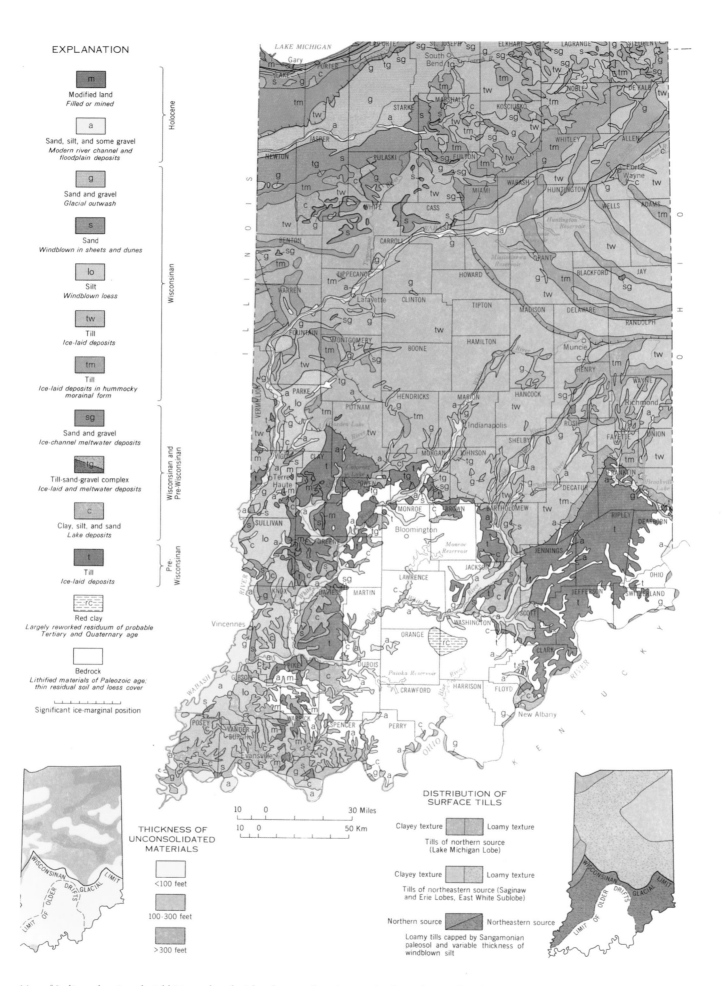

EXPLANATION

Holocene

m — Modified land
Filled or mined

a — Sand, silt, and some gravel
Modern river channel and floodplain deposits

Wisconsinan

g — Sand and gravel
Glacial outwash

s — Sand
Windblown in sheets and dunes

lo — Silt
Windblown loess

tw — Till
Ice-laid deposits

tm — Till
Ice-laid deposits in hummocky morainal form

Wisconsinan and Pre-Wisconsinan

sg — Sand and gravel
Ice-channel meltwater deposits

tg — Till-sand-gravel complex
Ice-laid and meltwater deposits

c — Clay, silt, and sand
Lake deposits

Pre-Wisconsinan

t — Till
Ice-laid deposits

rc — Red clay
Largely reworked residuum of probable Tertiary and Quaternary age

Bedrock
Lithified materials of Paleozoic age; thin residual soil and loess cover

Significant ice-marginal position

THICKNESS OF UNCONSOLIDATED MATERIALS

<100 feet

100-300 feet

>300 feet

DISTRIBUTION OF SURFACE TILLS

Clayey texture · Loamy texture
Tills of northern source (Lake Michigan Lobe)

Clayey texture · Loamy texture
Tills of northeastern source (Saginaw and Erie Lobes, East White Sublobe)

Northern source · Northeastern source
Loamy tills capped by Sangamonian paleosol and variable thickness of windblown silt

Map of Indiana showing glacial history plus glacial and recent deposits.   *Taken from Indiana Geological Survey Map 26*

Glacial till showing assorted sizes of rock fragments from clay to small boulders, all in various stages of weathering and breakdown. Montgomery County, Indiana. *Photo by Marion Jackson*

27,300±1,100 years old, and oxygen isotope analysis of the shells suggests that water temperatures then were perhaps only slightly cooler than exists in the Wabash River today. Yet, only four miles distant are remains of a forest where carbon dating indicates that ice pushed over the trees 21,660 years ago!

The latest Wisconsinan (Woodfordian) glaciation of Indiana clearly is the best-known; after all, these deposits are at the surface in more than half of Indiana! Interpretations, however, are not always simple and unequivocal. At varying times, ice masses moved south from the Lake Michigan basin (Michigan Lobe ice) and from the Huron-Erie basins (East White Lobe ice). There is an apparent lack, however, of time synchrony between the lobes. Thus, in Indiana these deposits are interleaved, with Huron-Erie ice advancing far westward in north-central Indiana over terrain formed previously by glaciers of the Michigan Lobe.

> Nothing goes unrecorded. Every word of leaf and snowflake and particle of dew, shimmering, fluttering, falling, as well as earthquake and avalanche, is written down in Nature's book, though human eye cannot detect the handwriting of any but the heaviest. . . . Glaciers make the deepest mark of any eroding agent, and write their histories in inerasable lines.
>
> —*John Muir, "Sierra Fragments" (1872), in* John of the Mountains *(1938)*

The late Wisconsinan glacier left a specific landform, the Shelbyville Moraine, which ostensibly marks a line of maximum extension, commonly known as a *terminal moraine*. Although this moraine appears on Indiana's glacial map as a continuous entity, it apparently is composite, built in three stages by non-synchronous ice lobes.

The first Woodfordian glacier came from the northeast, covered perhaps two-thirds of the state, and formed the middle section of the Shelbyville Moraine. Radiocarbon dates, from organics beneath these deposits, indicate that ice reached the terminal position about 21,000 years ago.

A brief, short-distance retreat was followed by a readvance which picked up new, additional material as it went. When this Erie Lobe glacier fell back, perhaps this time out of the state, the vacuum quickly was filled by the advance of a Michigan Lobe glacier, which deposited a strangely pinkish-tinged drift which forms that part of the Shelbyville Moraine in western Indiana north of Terre Haute. The line of maximum advance extended northeastward, through Lafayette, but farther northward the limits are obscured under younger drifts. We think that retreat of this ice soon was followed by a new resurgence from the Michigan Lobe, which left a moraine of sorts that passes from Alamo through Crawfordsville, then swings northwestward. Radiocarbon dating places these events at around 20,000 years ago.

As Michigan Lobe ice melted, Erie Lobe ice re-entered the state. In east-central Indiana, ice advanced beyond the limits reached earlier and formed the eastern section of the Shelbyville Moraine. In west-central Indiana, the ice margin passed through Crawfordsville. Deposits at Crawfordsville and Lafayette suggest that a very brief retreat was followed by readvance to the original terminal position.

Another incursion from the northwest then left the so-called Snider Till, which blanketed northwestern Indiana. The Snider is the most recognizable late Wisconsinan deposit in the state. Though relatively thin, the Snider is silty clay, characterized by a distinctive blue-gray color, and has internal orientation or imbrication of pebbles; we think this indicates a true *basal till,* emplaced at the ice bottom by active, vigorous ice. Current theory holds that Snider ice meltwaters were first dammed as a *proglacial lake* in Tippecanoe and adjacent counties, and that the middle reach of the modern Wabash River came into existence when lake waters succeeded in breaching a narrow channel southwest of Lafayette through a re-entrant in the buried northern extension of the Knobstone Escarpment. Today, this event is seen as a narrowing of the valley from a width of 5 to 7 miles, with a river bottom in glacial materials at Lafayette, to a width of less than one-half mile and a bedrock-floored channel at the Tippecanoe–Warren County boundary, less than 10 miles downstream.

After the Snider ice melted, Erie Lobe ice made a quick, final foray across the state. Moving almost directly east to west, this surge event apparently allowed ice to advance more than 200 miles in no more than a few hundred years, though confined to a front no more than 50 miles wide. The southern limits of this Earl Park event have been fairly well established, but the northern boundary (perhaps obscured by dune sands?) still is undefined. Though the Earl Park surge was insufficient to greatly alter the course of the Wabash River, maps clearly show that lesser streams, especially in Clinton and Tipton counties, have the east-west orientation of the Earl Park ice, whereas minor streams on older terrain tend toward a northeast-southwest flow orientation.

Apparently Earl Park ice melted as quickly as it came. Landforms, in fact, suggest that the ice became stagnant, melted in place, and released copious floods of meltwaters. Kames and crevasse fillings are abundant, as are large-scale scour channels. The saga does not end here. We still know relatively little about the antics of later ice events, which seem responsible for deposits of the upper Wabash Valley region, and especially the arcuate moraines (most are barely distinguishable as landforms in the field) of northeastern Indiana.

We can say with assurance that ice had left the state completely by about 13,000 years ago. By this time, however, the development of the Great Lakes had begun. Because at various times early in the history of Lake Michigan there were "high water stands" of early lake stages, much of the Calumet region, north of the Valparaiso Moraine, was periodically flooded. A similar situation existed northeast of Fort Wayne, where initial stages of what now is Lake Erie flooded as far west as New Haven, Indiana. Clearly, the Ice Age was not yet over for those areas! It was not, in fact, until after about 11,000 years ago that the glacial lakes had receded to levels not significantly differing from the lakes of today.

Spillway cut at Cagle's Mill Dam showing successive glacial deposits and soils which were derived therein. The gray bands across the slope are soils formed in early glacial deposits; whereas the trees at the top of the slope are rooted in soil of Wisconsinan glacial age. *Photo by Marion Jackson*

This extensive series of ridges and valleys near Layton Mills in Decatur County represents areas where meltback rates matched glacial advance and, in the process, huge amounts of glacial till were trundled forward for deposition at the ice margin.   *Photo by Richard Fields*

AN INHERITANCE OF NATURAL LAKES

Ice of the Past! Of an age when frost
In its stern clasp held the lands of the South,
Dressed with its mantle of desolate white
Mountains and forests, fair valleys and lakes!

—*Karl Schimper, an ode published with his talk "Ueber
die Eiszeit," in* Eclogae Helvetiae *(1837)*

Proglacial lakes were formed directly abutting the ice front at times and places where briefly there was no available exit for glacial meltwater. None of these lakes remain today in Indiana, but several are worth noting, for their locations are marked by flat terrain (the bottoms of the old lakes), wisps of old shorelines, and abandoned channels marking the line of eventual exit and draining.

Glacial Lake Flatwoods formed in Owen and Monroe counties when Illinoian-age ice advanced across the present White River and climbed the bluffs in and around the vicinity of McCormick's Creek State Park, east of Spencer. Today, a badly degraded morainal ridge crowns the bluff there. This moraine seems to extend eastward, across northern Monroe County south of Bean Blossom Creek. The old Flatwoods lake plain still is evident west of Ellettsville, as is the former outlet, a terraced gap in a bedrock notch near the southwest end of the old lake, where the water eventually drained into the basin of Richland Creek.

Farther north, especially around Clayton and Belleville in Putnam County, are relict plains and faint shorelines of both an Illinoian lake (Glacial Lake Quincy) and a partly overlapping feature of Wisconsinan age (Glacial Lake Eminence). However, the former lake apparently found a southern outlet, whereas the latter exited along Cataract Creek and was at least partly responsible for the forming of Cataract Falls. Eventual discharge of both lakes was to the lower Wabash Valley.

Northern Indiana, especially north of the Wabash River, contains abundant *pit lakes* (if on an outwash plain), such as Bass Lake in Jasper County, or *kettle lakes* (if on ground moraine or nestled in a morainal upland), such as Lake Wawasee, Elkhart County, or Lake James, DeKalb County. Many, perhaps a majority of, northeastern Indiana lakes fit the latter category. Both types form by gradual meltdown, in place, of buried or stranded ice blocks, left intact during the final destruction of dead or stagnant ice.

Former Beaver Lake, mostly in the four northern townships of Newton County, was of glacial origin, though neither a pit nor a kettle. In the year 1834, this shallow lake occupied 28,500 acres. Drainage ditches and channelization of the adjacent Kankakee River reduced the area to 10,000 acres by 1917, and today the lake is completely dry. Strong southwest winds, however, can whip relentlessly across the desiccated lake bottom, and these winds are capable of creating almost instantaneous "brownouts" of airborne silts (modern loess) across Interstate 65. Because the original timberlands, tall

Glacial lakes formed when ice blocks that became separated from the main ice mass melted, then filled the basins they had occupied. Seven Sisters Lakes in Steuben County is one of our best-preserved sequences of such natural lakes. High-altitude oblique aerial shown here of the Wing Haven Nature Preserve landscape.
Photo courtesy of the Indiana Geological Survey

grass, and postglacial wetlands are gone, the area no longer resembles the original refugium for plants and animals that remained here at the close of the Ice Age.

The lifespan of all glacial lakes resembles a human existence. Born of the ice, they flourish briefly, enter a period of maturity and slow decline, and die when an influx of eroded sediment from the surrounding landscape fills the basin. The process is enhanced by slow, additional infill of decaying vegetation or shelly material from minute organisms that flourished in the lake. Inasmuch as those Indiana lakes farthest south are also the oldest, generally these have progressed most in the extinction process; good examples are Cates Pond in Warren County and Lake Cicotte west of Logansport. Post-settlement agricultural practices, residential developments, and other land use, superposed on terrain adjacent to these natural lakes, has tended to speed up extinction as well as inducing pollutants that deteriorate water quality much more quickly than occurred naturally.

A RIVER RUNS THROUGH IT?

A great piece of Indiana's geological folklore is the story of a "buried river," "buried valley," or "Teays Valley," that presumably transected the state prior to the advent of the Great Ice Age. This myth is perpetuated, perhaps inadvertently, even in recent maps in *National Geographic* magazine.

Let us trace this folktale. About 1898, W. D. Tight noted clear evidence of a group of high-level abandoned surface valleys in southeastern Ohio and adjacent parts of West Virginia, and pub-

lished his synoptic interpretation of these features. This and other studies eventually and clearly established the former existence of a northward-flowing, major pre-glacial stream in a valley higher than the channel occupied by the present-day south-flowing Scioto River of central Ohio. Tight called this ancient river the Teays, for the little community of Teays Siding, east of Huntington, West Virginia.

Because this stream apparently was directed northwest at the point where the old channel disappears beneath glacial drift at Chillicothe, Ohio, it was assumed by later writers that the Teays had continued in that direction, across western Ohio and Indiana, becoming part of the equally well-known, now-buried Mahomet Valley in east-central Illinois. Nobody seemed to note the obvious fact that the Teays, a maturely developed meandering stream, was merely in a northwestward-pointing meander loop at the point of burial. Thus, for nearly 100 years, maps and reports have persisted in showing a Teays-Mahomet River, flowing westward across Indiana, from the central Appalachians to the Mississippi River. Presumably, however, this river was "put out of business" forever by one or more early ice incursions which filled, plugged, or buried the channel under glacial debris.

This delightful, attractive scenario has persisted, almost unchanged and unchallenged, for much of the twentieth century. Unfortunately, the story is seriously flawed, for fundamental tenets about topographic control of landforms (such as this surface stream) by rock structures, rock types, and other geologic conditions seemingly were ignored. Perhaps unwavering devotion to the original story was bolstered by proof from drilled wells that a deep-cut channel or gorge in bedrock does exist at about the position of the postulated extension for a "Teays channel" across western Ohio and Indiana.

Many glacialists no longer believe this classic story; in fact, substantial proof supports a more solid and geologically rational interpretation. In essence, there never was a Teays extension across Indiana; the Teays of West Virginia–Ohio flowed, via some yet unknown route, into what in pre-glacial times was the Erie Basin lowland, which later was deepened (by the ice sheets) and filled with water.

The Mahomet Valley of Illinois existed also, as shown on subsurface geologic maps, draining westward from the Illinois-Indiana border to meet the ancestral Mississippi River where Havana, Illinois, is located today. Likely there was an ancestral Salt River, more or less paralleling the Teays, that flowed from Kentucky to the Michigan Lowland, an area also later dug deeper by the glaciers to form the major depression today occupied by Lake Michigan.

What created the deep, transverse valley "buried" across western Ohio and much of Indiana (which exists as an artifact of mapmaking) was somehow a result of invasion by one or more pre-Illinoian-stage ice sheets that moved into northeast Indiana and northwest Ohio. This "buried river" across Indiana clearly is not the Teays of folklore, nor the traditional Mahomet from farther west. In reality, it is an ice-marginal channel, formed and cut by consolidating and diverting fragments of older drainages, during a time or at times when glacial advance and melting were in balance. This stabilized, probably curvilinear ice front produced the copious meltwaters that did the cutting.

Although this early glacial cross-Indiana channel as yet has no valid name, I doubt that the name "Teays" soon will be expunged from either oral or written reference by the lay public. There is a century of tradition, habit, and misunderstanding to overcome, so change will be slow. Greatly helpful, of course, would be a catchy, acceptable name for this ancient "river" (neither Teays nor Mahomet) that can be traced across the state.

EXOTIC PEBBLES AND ERRATIC BOULDERS

As a huge stone is sometimes seen to lie
Couched on the bald top of an eminence.

—*Wordsworth,* Resolutions and Independence

The geological terms *exotic* and *erratic* refer to rock fragments which occur naturally at a place far removed from their place of origin. Some pebbles or cobbles are of such unusual composition or appearance that we know of only a single source of this rock type. An excellent example in Indiana is the abundant "pudding stones," composed of angular fragments of red jasper in a matrix of very white, fine-grained quartz. "Pudding stones" seem most common as semi-rounded cobbles about the size of a human fist, and are seen in most gravel pits and in many farm fields. Because this particular rock type is known to come from a single, clearly Canadian source northeast of Lake Superior, these exotics are excellent proof of ice transport; no other geologic agent exists that could move such vast quantities of a special rock so far, and then disperse them so broadly across the landscape.

The term *erratic* increasingly is being restricted to very large boulders, many weighing tons, and equally "far from home." In some places they are so numerous that cultivation has been impossible, and areas of boulder-strewn, grass- and hawthorn-covered terrain have been used only for limited grazing. These areas are called "barrens."

In certain areas the boulders are limited to long, narrow zones called *boulder belts.* Some glacial geologists think these really are water-washed moraines, wherein glacial meltwaters winnowed the fine-grained sediment, leaving behind only boulders too heavy to move. Elsewhere, enterprising farmers have laboriously moved great numbers of large granite, greenstone, chert, or limestone boulders from plowed fields, leaving them in heaps or in rows along fence lines, thus the term *farmer's moraine.*

The surface of the ground is thickly strewn with boulders of various kinds, chiefly granite, gneiss and other metamorphic rocks. . . . Upon these interesting but unprofitable relics of glacial power the farmers have raged relentless war, bursting them with fire and the dynamite, and hauling them into heaps or using them for rough stone fences.

—*W. H. Thompson, "Marshall County," in* 15th Annual Report *(1886)*

It is interesting that the early glacialist T. C. Chamberlin seemed to limit use of the word *erratic* to pieces of ore or metal transported south from northern Michigan or Canada. Indeed, fragments of native copper, iron ore, and diamonds have been found in Indiana glacial deposits. Small quantities of very finely disseminated gold can still be panned at various places around the state, especially in Morgan and Johnson counties. None is now known in paying amounts, but the search for "color" makes for a day of fun and hard field work!

Using fancy laboratory techniques, today we can analyze rock composition much more quickly and accurately than in the past. Thus, erratics now are undergoing a renaissance of usefulness, for, as Chamberlin and others realized, they can tell us much about directions of ice flow and transport of glacially entrained sediment.

WHAT THE GLACIERS LEFT US

Every geological event leaves a major imprint on the landscape. The Great Ice Age was no exception; and, as expected, there is both a "downside" and an "upside." In a negative sense, repetitive ice

Large boulders, termed *glacial erratics,* were transported by moving ice masses from Canada to Indiana, and left as glacial "signatures" in farm fields. *Photo by Wilton N. Melhorn*

invasions tended to smooth out, or equalize, preexisting variations in landforms and their elevations. Although total thickness of the glacial debris which covers much of Indiana is amazingly thin—there are great areas where drift thickness does not exceed 25 to 50 feet—the general effect has been to produce broad expanses of scenically boring, flat to only modestly irregular tracts of terrain.

There is much, much more on the upside! Historically, Indiana is an agricultural state, lying near the eastern end of the "world's breadbasket," the Glaciated Lowlands province of the United States that extends from Ohio to the Missouri River. The glaciers and their meltwaters, in addition to leveling the terrain, also provided vast quantities of pulverized debris, rich in nutrients such as nitrogen, iron compounds, lime and phosphate, and many trace elements. Mixed with natural organics, the "loam soils" of the soil scientist are, for the most part, really derived from sands, silts, or clays of glacial origin. The price paid for scenic dreariness is more than compensated for by economic enrichments provided by glaciers of the Great Ice Age.

Furthermore, the sequence of glacial events left two other enviable commodities—groundwater and non-metallic mineral deposits such as gravel, molding sands, even brick and tile silts or clays. The best gravel deposits are situated wherever free-flowing meltwaters could stratify and sort the outwash by grain size. Gravel tends to be an abundant, low-cost commodity in Indiana, and thus rarely is fully appreciated. In many places elsewhere in the United States, some of our poorer, "dirty" gravels would command a premium in the marketplace.

And what of groundwater? The same meltwater processes that stratified the sand and gravel outwashes made these excellent aquifers, areas of underground storage for fresh water, derived first perhaps from the ice itself, but kept replenished by later additions

During glacial recessions and prior to vegetation of glaciated landscapes, winds picked up silt-sized particles (termed *loess*), then redeposited these, commonly as annual, laminated layers, shown here. Many of our finest agricultural soils were formed, partly or wholly, within loess deposits. *Photo by Wilton N. Melhorn*

Vegetation and its associated animals exist immediately adjacent to glaciers, especially when the ice is retreating. *Photo by John O. Whittaker*

from rainfall and overflow from streams in flood. Even the average rural household, in perhaps three-quarters of the state, has little difficulty in getting modest but sufficient quantities of good-quality, fresh water at relatively shallow depth from local aquifers within the local glacial deposits. (See also chapter 5, "Lifeblood of the Land.")

AFTER THE GREAT ICE AGE

Because the Ice Age obviously lasted longer in some parts of the world than in others, glacialists have arbitrarily drawn an imaginary line through the geologic time scale at 10,000 years ago. This line marks the passage from the Ice Age to the Holocene or Recent. What was Indiana like then, and what has happened since?

In Indiana, the ice was long gone by 10,000 years ago, unless some isolated buried blocks still melted slowly away in the northern part of the state. The "high" lake stands in the Lake Michigan basin probably had receded to near the present "normal" levels, because the same outlets for the lake operated then as exist now. The frozen-ground tundra and boreal forests that, in quick succession, probably followed final collapse and meltdown of the late Wisconsinan ice likely also were gone, though remnant vestiges of northern forest today remain in secluded alcoves, or *refugia*. An excellent example is seen in eastern hemlock, eastern white pine, and Canada yew stands along Big Walnut Creek in Putnam County and Sugar Creek in Montgomery County. These protected vegetational "islands" clearly attest to the character of past climate and flora in the state.

> A pine tree stands so lonely
> In the North where the high winds blow,
> He sleeps; and the whitest blanket
> Wraps him in ice and snow.
>
> —*Heinrich Heine,* Ein Fichtenbaum steht einsam

During the early Holocene, average climates warmed, perhaps markedly, with periodic return to cooler, perhaps damper condi- tions. By about 4,500 years ago, we had reached the zenith of what universally is called the Altithermal (or Climatic Optimum). This time of "warm" climates likely was marked most by extremes of temperature and erratic rainfall patterns; perhaps averages did not differ greatly from what we have today.

About 3,000 years ago, and again about 700 years ago, there was a worldwide return to much cooler climates. The most recent episode has been called the Neoglacial, or Little Ice Age. Most books give the dates as A.D. 1450 to 1800, though my preference spans a longer time, from circa A.D. 1200 to about 1880. Although the Neoglacial brought no return of ice to Indiana, as happened in the mountains of western North America, it must have been a time of extreme winter cold in the state, as suggested by existing climatic records from the latter part of the nineteenth century.

Today, then, we merely are in another interglacial stage. How long will it last? No one knows. Perhaps another few hundred years will see a return to a situation when climates again deteriorate. Or will it be 1,000, even 10,000 years? All we can say, based on analogues provided by the known average duration of past interglacials, is that probably we have now passed the midway point in the current episode of deglaciation. Inevitably, someday Indiana will again be locked in the grip of a new Ice Age, with social and economic implications too devastating to contemplate. Perhaps it is fortunate that none of us will be around when this occurs.

> Some say the world will end in fire,
> Some say in ice.
> From what I've tasted of desire
> I hold with those who favor fire,
> But if it had to perish twice,
> I think I know enough of hate
> To say that for destruction ice
> Is also great
> And would suffice.
>
> —*Robert Frost,* Fire and Ice

3. The View from the Window: Physiography

Henry H. Gray

We see through a glass, darkly.
—*I Corinthians XII*

All over Indiana, windows look out upon small segments of the Hoosier landscape. Each of these scenes is unique, if only in detail; collectively, they sum to a total view. Windows at Gene Stratton Porter's "Cabin in the Wildflower Woods" near Rome City in northern Indiana frame landscapes of low hills, lakes, and marshes. Windows that inspired painter T. C. Steele at his "House of the Singing Winds" near Belmont in Brown County look out upon rugged scenes with steeper wooded slopes. Windows at Ernie Pyle's birthplace near Dana open to a panorama of prairie. These places are state historic sites; we may go there and see these views, which are fragments of the total. What we need, however, for a fuller understanding of Indiana's landscapes is a larger perspective.

From the top of the Monument on the Circle at Indianapolis, or better still from one of the taller buildings downtown, we can get a larger view of the surrounding landscape. The city spreads in all directions beneath, and beyond the city—on a clear day—expands a broad perspective of the Indiana countryside. Our impression will be that it is flat. Only a few small rises in the land, mostly to the southwest, break the otherwise level horizon.

We are here entering the field of physiography, the descriptive study of landscapes. A related science, geomorphology, endeavors to find how landscapes were created. Descriptively, Indianapolis is in a physiographic region known as the Tipton Till Plain. Geomorphically, this till plain is a surface created primarily by the depositional activity of the latest of the glaciers to invade Indiana, that of Wisconsinan age. There are other till plains in Indiana, but none has the same geologic history or is as extensive as this one. (See also Part 2, "The Natural Regions of Indiana.")

We need, however, to rise to an even broader view. Can we see the entire state from a single viewpoint? Certainly, if we are far enough above Earth. For this we need a satellite or spaceship image. Only a few years ago this would have been in the realm of science fiction, but now we have many "snapshots from space" from which to choose. State boundaries are not painted on the ground, but cities, highways, rivers, and lakes are conspicuous and will provide orientation. And from this perspective, Indiana does look flat!

From such an altitude even the mightiest of mountains is brought low, but in this satellite view we can nonetheless see a lot. Most of Indiana is drained by the Wabash River and its tributaries, and certainly they can be seen. The larger lakes, especially Lake Michigan, also are obvious. Even the checkerboard of farm fields can be made out in many places. The spongy-looking areas are forested, and the darker tones represent areas of wet soils. If the rivers were in flood, we could see that in wide areas of bluish tones. Barren lands—strip mines, for example—generally show up in lighter colors, as do large paved areas and cities.

Before we descend from the heights for a closer view, notice the difference between northern and southern Indiana. The line of Interstate 70 as it transects the state from Terre Haute to Indianapolis to Richmond will serve as a convenient, if arbitrary, boundary. North of this line is a broad, open area dominated by farms, which of course means relatively level landscapes. This is the Tipton Till Plain, the breadbasket of Indiana, the source of the major part of our state's agricultural product. Farther north is a complex of lakes, fields, and forests. South of Interstate 70, however, we see belts of farmland and of forest that trend more or less north-south. Let us now descend to Earth so that we can examine these landscapes more closely, but keep this overall view in mind.

UPLANDS, LOWLANDS, AND PLATEAUS

When David Dale Owen first began to describe the geology of Indiana in 1837, he organized his discussion as if it were a trip down the Ohio River, then the most dependable artery of transportation. We too shall begin in the southeast corner of the state, but our trip will be traced along U.S. Highway 50 from Lawrenceburg to Vincennes. A glance at the satellite image shows that this route covers all of the north-south belts of farmland and forest that make up southern Indiana.

These belts of distinctive topography were no doubt noted by Owen, but it was not until 1922 that this more recent science, physiography, was first given its due. Clyde Malott, professor of geology at Indiana University, so well described the physiographic regions of Indiana in the *Handbook of Indiana Geology* that our concepts of these regions have changed little since. In southern Indiana there are, Malott said, three hilly belts called uplands, two limestone plateaus, and two lowland regions. Our tour will cross these in order.

FROM THE MISTS OF TIME: THE OHIO RIVER

Before we embark on our westward journey, however, a look at the valley of the Ohio River is in order. In defining the south border of our state, the Ohio crosses each of Malott's seven physiographic regions. Through the hill belts and across the limestone plateaus, the river is deeply entrenched; it is less prominently incised across the lowlands, where its valley spreads more widely.

But how came the Ohio to cut across the grain of the southern Indiana topography in this manner? Some 750,000 years ago, one of the earlier glaciers (but probably not the earliest) overspread the Midwest, disrupted then-existing drainage, and filled a deeply incised bedrock valley that crosses northern Indiana, the one that has long been called the Teays or Teays-Mahomet. By filling the old drainageways with glacial and related deposits, the ice sheet reversed many of the streams that had flowed northward to enter the Teays-Mahomet and created an entirely new major stream, the Ohio River. Here history repeated itself: the Teays-Mahomet was not a simple pre-glacial system, but probably was created in a similar way by the action of a still-earlier glacier (see also chapter 2, "Indiana on Ice").

One of the streams affected by this major reordering of the landscape was the ancestral Kentucky River, which once flowed northward past Lawrenceburg into Ohio, ultimately to join the Teays-Mahomet many miles to the north. When the glacier blocked

Infrared satellite view of Indiana showing vegetation in red, water in blue, bare soil in white or gray, and clouds as white "popcorn." Note the large tracts of forest vegetation in south-central and southeastern Indiana, and especially as represented by Jefferson Proving Ground north of Madison.

Ohio River Valley from overlook at Hanover College looking downstream.   *Photo by Marion Jackson*

that route, the segment of the Kentucky from Carrollton, Kentucky, to Lawrenceburg was, in effect, turned around to become part of the Ohio. Remnants of the old valley show the level to which the ponded waters rose before they found a gap near Madison that allowed them to spill into an existing valley that led past Louisville and westward. In evidence of this, the valley of the Ohio is at its narrowest at Madison.

Some time after the Ohio River was assembled in this piecemeal fashion, by streams finding their way through uplands and lowlands and around the edge of the glacier, the Ohio deepened its valley to some 100 feet below the present level. Probably it accomplished this through the erosive power of large volumes of "hungry" water, water not overloaded with sediment, the discharge of a healthy advancing glacier. When the glacier stopped pressing its margin southward, it probably stagnated—it ceased moving, and its meltwater streams became heavily charged with sediment that had lain trapped, mainly in basal layers of the ice. Gorged with this sediment, the river changed to a depositing, rather than eroding, mode, and partly filled its valley with sand and gravel deposits collectively called outwash. Small tributary streams that did not carry a heavy load of outwash were ponded by the deposits in the main valley, and in the lakes so formed, finer sediments such as silt and clay were deposited.

The cycle of erosion and deepening, deposition and filling, was repeated with each of several glaciers, leaving terraces of sand and gravel to mark the various levels to which the valley has been filled. Parts of Lawrenceburg and Aurora are sited on such terraces; the valley of Hogan Creek, just west of Aurora, is underlain by silt and clay lake deposits some 100 feet thick.

OUR JOURNEY BEGINS

Looking down the Ohio, as we leave it, we can see on both sides of the valley bedrock ramparts that embrace a relatively flat and narrow valley floor, but as we begin our journey westward, we leave the valley behind. Ascending some 400 feet, through roadcuts that expose shale and limestone of Ordovician age (see also chapter 1, "Of Time, Rocks, and Ancient Life"), we reach the upland surface. The highway winds westward following the ridge crests, and on either side here and there we can see below us the heads of valleys that drain northward to Hogan Creek and southward to Laughery Creek, thence to the Ohio.

This is the physiographic region called the Dearborn Upland, and it is characterized by sprawling ridges, steep slopes, and deep branching valleys. The earlier glaciers were active here, but in the time since, there has been so much erosional activity that their mark upon the land has been mostly fragmented and subdued. Remnant deposits indicate, however, that three, four, or perhaps more glacial events helped to shape this countryside.

We reach Laughery Creek and Versailles State Park just east of Versailles. Commencing near Batesville, Laughery Creek flows about 25 miles generally southward, then anomalously turns to flow northeastward. Complexities in the glacial history of the terrane no doubt explain this perverse behavior, but the exact reasons are unknown. At this point, however, the valley of Laughery Creek marks our entry into the next region westward.

Rising to the upland at Versailles, we see around us a much broader upland than we have seen before. This region, the Muscatatuck Regional Slope, is a tilted limestone plateau incised here and there by limestone-walled canyons. We will see little of the underlying bedrock, which is of Silurian and Devonian age, because of the pervasive upland blanket of glacial deposits, but limestone and dolomite underlie the floors and valley walls of most of the streams, both small and large.

Much of the Muscatatuck Regional Slope is so flat that water ponds on the surface, and the soils show evidence of being soggy much of the year. Some areas are, therefore, left in seasonally wet woodlands called flatwoods. At North Vernon we cross the canyon of the Vernon Fork of the Muscatatuck River. From here westward for a few miles the black New Albany Shale shows in roadcuts where the overlying glacial deposits are thin. About six miles west of North Vernon, the topography noticeably becomes not just flat but nearly level, and we enter the Scottsburg Lowland, probably unaware that since leaving Versailles we have descended more than 350 feet.

A SIDEWARD GLANCE

Arterial highways follow the Scottsburg Lowland southward to Jeffersonville and the Falls of the Ohio River—the only place from its origin at Pittsburgh to its junction with the Mississippi that the entire bed of the Ohio River from one bank to the other is underlain by bedrock. Why? Because here the valley was filled to its full width by outwash deposits from the several glaciers farther north, most recently from the Wisconsinan glacier, which dumped a mighty load of sand and gravel down the Miami River and into the Ohio. These deposits buried a bedrock ledge, and when the Ohio once more began to erode its channel downward, it failed to find its earlier course, which underlies the city of Louisville; instead, it superposed itself on this ledge, thereby exposing reef-like beds of richly fossiliferous limestone, now a major attraction of the Falls of the Ohio State Park (see also chapter 1, "Of Time, Rocks, and Ancient Life").

A TALE OF TWO RIVERS

The Scottsburg Lowland west of Seymour is dominated by the Muscatatuck River to the south and the East Fork of the White River to the north. These two streams are very different in their behaviors. The Muscatatuck flows in a course that can best be described as kinky. Soggy, mostly wooded areas adjacent to the stream give evidence of frequent and extended flooding, a result in part of the very low gradient of the river. The East Fork, in contrast, swings smoothly in sweeping meanders. On maps and aerial photographs it is apparent, from the number of oxbow lakes and crescent-shaped sloughs, that these meanders are not fixed but must have moved actively in the relatively recent past.

The meanders on the East Fork are, in fact, moving almost perceptibly even today, and both the railroad and the highway have had to build bulwarks against their downvalley sweep. Especially in time of flood, the stream impinges sharply on the outer bank of each meander, undercutting it, while simultaneously, in the less rapidly moving water along the inner bank, the stream deposits the sediments that it has just excavated from the meander scar next upstream. In this way the meander sweeps slowly across the valley floor and downvalley, sometimes in the process cutting through entirely to the next downstream bend and in so doing creating an oxbow lake in the abandoned channel segment.

But why does a stream meander? There is no simple way to explain it, but it is definitely the preferred *modus operandi* of streams having a certain gradient and sediment load, and is best expressed where the stream has sandy sediments to rework. The East Fork drains the

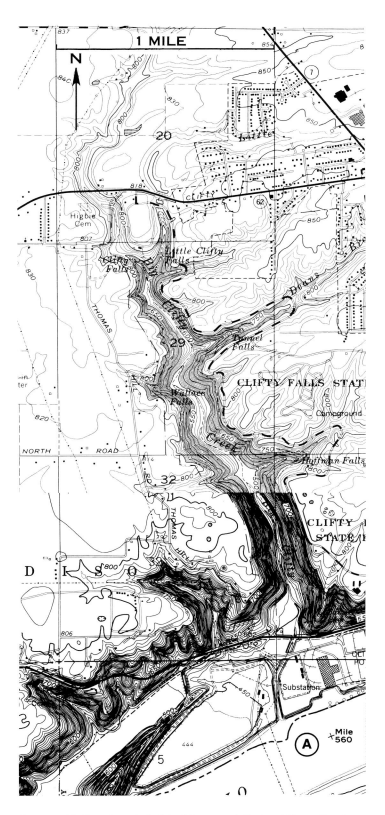

Area near Madison is typical of the Muscatatuck Regional Slope. Gentle westward slope of the upland surface is interrupted by the deep canyon of Clifty Creek. To read a contour map such as this one, it helps to visualize each successive contour line as the hypothetical shoreline of a sea risen to the stated altitude; vertical interval between contours on this map is 10 feet. *Reduced from U.S. Geological Survey Clifty Falls and Madison West Quadrangle maps*

Since the time of formation of the Ohio River (A), the several falls in Clifty Falls State Park have been gradually eroding their way upstream.

Aerial view (looking southward) of Clifty Canyon of Clifty Falls State Park and flat farmland of the Muscatatuck Regional Slope near Madison, Indiana. *Photo courtesy of the Indiana Geological Survey*

relatively youthful Wisconsinan glacial terrane to the north and reworks its way across a vast tract of sandy outwash deposits. The Muscatatuck, which did not carry outwash in Wisconsinan time, was blocked and ponded by sand deposition along the East Fork, and its valley is filled mainly with stiff and hard-to-erode silt and clay that settled in the quiet waters of a slackwater lake. In such materials streams find it difficult to express a meandering habit.

Along the route from Seymour to Brownstown are many low rises crowned by sandy soils. These are dunes, now mostly stabilized by vegetation. During late Wisconsinan time, however, when the East Fork, swollen by glacial meltwater, was spreading its huge valley train of sand and gravel, dunes were built along the leeward margin of the valley. Dune building was most active in winter when diminished meltwater supply left large areas of sand exposed to the wind. Sand movement continues today, mostly from fields freshly plowed in the spring.

Some time before we reach Brownstown, a change is visible in the skyline ahead. Ranges of hills appear to the west and south, rising in aspect as we approach. Nearest, to the south of us at Brownstown, are the Brownstown Hills, and south of those hills is the valley of the Muscatatuck, not so broad as the valley of the East Fork to the northwest. These low areas are underlain by soft rocks, shales that are less resistant to erosion than the limestones to the east or the siltstones that underlie the hills.

CLIMBING THE STAIRS OF THE AGES

In progressing westward since the beginning of our journey, we have been ascending the rock section; the rocks dip slightly to the west (see also chapter 1, "Of Time, Rocks, and Ancient Life"), and we are, in a sense, climbing a flight of tilted stairsteps. The rock strata we left behind us at Aurora are now some 1,000 feet beneath us, and as we cross the lowland area we also cross from rocks of Devonian age to those of the Mississippian.

Let us now continue westward across the valley of the East Fork to the foot of the massive Knobstone Escarpment. For some time we have been paralleling the tracks of the former Baltimore and Ohio Railroad, the first railroad to cross Indiana, completed in 1857. Here, however, we leave them, and for a simple reason. The railroad can easily fit into the narrow valley through which the East Fork of the White River, now joined by the Muscatatuck, plunges through the escarpment and into the Norman Upland. The highway, needing a wider right-of-way and being less constrained to a water-level route, ascends the escarpment to the upland surface.

The Knobstone Escarpment is the most prominent physiographic feature in Indiana. Rising some 600 feet above the Ohio River at New Albany, it extends northward into Scott County, where it turns westward to form the southern arm of the great re-entrant that cradles the Brownstown Hills. At the western apex of that re-entrant, where the East Fork of the White River leaves the Scottsburg Lowland, the escarpment turns once more northward. It passes a few miles west of Columbus and, continuing northward, becomes gradually obscured by the thickening cover of glacial deposits, though it can be sensed vicariously in a rise in the topography at Danville and Belleville, some 50 miles to the north. Southwest of Lafayette the escarpment is totally buried, but it is expressed in the bedrock surface beneath thick glacial deposits.

A BACKWARD LOOK, AND MORE MISTS OF TIME

Before we ascend the escarpment, however, let us pause to look back across the lowland so that we can put into perspective some of the features of the region through which we have just passed. If we can rise to the occasion, so to speak, and can imagine ourselves looking eastward from a vantage point of some height, we can perhaps visualize some of the processes that have shaped the features that we have just seen.

The earliest history of these landforms is shrouded in the mists of time—of that, more later. More easily visualized, however, are the geologically more recent events, those of half a million years ago and less: first, the lowland filled with ice of a wasting glacier, ice that just tops the crest of the escarpment south and west of us; then, on the gradual disappearance of that glacier and as the Knobstone Escarpment and the Brownstown Hills emerge from the thinning mass of

ice, a flood of meltwater that diminishes as the glaciers recede; and much later, another flood of meltwater issuing from a glacier to the north, one that terminates a little south of Columbus. This later torrent, however, occupies only the valley of the East Fork; south of the Brownstown Hills, the valley of the Muscatatuck contains only a placid, muddy lake. And finally, in today's scene, we see the meandering East Fork, now only a shrunken remnant of its former self, and the still-active dunes along the east margin of the valley.

We have just dipped into the immediate past of Indiana's present yet ever-changing landscape. What about earlier landscapes—what might Indiana's surface have looked like millions of years ago? We know that through hundreds of millions of years of Paleozoic time, what is now our state lay near sea level, sometimes partly or totally emergent, sometimes partly or totally submerged (see also chapter 1, "Of Time, Rocks, and Ancient Life"). Our concepts of those landscapes are mostly speculative, but certainly they were vastly different from today's.

Sometime late in Paleozoic time, about 200 million years ago, Indiana emerged from the sea for the last time. There is no trace remaining of the landscape that then developed and that eventually evolved into our current scene. We can only speculate that major streams on this surface flowed southwestward toward the sea, as indeed they did in Pennsylvanian and earlier times, and as indeed they do now.

There is, however, a landscape recorded in the rocks that gives us

Aerial view of the Falls of the Ohio State Park area near Clarksville during the drought of August 1991. Low river levels expose expanses of the fossil-rich limestone reef of Silurian age which forms the falls. *Photo by Hank Huffman*

The View from the Window / 33

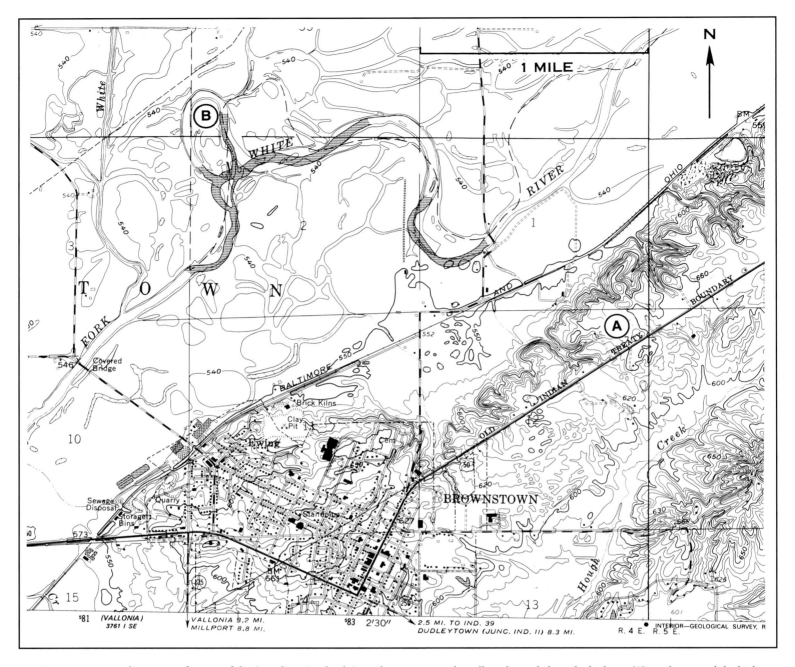

Brownstown area shows many features of the Scottsburg Lowland. Irregular contours at the valley edge and along the highway (A) are dunes, and the high area near the southeast corner of the map is the edge of the Brownstown Hills, which in their central part rise almost 450 feet above the valley floor nearby.
Reduced from U.S. Geological Survey Brownstown Quadrangle map

Tracery of the 540-foot contour along the East Fork of the White River delineates the many channels the stream has cut and abandoned. The stippled portion of the river's course indicates new channel cut since the map was first drawn in 1959 and before the date of revision, 1981. An oxbow lake is now in the process of formation as one meander (B) is cut off and abandoned.

a glimpse of what these earlier landscapes might have been. Between the rocks of Mississippian age and those of Pennsylvanian age is an irregular surface, a disconformity, that represents such a landscape. After the Mississippian rocks were deposited, the land was uplifted and eroded into uplands and lowlands not unlike those of today. Resistant rocks upheld hilly tracts; softer rocks formed lowlands. A network of streams, now limned by valleys on this surface, flowed southwestward and cut across the grain of this landscape.

But this ancient scene was interrupted. Probably the land subsided somewhat; certainly this landscape was inundated by a new flood of sediments, deposits of Pennsylvanian age that buried the

hills and valleys and that in this manner preserved for later study by geologists this particular landscape from among the many others that might have been preserved but were not.

Our geologic record is far from complete. It's like trying to read a book from which many pages, even whole chapters, are missing, and many of the remaining pages are torn, stained, and illegible. But what was surely once an emergent coastal plain has been slowly etched into our present landscape. We should keep in mind, however, that even this landscape—these "everlasting hills"—is just the latest page in a book not yet complete, and that some future geologic event will destroy or bury it and begin a new chapter in Indiana's geology.

The "Knobs" which form the transition escarpment from the Scottsburg Lowland to the east from the Norman Upland (Highland Rim Natural Region) to the west represent the only near-mountains in Indiana.   *Photo taken northeast of New Albany by Richard Fields*

OUR JOURNEY RESUMES

U.S. Highway 50 ascends the Knobstone Escarpment through a series of roadcuts that expose siltstone and shale, the record of a great delta that overspread this area in Mississippian time. The rocks lie close to the surface, partly because the slopes are steep, but partly also because the glacial deposits here are thin as we approach an indefinite line that marks maximum extent of the ice. The escarpment, which stands in high relief because the rocks that uphold it are resistant to erosion, was for the same reason a mighty impediment to the glaciers that passed this way; only the most powerful of the ice advances was able, barely, to surmount the escarpment here.

The Norman Upland, which we now are crossing, is plateau-like in this area, but to the north, where Salt Creek and its tributaries dissect it, most of the upland is in steep slopes. Brown County State Park is an example. Southward from us, however, the belt of rugged upland narrows, and southwest of New Albany it consists mainly of the dissected front of the Knobstone Escarpment. Except around its eastern fringe and at its northern margin, the Norman Upland was not glaciated.

The plateau surface and the highway drift downward a bit, and we pass almost imperceptibly into the next physiographic region west-

ward, the Mitchell Plain. North and south of here the boundary is somewhat more distinct. Bedrock beneath the Mitchell Plain is limestone of Mississippian age, and the soils are clayey and red. Where we approach Bedford, the limestone is sufficiently thick to allow the development of caves, sinkholes, sinking streams, underground drainage, and other evidence of a type of landscape called karst.

Limestone differs from other rocks in the way it weathers because limestone is soluble in water, especially in water that has become slightly acidic in its passage through the atmosphere and the soil. The result is a system of underground drainageways, the largest of which are caves (see also chapter 7, "Underground World"). Collapse of a cave roof may lead to the formation of a sinkhole at the surface of the ground above, but most sinkholes were formed by soil subsiding and washing into underground channelways that are not large enough to be called caves. Sinkholes in the Mitchell Plain probably are numbered in the millions.

ANOTHER SIDEWARD GLANCE

West of Bedford the plateau surface is so intensely pitted by sinkholes that all drainage is underground. A few miles south of us is

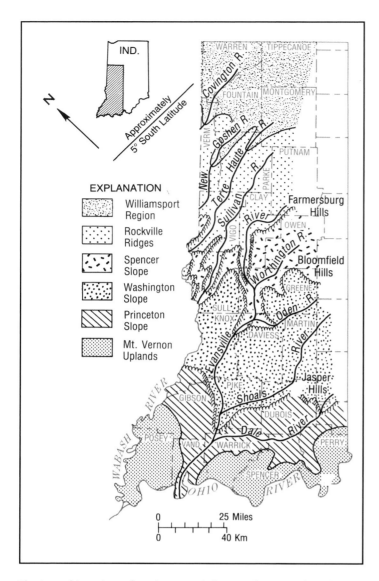

Physiographic regions of southwestern Indiana as they were about 325 million years ago, just before deposits of Pennsylvanian age began to overspread this land surface. Details differ, but this landscape is broadly similar to the present one—for example, the Evansville River is a counterpart to the lower Wabash.　*From Indiana Geological Survey Occasional Paper 55*

Indiana then had a different geographic position on the globe; movement of the North American Plate since the time represented by this map has brought Indiana to its present position.

Spring Mill State Park, whose springs and caves and sinkholes are typical of the Mitchell Plain, and a few miles south of that, near Orleans, is the famous Lost River, a stream that sinks and flows underground through "caverns measureless to man" for about eight miles before emerging, again to become a surface stream. The abandoned surface stream course, known as the dry bed, which marks the path the stream took before it was captured by underground routes, now is occupied only at high-water stages.

ONCE MORE INTO THE HILLS

We now approach another escarpment, sometimes called the Chester Escarpment because it is underlain by rocks of the Ches-

terian Series, rocks that form the upper part of the Mississippian System in Indiana. At this point we enter another belt of hills, the Crawford Upland. Sandstone, limestone, and shale make up the bedrock; some of these rocks are resistant and form ledges on the hillsides and rimrocks at hill crests. From here to Shoals, Mississippian rocks underlie the slopes and Pennsylvanian rocks cap the ridges.

At Shoals we cross the East Fork of the White River for a final time. Here the deeply buried bedrock valley runs in a loop east of town, and here, just as at the Falls of the Ohio, the river in its random wanderings superposed itself on a ledge of sandstone bedrock, which we can see at low water just below the highway bridge.

From Shoals to the Wabash River, the bedrock we see is Pennsylvanian in age. In some of the roadcuts between Shoals and Loogootee are exposures of thin beds of coal, but major producing areas are farther west. Where we cross Boggs Creek, a little east of Loogootee, we pass some small and inactive gravel pits. There is no commercial gravel in the main body of outwash along the East Fork here; whence came this gravel?

We are about to re-enter terrane built by one (or more) of the pre-Wisconsinan glaciers. Perhaps half a million years ago, meltwater from along the margin of this ice from as far north as Bloomington passed this way en route to the Ohio River near Evansville, bringing with it the usual sand and gravel outwash. The ice did not stay in place long enough to establish a major connected stream, but all along the former ice margin are minor drainage diversions and deposits marking its place. The age of the deposit here is demonstrated by the thick layer of soil that has formed on it.

At Loogootee, the railroad that we followed across southeastern Indiana at last escapes from the valley of the East Fork of the White River and ascends slightly, as we do, onto an area of gently rolling terrane. This is the westernmost of southern Indiana's physiographic regions, the Wabash Lowland. We also here re-enter the glaciated area.

UPLANDS VS. GLACIERS

It is no coincidence that the uplands through which we have just passed escaped glaciation. It would be an oversimplification to say that the Norman and Crawford uplands acted as cleavers to part the ice, though a look at the map might so suggest. Nevertheless, from Bloomington southward the several glaciers that crossed the Ohio River to the southeast and that extended almost to the Ohio in the southwest avoided, for the most part, these uplands.

We know, of course, that the glaciers descended upon Indiana from the north (see also chapter 2, "Indiana on Ice"). We may further look upon the map of the Midwest and note the ice-carved basins of the Great Lakes, of which Erie and Michigan perhaps seem the most obvious routes for the glacier from Canada to Indiana. What is less obvious is that, for whatever reason, most of the drift deposits even in southwestern Indiana came by the eastern route, not the northern; only the drift near the western margin of the state came by way of the Lake Michigan basin. Thus the concept of the highlands acting as a cleaver may not be inappropriate, but details of the mechanics of ice movement still elude us.

WESTWARD ONCE AGAIN

A little beyond Washington we cross the main stem of the White River, which is on its way to its junction with the East Fork not far away. The White, like the East Fork, drains largely glacial terrane from as far east as Muncie, and as a consequence has a broad sandy bottom replete with meanders and oxbows. A belt of dunes lines the

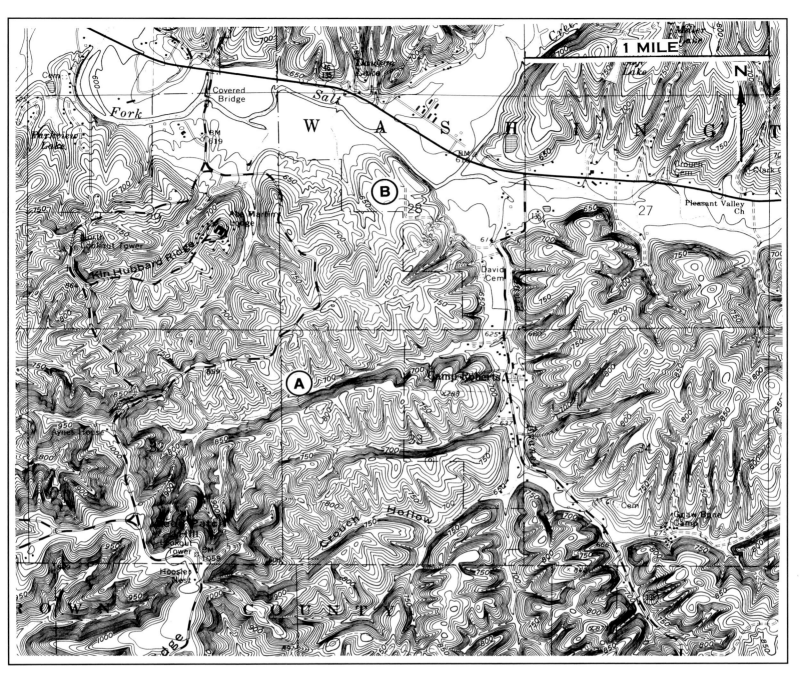

Hills in Brown County State Park just southeast of Nashville are typical of the Norman Upland. Weed Patch Hill rises about 450 feet above the valley floor of Salt Creek, and steep slopes, shown by close-set contour lines, abound.   *Reduced from U.S. Geological Survey Nashville Quadrangle map*

Several of the smaller valleys shown here (A) are asymmetrical; that is, they are steeper on the south side than on the north. This is attributed to frequent freeze-thaw cycles on the warmer north side of the valley; the south side stays frozen much of the winter. An intermediate erosion level shown by terraces along Salt Creek (B) relates to an early glacial episode; Salt Creek carried drainage from one of the earlier glaciers, which terminated in the northern part of Brown County.

The karst plain southwest of Orleans in Orange County is pockmarked by numerous sinkholes which lead into the cavern system within the limestone bedrock.   *Photo by Richard Fields*

east margin of the valley. Where U.S. Highway 50 crosses the river, the sandy outwash beneath the valley floor is 150 feet thick, a testament to the great volumes of glacial meltwater once carried by the ancestor of the White River.

A blanket of till, the direct deposit of glacial ice, blankets the bedrock on most of the low hills between the White and the Wabash, and capping this is a layer of windblown silt, or loess. A belt of upland loess more than 6 feet thick and 10 to 25 miles wide parallels the Wabash River from its mouth upstream to Terre Haute. The silt is increasingly coarser westward and grades into sand in the dunes that line the east edge of the Wabash Valley; loess of lesser thickness overlies most of the uplands across southern Indiana. It all was blown from the outwash deposits along the Wabash, the White, and the East Fork, and it is an important component of many of the soils of southern Indiana (see also chapter 4, "Cradle of Life").

Historic Vincennes, the Wabash River, and the end of our southern journey lie ahead, but we need also to glance at some of the unusual features of the Wabash Lowland called island hills. Dotting the lower Wabash Valley are low bedrock knobs that rise just above the flood of river-deposited sand that surrounds them. Some of these hills are conspicuous; some are almost buried; and there are still other similar knobs that lie completely engulfed in sand and are known only from subsurface geologic studies. The Wabash River, having its origin far to the north, carried sand-rich glacial meltwater

for an even longer time than did the White or its East Fork. And as a final event, a catastrophic burst of water, the Maumee Torrent, filled the entire valley when, far upstream, the waters of a great glacial lake were suddenly released!

And now let us set our attention northward.

> Far north, far north are the sources.
> —*Stephen Vincent Benét, "Ode to Walt Whitman"*

Some of the glaciated parts of southern Indiana could be considered till plains, but when we use that term in Indiana we usually mean the Tipton Till Plain. The vast flat areas north of Indianapolis, especially near the town of Tipton, are most typical of the till plain, but to experience its many aspects we must travel rather widely.

OVERSIZED VALLEYS AND UNDERSIZED STREAMS

North of New Castle the Blue River, like many others in Indiana, flows in a valley that seems oversized. Indeed, the valley was shaped by meltwater discharge, and the stream today is but a tiny remnant of its former self. This valley is part of a complex that formed along the margin of a wasting glacier. Intermixed slices of till and gravel mark this as the site of a group of sub-ice tunnels, or of ice-walled channels that carried meltwater from inner parts of the glacier to its

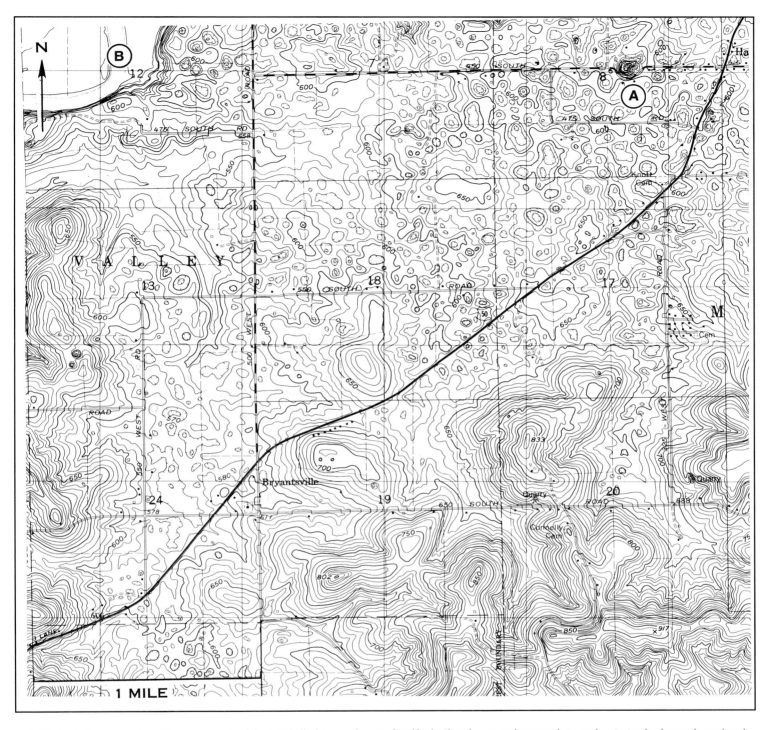

Sinkholes in karst area along the west margin of the Mitchell Plain southwest of Bedford. Closed contour loops with inward-pointing hachures show closed depressions on the ground. A particularly deep one (A), marked by many contours, each of which signifies a 10-foot difference in altitude, has caused a road to diverge around it.   *Reduced from U.S. Geological Survey Bedford West Quadrangle map*

General level of the plateau surface is 100 feet or more above the valley of the East Fork of the White River (B). Hills on the south and west portions of this map define the Chester Escarpment—the eastern boundary of the Crawford Upland—which here rises to an altitude of nearly 900 feet.

margin, whence the meltwater flowed down what is now the valley of the Blue River. To the east, other such features were the source of meltwater streams that flowed down valleys that now hold the various forks of the Whitewater River.

To experience another aspect of the Tipton Till Plain, we must travel westward and follow U.S. Highway 41 north from Terre Haute. For some miles this highway follows the valley of the Wabash River,

but at the old mining town of Lyford it turns from the valley, and in a series of ups and downs arrives at the Tipton Till Plain as we approach Rockville. Still farther north we cross another series of valleys before we ascend once more to the till plain a few miles north of Sugar Creek.

Here along its western edge, the Tipton Till Plain is dissected by streams that drain to the Wabash River. Sugar Creek, for example,

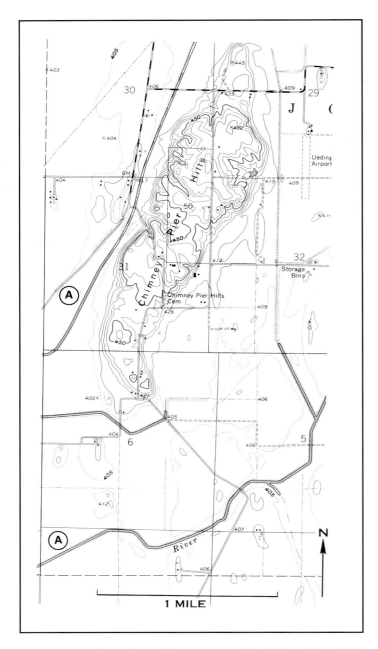

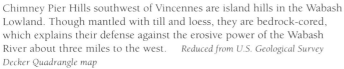

Chimney Pier Hills southwest of Vincennes are island hills in the Wabash Lowland. Though mantled with till and loess, they are bedrock-cored, which explains their defense against the erosive power of the Wabash River about three miles to the west. *Reduced from U.S. Geological Survey Decker Quadrangle map*

The valley floor is so flat that supplementary five-foot contours (dashed lines) have been used; sluggish natural drainage has been replaced by ditched channels (A).

originates many miles to the east near Tipton and has excavated a valley that deepens westward as it nears the Wabash. In some places the creek flows in broad, open valleys where, in cutting downward since the Wisconsinan glacier left this land some 17,000 years ago, it had to cut only soft glacial deposits. In other places, however, the creek cut downward into sandstone and siltstone bedrock and so created the scenic bluffs and canyons that make the Shades and Turkey Run state parks famous.

All the features of the Tipton Till Plain either are glacial in origin or were formed by stream erosion in late to post-glacial time (see also chapter 2, "Indiana on Ice"). Isolated gravel hills called kames dot the landscape; the hills southwest of Indianapolis, already remarked upon, are kames. These were formed by meltwater pouring off the top of the glaciers. Low ridges—end moraines—mark places where for a time the terminus of the glacier remained more or less stationary, melting about as fast as it advanced; these are most conspicuous south of Fort Wayne and near Bluffton and Marion. And in the

Aerial view of farmland of the Tipton Till Plain (Central Tillplain Natural Region) shows the featureless terrain of that productive agricultural region.
Photo by Lee Casebere

Noblesville and Anderson areas are networks of meltwater discharge channels that now are abandoned and carry no present stream of any size.

MORE TO TELL OF THE TILL PLAIN

The Tipton Till Plain is so broad and diverse that we simply cannot see it all, because we must again look northward along U.S. Highway 41. Where we cross the Wabash River at Attica, the lower valley walls are cut in the same siltstone bedrock that we saw as we ascended the Knobstone Escarpment. From Terre Haute northward we have been transiting older and older bedrock, descending the stairs of time, but the drift cover has obscured the rocks except in some of the deeper-cut valleys.

At Attica the Wabash is in a post-glacial valley; it is cutting across a bedrock divide that lies between the Teays-Mahomet Valley on the north, where the drift is as much as 400 feet thick, and the buried

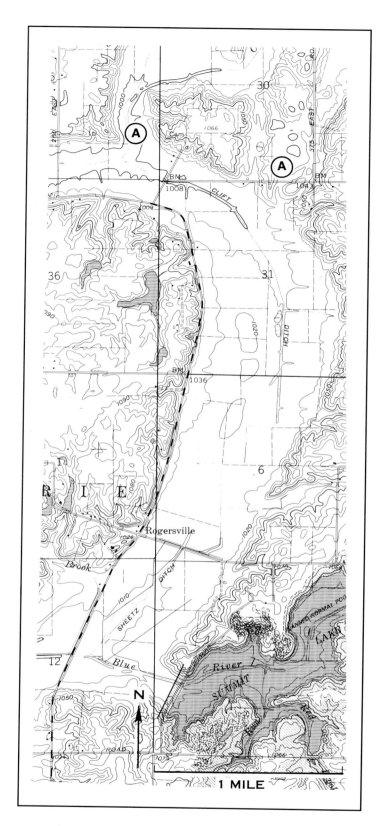

Deep and nearly abandoned valley in which both the Blue River and Buck Creek now head, flowing in opposite directions, was excavated by a much larger stream, part of a tunnel-valley system that discharged from a rapidly wasting glacier. *Reduced from U.S. Geological Survey Mount Pleasant Quadrangle map*

Some of the tributary valleys (A) were part of the meltwater discharge system; the valley that Summit Lake now occupies may have been excavated by post-glacial erosion.

bedrock valley of the lower Wabash. The stream was placed here by interaction of the Lake Michigan and Huron-Erie lobes of the Wisconsinan glacier as these ice masses wasted; in cutting downward since, the Wabash has, so to speak, accidentally discovered that it must excavate bedrock in this area.

A little south of Boswell we cross the buried Teays-Mahomet bedrock valley system. You didn't see it? Neither has anyone else; it requires deep drilling or geophysical studies to detect such features, but it is well to remember, especially as we cross some of these areas that are featureless on the surface, that beneath us are other sets of physiographic features dating from earlier geologic times—some pre-glacial, some dating to one or another of the older glaciations.

We continue northward over the Tipton Till Plain. Where U.S. Highway 52 joins, just west of Fowler, a cluster of kames lies to the east. Gravel pits expose the tumultuous structure and coarse gravelly texture of these deposits, evidence of their origin by meltwater pouring off the top of the ice.

Near Kentland and over a wide area extending northeast to Remington, Monon, and Rensselaer, bedrock is at shallow depth; this is a bedrock plateau of Silurian and Devonian limestone. Several limestone quarries take advantage of the thin drift cover. As we approach Morocco, a slight rise marks a morainal belt, called the Iroquois Moraine. Its east-west trend suggests that it was built by the Lake Michigan Lobe of the glacier, but its surface materials are of eastern derivation. Drilling provided the answer: The bulk of the moraine is indeed drift of the Lake Michigan Lobe, but after the moraine was built, a later advance of ice of the Huron-Erie Lobe covered the moraine with a veneer of eastern-source till only a few feet thick.

Continuing north, just beyond Morocco we leave the Tipton Till Plain and enter a cluster of dunes that mark the margin of another physiographic region, a complex area called the Northern Lake and Moraine Region. The dunes are marginal to a broad sand plain that marks the floor of a shallow lake of late glacial time, but the dominant landforms today are the numerous small dunes, all of which indicate a western source for the wind that built them, scooping sand from the dry lake floor.

Lake Village memorializes a small former lake, one of many historic remnants of a far larger lake of glacial time, but ditching of the Kankakee River (just ahead) has lowered the water table, and the lakes are now dry. The Kankakee itself is a sluggish and ineffectual stream nowadays, but in late glacial time it carried meltwater from a 100-mile perimeter of the ice, from as far northeast as present-day Kalamazoo, Michigan.

Ahead now as we cross the Kankakee is the front of the Valparaiso Moraine, one of the most impressive glacial features in Indiana. From Lowell to Valparaiso to LaPorte it swings in a massive arc around the toe of Lake Michigan. Clearly it was built by ice of the Lake Michigan Lobe during a late phase of the latest, or Wisconsinan, glacier.

Where we cross the moraine we are on ice-built terrane, but just east and west of us, as well as at Valparaiso, valleys of great complexity cut the moraine. Like the valleys near New Castle, these originated either as sub-ice tunnels or as ice-walled channels, and they conveyed meltwater from inner parts of the glacier to the perimeter of the ice. Where they exited the moraine and entered the broad valley of the Kankakee, these meltwater streams built huge fan-like deposits of sand and gravel such as we can see at the edge of glaciers today. In some areas, the surface of these fans is pitted by numerous depressions made where blocks of ice were incorporated into the sediment and later melted.

A few miles north of Crown Point we drop from the moraine onto a plain that was shaped by a succession of Ice Age predecessors of

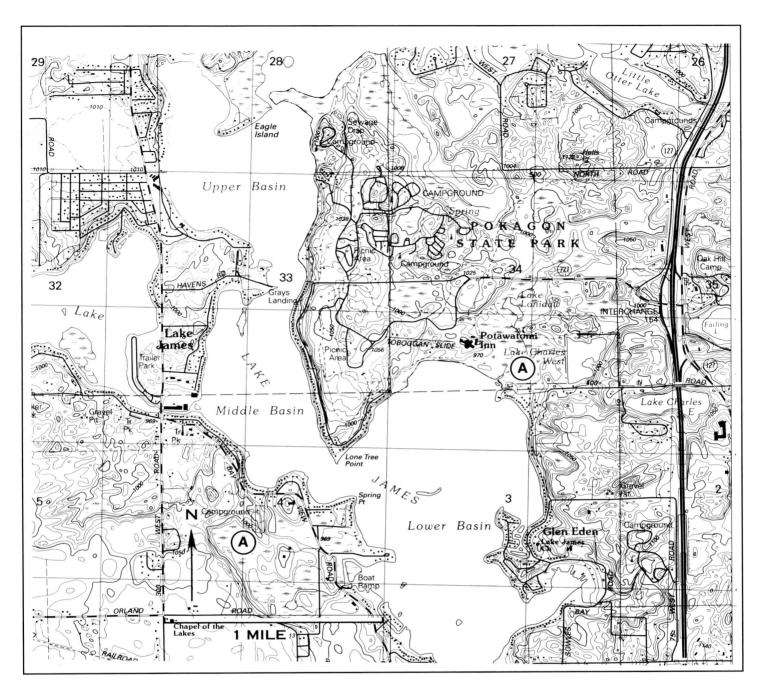

Pitted and uneven nature of the topography around Lake James and Pokagon State Park is typical of the Northern Lake and Moraine Region. Most of the basins were formed by the melting of large blocks of ice buried in thick glacial deposits.   *Reduced from U.S. Geological Survey Angola West Quadrangle map*

Swampy areas (A) once were lakes or parts of lakes, but now have been filled by the detritus of generations of plants, forming peat. Only the deeper basins remain unfilled.

Lake Michigan. The first of these was a crescent-shaped lake held in on the south by the moraine, on the north by the lobe of ice. Each successive larger and lower stage left its mark as a sandy strand of beaches. Early lake stages drained mainly by way of the Illinois River, but when the ice retreated sufficiently to open up the Straits of Mackinac, far to the north, the lake found its way to its present level—where it now builds (and erodes) beaches. In some places sand blown from these and older beaches has built massive sets of dunes, as at Indiana Dunes State Park and Indiana Dunes National Lakeshore.

OTHER SCENIC NORTHERN ASPECTS

To experience other aspects of the Northern Lake and Moraine Region, we must travel elsewhere. If we turn eastward and follow the blue highways to Lake Maxinkukee, to Lake Wawasee, and to Lake James and Pokagon State Park in the northeastern corner of the state, we can begin to understand the topographic complexity of this area.

Some years ago, geologists conceived these random hills to have been built at the interfaces between three coexisting lobes of ice, the Lake Michigan Lobe on the west, the Saginaw Lobe centrally, and the

Wabash River looking upstream near Logansport during a February 1959 flood. During the Maumee Torrent at the close of the Ice Age, floodwater volume and speed of flow were several times greater than during modern floods.   *Photo by William A. Oates*

Huron-Erie Lobe on the east, but the geologic history of this region is now known to be much more complex than that. In most areas the deposits of the various lobes overlap in such a way as to indicate much backing and filling as the ice of one lobe became more active and overrode both deposits and ice of an adjacent less-active lobe. The result is topographic chaos; the only simple elements of the topography are some of the valleys that mark meltwater discharge routes associated with the final glacial events.

> Great floods have flown from simple sources.
> —*Shakespeare,* All's Well That Ends Well

In the southeastern corner of the Northern Lake and Moraine Region, the last glacial episode that directly influenced Indiana built as its final mark on the land the massive Fort Wayne Moraine, which forms two sides of a triangle with its western apex at Fort Wayne. Following this, the ice melted rapidly, and an ancestral phase of Lake Erie was formed between the moraine and remnants of the ice to the

east. A seemingly benign event, but watch out! There is one last dramatic happening to describe. Remember the Maumee Torrent, which we touched upon at Vincennes?

This lake stage rose until it overtopped the moraine at Fort Wayne, probably at the position of a tunnel valley through the moraine. Erosion of the outlet rapidly lowered the level of the lake, and many cubic miles of icy water were suddenly released to create the most powerful single flood event the Wabash Valley has ever known. Channelways and deposits of this flood, well above the level of any flood since, mark the plain of the Wabash River all the way to its junction with the Ohio.

The Maumee Torrent was the last major dynamic geologic event to shape Indiana's landscape. Relentless, but slower, erosional processes continue, hastened now in many places by man's activities. And here this narrative must end—but not without a return look at our state from space, where now we find that we can see vastly more in the landscape than we could before.

4. Cradle of Life: Soils

Donald P. Franzmeier

Soil is a nutritive platform, the Mother Earth for all life. It's a stage that holds up every actor on the Earth and nourishes them.

—*Francis D. Hole, University of Wisconsin*

Soil is one of Indiana's major natural resources, and we are the custodians of this resource for a relatively brief time in its overall life. We use soils to grow food for ourselves and our livestock, and wood for our houses, furniture, and paper; to support the buildings we live and work in and the roads we drive on; and to receive and purify many of our waste products. Soils are the source of many antibiotics. Soil also forms the base of the food pyramid which supports all native vegetation, lower animals, and wildlife living in terrestrial habitats. All water that enters our aquifers first passes through the soil, and all runoff that enters our streams and lakes first flows over, and is influenced by, the surrounding soils. The better we understand our soil and land resources, the better we can care for them, and the better will be the resources that we leave for future generations.

SOIL FORMATION FACTORS

$$s = f(cl, o, r, p, t, \ldots)$$

—*Hans Jenny*, Factors of Soil Formation *(1941)*

Jenny's environmental formula for soil formation states that any soil property (*s*) is influenced by the environmental factors climate (*cl*), organisms (*o*), relief (*r*), and parent material (*p*), during a certain period of time (*t*). The relationships inherent in this expression have clarified the interaction between soils and environment for generations of soil scientists and ecologists. Students remember the factors using the mnemonic "*clorpt.*"

Parent materials. Soil parent material is the substance from which soils form. The original source of most soil parent materials in Indiana is the underlying sedimentary bedrock. Some soils developed directly on these rocks; others developed on bedrock material that was ground, mixed, and transported by the action of glacial ice. Some of this glacial material was further transported and sorted by water and wind.

The size of particles has a great influence on the properties of rocks and soils. The finest particles are clay size (less than 0.002 mm in diameter). Clay particles make soils plastic and sticky. They retain many plant nutrients and hold water tightly, so tightly that much of it is not available to plants. Silt particles (0.002 to 0.05 mm) give the soil a "floury" texture. They hold much water, most of which is available to plants. Sand particles (0.05 to 2 mm) hold few nutrients and little water, but tend to make the soil easy to work. The term *soil texture* refers to various mixtures of sand, silt, and clay. The *loam* texture class comprises significant amounts of sand, silt, and clay; sandy loam, for example, contains mostly sand particles, but also some silt and clay.

Soils that result from bedrock parent material weathering in place are termed *residual*. Many soils in southern Indiana developed from local sedimentary rocks. Sandstone is very resistant to weathering and forms large highland areas and local cliffs and outcrops. Siltstone and shale, composed of silt and clay particles, respectively, weather more readily than sandstone and thus form lowland areas. Limestone is a sedimentary rock composed mainly of calcium and magnesium carbonate minerals. Acid groundwater dissolves fissures and caverns in limestone bedrock through which water moves easily after it percolates through the soil. Sedimentary rocks occur in various combinations, such as sandstone with shale, siltstone with shale, and shale with limestone.

A glacier is a large mass of ice, so thick that it flows like a liquid, but very slowly. As it moves, it grinds up and transports the material beneath it, which it then deposits as *till*, a mixture of clay, silt, sand, gravel, and boulders.

During the Ice Age, the ice mass extending into Indiana was a few thousand feet thick and hundreds of miles long, covering all of Indiana except the south-central part. There were probably several major glaciations, but the last two, the Illinoian and Wisconsinan glacial advances, deposited the materials on which our soils developed. Around 12,000 years ago the glacier left the state, and has been absent since (see also chapter 2, "Indiana on Ice").

When the ice melted, the water carried ground rock material away from the glacier and down the streams and rivers. The coarser-textured material was deposited from faster-moving water as *outwash* to form outwash plains and terraces, and the finer material was deposited from slowly moving and still water in lakes as *lacustrine deposits*. Before these deposited materials were stabilized by vegetation, some of them were picked up and moved by the wind. The finer sand particles were carried a short distance and deposited as *eolian sand* in dunes. The silt-size particles were transported a longer distance and deposited as *loess*. There is some loess in the surface layers, or horizons, of most soils of the state, and some soils consist entirely of loess.

After the glaciers melted from Indiana, some other parent materials were deposited or formed. *Peat* is plant material that accumulated and was preserved underwater in lakes. Partially decayed peat is called *muck*. *Alluvium* is sediment that was deposited by water in recent times. It might cover an extensive area on a floodplain or a small area in a local depression.

Relief. Two important factors in the formation of soils are shape of the land surface (topography) and the depth of the water table. Topography determines how water moves over and within the soil. Internal drainage and depth to the water table greatly affect soil properties and the uses to which it can be put.

The bedrock of Indiana dips slightly to the west, but so gently that it seems to be horizontally bedded. Alternating layers of more and less resistant rocks and this dipping of the bedrock are responsible for major topographic differences across the southern part of the state. The more resistant rocks form highland areas, and the more weatherable rocks form lowlands. The east edges of the resistant rock areas are marked by escarpments characterized by steeply sloping soils. The glaciers left deposits in the northern two-thirds of the state which covered the more rugged topography of the south and smoothed the landscape by grinding down the hills and filling the valleys (see also chapter 3, "The View from the Window").

In slightly more than half of Indiana's soils, the water table is within 18 inches of the surface for at least a few months of the year. One indication of the presence of a high water table is soil color. Iron and manganese compounds are responsible for much of the color of subsurface soil horizons. These elements change chemical characteristics subject to the presence or absence of oxygen.

A well-aerated soil is a uniform reddish to brownish color because of the presence of oxidized iron compounds. When the soil becomes waterlogged, however, oxygen is excluded from the soil pores, and the iron and manganese compounds are reduced, become much more soluble, and can move in the soil. The area they move from becomes gray, the color of the other soil minerals. If they move entirely out of the soil, the whole profile becomes gray. More commonly, a fluctuating water table results in a mottled appearance with spots of gray, brown, and black, often within a distance of an inch or less.

Soil scientists use these color patterns to evaluate the water and oxidation-reduction status of a soil. In the profile sketches that follow, significant wetness and reduction features are indicated by broken vertical lines. The depth to these features is critical for many soil uses, such as drainage of farmland, drainage around basements and footings of buildings, home waste disposal, and preservation of wetlands.

Plant roots need air to grow, and most plants do not thrive in waterlogged soil. For efficient crop production in these soils, the water table that is high mainly in the late winter and spring is lowered by underground drainage systems, most commonly by 3- to 4-inch diameter perforated plastic drain tubes placed about 3 to 4 feet deep within the soil profile and 50 to 150 feet apart. These drains commonly empty into larger tubes and then into ditches that are dug and maintained by landowners in a cooperative venture. Most soils with seasonally high water tables (including many former lakes and wetlands) that are used for crop production have been drained in this manner, and are now farmland. Beaver Lake in Newton County, which occupied 28,500 acres in 1834, was drained, and now most of it is farmed. Today, however, the installation of new farm drain systems is strictly regulated to preserve our undrained wetlands. These areas function to replenish groundwater, provide habitat for wildlife, and serve as flood-control reservoirs.

Many houses in Indiana are built without access to sewer systems and depend on individual treatment systems to purify their sewage. This is commonly done with a septic tank with drains connected to an effluent absorption field that is constructed similarly to a farm drainage system, but operates in reverse—water is added to the soil. Soil conditions, especially the depth to wetness features and the presence of a tight layer that limits percolation of water, are critical to the design and function of these facilities.

Two very important attributes of soils are their position in the landscape and their profile characteristics. The relation of these attributes is shown in a set of block diagrams with profile sketches of a few Indiana soil series. Soil landforms come in many different sizes, and their size is significant. In the block diagrams, large *landscape units,* such as till plains, moraines, bevels, and terraces, are shown in uppercase letters on the land surface. These features can be seen while driving through an area. Distinctive but smaller parts of a landscape unit, called *landscape components,* are shown in lowercase letters in the block diagrams. Examples include swells (convex areas) and swales (concave areas) of nearly level till plains and the hillslopes components.

The term *bevel* is used to describe landscape features just as it is used in woodworking. If a flat board with 90° corners at all edges is planed at 45°, the newly cut surface is a *bevel*. Similarly, a newly

formed flat land surface may have rather square edges, which are subsequently cut down through geologic erosion. The overall cut surface is like a bevel, but on close examination the beveled edge is cut by many ravines and is quite irregular. As in woodworking, the beveled edge is younger than the surface into which it was cut.

Hillslopes consist of several components. The *summit* is the uppermost part of the hillslope. Downward from the summit is the *convex shoulder,* the *linear backslope,* the concave *footslope,* and the *toeslope* on alluvial fill. Not all of these components are present in every hillslope, however. For example, in a small hillslope profile, the backslope might be missing, and the shoulder joins the footslope.

Climate. Soils have been affected by the climate of their environment during the entire time of their formation. After the glaciers retreated from Indiana, the climate of the region was cool and moist. Then it gradually became warmer and drier until around 5,000 to 3,000 years ago, when the direction of climatic change reversed and the state became somewhat cooler and more moist.

In the present climate, precipitation is greater than evapotranspiration (the water evaporated from the soil surface and transpired by plants growing on it). The excess water soaks into the soil or runs off the surface. Both of these processes are important to soil development.

Percolating water dissolves materials in the soil and moves them downward in the soil profile or out of the soil entirely. It also displaces solid particles such as clay downward in the soil. Runoff causes erosion and shapes the landscape surface. Although there is an excess of precipitation during average years, there is usually a time during the summer when plants experience some drought stress. Some years the drought is severe enough to kill some kinds of plants.

Vegetation. The vegetation that grew on a soil during its formation also influences the properties of that soil. The vegetation throughout Indiana was influenced by the last glaciation, either because this large mass of ice covered the area and destroyed the plants or because it influenced the climate for miles around it.

The landscape was barren after the glacier left. Vegetation again covered the area by the process of plant succession, which was initiated by the invasion of lichens, mosses, sedges, grasses, and broad-leaved herbs. Soon thereafter, deciduous shrubs moved into the cool, inhospitable areas. Some of them fixed nitrogen, which is necessary for plant growth but is not present in the ground-up rock. Then coniferous trees that thrive in a cool climate, such as spruce and fir, moved in. As the climate became warmer and drier, spruce and fir were replaced by pines, and eventually by deciduous forest species, probably similar to those growing in some undisturbed areas of the state today. As the climate grew warmer and drier still, prairie vegetation moved in from the west. When the climate again became cooler and wetter during the last few thousand years, forest vegetation largely replaced prairie (see also chapter 10, "In the Glacier's Wake").

When European settlers arrived in Indiana, most of the land was covered with hardwood forest, with some prairie vegetation in the western part of the state. The natural vegetation has a very important influence on the kinds of soil horizons formed. Prairie soils have deep dark surface horizons. In contrast, many woodland soils have a thin organic mat, a thin dark horizon, and then a light-colored, leached horizon.

The settlers cut the trees of the forest and plowed the prairie for farmland, so very little original vegetation remains. Marks of this vegetation, however, are still evident in the soil landscape. In the areas that were forested, the surface soil horizons are generally light in color and a few remnant woodlots remain, but in the former prairie area, the soils tend to be darker and the only trees are those planted around homesites.

Time. The time of soil formation refers to the age of that land surface. In Indiana, some of the rocks are many millions of years old, but younger surfaces were cut into these rocks or they were covered by younger materials, so the surface age is much younger. Many land surfaces date back to glacial times when glacial till, outwash, and loess covered most of the northern two-thirds of the state and loess covered much of the southern part. Some surfaces, however, are older. The youngest surfaces are those on floodplains and in bogs where organic soil material has accumulated. Older soils show more distinctive horizon features than do younger soils.

Soil properties, horizons, and series. Different combinations of the soil-forming factors result in different soil-forming processes. Through these processes, soils form distinctive horizons. The nature of these horizons is used to define the different kinds (genera) of soils, called soil series. Properties important in characterizing soil series include texture (size of particles), color, structure (arrangement of particles), consistence (hardness), and pH (acidity-alkalinity). The soil series plus the textural class of the surface horizon is the soil phase (species), e.g., Miami silt loam. Profile sketches outside the block diagrams illustrate the major kinds of soil horizons in some important soils.

Just as a distinctive set of soil properties characterizes a soil horizon, a certain set of soil horizons defines a soil series. Soil series are named after locations where the soil was first identified. For example, the Chalmers, Brookston, and Princeton soils, illustrated in the diagrams, are named after Indiana communities. Map units in soil surveys are named for the major soil series they contain, plus the slope gradient and the degree of erosion. Published soil surveys provide detailed information about soil profile and landscape characteristics of all map units, and also predict how the soils will respond to various uses.

THE SOIL REGIONS OF INDIANA

The simple story of the soils of Indiana is largely one of glacial action. Thousands of years ago great ice sheets hundreds of feet thick spread over most of the state, scraping down hills, filling valleys, and grinding the rocks to gravel and flour.

—*T. M. Bushnell,* The Story of Indiana Soils *(1944)*

Sandy soils (Regions 1 and 4). In Soil Regions 1 and 4, sandy material was deposited by water, and some of this material was subsequently moved by wind and piled into dunes. At the southern tip of Lake Michigan, sand was deposited on the beach and then blown into high dunes. This area is part of the Calumet Lacustrine Plain physiographic region (see block diagram). Soils formed on these dunes (e.g., Oakville) are relatively young and have weakly developed horizons. Black oak and white oak were the dominant pre-settlement trees on these soils, whereas such mesic species as sugar maple and American beech occupied the coves among the dunes. The soils in the low-lying sandy lake plains (e.g., Maumee) have dark surface horizons and B horizons that are gray because of their wet and reduced condition.

South of Lake Michigan in the Kankakee Outwash and Lacustrine Plain, sandy materials were deposited when the ancestral Kankakee River meandered over the sandy lake plain. The wind piled some of this material into dunes that are smaller and have stronger soil development than in those along Lake Michigan. In many soils the subsoil has thin bands, called *lamellae,* that are finer in texture than the surrounding material (see Chelsea profile).

The low-lying Maumee and Morocco soils of Region 1 have been farmed for many years, while the soils on the dunes were left in forest. More recently, the trees were bulldozed from some of the dunes and the soils were irrigated and planted to crops. These soils are very poorly suited to crop production, however, because they are highly wind-erodible and their water holding capacity is very low. The low-lying sandy soils, which are saturated with water in the subsoil several months of the year (see profile sketches), have been drained to lower the water table and permit crop production.

Soil Region 4 occurs in north-central and southwestern Indiana. In this region, sandy outwash materials were deposited on outwash plains or terraces; the wind then moved some of the sandy material into dunes. In contrast to those of Region 1, almost all soils of Region 4 lack wetness features. The soils on dunes also have a higher available water-holding capacity and better nutrient-holding ability than those in Region 1, and can be used effectively for crop production. Many of these soils along the lower Wabash and White River valleys are used for growing cantaloupes, watermelons, and tomatoes. Other soils of the region are used for more conventional farm crops such as corn, wheat, and soybeans.

Soils on water-deposited materials (Regions 2 and 3). These soils formed in glacial outwash, lacustrine (lake) deposits, and alluvium in various parts of the state. Soils formed in outwash deposits occur on two landscape units, *outwash plains* and *terraces.* Outwash plains are generally on upland positions, while a terrace is enclosed in a

Chelsea soil profile developed in dune sand in the sandy lake plain region of northwestern Indiana.   *Photo by Donald P. Franzmeier*

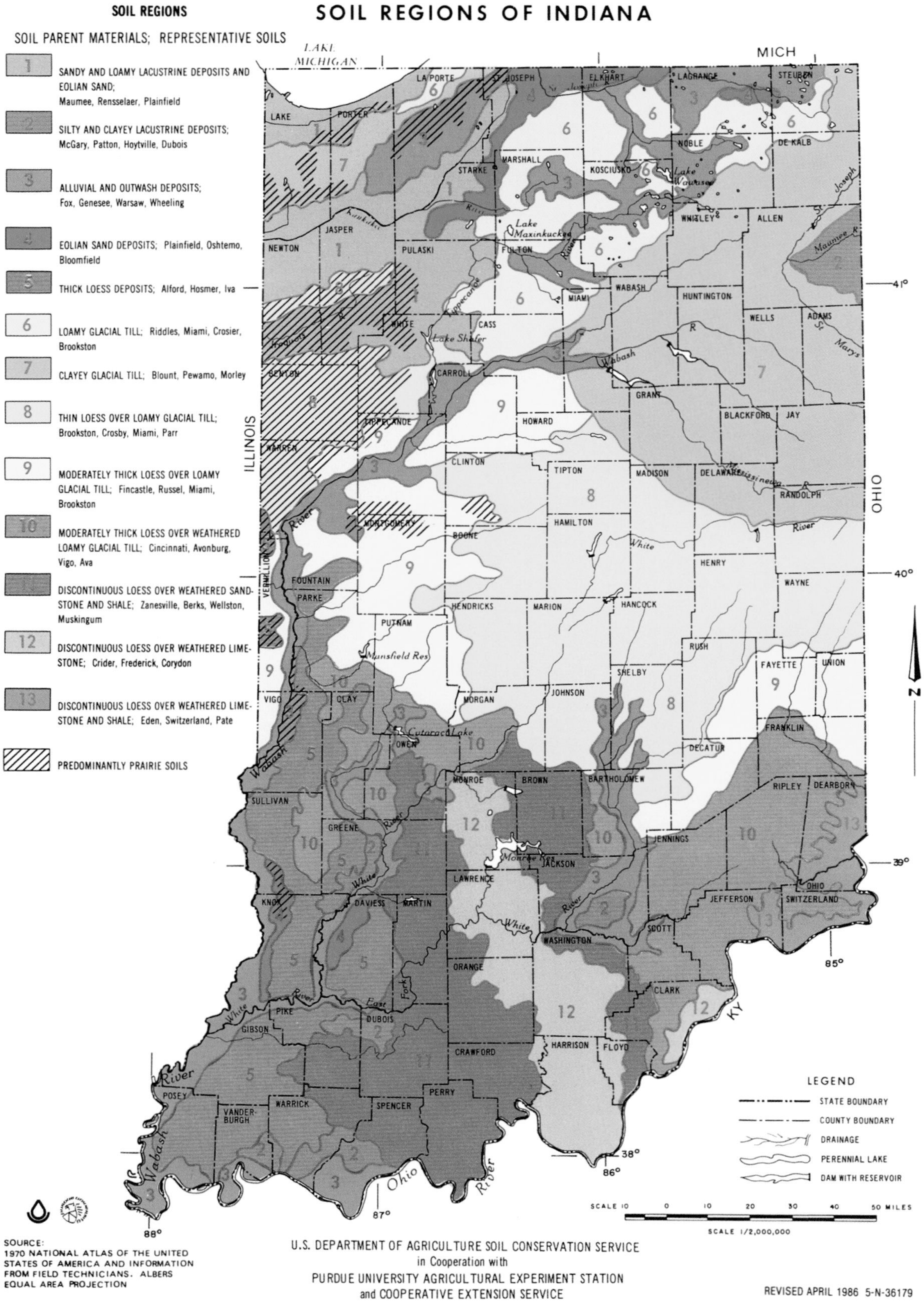

SOIL REGIONS OF INDIANA
SOIL REGIONS
SOIL PARENT MATERIALS; REPRESENTATIVE SOILS
1 SANDY AND LOAMY LACUSTRINE DEPOSITS AND EOLIAN SAND; Maumee, Rensselaer, Plainfield
2 SILTY AND CLAYEY LACUSTRINE DEPOSITS; McGary, Patton, Hoytville, Dubois
3 ALLUVIAL AND OUTWASH DEPOSITS; Fox, Genesee, Warsaw, Wheeling
4 EOLIAN SAND DEPOSITS; Plainfield, Oshtemo, Bloomfield
5 THICK LOESS DEPOSITS; Alford, Hosmer, Iva
6 LOAMY GLACIAL TILL; Riddles, Miami, Crosier, Brookston
7 CLAYEY GLACIAL TILL; Blount, Pewamo, Morley
8 THIN LOESS OVER LOAMY GLACIAL TILL; Brookston, Crosby, Miami, Parr
9 MODERATELY THICK LOESS OVER LOAMY GLACIAL TILL; Fincastle, Russel, Miami, Brookston
10 MODERATELY THICK LOESS OVER WEATHERED LOAMY GLACIAL TILL; Cincinnati, Avonburg, Vigo, Ava
11 DISCONTINUOUS LOESS OVER WEATHERED SANDSTONE AND SHALE; Zanesville, Berks, Wellston, Muskingum
12 DISCONTINUOUS LOESS OVER WEATHERED LIMESTONE; Crider, Frederick, Corydon
13 DISCONTINUOUS LOESS OVER WEATHERED LIMESTONE AND SHALE; Eden, Switzerland, Pate
PREDOMINANTLY PRAIRIE SOILS
LAKE MICHIGAN
MICH
ILLINOIS
OHIO
KY
LAKE
PORTER
LA PORTE
ST. JOSEPH
ELKHART
LAGRANGE
STEUBEN
NOBLE
DE KALB
STARKE
MARSHALL
KOSCIUSKO
WHITLEY
ALLEN
NEWTON
JASPER
PULASKI
FULTON
MIAMI
WABASH
HUNTINGTON
WELLS
ADAMS
WHITE
CASS
CARROLL
BENTON
GRANT
BLACKFORD
JAY
TIPPECANOE
HOWARD
WARREN
CLINTON
TIPTON
MADISON
DELAWARE
RANDOLPH
MONTGOMERY
HAMILTON
BOONE
FOUNTAIN
VERMILLION
PARKE
HENDRICKS
MARION
HANCOCK
HENRY
WAYNE
PUTNAM
RUSH
FAYETTE
UNION
VIGO
CLAY
MORGAN
JOHNSON
SHELBY
FRANKLIN
OWEN
DECATUR
MONROE
BROWN
BARTHOLOMEW
RIPLEY
DEARBORN
SULLIVAN
GREENE
JENNINGS
OHIO
SWITZERLAND
JACKSON
LAWRENCE
JEFFERSON
KNOX
DAVIESS
MARTIN
WASHINGTON
SCOTT
ORANGE
CLARK
PIKE
DUBOIS
GIBSON
HARRISON
FLOYD
CRAWFORD
POSEY
VANDER-BURGH
WARRICK
SPENCER
PERRY
Lake Wawasee
Lake Maxinkuckee
Lake Shafer
Mansfield Res
Cataract Lake
Monroe Res
Kankakee
Tippecanoe
Wabash
White
Mississinewa
Maumee R
St. Joseph
St. Marys
East Fork
Ohio River
41°
40°
39°
38°
85°
86°
87°
88°
N
LEGEND
STATE BOUNDARY
COUNTY BOUNDARY
DRAINAGE
PERENNIAL LAKE
DAM WITH RESERVOIR
SCALE 10 0 10 20 30 40 50 MILES
SCALE 1/2,000,000
SOURCE:
1970 NATIONAL ATLAS OF THE UNITED STATES OF AMERICA AND INFORMATION FROM FIELD TECHNICIANS. ALBERS EQUAL AREA PROJECTION
U.S. DEPARTMENT OF AGRICULTURE SOIL CONSERVATION SERVICE
in Cooperation with
PURDUE UNIVERSITY AGRICULTURAL EXPERIMENT STATION
and COOPERATIVE EXTENSION SERVICE
REVISED APRIL 1986 5-N-36179

Soil Regions of Indiana. Almost all of Indiana's soils formed under deciduous forest vegetation except those areas in the western part of the state where prairie was prevalent. *Map courtesy of Purdue University / Natural Resources Conservation Service*

river valley. Typically, coarse material settled out of the outwash streams before finer material, hence these soils formed in loamy material over sandy and gravelly material (e.g., in the Fox, Ockley, and Wea soils).

The soils are mainly on broad, flat areas with some swells. At some depth below the outwash, in many places there is a less permeable layer that holds up the water. If that layer is near the surface, the soils are more poorly drained, and if it is deeper, the soils are better drained, even on nearly level slopes (see Ockley photo and Fox and Ockley sketches). The Fox and Ockley soils formed under forest vegetation, mainly American beech, sugar maple, and white oak, and Wea formed under prairie.

Most of the soils that formed in outwash are used for crop production. Where the water table is close to the surface, crop yields are consistently high, and these soils rank among the most productive in the state. Where the water table is deep, crop yields can be severely reduced in a dry year, and many of these soils are irrigated. Soils on outwash deposits that have a coarse-textured surface horizon are subject to wind erosion and should be covered at all times.

In contrast to outwash that was deposited from moving water, finer-textured sediments were deposited as lacustrine deposits from meltwater streams that had become ponded in lakes or in slackwater terraces some distance from the major stream. The resulting landscape units are lake plains. These soils range in texture from loamy to clayey and frequently have wetness features. Soils on swells (e.g., Nappanee) have light-colored surface horizons, while surfaces of those in swales (Hoytville) are dark-colored. Beech, maple, white oak, and hickory were the dominant species on these soils.

Most of these soils have been drained by tile lines and are highly productive for row crops. Some of them are difficult to drain, however, because they are so high in clay or because they lie so low in the local landscape that it is difficult to find an outlet for the underground drainage lines. Such soils are considered to be wetlands.

The major floodplains form part of Soil Region 3, but smaller floodplains occur along numerous small streams throughout the state. As a result of differences in texture, carbonate content, pH, organic matter content, stoniness, and other properties, there are many different kinds of soils on floodplains.

Soils formed in thick loess (Region 5). In Soil Region 5 along the Lower Wabash and White rivers in the Wabash Lowland, loess is thick enough that the entire soil formed in it. Most of these soils are hilly, but some are on broad flats. In many other parts of the state, loess is the parent material of the upper parts of many soil profiles.

Loess is an ideal soil parent material. It is loose, and most soil horizons formed in it have a relatively large percentage of pore space, permitting water to move through these pores readily and roots to penetrate with few restrictions. The silt particles of loess hold much water after a rainy period, and plants can absorb most of it, so these soils have a high available water-holding capacity. Silt-size particles, however, are most subject to water erosion. Sand grains, in contrast, are heavy enough that they are not easily moved by water flowing over the soil, and clay particles attach to each other and to organic matter to form aggregates that also are not readily transported.

Alford soils formed where loess is more than about 7 feet thick, whereas soils with fragipans (e.g., Hosmer) formed in loess of intermediate thickness (4 to 7 feet). Fragipans are dense, brittle subsoil horizons that restrict water movement and root penetration. They commonly are 20 to 30 inches thick and begin at depths from 20 to 50 inches. They consist of large prisms surrounded by light-colored, silty zones that form a polygonal pattern when viewed in a horizontal section. Fragipans tend to be deeper in more poorly drained soils. They are depicted by the funnel-shaped pattern in the Hosmer profile sketch.

Originally these soils were forested, primarily black and white oak and American beech, but most of the deep loess soils, especially the flatter ones, are now farmed. Some of the sloping soils are used for fruit trees such as apples and peaches, and some are in pasture. It is important to keep these soils covered at all times to reduce erosion. This can be done by using crop rotations that include perennial crops, leaving crop residue on the soil, and growing winter cover crops.

Soils formed in Wisconsinan glacial till (Regions 6, 7, 8, and 9). Around 21,000 years ago, the Wisconsinan glacier advanced to the southern limit of Soil Region 9. It ground up and mixed most of the material over which it moved, so most soils previously formed were destroyed. The glacier left a nearly level to undulating surface, called a *ground moraine* or *till plain,* in the areas where it kept moving, and an undulating to hilly surface, called an *end moraine,* where it stood still for a time near its outer margin. The large, nearly level glacial surface in central and northern Indiana is called the Tipton Till Plain.

Immediately after the glacier retreated, loess was deposited over these surfaces. On the till plains, loess filled in the low places in the landscape and thus tended to level out the surface, creating a loess surface that is smoother than the surface of the till below it.

In the forested part of the state, the soils in the concave *swales* (e.g., Brookston) are dark-colored and those on the convex *swells* (e.g., Crosby) are light-colored. Organic matter from tree leaves and understory vegetation was incorporated into the soil of the swales and preserved by the low-oxygen, wet conditions, thereby forming dark-colored humus.

On the swells, however, the water table was lower and the organic

Ockley soil profile developed in glacial outwash on terraces under forest vegetation.   *Photo by Donald P. Franzmeier*

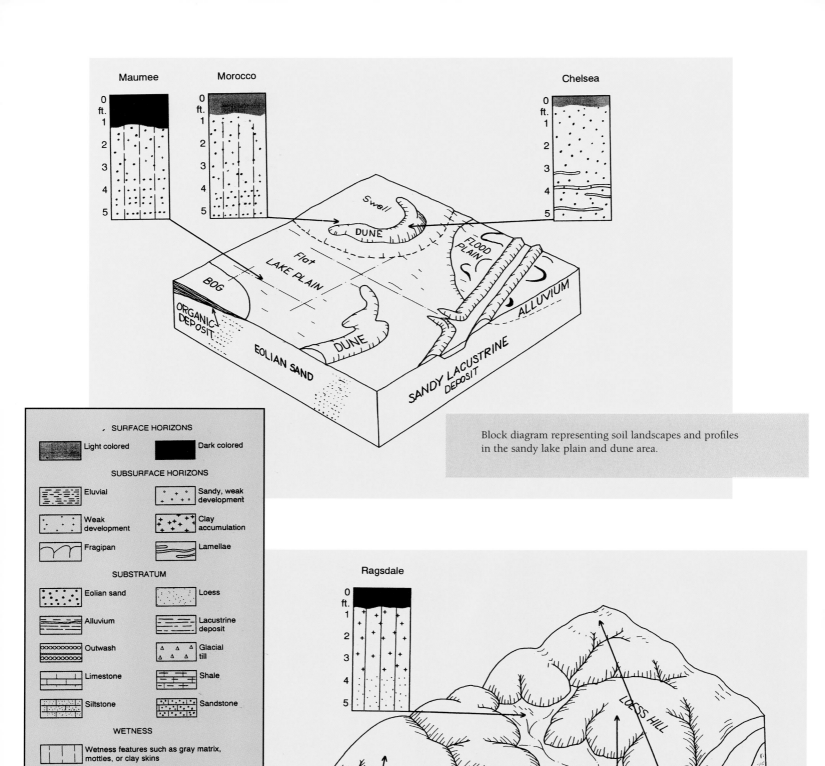

Maumee Morocco Chelsea

Block diagram representing soil landscapes and profiles
in the sandy lake plain and dune area.

SURFACE HORIZONS

Light colored   Dark colored

SUBSURFACE HORIZONS

Eluvial   Sandy, weak
                           development

Weak   Clay
development   accumulation

Fragipan   Lamellae

SUBSTRATUM

Eolian sand   Loess

Alluvium   Lacustrine
                          deposit

Outwash   Glacial
                          till

Limestone   Shale

Siltstone   Sandstone

WETNESS

Wetness features such as gray matrix,
mottles, or clay skins

Ragsdale

Princeton

Alford

Hosmer

Block diagram representing soil
landscapes and profiles in the
southern dune and loess area.

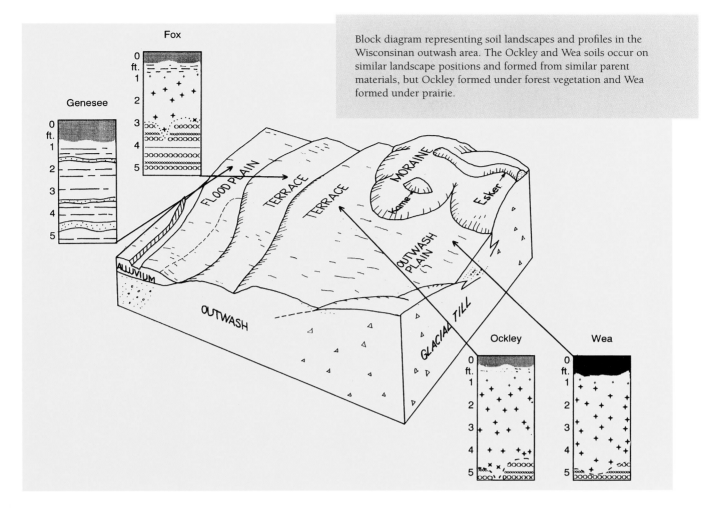

Block diagram representing soil landscapes and profiles in the Wisconsinan outwash area. The Ockley and Wea soils occur on similar landscape positions and formed from similar parent materials, but Ockley formed under forest vegetation and Wea formed under prairie.

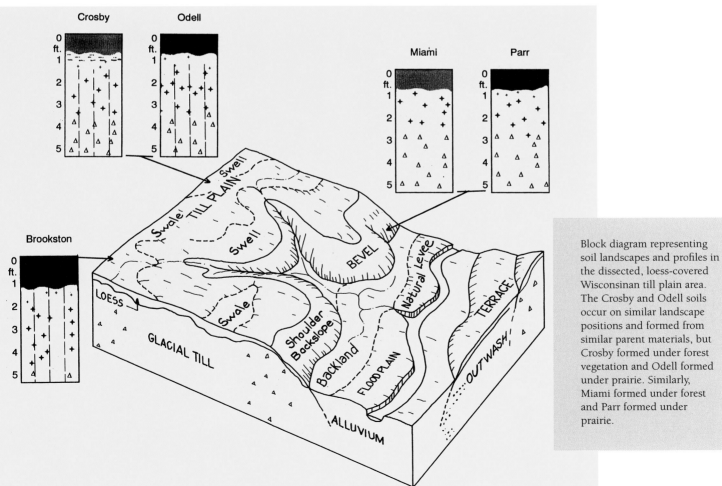

Block diagram representing soil landscapes and profiles in the dissected, loess-covered Wisconsinan till plain area. The Crosby and Odell soils occur on similar landscape positions and formed from similar parent materials, but Crosby formed under forest vegetation and Odell formed under prairie. Similarly, Miami formed under forest and Parr formed under prairie.

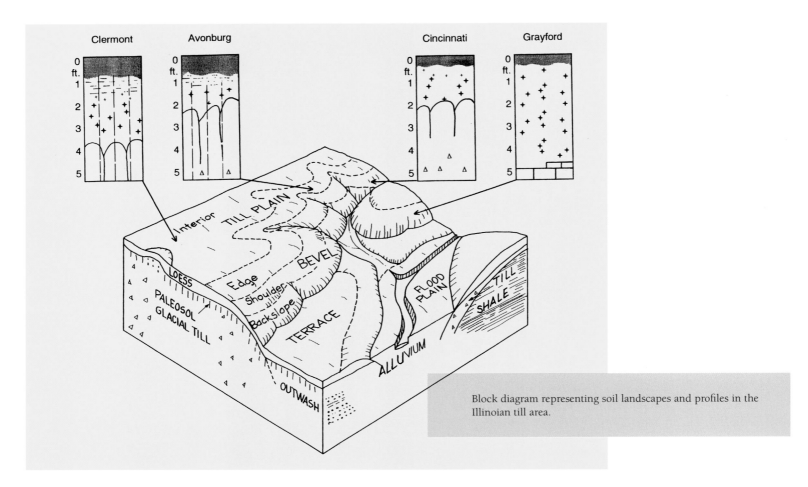

Block diagram representing soil landscapes and profiles in the Illinoian till area.

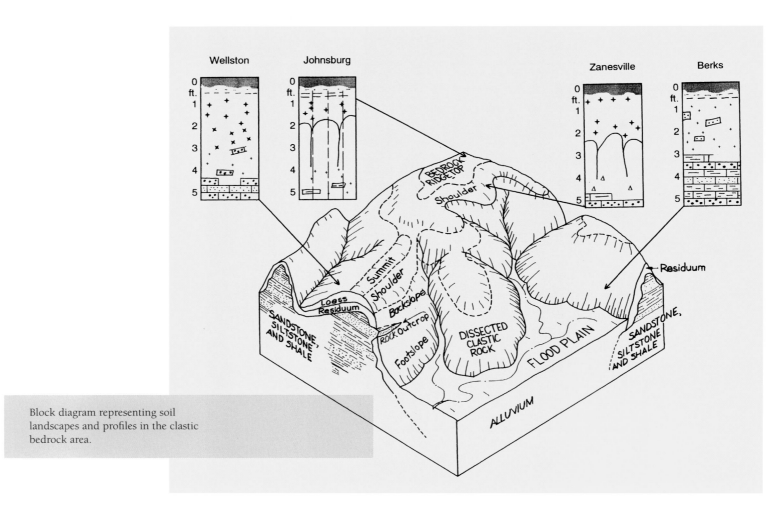

Block diagram representing soil landscapes and profiles in the clastic bedrock area.

Brookston soil profile, a poorly drained soil developed in glacial till in tillplain swales. *Photo by Donald P. Franzmeier*

by the glacier have not been leached from the soil as they have in some older soils. In most of the area, loess covers the till to different depths. Loess-derived soil horizons have a high water-holding capacity, and most of this water is available for use by plants.

Soils on the moraines are more hilly than those on the till plains, but in some moraines, especially those in Soil Region 7, the topography is barely distinguishable from that in the till plains. On the sloping soils, erosion by water is the most serious problem.

Soils on Illinoian glacial till (Region 10). Soil Region 10 has been called the Illinoian Till Plain, but recent investigations suggest that its glacial drift may have been deposited earlier than Illinoian time. This plain consists of broad, very flat surfaces cut by sharp ravines. Soils were formed on this glacial drift during the warmer interglacial time (Sangamon), and many of them were later eroded. This erosion surface was subsequently covered by about 40 to 100 inches of loess during Wisconsinan time.

The present soils on the loess-covered till plains have very light-colored surface horizons because they are very low in organic matter. Soil wetness features are near the surface in the Clermont (Cobbsfork) soils on the till plain interior. They become progressively deeper in the Avonburg soils at the edge of the till plain, and in the Cincinnati soils on the shoulder of the till plain bevel. Fragipans are present in these three soils, but they are lacking in Grayford soils on the steeper backslopes. Beech and white oak were the predominant species on all the soils. In addition, the wetter soils supported more tuliptree and sweet gum, and the better-drained soils, Avonburg, Cincinnati, and Grayford, had more sugar maple.

The soils on the broad flats of this till plain are used mainly for row-crop agriculture, but poor physical conditions and compaction by farm machinery are special problems. For best crop yields, these soils should be drained with an underground drainage system, but in many areas it is difficult to find an outlet for the water.

Soils formed in clastic bedrock (Regions 11 and 13). The glaciers did not override the bedrock highs of south-central Indiana, so in this region the rugged topography was not ground down and smoothed as it was in the northern part of the state. Soil Region 11 is on *clastic* rocks such as sandstone, siltstone, and shale. It includes the Norman Upland (east part of the region) and the Crawford Upland (west part).

Water does not penetrate these rocks readily, so it runs off and carves an open drainage system in which the streams form a dendritic pattern. These regions have narrow ridgetops and steep side slopes. Most soils on less than 12 percent slopes have fragipans, illustrated by the Johnsburg soil on summits and the Zanesville soils on shoulders. On the backslopes, Wellston soils are on the moderate slopes, and the shallow Berks soils are on the steeper slopes.

White oak, other oak species, and hickory were the common species at the time of settlement. Now, oak and hickory predominate on the south- and west-facing slopes, but beech and maple are more abundant on the north- and east-facing slopes, which receive less direct solar radiation.

Soils on more gentle slopes are used mostly for pasture, but some are in forest and some are cultivated. Where sloping land is farmed, water erosion is a serious problem. Farmers are advised to keep the soil covered all the time, by growing winter cover crops to protect it when row crops are not in place, and by leaving all the crop residue on the surface instead of plowing it down. Around 50 to 60 years ago, many of the steep slopes were farmed and were severely eroded. Some of these areas are now healing under forest or permanent pasture vegetation.

The topography in Soil Region 13 is similar to that in Region 11, but the rocks are mainly shale with interbedded limestone strata.

matter in the soil was not so well preserved, resulting in soils much lighter in color. This gives soils on the till plains a distinctive "salt-and-pepper" appearance, especially visible from the air during the spring planting period, when many have been tilled. In some areas, better-drained soils have been eroded, exposing the reddish-brown subsoil, thereby adding another color to the pattern.

The Miami, Crosby, and Brookston soils make up a soil *catena,* a sequence of soils that are similar in all environmental factors of soil formation except topography, and thus natural soil drainage. In the reddish-brown areas are eroded well-drained Miami soils, the light gray areas are somewhat poorly drained Crosby soils, and the dark areas are poorly drained Brookston soils. Beech, sugar maple, white oak, and red oak were common on all these soils; hickory, ash, and elm were more common on the wetter soils. In the formerly prairie area of a large part of west-central Indiana, all of the soils are darker than their forest counterparts, with fewer color contrasts.

Within the Wisconsinan till area, the soils differ mainly by the texture of the glacial till, the depth of loess over the till, and the depth to wetness features, which are related to topography. Much of the glacial till in these soil regions is dense and very slowly permeable to downward-moving water. Thus, the soils on the till plain are wet much of the year and need to be artificially drained to be used for crop production. Underground drains empty into ditches, which in turn flow into natural streams, thereby lowering the water table to accommodate spring planting.

The soils on the till plains of these regions are nearly all used for farming, largely for growing corn, soybeans, and wheat. These soils are the most productive in the state, or for that matter in the world. They have high natural fertility because the soils are relatively young, and many of the plant nutrients released from the rocks ground up

Zanesville soil profile developed from loess over bedrock in unglaciated southern Indiana.   *Photo by Donald P. Franzmeier*

Where shale is dominant, the soils resemble those in Soil Region 11. Where limestone strata are thicker, however, the soils tend to be better drained and resemble those in Soil Region 12.

Soils over limestone (Region 12). This region has a drainage pattern much different from that in Regions 11 and 13. Here percolating water penetrates the limestone and dissolves it to form an underground drainage network. Much of the surface drainage is into the bedrock through closed depressions called *sinkholes.* Most sinkholes drain out the bottom, but some hold water. There are very few surface streams, and they flow only during intense rains. This kind of drainage results in a topography dotted with sinkholes called a *karst plain.* Bedford soils, with more than 30 inches of loess on the karst plain, have fragipans, but they are lacking in the Crider soils of steeper slopes where the loess is thinner. Caneyville soils are shallow to limestone rock.

In general the slopes in Region 12 are moderately sloping, so much of the limestone region is used for pasture and crops. Like those in Regions 11 and 13, the soils are very erodible, so slopes should be kept under cover at all times. Most of the more steeply sloping soils are in forest.

USE OF OUR SOIL RESOURCES

History celebrates the battlefields whereon we meet our death, but scorns to speak of the plowed fields whereby we thrive.

—*J. Henri Fabré, French naturalist*

How we use our soil resources affects all people, not just those who currently own or manage the land. If we use them properly, they will last forever. If we misuse them, however, we can also ruin them

forever. We can misuse our soil resources by removing land from the natural system or the crop production system, thus decreasing the *quantity* of soil available for growing plants, and by mistreating the soil and decreasing its *quality.* We must be concerned about how much natural or productive land we turn over to our descendants and how good the soil is. The quantity of soil available for growing plants is determined mainly by our decisions about land use. The main processes that decrease the quality of soil in Indiana are soil erosion, soil compaction, and chemical contamination.

We abuse our land because we regard it as a commodity belonging to us. When we see land as a community to which we belong, we may begin to use it with love and respect. . . . That land is a community is the basic concept of ecology, but that land is to be loved and respected is an extension of ethics.

—*Aldo Leopold,* A Sand County Almanac *(1949)*

Land use. In Indiana, recent development has encroached onto farmland at urban perimeters and along roads and highways. Once land is used for a highway, shopping mall, factory, or home site, it will never again be returned to natural vegetation or used to grow crops. Thus, we are continually losing farmland and natural areas.

Also, it is much more difficult and expensive to supply public services, such as utilities, fire and police protection, and transportation, in sprawling developments than in areas with higher population density. People in countries that have fewer land resources relative to their population (in Europe, for example) have learned that more compact development is necessary if the living environment is to be maintained. Hoosiers should also be more concerned about urban sprawl and related land-use changes.

For example, we could make better use of land already within a city instead of converting surrounding farmland to urban uses. Our ancestors settled and created towns on the good soils; when we convert farmland to other uses, we are losing some of our most productive farmland. We must consider how to preserve these soil resources, as an increasing population will require more food, recreation, and open space. Each of the soil landscapes described in this chapter has characteristics which make it better suited to some uses than others. These characteristics should be used in directing our decisions and planning for our future environment. Indiana does not have a state land-use plan, so it is important that we support local planning efforts.

The soil is the basis for a $4 billion industry in Indiana. However, despite nearly a half-century of efforts to combat erosion, more than 100 million tons of soil are eroded each year through the action of wind and water. That is enough to make a mound two feet wide and one foot high stretching from Indianapolis through the Mississippi Delta, and well into the Gulf of Mexico.

—*Governor's Soil Resource Study Commission (1984)*

Soil erosion. Every year some soil forms from the geologic material below it. This amount of soil loss can be tolerated without reducing the thickness of the soil. Soil formation, however, is measured in terms of thousands of years, so the amount of soil loss that can be tolerated in any one year is negligible. Except on very flat land, soils exposed to rain and wind with no cover on them will erode.

Falling raindrops strike the soil with much force, detaching soil particles in the process. Erosion continues as rainfall accumulates on the surface and then runs off the soil, carrying with it these detached soil particles. Accompanying the removal of the soil itself are losses of fertilizers, agricultural chemicals, and native soil fertility which enter the state's waters causing turbidity, pollution, and premature eutrophication of streams, ponds, lakes, and reservoirs.

Soil cover, in the form of living plants or dead crop residue, greatly retards erosion. First, this cover breaks the impact of raindrops on the soil surface. Plant roots anchor the soil mass and create pores in the soil for water to enter, reducing the amount of runoff. Plant residue also forms small dams on the soil surface that slow down the runoff.

Thus, farmers should keep practically all soils under cover all the time. This can be done by keeping the land in forest, pasture, or forage crops (hay), using crop rotations that include forage crops, and keeping the soil at least partially covered when growing row crops. In Indiana, most farmland is used to grow row crops such as corn and soybeans that traditionally have been grown in cleanly tilled fields. Soil erosion can be controlled in these fields by using conservation tillage techniques which leave the soil surface covered at planting time. The practice of planting a new crop into a soil that still has all the residue on it from the previous crop is called "no-till." In cornfields, the required 30 percent cover necessary to control erosion can be accomplished by leaving the residue from the previous crop on the soil, and not plowing it down. Soybeans, however, produce less residue than corn, and it decays quickly, so former soybean fields might require the planting of a winter cover crop in early fall.

> An Indian watched as a pioneer settler was breaking prairie sod with a moldboard plow pulled by a yoke of oxen, then came to the scene of the plowing and stated in broken English, "Land wrong side up." The farmer, not comprehending, went back to turning the soil.
>
> —*Paraphrased from Ernest Swift, in* Conservation News *(mid-1960s)*

Wind also erodes soil, as can be seen by the dirty snow that sometimes falls and accumulates in Indiana. Soil cover also greatly reduces wind erosion. Another practice that reduces it is to break up the length of a field that is exposed to the wind with strips of green crops, fencerows, or windbreaks in the form of rows of trees and shrubs.

To make specific recommendations for managing soils, we need to know how various soil properties affect erosion. For example, the main factors that determine the amount of water erosion are the intensity of rainfall, the erodibility of the soil material, and the length and steepness of the slope. These factors are balanced by the practices the farmer uses, e.g., the amount of soil cover, tilling on the contour, etc. All these factors are represented in models that soil conservationists use to help the farmer select management practices that will reduce soil losses by wind and water erosion to tolerable levels.

Farmers and others can get technical help through the U.S. Natural Resources Conservation Service, the Indiana Department of Natural Resources, and the Purdue Cooperative Extension Service. Together they sponsor the "T by 2,000" program, which strives to control erosion within tolerable levels (T) by the year 2000.

Soil compaction. Plant roots need nutrients, water, and air to grow. Roots, water, and air all move through soil voids, spaces, or pores. If the soil has sufficient pore space, roots have room to grow, and water and air can move to the growing roots. If the soil is compacted by plowing or by heavy equipment being driven over it when it is wet, water and air cannot move readily through it. This is a special problem in Indiana because the soils are wet and most subject to compaction in the spring, when farmers do much of their field work.

Soil compaction is minimized by reducing the amount of traffic by tractors, plows, and other equipment through the field. The no-till method, used to combat soil erosion, also helps to reduce compaction because it reduces the traffic through the fields. Waiting to get on a moist field until it dries out also helps.

Use of chemicals. Modern farming methods include the use of chemical fertilizers to supply essential nutrients, herbicides to kill weeds, insecticides to control insect infestations, and fungicides to control diseases. When used properly, most of these chemicals do not damage the soils or the environment. Improper use, however, causes problems. For example, groundwater or surface waters can be contaminated by nitrate-nitrogen if nitrogen fertilizer rates are too high. Recommended nitrogen fertilizer application rates now match the amount of nitrogen known to be removed by the crop to be grown, so nitrate does not accumulate in the soil.

Reduced tillage greatly reduces the risks of soil erosion and compaction. The practice requires that weeds be controlled with chemicals instead of by cultivation, however. Many herbicides specifically kill a few kinds of weeds, so farmers can use small amounts of these chemicals only on the parts of the field where these weeds are a problem. Similarly, disease and insect problems can be controlled by smaller applications of specific chemicals.

Through integrated pest management (IPM), trained technicians scout a field, identify specific problems related to plant nutrition, soil compaction, weeds, insects, and diseases, and recommend the management practice or chemical application that should be used on certain areas of the field. Farmers who once tended to use large applications of chemicals to make sure that a problem was solved are now using these IPM techniques, which greatly reduce the amount of chemicals applied.

Application rates of many chemicals depend on soil properties, so farmers must have detailed knowledge about the kinds of soils in their fields. New techniques are being developed to farm by specific kinds of soils instead of by fields. This is accomplished by two different approaches. In one, a map of soil conditions is stored on a computer in the truck making the application, and the computer changes the application rate of fertilizer or pesticide as the truck moves through the field. In the other, an instrument mounted on the applicator truck senses a soil property, such as organic matter content, and a computer adjusts the application rate according to that property.

Soil biology. We have known for a long time that many kinds of small animals live in the soil, but they were mainly considered to be a curiosity. Farming practice emphasized chemical and physical processes. Now we have more appreciation for the biological processes.

An abundant and healthily functioning population of soil microbes is essential to many soil processes and soil-plant interactions. Nitrogen fixation, nutrient cycling, organic matter decomposition, and nutrient and water uptake all require suitable numbers of the appropriate bacteria, algae, protozoa, invertebrate animals, and mycorrhizal fungi. Many plant species simply cannot survive if their specific mycorrhizal symbiont is not present in the soil to sheath their roots, thereby facilitating nutrient and water absorption.

Earthworms are also receiving much attention, especially the large nightcrawlers. Their deep burrows allow water to percolate through the soil rather than running off the surface. Also, they mix the soil to considerable depth. In some soils, the subsoil contains more nutrients, such as calcium and potassium, than the surface horizon, and worms (ants also) can bring these nutrients to the zone where plant roots are most abundant.

Previously it was thought that compacted soil layers could be broken up by plowing them. Now it is known that breaking up one

"Salt and pepper" soil patterns on swell (lighter soils) and swale (darker soils) topography of a Wisconsinan-age glacial till plain. *Photo by J. E. Yahner*

Dark prairie soils of Benton County gridded in square-mile sections. *Photo by Marion Jackson*

Wind erosion of finer particles from fall-plowed depressional soil near Warsaw, Indiana. *Photo by Marion Jackson*

By weight or by volume, sediment eroded from soils is the most common water pollutant in Indiana. *Photo by Richard Fields*

compacted zone often causes compaction in another zone, usually lower in the soil where it is more difficult to treat. We have learned that often the most effective way to counteract compaction is to grow deep-rooted plants and encourage earthworms. We are also noticing that when the same crop is grown year after year, its yield is reduced, probably because the soil biological community is becoming less diverse. Finally, researchers are studying biological control of pests.

Preservation of wetlands. In recent years, the public has become much better informed about the importance of wetlands in replenishing groundwater supplies, hosting wildlife, and controlling floods. Consequently, the U.S. Congress has passed legislation that requires that certain wetlands be left in their natural state, or if a wetland is removed from its natural state, it must be replaced by equal land area that is converted to wetland.

Wetlands are defined according to soil, plant, and hydrologic criteria. Soils are an essential part of this determination because the morphology of a soil integrates the effects of soil wetness throughout the life of the soil—thousands of years. Climate varies considerably, so the length of time a soil is saturated and the depth of saturation vary greatly from one year to the next, but soil morphological properties are relatively constant. This makes soil a reliable indicator of wet conditions.

Responsibility for the soil resource. People are becoming more aware of the importance of using our soil resources, and other resources, in an ecologically sound manner. To accomplish this requires a better understanding of our soils and continued research in soil science and management. It also requires delicate adjustments to balance ecological concerns with the economic realities, because many of the ecologically sound practices are not cost-effective in the short term, and many of the seemingly economically sound practices are destructive in the long run.

Because the entire public will benefit from ecologically sound management techniques, their costs must be partially borne by the public rather than the landowner. This issue of how we use our soils is too important to be left in the hands of only scientists and agriculturists. Everyone's descendants depend on soil resources, so everyone should be concerned about them.

*   *   *

We can take no comfort at all in the fact that the problem [of exploitation of soil and water resources] is universal. Absurdly, nations fight wars over every inch of their political boundaries while mindlessly sacrificing whole regions to environmental degradation. Their patriots salute the flag and take up arms to defend the country against external enemies, while neglecting its environment and ignoring the real attacks being waged from within on the land they purport to love. Thousands of years are required for a soil to form in place, yet this amazingly intricate work of nature can be destroyed by man, with remarkable dispatch, in just a few decades. We must understand that, on the time-scale of human life, the soil is a non-renewable resource. So is a mature forest, a river, or an aquifer. They belong not only to those who are the titled owners at this moment, but to future generations as well. In an even more profound sense, both soil and water belong to the biosphere, to the order of nature, and—as one species among many, as one generation among many yet to come—we have no right to destroy them.

—*Daniel Hillel,* Out of the Earth *(1991)*

Water vapor over a reservoir, a visual confirmation of the hydrologic cycle in operation.   *Photo by Richard Fields*

5. Lifeblood of the Land: Water

John Simpson

All the rivers run into the sea;
Yet the sea is not full;
Unto the place from whence the rivers come,
Thither they return again.
> —*Ecclesiastes 1:7*

OUR WATER RESOURCE

Like our own bodies, Indiana is a living ecosystem. Water is its lifeblood.

Gaze at a map of Indiana, with its lakes, streams, rivers, and reservoirs, and watch the state come alive. The watery squiggles that splay throughout our 92 counties are more than lines on a map. Indiana's waterways serve as arteries, veins, and capillaries, those vital conduits that deliver nourishment.

Water joins air and land in a natural resources trio, the cornerstones of all life. Take away its water and Indiana becomes a midwestern Sahara, incapable of supporting nearly 6 million human residents. Our daily social, physical, economic, and environmental well-being depends upon water. Its value is beyond price.

No matter where you live in Indiana, you will find water in a variety of forms. Consider the following examples:

The Wabash River, stretching across the state's midsection, then southward along Indiana's western fringe, supplies water to historic cities such as Vincennes and Terre Haute. More than 350 miles of the Ohio River form Indiana's southern border, serving, among many other towns and cities, Evansville, Corydon, Jeffersonville, and Madison.

Southern Indiana's many farm ponds and surface mine pits provide quick and easy sweet spots to plop a bobber. Anglers have landed the state's largest bluegill, channel catfish, crappie, green sunfish, warmouth, white catfish, and yellow perch in such "honey holes."

In the northeastern region, scores of natural lakes dot Indiana's landscape where Ice Age glaciers plowed and cratered the earth.

In north-central Indiana, anglers find Indiana's best trout and salmon fishing along 63 miles of the St. Joseph River, which also serves industry and such major cities as South Bend and Mishawaka.

One of the world's largest industrial and commercial complexes exists along Indiana's 45-mile-long Lake Michigan shoreline. The 241 square miles of lake are a major water source for industries and public utilities.

Outdoor enthusiasts numbering in the tens of thousands visit the nine artificial lakes that the U.S. Army Corps of Engineers designed during the 1950s and 1960s for water control. This popular reservoir system covers almost 36,000 acres, with 10,750-acre Lake Monroe in south-central Indiana representing almost a third of that total. The state receives millions of tourism dollars at these sites.

Throughout Indiana, vast groundwater supplies stored in sand and gravel deposits and bedrock aquifers quench our dry palates and meet domestic and urban needs.

Man is but a reed,
the most feeble thing in nature,
The entire universe need not arm
itself to crush him . . .
a drop of water suffices to kill him.
> —*Pascal (1623–1662),* Pensées

Hoosiers fret that such stiff competition for the water resource is taking a toll, as pollution degrades water quality for humans and fish and wildlife. As one of the nation's top industrial states, Indiana faces injury from polychlorinated biphenyls (PCBs), heavy metals, and semi-volatile waste and sludge. As an agricultural giant, Indiana suffers from runoff of pesticides, animal waste, and eroded soil. Many of these problems began during the agro-industrial era of the 1940s and 1950s, when little data existed on the nature and impact of toxic substances. Fortunately, agricultural and industrial leaders are beginning to develop environmental initiatives concerning water resource protection.

In 1986, the Indiana Department of Environmental Management (IDEM) was founded; one of its major roles is to enforce water pollution regulations in regard to human health. For example, as many waterways receive municipal and industrial discharges, wastewater treatment is a major concern. IDEM sets standards to reduce pollutants into waterways.

To combat injury done to fish and wildlife resources, the Department of Natural Resources (DNR) began collecting financial damages in 1990 to fund restoration and purchase of new habitat. On a grassroots level, Hoosiers have taken to canoes, rowboats, and shorelines to patrol adopted waters that often wind past members' backyards. The DNR's Division of Outdoor Recreation has joined with such "river keepers" to strengthen and unify their efforts.

It is easy to take water resources for granted, but growing numbers of people now realize that such an attitude is unwise. Obviously, we cannot exist without water. Water has been vital to survival since the dawn of human history, and it will continue to meet the needs of our children only if we safeguard this precious resource.

INDIANA'S WATER AVAILABILITY

The earth holds a silver treasure
cupped between ocean bed and tenting sky.
Forever the heavens spend it,
in the showers that refresh our temperate lands . . .
Yet none is lost;
in vast convection our water is returned,
from soil to sky, and sky to soil,
and back again to fall as pure as blessing.
There never was less; there could never be more.
A mighty mercy upon which life depends,
for all its glittering shifts
water is constant.
> —*Donald Culross Peattie and Noel Peattie,* A Cup of Sky
> (1950)

Little Sugar Creek near West Terre Haute in Vigo County formerly ran rusty red from unsealed mine drainage upstream, and was essentially devoid of aquatic life. The problem has now been corrected, and stream conditions are much improved. *Photo by Marion Jackson*

Cattails and water lilies are aquatic plants that help purify water in nature, in addition to providing habitat for aquatic animals. *Photo by Richard Fields*

The clear, relatively unpolluted Tippecanoe River joins the murky Wabash in northern Tippecanoe County. *Photo by James Gammon*

The earth has a finite amount of water. When you sip from a water fountain, know that a dinosaur may have drunk that same sample of liquid a hundred million years ago. Or it may have been locked in glacial ice for a thousand years during the Pleistocene. Again, it may have moved through the internal plumbing of an Indiana white oak tree just last summer. Continual recycling and replenishment of water from ocean to land and back to ocean makes life possible and binds all living things together.

Indiana's share of water is decided by its location on the Earth. Our geographic position results in a continental climate with sharp hot and cold season differences and a wide range of temperature changes. Such variation determines how and when Indiana's water flows through the hydrologic cycle. In warm months, vegetation uses tremendous amounts of water, and soft soils absorb rainfall to replenish underground water supplies. In cold months, vegetation is dormant and frozen ground often is impenetrable, resulting in spring floods when soils finally thaw.

Indiana's water is in constant motion, most often noted through abundant flowing streams, rainstorms, and heavy snows. Statewide, Indiana averages 38 inches of precipitation annually, with nearly 10 inches less falling in the far northern counties than near Evansville. Variability in the amount of precipitation, combined with temperature changes, affects precipitation effectiveness and water availability.

Topography also determines Indiana's water availability. Indiana's Ice Age glaciers altered the topography, resulting in northern flatlands with slow surface runoff and dotted with many natural lakes. In southern Indiana, terrain is steep and rugged, and runoff is rapid and varied. Indiana's water resource, largely determined by its glacial

history, contains two major components: surface water and groundwater.

Surface water is, as the name implies, water on the Earth's surface such as streams, lakes, ponds, and reservoirs. Surface water includes rainfall runoff and seepage from underground aquifers into waterways, which, when combined, account for a major portion of stream flow.

Indiana's surface is drained mainly by streams that originate here. Notable exceptions are the St. Joseph River, which drains from Michigan into Indiana's Elkhart and St. Joseph counties, then flows back into Michigan. The St. Joseph and St. Mary's rivers in Adams and Dekalb counties drain from Ohio into Indiana. The 475-mile-long Wabash River is the major stream of the state, with a watershed area of 33,100 square miles, including 319 in western Ohio and 8,563 in eastern Illinois, plus two-thirds of Indiana. It forms the boundary between Indiana and Illinois for a total of 198 river miles.

Easily accessible surface springs furnished settlers with their first

THE HYDROLOGIC CYCLE

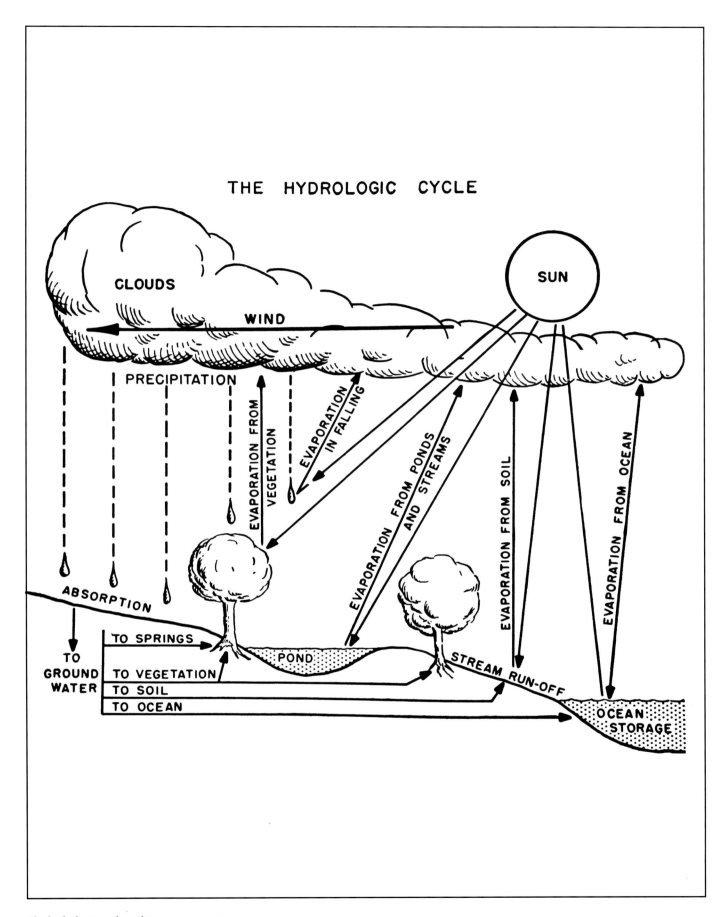

The hydrologic cycle and its measurement.

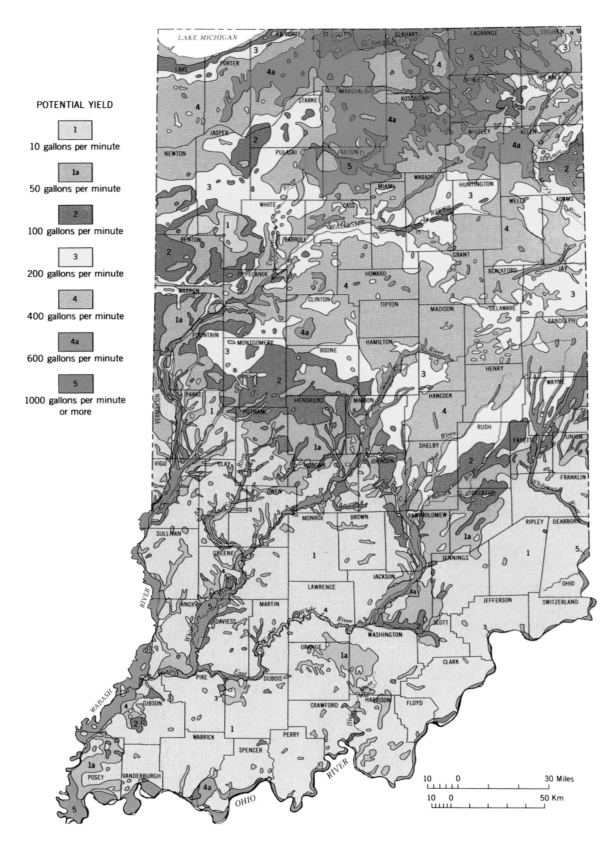

POTENTIAL YIELD

1	10 gallons per minute
1a	50 gallons per minute
2	100 gallons per minute
3	200 gallons per minute
4	400 gallons per minute
4a	600 gallons per minute
5	1000 gallons per minute or more

Generalized Groundwater Availability in Indiana   *Map courtesy of the Governor's Water Resource Study Commission as prepared by the Indiana Department of Natural Resources, Division of Water*

Cataract Falls in northern Owen County occurs in high-gradient stream as runoff water rushes back to the sea.   *Photo by Alton Lindsey*

water supplies, often determining the locations of their homes. However, when springs were unavailable, Hoosiers dug wells and bailed water from them by hand until drilling and pumping equipment expanded groundwater use.

Groundwater, located beneath the earth's surface, is a principal water supply for human consumption in much of the state. Indiana's groundwater is contained in unconsolidated sands and gravels or bedrock aquifers, nature's underground storage tanks. Historically, groundwater was prized for its purity and taste.

Unconsolidated aquifers are the most productive sources of groundwater in Indiana's river valleys. Ice Age glaciers created these aquifers as they sliced through the state, melting into large pockets of easily accessible underground water within sand and gravel deposits.

Heavy bedrock formations, untouched by the heavy ice, also absorb, store, and transmit water. Indiana's major bedrock systems are the Pennsylvanian, Mississippian, Devonian, Silurian, and Ordovician geologic strata, which increase in age from west to east across the southern part of the state. Groundwater is generally less available across southern Indiana than in central and northern regions.

Mineral water from deep within these bedrock aquifers made parts of Indiana famous in times past. The cities of Martinsville and French Lick once boasted the healing properties of their mineral

waters. Thousands of hopeful health-seekers, including Al Capone, flocked to these cities' posh resorts to sip and soak in the mineral elixir. Remnants of that era remain in Martinsville; their sports teams are named the Artesians after the freely flowing mineral springs located there.

Today, groundwater contamination is a puzzling concern, because it is hard to identify and more difficult to solve. Citizens are becoming increasingly aware of groundwater pollution and the need to protect this vital resource.

HISTORY OF INDIANA'S WATER USE

The same water that drives the mill, decayeth it.

—*Stephen Gosson*, The Schools of Abuse

Indiana's water resources are interwoven within its history of development and growth. When Indiana joined the Union in 1816, the state was primarily agricultural. Early farmers, then numbering under 100,000, molded the soil into their dream. During the settlement years, farmers painstakingly logged forests that once blanketed some 20 million acres of the state, and later on they irrigated some of those lands to grow crops. Rivers and streams powered gristmills. Fishing provided a ready food source. Hunters and trappers found plentiful game along Indiana's waterways, providing them with food

Abundant introduced watercress growing in crystal-clear spring water.
Photo by Richard Fields

Water-based recreation in Indiana often centers on human-built reservoirs around the state. *Photo by Richard Fields*

and income. Homesteaders used springs and wells to fill most of their domestic needs.

Early settlers used rivers and streams, the frontier highways, to transport themselves, their supplies, and their crops to market. In the early nineteenth century, a crisscrossing network of canals was envisioned as a better method of water transportation. In 1832, construction began on the Wabash and Erie Canal to connect Lake Erie with the Ohio River. The canal, completed in 1843, cost $6,437,809.

The 468-mile Wabash and Erie Canal was the longest canal in the United States, but its heyday was brief. Financial woes and competition with improved railroad travel and freight shipment led to the canal's decline; it ceased operations in 1874. The Wabash and Erie Canal now appears a failure, but historians say that it played a vital role in opening up the state. Sections of the canal bed and towpath are still visible at several locations along its former route of travel.

The Whitewater Canal operated from 1832 to 1865 in southeastern Indiana from Hagerstown to the Ohio River. Remnants of this and other canals, most notably the Central Canal in Indianapolis, exist today. These waterways mark an important era in Indiana's history.

Hoosiers strategically set up housekeeping near Indiana's springs, streams, and rivers for easy access to drinking water, water power, and transportation. Several of these early hamlets now thrive as major cities: Evansville, Fort Wayne, Indianapolis, South Bend, Terre Haute, Jeffersonville–New Albany, and Vincennes.

TODAY'S WATER RESOURCE NEEDS AND USES

The trouble is not whether water supplies are running out, but whether people are outrunning the supplies. Water supplies have finite limits, but the demand of people on the supplies has no known limit.

—*Raymond L. Nace, Research Hydrologist, U.S. Geological Survey*

In Indiana today, water serves a variety of needs: navigation; industrial, domestic, and agricultural use; sport fishing and water recreation; and fish and wildlife. Let us take a look at each.

Navigation. As part of the Great Lakes–St. Lawrence navigation system, Lake Michigan is an invaluable transportation corridor for shipping cargo inland and to the Atlantic Ocean. Indiana's commercial harbors provide easy access to this major waterway.

In southern Indiana, 350 miles of the Ohio River is part of the Ohio-Mississippi navigation system. The Ohio River floats shippers to the central and south-central United States as far as the Gulf of Mexico. Both navigation systems provide efficient, low-cost transportation.

Industrial, domestic, and agricultural use. The production of energy places a significant demand on water resources. Electrical power generation requires the largest single water withdrawal, largely for coolant water. Generating plants are located along such major waterways as the Ohio, Wabash, White, and Kankakee rivers, and along the Lake Michigan shore. Often heated effluents elevate the temperature of receiving streams or lakes, sometimes keeping waters ice-free in winter, thereby enhancing their wildlife value for some species; temperature-sensitive species may be harmed by the warmer waters.

Self-supplied industrial water accounts for the second-largest withdrawal use. Indiana ranks among the nation's highest users of industrial self-supplied water. Industries in Lake and Porter counties and along Lake Michigan are major surface water users. Elsewhere in Indiana, industries draw upon groundwater supplies.

Public water supplies are the third-largest user of water. Seventy percent of Indiana's population takes its water from such surface and groundwater supply systems.

Agricultural irrigation is a rapidly increasing use of water. Farmers usually irrigate on coarser-grained, well-drained soils that do not hold soil moisture well. These areas suffer deficient soil moisture during peak growing seasons, and irrigation improves agricultural yields. While irrigation accounts for only 1.4 percent of Indiana's total water use, it is the major use in some areas.

Sport fishing and water recreation. Sport fishing has significant economic impact in Indiana. Hoosier fishermen spend more than $500 million per year for food, lodging, equipment, and fishing and boating license fees. Commercial boating and fishing are prevalent on Lake Michigan. The Lake Michigan sport fishing industry nets at least $30 million per year. As a result, fishing generates thousands of jobs within the state; license and excise taxes on equipment are returned to Indiana fisheries and lake management.

People today possess a comparatively high degree of affluence and leisure time. Where early settlers used rivers, lakes, and streams for survival, Indiana now experiences a major demand for boating, waterskiing, and swimming recreation.

Fish and wildlife. Fish and wildlife cannot survive without clean water, and water, in turn, is cleansed in nature by organisms. The health of Indiana's waters relies upon an intricate cycle. Stream and wetland habitats support the highest diversity of plants and animals in the state. Walk along any healthy stream or wetland, and your footprints will mingle with those of white-tailed deer, beaver, mink, muskrat, raccoon, opossum, ducks, geese, great blue herons, and a variety of other animals. Look closer on your journey and you will find an array of insects, amphibians, reptiles, freshwater clams, mussels, and crayfish. All species depend upon water, and upon one another. Should one species fail to thrive, others will suffer—especially humans.

Prodded by an environmental ethic born in the 1960s, our citizens now work harder than ever to protect Indiana's water resources. Indiana is a system much larger than our own body. As we care for our physical beings, we should come to understand that we cannot abuse Indiana or taint its lifeblood. For all life, water is priceless.

If there is magic on this planet, it is contained in water.
—*Loren Eiseley,* The Immense Journey *(1946)*

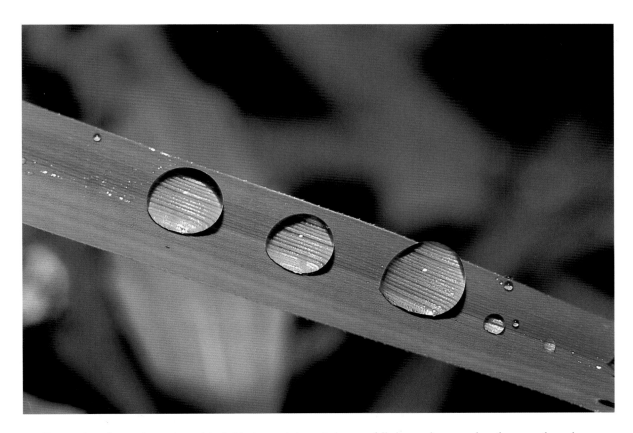

Evaporation of water leaves impurities behind, permitting raindrops to fall clear and pure, unless they pass through a polluted atmosphere.   *Photo by Richard Fields*

Sandhill cranes stop over at Jasper-Pulaski State Wildlife Area during their spring and fall migrations, making good use of the extensive wetlands during their visit. *Photo by Mark Romesser*

6. An Endangered Natural Resource: Wetlands

Eric Myers

At last a glint of sun reveals the approach of a great echelon of birds. On motionless wing they emerge from the lifting mists, sweep a final arc of sky, and settle in dangerous descending spirals to their feeding grounds. A new day has begun on crane marsh.

—*Aldo Leopold, "Marshland Elegy," in* A Sand County Almanac *(1949)*

Standing against the bright periwinkle skyline of a frosty October morning, a gray-brown sandhill crane stretches to his full height of three and a half feet. Bending low, he jumps gracefully into the air. The crane settles back lightly, bows again, and picks at bits of leaves and twigs with his long, sharp bill. He tosses the tidbits over his shoulders and leaps again on long, spindly legs. The bright red patch on his head flashes, and he stretches his wings. From wingtip to wingtip the spectacular bird measures seven feet. Sandhill cranes surround him and watch, then others join the ritual dance. Hundreds of leaping cranes begin a wildlife ballet, one of the most fantastic wetland sights in Indiana.

More than 15,000 sandhill cranes congregate at Jasper-Pulaski Fish and Wildlife Area in northwestern Indiana in the spring and fall of each year. Jasper-Pulaski contains one of Indiana's largest remaining wetlands—1,000 acres of marshy flatlands on an 8,000-acre property—providing one of the nation's most important stopover sites for the eastern population of this Indiana-endangered bird. During migration, the birds leave their nesting grounds in Minnesota, Michigan, Wisconsin, and southern Canada and arrive at Jasper-Pulaski in September, October, and November. Cranes roost at night on shallow wetlands and feed in the surrounding croplands during the day. They remain until late November and early December, when they fly to wintering grounds in southern Georgia and Florida.

During late February and all of March, the birds leave their wintering grounds and start spring migrations north to return to summer nesting areas. Cranes also stop at Jasper-Pulaski during the spring, but in fewer numbers than in the fall.

This cry of the Sandhill crane is a veritable voice of Nature, untamed and unterrified. . . . Its resonance is remarkable and its carrying power is increased by a distinct tremolo effect. Often for several minutes after the birds have vanished, the unearthly sound drifts back to the listener, like a taunting trumpet from the under-world.

—*George Gladden, "Sandhill Crane," in* Birds of America *(1936)*

Sandhill crane populations in the eastern United States had declined to dangerously low numbers because of habitat destruction and human disturbance in the early to mid–1900s. The large marsh areas necessary for nesting were being drained for human development. The cranes' available feeding and nesting areas decreased, and the birds stopped nesting in Indiana around 1929. In the 1930s and 1940s, state and federal agencies counteracted the decline of these magnificent birds by protecting them under governmental regula-

tion. At about the same time, nesting and feeding refuges such as Jasper-Pulaski Fish and Wildlife Area were established.

Thanks to wetland protection and wildlife regulation, numbers of sandhill cranes stopping at Jasper-Pulaski Fish and Wildlife Area have increased from less than 1,000 in the 1950s to more than 15,000 in recent years. Beyond their beauty, sandhills are also a valuable lesson to the more than 30,000 Hoosiers who trek annually to Jasper-Pulaski to see firsthand the benefits of wetlands.

In recent years, Americans have learned that wetlands are vital to the balance of the environment, but such wet areas were once considered wastelands, a mistake by Mother Nature. Humans tried to correct that mistake by filling in or draining wetlands for agricultural and human development. Needless to say, we were wrong.

WHAT IS A WETLAND?

The creeks overflow: a thousand rivulets run
'Twixt the roots of the sod; the blades of marsh-grass stir;
Passeth a hurrying sound of wings that westward whirr;
Passeth, and all is still; and the currents cease to run;
And the sea and marsh are one.

—*Sidney Lanier,* The Marshes of Glynn *(1878)*

Today, wetlands join rainforests and a variety of other diminishing habitats that illustrate the importance of ecological maintenance for wildlife and humans. Many people will readily admit that wetlands are important, but few understand what a wetland is or its ecological value.

If you live in Indiana's natural lakes region, you probably picture wetlands as the marshy area surrounding those beautiful lakes. If you live in southwestern Indiana, you may think of Hovey Lake's Cypress Swamp along the Ohio River.

Indiana's wetlands are "in-between places" that provide a transition between land and water. Wetlands include swamps, bogs, fens, marshes, seep springs, sloughs, bottomlands, potholes, wet meadows/prairies, and the deepwater areas of lakes, reservoirs, rivers, and streams. They are a precious ecological resource, hosting a varying combination of plants and animals which are adapted to living in wetland conditions for all or part of the year. In fact, wetland habitats contain the highest diversity of plants and animals, including endangered species, in Indiana.

To humans, wetlands are important for flood storage and control, water quality, controlling shoreline erosion, and recreation. They also dilute, dissipate, and neutralize pollutants, thereby serving as the ecological equivalent of giant kidneys.

According to the U.S. Fish and Wildlife Service's classification system, three of the five major wetland types are found in Indiana:

Lacustrine. Lacustrine refers to permanently flooded lakes, rivers, and smaller basins containing water deeper than six feet. Chain O'Lakes State Park in northern Indiana is an example of this wetland type. Lacustrine wetland accounts for 16 percent of Indiana's remaining wetlands.

Palustrine. Palustrine wetlands are shallow-water wetlands con-

Sedge tussocks form hummocks in Jasper-Pulaski wetlands.   *Photo by Richard Fields*

Showy marsh marigolds have many reproductive parts that typify the buttercup family.   *Photo by Delano Z. Arvin*

taining water-loving plants. They are usually less than six feet deep. This type includes ponds, marshes, bogs, bottomland forests, mudflats, and sandbars. Palustrine areas are by far the most abundant wetlands type in Indiana, accounting for nearly 80 percent of all wetlands.

Riverine. Riverine wetlands are river and stream systems containing flowing water in a channel. Mallard Roost, located on the south branch of the Elkhart River in northern Indiana, supports this type of habitat, which accounts for 5 percent of Indiana's wetlands.

THE BENEFITS OF WETLANDS: WHAT OUR FOREFATHERS DID NOT KNOW

Education, I fear, is learning to see one thing by going blind to another. One thing most of us have gone blind to is the quality of marshes. I am reminded of this when, as a special favor, I take a visitor to Clandeboye, only to find that, to him, it is merely lonelier to look upon, and stickier to navigate, than other boggy places.

> —Aldo Leopold, "Clandeboye," *in* A Sand County
> Almanac *(1949)*

In Indiana and across the nation, wetlands perform functions important to humans and wildlife. As a landform, they serve as a giant sponge, storing excess water then releasing it gradually. Wetlands thereby cleanse and slow flood waters and reduce flood peaks; additionally, they stabilize and prolong the duration of stream flow.

This benefit is evident along portions of the Little Calumet River, which flows through northwestern Indiana. Urbanization, filling, and drainage of natural wetlands have resulted in one of the worst areas of flooding in the state. In the 1980s and 1990s, the Little Calumet River Basin Development Commission began acquiring 1,350 acres of wetlands to help alleviate flood damage. Wetlands along the river will be woven into a major regional greenway, providing hiking, biking, and nature study opportunities in that heavily urbanized area.

Wetlands maintain water quality by filtering pollutants and sediments from the waters that flow through them. At Marsh Lake in Steuben County, human-constructed wetlands filter wastewater effluent and serve as a natural wastewater treatment system.

Lake Maxinkuckee in Marshall County is one of Indiana's largest natural lakes. Many wetlands associated with the lake and its tribu-

tary streams have been lost to filling for development and draining for farming. With fewer wetlands, the lake was affected by fertilizer-laden sediment and chemicals entering the watershed from farmland and other sources. Concerned residents, farmers, and community leaders have joined with the Department of Natural Resources, Division of Soil Conservation Lake and River Enhancement Program, along with the Division of Fish and Wildlife, to restore wetlands to help filter pollutants before they reach the lake.

Indiana's wetlands play a major role in erosion control along stream banks and around lakes by holding and stabilizing soils, moderating wave action, and trapping sediments. Nowhere is this benefit more evident than in the wetlands lining the shores of numerous lakes in northern Indiana. Here, wetlands buffer the impact of waves created by the wakes of boats and the wind.

> By morning, the coots are gone—all that can fly—and so are the grebes and most of the ducks that do not like ice. . . . Muskrats sit beside open holes. New lodges and feed houses appear over the marshes. Faint, muddy prints of both muskrats and minks mark the new ice. Lake shore ice, in particular, may have a little blood, some bits of vegetation, fish scales or skin about the rocks and openings where minks and muskrats feed.
>
> —Paul L. Errington, "Of Marshes and Fall," *in* Our
> Natural World *(1965)*

Wetlands provide an abundance of food, cover, and habitat for fish and wildlife. The DNR estimates that more than 900 species of North American vertebrate animals rely upon wetlands at some point in their lives. Muskrat and beaver are totally dependent on wetlands. Most freshwater fish also are wetland dependent, because many species feed in wetlands or upon wetland-produced food, and use wetlands as nursery grounds. Almost all important sport fish in Indiana spawn in aquatic portions of wetlands.

Considering the millions of acres of wetland that have been altered or destroyed in Indiana, it is not surprising that large numbers of wetland-dependent plant and animal species have become rare and endangered in Indiana. The Indiana DNR reports that more than 120 plant species and 60 animal species that are wetland dependent fall into categories of rare, endangered, threatened, or species of special concern.

Because of their beauty and aesthetic qualities, wetlands often are key features of public parks, greenways, and outdoor education areas. Recreational activities in or around wetlands include hunting, trapping, fishing, canoeing, boating, nature study, and birding. More than 1.5 million Hoosiers annually visit 17 state fish and wildlife areas to enjoy wetland-related activities.

Clearly, wetlands perform a variety of valuable functions. Although they are an integral part of the ecosystem, the range of values they represent is not fully understood. National studies are currently under way to determine the role of wetlands in groundwater recharge and the cleansing of public water supplies. In Indiana, at least 60 municipalities have public wells in or very near wetlands. It is apparent that without wetlands, the health of our water resources is in jeopardy.

THE HISTORY OF INDIANA'S WETLANDS

As Ice Age glaciers retreated from the northern half of Indiana thousands of years ago, wetlands came into being. Glaciation shaped Indiana's topography and influenced the patterns of human development, especially in this portion of the state.

Prior to settlement, Native Americans revered wetlands that provided habitat for fish, furbearers, waterfowl, and other birds. This

Streams, rivers, reservoirs, and natural lakes of Indiana. *From Richard S. Simons,* The Rivers of Indiana *(Bloomington: Indiana University Press, 1985)*

Floating-leaved and emergent aquatics grow intermixed in the clear waters of the Tefft wetlands.   *Photo by Richard Fields*

abundance of wildlife significantly shaped the settlement pattern of Indiana, as settlers and trappers found plentiful food, clothing, and profit along or in the wetlands of this new territory.

As settlers cleared and plowed Indiana into an agricultural state, their attitude toward wetlands changed. By the mid-1800s and early 1900s, wetlands were thought of as wastelands. Finding that rich, hydric soils were highly productive, farmers began to drain wetlands and convert them into tillable land. By 1880 more than 1,100 tile factories operated in Indiana, Illinois, and Ohio, and within two years, Indiana farmers had installed more than 30,000 miles of clay drainage tile.

The impact of this process is emphasized in a 1914 article in the *Indiana Bureau of Legislative Information Bulletin.* Entitled "Drainage and Reclamation of Swamp and Overflowed Lands," it said in part: "The past ten years have witnessed an extraordinary revival of interest in the drainage and reclamation of our non-arable swamp lands, and it is safe to predict that no movement will be attended with more beneficial or far-reaching consequences."

More than 80 years have passed since the Bureau of Legislative Information urged Hoosiers to accelerate the reclamation of Indiana's swamplands. In retrospect, past wetland drainage and reclamation efforts benefited the agricultural economy. But the far-reaching consequences have been to greatly diminish Indiana's wetland resources, water quality, fish and wildlife, and the stability and health of the environment. Over the past century, well-intentioned public and private efforts to provide flood protection, greater agricultural production, and better highways have led to the drainage or filling of wetlands for farming, urban development, and industry.

Marshes are characterized by herbaceous plants, frequently by emergent aquatics such as cattails.   *Photo by Perry Scott*

Muskrats are common residents of most wetlands. They build their lodges above the water level, entering them via underwater tunnels.   *Photo by Richard Fields*

Wetlands are truly one of Indiana's endangered natural resources. Of the original 5.6 million acres of wetlands that covered about 24 percent of Indiana two hundred years ago, only about 800,000 acres or about 15 percent remain today. The distribution and density (percent acreage) of wetlands and deepwater habitats in Indiana vary by county (see map).

The loss in historical wetlands acreage is represented by the Grand Kankakee River, which prior to channelization meandered to such an extent that it was almost impossible to tell in which direction the river flowed. The area was so inhospitable that gangsters once used it as a hideout. So extensive was this wetland that in excess of 500,000 acres would be flooded during high flow.

WHAT GOVERNMENTS AND PEOPLE CAN DO

It is clear that as wetlands continue to be depleted, increased efforts are needed at national, state, and local levels to protect this endangered natural resource. At the national level, Executive Order 11990 (no net loss) was instituted in 1977. This was followed by the 1985 Farm Bill, which authorized the Conservation Reserve Program, as well as the Wetlands Conservation Provision (Swampbuster). The Wetland Reserve Program was authorized in the 1990 Farm Bill, and the Wildlife Habitat Incentive Program in 1996.

At the state level, the Indiana DNR established the Wetland Conservation Area Program in 1967. This acquisition program has protected more than 4,000 wetland acres to date. In 1988, the U.S. Fish and Wildlife Service and the Indiana DNR created a nationally recognized wetland program that targets marginally productive farmlands for wetland restoration. This cooperative effort has restored about 1,000 wetlands throughout Indiana, consisting of approximately 6,000 acres.

In 1993, the Indiana General Assembly established the Indiana Heritage Trust, funded by environmental license plate sales. This DNR land acquisition has protected more than 8,000 acres purchased from willing sellers. The Indiana Wetlands Conservation Plan was developed in 1996 by a work group including farmers, environmentalists, business leaders, conservationists, and government officials.

At the local level, Indiana communities such as Auburn and La Porte have established wetland ordinances to amend existing zoning regulations for the draining or filling of wetlands.

To ensure wetlands protection, the Indiana Wetlands Conservation Plan has identified areas that must be improved:

Public-private partnerships. The Indiana DNR is working to strengthen public-private partnership programs such as the Classified Wildlife Habitat and Riparian Lands program to provide landowners with financial incentives to conserve wetlands. The state agency has forged partnerships with private organizations to ensure wetlands protection as well. These partnerships include the Indiana Grand Kankakee Marsh Wetland Restoration Project, which is part of the North American Waterfowl Management Plan. Other entities include the North American Wetlands Conservation Council, Ducks Unlimited, The Nature Conservancy, and numerous businesses and industries.

The need for improved coordination, efficiency, and consistency of local, state, and federal regulations is evident. Laws currently in place to protect wetlands have seen a mixture of success and failure. For example, the federal Clean Water Act regulates the placement of dredge and fill material into wetlands, which accounts for the majority of wetland destruction. However, Indiana's Flood Control Act and Public Freshwater Lake Law consider wetlands only within their jurisdiction. More than 50 percent of wetlands are beyond the

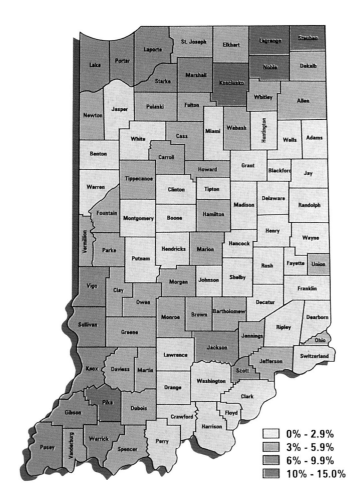

Distribution and density (percent acreage) of wetlands and deepwater habitats in Indiana by county, based on the National Wetland Inventory. *Map by Shelley Liu, IDNR-MIS, 1996*

jurisdiction of existing state law. So as to protect these at-risk wetlands, incentives for the conservation, restoration, and creation of wetlands need to be offered.

Wetlands information. To make better regulatory decisions and ensure that scarce funds are well spent, there is a need to have comprehensive, accurate, and up-to-date scientific information on Indiana's wetlands resources.

Land acquisition. Finally, many cases exist where acquiring high-quality wetlands from willing sellers is the only means of protection. To accomplish this, consistent funding sources like the Indiana Heritage Trust Program are needed.

Education. Wetland protection requires the commitment, cooperation, and education of public agencies, elected officials, private landowners, and all residents. Unfortunately, many people view wetlands only as mosquito breeding sites. An expanded effort is needed to inform and educate the public about wetlands and their preservation.

We have misused and misunderstood our wetlands for nearly a century. Nature has built wetlands for millions of years, but people have destroyed them in a few short decades. We cannot begin to recover all wetland habitats and the plant and animal species that once flourished in them. But we can take action to stop the destruction of what remains, and to restore some sites by reflooding.

Some day my marsh, dyked and pumped, will lie forgotten under the wheat, just as today and yesterday will lie forgotten under the years. Before the last mud-minnow makes his last wiggle in the last pool, the terns will scream good-bye to Clandeboye, the swans will circle skyward in snowy dignity, and the cranes will blow their trumpets in farewell.

—*Aldo Leopold, "Clandeboye," in* A Sand County Almanac *(1949)*

Newly formed wetlands now occur in the upper reaches of Lake Monroe reservoir where sediments eroded from surrounding uplands have shallowed its waters.
Photo by Richard Fields

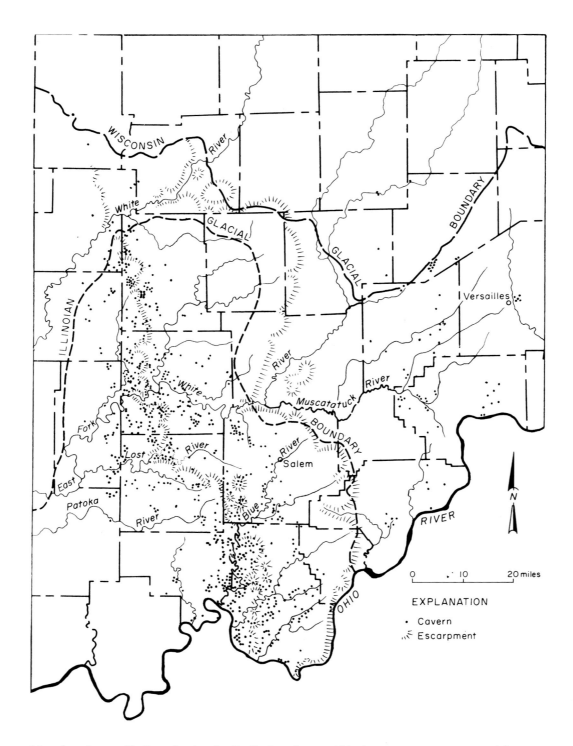

Map of south-central Indiana showing the distribution of caves within the state, stream patterns, and the location of the Lost River.

7. Underground World: Caves

James H. Keith and Richard L. Powell

Continuing forward, you notice that the air is becoming cooler. Mosses and ferns grow thicker and deeper on the rock walls of the valley . . . there is a no-daylight world just ahead. Peering into the gloom, you can see nothing distinctly. The pathway and the stream that it follows disappear into darkness. You have reached the entrance of a cave.

—*Charles E. Mohr and Thomas L. Poulson,* The Life of the Cave *(1966)*

GEOLOGIC SETTING AND FORMATION OF INDIANA CAVES

Nowhere in Indiana is there land or water surface that has not been seen by a farmer, a woodsman, a hunter, or a fisherman, but there are probably hundreds of miles of underground passages that are yet to be discovered. The two longest caves in Indiana each consist of about 20 miles of mapped passages. Several caves of the more than 2,200 known in Indiana have more than 10 miles of mapped passages. However, most of them, as far as we now know, can be explored for only a few hundred feet at most. While many of the passages consist of crawlways, some are large enough to accommodate two semitrailers side by side, and a few underground rooms are larger than football fields.

Most of the caves in Indiana are located in the southern third of the state, generally south of the maximum extent of Wisconsinan glaciation. The major cave area of Indiana is located in a region of relatively flat-bedded limestones of Mississippian age (about 350 million years old) that extends from Greencastle south-southeastward to the Ohio River and includes both the Mitchell Plain and the eastern part of the Crawford Upland physiographic units. A second cave area is located in southeastern Indiana, where older limestones of Silurian and Devonian ages occur.

The caves of Indiana have formed (some are still growing) in limestone bedrock owing to movement of water along particular routes through the rock over long periods of time. Four conditions are necessary for the development of a cave: slightly acidic groundwater or precipitation; soluble bedrock; openings in the bedrock through which water can move; and a gradient that can provide direction and speed to the flow of water. Differences in these conditions, varying from location to location and over time, created the variety of cave passages we see today.

Because of absorption of carbon dioxide from the atmosphere and the uptake of humic acids from soil and decaying plant litter through which most precipitation passes once it reaches the earth, groundwater tends to be slightly acidic, even without taking into consideration the phenomenon described today as "acid rain." The acidic water can dissolve small amounts of limestone by a process known as solution as it moves through openings in limestone.

Limestone bedrock in this region generally consists of horizontal layers of fine-grained rocks and layers of coarse-grained rocks that may be either dense or porous. Fine-grained layers of limestone are commonly more soluble in the presence of slightly acidic groundwater than are coarse-grained layers. Layers of rock are often broken by two sets of joints, which are usually vertical or nearly vertical cracks forming an approximate right angle to one another. The compass orientation and density of joints will vary from one layer of limestone to the next, so joints in one layer of limestone will not necessarily coincide with joints in adjacent layers. Thus, slightly acidic groundwater can flow laterally along joints within a layer, dissolving the limestone and leaving a slightly larger opening through which water can pass more easily. Where a joint is encountered in a lower limestone layer, the water can move vertically into that layer.

A given amount of acidic water can dissolve only so much limestone, so continued solutional enlargement depends upon fresh supplies of water. Rapidly flowing water will retain its acidity over a longer distance than will slowly flowing water. Joints that receive large amounts of fast-flowing water enlarge more quickly and allow progressively more water to enter. The most rapid flow of water is toward a lower elevation, often to one or more outlets or springs which flow into a surface stream. This route enlarges, first to widened joints, then to tube-like conduits, and finally to passages large enough to be entered by humans.

The main passage that feeds a spring enlarges to a size at which it is capable of draining water from the entire cave system. Most cave passages in Indiana either contain small streams or are relatively dry, except perhaps after a severe rainstorm or a sudden melt of thick snowfall. At such times, they may flood to the ceiling.

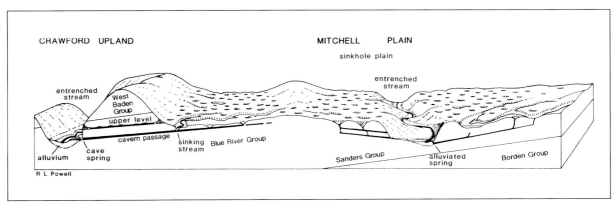

Cross-section of limestone belt of southern Indiana showing interrelationships of above- and below-ground landscape features.

KARST FEATURES AND CAVE FORMATIONS

The process of limestone dissolution that forms most caves leads also to the development of a distinct landscape type on the ground surface called *karst* terrain, named after a region in Yugoslavia where it was first described and studied. A number of distinctive karst features result from the process of cavern formation below.

Sinkholes may result from the continued intake of water at the ground surface along a joint or intersection of joints. Water eventually widens the joint into a crevice, and the overlying soil surface forms a characteristic funnel-shaped depression. One area of karst topography in Orange County has more than a thousand sinkholes per square mile. Sinkholes often serve as cave entrances.

Sinking streams can form where surface streams encounter and enlarge a joint or crevice to the point where all or part of the flow is diverted underground. This often results in the abandonment of the surface stream channel downstream from this point except during floods. Lost River in Orange County is a world-renowned example of a sinking stream.

Springs are the typical outlets for cave waters. They may range from a small opening in a hillside that flows only when it rains to a large cavern entrance that is an outlet of an underground river discharging hundreds of gallons per minute. Spring openings may be collapsed or be too tight to afford access to the cave beyond. Some springs issue from large, flooded cave passages that can be entered only by teams of trained, experienced divers.

Within caves, the water can dissolve only so much limestone before it becomes saturated. At that point, it may flow out of the cave without accomplishing any more solution. Water saturated with dissolved limestone may also seep through ceiling cracks from rock strata above, at which point a small amount of dissolved carbon dioxide may escape, lowering the acidity of the water and causing the deposition of a small amount of dissolved limestone. When this occurs at the ceiling, a pendant of deposited limestone, called a stalactite, develops with time. When the water drips to the floor, additional limestone may be deposited, forming a mound or a column called a stalagmite. The pure material is usually white, but impurities may color the deposits brown, black, or even red. Variations of these formations can assume fantastic shapes with equally fantastic names such as bacon rind, rimstone, palettes, soda straws, and stalactoflats. Such features are often the chief attractions of commercial caves.

THE CAVE ENVIRONMENT AND CAVE LIFE

The basis of the food chain of most natural ecosystems is green plants, which get energy from the sun. Except near entrances, caves are entirely without light, and there is no plant life unless bacteria and fungi are considered to be plants, so caves lack an important primary energy source. Energy has to be imported in the form of dead and decaying organic material. This usually consists of fine bits of plant detritus (leaves, stems, and twigs) washed in through sinkholes and sinking streams or blown into entrances by wind. Other energy sources are the dead bodies and droppings of animals that feed outside the caves, then return for rest or refuge, such as packrats, bats, or cave crickets. These sources of energy are often low in nutrients, may be imported infrequently, and are either spread thinly or localized in widely separated areas.

Air temperature in caves is usually near the mean annual air temperature outside—about 55°F in Indiana—and relative humidity is usually high—between 85 and 100 percent. Most people think of caves as having a constant air temperature and relative humidity. In some caves and cave systems, a patient observer might find areas where air temperature and relative humidity vary little from year to year, but they are almost never suitable environments for full-time cave dwellers. They are usually too far from entrances and streams, the sources of water and food.

There is enough variation in the physical environment of a cave to force cave-dwelling animals to adjust from time to time. The largest variations in air temperature and relative humidity are found near cave entrances. In summer, cave air usually flows out of entrances at stream exits, extending the cool, moist cave environment nearer the entrance. In winter, the flow often reverses, and colder, drier outside air may extend into the cave for a considerable distance. Many cave-dwelling animals are sensitive to drying, and to large changes in air temperature and air movement. Those animals that may be found near a cave entrance in summer must either move deeper into the cave in the winter or die.

It is not rare in Indiana for caves to flood during storms, most commonly in late fall, winter, and early spring when the soil and bedrock are saturated with water. Flooding probably has the greatest effect on the physical cave environment. Cave air temperature can be changed several degrees Fahrenheit by the temperature of incoming water, and the periodic saturation of rock and mud maintains a high relative humidity. More important, energy resources are replenished when suspended organic particles and detritus are deposited in and along stream passages. Flooding has other effects on cave animals. They can be swept from the cave, then usually die quickly, or they may drown or be injured or killed by turbulent water.

> In food-rich areas above ground, animals are likely to be specialists, eating only certain kinds of plants or other animals that are abundant and easy to find. But most cave-dwellers cannot afford to be "choosy." . . . Cave animals, in short, must be opportunists and take advantage of whatever food is available . . . nearly all the cave's inhabitants are omnivorous.
>
> —*Mohr and Poulson,* The Life of the Cave

Animals living in caves on a full-time basis can complete their life cycles successfully by relying on food supplies that are low in available energy, and that are not always easily found or exploited. Cave-dwelling animals consist of both aquatic and terrestrial vertebrate and invertebrate species. They are divided into four groups based upon how they use caves.

Accidentals are animals that have wandered into caves, entered to forage, or become trapped or lost. They are generally not adapted in any way to a subterranean life, and they cannot survive for long in a cave environment. Typical accidentals are raccoons, frogs, and turtles.

Trogloxenes are not adapted to cave life to the extent that they can complete their life cycles there; they must go outside or to nurseries to forage and reproduce. Some bat species use caves for hibernation, and may number in the hundreds of thousands. Packrats, cave salamanders, and cave crickets are other Indiana trogloxenes. Trogloxenes contribute to the cave food base by leaving droppings, dead bodies, and organic debris.

Troglophiles complete their life cycles either in caves or outside of caves in suitable environments, most often the soil. Most caves contain at least a few members of this group. Terrestrial Indiana troglophiles are invertebrates, and include earthworms, ground beetles, rove beetles, orb-web spiders, terrestrial isopods (sow bugs), collembola (springtails), and millipedes. Aquatic troglophiles include crayfish, fish such as sculpin, and surface-adapted amphipods (scuds). Most have functional eyes, sometimes reduced in size.

Troglobites complete their life cycles only in caves. They do not occur in every cave and may be difficult to find where they are present. Terrestrial troglobites in Indiana are invertebrates, and

The above-ground channel of Lost River meanders across the Mitchell Plain south of Spring Mill State Park.
Photo by Richard Fields

The Orangeville Rise in Orange County, where the Lost River returns to the surface.   *Photo by Marion Jackson*

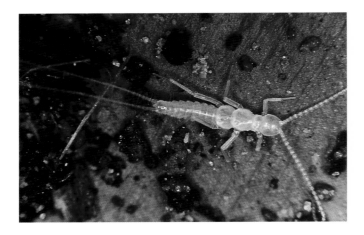

The bristletail is a tiny detritus-eating cave-dwelling insect. Note the lack of color and functional eyes.   *Photo by Thomas Poulson*

include cave beetles, cave spiders, cave millipedes, pseudoscorpions, springtails, and bristletails. Aquatic troglobites include the northern cavefish, the cave crayfish, isopods, amphipods, and flatworms. Troglobites either have no developed eyes or they have eyes that do not function. They may have other adaptations to cave life such as reduced pigmentation, long, thin limbs, increased senses of smell and touch, slowed growth and development, and reduced egg laying.

Dead and decaying organic detritus is the base of most cave food chains. Animals feeding on detritus are called detritivores. Terrestrial detritivores include millipedes, bristletails, collembola, and earthworms. In aquatic environments flatworms, isopods, and amphipods perform that function. Detritivores form a base for carnivores. The cave beetle and the cave spider are the common terrestrial carnivores in caves where they occur, feeding mainly on collembola and bristletails. Aquatic carnivores are crayfish and the northern cavefish. They feed on isopods and amphipods, and occasionally on one another.

A number of rare and endangered animals are found in caves, and some are protected by federal and state laws and regulations. These include the Indiana bat, which is on the federal list of endangered species. The northern cavefish has been determined to be a state endangered species in Indiana.

HUMAN USE OF CAVES

While utilization of limestone cave interiors by prehistoric Native Americans was fairly common in the eastern United States from central Kentucky southward, archaeologists have discovered little evidence to show that they used such caverns for shelter in Indiana. In 1990, archaeologists Pat and Cheryl Munson published their findings on the utilization of Indiana caves by Native Americans and early settlers in Indiana, and discussed the findings of other investigators. There is evidence that a pit in one small cave in southern Indiana was used for burial purposes.

There is also well-documented evidence of extensive exploitation of Wyandotte Cave. Flint nodules were mined in Wyandotte Cave between 2200 B.C. and 240 B.C. The mineral aragonite was mined during a period lasting from approximately A.D. 1 to A.D. 690, mostly around and from a large formation today known as the Pillar of the Constitution, located several thousand feet from the entrance. Artifacts made of this aragonite have been found at sites in Indiana, Illinois, Iowa, Ohio, and Tennessee.

Early settlers noted cave entrances as landmarks, and springs provided early supplies of domestic and urban water, and water power for gristmills. Some caves were the subject of fantastic tales of candlelight exploration or hunters cornering bears in black passages. Early records relating to caves by white explorers, land surveyors, and settlers in Indiana refer to mining saltpeter from cave dirt for gunpowder. One "saltpeter" cave in Monroe County may have been prospected as early as 1776. Saltpeter Cave, near Wyandotte Cave, provided saltpeter for early settlers and for the War of 1812. It may have been mined as late as the Civil War to provide gunpowder for northern troops. Epsom salts were collected from Wyandotte Cave about the time of the War of 1812.

Indiana caves have been the subject of many popular accounts and scientific studies. Wyandotte Cave received much popular acclaim in the mid–1800s as a place for the adventurous to visit and explore, and was claimed by some to be at least as extensive as Mammoth Cave in Kentucky (now the world's longest). Scientific reports and descriptions of caves in Indiana began in 1862 with Richard Owen's accounts of Wyandotte Cave and certain caves in the Lost River area of Orange County. A number of reports and studies of Indiana caves and their fauna were published by the Indiana Department of Geology and Natural Resources throughout the 1870s, 1880s, and 1890s. Around the turn of the century, Indiana University professor Carl Eigenmann published extensively on studies of cavefish anatomy, physiology, and behavior that he conducted at Donaldson Cave in what is now Spring Mill State Park. A. M. Banta's classic study of cave ecology was conducted at Mayfield's Cave near Bloomington, Indiana, and was published in 1907. Published studies by Indiana University professor Clyde A. Malott between 1919 and 1952 provided valuable insight on the relationships and origins of sinkholes, sinking streams, and caverns.

It is not hard to become acquainted with the beauty and mystery of caves. There are excellent "show" caves in Indiana that are open to the public. Cave trips operated by the Indiana Department of Natural Resources are available at Upper Twin Cave in Spring Mill State Park and at Wyandotte Cave and Little Wyandotte Cave in Crawford County. Private caves include Bluespring Cavern Park southwest of Bedford, Marengo Cave in Marengo, and Squire Boone Cavern near Mauckport in Harrison County. Bluespring Cavern Park offers a lighted boat ride on an underground river. Wyandotte Cave and Marengo Cave are on the National Registry of Natural Landmarks. A small cave near Squire Boone Cavern is reportedly the final resting place of Squire Boone (Daniel Boone's brother), who operated a gristmill at the cave. The old mill is a national historic landmark. All of these caves offer lighted, guided tours, and can be enjoyed for a moderate cost.

> On the floor of this squirmway was a four-inch layer of mud, the consistency of axle grease. It oozed into their clothing at their wrists and pockets. They could feel it forcing its way into their shoes, but the sound of falling water was louder now. It drew them like a magnet as they picked up speed in spite of their unpleasant surroundings.
>
> —*Joe Lawrence, Jr., and Roger W. Brucker,* The Caves Beyond *(1955)*

There are more than 2,200 "wild" caves in Indiana. These should not be entered except with landowner permission, and should be attempted only by experienced groups of cavers. Those who put up with the rigors and discomforts of wild caving have the opportunity to explore a part of Indiana that only a handful of people have seen, and perhaps to discover unexplored caves and passages where no human has set foot before.

Interior of Rothrock Cathedral in Wyandotte Cave.   *Photo by Richard Fields*

Entrance to Donaldson Cave, Spring Mill State Park. Note large flow of water.   *Photo by Richard Powell*

Dedicated cavers will not knowingly vandalize caves by breaking formations, marking on walls, or killing cave animals. They tend to develop a deep appreciation for the cave's uniqueness and fragility, and know that when damage does occur, its effects are often permanent. Caves have few available mechanisms by which to "heal" themselves. The caver's approach to cave conservation is simple: "Take nothing but pictures. Leave nothing but footprints. Kill nothing but time."

Many cavers have scientific training, and map cave passages, study geology, trace groundwater flow, and study cave life. The relationship between caves, groundwater, and surface land use in karst areas is another field of study that is of immense academic interest. It has more immediate applications as well. It is being shown that karst areas, as well as the caves within them, are special areas that will require care, planning, and study as they continue to be developed and used.

From observation and studies, it is apparent that public health and safety, as well as the quality of the cave environment and groundwater in karst areas, can be strongly influenced by land use and events that occur on the surface. Since most groundwater in karst areas moves through openings in the rock, its flow is often faster, more concentrated, and less predictable than groundwater movement in non-karst areas. It is impossible to determine the locations and directions of flow of all of the underground conduits in an area, and in the event of a spill of a toxic substance, the effects could be rapid and unpredictable. Pollutants can travel many miles underground in an unknown direction in a single day, in a relatively undiluted state, making containment, cleanup, and public protection virtually impossible.

Urban and commercial developments often result in filling low spots and diverting surface water flow. Without adequate planning and protection, the amount and quality of surface water runoff into caves can be drastically altered. Activities such as farming and logging can result in increased sediment transport into caves if not done properly. Not only can this reduce the amount and quality of available groundwater, it can clog sinkholes, dry up or reduce the flow of cave streams, reduce the input of detritus and nutrients into caves, and choke cave passages and streams with mud and sediment. The result can be the impaired usability of groundwater in the area, as well as the possibility of local extinctions of cave-dwelling animals, particularly the aquatic forms.

Indiana's underground world abounds in beauty, mystery, and danger. It challenges the imagination and offers a reminder that natural systems are often very complex and fragile. We are only now beginning to appreciate our interrelationships with the underground world. We have much more to learn.

> On taking our leave of Wyandot [*sic*] Cave as we did in the gray twilight of the early dawn, and considering how simple the components were that went to make up the miles of wonders through which we had wandered, we enjoyed renewed admiration of Creative wisdom and skill. The myriad miracles in stone whereof we were the witnesses, were wrought by One to whom darkness and light are alike, and who loves beauty, whether in the tropical forest, in the sunset sky, or in the marble halls and crystalline gardens of this deep and lonely cave.
>
> —*Horace C. Hovey,* Celebrated American Caverns *(1882)*

A few of Indiana's "wild" caves have exceptional displays of formations.   *Photo by Richard L. Powell*

Lone tree and fence covered with rime (hoarfrost). Such ice deposits occur when objects are much colder than the moist air passing over them.   *Photo by Lee Casebere*

8. Our Changing Climate

James E. Newman

Oh, what a blamed uncertain thing
This pesky weather is!
It blew and snew and then it thew,
And now, by jing, it's friz!

　　　—*Philander Johnson*

CHARACTERISTICS OF INDIANA'S CLIMATE

A common expression in Indiana is, "If you don't like the weather, wait a little while and it will change." Since climate is a composite of weather, it should be no surprise to learn that Indiana's climate changes too.

One might ask, "Why is Indiana's weather so changeable?" In meteorological terms Indiana's changeable weather is related to the hemispheric storm track and jet flow associated with the mid-latitude westerly wind belt that passes over or near the state frequently. These large-scale weather producers transport cold air from the north and warm air from the south for short periods, making Indiana's weather highly changeable. South of the Ohio River and north in the Great Lakes Region, these short-term changes are not as frequent. This is particularly true during the late fall, winter, and early spring. Associated with the storm track are the highs, lows, and fronts that produce the changeable weather.

Indiana's climate is classified as temperate-continental and humid. Temperate climates normally exist between 30 and 50° north and south latitudes. Continental climates have a pronounced difference in average seasonal temperature between summer and winter. Climates are considered humid when the normal annual precipitation exceeds annual evapotranspiration.

The average annual temperature varies considerably across Indiana, from near 48°F (8.7°C) in the northeast to 57°F (13.7°C) in the extreme southwest. As a result, southern areas are classified as warm-temperate-continental and humid, while northern areas are classified as cool-temperate-continental and humid.

The average annual precipitation for Indiana is near 40 inches (102 cm), but there are a number of regional and seasonal differences within the state. The wettest seasonal period in southern areas is late winter; for northern and central areas, it is late spring. The driest month in southern areas is October; for northern and central areas, it is February. In northern and central areas more than half (54 percent) of the average annual precipitation occurs during the five-to-six-month frost-free growing season, whereas less than half (48 percent) occurs during the longer six-to-seven-month frost-free period in southern areas, so that southern areas experience more summer droughts.

These annual and seasonal differences clearly show that northern and central areas are strongly influenced by the prairie climatic norms to the west and north, while southern areas are more closely related to the climatic norms to the south.

Indiana's weather is similar to that of Illinois to the west and Ohio to the east. This is related to latitude plus similar topographical characteristics. There are considerable differences in both annual and seasonal weather events within the Great Lakes states of Michigan and Wisconsin to the north as well as Kentucky to the south. The main difference in states, both north and south of Indiana, is in summer and winter weather. To the north, winter weather extends at least a month longer, with persistent snow cover. The summer weather is cooler, with less rainfall and humidity. To the south, winter weather is confined to less than three months, featuring frequent rainy periods with little or no persistent snow cover. Summer-like weather conditions persist for four months or longer, with high daily temperatures and humidity.

Why does Indiana have such high humidity? Humidity, the amount of water vapor in the air, is related to the surface conditions from which the air came. This is why humidity is associated with wind direction. Winds from a southerly direction, having passed over the tropical waters of the Gulf of Mexico, are loaded with humidity. But winds from the west and north, having passed over the rather dry, high plains, carry relatively low amounts of humidity.

Indiana's weather is often very humid. This is particularly true during the summer months when the winds are southerly much of the time. The raw, humid weather during the colder seasons of late fall, winter, and early spring are associated with the rapid cooling of moisture-laden air.

Why does Indiana weather have so many thunderstorms and associated lightning? Historically, Indiana weather conditions have produced thunderstorms in every month of the year. Seasonally, they occur primarily in the late spring and summer months.

Thunderstorms develop during warm, humid weather conditions when air currents thrust upward violently. This produces associated violent downdraft thrust as well. Vertical type cumulus clouds are formed in this manner. These violent upward and downward air currents produce electrical fields of different polarities. When these cloud-accumulated electrical charges are of the opposite polarity to that at the Earth's surface, a cloud-to-ground lightning streak occurs. Electrical fields of different polarity often build up between clouds, thus producing cloud-to-cloud lightning—often referred to as "flash lightning."

When warm, humid air from the south overrides cooler, drier air from the north along frontal boundaries, a line of thunderstorms is often produced. Isolated thunderstorms develop when warm, humid air is overrun aloft by cooler, drier air from northern and western areas. This produces instability that causes the isolated "popcorn" type thunderstorms to occur during the summer season.

Why is Indiana a part of the national tornado path? The so-called "tornado alley" begins in the Texas-Oklahoma Panhandle area and extends northeastward through Oklahoma, Kansas, Missouri, Illinois, Indiana, and Ohio. The high frequency of tornadoes in these states is associated with the seasonal position of the storm track that is normally present during the peak tornado months of April and May. It is in these geographical areas that the cold, dense air from the north clashes with the warm, moist air from the south, often creating severe thunderstorms and associated tornadoes.

Tornadoes are formed within intense thunderstorm-type cumulonimbus clouds. Those that produce tornadoes normally build up to heights of 30,000 feet or more. These tornado-producing thun-

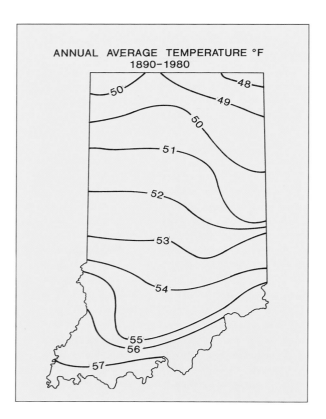

Isotherms of average annual temperature in °F for Indiana (1890–1980).

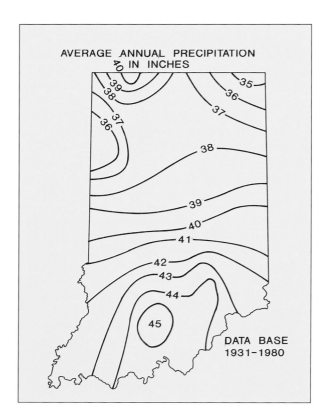

Isohytes of average annual precipitation in inches for Indiana (1931–1980).

derstorms have severe up- and downdrafts within them that usually produce some hail. Tornadoes are formed within the up- and downdrafts, in which the air currents begin to whirl into a vortex that produces a funnel-shaped extension from the mother cloud. Pressure is extremely low in the vortex center of the tornado funnel. Because of this, winds within the funnel can reach between 200 and 300 miles per hour, making the tornado the most destructive atmospheric condition on Earth.

Why is Indiana subject to ice storms? Ice storms, like most snow storms in Indiana, are caused by warm, moist air from the south overrunning cold air from the north along so-called warm fronts. But the difference between ice storms and snow storms is in the temperature of the air aloft. For precipitation to fall as snow, the air temperature aloft within the precipitating cloud layer must be below 32°F (0°C). In an ice storm the temperature aloft in the precipitating cloud is above 32°F. Therefore, the precipitation from the cloud falls as rain into a cold layer of air below 32°F. While passing through the cold layer, the rain droplets are supercooled. As a result, they freeze on contact with the cold ground surface, which must be below freezing as well. If the below-freezing layer of air near the ground is too deep, the falling rain droplets freeze into some form of sleet. This is why sleet is usually associated with ice storms.

Historically sleet and ice storms have occurred in Indiana in all the colder months from November into April. But the most likely period for ice storms across Indiana is during March. Warm, moist air from the south often overruns cold air at the surface during that month.

INDIAN SUMMER—A SPECIAL TIME IN INDIANA

By definition, "Indian Summer" may occur any time after the first autumn killing frost. This unique period of weather almost never occurs before October 10 or after mid-December, but may occur for two or three 5-to–10-day periods between these dates in a given season.

What are some of the unique characteristics of Indian Summer in Hoosierland? First, it normally occurs in two phases—an early phase which usually lasts 7 to 10 days around mid-october, and a later phase which may last up to two weeks in November. The early phase is followed by a 7-to–10-day stormy period in late October or early November. Also, this stormy period marks the first southward migration of geese and ducks in large numbers.

During the early phase of Indian Summer, daily temperatures normally climb into the 60s and drop to the low 40s and 30s at night. The humidity is low in the daytime. There is no precipitation except dew or frost at night. The skies are clear. Winds are light and variable. It is a good time to harvest soybeans or corn, take that hunting trip or late-autumn fishing outing, make that last camping trip, or go to that special football game.

The late phase of Indian Summer in November is similar, except that daily temperatures are usually in the upper 40s or 50s, with night temperatures dropping below freezing and producing a good frost each night. The sky is clear with a smoky, hazy appearance, and the sun has a reddish appearance much of the day except around high noon.

Certain large-scale atmospheric motions characterize Indian Summer. For instance, there is a general sinking motion in the atmosphere from excessive cooling during the short autumn days. This helps produce a weak high-pressure system, which normally dominates the weather map from the Rocky Mountains to the East Coast of the continental United States. Since average land and ocean temperatures tend to be nearly equal at our latitudes during the mid-autumn season, this leads to a slowdown in the movement of high-pressure systems and results in Indian Summer.

Explanations for its name include the early settlers' observation that the Indians recognized the summer-like weather as a time for storing late crops and readying their lodges for the coming winter, or the settlers' attributing the blue haze which is characteristic of the season to the smoke of fires set by Indians on the western prairies. Whatever the reason for its name, Indian Summer is a beautiful description of a delightful weather event.

SEASONAL AND GEOGRAPHIC VARIATIONS

When the hounds of spring are on winter's traces
The mother of months in meadow or plain
Fills the shadows and windy places
With lisp of leaves and ripple of rain.
     —*Swinburne, Chorus of* Atalanta in Calydon

The seasons. In a mid-latitude continental temperate transitional climate such as Indiana's, the astronomy-based concept of four equal-length seasons does not accurately coincide with the observed facts. As any resident well knows, spring does not automatically begin on March 21 each year. Plant growth does not follow the classical four-season concept very well either.

For many species of native plants and cool-season agricultural crops, the growing season is not confined to the frost-free period of the year. In fact, the total array of agricultural crops conforms far better to the concept of six seasons, in which both spring and autumn are divided into early and late subseasons, than to the conventional four.

The extreme seasons within the annual cycle determine what cultivated crop can be grown as well as which species survive within the natural vegetation. This is particularly true in mid-latitude temperate climates with distinct summer and winter seasons like those experienced in Indiana.

Winter temperature extremes largely determine overwintering crop survival. In addition, almost all overwintering crops such as winter wheat and tree fruits have a chilling requirement (vernalization) to induce flowering for grain or fruit development during the forthcoming growing season. Vernalization requires a certain level and duration of winter temperatures. This chilling requirement exists within natural vegetation species as well.

Winter precipitation often can determine crop and natural vegetation survival. For example, replacement of forests with prairie to the west of Indiana is related to dry winters, not dry summers. Lincoln, Nebraska, normally has about the same amount of precipitation from May to September as Indianapolis. Therefore, it is the summer rainfall that determines the Corn Belt.

The primary cause of droughts in Indiana is the lack of summer rainfall. But droughts do not develop overnight. It takes several weeks or more. Therefore, dry conditions can develop in any season or over several seasons—in some cases, years. Such was the case during the dustbowl years of the 1930s.

Droughts are devastating to annual summer crops such as corn and soybeans. Multiple-season droughts, particularly dry winters followed by a dry spring and summer, can and do eliminate some deciduous forest species in the northwestern areas of Indiana.

The growing season. The transitional nature of Indiana's climate is evident in the length of the so-called frost-free growing season, which varies from less than 150 days in the higher elevations of the northeast to more than 200 days near the confluence of the Ohio and Wabash rivers. The most dramatic change in seasons and local climates is found in the lakeshore areas bordering Lake Michigan. Here the average frost-free growing season varies from about 190

Cumulonimbus mammus clouds are foreboding as they sometimes coalesce into the funnel clouds of tornadoes.   *Photo by James E. Newman*

Funnel cloud over Indiana when a family of tornadoes hit the state on Palm Sunday, 1965.   *Photo by James E. Newman*

This thrifty 30-inch-diameter American beech tree in Hoot Woods, Owen County, was twisted off completely about 25 feet above the ground by an August 1980 tornado.   *Photo by Marion Jackson*

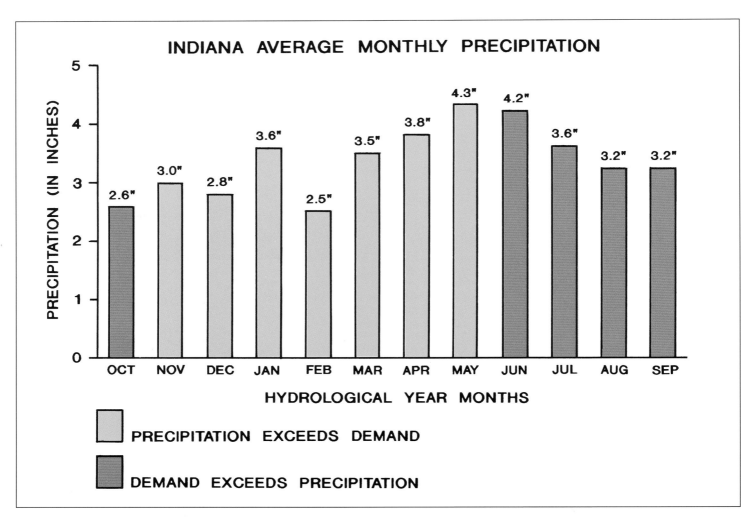

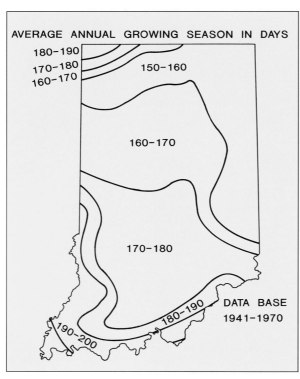

Average annual growing season length in days for Indiana (1941–1970).

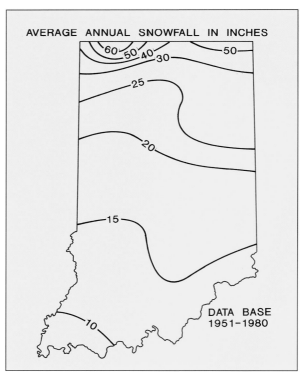

Average annual snowfall in inches for Indiana (1951–1980).

days near the shoreline to less than 160 days in the Kankakee River Valley 20 to 30 miles to the south. This change is also evident in seasonal temperatures, summer rainfall, winter snowfall, local winds, and cloudiness.

Local climates. Climate is greatly influenced by conditions at or near the Earth's surface. There are several natural and artificial features within Indiana that create unique "local climates." They include the Lake Michigan shore areas in the northwest, the major river valleys, the high plateaus in south-central and east-central areas, the larger natural lakes, reservoirs, and the large urban areas.

Local climates are usually created or influenced by unusual wind patterns such as lakeshore breezes, river valley winds, cold air drainage into depressions, and city "heat island" thermal cell winds. Since winds are normally a major influence in creating local climates, windbreaks and shelter belts (trees and shrubs spaced so as to break up surface winds) can often be used to modulate climates.

Perhaps the best example of a local climate influence in Indiana is the increased annual precipitation (especially snowfall) near Lake Michigan, thus producing a well-known snowbelt. This situation is well-known to meteorologists nationwide as the LaPorte precipitation anomaly. In addition to the increased snowfall that typically occurs leeward of large lakes, cloud seeding from air pollutants generated by the Chicago-Gary industrial complex causes greater than expected mean annual precipitation immediately downwind.

Microclimates. Since the amount of solar energy received per unit area of surface depends on the angle of incidence, topographic features of the Earth's surface, the presence and structure of vegetation, buildings, and street orientation, etc., microclimates are often created on or near the surfaces of water, land, and structures, and at the boundaries of living organisms. These small-scale climates are usually restricted to a few inches or a few feet immediately above or around surfaces, and may be either more or less extreme than the prevailing local or regional climates.

Microclimates are a product of differences in radiant energy exchange which creates temperature and moisture differences between specific surfaces and the surrounding atmosphere. In outdoor environments, microclimates exist around the surfaces of living organisms, within plant canopies, and near land and water surfaces. They are critical to the comfort and survival of both domesticated and wild plants and animals because the microclimate represents the actual conditions where organisms live.

WEATHER EXTREMES AND CLIMATE EVENTS

> Announced by all the trumpets of the sky,
> Arrives the snow, and driving o'er the fields,
> Seems nowhere to alight; the whited air
> Hides hills and woods, the river, and the heaven,
> And veils the farm-house at the garden's end.
> The sled and traveler stopped, the courier's feet
> Delayed, all friends shut out, the housemates sit
> Around the radiant fireplace, enclosed
> In a tumultuous privacy of storm.
> —*Emerson,* The Snow-Storm

Where and when extreme weather events will occur is difficult to understand, much less predict. One would expect that the coldest temperature ever recorded would be in the north and the hottest in the south, but this is not the case. The coldest official temperature was −35°F on February 2, 1951, at Greensburg. However, a new low temperature of −36°F occurred on January 19, 1994, at an unofficial station with official thermometers near New Whiteland. The hottest temperature ever recorded is 116°F on July 15, 1936, at Collegeville. The coldest January was in 1886, with the hottest July being in 1936.

The heaviest single official rainfall was recorded at Princeton on August 6, 1906, where 10.5 inches fell in 25 hours. The greatest single snowfall was recorded at Vevay, where 24 inches fell on December 9 and 10, 1917.

The most devastating single tornado, in terms of human casualties, struck on March 18, 1925, killing 70 people and injuring more than 200 in Posey, Gibson, and Pike counties. The largest number of tornadoes occurred on Palm Sunday, April 11, 1965, killing 137 people and injuring more than 500. The largest hailstones officially observed fell at Columbia City on March 28, 1969. They were up to 3 inches in diameter. The largest ice storm on record was on March 12 and 13, 1991, covering much of north-central Illinois, Indiana, and Ohio.

Killing frosts have been recorded in every month of the year. The latest official spring date is June 14, 1925, when a frost occurred in almost all northern border counties. A freak summer frost was recorded in northern Jasper County around Wheatfield on July 29, 1936, just two weeks after the all-time record high temperature occurred less than 20 miles away. Several late August frosts have been recorded over low muck soils in the Kankakee River Valley. One of the most spectacular early autumn frosts occurred on September 11, 1917, covering most of the northern, central, and eastern areas.

> There was a roaring in the wind all night;
> The rain came heavily and fell in floods;
> But now the sun is rising calm and bright;
> The birds are singing in the distant woods;
> And all the air is filled with pleasant noise of waters.
> —*Wordsworth,* Resolution and Independence

The greatest floods on the Wabash and White Rivers were recorded in March 1913. The highest flood levels on the Ohio River were recorded in February 1937. The wettest year was 1950, when the average annual precipitation totaled 50.5 inches statewide. The driest year was 1934, with a state average precipitation of 29.7 inches. During the past century (1890 to 1990), statewide droughts existed in 1894, 1895, 1901, 1914, 1930, 1934, 1954, 1956, 1977, 1983, and 1988. Smaller droughts, sometimes labeled "pocket droughts," affecting anywhere from a few townships to a few counties, have occurred in about half of the past 100 years.

Weather extremes and climate events as reported by the news media are often based on only the past 30 years or since April 1, 1948, the date when the National Climatic Data Center began recording climate data on computer systems. The extreme events listed herein are based on all known official climate records for Indiana dating back into the 1800s.

WEATHER SIGNS AND FOLKLORE

Since their survival depended upon a keen awareness of their environment, it is safe to assume that prehistoric peoples had considerable proficiency in forecasting the weather. Expressions of weather wisdom exist in the earliest writings and scriptures. People have always been intensely interested in weather and how it affects their daily affairs. Such knowledge has been passed down through many centuries in the form of proverbs and folklore sayings. The Temple of the Winds in Athens is positive proof that the classical Greeks associated weather with wind direction. Much later, a proverb by Francis Bacon, "Every wind has its weather," restated this wisdom. Bacon's proverb was greatly refined by the early American conservationist Izaak Walton with his verse to New England fishermen:

Satellite photograph of the southwestern Lake Michigan region showing cloud seeding downwind from the Chicago-Gary pollution sources. This phenomenon creates elevated precipitation levels in northwestern Indiana.
Photo courtesy of James E. Newman

Sugar maple forest in fog of a Floyd County nature preserve illustrates the cool, humid microclimate that occurs within the vegetation canopy during summer.   *Photo by Perry Scott*

When the wind is in the *North*
The skillful fisher goes not forth.

When the wind is in the *East,*
'Tis good for neither man nor beast.

When the wind is in the *South,*
It blows the flies in the fish's mouth.

When the wind is in the *West,*
There it is the very best.

Weather proverbs and folklore are based largely on observations of nature, including shifts in wind direction and sky conditions, with special emphasis on cloud type and cloud height. Other folklore expressions are based on observations of the presence or behavior of mammals, birds, fish, insects, or plants. Some are based on sky-sun and sky-moon observations as well as the positions of the planets and certain stars.

Since most weather folklore is based on natural events, the resulting forecasts are often accurate, particularly when they are applied in climatic regions where they originated. But the most common misuse of folklore expressions is the application under different climatic conditions from that of origin. A good example is found in these biblical verses:

When it is evening, ye say, *It will be* fair weather: for the sky is red. And in the morning, *It will be* foul weather to-day: for the sky is red and lowering.

—*Matthew 16:2–3*

These verses are meaningful in the subtropical trade wind latitudes where the prevailing winds are from east to west, but the reverse is

Dry plants and their shadows create snow artistry following a 1977 blizzard.   *Photo by Marion Jackson*

White pine tree during ice storm.   *Photo by Ron Everhart*

more likely at higher latitudes (e.g., Indiana) where westerly winds prevail.

The Native American tribes of the eastern U.S. described wind directions in terms of the sun, the moon, and the stars. Some of the best weather folklore published in almanacs of colonial America was very likely based on observations by Indians. The following verse probably originated from an Indian expression:

> If the wind backs against the sun
> Trust it not, for back it will run.

The truth of this verse lies in how wind directions shift with the passing of a low-pressure storm center. The sequence of changes in wind direction depends on the position of the observer with reference to the center of the passing storm. The verse relates how the wind will shift with a storm center passing south of the observer; if it passes to the north, opposite wind changes will occur.

The publication of almanacs began early in colonial America, with the *Old Farmer's Almanac* claiming to be the oldest continuous publication in North America. Almanacs were read second only to the Holy Bible itself by colonial and pioneer families. Since colonial and pioneer peoples were constantly exposed to the elements, any information related to the weather and the changing of the seasons was much cherished. In the absence of any formalized weather and climate services, weather information was developed from the provincial wisdom of an experienced local weather observer, and as a result, seasonal weather prognostication became the centerpiece of eighteenth- and nineteenth-century almanacs. The best information in almanacs today, as has always been the case, is the astronomical information, such as moon phases, tides, sunrise and sunset, etc. These data are accurate if properly interpreted for time and place.

EARLY WEATHER FORECASTING

> The hollow winds begin to blow;
> The clouds look black, the glass is low;
> The soot falls down, the spaniels sleep;
> And spiders from their cobwebs peep.
>
> —*Edward Jenner,* Forty Signs of Rain

Weather prognosticators that predate modern meteorology often were uncannily accurate. From careful observations over the years,

they learned that daily weather conditions reoccur in somewhat predictable sequences, i.e., fair and foul weather periods repeat over several days' time. Also, the time span of repeating weather events varies with the seasons, from as little as 2 to 3 days in the winter to as long as 10 to 14 days in summer.

Early amateur weather forecasters learned to read changes in the direction of the wind, barometric pressure, cloud types, temperature, and humidity to forecast the approach and departure of storms and fair weather periods that followed.

Storms are associated with centers of low atmospheric pressure called *lows*—gigantic whirlwinds of several hundred miles in diameter. Ascending light moist air in the center of the low causes winds to blow inward and upward around the center. Fair weather is associated with high pressure called *highs,* in which heavy-dry air at the center blows downward and outward.

If the storm center passes south of your location, the winds will shift from the east to northeast to north and finally to a northwesterly direction as the storm passes. The first clouds observed are usually some form of cirrus followed by altostratus, stratus, stratocumulus, and finally altocumulus as the trailing high pressure approaches. The pressure drops, then rises; temperature holds steady, then drops; and the humidity rises, holds steady, then drops.

If the storm center passes north of your location, the winds shift in an opposite manner—from the east to southeast to south to west, thence to northwest. In this case, the cirrus clouds are usually followed by some form of stratocumulus, then cumulonimbus (thunderstorms), and finally some form of cumulus-of-fair-weather as the trailing high-pressure center approaches. The pressure drops, then holds steady, and rises rapidly; temperature rises, then falls rapidly, and the humidity does likewise. In either case, the winds finally end up blowing from a northwesterly direction, signaling the arrival of fair weather. With these winds comes a rapid drop in temperature, lower humidity, and a clearing sky. These changing weather sequences are associated with the passing of a high- or a low-pressure center.

> The wind goeth toward the south, and turneth about unto the north; it whirleth about continually, and the wind returneth again according to his circuits.
>
> —*Ecclesiastes 1:6*

Associated with the passing of a low-pressure storm center and a high-pressure fair weather center are so-called *fronts* with rapidly changing weather conditions. A *cold front* is the dividing area between a departing low-pressure storm center and the approaching high-pressure fair weather center. A *warm front* is the dividing area between the departing high-pressure fair weather center and the approaching low-pressure storm center. Sky conditions change very rapidly along fronts. It is here that amateur weather-forecasting knowledge can be very useful.

EARLY CLIMATE RECORDS
AND CLIMATOLOGICAL DATA

The first organized and continuous climate records for Indiana were likely those of the early settlement at New Harmony. They began January 1, 1826, and extended unbroken to January 31, 1829, with spotty or seasonal observations through the remainder of the nineteenth century. At Richmond, continuous monthly precipitation was recorded from 1852 to 1868. A similar record existed at Spiceland in Henry County from 1863 to 1890. Elsewhere, early observations were recorded at South Bend, Collegeville, LaPorte,

Altocumulus clouds at leading edge of frontal system.
Photo by Richard Fields

Cumulus clouds of "fair weather" above northern Indiana.
Photo by Lee Casebere

Thunderheads often build to 30,000 feet or more before summer storms.
Photo by Russell Mumford

Logansport, and Greencastle. The larger cities as we know them today were not the first to record weather observations.

The longest continuous climate record in Indiana exists in Switzerland County at Vevay near the Ohio River. It began in 1872 and remains unbroken to this day except for minor station location changes. Currently this Switzerland County station is located at Markland Dam.

A volunteer weather service for the state was organized in the early 1870s by Professor W. H. Ragan of DePauw University at Greencastle. The Indiana State Weather Service was created in 1881 and placed in the charge of H. A. Huston, director of the Agricultural Experiment Station at Purdue University in 1882, where it remained until the U.S. Weather Bureau was organized within the USDA in 1891. The responsibility for weather observations and climatic records has remained primarily with the federal government ever since.

EVIDENCE OF CLIMATE CHANGE IN CLIMATOLOGICAL DATA

Men say the winter
Was bad that year.
Fuel was scarce
And food was dear
A wind with a wolf's head
Howled about our door.

> —*Edna St. Vincent Millay,* The Ballad of the Harp-Weaver

Continuous and accurate climatological records have existed since about the middle of the nineteenth century, less than 150 years. They show that climate has indeed changed over the past century and that detectable shifts have occurred over a decade or so. In general, on a global or hemispheric scale, mean annual temperatures increased between the 1890s and 1930s, then decreased from the 1940s to the 1980s, followed by the onset of a warming trend in the 1980s. The fact that the cooler 1970s were followed by the warmer 1980s is often cited as early evidence of the increasing influence of atmospheric gases on global climate, known as the greenhouse effect. On the other hand, similar decadal variations have been recorded during the past century.

Similar century-long climate trends exist in state records. An analysis of nine central Indiana climate records showed a warming trend of nearly 3°F in annual mean temperatures between the 1890s and the 1930s, followed by a cooling trend of about 2°F from the 1940s through the 1970s. But a sharp increase occurred in the 1980s, giving rise to the warmest decadal mean annual temperatures since the 1930s. These century-long trends are illustrated in the accompanying graph.

Indiana weather and climate records over the past century or so suggest that these climatic trends have affected weather events. For example, during the decade of the 1880s, the Ohio River was frozen in most years. Records from Cincinnati and Louisville mention river ice in 7 out of 10 years. River ice was recorded rather regularly up to about 1920. After 1920, ice was not recorded as a problem to Ohio River transportation until the 1970s, when it occurred during three winter seasons.

The decade with the most summer droughts was the 1930s, followed by the 1980s. The decade with the greatest annual average snowfall was the 1880s, followed by the 1970s and the 1980s. Collectively, these seasonal, annual, and decadal statistics strongly suggest that climate is constantly changing.

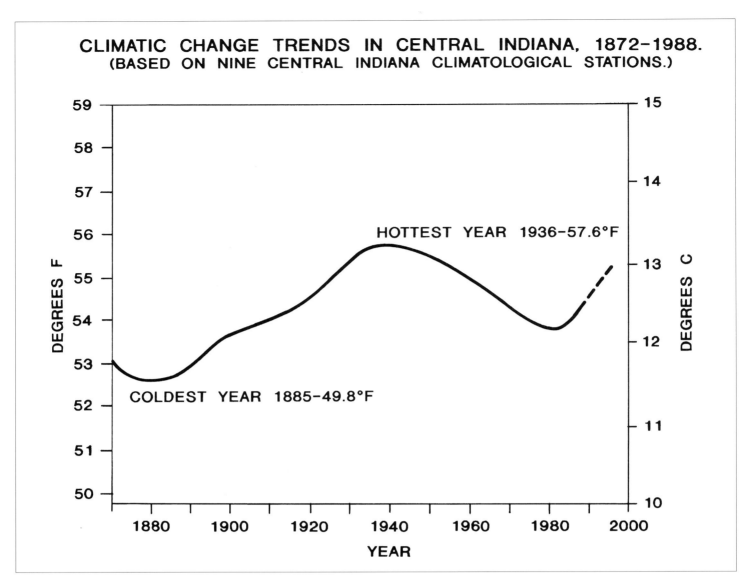

CLIMATIC CHANGE TRENDS IN CENTRAL INDIANA, 1872–1988.
(BASED ON NINE CENTRAL INDIANA CLIMATOLOGICAL STATIONS.)

HOTTEST YEAR 1936–57.6°F

COLDEST YEAR 1885–49.8°F

Climate changes in central Indiana.

CYCLIC VARIATION IN CLIMATE

There is little doubt that some relation exists between the sunspot cycle and terrestrial conditions, but it is very obscure . . . rainfall seems to have a tendency to be greatest at spot maximum but there are many exceptions. One of the most interesting relations is between sunspot relative numbers and the frequency of thunderstorms which are more frequent at sunspot maxima.

—C. E. P. Brooks, Climate through the Ages (1949)

Most people's knowledge of climate is based on fixed averages in weather statistics. This often leads to a lack of understanding of a changing climate in decision-making. As a result, much of the existing inadequate planning for water supply, flood damages, soil erosion, urban design, plus a host of other air, land, and water management problems are traceable, in part, to a lack of appreciation for variability in climate.

As any farmer can testify, no two growing seasons are alike.

Anyone who has made an analysis of Indiana's climatic records over several decades learns that intra-annual variability in temperature, precipitation, etc., is far greater than the variation in longer term averages. Yet many research reports reveal that cyclical patterns in seasonal weather and climate do recur.

The major cause of annual changes in seasonal weather and climate is well understood—latitudinal change in the zenith position of insolation during the earth's annual orbit of the sun. Beyond this annual cyclic change in energy balance there are several possible minor influences, including variations in solar activity, in sea surface temperatures over large oceanic areas, and in lunar and planetary orbits. Volcanic activity may be a minor influence, but has no cyclic input because of its discontinuous nature.

It is a historical fact that weather deviates from what is the climatological normal for weeks, months, and, on rather rare occasions, years. Such deviations in daily weather create droughts, floods, and unusual trends in seasonal weather conditions. The search for the possible causes of these observed anomalous weather

94 / James E. Newman

trends has centered on known changes in large-scale ocean surface temperatures, the extraterrestrial changes in solar output, and lunar influences.

Sea surface temperatures. The greatest influence on extended anomalous weather trends if associated with large-scale changes in sea surface temperatures, known as the El Niño. Sometime during the middle of the nineteenth century, fishermen discovered that the cold water current off the Pacific coast of Peru warmed rapidly around Christmas each year. They called this phenomenon El Niño, "the Christ Child" in Spanish.

It is now known that when sea surface temperatures are warmer than normal in the tropical areas of the Pacific Ocean east of the international dateline to the South American–Central American coasts, many areas within the continental United States, including Indiana and other midwestern states, receive extended periods of above-normal precipitation. The most recent occurrence produced the 1993 floods in the upper Mississippi and Missouri River valleys. The opposite trends in seasonal weather exist after El Niño conditions die out. This is particularly so when tropical sea surface temperatures in the eastern Pacific Ocean revert to normal or below normal. These conditions are known as the La Niño. When La Niño conditions exist, many areas within the continental United States, including the Midwest and Indiana, experience below-normal seasonal precipitation and above-normal seasonal temperatures.

The drought years of the 1930s often reduced Indiana crop production by as much as 50 percent. The most devastating drought year on record was 1936. Production was reduced from 10 to 50 percent during the La Niño years of 1983 and 1988. During the El Niño year of 1993, floods reduced crop production in Indiana by 5 percent to 10 percent and by as much as 50 percent in Iowa.

Natural vegetation is not normally influenced by short-period deviations in daily weather. But extended periods in seasonal and annual weather trends that deviate from the climatic normals of any geographic area usually affect natural vegetation and wildlife in a negative way. Further, natural vegetation and associated wildlife are more sensitive to weather trends in the extreme seasons of summer and winter than during the transition seasons of spring and fall.

Solar activity patterns. Differences in solar activity may be associated with short-term seasonal and annual variations in climate. Seasonal and annual periods with below-normal precipitation and above-normal temperatures are associated with low sunspot numbers over the past century.

Variations in solar activity are associated with a phenomenon known as sunspots, which increase to a maximum, then die out to a minimum in a predictable cycle that averages nearly 11 years. Sunspots are magnetic disturbances that reverse polarity between the solar hemispheres at the end of each 11-year cycle, thus producing a 22-year magnetic cyclic change. Fewer spots appear during the negative cycle than during the positive cycle that follows.

In addition to the commonly observed 11- and 22-year sunspot cycles, there is a longer cycle of 86 to 90 years, often referred to as the Gleissburg cycle. It consists of eight 11-year cycles, or four 22-year cycles, with an increasing number of sunspots occurring during each succeeding 11- and 22-year cycle. The last complete Gleissburg cycle began in 1870–71 and ended in 1957–58, and was the basis for the year to be designated as the International Geophysical Year (IGY).

The coolest decade in existing North American climate records was the 1880s. This cold decade occurred during or following the 11-year sunspot cycle with the lowest solar activity within the 1870–1958 Gleissburg cycle. The cold decade of the 1970s occurred during a similar period in the current Gleissburg cycle. The warm decade of the 1980s had a counter period in the 1890s as well.

There are numerous studies relating the Gleissburg cycle of solar activity to recorded impacts of possible climate change. Water levels of Lake Chad in the Sahelian area of Africa suggest that minor droughts lasting several years have occurred during the first and second decades of each Gleissburg cycle for the past 500 years.

The "Little Ice Age" in northern Europe, a period of unusually cool weather from about 1630 to 1710, was also a time of minimal sunspot activity, the timing and duration of which agrees rather closely with one complete Gleissburg cycle.

There is much evidence relating seasonal, annual, and multiple-year climate impact to sunspot cycles. The most intense interest in these relationships probably occurs here in the United States, where a repeating pattern of multiple-year droughts centered in the high plains of North America has occurred every 18 to 22 years for the last century. Before recorded historic accounts, evidence of these recurring droughts has been revealed by examinations of annual tree-ring growth, and they too have been associated with the double-sunspot cycle for the past two centuries. The National Center for Atmospheric Research linked levels of solar activity to small changes in atmospheric pressure at stratospheric altitudes in the polar regions. Such persistent minor pressure change could have an impact on the displacement of mid-latitude storm tracts.

> The distribution of the world's climates is too regular to be due to accidents of history. . . . The patterns suggest that we can understand the climate as a consequence of the earth's geography, particularly its rotation.
>
> —*Robert H. MacArthur,* Geographical Ecology Patterns in the Distribution of Species *(1972)*

Possible lunar effects. It has long been postulated that the moon affects the weather. Some weather folklore is based on the lunar monthly cycle. The gravitational effects of the moon on ocean tides are well understood, but lunar influences on atmospheric pressure, temperature, and precipitation are small and difficult to detect. There is some evidence that bimonthly increases in precipitation occur during the week following the "new moon" and "full moon," but they have been considered too minor to be worthy of serious attention. Recent studies reveal that such increases are more closely associated with the times the moon is closest and farthest from the Earth during its monthly orbit.

It is easy to observe that the moon orbits the Earth every 29.53 days, but other cyclic features of the lunar orbit are less evident. For example, the moon's orbit oscillates between 18.5° and 28.5° north latitude during an 18.6-year cycle, resulting in tidal cycles with a similar periodicity. Recently, a temperature change cycle of about 18.6 years in North America, eastern Asia, Japan, and western Europe has been reported. Other research has linked cyclic changes in sea surface temperatures in the Atlantic and Pacific oceans as tidal strength changes during the 18.6-year lunar cycle.

It has been known for several decades that annual grain production is cyclic for several major grain producing areas around the world. This is particularly true for the grain belts within the United States, where several studies have related an 18-to–20-year and a 9-to–10-year cycle in grain production to seasonal weather cycles of a similar length. It is now known that maximum 18-to–20-year United States corn yields correlate well with minimum declination of the 18.6 lunar orbit as well as the positive 11 years of a 20-to–22-year solar cycle. Just how lunar cycles and solar cycles influence the weather and crop production is now a central topic in climatic research.

Concurrent with the increasing aridity over the continent was cooling of the air . . . and brought a gradual southward shift of climate belts which culminated in the very severe glaciation of the Pleistocene. The actual cause of the glaciation is obscure, but there is no doubt that the glaciation was accompanied by a drop in average temperature, and an increase in annual precipitation.

—*S. Charles Kendeigh, "Paleoecology," in* Animal Ecology *(1961)*

Down through the ages, climate has changed continuously. Evidence for this is voluminous. The only questions open to debate are those concerning the possible causes.

Early geological time. It is possible that climate began to change soon after the appearance of the early forms of life, such as blue-green algae. The process of photosynthesis requires the splitting of water and carbon dioxide molecules by sunlight. This produced the first organic compounds and increased the oxygen in the atmosphere. The fossil storage of organic matter and the release of oxygen into the ancient atmosphere may have been responsible for the first greenhouse climate change. As oxygen increased in the atmosphere, a second life-supporting climate change began to develop. High in the atmosphere, perhaps 1 billion years ago, ultraviolet radiation from the sun split oxygen molecules, producing increasing amounts of ozone, thus creating the ozone shield which protected the terrestrial surfaces from harmful ultraviolet radiation, allowing living forms to invade land.

The next major climate changes likely occurred over several hundred million years during the rifting and drifting of the continents. The hemispheric and regional climates of some 200 to 300 million years ago, when the continents came together to form the one supercontinent known as Pangaea, must have been very different from those of the present. A main feature of the one-continent world was extremes in seasonal climate. It is likely that winters were very cold and the summers were very hot in the interior of Pangaea. (See also chapter 1, "Of Time, Rocks, and Ancient Life.")

Many violent shifts in global climate must have occurred between the breakup of the supercontinent about 100 million years ago and the beginning of the Ice Ages about 1 million years ago. Fossil records reveal that 50 to 75 percent of the existing species, including the dinosaurs, became extinct during this interval of time, and that there were periods of intense volcanic occurrences that dramatically changed the levels of atmospheric greenhouse gases. These elevated levels of greenhouse gases produced a tropical-like global climate. Atmospheric carbon dioxide was 10 to 100 times greater before glaciation than since glaciation.

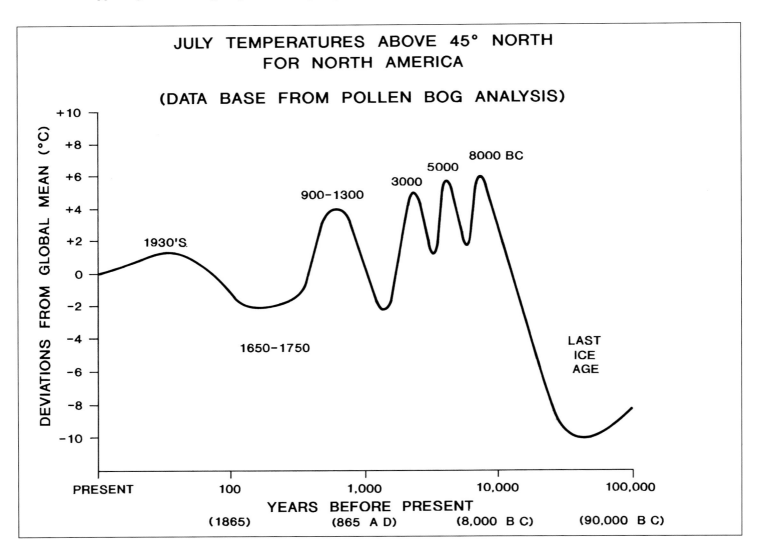

Climate changes from the Ice Age to the present, as based on fossil pollen analysis from bogs.

Pleistocene climates. The continued fossil storage of atmospheric carbon dioxide, methane, and other "greenhouse" gases produced a colder global climate trend that evolved into cycles of glaciation about 1 million years ago. Glaciers develop when accumulation of frozen precipitation exceeds its annual melting. As a general rule, it requires an annual mean temperature of 43°F (7°C) or less with a mean annual water-equivalent precipitation of 20 inches (50 cm) or more for glacial ice to accumulate. These conditions currently exist in parts of Greenland and Antarctica, and in higher-latitude mountainous areas.

There have been four distinct glacial periods during the past million years. During each of these, much of North America, Europe, and Asia was covered with glacial ice sheets. At least two of these continental glaciers, the Illinoian and the Wisconsinan ice sheets, covered much of Indiana (see also chapter 2, "Indiana on Ice").

Several theories have been advanced related to the possible causes of the repeated Ice Age climates. It is likely that the greenhouse gases reached their lowest atmospheric concentrations in the entire geological history of the Earth. For example, carbon dioxide may have been less than 200 parts per million at times during this Pleistocene era. This, coupled with variations in the orbital geometry of the Earth, appears to be the most creditable explanation of the climate changes that produced the reoccurring ice ages.

The Earth wobbles on its axis like a spinning top, requiring about 20,000 years to complete a wobble cycle. Also, the tilt of the Earth's axis varies from near 22° to about 25°. It takes about 40,000 years to complete an axis-tilt cycle, known to astronomers as the precession of the equinoxes. Further, the solar orbit varies from an almost circular one to a slight ellipse with a cycle of near 100,000 years. When these orbital characteristics line up to favor less solar heating during a year, the climate cools. Contrarily, when the orbital conditions favor more solar heating, the climate warms. This is particularly true for the high-latitude polar regions.

The sequences of climate change during the ice ages of the past million years strongly suggest that a minimum of solar heating has recurred about every 100,000 years, with lesser cycles of change near 40,000 and 20,000 years each. Presently, these orbital characteristics are in near neutral phase during the current intraglacial period.

The present intraglacial period. It is estimated that mean global temperature dropped to near 41°F (5°C) at the peak development of the Late Wisconsinan glacial epoch some 40,000 to 50,000 years ago. Temperatures began to rise dramatically about 25,000 years ago, marking the beginning of the post-Late Wisconsinan period. Pollen analysis from bog sediments reveals that summer temperatures must have risen rapidly beginning about 18,000 years ago, reaching a thermal maximum about 10,000 years ago (8000 B.C.) (see also chapter 10, "In the Glacier's Wake"). It is estimated that mean July temperatures in North America above 45° North Latitude (NL) rose 18°F (10°C) or more during this period.

The post-glacial climate of North America has oscillated several times between thermal maximum and thermal minimum periods over the past 10,000 years. Each of these periods lasted several centuries. Thermal maxima occurred near 8000 B.C., 5000 B.C., 3000 B.C., and at the beginning of the current millennium. There were thermal minima periods near 6000 B.C., 4000 B.C., and at the time of Christ.

There have been significant climate changes during the current millennium. The global climate began to warm in the ninth and tenth centuries, reaching a thermal maximum during the eleventh century. The Norsemen settled in Greenland during this period, in areas that since have been covered with glacial ice. A cooling trend followed in the fifteenth and sixteenth centuries, reaching a thermal minimum near the end of the seventeenth century. The last half of the seventeenth and first half of the eighteenth century is commonly referred to as the Little Ice Age in European history. By the end of the eighteenth century, a warming trend was under way which has continued through the nineteenth and twentieth centuries.

These climatic oscillations are well documented in written history for the past 100 years or so. Evidences for earlier post-glacial climate shifts are largely based on archaeological and fossil records. Native Americans left many archaeological evidences of climate change. For example, the disappearance at Mesa Verde and other inhabited sites in the southwestern United States and northern Mexico took place during the thermal maximum of the tenth through twelfth centuries. The growing of maize in tribal-designed gardens shifted southward in the Great Lakes region during the Little Ice Age. There are many other such examples across the North and South American continents.

These multiple-century climate variations of the post-glacial period have been estimated to be between 5 and 9°F (3 and 5°C) in mean annual temperature at the higher mid-latitudes and the polar regions. Estimated climate change at the lower latitudes is much less, deviating by less than 2 to 4°F (1 to 2°C) in subtropical areas and less than 2°F (1°C) in the tropics.

PRESENT AND FUTURE CLIMATE CHANGE

What dreadful hot weather we have! It keeps me in a continual state of inelegance.

—*Jane Austen*

In this era of environmental concern, one of the most pressing questions within the scientific community is that of possible irreversible changes in the global climate caused by the collective activities of the human race. We know that a number of atmospheric gases are being affected by human activities. The observed rapid increases in carbon dioxide, nitrogen oxides, and methane plus the release of chlorofluorocarbons (CFCs) that deplete the stratospheric ozone result from global atmospheric pollution. The rapid increases in atmospheric carbon dioxide (CO_2) in the past several decades could produce a global climate change as a result of an intensified greenhouse effect. (This is not a new concern created by overzealous environmentalists; it was first expressed by the famous chemist Arrhenius in 1896.) The impact on natural vegetation, crop production, and human activities can be both direct and indirect.

Increases in atmospheric CO_2 can affect the photosynthetic rate directly, resulting in increased biomass and crop yields. Decreased water use per unit of biomass occurs in many species when grown in enriched atmospheric CO_2 environments. This in turn results in greater water use efficiency. Further, transpiration losses are reduced by the partial closure of stomates in many species. This often increases temperature tolerance as well. These are the primary direct biological reactions to changes in atmospheric CO_2 levels.

Indirect effects of climate change are related to temperature, precipitation, or, more correctly, water balance, which involves nearly all factors that collectively make up climate. Similarly, any changes in the length of the growing season will in turn indirectly affect vegetative growth and biomass accumulation in general.

It is well known that atmospheric CO_2 has increased approximately 10 percent over the past three decades, from near 315 ppm in 1960 to near 350 ppm in 1989. Current projected rates of increase produce a doubling of pre–Industrial Revolution atmospheric CO_2 to about 600 ppm in the last half of the twenty-first century.

The increases of global distribution of atmospheric CO_2 vary with latitude. Since the largest amount of fossil fuel burning occurs between 35 and 55° NL, the mean annual values of atmospheric CO_2 are 2 to 4 ppm higher at these latitudes.

Numerous general circulation models (GCM) have been developed over the past two decades. They vary in complexity from a simple one-dimensional model to three or more with a number of feedback assumptions. The primary objective of many of these models is predicting terrestrial surface temperature rise associated with a doubling of atmospheric CO_2 to an assumed 600 ppm.

Because of the enormous heat-absorption capacity of the oceans, increases in mean global terrestrial surface temperatures resulting from rising atmospheric CO_2 are not likely to exceed 0.2°F (0.1°C) per decade during the late twentieth and the early twenty-first century. Currently, most model results reported show considerable variation in mean annual temperature across latitudes, ranging from 2°C in the tropics to 6°C or more in Arctic regions. The GCM temperature change predictions for the Southern Hemisphere are smaller, primarily due to ice-covered Antarctica. The latitudinal variations in estimated mean annual precipitation resulting from atmospheric CO_2 doubling vary considerably with latitude as well.

Water balance, or the difference between precipitation and evaporation (P minus E), is an important consideration in crop production and agriculture in general. In a sense the annual mean value of P – E expresses the combined effects of temperature and precipitation in a climate change scenario. Model results indicate that the tropics and subtropics would experience little change under atmospheric CO_2 doubling, but at 35 to 55° NL, model results predict a more humid annual water balance.

Almost all global, continental, and regional climate scenarios are based on the dynamic shifts in the inter-tropical convergence zones (ITCZ), the global wind belts, and the resulting storm tracks. Projections indicate a drier and warmer tropical rainforest climate in some regions and cool-wetter climate in others; some regions with a subtropical winter precipitation maximum will be cooler and wetter; while most mid-latitude grassland climates with a late spring and early summer rainfall maximum will be warmer and drier.

What impacts would such global shifts in climate have on vegetation and agricultural production? Based on existing knowledge and reasonable assumptions, the subarctic and high middle latitudes should benefit from a climatic warming. As a result of possible increased shifts in the ITCZ, there are likely to be both positive and negative impacts on vegetation growth in the tropical and subtropical latitudes. Similar mixed impacts are likely in the mid-latitude due to a possible shift in seasonal storm track positions. But atmospheric CO_2 fertilization and potential increase in water use efficiencies should produce some positive benefits in crop production on a local, regional and global scale.

In conclusion, climate as a natural resource is the range of conditions in the atmospheric environment over a period of time. It has never been static, fixed, or a given. It has always been changing in a rhythmic or cyclic manner over decades, centuries, and millennia. In the past, these changes have been credited entirely to natural causes. But the addition of human impacts through global air pollution can no longer be discounted.

Some people are weatherwise but most are otherwise.
—Benjamin Franklin

Early snowstorm accents autumn colors during October 1989. Such unseasonal weather may be one evidence of "our changing climate."
Photo by Delano Z. Arvin

Aerial view of Koontz Lake Nature Preserve, Starke County, shows the pattern of late lake succession and surrounding wetlands in a glaciated landscape. Native Americans hunted such habitats for millennia.   *Photo by Lee Casebere*

The Vegetation and Fauna: History and Development

9. Remembrance

Robert O. Petty

We cannot know how much we learn
From those who never will return,
Until a flash of unforeseen
Remembrance falls on what has been.

—*Edwin Arlington Robinson,* Flammonde

We remember a place in time—in human consciousness. We were there. A hundred centuries ago, we came upon a vast drowned land. It seemed we walked into a foreverness of lakes and marshes, the brief nights spinning into dawn. Children of the Pleistocene, we hunted the great herds, then with the fierce winter tracked them south. Far to the north and east, the blue-gray paternal ice still lay a half-mile thick. At summer's end and throughout the dwindling light of autumn, a great wind-howl roared from the frozen waste, swept over gravel tundra, across the withered sedge and stunted trees. Sounds of wind still haunt us with old meanings.

Each spring the wind brought storms and rains of pollen which drifted over the widening thaw of lakes. In early summer we crossed the melted ice country: horizons of boulder-strewn gravels, glacial till in mounds and ridges, and the long moraines—all of it like scattered bones of some beast too huge to imagine. We came upon a rise and beyond it saw forests, like long fingers, reaching out, something gripping that land, something invading. Forests of light and dark spruce, balsam fir and the brush of willows. Beyond that was quilted land, patches of pine, birch, and aspen—the coppice that followed fires. Fire and wind and freeze. The forces on the land were physical. We felt the terror of such fierce shaping forces when the gift of life meant simply to endure.

Lakes! Some were old drainageways dammed by vast moraines. In places the retreating ice stopped, melted, and readvanced, breaking through the old morainal dams, spilling the massive ponded water, and flooding the land again like an inland sea. The ancient sluiceways which those giant floods carved out are scattered everywhere across the landscape. We have kept our memory of so much water.

In time, all the southern lakes began to die. They dwindled, shrank, filled in, evaporated, year after year under endless wind and summer sun. They left the landscape mottled, ringed with sediments—"lacustrine" or dark organic soils—muck land from the shallows, fens, and bogs. Some lakes were choking out with plant debris and inwashed sediments, filling, a foot of peat each century. In other lakes, a foot of sediment might take a thousand years. Many artificial lakes receive a foot of sediment each year. And with drought and the spoils of erosion, lakes can die faster still. Yet, for many lakes, filling takes millennia. From its surface, it is still more than thirteen hundred feet to Lake Superior's rocky floor.

The "lake country" is, for the most part, all of the lands north of the Missouri and Ohio rivers whose valleys were carved out or entrenched by glacial meltwater. Freshly minted land—clear, shining, winter-cold, and geologically young. The ice has been gone little more than a hundred centuries, only twice as long as written words. To the older south, there are quiet waters too—but fewer and different—swamps and bayous, the great oxbows and sloughs; long chains of dams and human-altered watercourses.

Yet, somewhere at the edge of water, earthwise primal man has been wearing trails for the last three million years.

No traces left of all the busy scene,
But that remembrance says: These things have been.

—*Samuel Boyse,* The Deity

10. In the Glacier's Wake: Patterns of Vegetation Change Following Glaciation

Donald R. Whitehead

CHANGE: THE UNIVERSAL CONSTANT

Not in vain the distance beacons
Forward, forward let us range.
Let the great world spin forever
Down the ringing grooves of change.

—Alfred Lord Tennyson, "Locksley Hall"

In the past few decades we have become acutely aware that global climate is changing and that these changes will affect us and all plants and animals that share the Earth with us. If the world's climate changes in a significant way, then the patterns of distribution of many plants and animals will be altered as well. Our growing concern with global change has led to the development of climatic models to predict how future conditions may affect all aspects of our environment.

Increasingly scientists have begun to look backward in time to gain an understanding of how climatic change can influence the distribution of plants and animals and the composition of biological communities. Past response patterns of both individual species and entire communities can provide important insights concerning how the Earth's biota will respond to future changes.

This approach leads to some intriguing questions about the environmental changes experienced by the Indiana landscape since the beginning of glacial retreat about 18,000 years ago. We know a great deal about the character of the pre-settlement vegetation of Indiana from accounts written by early settlers and from the original land surveys. How does that landscape compare with what was present when the continental ice sheet extended about 50 miles south of present-day Indianapolis?

Both climate and vegetation in that glacial world differed dramatically from the conditions that the first European settlers encountered. But how different was the vegetation of that ice-dominated era? In addition, what sequence of vegetational change took place as the ice sheet underwent its oscillating retreat from 18,000 to 8,000 years ago? Were there yet additional changes in the last 8,000 years of this post-glacial time period? More specifically, what sequence of ecological communities preceded the pre-settlement wilderness of Indiana? How did the vegetation of 1816 come to be? Can we reconstruct this distant portion of Indiana's environmental history?

WINDOWS INTO THE PAST

The closer one looks the farther one sees.

—David Cavagnaro, "The Wonders of Nature," in
National Geographic Society Engagement Calendar
(1991)

Scientists can determine the character of past climates and biological communities by deciphering relevant prehistoric records that provide images of the past. Where do such archives exist? The answer is actually quite simple. The insights that we seek lie buried in the muddy or peaty sediments of every natural lake and bog in the northern half of the state.

Most of us are aware of the well-publicized finds of bones of long-extinct large mammals such as mastodons which roamed much of Indiana shortly after the glaciers began to retreat. A large number of these fossil bones have been unearthed during the excavation of mud and peat from depressions formed by the melting of large ice blocks which had been buried in the thick, unconsolidated sediments left behind as the glaciers retreated. Such remains were preserved both by the gradual accumulation of younger sediments on top of the animal and by the presence of water in the basin; both would retard decomposition and permit preservation.

Bog and lake sediments also contain remains of terrestrial plants and animals (both microscopic and macroscopic): pollen grains and spores from both terrestrial and aquatic plants; bodies of microscopic plants and animals that lived in the lake; fine organic fragments from the soil and leaf litter near the lake; mineral particles of many kinds, either blown in or washed in from the soils on nearby slopes; and various sorts of chemical compounds that were precipitated out of the lakewater (for example, the marl found in many northern Indiana lakes).

Sediment begins to accumulate as soon as a lake basin is formed (e.g., when the ice block melts), and it is added slowly and continuously throughout the lifespan of the lake. Thus the oldest (deepest) sediment provides information on conditions that existed when the lake was formed (in our case, shortly after the retreat of the glaciers began); sediment closer to the surface provides insights about conditions existing more recently (e.g., 6,000 years ago); and sediment now accumulating reflects present-day conditions in and around the lake.

Thus, lake and bog sediments can be thought of as a complex and comprehensive history book in which the events of the past have been recorded in many different languages, each language telling us about a different aspect of environmental history. The job of the scientist is to pick the appropriate pages (the layers of sediment corresponding to the time span of interest), select the most appropriate language, and make an accurate translation (the environmental reconstruction).

Since our focus is on the entire time period from ice retreat to the present, it is necessary to obtain a representative sample of the entire sedimentary record in a lake or bog by taking core samples with a hollow borer. In the case of a bog, the core can be taken directly from the peat surface. Lake sediments may be cored either from a boat or from the ice surface in winter. The complete sedimentary record of most Indiana lakes and bogs ranges from 5 to 10 meters in thickness.

Once obtained, the core can be sub-sampled at appropriate levels for both radiocarbon dating and analysis of the selected sediment component. Radiocarbon dating is an isotopic technique first developed in the 1950s and now capable of providing accurate ages of carbon-containing sediments back to about 50,000 years before the present (and even back to 100,000 years with sophisticated and expensive refinements).

The next problem is to select the sediment "language" most suitable for telling us about the plant communities of the past. Luckily, we have two choices: the first is pollen, the second larger

Binkley Bog is a late-stage result of the lake-filling process. Bogs are prime sites for the recovery of fossil pollens, which are necessary for post-Pleistocene vegetation reconstruction.   *Photo by Richard Fields*

plant fragments such as seeds, leaves and leaf fragments, cones, needles, etc. The larger fragments provide information on vegetation close to the shore of the lake, whereas pollen informs us about the plant communities located within a 20- to 50-square-mile region. Since our interest is in knowing what the past landscapes and early vegetation of Indiana looked like, it makes sense to rely heavily on the story that fossil pollen grains can tell us.

Pollen provides us with good information on the plant communities of the past, because many common trees, shrubs, and herbs are wind-pollinated. Since wind pollination is very inefficient, each plant must produce enormous numbers of pollen grains to ensure that at least a few will reach a compatible flower to fertilize it.

> Forest trees produce great quantities [of pollen]; a 10-year old branch system of beech produces more than 28 million, birch, spruce, and oak a little more than 100 million, and pine ca. 350 million. The production per hectare of forest runs into billions and Hesselman concludes that the spruce forests of southern and middle Sweden produce ca. 75,000 tons of pollen annually.
>
> —*Faegri and Iversen,* Textbook of Pollen Analysis
> *(1975)*

The quantity of pollen that is in the air during the flowering season can be staggering. On a late summer day in Indiana, literally billions upon billions of pollen grains may be in the air at a given time. A fraction of this "pollen rain" may settle on the surface of a lake or bog, where it can be incorporated into the sediments that are accumulating and preserved there, both because accumulating sediment "buries" the pollens and because the outer wall of a pollen grain is incredibly resistant to decomposition.

Sediments accumulating in present-day lakes in Indiana contain an assemblage of billions of pollen grains which reflects, reasonably accurately, the composition of the vegetation in the region near the lake. If the vegetation were to change at some point in the future (for example, in response to global warming), this change would be reflected in the "pollen rain" landing on the surface of lakes at that future time. A different suite of plant species might then be represented, and the species that had contributed pollen in the past might be relatively less or more common. Similarly, if past plant communities were different from those that surround us today, those differences would be reflected in the composition of the pollen rain that was trapped in the bottom sediments at that point in time.

It follows that the sedimentary sequence in a lake or bog contains

Close view of emerging leaves and catkins of black oak. Such wind-pollinated species produce enormous amounts of pollen, which fills the air during flowering season. *Photo by Ron Everhart*

a decipherable record (pollen profile) of the changes in plant communities that have taken place since the basin formed. That aspect of prehistory was recorded in the "pollen rain" that was deposited year after year. The core represents our sampling of the "history book"; the story that is "read" is written by pollen.

How is the pollen record translated? "Reading" is possible because the outer wall of a pollen grain often has a distinctive architecture that differs from one species to another. Thus many different types of pollen can be identified, sometimes to species (e.g., tamarack), sometimes to genus (e.g., oaks), sometimes to plant family (e.g., sedges or grasses).

A microscope is used to identify and tabulate 500 to 1,000 pollen grains extracted from each relevant level of the sediment profile. Completed counts are arranged into a pollen diagram, which is a profile of the changes in frequency of each pollen type through time. A generalized and abbreviated pollen diagram is presented from a lake site in northeastern Indiana. This diagram is characterized by significant changes in many pollen types. Early in the lake's history, the pollen profile is dominated by spruce. Later there are peaks for ash and hornbeam, followed by a higher peak for pine, and finally oak and other hardwoods dominate the upper levels. These differences suggest that the forest vegetation surrounding the lake changed over time from spruce domination to spruce-hardwoods to pine to pine-oak and finally to oak and other hardwoods.

> Dark behind it rose the forest,
> Rose the black and gloomy pine tree,
> Rose the firs with cones upon them.
>
> —Henry Wadsworth Longfellow, "Hiawatha's Childhood,"
> in The Song of Hiawatha (1855)

The abundance of spruce and fir in the lower half of the profile suggests a forest and climate radically different from that of today. For example, today the nearest populations of spruce and fir to Indiana occur in northern Michigan. In fact, the best "match" for the vegetation indicated by the early part of the pollen diagram occurs near the tree line in the vicinity of Hudson Bay, where open spruce-fir forests give way to arctic tundra.

A reconstruction of Indiana's entire post-ice forest history requires

many "complete" profiles from sites located throughout the state. Pollen diagrams available from the several lake sites in northern Indiana, the scattered mastodon excavation sites, and profiles from elsewhere in the Midwest provide us with an outline of Indiana's vegetational history. This outline indicates that our landscape has experienced numerous major changes in plant cover, some caused by climatic change, some by the highly individualistic responses of plant species to climate (for example, some species can disperse and migrate much more rapidly than others). In the following section a broad brush is used to develop a generalized picture of the most dramatic changes that our landscape has experienced over the last 15,000 to 16,000 years.

POST-GLACIAL VEGETATIONAL HISTORY

> Once the fierce Kabibonokka
> Issued from his lodge of snow-drifts,
> From his home among the icebergs,
> And his hair, with snow besprinkled,
> Streamed behind him like a river,
> Like a black and wintry river,
> As he howled and hurried southward,
> Over frozen lakes and moorlands.
>
> —Longfellow, "The Four Winds," in The Song of
> Hiawatha

From about 16,000 to 14,000 years ago, much of Indiana south of the waning glacial margin was covered with treeless vegetation, an arctic tundra of sorts with scattered patches of spruce and fir in southernmost Indiana. The existence of tundra vegetation is suggested by the high percentage of herbs represented in the pollen rain; in fact, some of the pollen came from species that now grow only in tundra environments. Furthermore, macrofossils (seeds and leaves) of tundra species have been found.

The tundra was replaced by a spruce-dominated "parkland" about 14,000 years ago, a landscape characterized by extensive open areas vegetated with grasses, sedges, and some tundra plants dotted with isolated patches of coniferous trees. The trees were mostly black and white spruce, but balsam fir and tamarack were also present. This type of vegetation dominated the Indiana terrain for about 2,000 years. There was undoubtedly a north-south gradient in the vegetation across Indiana: tundra with fewer patches of trees to the north, extensive forest with less open area in the south.

> Those pollen grains fell like rain onto the open water of this lake
> soon after the glacier receded. . . . The forest that had been
> driven south by the glacier was moving north on its very heels.
> Around the lake the hills were covered with the narrow spires
> of [conifers]. Probably little life had begun in the cold waters of
> the lake.
>
> —May Theilgaard Watts, "History Book with a Flexible
> Cover," in Reading the Landscape (1957)

Between 12,000 and 11,000 years ago, a few hardwood species immigrated from the south and shared the parkland environment with spruce. The immigrants included ash (of the black ash group), hornbeam and/or ironwood, elm, and some oaks. This "wavelet" of hardwood immigration was driven by the continued warming of climate. The northern forest stands probably contained more coniferous species in the north, more hardwoods in the south. A brief episode of cooling between 11,000 and 10,500 years ago resulted in a transient increase in spruce in the parkland and significant declines in the hardwoods that had just arrived.

At approximately 10,500 years ago, major changes occurred in the

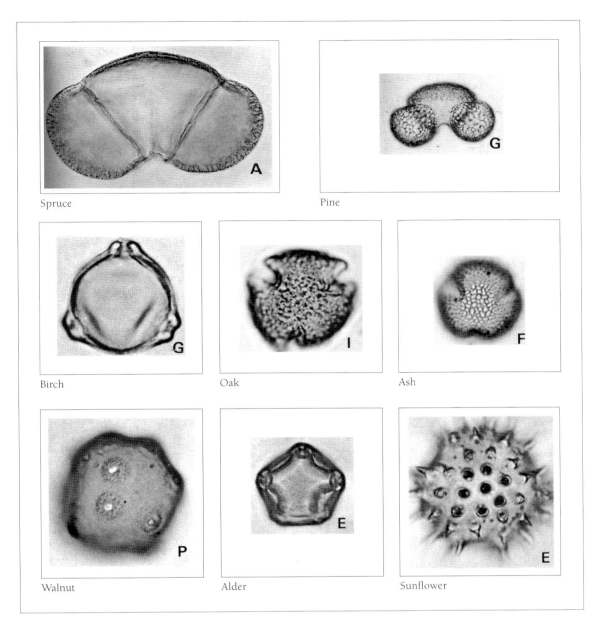

Spruce Pine

Birch Oak Ash

Walnut Alder Sunflower

Selected pollen shapes. *Adapted from* Key to the Quaternary Pollen and Spores of the Great Lakes Region, *published by the Royal Ontario Museum*

vegetation. Virtually all of the northern species disappeared (spruce, fir, tamarack, and tundra plants), the percentage of herbs such as grasses and sedges dropped sharply, and a variety of new immigrants began to dominate the landscape. The new surge of immigrants was led by pines (first northern species, such as jack and eastern white pines) and paper birch, but a wide spectrum of hardwoods also arrived and become established. This new hardwood assemblage included oaks, hickories, maples, elms, ashes, sycamores, walnuts, and hornbeams (and/or ironwoods). The forest composition was thus very diverse, with a mixture of pines and hardwoods, somewhat similar to what occurs in the lake states today.

In addition, the overall structure of the forest shifted from open parkland to closed forest with few, if any, open areas. This rapid and dramatic change in vegetation was driven by an acceleration in the rate of warming. This period of significant climate change and the accompanying changes in forest structure contributed in a major

way to the extinction of the large mammals that had roamed the open landscape.

The "pine invasion" was relatively short-lived. By 9,500 years ago, virtually all pine populations had declined dramatically and hardwood forests dominated the Indiana countryside. Although hardwood domination continued until the extensive land clearing of the nineteenth century, there was considerable variability in both space and time. This variability reflected the continual adjustment of plant communities to local ecological conditions and constant minor fluctuations in climate. The spatial pattern of communities was probably much like that described for pre-settlement Indiana, but the actual composition of the communities was different and also changed continuously through the entire 9,000-year time span.

For example, much of pre-settlement Indiana was covered by beech-maple–dominated forest. However, beech did not immigrate into Indiana until approximately 6,000 years ago. As a result, areas

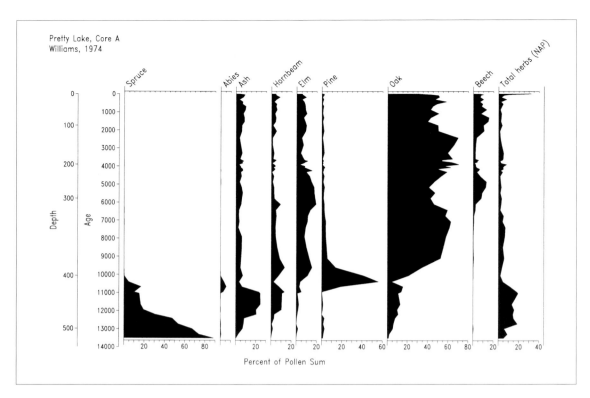

Pretty Lake, Core A
Williams, 1974

Pollen profiles for selected tree species and herbaceous plants (collectively) for Pretty Lake in Noble County, showing pollen sequences by depth, hence age.   *From Williams 1974*

that were ultimately dominated by beech-maple communities were probably vegetated by a complex hardwood forest with sugar maple as a dominant and elm, different ashes, hornbeam and ironwood, hackberry, basswood, black gum, and scattered oaks and hickories as associates. In addition, once beech immigrated and became established, it experienced at least two significant changes in frequency on the landscape (a "maximum" centered at 5,500 years ago and another about 1,800 years ago). Most of the other hardwoods also experienced periodic changes in abundance over the last 9,000 years, emphasizing how dynamic both vegetation and climate have been. Change was the rule rather than the exception during Indiana's past.

Extensive patches of prairie became established in northwestern Indiana by about 8,000 years ago, expanded somewhat in response to increasing temperature and aridity between 7,000 and 4,000 years ago during a time known variously as the Xerothermic or Hypsithermal Period, then contracted to their present positions about 3,000 years ago. Thus the vegetation mosaic of this restricted area appears to have been as dynamic as the forests of the rest of the state.

The forests gradually . . . were replaced by a vegetation of herbaceous plants, chiefly grasses. This vegetation persists today . . . on a triangular area in the center of the continent, with one side of the triangle along the Rocky Mountains . . . and its apex extending east to Indiana. . . . present day prairie [as a vegetation type] is preglacial in origin and . . . has undergone many vicissitudes during and following the glacial periods.

—*J. E. Weaver,* North American Prairie *(1954)*

The last major event recorded by the pollen record is the extensive land clearance that was initiated when European settlers arrived. This is indicated in the uppermost levels of every core by a decrease in pollen of woody plants and a phenomenal increase in pollen of herbs, especially weedy types. Not surprisingly, the explosion of weed pollen is dominated by ragweed, a fact easily confirmed by many who suffer from pollen-aggravated allergies.

Thus, our vegetational history is characterized by continual change, some caused by climate, some by the combined migrations of many individual species. Equally important, few if any close "matches" can be found between the modern vegetation of North America and the various communities of the past. This lack of correspondence suggests that communities of the past were unique; their composition was unlike that of any modern community. Thus, the magnificent forests that the first European settlers encountered came into being relatively recently and represent the most recent "shuffling" of the environmental cards—the end product of processes set in motion as the glaciers began to retreat.

This long process of continual change and shuffling of vegetation also provides an explanation for the occurrence of isolated patches of more northern species in the modern Indiana landscape—for example, the impressive stands of hemlock and white pine that are preserved in such natural areas as Turkey Run, Pine Hills, Hemlock Bluff, Hemlock Cliff, and Big Walnut. Eastern hemlock, eastern white pine, and Canada yew are "northern" relict species. They are common constituents of contemporary forests only as far south as central Michigan. However, all were quite common in Indiana between 10,500 and 9,000 years ago.

The subsequent warming of climate eliminated all such populations except those occurring in isolated protected "pockets" such as the cool-moist microclimates of north-facing sandstone bluffs and cliffs. These isolated stands provide us with a flavor of the plant communities that occurred over vast areas of Indiana thousands of years ago at a time when the climate was both cooler and moister. In fact, the bogs themselves, from which the corings were taken to

White pine and hemlock survive as relic species in cool, moist microclimates such as are found at Portland Arch (shown here), Pine Hills, and Turkey Run. *Photo by Lee Casebere*

obtain the pollen samplings, are dying remnants of an ice-margin landscape and climate that was once widespread across much of Indiana.

The uniqueness of the plant communities of the past and the truly kaleidoscopic character of the changes that have taken place are emphasized by distribution patterns for each plant type at intervals of 4,000 years from 18,000 years ago (glacial maximum) until 2,000 years ago. In this set of panels we can see how the distributions of many different species, all important constituents of either past or present forests, have changed over the past 18,000 years.

What is evident is that no two patterns are alike in space or time. Species have behaved in a distinctly individualistic way. They were in different areas during the glacial maximum, they migrated in different directions and at different rates. All of these unique shifts in distribution and migration patterns took place in the context of a climatic regime that was itself continually changing.

This complex pattern of change appears to have characterized all areas of North America and, very probably, all areas on the surface of the Earth. Vegetation and climate have always been changing in dynamic and complex ways. The future will be no different, except that the magnitude and rate of human-caused environmental changes are likely to be far greater than any experienced before. The future scenario will likely pose a significant threat to many species and communities, but in turn will favor others.

*   *   *

As we turned north on the Mineral Springs Road and crossed the tracks of the South Shore Electric on our way to the bog, I recalled the times our ecology class from the University of Chicago, led by Dr. Henry Cowles, had alighted there, each of us with a green metal vasculum (for specimens) hanging from one shoulder, and a knapsack full of lunch and a Gray's Manual hanging from the other. . . .

More than 50 years after the trip to the bog . . . I was arriving in an air-conditioned car. The drifts of bluets that I remembered were still in the meadow to the west of the road, the Michigan holly grew as abundant as ever in the ditches beside the road. . . .The bog has been designated a National Natural Landmark. I stood beside the marker with its bronze plate, proclaiming the name "Cowles Bog," and thought how he would have grinned his wide grin, and perhaps sat down on the marker to empty the sand out of his shoes. . . .

A most important factor in saving the bog was its inclusion for some years in Dune Acres, with police in the gatehouse refusing entrance to vehicles of any kind.

The cinnamon ferns were six-feet tall, and as abundant as ever. The sour gums, and yellow birches, and red maples were the same individuals I had known. Their root hummocks still displayed the same rich northwoods assortment of partridge-berry, cucumber root, star flower, goldthread. The woodthrush call was as mellow, and the tips of spicebush as tasty as ever. The bog, and its pitcher plants, sundew, sphagnum, and lady slippers, all have had the benefit of inaccessibility, and the protection of poison sumac and swamp rattlers. The display of cinnamon ferns has escaped the gatherers by their frailty, wilting when picked, dying when transplanted.

—May Theilgaard Watts, "The Bog-Revisited," in Reading the Landscape of America (1975)

Years before present (ybp)	14,000	10,000	6,000	Modern (500)
Pine				
Oak				
Hickory				
Spruce				

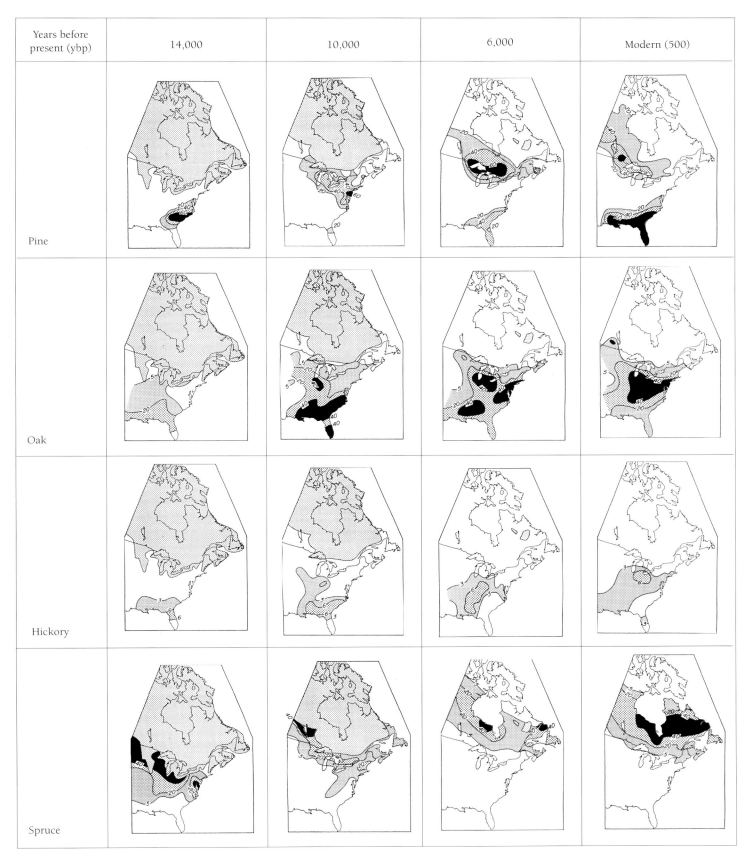

Changing pollen densities in eastern North America. These contoured pollen densities reflect the distribution of the species.
Adapted from a map published by the Geological Society of America

11. Origins: The Deciduous Forest

Robert O. Petty

All North American trees were bigger than most of those today, because they could grow undisturbed for centuries, till they reached their full natural size. In primitive times there was no need to cut them and nobody who wanted to.

> —*John Bakeless, "West to Pittsburgh," in* The Eyes of Discovery *(1950)*

It was the deciduous forest which nurtured and shaped technological man. No other vegetation on Earth has absorbed so utterly the impact of "the toolmaker" as the temperate summer-green forest of the Northern Hemisphere. We still live amid its remnants. How did that forest come to be?

For the most part, the forests we know are "woods." A woods is our name for a particular stand of trees, found today most frequently as a biotic island in a sea of domestic monoculture—a small fragment left from a vast green expanse, rich, varied, and ecologically resilient.

Given a score of years, cleared forestland is gradually transformed through a succession of early weed, forb, and grass to blackberry briars and goldenrod and, following that, a brush fallow of young saplings. Another 10 years, 20, a half-century, and once again a vigorous forest prevails, layered with small trees, shrubs, and flowering herbs. Most of the woods we know have developed in this way, as adaptive secondary growth, following disturbance.

The particular combinations of forest trees we walk among have an older origin. They have assembled variously across vast landscapes, advanced and retreated as climates shifted. Forests are still adjusting to the broad displacements caused by the recent glaciers. Finally, a forest has an origin which occurs over much longer geologic time, species by species, as adaptive forms evolve—a flower, a fruit—a way to move about and be. A forest then is a sum of origins.

It is difficult to imagine a world without flowers, yet we know that in the Earth's chronology, flowers are a relatively recent innovation. Nearly 200 million years ago, the Earth's domination by ferns and other spore-producing plants climaxed with the Coal Age floras. Later, by the time the dinosaurs were thriving, gymnosperms and seed ferns flourished across the continents. Some seed plants, such as the gymnosperms which today dominate the boreal forest (spruce, fir, and other conifers), produce naked seeds.

Botanically, a flowering plant, or angiosperm (producing enclosed seeds), is a plant which produces a fruit. A fruit develops from a flower and contains the seed. While the precise ancestor of the flowering plants is not yet clear in the fossil record (and may never be), most botanists agree that flowering plants probably evolved from an advanced type of seed fern more than 120 million years ago.

During this Late Mesozoic period, North America was uniformly warm and wet. A dense forest extended from Iceland to Alaska. Gradually, sea levels began to change. Continents were drifting. Soon the Earth was in upheaval, a revolution of mountain-making—the Himalayas, the Alps, the Andes, the Rockies. Older mountains such as the Appalachians were once again uplifted. The physiography of Earth was becoming intricately diverse. It was during this time that gymnosperm floras began to wane in the shadow of the rapidly evolving flowering plants.

To fill the newly fashioned environmental niches, new kinds of survival strategies were required. The ancestral woody plants perfected deciduous habits, devised shorter life cycles, while many were reduced to ephemeral herbaceous growth.

During the last 60 million years, three major environmental forces substantially affected the vegetation of North America. One of these was continued uplift of the Rocky Mountains, which produced a vast eastward rainshadow driving the mixed deciduous forest before it. A second force was the onset of lowering temperatures over the whole Northern Hemisphere, which together with altered precipitation patterns culminated in glacial climates. A third factor was the rejuvenation of erosion in the eastern landscapes by renewed uplift of the Appalachian Mountains. As a result of all of these forces, the mixed forest was segregated by a physiographic and climatic pattern.

> With the elevation of the western mountains . . . and the drying and cooling of the climate, the Arcto-tertiary flora retreated from the far North, and . . . there were changes in the composition of the Tertiary forest during this long period . . . but all these changes were conservative, and the present-day mixed mesophytic forests of the Cumberland Mountains of Eastern Tennessee have nearly the same composition and appearance as did the ancient forests.
>
> —*S. Charles Kendeigh, "Paleoecology," in* Animal Ecology *(1961)*

Following the most recent glaciation of some 20,000 years ago, deciduous trees left their glacial refugia, invading the wake of the retreating boreal forest. Slowly along the sheltered river courses where erosion inched its way into the boulder-strewn uplands, the mixed forest began to move. Wherever a fruit or seed could be carried, by wind or water, mammal or bird, seedling by seedling, the forest returned.

In the southeast, out of the Great Smoky Mountains, the forest crossed the Cumberland Plateau, spread along the floodplains of the Clinch River Valley, down the canyons of the Green and the Tennessee. In the north from along the Alleghenies, the new forest turned west, across glacial-minted soils, then moved down the vast meltwater drainage of the Ohio.

New forests, new genetic potential, new ecological affinities were once again segregating: forests of chestnut and oak; forests of oak, hickory, and yellow-poplar; forests of beech and maple; of maple and basswood; and in the north, these and other hardwoods mixed with hemlock and pine. A rich mosaic of coves, dry hillsides, bogs, and wetlands, soils lime or acid—adapted to each was a complex of forest species.

Three to four thousand years ago, climates became warmer and drier than they are today. Xeric oak forests were encroaching far to the east and north, crossing the St. Lawrence Valley into southern Quebec. During this time, which ecologists call the Xerothermic period, northern conifers and hardwoods retreated to local refugia where steep-walled valleys, north-facing slopes, moisture seeps, or cold air drainage preserved a vestige of their earlier climate.

They topped the rise and stood blinking into the sunset across the greatest deciduous forest there ever was.   *Photo by Richard Fields*

Gradually a cooler time returned. Oak domination of the forest weakened. The Greek and Roman world had come and gone when climates became steadily warmer once again. In the eleventh century, another xerothermic interval entrenched the oak forests into a distribution much like that of today. Again the climate cooled. In the seventeenth and eighteenth centuries, a "little ice age" brought the coldest winters since the major glacial retreat, 10,000 years before.

In the rich ground north and west of the Ohio, dry upland forests of oak and yellow-poplar were relentlessly invaded by mesic species, beech and basswood, sugar maple and ash. Forests were realigning their strategies everywhere across the eastern landscape. Along the tension zones of merger between different forest types, replacement succession was under way. A windthrow, a seedling at a time, across a thousand miles, the ancient, root-anchored forests were slowly changing once again.

In the late 1700s, settlers reaching a crest of the Wilderness Road in a notch of the Cumberlands stood blinking into the western light across the greatest deciduous forest that ever was.

For a moment Sayward reckoned that her father had fetched them unbeknownst to the Western ocean and what lay beneath was the late sun glittering on green-black water. Then she saw that what they looked down on was a dark, illimitable expanse of wilderness. It was a sea of solid treetops broken only by some gash where deep beneath the foliage an unknown stream made its way. As far as the eye could reach, this lonely forest sea rolled on and on till its faint blue billows broke against an incredibly distant horizon.

—*Conrad Richter,* The Trees *(1940)*

12. Walking in Wilderness

Alton A. Lindsey

WHAT WE LOST BY WINNING

Wilderness. . . . The word suggests the past and the unknown, the womb of earth from which we all emerged. It means something lost and something still present, something remote and at the same time intimate, something buried in our blood and nerves, something beyond us and without limit.

—*Edward Abbey,* Desert Solitaire *(1968)*

The human species originated in wilderness—the natural "Garden." To walk in wilderness challenges body and mind, stirs the ancestral memory, and eases the spirit. Above all, constellations still swing brightly in the night sky.

Early white explorers found strange peoples existing at the sufferance of Nature. In many cultures, Nature was revered as the universal Mother. The wilderness is both the broadest and the most concentrated expression of her creative and sustaining powers. As Charles A. Lindbergh wrote, all human accomplishments are trivial in comparison with Nature's. Yet today, except perhaps in and near the polar regions, Nature prevails on this planet only as permitted by humankind.

In medieval Europe, many were distracted from the God-given wonders around them by the dazzling vision of a better life after death. Likewise today, the world which is, in Wordsworth's phrase, "too much with us" is also too far removed from that of the natural creation. However, the present blindness and deafness toward Nature is from another cause than in the Middle Ages. The modern world is the hectic, congested, artificial one we created for ourselves and against most other life forms on Earth—a world in which "making a living" rates higher than does living itself.

In cities, suburbs, small towns, and increasingly even in rural areas, there remains close to us only a highly filtered, denatured Nature. Most people have little acquaintance even with that. Trees and shrubs, for example, are often our nearest neighbors, but the closeness is merely spatial, seldom involving the mind or spirit. The way a woody plant grows, so different from the growth plan of a human body, is quite simple in its easily visible engineering aspects. But does one person in a thousand understand the most elementary points of these plants' everyday operations?

There are many natural areas in the contiguous United States, but few of them qualify as true wilderness. The one "wilderness" in Indiana is an official or legal one. My friend after whom it was named, the late Charles Deam, a stickler for scientific accuracy, would not have considered it a real wilderness. What qualifies a tract as wilderness today? Units of true wilderness are large, usually quite remote, and lack roads and buildings. People are visitors there, not permanent residents. The word's derivation from the Old English *wilder* is significant. That meant "wild beast." It is the *animal life* which best indicates wilderness, since the dominant plant cover can vary from practically none in the polar regions to desert or grassland or old-growth forest. A practical, not purist, definition of wilderness in these times requires that not only large grazing and browsing animals range freely there, but also one or more species of their large natural predators. The large wilderness predators in the United States and Canada are cougar, bear, lynx, wolf, and wolverine.

Deer and pronghorn antelope do not require wilderness. Deer are far more abundant in Indiana today than in pioneer times, adapting themselves successfully to human-dominated ecosystems. Thoreau believed that wilderness is "another kind of civilization," thereby foreshadowing the ecosystem concept.

We must never conceal from ourselves that our concepts are creations of the human mind which we impose on the facts of nature, that they are derived from incomplete knowledge, and therefore will never exactly fit the facts, and will require constant revisions as knowledge increases.

—*A. G. Tansley,* Journal of Ecology 8: 120 (1920). *Tansley, a noted British ecologist, coined the term* ecosystem *in the mid-1930s.*

Wandering into the deciduous forest ecosystem of North America, aboriginal people used their intelligence to adapt their culture to given natural conditions, rather than to bend Nature to their ways.

Huge white and red oak stems in old-growth flatwoods—Wells Woods, a nature preserve in Jennings County.   *Photo by Perry Scott*

Thus, the preexisting order of Nature retained its dynamic equilibrium, shared by myriads of survival-seeking plants and animals. The word *ecosystem* covers this long-evolving web of reciprocities in life and its habitat, a successfully functioning structure of natural capitalism.

Charles Darwin, in closing his book *Origin of Species,* alluded to a small, now classic, example:

It is interesting to contemplate a tangled bank, clothed with many plants of many kinds, with birds singing on the bushes, with various insects flitting about, and with worms crawling through the damp earth, and to reflect that these elaborately structured forms, so different from each other, and dependent upon each other in so complex a manner, have all been produced by laws acting around us.

The Indiana wilderness of another time defined itself by the dominant tree species of its woodlands and the dominant herbaceous plants of its grasslands. A tall man seated on horseback in the best unplowed prairies of Benton County could tie the grass tops together over his head. The floodplain forests of the Lower Wabash Valley, with 200-foot tuliptrees, bald cypresses, and sycamores, equaled in grandeur the finest tropical rainforest. Straddling the border where eastern forest met and mingled with tallgrass prairie, Indiana had the best of both these vast domains.

The extensive wetlands of the Kankakee Valley constituted early Indiana's most striking wilderness, but it was not a suitable one for walking. The Potawatomi Indians enjoyed the rich resource base of the herbaceous marsh and the woody swamp plant life, the teeming fish, and the incredible flocks of waterfowl. However, this biological paradise finally succumbed to systematic farm drainage and to the straightening and deepening of the river—a process which changed "the lost lands" into farms with rich organic soils. Thus eradicated were two major lakes—Beaver Lake, which had occupied 28,000 acres, and English Lake, which had been a wide, 12-mile-long stretch of the Kankakee. Few residents of northern Indiana now realize the tremendous change made by artificial drainage. In wilderness times, more than half of the land north of the Wabash was flooded for at least six months of a year of normal precipitation. At flood times, freight canoes could readily be paddled across the portages separating major watersheds!

Voyageurs on the midwestern rivers were likely to encounter blockages of a sort never seen today. Floods dislodged trees and brush, which then jammed up a long stretch of stream as a natural, permeable dam. Termed an *embarrass*, this feature gave the name "Embarrass River" to several streams.

THE PRIMEVAL PRAIRIE

In our year of statehood, 1816, a superb observer, David Thomas, and one companion rode horseback across southern Indiana. Thomas was the first to correctly interpret the tallgrass prairie as due primarily to recurring fires, rather than too dry a climate for tree growth. On sites protected from fire grew the forests. Because grasses, unlike woody plants, have their growing points at ground level instead of at the tips, mowing your lawn or burning the prairie does not kill the grass. Fires occurred naturally by lightning strokes, or were set by Indians to maintain openings for better hunting. The prairie fires, though spectacular and hazardous, nevertheless benefited prairie species overall.

When a fire starts under favorable conditions, the horizon gleams brighter and brighter until a fiery redness rises above its dark outline, while heavy slow-moving masses of dark clouds curve upward about it. In another moment the blaze itself shoots up, first at one spot, then at another, advancing until the whole horizon extending across a wide prairie, is clothed with flames that roll and curve and dash onward and upward like waves of a burning ocean, lighting up the landscape with the brilliance of noon-day. A roaring, crackling sound is heard like the rushing of a hurricane. The flame, which in general rises to the height of twenty feet, is seen rolling its waves against each other, as the liquid, fiery mass moves forward, leaving behind it a blackened surface on the ground, and long trails of murky smoke floating above.

—*Judge James Hall, in Logan Esarey,* History of Indiana (1922)

In the Great Plains or high plains country farther west, the shortgrass vegetation type forms the climatic climax, for conditions are less moist. Its eastern edges met the tallgrass prairie along a transition zone that runs north-south through Fort Dodge, Kansas. From that boundary line as its base, a roughly equilateral triangle, the midwestern tallgrass prairie (east of the plains) occupied an area of greater precipitation, with its eastern point extending as far as halfway across northern Indiana. The climate and the humus-rich topsoil built by decayed roots and tops combined to make the best of the Corn Belt of our day. Waist height on a person is considered the dividing line between statures of shortgrass versus prairie communities. The dominant plants of the latter, in ideal sites, grew higher than another grass, corn, which, with soybeans, replaced most native grassland. Big bluestem, Indian grass, and others were mixed with herbaceous non-grass species of prairie which are called "forbs." Such were the asters, sunflowers, and goldenrods. A prairie in flowering season was one of Nature's loveliest exhibits.

Prairies covered about 13 percent of aboriginal Indiana. T. Scattergood Teas wrote that river bottomlands were covered with grass five to eight feet high and "so matted together that it was extremely difficult to force my way through it." On nearby high ground, stinging nettles reached to his shoulders. The many attractive prairies along the Wabash, well known among travelers and settlers, were probably brought about by Indian activity.

Whereas the soils of shortgrass plains have a limy hardpan 2 or 3 feet down, marking the depth of leaching, the rich black topsoil of virgin prairie sometimes reached 22 feet deep. The *first* plowing of the tough interlacing roots of tall grasses could be accomplished only by itinerant "breaking teams" of two men and six or eight yokes of oxen, with an unusually strong plow. One can still tell, by a simple difference in color tone and pattern, whether a bare field was formerly in prairie or timberland. Prairie soils appear rather uniformly dark over the ridges and knolls as well as in the hollows. Soils which developed under forest, however, are black in the low ground where profuse plant growth deposited more organic matter, but the high areas are lighter, usually brownish in Indiana. The mottled contrast shows up best from the air, but well enough from a car on the highways.

Along the transitional belt where forest and prairie met, a strange growth habit of bur oak and black oak adapted them to survive the frequent fires. The trunks lacked normal form, height, and position; they grew only underground, as short, heavy, keg-like structures, sending up aerial shoots which reached six feet at most before being killed back. Pioneer farmers called this "stooling out." Since the only way the obstruction to plowing could be eradicated was by grubbing it out by hand tools, the whole thing was termed a "stool grub."

Wildflowers such as horned bladderwort filled unspoiled wetlands with their ethereal beauty. *Photo by Perry Scott*

FORESTS AS NOTED BY TRAVELERS ABOUT 1800

David Thomas was the traveler whose observations in early Indiana yielded the best information on plant life in general. During his 57-mile trip from Vincennes to Fort Harrison, the site of present-day Terre Haute, he recorded 105 species of plants by technical and English names. He wrote that tree nuts, hazelnuts, and wild fruits were so profuse along the Wabash that farmers' hogs lived through the winters on these alone. In 1818, a farmer who had bought no food for his pigs received one thousand dollars for his pork production.

We came to a tall, gloomy forest, consisting almost wholly of large Beech trees, which afforded a most refreshing shade. The forest continued without intermission . . . the lofty crowns of the trees shut out the sky from our view. They were the most splendid forest I had yet seen in America.

> —*Prince Maximilian of Wied,* Report of Travels in Indiana *(June 1833)*

A justly famed explorer, C. F. Volney, stated that in July of 1796 he traversed the woods between Louisville and Vincennes without hearing any bird voice. Surely this indicates that a deep, dense forest prevailed there, but this condition was less general in pre-settlement Indiana than romantic moderns like to think. Patches of savanna were not uncommon, and the first surveyors identified some lands as "barrens."

Audubon was quite familiar with dense canebrakes on the Indiana side of the Ohio River. The cane, a species of bamboo, grew abundantly up the Wabash, reaching almost as far north as Vincennes. David Warden noted in 1819, "An extraordinary phenomenon is met with in the woods along White River,—natural wells, from 10 to 15 feet deep, formed by the decay of trunks and roots of large sycamore trees."

A Quaker of Wayne County, Charles Coffin, wrote in 1833: "There was a vast amount of fine walnut timber . . . which was used lavishly because it was easily split into rails and greatly wasted. In subsequent times it became exceedingly valuable."

Tall big bluestem grass and equally tall prairie dock characterized the prairies of northwest Indiana prior to agricultural development.
Photo by Marion Jackson

LOWER WABASH FLOODPLAIN FORESTS OF ROBERT RIDGWAY

Because the tall tales of frontiersmen often found their way into print, science is fortunate to have solid data and early photographs from Robert Ridgway, a Smithsonian biologist brought up in Indiana and Illinois. His careful measurements of gigantic trees in the Lower Wabash floodplains of Indiana are incontrovertible. He measured living trees by tape, *above* the butt swells, and their heights by triangulation. The average treetop level in the stands was 130 feet, but "the by no means infrequent monarchs," usually tuliptrees, sycamores, and bald cypress, attained 180 to 200 feet. As lumbering was still actively progressing in 1875, he measured by tape the lengths of the larger felled trees.

In 1919, the aging Ridgway gave his younger friend Charles Deam a remarkable set of tree and forest photos to preserve for science. One print shows a group of four huge tuliptrees, a species called "yellow-poplar" by those unaware of botanical relationships, on the floodplain south of Vincennes. Their diameters ranged from 5 to 7 feet. Twenty-five tuliptrees which he measured nearby averaged 6.2 feet in diameter; the greatest diameter for a living specimen was 11 feet, but a stump measured 12. Ridgway found tuliptrees very common on the Wabash floodplain, but they are not reported from that topographic feature today, because of increased flooding.

Little Cypress Swamp, across the Wabash from Mount Carmel, had been a 20,000-acre wilderness, but Ridgway saw those cypress trunks considered "worth cutting" being rafted away for shingles. His photograph of the "*average* size mature cypress" of those remaining shows a much larger tree than any present Indiana cypress. Several stumps measured 9 and 10 feet in diameter above the flaring butt. Cypress in that swamp were so densely crowded that "the intervening spaces are entirely taken up by the knees, the whole surface thus being an irregular wooden one, with soil or water only in the depressions." He completely exhausted himself by penetrating a few yards into the swamp.

Two neighboring walnut trees on drier ground were each 6 feet in diameter. Within 100 yards of them was a Shumard's red oak, 6 feet in diameter at 12 feet above the 12-foot-diameter base. Because it had grown up in a very dense stand, it was extremely tall. The denser the growth in a forest, the taller the trees. The explanation, curiously, is the scarcity of the bright light now well known to inhibit activity of terminal growing points of twigs. Hence, the younger trees that survive in deep woods, where the terminal growth is not kept down by light, reach towering heights.

Ridgway stated that these Lower Wabash stands were equal in grandeur to any of the tropical rainforests of Central America, with which he was also familiar. They surely constituted, until 1860–70, the most magnificent forests in Indiana. Nothing comparable exists

In southern Indiana, cliffs, deep ravines, and clear streams greeted the first explorers. Yellow Birch Ravine in Crawford County shown here.   *Photo by Lee Casebere*

Group of tuliptrees near Vincennes, ranging in diameter from 5 to 7 feet, photographed in 1888 by naturalist Robert Ridgway. Ridgway reported that all four were cut the following year.

in the state today. One pale approach is preserved on the floodplain parts of Beall Woods Nature Preserve near Keensburg, Illinois.

THE FORESTS OF
CHIEF POKAGON AND TECUMSEH

During almost all of the decade of millennia which followed the time of the Great Ice, trees ruled the land. Until the time when their felled trunks were notched for settlers' cabins or, more usually, rolled into ravines for burning, their shade and cycles controlled the life of terrestrial wilderness. Nearly all the individual trees that Little Turtle and Leopold Pokagon looked upon are long gone, yet an amazing stock of detailed information about aboriginal trees is found in reports by the surveyors employed by the General Land Office of the federal government.

When Indians of the deciduous forest ecosystem were forced westward into the high plains and deserts, they lost not only their land but their culture as well. Recently, their descendants have asked some reimbursement from the Great White Father, claiming that a probable 25 cents per acre distributed by the Indian agents, not to mention the firewater supplied by the traders, was not satisfactory, in hindsight, at least. Attorneys of the United States Department of Justice defend the government before the three-judge Indian Claims Commission in Washington; its rulings usually favor the claimants. During the 1950s and 1960s, it was said that the attorneys for the tribes were in the most profitable branch of legal practice.

> The confrontation of Indians and whites had in it the seeds of hopeless misunderstanding from the start. The two cultures had produced irreconcilable concepts of landownership, and once the first white man set foot on American soil, the drama unfolded with all the certain sweep of a Greek tragedy.
>
> —*Stewart L. Udall*, The Quiet Crisis *(1963)*

Fifteen cases in the early 1960s, chiefly from the Potawatomis and Miamis, were consolidated into one claim of $50 million for land in Indiana north of the Wabash River. Perhaps because Tippecanoe

County had once been the site of bad "Indian trouble" (or was it "whites trouble"?), the Justice Department asked a Purdue professor of forest ecology to organize and direct an investigation of the physical-biological Indiana of the treaty period and provide the results to both sides. Such data were expected to help determine the actual monetary value of the lands at the time of purchase. Thus, three modern botanists were enabled to look over the shoulders of the early, adventuresome surveyors who, like many teams during the years, had been privileged to observe and record conditions along the bounds of every square mile in the state.

Although George Washington's first profession was public surveyor, it was Thomas Jefferson who later wrote the system used for most of the United States surveys. Deputy surveyors, the educated woodsmen who bossed the field work, followed Jefferson's directions and achieved a massive, detailed description of old Indiana's physical features, the "natural productions," and the limited works of man—native and European. Starting in 1795, the work was done largely in the first quarter of the nineteenth century. A plat map was filled in for each township or town, comprising 36 sections or square miles.

A survey team traversed only the outer boundary of each square mile, with compass and chain. They filled in two preprinted forms. One recorded their running description along the entire survey line of the topography, drainage conditions, soil quality, and vegetation. Besides the ability to identify trees, most deputy surveyors knew some shrubs and wildflowers as well. In Indiana they recorded 73 species of trees, distinguishing 13 kinds of oaks.

A second, more important form involved only the section and quarter-section corners where stakes were driven. To enable later surveyors to locate these crucial points, from two to four identifiable witness trees were needed. Each of the selected four trees was blazed and "scribed" or marked, and the diameter measured by tape. Also recorded were the compass bearing of that tree from the point, and the taped distance from corner point to tree. (At the corners in prairie, they used different and more laborious methods.)

Our material was prepared for statistical analysis by computer. We applied to surveyors' data the same sampling method, and expressed quantitative results in the same terms, that ecologists now use in sampling and describing a living forest.

Our results on the ghost forests and other pre-settlement vegetation were summarized in map form, each of the three main forest types being distinguished by the few tree genera which dominate the community by virtue of numbers and size. The dominant species of the oak-hickory type are upland ones, not those of lowland depressions. (River floodplains average too narrow to be shown on a small-scale map.) That maple species which shares dominance with American beech in the beech-maple type is sugar maple or "hard maple," which settlers called merely "sugar."

Soil experts had classified soil types along a drainage gradient of 10 classes or "profiles," ranging from excessively drained to permanently ponded, of which the latter sites are typical wetlands. How does one decide, in mapping, which broad forest type to indicate when, in the field, the distinct topographies and vegetations are much finer-scale than can be shown on a map of the whole state? One emphasizes the forest which occurred, characteristically, but not exclusively or invariably, on gentle or moderate slopes of median or "normal" moisture conditions for that latitude and longitude. This is the part of the spectrum termed "well-drained."

A CLOSE LOOK AT A FEW PLACES

Some younger ecologists today also enjoy traveling in "the past lane." Let us note here a few of the many important findings they unearthed by settling as squatters on small holdings and working hard there to hack new knowledge out of their parcels of Indiana wilderness. (See the "Suggested Readings" list for their results, by senior authors' names as given here.)

James Keith mapped the relatively treeless "barrens" of the sinkhole topography of the Mitchell Plain in Harrison and Washington counties. After wildfires became uncommon following settlement, these prairie-like barrens gave place to forest growth, so that only the surveyors' records now reveal their background. Because the deputy surveyors were better at identifying trees than grasses and forbs, these records are less complete for species composition than those for original forests.

In an *Outdoor Indiana* article about Portland Arch Nature Preserve in Fountain County, Ron Campbell reported the results of his work with old survey data. He mapped findings which show that much of the terrain was previously in savanna and prairie.

The Lake Michigan dunes area was still, in the 1960s, unsurpassed in Indiana for natural interest. Local Hoosiers enlisted United States Senator Paul Douglas of Illinois for political help in setting up a National Lakeshore. Douglas confessed, "When I was young, I wanted to save the world, and when I was middle-aged I wanted to save the nation. But now that I'm old, I want to save the dunes."

> Standing on a hilltop, we see a landscape spread below us like a giant tapestry, the land of the small made big solely by connection of the many parts. Yet no one person, not even the most brilliant scientist, can see an entire ecosystem. . . . The web of life and the web of knowledge it has spawned, are visible only to the collective body of mankind.
>
> —David Cavagnaro, "The Wonders of Nature," in
> National Geographic Society Engagement Calendar
> (1991)

Cowles Bog near Dune Acres was named for Professor Henry Cowles of the University of Chicago, the first plant ecologist to do research in Indiana. In 1900, he was studying plant succession in what is now Indiana Dunes State Park. More recently, the co-discoverer of the momentous double helix structure of DNA, Nobelist James D. Watson, got his biological start as a young naturalist wandering the dunelands near his home in Chesterton.

Thorough study of the pre-settlement vegetation of that general area came with the work by John Bacone and his co-workers. In 1980 they offered two papers to the scientific community about this complicated mix of plant communities. Lake County, which had been predominantly prairie and savanna, has been so changed by civilization that the communities which were the most common earlier are the rarest today, retaining only a few small remnants of the original natural landscape.

At Indiana State University, graduate student Ellen Oliver Donselman, braving the tall timber of the Vigo County of 1814, compared the pre-settlement record (and modern interpretations thereof) with the nature and locations of the several vegetation types she found there in the field in 1974. Her detailed county cover map differs considerably from the county's vegetation as depicted on state vegetation maps, partly because the latter are so small-scale and generalized, but also because she based hers on both surveyors' records and present-day stands.

In 1814, the Wabash floodplains in Vigo County were dominated by elm, white oak, and hickory, which by 1974 had given way to more water-loving and flood-tolerant trees, especially silver maple and cottonwood. This is good evidence that flood crests were much lower and flooding less frequent at the earlier time, because of the effects of relatively unbroken forests then on the watershed. Next

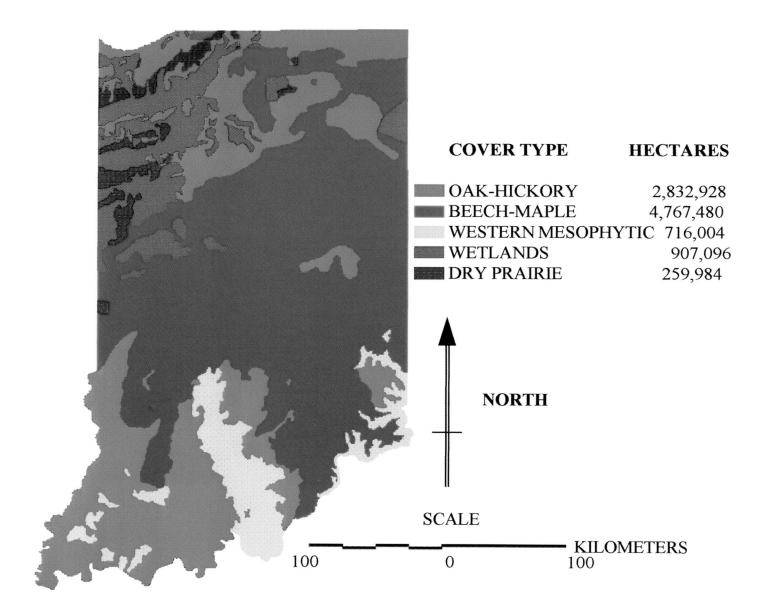

COVER TYPE	HECTARES
OAK-HICKORY	2,832,928
BEECH-MAPLE	4,767,480
WESTERN MESOPHYTIC	716,004
WETLANDS	907,096
DRY PRAIRIE	259,984

NORTH

SCALE

KILOMETERS

100   0   100

Generalized map of the main vegetation types of Indiana, as determined from records of the original federal land surveys and the modern soil maps. *Based on a 1965 research publication by Lindsey, Crankshaw, and Qadir, which appeared in the* Botanical Gazette. *Maps digitized by Martin A. Spetich of Purdue University, using ERDAS 7.7 GIS software*

higher up than the floodplain, almost the whole terrace in Vigo County had been in prairie. Donselman suggests that the effects of varied slope exposures determined the very mixed nature of the county's forests, which, of course, complicates mapping.

WHY WHAT TREES GROW WHERE

Trees, like people, show their preferences and tolerances just by being where they are—or were. We at Purdue hoped to go beyond what was needed by the Indians and Indian-fighting lawyers, not only mapping *where* forest types had typified parts of the state, but also turning the data from thousands of surveyors' corner points to finding out *why* a tree species grows where it does, today as well as yesterday, in its competitive struggle for a place in the sun and soil.

To do this, we needed another source of information besides survey records, to find the exact soil type and its associated factors that supported each individual tree the surveyors recorded.

The patterns of life, natural or managed, must fit patterns of soil fertility.

—*William A. Albrecht,* Transactions, *North American Wildlife Conference (1944)*

A large soil map for each Indiana county has been published in color by the Purdue Soil Survey. Through use of aerial photos and ground studies, the 357 soil types appear in fine detail as an intimate mix of types. We organized the wealth of data—old and newer—for the computer to digest, such as chemical factors, soil textures, slope,

Dense understory and huge red elm in old-growth forest along the Mississippi River floodplain are reminiscent of the early forest along the lower Wabash River.
Photo by Marion Jackson

water supply, and drainage, and the meaningfulness of each reading in the physiology of each tree species.

Because the surveyors recorded so few trees per mile of line, this aspect of tree growth and survival cannot be studied from survey records of a limited, local area. On a statewide scale, enough trees (of the dominant and common species) were recorded from specific soil types to yield reliable averages for each of the factors analyzed. It is hardly feasible to study the functioning of mature trees, which grow slowly and to large, inconvenient sizes, in the laboratory or greenhouse. Nor can entire forest communities or ecosystems be duplicated there. But this new approach, combining old survey records and modern soil maps, made possible the use of "experimental material" of unrivaled "naturalness" and ecosystem-wide scope. It was next best to being taken back in a "time machine."

Evidence from those lines of study combined with what we had learned from previous work on existing forests throughout Indiana

revealed a natural sequence of species. They fell along a gradient between two environmental extremes—a spectrum related to available moisture and the other soil factors that generally vary along with moisture differences. The relative positions of trees along this (basically) soil drainage-aeration gradient were as follows: MORE WATER, more clay, and less sand content, less leaching, less acid, more nitrogen—bald cypress, black willow, black ash, cottonwood, red maple, silver maple, sycamore, pin oak, honey locust, hackberry, buckeye, American elm, black walnut, ash-leaved maple, black maple, sweet gum, basswood, white ash, beech, sugar maple, tuliptree, red oak, the upland hickories, post oak, shingle oak, wild black cherry, white oak, chinquapin or yellow oak, black oak—LESS WATER and mostly opposite in soil traits given for the "more water" extreme.

Sugar maple trees so impressed the early settlers that they named a number of midwestern streams "Sugar Creek." This species, along

Watercourses were filled with beaver in the early days. Their valuable pelts spurred early exploration of Indiana and westward.   *Photo by Russell Mumford*

with the associated American beech, falls centrally in the above sequence. Both trees strongly favor not only a moderate moisture level with enough drainage for adequate air supply to their roots, but also a very high content of silt (the medium texture or particle size) in the soil. They shun soils with much sand, in contrast to the oak species in the study with the exception of post oak. Sugar maple and beech are found most typically on gentle or moderate, often east-facing, slopes, where the well-drained class on the soil drainage-aeration gradient is best represented. Consequently, the beech-maple forest type constitutes, in traditional ecological thought about succession, the theoretical ultimate climatic-climax status in Indiana, broadly considered. So much for the idea; conclusions on beech and sugar maple, for other factors among the dozen studied, need not be mentioned here, nor the conclusions about any of the other 27

tree species for which the results were shown to be statistically significant.

All the witnesses and attorneys in the Indians' case against the U.S. government were brought to Washington for a week of testimony and argument. Two principal Indian witnesses were heard and quizzed. A Potawatomi man, a supervisor in a Ford assembly plant, was the son of a chief, from whom he had inherited the tribe's copy of a pertinent treaty. Also testifying at length was an Indian anthropology professor, dressed in native garb and wearing her black hair in two long braids. About a dozen white attorneys of several firms, who had worked for four years preparing cases for the various tribes, were present. The Purdue findings were presented in detail, and questions were dealt with, more or less.

The final outcome proved a surprise to both sides. The claims commissioners judged that the tribes had failed to prove "aboriginal title" to any of the lands they claimed to own, but that the ancestors of all of them had merely used the land in common as wandering hunters, basically. This unexpected decision made all other considerations, including the Purdue research, irrelevant to the case. By following in the tracks of the surveying teams, we had advanced science a bit, without helping or harming the tribes of today. Neither the Indians nor the law firms representing them received any payment whatsoever. The federal government, though, refrained from claiming that the 25 cents per acre, or any interest on it, was owed by the Indians!

Henry David Thoreau might have predicted this outcome! Writing in his book *Walden,* he observed: "The very simplicity and nakedness of man's life in the primitive ages imply this advantage at least, that they left him still but a sojourner in nature. . . . He dwelt, as it were, in a tent in this world, and was either threading the valleys, or crossing the plains, or climbing the mountain tops."

The wilderness came to us from the eternity of the past. Let us have the wisdom and courage to project it into the eternity of the future.

Still, above all, swinging brightly in the darkened sky, the constellations wink down at Planet Earth.

Man always kills the thing he loves, and so we the pioneers have killed our wilderness. Some say we had to. Be that as it may, I am glad I shall never be young without wild country to be young in. Of what avail are forty freedoms without a blank spot on the map.

—*Aldo Leopold,* A Sand County Almanac *(1949)*

Looking into the crowns of two of the largest tuliptrees remaining in Indiana, Hemmer Woods, Gibson County.   *Photo by Marion Jackson*

13. Nature's Recovery Act: Nothing Succeeds Like Succession

Edwin R. Squiers

There is no forest primeval, no constant, unchanging vegetation.

—*Jack McCormick,* The Living Forest *(1959)*

The air was still and the dew lay heavy on the grass when the Indiana DNR helicopter picked me up on an August morning. Another ecologist and I would spend the day evaluating wetlands as possible additions to Indiana's Nature Preserves System. As we flew north out of Marion, the panorama of the Central Till Plain spread out before us. A gridwork of country roads, sprinkled with tidy farmsteads, bordered mile after mile of agricultural fields. From the air, in August, the northern two-thirds of Indiana appears to be one great expanse of corn and soybean fields, only occasionally interrupted by a pond or a woodlot of oak and hickory. On that morning, the wooded tracts reminded me of postage stamps meticulously arranged on envelopes of cropland on the countryside below.

Indiana's landscape was not always like this. The records of the original Government Land Office survey indicate that in the early 1800s the higher ground of the gently rolling Central Till Plain was blanketed by a majestic old-growth forest dominated by sugar maple and American beech, while swales were covered with dense swamp forests. Native Americans had occupied the region for several thousand years, but their impact on the landscape was small. Although they are known to have used fire as an effective tool for clearing undergrowth and opening the forest for travel, hunting, and small-scale farming, the idea of destroying the forest would have been unthinkable. To the Indians, the forest, like the stars, must have seemed infinite and eternal. It was neither. The steel axes and plows of European settlers would change the face of the land forever.

The wholesale cutting of the pre-settlement forest was perhaps the single most dramatic ecological event in the last thousand years of Indiana history. The land was cleared of trees to supply wood for fuel and building materials, to extend pasture and cropland, and to provide living space for a rapidly expanding nation. Today, Indiana's patchwork landscape is largely a product of the interaction between human-induced disturbance and the natural processes of succession.

BACKGROUND OF AMERICAN ECOLOGY

Since 'tis Nature's law to change,
Constancy alone is strange.

—*John Wilmot, Earl of Rochester,* A Dialogue XXXI

The fact that landscapes are dynamic rather than static is a newer idea than one might suppose. During the Middle Ages, the natural order of things was seen as established by divine command. The eighteenth century brought a flood of change. A renewed interest in philosophy and science, spurred on by an attitude of rationalism and skepticism, produced a fresh look at the natural order. This period of intellectual ferment, sometimes referred to as the Enlightenment, changed Western ideas about existing sciences and saw the birth of new fields of study. Modern ecology is a product of that age. In 1895,

Eugenius Warming, an Austrian trained as a plant geographer, introduced the science of plant ecology with the publication of *The Oecology of Plants: An Introduction to the Study of Plant Communities.* The last section of Warming's classic work described the processes of ecological succession, the transition from one kind of biotic community to another in a given habitat, and the "peopling" of new soil. Like other scientists of his age, Warming added to our understanding of the dynamics of the natural world.

The concept of succession was developed in this country by the "Father of American Ecology," a botany professor from the University of Chicago named Henry Chandler Cowles. Cowles's detailed study of the plant communities of the Lake Michigan dunes in northwest Indiana remains the classic model for many of the more recent studies of plant succession. Near the beginning of the twentieth century, he wrote: "The ecologist, then, must study the order of succession of plant societies in the development of a region, and he must endeavor to discover the laws which govern the panoramic changes. Ecology, therefore, is a study in dynamics."

Cowles's recognition that vegetation is dynamic, rather than static, and his development of the concept of ecological succession as a predictable, orderly process of change can be viewed as one of the most significant milestones in the quest to discern how nature works.

The topography along the Lake Michigan shore in northwest Indiana provided Cowles with the living laboratory that he needed to solve one of the basic problems facing those who would investigate succession: How do you study a process that takes hundreds, or even thousands, of years to occur?

Cowles understood that landscapes are dynamic and correctly deduced that Lake Michigan had been receding northward since the retreat of the continental glaciers of the last ice age. As a result, Cowles postulated that the landscape of old lakeshores and dune ridges became progressively younger the closer they were to current shoreline.

Given this perspective of the landscape, it is easy to see how he concluded that the communities of plants occupying these ridges could be studied as a time series, in which the youngest community was near the lake and the oldest one was far inland. Since the initial substrate for the whole area was dune sand, and the climate and topography throughout the region were similar, any differences in the plant communities occupying the ridges ought to be due to change over time, the processes of succession, and random events associated with dispersal and colonization.

Cowles's careful description of the changing vegetation of the dunes landscape provided ecology with its first clear example of the stages of succession, from the first colonizers of bare sand to the well-established forest communities of the oldest dune ridges.

The succession begins as the bare sand of the beach is colonized by dune-forming grasses, especially Marram grass. Spreading by deep-root rhizomes, the grass can stabilize the shifting sand in as few as six years and is often joined by sand reed and little bluestem grasses in the pioneer community on these low foredunes. Shrubby species such as willow and sand cherry are also early colonizers. Fast-

Wind shifts create blowouts in high dunes formerly stabilized by complex plant and animal communities. Sometimes the remains of ancient forests are exhumed by shifting sand dunes.   *Photo by Marion Jackson*

growing cottonwoods are usually the first trees to appear in the dune communities, but once the dune is fully stabilized, jack pine and white pine invade quickly, if a seed source is available.

The Marram grass declines in vigor as time passes, and is generally absent altogether at 20 years into the succession. The pines, in turn, are gradually replaced by a community dominated by black oak as the system reaches 100 to 150 years of age. The shrub layer also changes, as those species that require the high light intensity of the immature forest are gradually replaced by species whose seedlings can better tolerate the deep shade created by the closing canopy of forest trees.

Cowles believed that the ultimate fate of any succession sequence would be controlled primarily by climate and secondarily by topography. His explanation of the sequence favored the notion of *convergence* to a single regional final community termed the *climax*. With that in mind, he postulated that the black oak forest would proceed to a mixed oak and hickory stage before reaching the theoretical "climatic climax," a beech–sugar maple forest.

Research in the years that followed suggests that topography, soil characteristics, and biotic factors produce a *divergence* to several community types depending on local conditions. Later findings notwithstanding, Cowles's analysis of the dune systems of northwest Indiana remains the classic model for all of the more recent studies of plant succession.

While Henry Cowles may have been the first American to recognize the role of succession in shaping the landscape, it was Frederic E. Clements, a botanist with the Carnegie Institution of Washington, and later the University of Nebraska, who composed the first complete theory of plant succession. Where Cowles was an observer, Clements was a codifier, defining and advancing successional terminology and concepts.

Perhaps one of Clements's most valuable contributions was the expansion of the concept of succession to include natural changes that occur in aquatic communities. Both scientists saw succession as a gradual moderation of the environment. Just as Cowles's dry sand dunes are eventually replaced by cool, moist forests, so does a pond or lake slowly fill with sediment and plant debris to become a bog or fen and, given enough time, a moist forest. Cowles and Clements both referred to the terminal vegetation type as the climax, a final community shaped by the regional climate. Thus, the classic model of plant succession is one of repetitive, directional change where one vegetation type succeeds another in a generally linear fashion until a self-replacing climax community is reached.

Almost anywhere a piece of soil is laid bare and then left alone, there will be an orderly sequence of plant communities that, with the passage of years, will invade it and be replaced. For most parts of the country this succession of vegetation types is to some extent understood and predictable. The last stage of development, or "climax" in a region is capable of renewing itself indefinitely. In theory it should be able to hold on until the climate undergoes a change, then a different climax might appear.

—*Durward L. Allen, "Plants That Succeed," in* Our Wildlife Legacy *(1962)*

Foredunes being stabilized by marram grass in Lake Michigan dune succession. Wave action keeps beach free of colonizing plants.   *Photo by Perry Scott*

FARMLANDS, FIELDS, AND FORESTS

Once we understand that the landscape is a dynamic system, we can begin to understand the farmlands, fields, and forests of Indiana as a patchwork of successional communities of varying ages. Under "normal" conditions, the pattern of natural succession in the state begins with a disturbance that leaves the land exposed and relatively free of natural vegetation. Agriculture and forestry practices are the most common initiators of succession throughout the Midwest. Although some disturbances, such as farming, may continue for many years, once the disturbance ends, the succession begins. Because it is a natural process, succession occurs whether we wish it to or not. Indiana's variety of forests and fields are a product of this process.

The first plant community to occupy a denuded Indiana landscape is likely to be composed of "obnoxious weeds," more properly called pioneer species. First-year fields are usually entirely covered by annual species such as common ragweed, giant foxtail grass, horseweed, panic grass, yellow nut sedge, green amaranth, common lamb's-quarters, or shepherd's purse.

The secret of success for these "pioneers" is not how quickly they arrive after the disturbance ends but that they were there on the site even before the disturbance began. In fact, many early successional species have seeds that can survive in the soil for an extraordinarily long time. Millions upon millions of dormant seeds of these species are contained in every acre of Indiana topsoil. With lifespans measured in decades, they wait for the axe to fall or the plow to pass to create the ideal conditions for them to germinate, grow, and reproduce. This means that practically anything that we plant—whether lawns, vegetable gardens, crop fields, or tree plantations—is going to be invaded and displaced unless we apply some sort of "maintenance" such as herbicides, mowing, or cultivation to contain the invading army of annual plants.

Although these pervasive pioneer plants live for only a single summer, they produce huge numbers of seeds (often 200 to 300 pounds per acre) that fall to the ground and wait in a kind of suspended animation for the next disturbance. The rapid revegetation by abundant annuals acts as a kind of "dressing" on the "wound" of bare soil created by the disturbance. These fast-growing species hold the soil against erosion and slow the loss of nutrients and water from the system.

The colonizing annual plants rapidly give way to a more diverse community dominated by biennial and short-lived perennial herbaceous species. Queen Anne's lace, common mullein, evening primrose, and bull thistle are among the most common plant species on fields two or three years after the disturbance.

Queen Anne's lace, or wild carrot as it is sometimes called, is typical of this group of plants with a two-year "normal" lifespan. During the first growing season after germination, the plant forms a broad, prostrate rosette of leaves and spends much of its energy producing a long, thick taproot. This established root system and the food that it contains gives the biennial plant a decided advantage over annual species that must germinate from a seed and build a whole new plant each growth season.

This structural advantage allows the biennial to spend a significant amount of its second-year energy budget on the production of a tall stalk topped with many flowers. This reproductive activity is called bolting. Whereas many of the annual species are wind pollinated, most biennials use their brightly colored flowers to attract a host of insect pollinators. Thus, things really begin buzzing a couple of years into the process of succession.

I know the lands are lit
With all the autumn blaze of Goldenrod.

—*Helen Hunt Jackson*

Tall goldenrod is perhaps the most widely noticed old-field plant in Indiana. In late summer and early fall, the massed flowers of this species paint much of the state's landscape a brilliant yellow-gold. Tall goldenrod exhibits several characteristics that are typical of successful species at this stage of the succession: First, it is a long-lived perennial, flowering and producing seed year after year from the same root system; second, it spreads vegetatively, forming dense stands by extending underground stems called rhizomes; third, it is taller than most of its competitors and thus captures a greater share of the sunlight; and fourth, it produces leaves and stems filled with toxins that discourage insects from eating them and prevent seeds of other plants from germinating on soil littered with its leaves.

Other species common at this stage include Canada goldenrod, rough-stemmed goldenrod, fleabane, St. John's-wort, New England aster, black-eyed Susan, Canada thistle, and sodgrasses. These herbaceous perennials form the community that will replace the biennials in the fourth or fifth year of the succession and will remain relatively stable for a decade or more. Because large, well-developed clones of these species create an environment that hinders the germination and growth of other species, the succession may be slowed or stopped at this stage for many years.

The next major transition in the successional odyssey begins with the appearance of woody perennial shrubs and vines. These species appear to be successful for many of the same reasons as their herbaceous predecessors. If shrubs such as blackberry, dewberry, staghorn sumac, multiflora rose, elderberry, shrubby dogwoods, and hawthorn, or vines such as poison-ivy, Virginia creeper, wild grapes, and hedge-bindweed gain a foothold in a field dominated by aster or goldenrods, they will quickly overtop and replace them.

With the breakup of the clones of goldenrods and asters, the community often becomes a tangled "briar patch" containing many kinds of plants and a great variety of animals. This new diversity of habitats also seems to promote the growth of successional tree species. Closed canopies of sumac, for example, have been shown to choke out herbaceous species while at the same time favoring the growth of the trees that will constitute the dominants in the next stage of succession.

Tomorrow to fresh woods and pastures new.

—*John Milton,* Lycidas

If you look carefully at a "young" old field, you will find occasional tree seedlings among the wild carrot, goldenrod, or sumac. They have arrived as seed carried by the wind, buried by a small animal, or dropped conveniently fertilized by a passing bird. Generally suppressed and slow-growing at the earlier stages of succession, the tree species now begin to manifest themselves.

The first to become important are relatively short-lived, fast-growing species that thrive in the bright sunlight and patchy environment of the shrub and vine stage. The tree species associated with this successional forest in much of Indiana include white ash, red maple, wild black cherry, tuliptree, sassafras, black locust, and eastern red cedar. Lasting for 50 to 100 years, this stage marks the end of the old field and the beginning of the true forest ecosystem.

The forest continues to change. Oaks and hickories gradually rise to form a dense understory in the successional forest. While the particular mixture of oak and hickory may vary depending on the local conditions, the most common species in this association are white, red, and black oak and shagbark and pignut hickory. As the

Old-field succession dominated by tall goldenrod has islands of woody species invading the herbaceous community. Old-growth forest of Laughery Bluff Nature Preserve in Ripley County in background. *Photo by Marion Jackson*

trees in the canopy die, these longer-lived and moderately shade-intolerant forest species push their way upward and become the typical forest community that we see scattered across the Indiana landscape. These second-growth forests are the product of more than one hundred years of natural succession.

Will it end here? Do these oak and hickory forests represent the "stable self-maintaining climax" forest that Cowles and Clements envisioned? Probably not. In many cases the understory of the oak-hickory forests is populated by sugar maple rather than oak and hickory. Perhaps, in time, the forest of maple and beech that greeted European settlers will return—at least on well-drained mesic sites, it likely will. In any case, there is one thing that we can be sure of—given enough time, the biotic community and its associated environment will change.

PRIMARY SUCCESSIONS

Succession, quite obviously, is not confined to areas of soil laid bare by human activity, then left partially or wholly alone. Nature abhors a vacuum in the biological as well as in the physical sense, so anywhere that has unoccupied habitat within the survival tolerance of potentially invading populations, succession will occur.

For convenience in description and discussion, ecologists view successional processes as primary when they occur on new substrates largely devoid of organisms, and as secondary on sites that previously supported biotic communities, frequently with the soil formed earlier still in place. In addition to the succession patterns studied by Cowles and his successors at the Indiana Dunes, primary succession also occurs on recently deglaciated landscapes, on newly exposed rock surfaces, and in newly created aquatic habitats (see also chapter 10, "In the Glacier's Wake").

Long-headed cone flower is a successful old-field invader in certain habitats. *Photo by Paul Rothrock*

Primary successions frequently occur in severe environments where physical factors are most limiting. On such sites, invasion and successional change are often excruciatingly slow. For example, crustose lichens, typically among the first organisms to arrive on rock outcrops, gravestones, brick buildings, sidewalks, stone walls, and the like, may grow less than a millimeter per year, and may reach centuries in age. Replacement of the lichen stage by their moss, liverwort, or other successors may be equally deliberate. But eventually soil accumulates over pavement surfaces, allowing vascular plants and animals to invade more readily, as the physical extremes of wide temperature swings and alternating wet-dry cycles are ameliorated.

Given millennia, a complex forest or barrens community may develop over formerly bare, exposed rock surfaces. Numerous examples of such ecosystems are found in many parts of Indiana, especially along Sugar Creek Valley and in the hill country of the south-central and southeastern parts of the state, where rock outcrops are more in evidence.

LAKE AND STREAM SUCCESSIONS

Successional changes occur in aquatic environments as well, establishing the patterns of life in Indiana streams and lakes. Ecologists call these successions *hydroseres,* water substrates being their common denominator.

Successions occur in flowing waters, but if the gradient is steep and water flowage fast, at least in flood times, the beginnings of successional advance are flushed out periodically, keeping most

Lichens and mosses commonly initiate succession on rock outcrops, likely because they can tolerate such severe environments.
Photo by Perry Scott

Vegetation banding on a sand and gravel bar along the Wabash River increases in age from the water's edge landward.
Photo by Marion Jackson

stream successions perennially in pioneer stages. On the other hand, mature, slow-flowing streams such as the lower reaches of the White and Wabash rivers have well-developed stream-border communities that are the product of many years of slow successional change.

Starting with the open water of a lake or pond, another succession will progress as the body of standing water fills with accumulating sediments and plant remains. Eventually the lake will be converted to dry land by the shoreline communities migrating centripetally into ever-shallowing water, much as a camera shutter stops down.

Perhaps the best way to observe and understand the processes involved in succession along lake margins is to paddle a canoe shoreward from the center of one of northern Indiana's few remaining undeveloped lakes of glacial origin. Failing Lake at Wing Haven Nature Preserve in Steuben County is a prime location for such an experience.

A daytime visual experience is likely most instructive of nature's conversion of lakes to land, but as May T. Watts pointed out in her perceptive book *Reading the Landscape,* a nocturnal traverse can be similarly informative if one listens attentively to changes in the sequence of sounds on the canoe hull as forward progress is made.

> Was the sequence, *drip, slide, rustle?* No, there was something missing in that sequence. Something between the *drip* and the *slide.* There was an interval filled with a sort of tangled dripping, the stretch where submerged pondweeds enmesh the paddle and change the clean drip to a muffled spatter. The sequence was: *drip, spatter, slide, rustle.*
>
> —May Theilgaard Watts, "Coming Ashore," in Reading the Landscape (1957)

In the clear open water at lake center, only floating and free-swimming algae dominate the earliest pioneer aquatic community. Toward land, where the water shallows sufficiently yet remains clear enough for sufficient light to penetrate for photosynthesis to occur, a lovely intermingling of submerged vascular plants creates an underwater habitat that rivals an above-ground meadow in interest and complexity. Water milfoil, hornwort, pondweeds, elodea, bladderworts, and coontail create miniature aquatic forests, the water giving their fragile, limp bodies both form and nourishment. Animals, both invertebrate and vertebrate, abound in these mazes of vegetation. This zone yields the *spatter* from the canoe paddle.

Shallower and shoreward is a belt of floating-leaved aquatic plants, firmly rooted in the ooze but with their expansive rigid waxed leaves riding the unsteady surface, tethered in place by the miniature hawsers of their flexible leaf stems. Their large, showy flowers also float at the surface on their ring of canoe-shaped sepals. Water lily, spatterdock, and water shield are typical dominants of this community. Being coarse vegetation, they add considerable bulk to the lake margins, and upon decay they cause rapid shallowing and faster successional change. Here is the *slide* sound of the scabrous leaves rasping across the canoe bottom.

As the water shallows to two feet or less, tall emergent herbaceous species gain ascendancy in the successional sequence. Cattails, bulrushes, and tall sedges now crowd densely along the shore, forming near-impenetrable tangles at their bases, adding great quantities of decaying plant material with each fall freeze, thereby accelerating the progress of succession with their rapid accumulation. This marsh zone is the haunt of the rail and bittern, redwing and sedge wren, muskrat and mink, as well as the location of the *rustle* against the night-active canoe.

The land-water interface at the lake rim may be inhabited variously by either a shrub swamp of buttonbush, poison sumac, etc., in dense thickets, or at other sites by herbaceous sedge-spike rush–true

Canoeing shoreward in a natural lake with shoreline undisturbed by human activity would result in a traverse of most stages of aquatic succession.
Photo by Marion Jackson

rush meadows. Either community can tolerate "wet feet" but not extended periods of total submergence. As water levels lower, occasional tree seedlings become established.

Finally, on the wet soils surrounding the lake, a hydric forest develops, usually heavy in red maple, box-elder, elms and wet-site ashes, oaks and hickories. Clements called this a subclimax community, its continuance dependent on conditions too wet to be considered a "true" climax. With time, as the water table drops and mesic conditions ensue, in theory at least, the climax forest dominated by American beech and sugar maple could replace the lowland subclimax forest. This whole sequence of lake to land may take thousands of years to complete, but occupies only an eyeblink in geological time.

DOES EQUILIBRIUM OCCUR?

Thus the endpoint of both xerosere succession beginning on dunes and hydrosere succession beginning in a glacial lake could theoretically be one and the same (namely a beech- and maple-dominated forest community) for the climatic conditions that presently prevail in Indiana. In actuality, these results seldom occur. For succession to run that lengthy course would require stable conditions to prevail for millennia. Usually major changes occur in the climate or other environmental conditions within that time span, disturbing or interrupting the sequence and initiating one of the earlier stages of successional recovery.

One of the most fruitful and most interesting areas of research on successional change is long-term study of sections of some of the best remaining old-growth forests in Indiana to determine the nature of climax communities, if such exist. Scale-model maps of the exact locations of each tree in portions of these mature stands permit tree-by-tree comparisons of growth and survival of individual trees at decade intervals. In this way, changes in dominant species and long-term recovery from such disturbances as tree falls and windthrows can be evaluated.

Data from such studies involving 30- to 70-year total time spans reveal that old-growth (climax?) forests are not at equilibrium in species composition as once thought, but do, in fact, change substantially in ways and at rates that would not have been discerned by other than this detailed, patient research.

There is nothing permanent except change.

—*Heraclitus*, Fragment

THE NATURE OF BIOTIC SUCCESSION

This chapter has focused on plant ecology, which is not surprising because scientists who study community structure and succession usually concentrate on the vegetation. Plants commonly provide most of the biomass and physical structure of natural communities; they exert a strong influence on the environment within the community; and they are the base of both the grazing and detritus food chains. Perhaps equally important, plants do not hide or run away when you go into the field to study them, and this makes it relatively easy to collect data and detect change.

The succession of plant species is always accompanied by a succession of animal species. The kinds of plants present will

Tornado damage in forest near Romney, Tippecanoe County, will enable sunlight to penetrate to the forest floor, allowing shade-intolerant trees to reproduce in the light gaps.   *Photo by Alton Lindsey*

Animal populations also change with the succession of plant communities. Birds such as the cardinal, our state bird, eat and subsequently plant many seeds of plants typical of brushy old fields. They also nest there in small eastern red cedar trees or in woody tangles.   *Photo by Richard Fields*

determine the kinds of plant-eaters, and in turn, the kinds of these herbivores govern the kinds of predators that can be supported within the community. Thus, the early successional community of annual and biennial plants such as ragweed, foxtail grass, and wild carrot provides a feast for hordes of grasshoppers, leafhoppers, and aphids. These, in turn, become "dinner" for such predators as crab spiders, spotted red ladybugs, meadowlarks, and killdeer.

As the goldenrod and asters become abundant, bees, beetles, butterflies, and moths are joined by meadow-nesting sparrows and red-winged blackbirds. Mice and voles thrive among the dense perennial vegetation. Hawks appear overhead, joining a variety of snakes, foxes, and weasels in search of prey. Finally, as the trees begin to take over, the animal community changes to take advantage of the new sources of food. Nut trees, especially the oaks and hickories, support large populations of woodpeckers, jays, crows, white-footed mice, chipmunks, and tree squirrels. In fact, some of the earliest

commentary on the mechanisms of succession resulted from the observation of animals in the forest stage of the process.

Many of the animals associated with the plant communities typical of each of the several stages of succession are the most important vectors of pollen and plant fruiting structures. Without the animal components of successional ecosystems, a large majority of plant species would fail to set seed, or if that were accomplished, there would be fewer agents for transporting those seeds to sites favorable for their germination and growth.

To a very great extent, animals plant what they eat, then eat what they plant. Further, many plant species employ various techniques, including wide usage of chemicals and toxins (as mentioned earlier for goldenrod) which inhibit germination and success of invading species, thereby giving resident populations the competitive edge. This serves to prolong their tenure in the waves of invasion represented in the successional pageant of communities. Given free rein in nature, plants and animals go a long way toward management of the habitats in which they best fit.

All things change; nothing perishes.

—*Ovid,* Metamorphoses XV

EPILOGUE

Henry David Thoreau, best known as the author of *Walden,* wrote and spoke widely on issues of the environment. A keen-eyed naturalist and observer, Thoreau saw more than just the details of the world around him; he also saw the interrelationships. Watching a squirrel burying hickory nuts in a stand of hemlock, he concluded, "This is the way forests are planted." Here was one of the secrets of succession, bound up in these furry little creatures. The nuts, carried far from the parent tree, buried and forgotten, sprout to become the next generation of forest. In his lecture in 1860 entitled "The Succession of Forest Trees," Thoreau scooped Cowles, and even Warming, by describing one of the basic mechanisms of succession.

My own backyard is not Walden Pond, but the lawn chair under the big oak tree is a welcome haven. As I sit and watch the squirrels busily preparing for winter, I am reminded that Thoreau saw in the process of succession "the inextinguishable vitality of Nature," and that he suggested that prudent management practices would work with nature rather than against it. Sage advice for any age.

Off in the distance, I hear the drone of my neighbor's lawn mower. I am amazed at the time and energy he seems willing to expend on his front lawn in order to ensure that the natural process of succession will not occur. Fortunately, Thoreau has convinced me that mowing the lawn, certainly mowing it today, would be imprudent. Please pass the lemonade.

* * *

Observe constantly that all things take place by change, and accustom thyself to consider that the nature of the Universe loves nothing so much as to change the things which are.

—*Marcus Aurelius,* Meditations IV

The annual grass giant foxtail is a copious producer of seed, which accumulates in huge numbers in the soil. Most corn and soybean fields would be almost totally covered with giant foxtail each year if herbicides were not applied.   *Photo by Russell Mumford*

14. Aggressive Invaders: Exotic Plants

Paul E. Rothrock

A weed is no more than a flower in disguise.

—*James Russell Lowell,* A Fable for Critics *(1848)*

The prickly heat of another dog day of August was alive with cicadas. I had planned to pull out the lawn chair and sip some cool lemonade, but my wife, the "keeper of civilization," popped my idyllic bubble with the entreaty, "Honey, why don't you mow the grass today?" I objected feebly to undertaking this difficult work under such humid conditions. It was to no avail. After all, what would the neighbors think of an ankle-deep growth of grass and weeds in the front yard? My failure to confront the dandelion problem already had tongues wagging.

I dragged the push mower out of the garage and laid my muscle to the weekly job. The task of following a smelly, loudly whirring, dangerous machine in order to mangle perfectly healthy and beautiful plants had never seemed to be an intelligent pastime. As I worked I pondered, "Why do supposedly rational human creatures mow lawns?"

The "why" of lawn mowing has to do with being cultural animals, a curse said to have been laid on Adam and Eve. Is it not curious that the Genesis image is one of first humans who are unwilling to leave the vegetation alone? Why do we no longer simply enjoy the God-planted garden and its abundance in the manner of Adam and Eve? Rather, we toil and shape the land to conform to our perceived needs, whether physical or cultural.

As a part of shaping the land to our presumed needs, we move plants from one place to another. Indeed, our Indiana landscape has undergone radical transformation in less than two centuries (see also "Perspective: The Indiana That Was" and chapter 46, "The Wave of Settlement"). This transformation was not shaped by glacial activity, climatic change, or natural dispersal. Human immigrants, especially from Europe, carried a revolutionary image of how land should be managed: so trees were felled, burned, or sold as lumber; prairies were plowed; roads, railroads, and towns were built. As Indiana became the third most developed state in America, vast tracts of habitat suitable for the growth of introduced species were made available in the process.

My lawn mower blade hacks at plants that benefited from the transformation of Indiana from forest to artificial savanna or grassland—communities of plants which followed in the footsteps of the settlers—and alien species such as English ribgrass, Kentucky bluegrass, common dandelion, and common chickweed. Of the 2,265 plant species growing spontaneously in Indiana, probably 16 percent are the result of human introduction and are what we call "exotics."

CULTIVATED EXOTICS

Although some people may regard all exotic plants as nothing but weeds, pests, or nuisances, many are useful or beautiful. Few present-day crop and food plants were part of our pre-settlement Indiana flora. Corn originated in Mexico, soybeans in China, and wheat in the Mideast. Our vegetable gardens are full of exotics: tomatoes and potatoes from South America, peas from Asia, and herbs from the Mediterranean. Human activity has shaped these plants through a co-evolutionary process by gradually selecting genetic strains, hybrids, and polyploids with bigger seeds, sweeter taste, and greater ease of harvest. As these plants flourished under our protection, we simultaneously altered our way of living. Today, less than 1 percent of the world's humans continue to live as hunters and gatherers, the dominant lifestyle of only 300 human generations ago. Humans now direct an estimated 20 percent of the world's photosynthetic activity into raising exotic plants, testimony to the importance of exotics for human welfare.

As for diversity, what remains of our native fauna and flora remains only because agriculture has not got around to destroying it. The present ideal of agriculture is clean farming; clean farming means a food chain aimed solely at economic profit and purged of all non-conforming links. . . . Diversity, on the other hand, means a food chain aimed to harmonize the wild and the tame in the joint interest of stability, productivity and beauty.

—*Aldo Leopold,* The Round River *(1953)*

Raising plants for human consumption requires an incredible infrastructure to sustain them. Land grant colleges such as Purdue University are specifically charged with conducting research leading to new crop varieties and for controlling plant pests and disease. Other scientists search the world for new species of plants with economic potential or for new genetic material to use in breeding programs. When a new crop variety is developed, seed stock, usually hybrid, has to be produced by commercial seed producers. Agricultural equipment, chemical manufacturers, grain bins, processing plants, and distribution facilities round out the infrastructure necessary to bring food to market. Our extensively industrialized agriculture directly and indirectly employs one-fifth of the U.S. work force and consumes 17 percent of all fossil-fuel energy used in the United States.

EXOTICS OF PIONEER GARDENS

In the deep shadow of the porch
A slender bindweed springs,
And climbs, like airy acrobat,
The trellis, and swings
And dances in the golden sun
In fairy loops and rings.

—*Sarah Chauncey Woolsey ("Susan Coolidge")*

Every spring, seed catalogs, nurseries, and supermarkets display an enticing selection of exotics ranging from *Ageratum* to *Zinnia*. Fortunately, the majority of these ornamental species behave like neutered pets. They thrive where we plant them but seldom produce offspring which spread across the landscape. Some species, however, have the unfortunate habit of spreading into neighboring fields and roadsides. It is these plants that fit my definition of a weed as "a plant growing where it is not wanted."

Morning glories and corn are both alien species, but only the former reproduces successfully in nature.
Photo by Paul Rothrock

Pioneer gardens in Indiana boasted displays of morning glories, bouncing Bet, dame's rocket, flower-of-an-hour, and dayflower. All of these are now familiar weed species. Morning glories, originally from South America, spread their rapidly growing vines over unsightly tree stumps and outhouses on nineteenth-century homesteads. Before widespread herbicide usage, sometimes they would so tightly intertwine the edges of some cornfields that you could shake a single cornstalk and watch the vibrations ripple through the entire row!

Bouncing Bet was both a handsome and useful plant, with its leaves and roots containing saponin, a gentle soap once used to wash wool. Now its cleansing properties are forgotten and the plant has taken up refuge in roadside ditches. Of the early ornamentals, orange daylily has the puzzling behavior of failing to produce fertile seed, and yet it appears frequently across the state. More likely daylilies have been planted freely since pioneer days and simply persist by their many rhizomes and tuberous roots. Even in shade they persevere indefinitely in vegetative condition.

Early settlers raised many plants for their now-forgotten medicinal value. Common weeds such as catnip, yarrow, motherwort, and heal-all had medicinal properties recognized by the U.S. Pharmacopoeia. Catnip can make a tea soothing to the nerves, while motherwort may serve as a tonic in heart diseases. Yarrow leaves have the capability of stanching blood flow from small cuts, and they can serve as an astringent. And, of course, heal-all can provide a salve for cuts.

Continued use of herbal remedies in less-developed regions of the world attests to the power of plant chemicals as well as to the dangers inherent in their indiscriminate use. In Indiana, the herbal industry continued well into the twentieth century. Two herbs, spearmint and peppermint, are still grown commercially in the northern part of the state, with Indiana leading the nation in the production of these mint oils. Gene Stratton Porter has preserved a delightful slice of our herbal history in her love story *The Harvester.*

Pioneer gardens also had fiber and food plants. Members of the family Umbelliferae, wild carrot and parsnip are so familiar in our flora that we seldom recall their cultivated origin from Eurasian ancestors. Dandelion, chicory, and dock are other pioneer food plants gone to weed. Dandelion (*dent de lion* in French, referring to the peculiar toothy leaves) was an herb traditionally valued for its vitamin-rich greens and medicinal effects. Dandelions do not seem to be a bother in their native Europe because they are avidly collected for food. Eighteenth-century herbalists commented: "They are no bad ingredient in salads. The French eat the roots, and the leaves blanched, with bread and butter." Someone has suggested that if dandelions were difficult to grow, they would be enthusiastically cultivated by gardeners for their showy flowers and edible greens.

Like dandelion, chicory has served as a source of cold-season greens; it also has valuable roots. Even today, dried and roasted chicory roots are sold as a substitute or blend for coffee.

Fiber for bagging, rope, and cordage was essential for agriculture, manufacturing, and home use in our young nation. Two species, hemp and velvetleaf, were introduced to overcome the apparent lack of suitable North American species. Although its intoxicating nature went unappreciated in this country until after 1900, hemp was grown in America as early as 1611. Even as late as World War II, the U.S. government encouraged the cultivation of hemp for fiber. Today some northern Indiana weed patches still contain spontaneous hemp plants, a by-product of World War II rope production.

Velvetleaf was an early introduction from China. Although grown for more than a century as a potential fiber plant, it never seemed able to displace hemp and imported fibers. Unfortunately, while the fiber potential of this species failed to catch on, by the 1870s velvetleaf had become a major weed problem in midwestern cornfields. Currently Purdue scientists estimate that it infests 20 percent of corn acreage and an astounding 65 percent of soybean acreage. The resulting costs for velvetleaf control probably exceed $40 million per year in Indiana.

The early settlers in Indiana introduced plants for food, medicine, fiber, and beauty. They also brought with them much livestock—cattle, sheep, hogs, horses, and mules—which needed an abundance of pasture and hay. The limited natural grassy openings were quickly supplemented with tame pastures containing a nutritious mix of European grasses. Today, Kentucky bluegrass, orchard grass, redtop, tall fescue, and timothy blanket more than 2 million acres of Hoosier pastureland. One fescue in particular, an aggressive polyploid known as Kentucky 31, dominates thousands of miles of grassland maintained along Indiana highways.

SOME BIG MISTAKES

Our rash introduction of hundreds of plant species was bound to have some unintended and unwanted consequences. Indeed, mistakes in plant introduction make for some horrifying bedtime reading. My local area has two of the most hated plant mistakes: multiflora rose and Johnson grass. Multiflora rose was for many years recommended for use as "living fences" suitable for wildlife cover and the prevention of soil erosion. Now its bountiful hooks grab my attention whenever I walk the shortcut to town. Of course, no human planted it in these particular old fields and hedgerows. The red hip-fruits of autumn act as flags to attract the attention of hungry birds. Like many fleshy fruits, the seeds are ingested whole and pass through the animal's gut unharmed. Later the seeds are defecated, complete with a bit of nutrient-rich organic residue. Bird dispersal similarly has spread other familiar exotics such as Russian olive, Tartarian and Japanese honeysuckles, white mulberry, and glossy buckthorn.

I understand they are strongly recommending now that all the old cemeteries be planted with multiflora rose. When Gabriel sounds his horn, I am afraid some will be stranded and not be

Dandelions may be a troublesome lawn weed if uncontrolled. They flower almost any month of the year. In Europe, they are widely eaten as human food.   *Photo by Richard Fields*

Meadow fescue, once eagerly planted by farmers, is perhaps the most widespread invading plant species in the state, and is extremely difficult to eradicate once it is established.   *Photo by Paul Rothrock*

able to get thru the roses. Please do not recommend the multiflora rose except to the bonfire.

> —*Charles C. Deam, Letter to Professor Daniel DenUyl, Purdue University (1940s)*

Another weed of our area, Johnson grass, has the dubious honor of being declared one of the world's ten worst weeds. In the United States, this grass was introduced before the Civil War as a forage grass that would regularly produce amazing amounts of hay. Unfortunately, it also forms an amazing amount of tenacious rhizomes which are nearly impossible to eradicate. Since even small rhizome fragments can readily resprout, herbicides have proven to be the most effective way to control and eradicate this weed.

Johnson grass shares the same savage rhizomatous habit with several other weeds commonly found in vegetable gardens—quackgrass, horse nettle, and Canada thistle. My own experience with quackgrass has been an especially trying episode. Its sharply pointed rhizomes can grow through the flesh of potato or carrot, and under favorable (or should I say unfavorable) conditions it can form a meter-long mat with innumerable nodes in just a single season.

With all these mistakes in plant introduction, it is at least some consolation that many exotics were accidental introductions. But how did plants walk across the oceans and continents to central North America?

Weed seeds are silent travelers. Some arrive in packing material or soil of nursery stock; others stow away in the intestinal tracts or bedding material of farm animals shipped from Europe. However,

probably the majority came as contamination of crop seed. In essence, they were harvested with good seed and efficiently carried from one site of favorable growth to another many miles away. Before the advent of weed screening, common passengers in crop seed included clovers, Canada thistle, and curly dock. Even just a "few" weed seeds per pound of crop seed can represent a major introduction: if an average pound of oats is calculated to contain a mere 30 mustard seeds, a seeding rate of three bushels of oats per acre will include 2,800 mustard seeds.

Stock feeds provide another major vector for plant introduction because weed-seed screenings are often added as a cheap yet nutritious filler. Attempts are now made to destroy the viability of weed seeds by grinding and/or cooking. However, a particularly appalling example from 1954 provides food for thought. A boxcar shipment of animal feed was found to contain 40 percent weed seed and 60 percent cracked wheat. From this statistic, one can estimate that the boxcar as a whole contained 4 trillion viable weed seeds. In this case, 23 species of seed were identified, including another of the world's 10 worst weeds, barnyard grass.

TAXI SERVICE, PLEASE

Although the role of railroads in long-distance seed dispersal is well documented, the continued success of a weed species in a locality requires an ability for new seeds to taxi away from the parent plant. Imagine a situation in which a single plant can produce 300 seeds per year, and all 300 seeds germinate and in turn produce 300 seeds. In this scenario, if no dispersion of seeds occurs, 90,000 seeds would envelop the small clump of plants. In real life it is apparent that such a surplus of seed would cause monumental problems. Rodents might feast on the seed larder or, if the 90,000 seeds germinated, competition for water, nutrients, and light would be intense. On the other hand, as distance from the parent increases, new seedlings have a greater likelihood of escaping parent-associated mortality. By the way, the 300 seeds in this example would be a very modest level of production, since many vigorously growing weeds can produce tens of thousands of seeds per plant.

Field weeds often rely upon wind to whisk seeds away. Canada

Multiflora rose was promoted as a wildlife cover and food plant in years past. It is now unlawful to plant it, but natural reproduction keeps it abundant in much of the state.   *Photo by Paul Rothrock*

Thistles, being insect-pollinated and wind-dispersed, are among the most successful and widespread of cropland and old-field species.   *Photo by Russell Mumford*

thistle and common dandelion have modified a part of each flower into a feather-like pappus which parachutes the seeds away. Curly dock has winged fruits, while great mullein has fine, light seed. To further enhance the chances of catching a waft of breeze, these plants hold their buoyant parcels as high in the air as possible. Dandelions have a particularly plastic flower stalk; one day the developing head of seed is nestled safely at ground level below the cutting height of my lawn mower, while the next day a spherical fluff ball stands 20 centimeters above the freshly cut grass.

One Indiana city, Terre Haute, still bears the marks of a most unusual episode of wind dispersal of exotic seeds. During the late nineteenth century, the winged fruits of the *Ailanthus* or "tree-of-heaven" were used as excelsior in shipments of glassware from the Orient to the Root Department Store. When the store caught fire, the firestorm carried the seed-bearing samaras aloft, resulting in a para-trooper-like invasion across much of the downtown.

Fur, feathers, socks, and wool slacks can also taxi seed packages to new neighborhoods. Beggar tick barbs and cocklebur hooks make these Composite family members especially mobile. I remember using spiny burdock balls as ammunition in boyhood war games. *Zing-g-g!* They left little doubt as to who got "shot" and how fatal the wound.

Some exotic species have less than obvious means of dispersal—no hooks, no barbs, no wings, and no plumes. Velvetleaf, for example, has relatively large seeds with little prospect of catching a breeze. These seeds can move from field to field on muddy feet and agricultural machinery as well as in the "bellies" of combines. Maybe they can even float from place to place during heavy rains, though this mechanism has been little studied.

SLEEPING BEAUTY?

Success in reaching a site for colonization represents only the first hurdle in the life of any plant, exotic or native. It must be followed by the critical step of germination and seedling establishment. For many exotic species this is an especially tenuous step, since they are annuals which have only one growing season to journey from germinating seed to successfully reproducing adult.

Not surprisingly, nature's vagabonds have an intriguing bag of tricks to ensure that their seeds germinate under optimal conditions. One strategy is a complex "sleeping-beauty act." Seeds become dormant upon maturity and lie asleep in the soil until the right "kiss" awakens them from their slumber. The basis and duration for seed-sleep varies from species to species, from seed to seed within a plant, and even from season to season for a single seed.

For this reason, a single "kiss" will seldom trigger germination of all seeds. A series of highly specific environmental and genetic cues have to be met. Has the embryo advanced far enough in development? Have chemical inhibitors been degraded or removed? What is the carbon dioxide concentration? Is soil moisture high enough?

As demonstrated by a mustard called mouse-eared cress, light and temperature provide especially critical cues for germination. In the field, cress seeds germinate most readily in the fall, produce an overwintering rosette of leaves, and complete their life cycle in the spring. When seeds are first shed in May, they are innately dormant. No amount of environmental tinkering can awaken the beauty within. By August, however, these seeds have entered a new phase of dormancy. Under laboratory conditions, seeds exposed to light and tricked with cool temperatures (less than 15°C) can germinate, but

Velvet leaf, a native of Asia, arrived in North America both as a deliberate introduction as a potential fiber plant crop, and as a seed-grain contaminant. It is especially troublesome in fields of soybeans, a crop plant also introduced from Asia.   *Photo by Paul Rothrock*

seeds in darkness or under warm conditions stubbornly maintain their sleep.

As autumn approaches, their temperature requirements become less and less finicky, allowing many seeds in the field to germinate. Nonetheless, buried seeds (i.e., seeds kept in darkness) by and large remain dormant. With the onset of winter, the non-germinated mouse-ear cress seeds enter yet a third phase of dormancy, in which any germination is again blocked by unfavorable temperatures until after the next midsummer.

My side yard has an unusual patch of exotic vegetation where we recently ran some new underground pipe. Only on that strip grows a dense patch of a mint called henbit. I had wondered where it came from since I had not previously seen it around the yard. Because of seed-sleep, some weed species spend most of their lifetimes as part of a seed pool or seed reservoir in the soil. In fact, a square meter of arable soil may harbor 30,000 dormant seeds. Twenty years before my lawn was lawn, it was part of a dairy farm, a favorite henbit habitat. The scratching of the soil brought those old seeds to the surface, exposed them to light and suitable temperature conditions, and released them from their slumber.

If the soil had not been stirred, the henbit seeds might have slept on for many more decades. In the world of seedpools, the Rip Van Winkles of seeds are those of chickweed, lamb's-quarter, and knotweed, whose seed-sleep has been measured in centuries.

Purple loosestrife has showy flowers that cause some wetlands to become seas of color, but it is a very serious pest in many wetland nature preserves.
Photo by Lee Casebere

And so it criticized each flower,
This supercilious seed;
Until it woke one summer hour,
And found itself a weed.

—*Mildred Howells,* The Difficult Seed

THE LINE OF BATTLE

In the popular jargon of natural history, the phrases "nature's tooth and claw" and "survival of the fittest" are often heard. While plants do not have teeth or talons, they are not devoid of weapons. Likewise, as is true of all living things, plants have survival strategies that work well under particular environmental conditions. What basic strategy allows exotics to gain their unwelcome rootholds on our territory?

Studies of genera with both weedy and nonweedy species, such as the genus *Portulaca,* reveal interesting life contrasts. Weedy portulaca, also known as purslane, is a generalist with an ability to respond to a wide range of conditions. This plasticity to environmental variation eases the transition to a new continent or region. Compared to non-weedy portulaca, purslane tolerates a wider range of light intensity, photoperiod, temperature, and soil types. It also has quick early growth and directs a much larger percentage of its energy into reproduction. In fact, because of succulent water-retentive leaves, purslane can ripen seed even after being pulled up or put into a plant press for drying.

Weedy generalists do best on productive sites where occasional disturbance reduces the number of specialized competitors. If a productive site is seldom disturbed, native plants can usually attain the advantage. Native species promote a counterstrategy of delaying reproduction and investing most of their available food energy in new vegetative structure. As a result, exotic weed species are usually replaced by native species during natural community succession.

Unfortunately, the succession "law" is broken by about 6 percent of our approximately 350 species of introduced species. These aggressive invaders have the ability to overpower even intact natural communities. Four species—purple loosestrife, glossy buckthorn, Japanese honeysuckle, and garlic mustard—represent the front line of battle for managers of natural areas.

Purple loosestrife was first noted along a small stream in Marion County in 1925. Unfortunately, this plant, with little value to wildlife, has now marched across many open wetlands in the northern part of the state. Glossy buckthorn, reported from only two counties in Deam's 1940 *Flora of Indiana,* has invaded peaty bogs and fens and rare moist-prairie habitats. Forming a dense canopy of leaves, it often shades out some of the state's rarest native plants. Japanese honeysuckle, with only two confirmed escapees in Deam's flora, has now been reported from mature woodland communities in at least 20 southern counties. Garlic mustard is our newest problem exotic. Not even known in the state until after 1940, it is quickly becoming established in numerous old-growth forests. The somewhat open oak woodlands of Pokagon State Park are particularly overrun with garlic mustard.

In agricultural settings, the weed battle has long been fought with mechanical control methods and more recently with herbicides. The selective broadleaf herbicide 2,4-D was the first modern herbicide and remains the weapon of choice in "dandelioncide." With mounting concern over chemicals in the environment, as well as the need to find alternate ways to control exotics in natural habitats, ecological and integrated pest management control measures are being investigated. USDA scientists hope, for example, to be able to learn how to use natural insect predators to check the spread of purple loosestrife.

> A particularly obnoxious plant in open wetlands is purple loosestrife. . . . Although attractive when in flower, it has almost no value to wildlife and can spread to the point of becoming the dominant vegetation in a marsh. . . . It is now illegal to plant or spread purple loosestrife in Indiana and in many other states throughout the Midwest.
>
> —*Lee Casebere, "Alien Invaders," in* Outdoor Indiana (1989)

Will this battle between human and plant have an end, or can a truce be reached? The landscape is too dynamic and too intensively managed for the likelihood of a truce. Since the glaciers receded, waves of new species have made their way into the state. The exotics are only the most recent surge of immigrants and, like us, they are here to stay. Also like us, they will continue to adapt to their new home. Already we can see this happening in the evolution of scores of new herbicide-resistant weeds and weeds that mimic the behavior of the crop with which they grow. Exotics have a bright future among us.

As for my own battle to restrain exotic species in a suburban landscape, this week's lawn-mowing skirmish is over. There were no heroes or defeats, no final victories. My weed antagonists, with their rosette form or creeping habit, were only slightly wounded by the blade of the mower. Exhaustion prevents me from mounting a counterattack until the weed threat is again great enough to upset domestic tranquility. For the moment, it's time to find a cool vantage point under my Norway maple tree. From there I can finally enjoy a well-deserved lemonade and survey the temporary manicured beauty that I have created.

> No one really knows how many species have been spreading from their natural homes, but it must be tens of thousands, and of these some thousands have made a noticeable impact on human life. . . . If we look far enough ahead, the eventual state of the biological world will become not more complex but simpler—and poorer. Instead of six continental realms of life . . . there will be only one world.
>
> —*Charles S. Elton, "The Invasion of Continents," in* The Ecology of Invasions by Animals and Plants (1958)

Bush honeysuckle, with its bird-attracting red fruits, has become a widespread plant in forest understories, where it competes successfully with native forest shrubs.   *Photo by Paul Rothrock*

15. Indiana's Vertebrate Fauna: Origins and Change

Ronald L. Richards and John O. Whitaker, Jr.

A prehistoric mastodon
Did not have its glasses on.
It fell across a cliff and died,
Was covered with silt and fossilized.
Now quarts of midnight oil are burned,
Recording all that has been learned.

—Anonymous whimsical poem

BEFORE HUMANS APPEARED

The land that is now Indiana did not always have vertebrate animals. Remains of vertebrates began to occur, sometimes in abundance, as plates and spines of an ancient group of fishes known as the placoderms, or as teeth and spines of ancient sharks in Devonian- and Mississippian-aged rocks. The dark Pennsylvanian-aged shales of Parke County's Mecca Quarry have yielded an abundance of bizarre primitive bony fishes, sharks, and other cartilaginous fishes, along with remains of their meals as "gastric residue masses." Revealing not the preferred crustacean prey but mixtures of scales and bones, these masses are mute evidence of thousands of cannibalistic fishes feeding upon one another after becoming concentrated in seasonally shrinking inland pools some 300 million years ago (mya) on the former coal forest floor. Seen best in X-rays, all of the fossils recovered preserve fishes that were mutilated or bitten in half by other fishes, some of them rather large: A slab from nearby Logan Quarry preserves 8 ½ feet of a 15-to-16-foot shark. But these ancient marine faunas have little relation to those of our modern terrestrial and aquatic communities.

Perhaps great strides toward the development of modern communities were taken along a Pennsylvanian-aged tidal flat, as 12-to-18-inch long amphibians, treading atop burrowing crustaceans, sprawled onto wet tidal sediments in search of insects within view of a humid, equatorial swamp. Rocks from Martin County have yielded impressions of their four-toed front and five-toed rear feet lithified into the crisscrossing trackways, complete with the furrow of their dragging tails. Their bones, however, still elude us.

Yet the Pennsylvanian strata of western Indiana also have revealed different trackways with five-toed, clawed digits, testifying to a much greater event—the presence of reptiles with dry, weather-resistant skin, and having the capacity either to lay eggs independent of water or to bear live young. First discovered in 1874, those few clawed footprints preserve but a small episode of a much larger event, the establishment of vertebrates on land. Their descendants gave rise to dinosaurs, and ultimately to the birds and mammals that populate the world today.

Rocks from the Age of Reptiles (225–65 mya) or for most of the Age of Mammals (65–2 mya)—and hence any fossils from these periods—have long since been eroded away, or they are buried deeply below later sediments. Thus, a great void of fossils occurs in Indiana from those 300 million-year-old Pennsylvanian trackways to the final 100,000 years where once again fossils are available from which to interpret the dramatic changes that have occurred in the vertebrate fauna of our state.

The deeper I delve into natural science the easier it is to see that every created thing has its use . . . and that upon Nature keeping her own balance depends the security of the whole.

—Gene Stratton-Porter

Long-term climatic, geological, and biological processes such as evolution, intercontinental movements, extinction, and various interrelationships among species have greatly affected the composition of our vertebrate fauna. At times during the Age of Mammals (beginning some 65 mya), North America was connected to Asia across the Bering Strait and to South America by the Isthmus of Panama, allowing for extensive intercontinental movements of animals.

Climates in some epochs were uniformly warm-wet throughout the year; at other times pronounced seasons occurred. Habitats underwent considerable vegetational change as well, from the late Cretaceous period, when ginkgos, cycads, conifers, and ferns stood among the rapidly evolving flowering plants and deciduous trees, to recent times, with our familiar prairies, wetlands, and forests.

Under such a range of conditions, and during such a vast period of time, the vertebrate species that composed our faunas changed greatly—sometimes slowly, sometimes in bursts of evolution—to become the assemblage of species we know today.

Fossils of early species of sturgeons and gars, two of Indiana's most ancient vertebrates, appeared during the Cretaceous period near the end of the Age of Reptiles, when dinosaurs last roamed the continent. Bowfins and minnows had evolved earlier in Europe, with bowfin fossils unknown in North America until Eocene times (60 mya). Pike and painted turtles appeared some 35 mya.

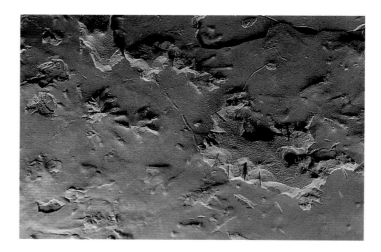

Crisscrossing trackways, discovered in Martin County rocks, record the movements of ancient amphibians about a Pennsylvanian-age tidal flat. Each footprint is about an inch across. Collection of the Indiana State Museum. *Photo courtesy of the Indiana State Museum*

First recognized in Oligocene deposits of Europe (35 mya), Indiana's oldest group of existing mammals, the mouse-eared bats (genus *Myotis*), did not appear in North America until late in the Miocene epoch (about 11 mya). Surprisingly, although the opossum family originated in North America in Cretaceous times, modern opossums moved into North America from South America during the Pliocene, only about 3 mya. The tree squirrels, known from the Oligocene of Europe, were latecomers, arriving in North America only a half-million years ago.

The Miocene epoch (24 to 5 mya) was an important period, producing numerous fish, amphibian, and reptile species similar to those in Indiana today. Several modern species were also present. The leopard frog and eastern spadefoot toad may be the oldest identified vertebrate species that presently inhabit the state. The woodchuck, which is known from deposits 11 million years old, appears to be the oldest modern mammal species that now resides in Indiana. The Miocene closed with a "time of great dying" when about three-fourths of the mammalian genera became extinct.

> Species are only commas in a sentence . . . one merges into another, groups melt into ecological groups until the time when what we know as life meets and enters what we think of as non-life. . . . And the units nestle into the whole and are inseparable from it.
>
> —*Ed Ricketts and John Steinbeck,* The Log from the Sea of Color

The Pliocene epoch (5–1.8 mya) saw the first appearance of numerous modern species of fishes, snakes, and mammals. Of the new mammal genera, approximately two-thirds evolved in North America, a few were immigrants from South America, and most of the remaining were immigrants from Eurasia. About a third of the mammalian genera became extinct at the end of the period.

THEY FOLLOWED THE ICE

The Pleistocene epoch (1.8 million–10,000 years ago) was a time of massive glaciation in northern and temperate regions, during which glacial ice advanced and melted several times during the last million years in what now is Indiana. Glacial movements had a profound effect on Indiana's flora and fauna. During advances some plants and animals died or failed to reproduce, but many emigrated or repopulated in suitable environments south of the ice which had altered, but not necessarily inhospitable, environments (see also chapter 2, "Indiana on Ice").

Glacial oscillations with corresponding sea level changes were accompanied by times of vertebrate movements into North America from Central and South America and from Eurasia, as lowered sea levels exposed continental connections, most notably the Bering land corridor. In addition, there were numerous extinctions of mammals (about one-fifth of the species) some 500,000 years ago, and again at 10,000 to 11,000 years ago, when about one-fourth were lost. During the latter period, heaviest losses were to the larger mammals, eliminating more than half of the 110 North American species fox-sized or larger, including at least 13 Indiana species. The present fauna of Indiana is impoverished when viewed against the diversity of our Ice Age fauna.

> An organism without an environment is inconceivable. A successful organism without a suitable environment is an irrational thought. An organism unable to adjust to a *changing* environment becomes an extinct organism.
>
> —*Frank E. Egler,* American Scientist *(1964)*

Contrary to what is commonly believed, as glaciers recede, both plants and animals quickly move onto de-iced landscapes, rapidly colonizing the glacially minted substrates at the ice margin. Valley glacier on slopes of Mr. Rainier shown here.   *Photo by Marion Jackson*

Our earliest glimpse of Ice Age life in Indiana comes from brittle bones and teeth at least 75,000 to 125,000 years old that were preserved in an ancient crevice in Monroe County. Today this site is hardly recognizable as the wall of a former cave, once entered through a narrow crevice from above. But during the warm Sangamonian interglacial, it served as a den for such large feline carnivores as the beautiful rosette-patterned jaguar and powerful, stalking sabertooth. Their remains were found alongside those of their apparent prey—the extinct Leidy's peccary, a formidable North American relative of the swine.

Other remains include those of the dire wolf, the horse, and such small mammals as the hairy-tailed mole and spotted skunk (neither of which is now present in Indiana). Representing more familiar animals are the remains of woodchuck, prairie vole, white-tailed deer, striped skunk, and coyote, as well as the plains pocket gopher (its habitat now limited to northwestern Indiana) and the eastern woodrat (presently found along the Ohio River bluffs of Harrison and Crawford counties).

While we can only speculate on the actual habitats of extinct mammals such as the sabertooth and peccary, they likely lived in a region cloaked with grasses interspersed with forest on a landscape not too different from present-day southern Indiana. It is not difficult to imagine a huge, solidly built jaguar dragging a young peccary carcass down through the snagging, rocky entrance of the cave, to feed in the twilight there, while crouched upon a cool slab of Salem limestone.

But the best indicators of past environmental conditions are the associated remains of such small grassland mammals as the prairie vole, southern bog lemming, and plains pocket gopher, since we can study where and how the living relatives of these animals exist today. The types of animals present indicate that, in the midst of the generally cool ice ages, interglacial periods were decidedly warmer than today.

Throughout the United States, Ice Age communities often contained assemblages of organisms that no longer coexist, and that often appeared to have different ecological tolerances. For example, the heather vole, a rodent of the boreal forest region of Canada and western United States, occurs in several Indiana fossil deposits with

American mastodont
Mammut americanum
x

Harlan's musk-ox
Bootherium bombifrons
x

Dire wolf
Canis dirus
x

Giant beaver
Castoroides ohioensis
x

Tundra (modern) musk-ox
Ovibos moschatus
M

Giant short-faced
Arctodus simus
x

Jefferson's ground sloth
Megalonyx jeffersonii
x

Pleistocene jaguar
Felis onca augusta
M C

Pleistocene horse
Equus
x

Tapir
Tapirus
x

Large

The large animal remains found in Indiana date from 10,000
years of the North American Ice Age. Most of the large anima
years ago. At that time, some animals like the tundra musk-c
the bison and black bear, changed into smaller forms at the e

imals From Indiana's Ice Age

black bear
ricanus

Long-snouted peccary
Mylohyus nasutus
x

Flat-headed peccary
Platygonus compressus
x

Leidy's peccary
Platygonus vetus
x

Beautiful armadillo
Dasypus bellus
x

Jefferson's mammoth
Mammuthus columbi jeffersonii
x

Stag-moose
Cervalces scotti
x

Sabertooth
Smilodon fatalis
x

Giant land tortoise
Geochelone
x

Caribou
Rangifer tarandus
M

Ancient bison
Bison bison antiquus
C

000 years old. This represents only the later part of the 1.8 million
the mastodont, mammoth, and sabertooth, became extinct by 10,000
and jaguar migrated to the north and south. Other animals, such as
e Age.

 EXTINCT   **MIGRATED**   **CHANGED - DEVELOPED INTO SMALLER VARIETIES**

Indiana State Museum
202 North Alabama Street
Indianapolis, IN 46204
(317) 232-1637
Free Admission

Mammalian species recorded from Indiana, Ice Age to present

	Interglacial		Glacial	Prehistoric	Settlement	Present
	(125,000 YBP*)	(75,000 YBP*)	(10,000 YBP*)		(A.D. 1800)	

Species	Range / Dates
Woodchuck; Southern bog lemming; Prairie vole; Woodrat; Pocket gopher; Gray fox; Coyote; Bobcat; Striped skunk	Interglacial → Present
Horse; Dire wolf	Interglacial → Glacial
Hairy-tailed mole	Interglacial → Prehistoric
Black bear	Interglacial → 1850
White-tailed deer	Interglacial → 1934—
Spotted skunk	Interglacial → —1920
Jaguar; Sabertooth; Leidy's peccary	Interglacial (early)
Common and Star-nosed moles; Pygmy, Smoky, Masked, Least, and Short-tailed shrews; Myotis and Big brown bats; Pipistrelle; 13-lined, Gray, Red, Fox, and Flying squirrels; Chipmunk; Meadow and Pine voles; Jumping mouse; Cottontail; Long-tailed weasel; Muskrat; Peromyscus; Mink; Badger; Raccoon	Glacial → Present
Arctic and Long-tailed shrews; Jefferson's ground sloth; Northern bog lemming; Heather and Yellow-cheeked voles; Giant beaver; Snowshoe hare; Mastodon; Jefferson's mammoth; Hay's tapir; Flat-headed and Long-nosed peccaries; Caribou; Stag-moose; Ancient bison; Harlan's muskox; Barren ground muskox; Giant short-faced bear; Red-backed vole; Beautiful armadillo	Glacial (segment)
Rice rat	Glacial → Prehistoric
Fisher	Glacial → 1859
Porcupine	Glacial → 1918
River otter	Glacial → 1942 1993—
Beaver	Glacial → 1840 1932———
Big-eared bat	Glacial → 1962
Opossum; Southeastern shrew	Prehistoric → Present
Elk	Prehistoric → 1830
Mountain lion	Prehistoric → 1851
Plains bison; Canada lynx; Red wolf	—1830–1832
Timber wolf	Prehistoric → 1908
Wolverine	—1852
Silver-haired, Red, and Hoary bats; Franklin's ground squirrel; Swamp rabbit; Red fox; Least weasel	Settlement → Present
House mouse; Norway rat	1800———
Black rat	1845
Evening bat	1942———
Western harvest mouse	1969———
Gray bat	1982———

*YBP = years before present

Note: Table 2 indicates the first and last occurrence of a species in Indiana, though the species may not have continuously inhabited the state during that period; most glacial records are less than 35,000 years old. The lack of early dates for many species is due to a lack of identified fossils, and does not necessarily indicate that a species was not present in earlier periods.

Mammalian species recorded from Indiana, Ice Age to present

the plains pocket gopher, an animal of open regions of the central United States. The ranges of the two animals are virtually exclusive today. These mixed assemblages seem to have occurred because Late Pleistocene climates were more equable than at present, with winters often less cold and summers less hot, resulting in less climatic restraint.

Since each species responds individually to environmental changes through its own physiological tolerances, habitat requirements, and competition, rather than collectively, animal communities are not of fixed composition. Instead they restructure in response to environmental change, including the influx or exodus of species. Knowing this, and given the possibility that human-induced environmental alternations could approach those that occurred as a result of glaciation, ecologists should carefully select and design natural areas to be preserved, including adequate habitat linking them. This will permit species to track environmental change and not be as vulnerable to extirpation, as is the case for smaller "island" preserves.

Much of Indiana's vertebrate story is preserved in sediments of Wisconsinan glacial age. At its maximum, about 18,000 to 20,000 years ago, Wisconsinan ice spread southward only through the northern two-thirds of Indiana, sparing the caves and hill country of the south. Many of these caves accumulated animal remains for thousands of years. Perhaps the best (and certainly the longest) faunal sequence is from Megenity Peccary Cave in Crawford County, where the largest sample in existence of the extinct flat-headed peccary has been recovered.

The oldest bones dated have an age of 50,700 years B.P. (before the present), but the deeper deposits extend back thousands of years beyond the range of radiocarbon dating. Older remains include an undated shell fragment of a giant land tortoise. Because they develop fatal enteritis in cold conditions, resulting in the inability to digest food, giant tortoises cannot survive in cool environments. This suggests that winters must have been frost-free (i.e., an interglacial period) when this tortoise inhabited Indiana.

Several chambers in Megenity Peccary Cave preserved different parts of the fossil sequence. One room contained remains of heather and red-backed voles, fisher, and plains pocket gopher in strata about 31,000 years old. These animals suggest open parklands with stands of conifer forest and perhaps an understory of heath. That was also the time when at least two adult peccaries tumbled over a 20-

The flat-headed peccary, a browsing pig-like animal, was apparently prevalent in Indiana during the Ice Age. This fine skull is from a Crawford County cave. Collection of the Indiana State Museum.
Fred Lewis photo, courtesy of the Indiana State Museum

foot precipice onto the muddy cave floor below. Neither died immediately; they crawled up on a clay bank, where, alongside remains of voles, fisher, and gophers, their bones were eventually buried and preserved. These remains and those of more than 400 other flat-headed peccaries were but incidental losses from the herds that sheltered in the entrance and nearby passages of the cave over thousands of years. Far greater losses were probably inflicted through the rigors of daily existence and by such predators as coyote, dire wolf, and large cats. A second chamber in the cave preserved the fine skull and skeleton of a dire wolf entrapped with accompanying peccaries, black bear, river otter, and snowshoe hare at the bottom of a 20-foot-deep pit some 25,500 years ago.

> Nature is often hidden, sometimes overcome, seldom extinguished.
>
> —*Francis Bacon,* Of Nature and Men

Higher in the chamber's sediment column (14,100 B.P.), an abundant and diverse assortment of frogs and small mammals such as yellow-cheeked, heather, and red-backed voles, northern bog lemmings, and arctic shrews was found. None of these mammals is present in Indiana today, but all occur farther to the north. The yellow-cheeked vole is found today in open conifer forests near the edge of the tundra some 1,200 miles to the north.

At the same time (14,000–15,000 B.P.), bones were accumulating at the Prairie Creek site in Daviess County. Formed in a glacial lake that teemed with fishes, frogs, snakes, turtles, muskrat, and mink, this deposit was later flushed from the basin and redeposited downstream in the bed of Prairie Creek. Animals in nearby habitats included the Jefferson's ground sloth, mastodon, dire wolf, giant beaver, long-snouted peccary, and beautiful armadillo, all of which are now extinct, as well as yellow-cheeked and red-backed voles. Pollen studies suggest mixed stands of deciduous and boreal forests surrounding the marshes and meadows.

This deposit contained thousands of turtle bones, suggesting summers as warm as those of the Central Great Lakes region today, since turtle eggs require extended summer warmth to hatch. The presence of the copperbelly water snake and hieroglyphic turtle, both temperate and southern forms today, further suggests relatively mild conditions beyond the ice.

The remains of isolated mammoths, mastodons, and musk-oxen are often found in sand and gravel deposited by rivers and streams that once flowed from the base of stagnating ice fields. Some remains, such as those of a Jefferson's mammoth found at Alton in Crawford County, were deposited in quiet-water "overbank" sediments along a major river. Others, such as many of our heavily abraded musk-oxen skulls and numerous mastodon bones found by mussel fishermen in the East Fork of the White River, were deposited in active glacial river beds, transported perhaps many miles from the original death site.

During the final phase of Indiana's Ice Age, glacial meltback produced large stagnating ice fields, often leaving remnant ice masses partially buried in sediment. When these ice blocks melted, the resulting depressions or "kettles" often filled with meltwaters, developing lake and marsh communities. Over time, the lake basins filled with sediment and plant remains and developed into bogs or fens. Layers of marl (calcareous clay) frequently occur near the base of the kettle lake deposits and are often stippled with a bewildering array of snails and minute clams. Marl occasionally harbors the remains of fishes, turtles, and even mastodons. The upper peaty soils of the vegetation-choked, marshy lake basins usually produce muskrat, beaver, deer, elk, and turtle bones, and occasionally the remains of large extinct mammals.

Folklore relates that most bogs larger than an acre or so probably

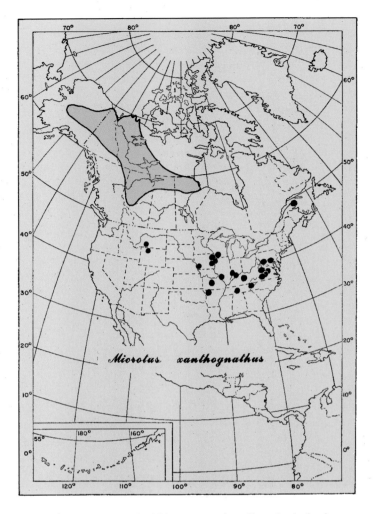

During the Ice Age some 14,000 years ago, the yellow-cheeked vole was displaced more than 1,200 miles south of its modern range into Crawford County, Indiana, and to other midwestern localities. Modern range in yellow, fossil localities as black dots.

contain the bones of at least one mastodon, perhaps a truism since more than 250 mastodon sites are known in Indiana, with many from lake and bog deposits.

At the Kolarik locality in Starke County, a mastodon skeleton was uncovered by a dragline operation in a peat deposit. About 11,000–12,000 years ago, this northern Indiana site was a small kettle lake surrounded by open spruce parklands. Lined with luxuriant pondweed and other vegetation, it teemed with snails, clams, and other invertebrates. Darting about the lake were huge northern pike, while yellow perch and sunfishes hovered among the concealing vegetation. Meadow voles networked their runways among the surrounding grasslands, while leopard frogs sat camouflaged along the shore.

How the mastodon became buried is unknown. Perhaps it died in summer and its bloated carcass floated about the lake, sloughing off parts of the skeleton. This could account for the absence of its huge skull, dense lower jaw, and massive rear leg. Or perhaps the animal died in winter, cracking through thin ice into the frigid water below. We are probably overlooking clues on many sites that will provide us with future answers.

> In Nature's infinite book of secrecy
> A little I can read.
>
> —*Shakespeare*

With more than 22 species of large mammals, Indiana's Ice Age fauna might have appeared as diverse as that of the historic African plains. Jefferson's mammoth was common; its teeth and bones have been found at more than 100 sites. While the mammoth and the mastodon look similar, only the mammoth is a true elephant.

The teeth bear this out. Mammoth teeth, like modern elephants', are composed of a long row of plates, resulting in a file-like crown adapted for grazing. Over hundreds of thousands of years, these teeth progressively developed into efficient vegetation-shearing rasps to reduce abrasive grasses into pulp. Teeth of the mastodon are quite different, bearing a series of conical tubercles used for chopping and crushing bark, twigs, and leaves while browsing. Mammoth remains are less abundant in Indiana than those of mastodons, probably because there was less grassland during glacial periods to serve as

Isolated remains of mastodons are known from more than 250 localities in Indiana. More complete skeletons, such as this composite skeleton mounted in the Joseph Moore Museum, Earlham College, are much less common.
Fred Lewis photo, courtesy of the Indiana State Museum

Mastodon teeth are perhaps the most commonly recovered of Ice Age fossils from Indiana. Tooth tubercules permitted effective browsing on woody vegetation. Collection of the Indiana State Museum.
Fred Lewis photo, courtesy of the Indiana State Museum

Mammoth teeth are also commonly recovered from Indiana deposits. Composed of a series of enamel-coated plates, they allowed for sustained wear during the shredding of abrasive grasses. Collection of the Indiana State Museum. *Fred Lewis photo, courtesy of the Indiana State Museum*

mammoth habitat than open conifer forests and swamps where mastodons were apt to populate.

Judging from the large number of fossils recovered, northern Indiana was also excellent habitat for another huge resident, the giant beaver. With characteristic "flutes" on the large incisor teeth and a longer, narrower tail than that of the modern beaver, large specimens reached nearly nine feet in length. This beaver may have behaved more like a giant muskrat than a beaver, since there is little evidence that it built dams or felled trees.

The long-snouted peccary, with a long, slender face and similarly proportioned legs, was nearly the size of a small white-tailed deer. Its remains have been found at a few Indiana localities. Remains of the stag-moose, represented in Indiana by portions of several antlers,

attest to an animal which possessed a moose's body and the muzzle of an elk. Harlan's musk-ox, with notable downward and forward-facing horns, was rather common in Indiana. The ancient bison, a direct ancestor of the modern plains bison, is represented in Indiana by one magnificent skull, displaying horncores that project characteristically at right angles.

One of the most complete skeletons in existence of perhaps the most powerful predator of the Ice Age was recovered from northern Indiana. The giant short-faced bear was as tall as a small horse, standing an incredible five feet, two inches at the shoulder while walking on all fours. Like many bears, it could feed on vegetation, but its long legs and powerful jaws also gave it the speed, vision, and armament to prey upon such large animals as bison or sloth.

Fossil horse remains from Indiana are few, partly because they are easily mistaken for modern horse remains, and because Indiana has not had a long history of open grassland environments.

Fossil teeth of tapirs and shell plates of armadillos suggest mild climates during parts of the ice ages. Fossils recovered from adjacent states suggest that other animals, now gone, were present in Indiana's Ice Age, including the water shrew, northern flying squirrel, grizzly bear, pine marten, Harlan's ground sloth, and wide-browed bison.

An interesting feature of Ice Age faunas is that some species were larger than their modern counterparts. The ancient bison, the beautiful armadillo, the black bear, the jaguar, and the giant beaver were notably larger than today's plains bison, nine-banded armadillo, recent black bear and jaguar, and modern beaver. The reason for such size differences is not clear but may be related to seasonal availability of food, the density of populations in some herbivores, and, in the case of carnivorous mammals, the size of both available prey and competing predators.

The glacial lake and bog deposits of northern and central Indiana and the cave sediments of the south give a unique perspective on the vertebrate life of the Ice Age. Although several fossil finds are reported to museums and universities each year, many still are destroyed by human activity and go unreported.

HAPPY HUNTING GROUND

We remember a place in time—in human consciousness. We were there. A hundred centuries ago we came upon a vast drowned land. It seemed we walked into a foreverness of lakes and marshes. . . . Far to the north and east the blue-gray paternal ice still lay a half-mile thick at summer's end . . . a great wind-howl roared from the frozen waste, swept over gravel tundra, across the withered sedge and stunted trees. Sounds of wind still haunt us with old meanings.

—*Robert O. Petty, from an unpublished manuscript*

Major changes occurred around 10,000 to 11,000 years ago, one of the most dynamic periods in Indiana's prehistory. A rapidly changing climate, mass extinctions, biotic reorganization, and the arrival of humans occurred in less than two millennia. No longer did mastodons browse in the swampy lowlands, giant beavers plunge into vegetation-choked lakes, or mammoths lumber through windy grasslands. Dire wolves no longer trembled nervously downwind of browsing peccaries, scanning the herd for injured animals or stray young.

The climate was now warmer and with greater seasonality. Forests became increasingly dominated by deciduous trees such as oak, hickory, beech, and maple. Paleo-Indian hunters were now present, having arrived at least 13,000 years ago.

Massive extinctions had suddenly eliminated many of the large mammals. In contrast to the situation in earlier epochs, there were no new species to take their places. There were also drastic range alterations for many other mammals. Gone were the arctic shrew, heather and yellow-cheeked voles, and northern bog lemming, as well as the caribou and tundra musk-ox—all displaced to the north, soon to be followed by the red-backed vole, hairy-tailed mole, and snowshoe hare.

There are several possible explanations for the extinction of large mammals at the end of the Ice Age, with environmental change and overhunting by Paleo-Indians leading the list. The evidence that major environmental changes occurred and that biotas were reorganized is overwhelming.

There are few good associations of ancient humans with extinct animals east of the Mississippi River. A characteristic tool of Paleo-Indians is the Clovis point, which has been recovered by archaeologists at several western mammoth kill sites.

> They lunged their spears. . . . Realization came slowly to the exhausted men. In the sudden silence, the hunters looked at each other. Their hearts beat faster in a new kind of excitement. . . . They did it! They killed the mighty mammoth! . . . [They] had killed the gigantic creature no other predator could.
>
> —*Jean M. Auel,* The Clan of the Cave Bear *(1980)*

Clovis points are frequently found in Indiana, but neither they nor any other cultural debris has been found with remains of Ice Age animals in the state, although it is widely believed that these Native Americans hunted large now-extinct mammals in Indiana (perhaps contributing to the animals' extirpation), or at least scavenged their carcasses.

The 10 millennia that have elapsed since the Ice Age are the dark ages of Indiana's vertebrate history. The story is traced largely by remains from archaeological sites and from undated cave deposits. Although climates changed some during this period, we are not certain how much such changes affected Indiana's vertebrates.

From their earliest entry into North America, Native Americans had some dependency upon vertebrate animals. Such contingency ranged from hunting and gathering societies that relied heavily upon vertebrates for food to agricultural societies that used vertebrates as a supplement to their harvest.

In Indiana, animal remains have been recovered from Native American sites dating back thousands of years and up to the time of European settlement. What species were utilized? Were there major effects upon the animal populations? Generally, the largest vertebrates were used, since they produced the greatest meat yields. Archaeological sites often abound with bones of white-tailed deer, raccoon, gray and fox squirrels, beaver, and muskrat, along with some remains of black bear, elk, eastern cottontail, woodchuck, and Virginia opossum. Noteworthy is the presence of the domestic dog, brought with Native Americans from Asia. Leading the list of birds are wild turkey, Canada goose, and larger ducks. Remains of the passenger pigeon, now extinct, are also commonly recovered.

Other species are usually present, with snapping, softshell, and eastern box turtles almost always the most abundant of turtle remains. Bones of large fish such as bowfin, buffalo, catfish, gar, bullhead, sucker, bass, and freshwater drum are sometimes common in middens. Moles and various mice appear in small numbers. The bones of some species were used as tools or implements, such as deer shin-bone awls and box-turtle bowls, or as decorations, such as carnivore teeth or jaw pendants.

We gain a different perspective of Indiana's prehistoric fauna by examining natural (non-cultural) sites. From 8,000 to 4,000 B.P. the Plains States endured a warm, dry period referred to as the Hypsithermal Interval. According to pollen records, prairie achieved its maximum extent into northwestern Indiana about 5,000 years ago. We have no dated natural faunas from this period, so we are uncertain of the impact of prairie upon vertebrates in Indiana.

Surprisingly, we actually have stronger indicators of open environments (e.g., the bones of thirteen-lined ground squirrels and plains pocket gophers) during the Ice Age than at any period since. Deposits from 4,140 to 2,880 B.P. from the Prairie Creek site show essentially the same fishes, snakes, turtles, birds, and mammals as are present today, although Blanding's turtle and the star-nosed mole were south of their modern Indiana ranges. Numerous fossils of this same period from Freeman's Pit in Monroe County (2,315 B.P.) also show a modern fauna, including the porcupine, spotted skunk, and black bear, all of which are extirpated today.

While most faunas of this period include present-day Indiana species, several animals were distributed differently than they are now. Throughout prehistoric times and earlier, the eastern woodrat was found throughout Indiana's cave region (as far north as Shelby County), well north of its present Ohio River bluff distribution. The opossum arrived from the south in the last 10,000 years. Although remains of the red fox are known from numerous sites of late glacial age in many other eastern states, its range seems to have shifted to the north during the prehistoric period. There are few if any prehistoric or older records for Indiana.

The modern plains bison appears to be a rather late addition to Indiana's fauna, arriving from the western plains between about A.D. 1450 and 1600, as evidenced by a few remains at archaeological sites and by numerous historical accounts. The scanty remains from natural sites are undated.

Although the rice rat does not exist in Indiana today, bones in two caves and from the Angel Mounds archaeological site in southwestern Indiana proclaim its past presence. Some believe that it was a pest in corn-growing Native American communities. Most elements of our present fauna were probably in place about 9,000 to 10,000 years ago, around the close of the Ice Age.

Apparently Native Americans had little permanent effect upon vertebrate populations in Indiana. They do not appear to have affected populations of the passenger pigeon, Carolina parakeet, beaver, elk, black bear, mountain lion, and others which declined rapidly following European settlement.

> Whatever befalls the earth befalls the sons of the earth. Man did not weave the web of life, he is merely a strand in it. Whatever he does to the web, he does to himself.
>
> —*Chief Seattle*

CHANGING LANDSCAPES

Pre-settlement Indiana was cloaked in either extensive forest, predominantly beech-maple in the north and oak-hickory in the south, or prairie, especially in the northwest and along waterways. Wetlands were extensive, with swamps in the forested areas and marshes in the prairies.

European settlement ushered in the beginning of a series of changes to the vertebrate fauna that are still in progress, the ultimate results of which may not be known for many years. Clearing the land for farming destroyed much of the original forest and most of the prairie, especially in the northern part of the state. Native animals that could not adapt either emigrated or were extirpated. Fewer changes occurred in the unglaciated south-central portion of the state. The red fox appears to have expanded its range southward again with the clearing of forests. The thirteen-lined ground squirrel

Passenger pigeons, which formerly occurred in incredible numbers in Indiana, were gone from the state by 1902, and from the Earth by 1914. This specimen was taken in Wayne County, Indiana, prior to 1869.
Fred Lewis photo, courtesy of the Indiana State Museum

Wild turkey, once extirpated from Indiana, were reintroduced and now occur in widespread, huntable populations.
Photo by John Maxwell

Prairie-chickens persisted in Indiana until the 1970s, but no longer occur here, largely because of wide-scale land-use changes.
Photo by Marion Jackson

Ringneck pheasants were widely introduced in many areas of North America, including Indiana. They still occur here in huntable numbers, but are less common now than formerly. They may partially fill the niche vacated by the prairie-chicken.
Photo by Delano Z. Arvin

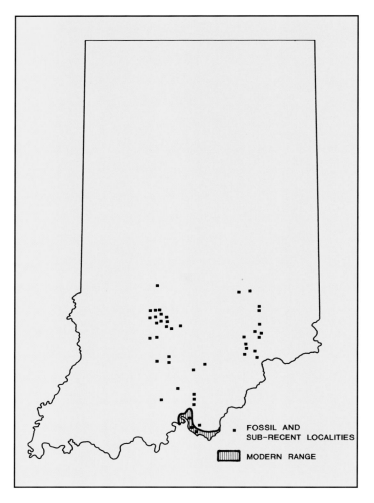

Currently the eastern woodrat occupies but a small part of its former range in Indiana

FOSSIL AND
SUB-RECENT LOCALITIES

MODERN RANGE

mountain lion (1851), wolverine (1852), fisher (1859), harlequin darter (1890), crystal darter (1892–95), mud snake (1894), stargazing darter (1900), timber wolf (1908), Great Lakes muskellunge (1910), porcupine (1918), spotted skunk (1920), river otter (1942), big-eared bat (last record 1962), and southeastern bat (last record 1971). The smallmouth bass, nearly exterminated around the turn of the century, is in trouble today because of increased pollution. The alligator snapping turtle was supposedly extirpated in 1935, but unexpectedly, a specimen was caught in the White River at Martinsville in 1991.

Birds that no longer nest here include the Carolina parakeet (1845; extinct ca. 1920), ivory-billed woodpecker (1859), Eskimo curlew (late 1800s), common loon (1893), trumpeter swan (1897), wild turkey (about 1900, but now successfully reintroduced), whooping crane (1905), passenger pigeon (extinct 1914), common tern (1936), Wilson's phalarope (1941), double-crested cormorant (1953), piping plover (1955), Forster's tern (1962), and greater prairie chicken (1972). The prairie chicken occurred in the northwestern half of the state at the turn of the century, but survived in only seven counties by 1950, with the last bird disappearing in 1972.

> The destruction of the wild pigeon and the Carolina parakeet has meant a loss as sad as if the Catskills or the Palisades were taken away.
>
> —*Theodore Roosevelt, Letter to Audubon Society president Frank M. Chapman (1899)*

There are secondary effects from removal of some species. Both the beaver and the white-tailed deer were extirpated from Indiana by

profited from land clearing, building large populations on mowed areas and expanding its range from the northwestern third of the state in 1909 to include the northern half by 1982. This was not its first expansion, for Ice Age cave fossils are known from several counties bordering the Ohio River.

Another human effect was the killing of animals for food or for protection of family, domestic animals, or crops. The black bear, mountain lion, timber wolf, river otter, beaver, white-tailed deer, and elk had maintained good populations prior to being eradicated.

Pollution has had a major impact. Factory wastes, fertilizers, pesticides, and other pollutants implanted in the soil, then concentrated in the waterways during recent decades, have greatly reduced habitat quality, and the related diversity and abundance of animals that rely upon those environments.

> The story of our nation in the last century as regards the use of forests, grasslands, wildlife and water resources is the most violent and the most destructive of any written in the long history of civilization.
>
> —*Fairfield Osborn, Our Plundered Planet (1948)*

An overall result of human activity has been the expansion of human habitat with a resulting decimation of natural habitats and reduction of vertebrate diversity. Many species have disappeared from Indiana in recent years. These include the bison (1830), elk, red wolf, and lynx (1832), black bear (1850, but one report in 1888),

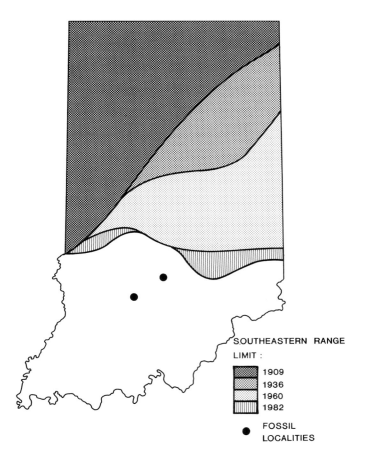

SOUTHEASTERN RANGE
LIMIT :
1909
1936
1960
1982

● FOSSIL LOCALITIES

Expanding distribution pattern of the thirteen-lined ground squirrel southeastward across Indiana during the twentieth century.

the turn of the century, but were reintroduced. Today, with an increase in forest-edge habitat and the absence of such large predators as wolves, mountain lions, and Native American hunters, deer have again become abundant. They have become major pests in some areas, particularly in state parks, where no hunting is allowed and overbrowsing of plants is serious. Often cascading changes occur in ecosystems as a result of removal of keystone species, especially large predators. Long-term, the consequences are often serious, but largely unrecognized.

The wild turkey is another reintroduced species which now is present in huntable populations in many counties. Attempts are being made to reintroduce the bald eagle, peregrine falcon, and river otter, and some consideration has been given to reintroduction of the porcupine and muskellunge.

Certain species have become more abundant with human restructuring of natural environments, including the prairie deer mouse, which requires areas of very sparse vegetation. Before settlement, it probably occurred mainly in the dry, open sandy barrens. Today it is one of only two species that are common in the cultivated cornfields of the Midwest and the only one that remains when the crops are harvested or the land is plowed. Some of our most common bats now normally live in buildings. One wonders where they roosted before there were buildings. Perhaps they were less abundant then.

NATURAL EXPANSIONS

The western harvest mouse rapidly extended its range across northern Illinois in the 1950s and 1960s, reached Willow Slough Fish and Wildlife Area in Newton County, Indiana, by 1969, and had invaded seven Indiana counties by 1975, and several more by 1996. Possibly another recent immigrant is the gray bat, although cave remains suggest that it may have occurred here all along. A maternity colony of about 400 individuals was discovered in an abandoned quarry in Clark County in 1982, suggesting that this colony was established by the early 1970s.

The house finch, a native of western North America, became established in the east, and as of the last few years commonly nests in Indiana. Originally from Africa and now common in southern states, the cattle egret is occasionally sighted in Indiana and may become established as a nesting species if it has not already.

> Civilization is a state of mutual and interdependent cooperation between human animals, other animals, plants and soils, which may be disrupted at any moment by the failure of anyone of them.
>
> —*Aldo Leopold,* Game Management *(1933)*

Presently extending their ranges into Indiana are several native North American species of fish, including the white perch, alewife, sea lamprey, and three-spine stickleback, which arrived in Lake Michigan via the lower Great Lakes from the eastern seaboard. The Welland Canal, completed in 1929, gave them open passage. The sea lamprey was discovered in Lake Michigan in 1936, and the alewife was first taken in Indiana waters in 1958, whereas the white perch and stickleback have arrived within the past 15 years. The suckermouth minnow occurred mainly west of the Mississippi River before 1800, but David Starr Jordan took it from the White River in 1876; by the early 1940s it was widely distributed in Indiana.

ALIEN ANIMALS

Exotics often escape or are liberated from captivity. Monkeys, lions, alligators, boa constrictors, parrots, and many other species

The house finch is native to the western United States, but is now common in much of Indiana.   *Photo by Michael Ray Brown*

have been found living in the wild in our state. Most do not become established. Exotics should not be introduced because it is not possible to predict how they will interact with native forms. Introductions of some exotic species such as the rabbit into Australia and mongoose into Hawaii have led to biological disasters.

The carp was introduced into Indiana in the late 1870s, and the goldfish about a decade later. Goldfish were used extensively as bait in the 1930s and 1940s. Carp have done well on their own, but goldfish establish reproducing populations only in highly polluted waters where other fish are scarce.

Some exotics have been successfully introduced. The ringneck pheasant was a welcome addition for the hunters and birders of our state, as the brown trout has been for fishermen. Pheasant releases were initiated in Indiana in 1899, culminating in their establishment as a game species. Dating from a shipment to a fish hatchery in Michigan in 1885, the brown trout was introduced in Indiana and still exists in very few self-reproducing populations.

An efficient plant feeder, the grass carp was brought into the United States by the U.S. Fish and Wildlife Service in 1963 for possible use in aquatic plant control. Escapees made their way into Indiana through the Ohio River, and were also illegally stocked in ponds. Recently the ban on grass carp was lifted in Indiana.

Several other fish species have been intentionally introduced, including brook and rainbow trout, coho and chinook salmon, striped bass, and rainbow smelt. Native to northeastern North America, smelt were stocked in Crystal Lake, Michigan, in 1921, but soon dispersed into Lake Michigan. They reached Michigan City, Indiana, by 1930, entering the commercial catch by 1937.

Accidentally introduced to Indiana were a number of unwelcome pests—exotic birds and rodents. The former include the European starling, which was first seen in 1919; the English or house sparrow, which was first reported in 1867; the rock dove, our familiar pigeon, whose time of arrival is unknown; and the house finch, which took up residence in just the last few years.

> It is easy for people to hate starlings, we dislike their aggressive behavior toward birds of milder manner, their gluttonous consumption of farm and garden products intended for human nourishment, their habit of congregating in massive, noisy flocks to feed or roost; and even their swaggering walk. But, most of all, people despise starlings for their unbounded fecundity, because starlings do nothing in moderation.
>
> —*George Laycock,* The Alien Animals *(1966)*

Accidentally introduced rodents include the black rat, collected at Indianapolis in the 1800s, which did not become established; the Norway rat, which inflicts millions of dollars in damage annually to stored food and occasionally injures humans; and, of course, now the most abundant small mammal in Indiana—the house mouse. Though often pesky infesters of houses, house mice also inhabit corn, wheat, and soybean fields of the state where cover is adequate, and are beneficial when in those habitats by feeding heavily on cutworms and other insect larvae and on weed seeds.

OVERVIEW

The present vertebrate fauna of Indiana is the result of evolution, migration, interaction of species, and extinction, all in context with changing environments and the activities of humans. Though some of these species are geologically quite ancient, most of the current vertebrate association is relatively recent—less than 10,000 years old. A small component is less than 200 years old. Vertebrates displayed great diversity during the Wisconsinan glacial phases, followed by massive extinctions and biotic reorganization at the end of the Ice Age. Vertebrates appear to have "held their own" during the prehistoric millennia, only to suffer selective annihilation, abundance, and distribution changes beginning with the settlement period.

Human population increase and technological advance have brought about not only "environmental" compromises in the expanding human habitat, but also some of the most critical problems facing natural vertebrate communities: decreasing diversity and habitat reduction. Thirty-two vertebrate species have been extirpated from Indiana in the last two centuries, and many others are now endangered or threatened.

Human activities have imposed some of the swiftest, most critical limiting factors to natural vertebrate communities in their history, despite our increasing conservation efforts. The species that we have lost can never be replaced. Will we enter the twenty-second century with many vertebrates other than the house mouse, Norway rat, starling, and carp? Will Indiana eventually become a land that only "once upon a time" had wild, free-ranging vertebrate animals?

> Living as we do in a world which has been largely denuded of all the large and interesting wild mammals, we are usually denied the chance of seeing very big animals in very big numbers. If we think of [bison] at all, we think of them as "the [bison]" (in a zoo) and not as twenty thousand [bison] moving along in a vast herd.
>
> —*Charles Elton,* Animal Ecology *(1927)*

Part 2: The Natural Regions of Indiana

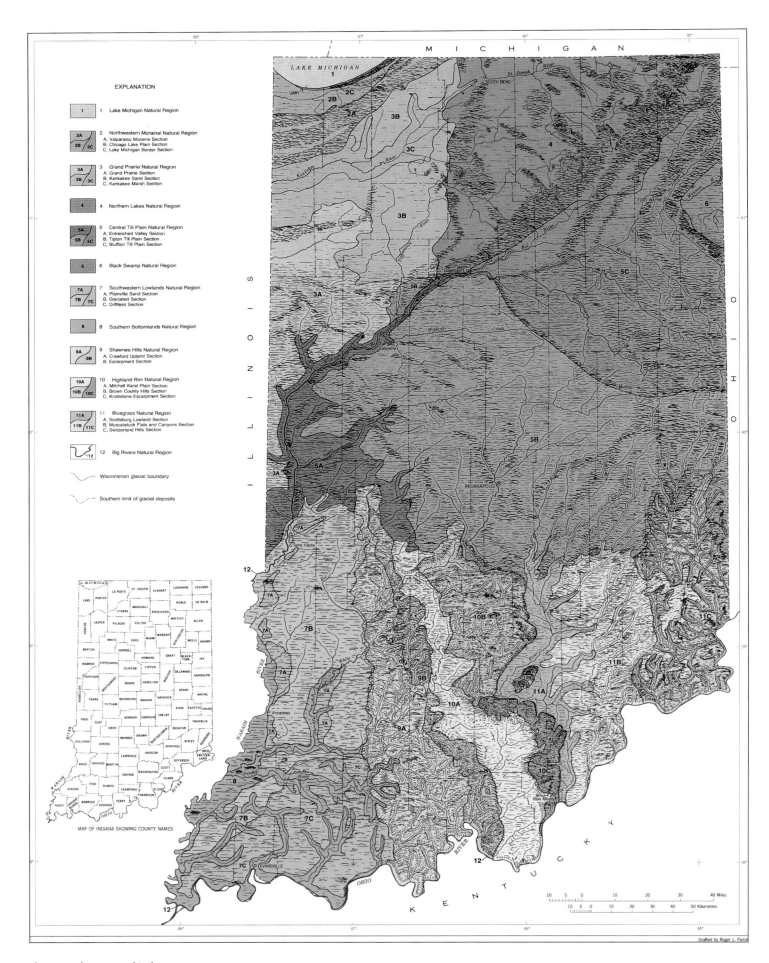

EXPLANATION

1 Lake Michigan Natural Region

2 Northwestern Morainal Natural Region
   A, Valparaiso Moraine Section
   B, Chicago Lake Plain Section
   C, Lake Michigan Border Section

3 Grand Prairie Natural Region
   A, Grand Prairie Section
   B, Kankakee Sand Section
   C, Kankakee Marsh Section

4 Northern Lakes Natural Region

5 Central Till Plain Natural Region
   A, Entrenched Valley Section
   B, Tipton Till Plain Section
   C, Bluffton Till Plain Section

6 Black Swamp Natural Region

7 Southwestern Lowlands Natural Region
   A, Plainville Sand Section
   B, Glaciated Section
   C, Driftless Section

8 Southern Bottomlands Natural Region

9 Shawnee Hills Natural Region
   A, Crawford Upland Section
   B, Escarpment Section

10 Highland Rim Natural Region
    A, Mitchell Karst Plain Section
    B, Brown County Hills Section
    C, Knobstone Escarpment Section

11 Bluegrass Natural Region
    A, Scottsburg Lowland Section
    B, Muscatatuck Flats and Canyons Section
    C, Switzerland Hills Section

12 Big Rivers Natural Region

Wisconsinan glacial boundary

Southern limit of glacial deposits

MAP OF INDIANA SHOWING COUNTY NAMES

Drafted by Roger L. Purcell

The Natural Regions of Indiana   Map by Michael A. Homoya

16. The Natural Regions of Indiana: An Introduction

Michael A. Homoya

The book of nature is open for all to read, yet few look into it; fewer try to understand what is written.

    —*Goethe*

When typical interstate travelers are asked to describe the landscape features that they observed during their pass through Indiana, they commonly answer with such terms as "flat," "monotonous," or even "boring." But those who have driven the back roads will vigorously disagree with such assessments, because upon closer inspection, Indiana is rich in topographic, geologic, and biological diversity. These "back road" looks, taken by the many people who have lived in and/or studied our state, have been compiled, analyzed, and ultimately organized by ecologists into units entitled "natural regions."

Natural regions are large delineations of the landscape where a distinctive and somewhat cohesive combination of natural features occurs. Such features include physiography (landforms) and types of soil, exposed bedrock, climate, vegetation, flora, and fauna. Subsets of these regions are called "sections." Sections of a natural region have enough differences between them that recognition is warranted, but the differences are not as great as between regions. Another useful subdivision is made at the natural community level. Natural communitites are assemblages of plants and animals interacting with their environment. They are what is seen in the immediate vicinity, in contrast to the "outer space" view needed to see a natural region. Examples of communities are mesic upland forest, wet prairie, glade, bog, and sandstone cliff.

To understand how all of these divisions relate to one another, let us construct a table model and fashion it in the shape of Indiana. The tabletop represents our portion of the earth. On the table we position 12 differently shaped puzzles, all meeting evenly along their edges to cover the entire table. Each puzzle represents one natural region. Within the puzzles are several colored puzzle pieces, where green represents forest, yellow equals grassland, blue equals water, and so forth. These pieces are the natural communities, and they also match along their edges to complete the puzzle picture. If we could, we would draw all of the kinds of plants and animals found in these communities, but this would be impossible at this scale. Thus we have a hierarchy: natural regions and sections composed of natural communities, and natural communities composed of natural features (plants, animals, soils, etc.).

Even though natural regions contain a combination of natural features more or less confined within their boundaries, there is also considerable overlap between them, making actual delineation of the units perhaps as much art as science. This is because the natural communities normally occur along a continuum of environmental conditions, rarely stopping at the conceptualized boundary line established by the cartographer. That is why, in our puzzle example, a certain colored piece, representing a particular community type, may be found in more than one puzzle. Thus, it is extremely difficult to point to a location on the ground and state, "This is the boundary between communities and regions." In reality a natural region is a concept of how one views the landscape. The map presented here is how I perceived it; another ecologist may draw somewhat different lines.

Even with their large size, the natural regions and sections are distinctive. Consider the Brown County area, for example. Many people are familiar with this scenic, rugged hill country. These hills are underlain by Mississippian-aged sandstone, siltstone, and shale, the soils are acidic, and the common trees are American beech, sugar maple, white ash, and many oaks and hickories, especially chestnut oak. The painted sedge, a grass-like plant absent in most of the state, is a dominant groundcover over many of the dry slopes here. Although each of these features—the rugged hills of Mississippian-

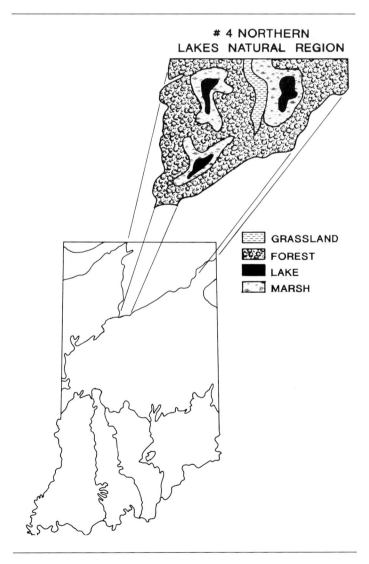

Natural Region—Section—Community Type hierarchy and mapping patterns of a natural region. Several of the natural regions contain sections, but the Northern Lakes Natural Region, shown here, does not.

age siltstone, the acidic soil, the painted sedge, and the forests of deciduous trees—occurs elsewhere in the state, it is the combination of them, and the degree to which they cover the landscape, that is found only in the Brown County Hills Section of the Highland Rim Natural Region.

Many of you may never have ventured off the main roads to see the real Indiana. If you have the opportunity, by all means do so. But if you are unable, you can nevertheless gain an understanding of what is out there by reading the following twelve chapters. Written by members of the Division of Nature Preserves, Indiana Department of Natural Resources, they provide that "back roads" look for you. Enjoy your trip!

I'll follow you, I'll lead you about around through bog, through bush, through brake, through brier.

—*Shakespeare*, A Midsummer Night's Dream

For additional information about Indiana's natural regions, see also volume 94 of the *Proceedings of the Indiana Academy of Science* (1985).

The Southern Hill Country

17. Limestone Ledges and "Crawfish Flats": The Bluegrass Natural Region

Ronald K. Campbell

THE NAME OF THIS NATURAL REGION was chosen to reflect its similarity to the Bluegrass Region of north-central Kentucky. While the reference is to the presence of Kentucky bluegrass, there is some doubt as to whether this species was native to the area or whether it was somehow introduced into Kentucky by early explorers and traders. Regardless of how the plant arrived, bluegrass is now a widespread species in this region, and elsewhere.

> It is time now to ponder the fact that the . . . lands, when subjected to the particular mixture of forces represented by the cow, plow, fire and axe of the pioneer, became bluegrass. What if the plant sucession . . . had given us some worthless sedge, shrub, or weed? . . . We do not even know where the bluegrass came from—whether it is a native species, or a stow-away from Europe. . . . In short . . . the pioneer simply demonstrated what successions inhered in the land.
>
> —*Aldo Leopold,* A Sand County Almanac *(1949)*

The entire Bluegrass Natural Region was glaciated during the Illinoian glacial period, and its northern boundary approximates the southern boundary of the Wisconsinan glaciation. The bedrock is overlain with a relatively thin layer of glacial drift.

Numerous scientists have recognized the uniqueness of this region. Charles Deam in his *Flora of Indiana* noted that an Appalachian flora was present and pointed out that there are level, poorly drained "flats," which are dominated by beech, tuliptree, and black gum on the higher sites and by sweet gum, red maple, swamp chestnut, swamp white, and pin oak in depressions. Lindsey, Schmelz, and Nichols, in *Natural Areas in Indiana and Their Preservation,* referred to this natural region as the Southeastern Till Plain Beech-Maple Division.

In pre-settlement times, this region was mostly forested, but it contained examples of glade, cliff, and barrens communities as well as a number of aquatic habitats. Two animals that are essentially restricted to this natural region are the dusky salamander and variegated darter. Another is a rare earthworm, *Diplocardia udei,* which has been found in Indiana only twice. This species is normally associated with the mixed mesophytic forests of the Appalachian Plateau.

Ron Campbell is now deceased. He worked with Indiana Division of Nature Preserves for several years.

SWITZERLAND HILLS SECTION

> In this dense forest mass, the weaker saplings soon died. The big trees that survived stood fairly close together. One early account says you could not shoot an arrow in any direction for more than twenty feet eithout hitting a tree. . . . The sombreness of the forest, which by day was dark and silent, made travel through it rather gloomy.
>
> —*John Bakeless,* The Eyes of Discovery *(1950)*

Since many of the earliest settlers first entered Indiana from the Kentucky Commonwealth or from Ohio Territory, this rugged landscape located in the far southeastern corner of the state was their first glimpse of what is now Indiana. The Switzerland Hills Section is

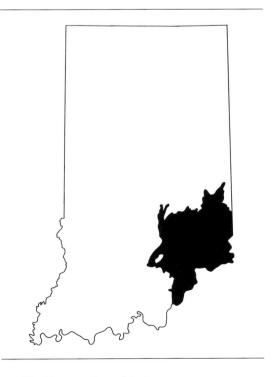

The Bluegrass Natural Region

Landscape and general terrain typical of the Switzerland Hills section of the Bluegrass Natural Region.   *Photo by Richard Fields*

sharply defined on its western boundary by the Laughery Escarpment. This escarpment, which approximates the boundary between the Ordovician rocks of this section and the Silurian rocks associated with the Muscatatuck Flats and Canyons Section, is about 1,100 feet above mean sea level in elevation. It is the drainage divide between westerly flowing streams of medium gradient such as the East Fork of the White River, and the southerly and easterly flowing Indian-Kentuck Creek, Laughery Creek, and Whitewater River. This section has been deeply dissected by streams, and the bottoms of the valleys may be 450 feet below the uplands. Some of the highest elevations in the state are also found here. While the topography is hilly, cliffs are not common. Soils are derived both from drift and from residual soils from Ordovician limestones and soft shales. Soil profiles are very thin with bedrock near the surface.

The most notable natural community of this section is the mesophytic forests associated with ravines. This community differs from many of the forests of Indiana in that about a dozen species of trees may dominate a given stand. Typical dominants include American beech, white ash, blue ash, sugar maple, white, chinquapin oak, red oak, shagbark hickory, tuliptree, Ohio buckeye, and black walnut.

Tree species with Appalachian affinities such as yellow buckeye and white basswood are occasionally found in the mixed forests of this section, and black locust, a tree common today in many parts of the state, was originally restricted to this section in pre-settlement times.

The ravine salamander is most common in this section, usually found under limestone slabs on forested slopes. These animals normally avoid dry ridgetops and overly wet sites.

MUSCATATUCK FLATS AND CANYONS SECTION

This region slopes gradually downward from the Switzerland Hills Section on the east to the Scottsburg Lowland Section on the west at about 12 feet per mile. Its northern portion has been covered with a layer of drift which is up to 150 feet thick, obscuring any sharp transition to the Central Till Plain Natural Region.

The uplands are mostly level to gently undulating plains dissected by steep-sided, moderately deep valleys where streams have cut their way down through the bedrock and overlying soils. Minor areas of karst topography with sinkholes and caves are found along the valley borders. Bedrock consists of Silurian- and Devonian-age limestones and dolomites.

Sullivantia is a delicate cliffside wildflower that is endemic to steep limestone rock faces of the Bluegrass Natural Region.
Photo by Perry Scott

Partridge-berry, a showy, creeping evergreen shrub, has a brilliant red edible fruit.   *Photo by Delano Z. Arvin*

Running buffalo clover (*trifolium stoloniferum*), one of Indiana's rarest wildflowers, is known only from Ohio County. It is the only Indiana plant species on the federally endangered species list. This clover, which once grew from Kansas to West Virginia, apparently was dependent on large mammals, such as bison, both for seed dispersal and for creation of the lightly disturbed microhabitats necessary for its establishment and survival.
Photo by Michael Homoya

Although not restricted to the Bluegrass Natural Region, the ravine salamander is typically found in that part of Indiana.
Photo by Sherman A. Minton

Dwarf ginseng is found here in selected woodlands, but also occurs in northern Indiana.   *Photo by Delano Z. Arvin*

It is not known for certain if black locust occurred in the state naturally, since the settlers frequently planted it early on, but there are records for far southeastern Indiana as early as 1817.   *Photo by Perry Scott*

Except at the northern end of the section, drift is relatively thin. In most places it averages 20 to 25 feet thick, but in some upland areas as little as 5 to 10 feet. The major soils are acidic and poorly to moderately drained. Many of the soils in this section are underlain by a fragipan, creating a perched water table near the soil surface. These wet soils, locally called "crawfish flats," are a favored habitat for crayfish, which build clay "chimneys" aboveground, sometimes at a density of thousands per acre.

Streams are moderate in both gradient and speed of flow, usually over beds of solid pavement-like limestone. Typical examples include Graham Creek and Big Creek.

> American beech heavily dominates the tree stratum in both Commiskey and Tribbetts Woods. Red maple and sweet gum replace sugar maple, the usual co-dominant . . . on these acid, poorly-drained planosol soils. . . . Both stands are remarkable for their low densities, high basal areas, large average tree size, and tall trees. . . . Both stands have high canopies and long, clear boles. . . . Eight trees taken at random averaged 133 feet in height.
>
> —*Marion T. Jackson and William B. Barnes, "Old-growth Forests in Jennings County, Indiana," in* Proceedings of the Indiana Academy of Science *(1975)*

Poorly drained and frequently ponded flatwoods, as shown here at Versailles State Park, characterize the widespread "flats" of the Bluegrass Natural Region. *Photo by Lee Casebere*

The most characteristic natural community type found in this section is flatwoods. Typical dominant plants of the flatwoods include American beech, red maple, sweetgum, pin oak, swamp chestnut oak, white oak, black gum, and tuliptree. In the canyons, the mixed mesophytic forest communities are similar to the forests found in the Switzerland Hills Section; they may contain Canada violet, longspur violet, and crinkleroot. Other communities found in this section include limestone glades and limestone gravel washes.

Sullivantia is a plant found only in the canyons of this section of the state. It is sparsely distributed throughout its range. Another plant found in the forests of the canyons of this section is the golden St. John's-wort, reported in the state only from Jefferson County. A third rare species, occurring in limestone glades, is Michaux's leavenworthia, which occurs only in Clark County.

A number of plants that occur in the northern part of the state, but in the south are restricted to this region, include fox grape, bluntlobed grape fern, swamp dewberry, dwarf ginseng, and false lily of the valley. These species are found on the plain, and American pennywort, wide-leaf ladies'-tresses, and pedunculate sedge occur in the canyons.

SCOTTSBURG LOWLAND SECTION

Before Indiana's landscape was modified by glaciers, this region extended northwest as far as southern Pulaski County. Even today, the present northern boundary of this section is obscured by as much as 150 feet of drift which overlays the area so that it blends imperceptibly into the Central Till Plain. Elevations in this section range from about 750 feet above mean sea level in the north to around 500 feet near the Ohio River.

The major physiographic features are wide alluvial and lacustrine plains bordering the major streams, and bedrock which consists of relatively non-resistant shales of late Devonian and early Mississippian age. Even though the overlying mantle of soil is thin, there are few rock outcrops, except at the Falls of the Ohio near Clarksville.

The Falls area is of particular interest because it contains the fossilized remains of a Devonian coral reef. More than 600 species of fossils of fish, coral, and other sea creatures have been found here; two-thirds of this number represent "type specimens," i.e., the model specimens used in describing a species for the first time.

Soils in this section are acid to neutral silt loams, with sizable deposits of wind-blown sand bordering the east margin of the East Fork of the White River.

Rivers and streams, such as the Muscatatuck River and Silver Creek, are normally rather slow-flowing with silty bottoms. Wetland communities consist of swamps, acid seep springs, and ponds. Characteristic species found in the swamp forest include swamp cottonwood, red maple, pin oak, river birch, green ash, stiff dogwood, and buttonbush.

> We forded the Muskakituck [sic] river at Vernon, which stands on its head waters, and is a country [sic] seat. We then directed our course to Brownstown, on the east branch of the White river. . . . We had been hitherto journeying through dense forests, and except when we came to a small town, could never see more than about ten yards on either side.
>
> —*S. A. O'Terral,* A Ramble of Six Thousand Miles through the United States of America *(1832)*

Floodplain forests are common along the major rivers and streams and are characterized by sweetgum, swamp chestnut oak, swamp white oak, black gum, shellbark hickory, and sometimes pecan. Herbaceous plants characteristic of this section include Muskingum and Louisiana sedge, Virginia dayflower, lizard's tail, and woodreed.

Areas of upland forest are present and are similar to those of the Muscatatuck Flats and Canyons Section.

The northern studfish is known only from this section of the state. It inhabits clear, fast-flowing streams with gravel or sandy bottoms.

One plant was historically restricted to this section of the state. Short's goldenrod was collected in 1844 by Dr. Asahel Clapp from the north shore of the Falls of the Ohio. While it still exists at one site in eastern Kentucky, it has been extirpated from Indiana.

Species which occur in other parts of Indiana but are limited in the southeastern part of the state to this section of the Bluegrass Natural Region include the attractive northern copperbelly snake, the eastern ribbon snake, and the southern pale green orchid.

Clifty Falls in Jefferson County is one of the highest and most scenic waterfalls in Indiana.
Photo by Lee Casebere

Knobstone escarpment rises some 600 feet above the Scottsburg Lowland to the east (left in picture, which looks south). The Driftwood Fish Hatchery and Starve Hollow Lake are visible in the valley. Forest opening in foreground is Knobstone Barrens Nature Preserve.   *Photo by Richard Fields*

18. Sinks, Slopes, and a Stony Disposition: The Highland Rim Natural Region

Michael A. Homoya and Hank Huffman

INDIANA'S HIGHLAND RIM NATURAL REGION is a large, mostly forested landscape extending from the Ohio River northward to approximately the Wisconsinan glacial maximum. The rim is an impressively rugged, wild, and biologically rich portion of our state's landscape. It is mostly unglaciated and shaped by the underlying and exposed bedrock. Topography and vegetation make the Highland Rim a distinctive unit not only in Indiana's landscape, but in the larger picture of North American landforms as well.

Our region is named for the Highland Rim Physiographic Region, a major section of the Interior Low Plateaus Physiographic Region. Extending northward from northern Alabama to Indiana's Morgan County, it contains some of the most rugged terrain east of the Rockies. It forms a "rim" above much of the landscape adjacent to it, hence the name Highland Rim.

Three units compose Indiana's Highland Rim: the Mitchell Karst Plain, Brown County Hills, and Knobstone Escarpment sections. All are underlain by limestone, siltstone, sandstone, and shale of Mississippian age. Limestone is the predominant bedrock of the Mitchell Karst Plain, whereas siltstone, sandstone, and shale are the principal rocks of the other two sections. Because of these differences in bedrock, the surface landforms, soils, and vegetation are also different. The section most unlike the others is the Mitchell Karst Plain, a land of great contrast.

MITCHELL KARST PLAIN SECTION

Named after a town in the heart of its range, the Mitchell Karst Plain is in many ways two landscapes—one seen, one unseen. This is because much of the karst plain world is a subterranean one. Sinkholes, the principal feature of karst, dot the surface like holes in Swiss cheese, testifying to the extent of cavernous passageways that snake through the fractured and dissolved limestone.

The cone-shaped sinkholes funnel water and debris into the darkness below, providing life to a group of cave residents that rarely if ever see the light of day. Most are small invertebrates, such as blind crayfish, cave isopods, and cave crickets, but a few vertebrate species are also here, most notably blind cavefish, cave salamanders, and bats.

Sinkholes are important also in shaping surface communities. Many sinkholes become plugged with soil or debris, preventing water from draining into the cavern system below. Consequently, the sinkhole fills and becomes a pond or, if shallow, a swamp. Sinkhole ponds and swamps are exceptionally rich in wetland species, and are notable for the presence of several Coastal Plain plants, including netted chain fern, sweetspires, log sedge, giant sedge, and horned-rush.

Ironically, these same sinkholes are responsible, at least in part, for creating an environment conducive to vegetation adapted to drought and fire. Because numerous sinks trap most of the precipitation, few surface streams form. As a result, there are (or at least were prior to settlement) few natural barriers to halt oncoming fires. Fires, thought to have been set annually by Native Americans, or occasionally by lightning, were important in suppressing dense tree growth. The lack of firebreaks coupled with the fact that much of the karst plain possesses flinty, dry soils contributes to the formation of a landscape feature called barrens (large trees in continuous canopy were absent; hence "barren" of forest). Barrens, a kind of natural community characterized by usually dry, rather infertile soils and a mosaic of herbs, shrubs, and scattered trees adapted to drought, occurred in the years prior to settlement over a large area of the karst plain from central Washington County south through Harrison County to the Ohio River. The town of Central Barren now marks a location near the center of the former barrens.

> [The barrens] are by far the finest field for a botanist that I ever beheld. A much greater number of species are found in the same space than I have observed in any other place. It is indeed like a botanic garden but much more interesting.
>
> —*Letter from Dr. Asahel Clapp of New Albany, Indiana, to Dr. John Torrey of New York, March 15, 1836*

Only a few remnants of the barrens exist today. One still exhibits the gnarled post and blackjack oaks in isolated copses within a patchwork of wildflowers and Indian grass, little bluestem, shining sumac, New Jersey tea, and prairie willow, giving us a glimpse of former times.

The Highland Rim Natural Region

Karst landscapes of the Mitchell Plain south of Spring Mill State Park sometimes have up to 1,000 sinkholes per square mile, many of which drain the land internally into caves. The sinks show up well in these crop fields during the drought of 1991.   *Photo by Richard Fields*

A related community, the limestone glade, reaches its greatest expression in more rugged areas of the Highland Rim. A glade, commonly defined as a natural opening in a forest where bedrock is at or near the surface, is a rare community type in Indiana. Glades are usually on steep south-facing slopes, typically situated above a cliff. The thin soil layer, along with direct exposure to the sun, makes a glade a very hot, exceptionally dry place. Limestone glades are the most diverse of the glade types found in Indiana. They contain many species commonly found in prairies, e.g., prairie dock, rattlesnake master, and blazing star. Some specialties found in glades, but not prairie, are crested coralroot, anglepod, and axe-shaped St. John's-wort.

Even with the barrens and numerous sinkhole wetlands, the Mitchell Karst Plain is primarily characterized by oak, hickory, and beech forest. Much of the same diversity found in the other sections of the Highland Rim can be found here, except that chestnut oak forest and its associates are largely absent.

BROWN COUNTY HILLS SECTION

Along the eastern edge of the Mitchell Karst Plain Section, the limestone bedrock thins and subsequently disappears as the topography abruptly changes to deep valleys and pronounced uplands. North of the East Fork of the White River, this rugged area covers portions of Jackson, Lawrence, Bartholomew, Monroe, and Morgan counties and all of Brown County, whence the name "Brown County Hills."

Over the ages the shale, siltstone, and sandstone bedrock of this region has been deeply eroded, or dissected, to form a complex of steep, V-shaped valleys and ravines which separate prominent ridges and hills, or "knobs." Most of the ridges and hills bear steep slopes all the way to their narrow, rounded crests, but a few of the more massive ridges are topped by level flat areas, the most notable example being Weed Patch Hill in the center of Brown County State Park.

Approximately half of the region was glaciated early in the Pleistocene, but the Wisconsinan ice sheets occurred only along the northern fringe of the Brown County Hills. Today an occasional large rounded boulder, or glacial erratic, can be found in stream beds far up some northern valleys. That portion of the Brown County Hills Section which remained unglaciated throughout the ice ages, particularly central and southern Brown County, has the most deeply dissected topography, with the region's highest hills, deepest ravines, and steepest slopes.

The Brown County Hills are characterized by a diverse but repeating mix of natural vegetation. Black walnut, wild cherry, and sycamore occur along streamsides. Adjacent lower slopes and sheltered north-facing slopes harbor a mesic forest dominated by a variety of mesic species and an equally rich ground layer of ferns and wildflowers. On drier ridgetops and sunny south-facing slopes, white, black, and chestnut oak and shagbark hickory dominate. A number of the steepest, highest, and driest ridgetops or knobs are dominated by chestnut oak, which sometimes forms nearly pure stands. These "chestnut oak knobs" have a distinctive shrub layer characterized by greenbrier, black huckleberry, and dryland blueberry, and often a thick ground layer of painted sedge, a species common throughout the Brown County Hills but rarely found elsewhere.

Yellowwood trees are restricted to only Brown County in Indiana. This legume has very showy flowers in spring, making it a prized ornamental.
Photo by Marion Jackson

Rose gentian is a spectacular summer wildflower in old fields of the region.
Photo by Perry Scott

Trailing arbutus is a lovely fragrant low shrub in the heath family that is found occasionally on dry hillsides in southern Indiana.
Photo by Delano Z. Arvin

Flowering raspberry, with its showy rose-purple flowers, is a rare shrub in Indiana, but abundant at Hemlock Bluff Nature Preserve.
Photo by Lee Casebere

Goat's-rue is one of the many showy wildflowers found in glade habitats.
Photo by Perry Scott

Fire pink is well named for its brilliant flowers in late spring. It is most common on steep slopes or cliff sides.
Photo by Perry Scott

Perhaps nowhere in the state can the influence of topography upon vegetation be as clearly and easily seen as in the Brown County Hills. On the highest hills in the most rugged areas, where the upper reaches of steep ravines begin, a hike along a narrow, dry ridge crest crowned by chestnut oak reveals dry south-facing slopes on one side dominated by oaks and hickories with an understory of sedges and thick with briers. An about-face brings the opposite north-facing slope into view with rich mesic cove forest, occasional pawpaw thickets, abundant wildflowers, and ferns.

Other than on the chestnut oak knobs, few rare or unusual plant communities are found within the mosaic of mesic and oak-hickory forests. Several small stands of eastern hemlock occur along steep slopes bordering streams at scattered locations, often accompanied by the rare and attractive flowering raspberry. A few small siltstone glades occur on the top of dry, exposed southwest-facing slopes in an outlier of this section known as the Brownstown Hills, in south-central Jackson County. These glades are not as rich floristically as those found farther south in the state, but they do harbor typical glade plants such as little bluestem and goat's-rue.

Natural bodies of water and wetlands were scarce in the Brown County Hills, being limited primarily to creeks and small intermit-

Siltstone glades, as shown here at Brock-Sampson Nature Preserve in Floyd County, usually have plants adapted to drought under blackjack and chestnut oaks. *Photo by Lee Casebere*

tent streams. One significant seep spring existed prior to its inundation by Monroe Reservoir. On the crests of several ridges in Brown County, a few small depressional wetlands or ephemeral ponds occur, often referred to by local residents as "bear wallows."

Rare plants of the Brown County Hills include the green adder's-mouth orchid, the large whorled pogonia, and the attractive trailing arbutus, all of which occur on a few dry, forested hillsides. All three also occur in far northern Indiana in quite different environments. Nodding yellow ladies'-tresses orchid is restricted in Indiana to the Brown County Hills, where it is sometimes found in dry oak woodlands and abandoned fields.

The most notable rare species is the yellowwood tree. More typical of the Ozark and Southern Appalachian mountain forests, where it was discovered by André Michaux, yellowwoods are found in Indiana only in Brown County. This understory tree occurs in the diverse mesic forest of sheltered, steep, northeast-facing slopes at the head of rugged hollows. A legume, the yellowwood blooms sporadically in spring, producing beautiful panicles of cream-colored blossoms.

An icy rain was falling . . . on the last day of February, 1776 when André Michaux stopped his horse . . . to examine a curious tree. True, the leaves must have been off it then; it stood winter-naked, but with its smooth silvery gray bark shining like some wood nymph through the drear forest. With his experienced plantsman's eye . . . [he] now added to his long list of first discoveries of American tree species what is one of the rarest trees of eastern North America. For the Yellowwood has a most restricted range, and even within the described range it is often a distinctly rare tree . . . the only American species of this strange genus which is best represented in the mountains of China and Japan.

—*Donald Culross Peattie*, A Natural History of Trees of Eastern and Central North America (1948)

The heavily forested Brown County Hills harbor a rich diversity of forest wildlife typical of southern Indiana, including several rare animal species. The timber rattlesnake, once found throughout a large portion of southern Indiana, is now state endangered. Isolated wild areas of Brown County are one of its last refuges. Extensive forests of the Brown County Hills provide habitat for a number of forest interior birds such as the wood thrush, ovenbird, worm-eating warbler, Kentucky warbler, black and white warbler, and Acadian flycatcher, all once common throughout Indiana's unbroken forest.

Owing to the large portion of publicly owned forestlands, the Brown County Hills presently retain more of the unbroken natural character of the original pre-settlement landscape than any other natural region in the state, and will continue to provide a glimpse of Indiana's original wilderness for generations to follow.

KNOBSTONE ESCARPMENT SECTION

Named after the stony sugarloaf hills that define it, the Knobstone Escarpment Section occupies the narrow eastern edge of the Highland Rim from the Ohio River north to the White River. Its steep-sided slopes and flume ravines, which drop precipitously along the edge of the rim, create an impressive landform unparalleled in the state. While the bedrock types, topography, and vegetation are the same as in the Brown County Hills Section, there are sufficient differences in the flora and fauna to warrant separation.

For example, the dry forests here are draped with Virginia pine in addition to black, white, scarlet, and chestnut oak and pignut and shagbark hickory. Although today Virginia pine is found in numerous southern counties, mostly in plantations or as pioneers in old fields, it is native in Indiana only to the Knobstone. Other trees of greater occurrence in the Knobstone than the Brown County Hills include post and blackjack oak, cucumber magnolia, and American chestnut. The latter (for the most part now existing only as stump sprouts) can be found more frequently in the Knobstone than anywhere else in the state.

Other specialties of the Escarpment are rattlesnake hawkweed, Deam's foxglove (an Indiana endemic; see also chapter 35, "The Diversity of Indiana's Flowering Plants"), stout-ragged goldenrod, and Harvey's buttercup. Another notable difference between the two sections involves the painted sedge, which is ubiquitous over much of the Brown County Hills. In the Knobstone it is absent to very local.

There are no such ironies with the animals of the natural region. Several species of animals from the south "sneak" into Indiana only in the southern Knobstone Escarpment, such as the scarlet snake, crowned snake, and red salamander.

Nowhere in the state are there as large or as many siltstone glades as what occur in the Escarpment. These glades—natural forest openings with a substrate of siltstone—typically occur on south-facing slopes near the peaks of the knobs. Their dry, sterile, rocky soil and low diversity, along with adjacent scrub forests of gnarled, limby blackjack and chestnut oak, give the glades a desert-like quality.

They are nonetheless colorful and fascinating areas, with scattered clumps of bird's-foot violet, goat's-rue, St. Andrew's cross, and northeastern beard-tongue, all occurring as if in a perfectly designed rock garden.

Perhaps the most impressive aspect of the Knobstone Escarpment is the view it affords to those scanning the horizon from one of its peaks. It is then that, upon observing what seems to be a mile drop to the Scottsburg Lowland below, one can appreciate the word *Escarpment*. Truly, these magnificent miniature mountains are special. Indeed, they are *nonpareil!*

> My nerves had thrilled at the name of the Knobs. . . . But these heights would interest without the aid of philosophy. . . . From the north, northerly round to the southeast, the line of the horizons was as smooth as if ruled by pencil; but wild mountain heads projected in the opposite direction. . . . The sides of these hills are deeply gullied, and the peninsulated points appear like ribs attached to the vertebrae. . . . This landscape though obscured by the rain, was rendered more awfully grand by the thunder and lightning which now flashed and rolled over us.
>
> —*David Thomas,* Travels through the Western Country *(1816)*

19. Land of the Cliff Dwellers: The Shawnee Hills Natural Region

Michael A. Homoya

THOUSANDS OF YEARS AGO, prehistoric Indians used them for shelter against the harsh elements. Early European settlers also found them useful, constructing sheds, livestock pens, and houses against their walls. Many wild animals, such as fox, woodrat, vulture, and phoebe, have enjoyed the protection that they offer for denning and nesting sites. And a myriad of plants, especially many members of the fern families, have adorned their craggy surfaces for untold ages.

What are these features upon which so many have dwelled? They are massive vertical or near-vertical cliffs of bedrock. These cliffs, composed primarily of sandstone or limestone, commonly drape the steep valley slopes and ridgetops in the rugged, mostly unglaciated landscape of south-central Indiana. This area of the "Southern Hill Country" is known as the Shawnee Hills Natural Region.

Shawnee Hills is a name given to a much larger area than our natural region in Indiana, including portions of Kentucky and Illinois. The segment consists of a more or less contiguous belt of rugged hills and cliffs that begins in Putnam County, Indiana, extends southward across the Ohio River at Perry County, Indiana, into Kentucky, thence south, and then west into southern Illinois.

At a place called French Lick, is a very large pigeon roost. Several acres of timber are completely destroyed, the branches even the thickness of a man's body being torn off by the myriads of pigeons that settle on them. Indeed the first time I saw a flight of these birds, I really thought that all the pigeons in the world had assembled together, to make a common emigration. These pigeons do a great deal of mischief; for as they clear immense tracts of forest, of all the mast, acorns, etc., numbers of the hogs, which run at large in the woods, are in consequence starved to death.

—*William Newnhane Blane,* An Excursion through the U.S. and Canada during the Years 1822–23 by an English Gentleman

The Shawnee Hills in Indiana can be divided into two distinct sections, most easily distinguished by the type of bedrock composing the cliffs. The Crawford Upland Section, the larger of the two, contains sandstone cliffs of Pennsylvanian- and Mississippian-aged strata. The Escarpment Section, where Mississippian limestone predominates in the cliffs, is restricted to a rather narrow band of terrain along the region's far eastern edge.

CRAWFORD UPLAND SECTION

It is in the Crawford Upland Section that we find our state's most massive and spectacular sandstone cliffs. They may occur as bold vertical cliff faces; as rough, broken, detached blocks; as sinuous borders of stream-carved canyons; or as walls of magnificent natural amphitheaters. These various landscape features are not only appealing to the eye, they are important habitats for the many plants that utilize cliff environments.

Three species in particular call the sandstone cliffs of the Shawnee Hills home: French's shooting star, small-flowered alumroot, and filmy fern. These three cliff dwellers are so dependent on sandstone cliffs for habitation that they are never found growing in other environments. The filmy fern and French's shooting star are even more specialized—they occur only in and around sandstone overhangs (also known as shelterbluffs or rockhouses) or shaded ledges and grottoes.

Ferns in general are especially well represented on sandstone cliffs. The shield ferns and spleenworts constitute most of the ferns found on cliffs, but other notable ones include polypody, hay-scented, and Christmas fern.

ESCARPMENT SECTION

Limestone cliffs, occurring most prominently in the Escarpment Section, have a distinctive plant life as well. Only a few of the plants growing on sandstone cliffs are found on limestone, and vice versa. Limestone cliffs provide high levels of calcium and an alkaline environment which some plants apparently need. Included are wall-rue fern, black-stemmed spleenwort, hairy alumroot, black-seeded sedge, and spreading rockcress.

The Shawnee Hills Natural Region

French's shooting star is a rare cliff-dwelling wildflower that is found in crevices of sandstone overhangs.   *Photo by Perry Scott*

An Appalachian native shrub that occurs along cliff faces and r of the region is the lovely mountain laurel, with its petticoat-lil
Photo by Marion Jackson

Scarlet tanagers are treetop nesters whose melodious territorial songs reverberate from dense forests during summer.   *Photo by Delano Z. Arvin*

Dutchman's breeches, so named for their floral structure, resemble a Hollander's pantaloons hung out to dry.
Photo by Lee Casebere

In an area of the state renowned for its showy wildflower displays, among the most welcomed in early spring is the glistening white bloodroot.
Photo by Perry Scott

The rare timber rattlesnake still occurs at some locations withir rugged hill country of southern Indiana.   *Photo by Richard Fields*

A verdant seep spring in Martin County. This unusual forested wetland in southern Indiana is habitat to lush ferns (including royal ferns as tall as a person), uncommon sedges, and a rich variety of wildflowers.   *Photo by Lee Casebere*

Beautiful waterfalls tumble from sandstone overhangs at Yellow Birch Ravine Nature Preserve in Crawford County.
Photo by Lee Casebere

One of the rarer and more interesting inhabitants of the limestone cliffs is a soft, furry mammal, the eastern woodrat. Also known as the "packrat," this attractive creature constructs nests of sticks (and anything else it can drag in!) in crevices of the towering limestone cliffs that border the Ohio River. Nowhere else in the state can the woodrat be found currently.

Some of the same crevices that harbor the woodrat also provide homes for snakes and vultures. The northern copperhead and the increasingly uncommon timber rattlesnake, along with a variety of other snakes, seek refuge as well as prey in the fractured cliffs. Both black and turkey vultures utilize the dark recesses of the larger crevices to raise their homely young. Although they and the snakes may not be as glamorous as some organisms, they nevertheless are valuable to the health and well-being of the natural region, and should be vigorously protected.

The recent discovery of the green salamander in the Shawnee Hills adds to the number of known cliff dwellers. This salamander enjoys the dark, damp fissures of rock faces, emerging only under the cover of darkness and high humidity. It is another of the organisms with Appalachian affinities that reach the western edge of their range here.

Many significant natural communities other than cliff communities occur in the Shawnee Hills. Extensive forests exist in many of the more rugged sections of the region. There are two principal forest types: dry upland forest and mesic upland forest. Typically, forests of dry upland slopes are composed of a canopy of black, white, scarlet, and chestnut oaks plus pignut and shagbark hickories. Post, chinquapin, and blackjack oak and blue ash occur locally. Understory species include such shrubs as deerberry, lowbush blueberry, farkleberry, and huckleberry, plus such herbs as dittany, elm-leaved goldenrod, creeping bushclover, forked panic grass, and greenish sedge.

A rare and very special natural community type associated with dry forest is the glade. In the Shawnee Hills, there are two principal types of glades—sandstone and limestone. Each is very different with respect to the plants present. Sandstone glades typically have acid-loving species, while limestone glades have plants that require alkaline conditions.

Some of the characteristic species found in sandstone glades are slender knotweed, poverty grass, goat's-rue, pineweed, panic grass, farkleberry, and, locally, prickly pear cactus. Limestone glades typi-cally are richer floristically (see also the glade discussion in chapter 18, "Sinks, Slopes, and a Stony Disposition").

At the opposite moisture extreme from glades are seep springs. A few small but excellent examples of acid seep springs occur in the Shawnee Hills. Their flora is seemingly out of place here, as many of the seep spring species are more likely to be found in a northern bog than in southern Indiana hill country. Dense growths of majestic cinnamon and royal ferns, along with sphagnum moss, sedges, orchids, and poison sumac, help to create the bog-like appearance (see also the seep springs discussion in chapter 23, "Forested Swell and Swale").

True springs are far more common in the Shawnee Hills than are seep springs, with Indiana's largest, Harrison Spring, occurring here. Many of these springs are part of an extensive cavern system that also produces some of our state's longest caves, most notably Wyandotte Cave. Indiana caves are utilized by a number of cave creatures, from troglobitic crayfish to bats, our most notable species being the Indiana bat. Although hibernating in the tens of thousands in a few of our caves, it is nevertheless a federally listed endangered species, due in part to the low number and vulnerability of caves suitable as hibernacula.

Of all the diversity and beauty that exist in the Shawnee Hills, perhaps the mesic forests are the most scenic. These forests, which are typically dominated by American beech, sugar maple, tuliptree, red oak, and white ash, harbor some of the best displays of wildflowers to be found anywhere. A few of the mesic cove forests have floral assemblages and scenery as outstanding as those of the southern Appalachians.

For example, imagine sitting along a boulder-strewn, briskly flowing stream situated deep within a cliff-lined cove. Everywhere there are wildflowers, ranging from the intense red of firepink to the delicate hues of waterleaf and wild geranium. On the bordering lower slopes you are surrounded by the tropical-looking umbrella magnolia, while on the higher slopes occur the much-esteemed mountain laurel and sourwood, both uncommon in Indiana. Not far away grow Allegheny spurge, barren strawberry, yellow birch, and eastern hemlock. It is these species, plus multitudes of animals and other plants, that make the Shawnee Hills so special. How fortunate we are that at least a portion of Indiana is a land of the cliff dwellers.

The Southern Lowlands

20. A Taste of the South: The Southern Bottomlands Natural Region

D. Brian Abrell

A VISIT TO THE SOUTHERN BOTTOMLANDS on a midsummer's day can be a sultry experience. Heat and humidity seem to pour onto your body from all directions, with an intensity that can drain your energy. A localism for the condition is "close."

The environment here seems nearer that of the Gulf Coast than that of the Great Lakes. As a result, some of the vegetation and animal life have responded in like manner. In this region numerous species have affinities to the Lower Mississippi Valley and Gulf Coastal Plain. It is this southern flavor that distinguishes this bottomland region from floodplains along other rivers and major streams of southwestern Indiana. Although both glaciated and unglaciated areas are present, impact of the ice has had little effect on the biotic composition of the region.

> All the land of this territory, with the exception of a small range of hills, which run from the Ohio northerly for about 100 miles, and the low grounds south of the mouth of White River, 20 miles below this, on the Wabash may be considered second to none in the world. The first rate lands lie on the Wabash . . . the most beautiful stream in my recollection.
>
> —*Caleb Lownes, "From Old Vincennes, 1815," in* Indiana Magazine of History *57: 141–54*

Frequent flooding is the lifeblood of many of the natural communities. Flooding produces an influx of needed moisture and nutrients, as well as new and potential residents in the form of seeds and aquatic life. Control structures built in the last few decades have had an impact on flooding in many areas, reducing the frequency and volume of water and altering the normal life patterns of the affected bottomland communities.

The dominant natural community of the region is bottomland forest. The silt loam soils and seasonal inundation provide a nutrient-rich substrate. Large-diameter trees towering 150 to 180 feet above the forest floor once covered vast tracts of the bottomlands. In sheer size and abundance, these trees had few rivals in eastern North America.

If the forest is viewed from a high bluff, it presents the appearance of a compact, level sea of green, apparently almost endless, but bounded by the line of wooded bluffs three to seven miles back from the river; . . . the general level broken by occasional giant trees.

> —*Robert Ridgway,* Notes on the Vegetation of the Lower Wabash Valley *(1872)*

Although much reduced in size, many bottomland forest stands still exist. Subtle changes in elevation of only a few feet result in notable differences in the moisture conditions of the soils. As a result the bottomland forests are a mosaic of varying species composition. Lower sites may often have prolonged periods of standing water, supporting such characteristic species as pecan, shellbark hickory, silver maple, sycamore, green ash, and sugarberry.

Slightly better-drained sites may be dominated by swamp white,

The Southern Bottomlands Natural Region

Cypress swamps were formerly widespread in southwestern Indiana and extended north almost to Vincennes. Deciduous forests along the lower Wabash River were among the finest in the world. Hovey Lake shown here.   *Photo by Russell Mumford*

swamp chestnut, and Shumard's red oak, shellbark hickory, and hackberry. Level sites with higher elevations are flooded far less frequently; however, the poorly drained soils result in prolonged periods of standing water. These "flatwoods" contain post oak and cherrybark oak, in combination with the other bottomland trees.

A variety of herbaceous species distinctive to the region are found among the bottomland forest. The spider lily, unique in the size and grandeur of its brilliant white flowers, prefers the fringes of wet sites. Mistletoe is a parasitic evergreen shrub whose preferred habitat is the upper branches of large trees. On occasion it grows in sunlight on smaller trees, but generally it remains hidden from view in its canopy habitat. Birds are the primary dispersers of seeds; they wipe the sticky seeds from their beaks on the upper tree branches. Mistletoe is best viewed in winter, when its green leaves and branches contrast sharply with the drab colors.

Another plant characteristic of the bottomland timber is the woolly pipe-vine. Taking advantage of the forest edge and light openings, this liana makes its way to the canopy by using trees and shrubs on which it climbs as both ladder and support. In late May the woolly, heart-shaped leaves hide a most peculiar flower—small, greenish-yellow, and shaped like a Dutchman's pipe bowl with a strongly crooked stem.

Among the bottomland forests and islands, extensive canebrakes were formerly encountered. Hundreds of acres were often domi-nated by giant cane. Although still common, cane is now restricted to small tracts. Giant cane is a bamboo, which makes it one of the more distinguishable grasses. On rich sites, this woody grass can grow to a height of 10 feet or more. After flowering but once about every 25 years, the entire population sets seed and dies, a life cycle similar to those of a number of Asian bamboo species.

The river valleys everywhere, beginning with the Ohio, and on southward, were covered with a luxuriant growth of cane, the "brakes" often extending for miles in every direction. No one, for the last hundred years, has seen anything like the tremen-dous growth of these primitive canebrakes. Brakes still exist, but they are poor and pitifully reduced descendants of the luxuriant growth whose tasseled tops once waved over mile upon mile of fertile plains. The fertility of the land on which they grew destroyed them quickly. They disappeared early because the first white settlers were quick to realize that a flourishing canebrake was a sign of first-class farm land.

—*John Bakeless, "The Wild Middle West," in* The Eyes of Discovery *(1950)*

The endangered swamp rabbit makes use of the cane, oxbows, and swamps of these bottomlands. Only in appearance does this rabbit resemble the eastern cottontail, because behavior and pre-ferred habitats clearly separate them. The swamp rabbit is strictly a

The swamp rabbit, the most endangered species of mammal in the state, is confined to the Southern Bottomlands Natural Region. Its habit of defecating on logs indicates its presence.   *Photo courtesy of the Division of Nature Preserves*

Dead-flat landscape of the Little Cypress Swamp area near the confluence of the White and Wabash rivers in Knox County.
Photo by Richard Fields

Featherfoil, which usually grows with stems submerged in the standing water of cypress swamps, produces distinctive, showy flowers in April.
Photo by Lee Casebere

Prothonotary warblers are the only eastern warblers that nest in tree cavities or crannies in standing snags along streams or at swamp borders.
Photo by Michael Ray Brown

Spider lilies sport one of the largest single blooms of any midwestern wildflower. They are relatively abundant in ideal habitat in late summer.
Photo by Lee Casebere

Close view of feathery needles and globular immature cones of bald cypress. Entire branchlets of this deciduous conifer turn rusty brown in autumn, then drop in winter.
Photo by Marion Jackson

bottomland species, making use of the low cane ridges for food and shelter, but it also ranges easily through swamps and sloughs. It is a good swimmer, often using this ability to escape predators and floods. If unable to escape floods by swimming, it will climb into masses of vines or hollow trees above the flood waters. The ability to thrive in what appears to be inhospitable rabbit habitat and to demonstrate non-rabbit behavior has given rise to many tales about swamp rabbits by local residents.

Several other distinctively southern plant species are found in the bottomland forest, notably bloodleaf, acanthus, and climbing dog-bane, with its pungent, far-reaching odor. A rare sedge of the region is social sedge, seldom encountered, but where it does occur it is usually abundant, with colonies of hundreds of the tufted plants forming extensive carpets.

Amid the bottomland forests are bodies of standing water created by the shifting channels of the rivers and maintained by the frequent floods. These areas are variously referred to as oxbows, ponds, or sloughs. Water depth and duration are highly variable, depending upon the frequency of floods and depths of the basins. Swamp privet and catbird grape are often found along the edges of these areas. Where shallow areas often go dry, swamp privet will sometimes form dense stands covering large areas. In these same areas the catbird grape will take advantage of the sunlight, blanketing areas with a dense tangle of vines. The new stem growth of this grape is a distinctive bright red.

The most distinctive southern influences are found in the swamps of this region. It is here that the straight reddish-brown boles of the bald cypress stand in contrast to the crooked gray trunks of swamp cottonwood, which often forms almost pure stands. In the early summer the cottonwood trees shed their downy, filament-borne seeds in such numbers that the swamp appears to be covered with snow. Birds take advantage of the event and line their nests with the soft filaments. Pumpkin ash, overcup oak, and water locust co-occur in swamp habitats.

Little Cypress Swamp across the Wabash from Mt. Carmel was estimated to be 20,000 acres in area. Most of which is timbered more or less with Bald Cypress. . . . The finer trees have been cut and rafted off for shingles, so that the remnant was undoubtedly a poor sample from which to judge the character of the original growth. Certain it is that several stumps *where cut off* measured nine and ten feet across, while one was usually if not always cut at the beginning of the cylindrical position, some of those felled far exceeded in dimensions any now standing.

—*Ridgway,* Notes on the Vegetation of the Lower
Wabash Valley

The cycle of wet and dry that takes place in many of the swamps is an important occurrence on which certain species base their life cycles. The featherfoil makes use of dry periods of the lake in summer and fall. As the water becomes shallow or disappears, this fall annual is able to generate next year's plant from fall-grown rosettes.

The eastern mud turtle also has a life cycle tied to the hydrologic cycle of the swamp. The mud turtle prefers shallow, quiet water and must make use of the periods of abundant water. During these few months, growth and mating must take place. Once the dry season comes, the turtle burrows deep into the damp earth and aestivates until the next wet season.

No other creature evokes a sense of the south more than the cottonmouth moccasin. The life of this snake, which never was common and now occurs only in remnant populations, is intimately tied to the bottomlands and the habitats that they supply. Like the mud turtle, the cottonmouth survives by adaptation to the periods of water abundance. But unlike the turtle, as the dry periods come the snake can travel to areas where water is still plentiful. Winter brings the cottonmouth's search for habitat and prey to an end, for at this time a long period of hibernation is required. Snakes gather in large numbers at long-used hibernacula located above potential winter flood waters. Here they lie in a torpid state awaiting warm spring days.

Many of the animals and plants of the Southern Bottomland Region of Indiana have strong ties to the south. In the bottomlands, life cycles of each species not only are determined by the seasons, but are tied just as strongly to the hydrologic cycle of the region.

21. Sandhills and Old Till: The Southwestern Lowlands Natural Region

Roger L. Hedge

THE RUGGED HILLS AND CLIFFS of the Crawford Upland grade westward into this large region of the Wabash River lowlands. Pre-Wisconsinan glaciation sculpted all but the southern portion of this natural region, leaving in its wake broad valleys and an occasional hill on otherwise level uplands. In some upland areas near the Wabash and White rivers, windblown sands were deposited, forming extensive dune ridges. This natural region is bounded on the north by the Wisconsinan glacial border, on the east by the Shawnee Hills Natural Region, on the south by the Ohio River, and on the west by the Wabash River. The region is divided into three distinct sections: Plainville Sand, Glaciated, and Driftless.

PLAINVILLE SAND SECTION

The Plainville Sand Section is a small area that is characterized by a series of scattered sand ridges and dunes that parallel portions of the eastern margins of the Wabash and White rivers in southwestern Indiana. These dunes show their greatest expression along the Wabash, stretching from north of Terre Haute to south of Vincennes. In some locations in Knox County, they are more than a mile wide.

This is a dry prairie, made xeric by the rapid internal drainage through the sand substrate. Directly beneath the clumps of little

bluestem the soil is of the black prairie type, whereas between grass clusters the sand is scarcely darkened. This indicates that the grass clumps have remained in the same pattern for many decades.

—*Lindsey, Schmelz, and Nichols, "Little Bluestem Prairie," in* Natural Areas in Indiana and Their Preservation *(1969)*

Virtually everything we know about the flora of these areas is taken from historical accounts. In the early 1800s, the state's first land surveyors came upon these sandy ridgetops and found grassy clearings with scattered, stunted trees, briefly describing them in their field notes as "barrens, some oak, hickory, grassy."

The sand barrens, as we refer to them today, were probably dominated by many of the same grasses and forbs that are also found in our native prairies. Sparsely scattered here and there among the tall grasses and drought-loving wildflowers were stunted, gnarled oak trees, their contorted ghost-like forms a result of the harsh, dry, conditions of the barrens.

But what made this plant community unusual was a colorful assemblage of several species that are more common in southern and western states, such as beard grass, rose gentian, sand and black hickory, and the showy clustered poppy-mallow. All of these plants were restricted in Indiana to the sand barrens of this region.

It should come as no surprise that areas with such interesting plant life often appeal to unusual animals as well. Prairie fauna common to northwestern Indiana such as the bull snake, the six-lined racerunner, and the relatively rare ornate box turtle also occur here in the sand barrens.

Today we can only imagine the former splendor of these prairie-like communities, as only a few acres of barrens vegetation remain. The existing remnants contain big bluestem, little bluestem, Indian grass, New Jersey tea, and blackjack oak, among other species. Marsh, swamp, and wet prairie are among the natural communities occupying low-lying areas between the dune ridges, but these are only a shadow of their former extent and diversity. The sandy soils on the ridges just east of the Wabash River are now excellent sites for growing Indiana strawberries, cantaloupe, watermelons, and fruit orchards.

DRIFTLESS SECTION

In the southern portion of the region lies an area beyond the reach of glaciation, an area that gives one a real sense of the south. The Driftless Section boasts the highest average summer temperatures and has the longest growing season of any section in the state. Because the area was not leveled by glaciation, modest hills and wide valleys have persisted, giving rise to a variety of natural communities that include forest, swamp, marsh, sandstone cliff, stream, and seep spring. Upland forests are similar in composition to those throughout the region, except that drier stands in this section have more post, southern red, and blackjack oak, and, in some areas, chestnut oak.

The Southwestern Lowlands Natural Region

Aerial view of sandhill landscape southwest of Washington in Daviess County. This region originally was primarily forested, but with barrens well represented in certain habitats. *Photo by Richard Fields*

Distinctive to this section is the occurrence of southern flatwoods dominated by post oak, which occur on the terraces and old lake plains of the Wabash and Ohio rivers. The moist acid soils here support a very different flora from that of all other Indiana flatwoods. Prairie species such as bluestem, prairie dock, and blazing star occur in the midst of southern bottomland species, including shellbark hickory, sweetgum, black gum, green ash, and such oaks as cherrybark, Shumard's, swamp white, and pin.

As you tramp the woods with stick and dog, one oak proclaims its unmistakable identity at a glance and at a distance. At least it does so if there is any free wind plowing through the summer foliage, for on the slightest provocation this beauty among the Oaks shows its white flounced petticoats—the silvery undersides of the blades which contrast so markedly with the upper surface. Hence the Latin specific name of bicolor.

> —*Donald Culross Peattie, "Swamp White Oak," in* A Natural History of Trees of the Eastern and Central United States *(1948)*

These flatwoods are home to at least two species that occur nowhere else in the state: black quillwort and pinkroot. In early summer, even an outdoor novice can readily spot the brightly colored scarlet and yellow tubular flowers of pinkroot. By comparison, the quillwort is an obscure non-flowering plant, whose long, narrow leaves give it a superficial resemblance to a wild onion.

Barrens occur in some of the post oak flatwoods. These too are distinctive in that they lack the characteristic prairie flora known to occur in most other barrens. The vegetation here consists mostly of lichens, mosses, grasses, and sedges. These communities are very hot and dry during most of the year, but in early spring they collect water and form shallow open pools. Later in the spring, these pools take on a very different appearance when plants such as fox sedge and slender spike rush reach their maximum growth. By midsummer, these plants are replaced by poverty grass, little bluestem, and a variety of interesting annuals, including the very rare elliptical rushfoil.

GLACIATED SECTION

As the name implies, the Glaciated Section, which forms the northern two-thirds of this natural region, was shaped and leveled by Illinoian glaciation and thus shows the least topographic relief of any of the three sections. Although most of the area was forested, wet prairie and marsh were also common. Lowland forests were common as well, and today's poorly drained flatwoods contain shagbark and shellbark hickory, pin and shingle oak, red and silver maple, hackberry, and green ash.

Another interesting feature of this section is the occurrence of black ash swamps. Black ash is more commonly associated with wet, swampy woods of the lake region in northern Indiana, but some of the flat, poorly drained, glaciated soils of this section provide favor-

Woodland pinkroot (also called Indian pink) is an endangered species in Indiana.   *Photo by Perry Scott*

Hoary puccoon, with the scientific name of *Lithospermum* for its rock-hard seeds, is a showy early spring wildflower at selected sites.
Photo by Perry Scott

The beautifully marked crayfish frog is a state-threatened amphibian found in crayfish burrows of southwest Indiana. Their pig-like vocalizations are heard at the time they lay their large clutches of eggs in temporary ponds during April.   *Photo by John O. Whitaker, Jr.*

able habitat for this species. Even these hard-to-use wetlands, however, have been drained, so that few remain.

It is believed that the greatest amount of prairie occurring south of the Wisconsinan glacial border in Indiana was found in this section. South and east of the Grand Prairie Natural Region, and well within a forest climate, prairie openings were maintained by recurrent fires set naturally or by Native Americans. A particularly noteworthy wet prairie, known as the Heckland Prairie, was located northeast of Terre Haute. It probably covered several square miles and contained a number of rare plant species including prairie blazing star, Canada burnet, and Carolina tassel-rue. The tassel-rue is no longer found anywhere in the state. A few isolated remnant prairie species can still be found today along old railroad lines. The prairie kingsnake and the crayfish frog are animals that are associated with this section. Both species have persisted in former prairie areas.

Although little remains of these prairies today, in all probability they were very similar in composition to the large expanses of grassland that occurred in northwestern Indiana—an area aptly named The Grand Prairie Natural Region.

Barrens with a heavy scatter of post oak overstory.   *Photo by Perry Scott*

Sand ridges, especially along the eastern margins of river valleys, frequently were barrens with vegetation of medium height and dominated by little bluestem grass. Little Bluestem Prairie Nature Preserve in Vigo County is one of the few surviving examples of this community type.
Photo by Marion Jackson

Controlled burn at Hoosier Prairie Nature Preserve in Lake County. Periodic burning controlled woody invasion into Indiana prairies in pre-settlement time.   *Photo by Lee Casebere*

The Central Flatlands

22. Where Tallgrasses Waved: The Grand Prairie Natural Region

Thomas W. Post

A PENINSULA OF GRASS, originating farther west and extending eastward, originally spread into northwest Indiana. This was a lobe of the tallgrass or Grand Prairie often associated with Illinois and Iowa. It was here that westbound explorers in Indiana first saw the sweep and expanse of grasslands that stretched westward to the Rocky Mountains. In seeking to describe this treeless, grassy plain, they referred to it as an ocean of green with waves of rippling, wind-blown grass.

> Everywhere, as far as the eye could read, there was nothing but rough, shaggy, red grass, most of it as tall as I. . . . As I looked about me I felt the grass was the country, as the water is the sea. The red of the grass made all the great prairie the colour of wine-stains. . . . And there was so much motion in it; the whole country seemed, somehow to be running.
>
> —*Willa Cather,* My Antonia *(1918)*

The Grand Prairie Natural Region of Indiana is divided into three sections: Grand Prairie, Kankakee Sand, and Kankakee Marsh.

GRAND PRAIRIE SECTION

The heart of the Grand Prairie in Indiana was Benton County, with reaches extending into Newton, Jasper, White, Tippecanoe, and Warren counties. This was the domain of big bluestem grass, described by early travelers as growing so tall on moist, fertile sites that horseback riders could tie stems together over their heads. Normally this grass grew five to six feet high, still tall enough to hide a person, or to lose your way if no trails were present.

To the Native Americans this was the land of *Mas-ko-tia,* the place of fire. For to speak of prairie is to recognize the importance of fire. Lines of flame and smoke stretching for miles were recorded by early travelers and settlers. The prairie vegetation, dry-curing on the stem from sun and frost in the late autumn, made excellent fuel. Let a spark from a campfire, an Indian hunting band, or a bolt of lightning serve as an ignition source, and away the fire would race in front of a strong wind until it met some natural barrier.

"It was the most glorious and awful sight I ever beheld," wrote Elias Pym Fordham, an English settler in Indiana. "A thousand acres of Prairie were in flames at once; the sun was obscured, and the day was dark before the night came. The moon rose, and looked dim and red through the smoke, and the stars were hidden entirely. Yet it was still light upon the earth, which appeared covered with fire. The flames reached the forests, and rushed like torrents through. Some of the trees fell immediately, others stood like pillars of fire, casting forth sparkes [sic] of light. Their branches were strewed in smoking ruins around them."

> —*John Bakeless, "The Wild Middle West," in* The Eyes of Discovery *(1950)*

The Grand Prairie Natural Region

From the blackened ground, using the ash as a natural fertilizer, the prairie sprang anew the following growing season. By the end of the following autumn there was little to suggest that a fire had gone through. The prairie would then be ready again to be cleansed by burning, should a spark be present. It was this scouring by fire that limited timber to small, isolated groves that appeared as islands in this sea of grass.

Wide, open skies and far horizons were the visual characteristics of the prairie. Prevalent grasses included big bluestem, little bluestem, Indian, switch, and side-oats gramma. When travelers stopped to look at plants typical of the prairie, they were amazed at the variety.

In spring the prairie would be painted by such colorful flowers as prairie violet, puccoon, shooting star, yellow and red paint-brushes, and cream indigo. Gradually these would give way to a kaleidoscope of colors and shades in summer, from the purples of leadplant, prairie clover, and coneflower to the whites of feverfew and mountain mint, all punctuated by spikes of lavender blazing stars and the yellows of the prairie dock. Gradually fall would bring with it the yellows of goldenrods, the whites and delicate blues of the asters, and finally the burnished bronzes of the prairie grasses. A careful search among the stems of grasses might reveal the deep violet of the prairie gentian.

Literally hundreds of plant species occurred on the prairie. It was not unusual to find twenty different species growing in one square meter of ground. This lush expanse of grassland provided habitat for a variety of animals. Chief among them was the bison, commonly called buffalo. Disappearing from the Indiana prairies in the early 1800s, this animal epitomized the prairie.

> I can remember exactly how the country looked to me as I walked beside my grandmother along the first wagon-tracks on that early September morning . . . for more than anything else I felt motion in the landscape; in the fresh, easy-blowing morning wind, and in the earth itself, as if the shaggy grass were a sort of loose hide, and underneath it herds of wild buffalo were galloping, galloping.
>
> —*Cather,* My Antonia

The prairie-chicken was another animal so closely associated with the prairie that as this habitat disappeared so did these birds, being last seen in our state in the early 1970s. Characteristic animals still to be found in prairie remnants include the prairie kingsnake, smooth greensnake, Franklin's ground squirrel, and dickcissel.

KANKAKEE SAND SECTION

Occurring north and south of the Kankakee River is the Kankakee Sand Section, which covers parts of LaPorte, Starke, Pulaski, White, Jasper, and Newton counties. Glacial meltwaters flushed large amounts of sand down the valley of the Kankakee; this material was later wind-worked into ridges and hills. Communities in this section were transitional, ranging from wetlands to prairies to savannas to tracts of timber which contained plants and animals more typical of eastern deciduous forest. Jasper County serves as a good example of this mix, as early accounts described the county as 50 percent prairie/marsh, 40 percent scrub oak/oak openings, and 10 percent forest.

An interesting natural community that occurs here is the sand savanna, with its widely spaced black and white oaks. Goat's-rue, bracken fern, lupine, Pennsylvania sedge, bird's-foot violet, huckleberry, and blueberries are representative ground-layer species. Located in proximity to the fire-swept prairies, this community was also influenced by fire, which helped maintain its openness. Early settlers commented on how quickly these openings disappeared once fires stopped sweeping into them.

> The prairie island and its grove are like the hammock in the everglades, like an atoll in the sea, like an oasis in the desert. It is something worth floundering and sweating for, a spot where a man can throw himself down and drink the wind and bathe in shade, where, as the blood stops pounding in his temples, he can begin to hear the birds singing deeper in the woods.
>
> —*Donald Culross Peattie,* A Prairie Grove *(1938)*

Sand facilitates burrowing by animals typically found in this region. The ornate box turtle, plains pocket gopher, bull snake, and glass lizard (which has no legs and looks like a snake) are representative.

Scattered among the ridges were wetlands ranging from open grassy sites dominated by bluejoint and cord grasses with cowbane, blue-flag iris, and marsh phlox to wooded areas dominated by northern pin oak and black gum, with royal and cinnamon ferns in the understory.

Very localized wetlands contain an assemblage of plants more typically found on the Atlantic coastal plain. On wet sand/mudflat areas, such interesting plants as floating bladderwort, yellow-eyed grass, black-fruited spikerush, and large beak rush occur. These wetlands of the Kankakee Sand Section graded into and were hydrologically connected to the marshes of the Kankakee Marsh Section, the third section of the Grand Prairie Region.

KANKAKEE MARSH SECTION

Au-ki-ki, the Potawatomi name for the Kankakee River, meant "beautiful river." For the European hunters and trappers, it was the "Grand Marsh" or "Hunter's Paradise." For people who wished to farm or travel through it, the area was made nearly impenetrable by water and mosquitoes.

Stretching from just west of South Bend to the Illinois line, the Kankakee flowed in a meandering path, frequently cutting back on itself so that it was said to have 2,000 turns in 250 miles of stream distance to traverse the 90-mile length of the valley. Lakes of various sizes were also associated with the river, with Beaver Lake in Newton County being the largest lake in pre-settlement Indiana.

This huge area, originally one of the largest freshwater marshes in the country, teemed with wildlife above and below the water. Hunters and anglers came from throughout the United States and abroad to hunt and fish the marshes and sloughs. Fish included walleye, largemouth bass, northern pike, bluegill, crappie, perch, and channel catfish. Waterfowl such as ducks and Canada geese were exceedingly numerous, as were tall wading birds, the great blue herons and sandhill cranes. The marshes were one of the best wood duck breeding areas in the nation. Hunter takes of 50 or more ducks per day were not uncommon. Such furbearers as muskrat, mink, otter, beaver, raccoon, and red fox provided income during cold winter months when the marshes were frozen.

Because of the variety of habitats available, the vegetation was equally diverse. Calm waters of bayous, sloughs, and oxbows were covered with yellow and white water lilies, water shield, and arrowhead. Wet prairies and shallow marshes were covered with bluejoint grass, sedges, and rushes. Timbered areas ranged from shrub swamps dominated by buttonbush and willows to heavily wooded swamp forests with silver and red maple, pin oak, green ash, cottonwood, and river birch.

Big bluestem or turkey-foot grass, which reached 6 to 8 feet high on prime sites, was an indicator grass species of tallgrass prairie.
Photo by Marion Jackson

Prairie dock is an indicator forb species of tallgrass prairie. It grew almost as high as the tallest grasses.
Photo by Perry Scott

St. John's-wort adds brilliant fall color to Tefft Savanna, Jasper County.
Photo by Lee Casebere

The glass lizard or ophisaur, although snakelike, is a true lizard. It is so named because the end of the tail may break off if caught by a predator.
Photo by Delano Z. Arvin

Lark sparrows (males, especially) have distinctive "quail-like" color markings on the head. They were frequent nesters in the original prairies.
Photo by Michael Ray Brown

Marsh blazing star (or prairie gayfeather) is one of the most showy of prairie wildflowers.   *Photo by Lee Casebere*

Although the great swamp around us was ditched and tamed, the fireflies spoke of its former wildness. We gave up all attempts to estimate how many hundreds of thousands of insect lamps we saw that night. They trailed above the wild roses of the roadside, across cut-over clover fields that perfumed the soft night air, against the black backdrop of stretches of woodland, above their own reflected lights along the water-mirrors of the drainage ditches.

> —*Edwin Way Teale, "River of the Fireflies," in* Journey
> into Summer *(1960)*

All that is left of the Grand Prairie Region are scattered small remnants of prairie in old cemeteries or along railroads. Most marshes have been drained for agriculture, and many remaining oak openings now contain houses. Glimpses of what the Kankakee Marsh and Sand sections once were like are possible at Kankakee, Jasper-Pulaski, LaSalle, and Willow Slough fish and wildlife areas. Quietly walking through the woods or standing at the edge of a marsh gives one an impression of what the original natural communities were like.

But after long hunting I have found, upon the edge of my island grove, one slim paring of forgotten virgin prairie . . . it was unsullied by a single foreign weed. Between field and field of grain, it grew with a varied flourish; close set, coarse-stemmed, the rank flowers spread amid the whistling grasses. . . .

I sat down there and looked away from the farms. I lay down and looked up at the sky. . . . I know the prairie was once all thus, and I tried to remember how it must have been. There would have been no feeling of fences around me, but only forest and grass, grass and forest, and rivers winding through.

> —*Peattie,* A Prairie Grove

Prairie/savanna transition at Beaver Lake Nature Preserve in Newton County. Beaver Lake was once the largest lake in Indiana. It was drained completely for agriculture, but prairie vegetation has become reestablished on a portion of the old lakebed.   *Photo by Hank Huffman*

Interior of beech-maple–dominated old-growth forest at Big Walnut Nature Preserve in Putnam County.
Photo by Lee Casebere

23. Forested Swell and Swale: The Central Till Plain Natural Region

Roger L. Hedge

The Beech-Maple Forest region, as we see it today, is mostly farm country. Those forest communities which occupied the better soils have suffered most. Drainage projects have made available large areas of former swamp forest . . . of which the oak-elm-ash-maple is most general. Much of the flat to rolling country, except where too wet, was beech-maple forest. . . . In this in spring was a vernal flora somewhat comparable in luxuriance but not in number of species to that of the mixed mesophytic forest. . . . We visualize a large area of flat to rolling country diversified by occasional fairly deep and youthful valleys in its marginal parts, where transitional forests occur.

—*E. Lucy Braun,* Deciduous Forests of Eastern North America *(1950)*

The Central Till Plain Natural Region, encompassing the central portion of Indiana, is our largest natural region. The northern perimeter of this vast area generally follows the Wabash and Eel river drainages, stretching in an arc southwesterly from the Ohio state line in eastern Dekalb County to the Illinois border in Vigo County. Its southern boundary is roughly delineated by what was the southernmost extension of the Wisconsinan ice sheet. Nearly all of the region was thickly covered and reshaped by this recent glacial advance, which retreated some 10,000 to 16,000 years ago.

With the exception of portions of west-central Indiana, the Central Till Plain is largely a level to gently undulating, somewhat monotonous landscape that was formerly heavily forested. Its deep, fertile glacial soils supported great forests of beech and maple, oak and ash and elm. In pre-settlement times, such forests spanned the width of the state, meeting the open prairies farther north and west.

Flatwoods (forests occurring on relatively level and often poorly drained soils) were easily the most common forest type present, with mesic upland forests and ephemeral swamps well represented. There were also various wetland communities along river valleys. Today there are still some fine examples of these natural communities that give us an idea of the original character of this region.

TIPTON TILL PLAIN SECTION

The flatwoods community is best represented in the Tipton Till Plain and Bluffton Till Plain sections of the Central Till Plain Natural Region. The poorly drained soils of flatwoods support pin, swamp white, bur, and Shumard's oaks, along with red maple, green ash, American elm, and sycamore. Characterizing better-drained sites are American beech, sugar maple, tuliptree, white oak, white ash, and shagbark hickory. Trout lily, waterleaf, and bloodroot are among the colorful spring wildflowers that put on fine displays in these more mesic sites.

Large sycamores invariably had hollow trunks, some so large that farmers cut them down carefully and used them as pig-sties and well-houses. Smaller sycamores furnished grain-bins and

casks. A very big sycamore could shelter a fairly large number of men—one traveler says twenty or thirty.

—*John Bakeless, "The Wild Middle West," in* The Eyes of Discovery *(1950)*

Shallow depressions that are seasonally wet are fairly common in flatwoods. Deeper, more permanent ponds are the favorite haunt of the shrub buttonbush, and locally winterberry. These woodland ponds sustain a variety of amphibians, such as western chorus frogs and spring peepers. While their noisy choruses fill the air on warm spring nights, small-mouth, spotted, and tiger salamanders quietly make their way to these depressions to mate and lay their eggs.

Mesic upland forests are especially diverse communities which are common throughout the region. American beech, sugar maple, tuliptree, white ash, and red oak are the dominant trees. Rich mesic forested slopes support some of the finest displays of spring wildflowers found anywhere. As spring unfolds, the list of colorful plants includes yellow and white trout lily, bloodroot, Dutchman's breeches, sharp-lobed hepatica, celandine poppy, cut-leaved toothwort, and wild geranium.

The Central Till Plain Natural Region

BLUFFTON TILL PLAIN SECTION

The Bluffton Till Plain Section in the northeast portion of the region was one of the last areas of Indiana to be covered by glacial ice. A characteristic series of moraines were left in the wake of the Ontario-Erie Lobe of the Wisconsinan ice sheet. These morainal features, more common here than in the adjacent Tipton Till Plain, give the landscape a mostly level to slightly rolling appearance. The clayey soils here have resulted in the predominance of poorly drained flatwoods and forested swamps.

The flatwoods in the Bluffton Till Plain contain tree species typically found throughout the Central Till Plain Region. Ephemerally wet depressions are common in the flatwoods. Species associated with these poorly drained sites include bur and swamp white oak, red maple, green ash, and buttonbush. With slight increases in elevation come significant changes in species composition. Sugar maple, beech, and white and red oak are among the dominant overstory species that occur on better-drained sites throughout the flatwoods community.

Forested swamps were formerly more common in this section than in the other two. Species composition varies with the extent and duration of flooding, but red maple, sycamore, buttonbush, and willow represent some of the more prevalent species. Swamp cottonwood may be found here on the borders of woodland ponds, but would be a rare find in the other two sections of this natural region. Also found here are a number of interesting wetland plants with northern affinities, including northern St. John's-wort, cottongrass, foxtail sedge, star sedge, mud sedge, and pitcher plant. There are also two species found here that are more typical of the swamps of southern Indiana: swamp St. John's-wort and log sedge.

ENTRENCHED VALLEY SECTION

Portions of the Entrenched Valley Section in west-central Indiana are remarkably different from the more typical level, forested plain in the other two sections. The Entrenched Valley is notable for its striking erosional features, particularly along the Wabash River and Big Pine, Big Walnut, and Sugar creeks.

Glacial meltwaters and the resulting drainage patterns have carved deep canyons into the land surface, exposing bedrock of sandstone, limestone, siltstone, and shale. In some areas, sandstone cliffs tower from 50 to more than 100 feet above the valley floor and have such colorful names as Inspiration Point, Devil's Backbone, Lover's Leap, and Falls Canyon. Various-sized glacial boulders of granite, basalt, and gneiss are found at the bottom of heavily forested ravines in many of these areas. Many of these materials were carried from Canada and the northern United States and were deposited here when the ice melted.

Aerial view of farmland of central Indiana with small, fragmented remaining woodlots. Although the land appears flat from the air, it usually is a gently undulating series of swells and swales.   *Photo by Richard Fields*

Like these glacial erratics, much of the plant life here is more common in northern or boreal regions. Relict stands of eastern hemlock, white pine, and Canada yew cling precariously to cliff edges, favored by the cool, moist microclimates found there. Other northerners that may be found in this area are Canada blueberry, wild sarsaparilla, shinleaf, Canada mayflower, and roundleaf dogwood. These plants probably occurred commonly in the surrounding uplands during post-glacial times when the climate was much cooler than today. As the climate gradually warmed, these species were eventually replaced by hardwood trees and are now restricted to the cooler cliffs and ravines.

> This is the forest primeval,
> The murmuring pines and the hemlocks,
> Bearded with moss, and in garments green,
> Indistinct in the twilight,
> Stand like Druids of eld,
> With voices, sad and prophetic,
> Stand like harpers hoar,
> With beards that rest on their bosoms.
>   —*Henry Wadsworth Longfellow,* Evangeline

A variety of ferns scale the mossy canyon walls. The tiny walking fern and delicate maidenhair spleenwort may go undetected among other, more showy herbaceous plants such as fire pink and wild columbine, but the larger and more prolific bulblet and lacy wood ferns are quite conspicuous. Other cliff-dwelling species include common polypody, Christmas, marginal shield, and maidenhair ferns, and the fern ally, shining club moss.

Eastern phoebes and northern rough-winged swallows build their nests in the rocky nooks of overhanging sandstone cliffs. Zigzag, long-tailed, and cave salamanders, earth snake, and northern copperhead reach the northern extent of their range in Indiana in the Entrenched Valley Section.

Circumneutral seep springs are unusual natural communities best represented in this section. Usually less than half an acre in size,

Cool, moist ravines within the Entrenched Valley Section harbor such northern relict species as eastern hemlock and Canada yew. Shown here is Pedestal Rock Nature Preserve.   *Photo by Lee Casebere*

Spicebush is a showy shrub throughout most Central Tillplain forests. *Photo by Richard Fields*

Gray squirrels occurred in unbelievable numbers in the pre-settlement forests of central Indiana, but occur there only rarely today. They have been almost completely replaced by fox squirrels, which are typical of forest edge and forest fragment habitats. *Photo by Russell Mumford*

Red-headed and several other woodpecker species are still numerous in many tillplain forests. *Photo by Delano Z. Arvin*

Forbes' saxifrage (endangered in Indiana), ferns, and liverworts adorn a cliff face at Portland Arch Nature Preserve in Fountain County. *Photo by Perry Scott*

Great blue herons still nest in a rookery at Calvert-Porter Nature Preserve in Montgomery County, as they have for decades, perhaps centuries. *Photo by Mark Romesser*

Sharp-lobed hepatica is one of the earliest and showiest of spring wildflowers along ravine faces of the region. *Photo by Perry Scott*

these relatively open wetlands are typically found below glacial moraines or terraces adjacent to larger drainages. The water seeps from the ground at the base of a nearby wooded slope and spreads through the dark soil into the forest opening it has helped to create. The cold, slightly alkaline water provides the setting for a unique assemblage of luxuriant and varied plant life, including skunk cabbage, marsh marigold, swamp wood betony, white turtlehead, Pennsylvania saxifrage, and queen-of-the-prairie. Nannyberry and black ash often occur around the perimeter of the seep.

> The original vegetation, despite a few . . . prairie tracts near the western end . . . was overwhelmingly beech-maple forest on the median, well-drained . . . soils. Today, the oak-hickory constituting most farm woodlots represents a subfinal successional type.
>
> —*Lindsey, Schmelz, and Nichols, "Tipton Till Plain Beech-Maple Division," in* Natural Areas in Indiana and Their Preservation *(1969)*

A very rare natural community known to occur in Indiana only in the Entrenched Valley Section is the gravel hill prairie. Never common in Indiana even in pre-settlement times, this community type exists today only as a few small remnants. These unusual grasslands occur in small oak-dominated forest openings on high gravel bluffs along some of the larger drainages in the northwestern portion of this section. They owe their precarious existence to the harsh environmental conditions resulting from excessively drained gravelly soils and steep topography.

Gravel hill prairies are restricted to south-, west-, and southwest-facing slopes, which exposes them to the drying effects of more direct sunlight and greater wind velocities. Consequently, these conditions have contributed to an original blend of both tallgrass prairie plants and plants from the drier mid-grass prairies farther west. These latter "western" plants, considered rare in Indiana, include androsace, gromwell, western wallflower, and plains muhly grass.

As one can see, central Indiana harbors yet today a surprising diversity of plant and animal life, and other natural treasures that offer us a glimpse into the past—and of the rich natural heritage once familiar to our ancestors.

Mud Pine Creek Hill Prairie represents one of the rarest community types in Indiana.   *Photo by Lee Casebere*

Panorama photograph of the community type and site conditions typical of northern Indiana swamp forests. Since no high-quality old-growth stands are known to remain in the Black Swamp Region, this photograph was taken at another site elsewhere in the state. Human at far left gives scale.   *Photos by Marion Jackson*

24. The Bed of a Glacial Lake: The Black Swamp Natural Region

Richard Dunbar

This "Black Swamp" was a scope of country extending through western Ohio. It was low and flat, thickly timbered and had a very fertile soil. The roads were new, the country sparsely settled, and the mud at that season of the year was in many places nearly hub deep. All this region is now cleared up, ditched, and under cultivation, and is splendid farming country. But at that time traveling was tedious. One day a distance of only three miles was made, due to a broken axle tree in the "Big Wagon."

> —*Aaron Work of his family's trek by covered wagons from southeastern Ohio to settle in Elkhart County, Indiana, in 1842*

Eastward from Fort Wayne toward the Ohio state line is the region of Indiana that has changed the most since settlement. East of New Haven, the land is almost tabletop flat. This area was once a part of the great Black Swamp that covered much of northwestern Ohio and extended westward into Indiana as a broad triangle with its apex at Fort Wayne. The extreme flatness is a marked change from the rolling glaciated lands found elsewhere in northeastern Indiana, yet this level landscape is as much a product of the glaciers as are the rolling moraines and till plains.

The Ontario-Erie Lobe of the Wisconsinan ice sheet formed the Fort Wayne Moraine at the western margin of its advance. When the glacier receded, meltwater was trapped behind the moraine, forming

The Black Swamp Natural Region

Lake Maumee, the much larger predecessor of modern Lake Erie. Silt deposits which had accumulated on the bottom of this lake were exposed when Lake Maumee eventually cascaded through a break in the Fort Wayne Moraine—known to geologists as the Maumee Torrent (see also chapter 3, "The View from the Window"). The flat terrain and highly productive farmland located east of New Haven in Allen County are products of lacustrine sediments from this vast glacial lake.

The soils left behind by glacial Lake Maumee were clays and silt loams with poor internal drainage, and flat terrain greatly retarded surface runoff. A dense swamp forest dominated by American elm, black ash, and red and silver maples formed on the old lake bed.

When the settlers arrived, the forest community was rapidly cleared, and through aggressive drainage programs almost all of the swampland was converted into agricultural fields. Most of the few woodlots that remain have been cut numerous times over the years. Trees in these stands are young enough that their roots never grew in the wet soils of the Black Swamp. The decimation of American elms especially, but also some red elms, by Dutch elm disease removed the large canopy trees of those species, which must have been an important component of the original forest of this natural region.

Now we can only imagine what the Black Swamp was like: large areas of standing water in spring, perhaps shrinking to small ponds by late summer; trees several feet in diameter reaching high into a dense canopy, which excluded almost all sunlight; trees falling to earth when the wet soil would no longer support their weight, creating a jumble of fallen logs and dead wood; the air thick with mosquitoes during much of the summer. The swamp environment was doubtless intimidating to the first settlers. Could they have imagined that one day the swamp and its forest would be gone, and highly productive farm fields would dominate that entire landscape?

Rain-sprinkled green ash leaves, a common canopy tree in the Black Swamp.
Photo by Perry Scott

Mosquitoes likely actively discouraged settlement of this region in the early years.
Photo by Lee Casebere

White baneberry, also called doll's eyes from the size and color of its toxic fruit, is a showy spring wildflower.   *Photo by Delano Z. Arvin*

The Northern Lakes and Moraines

25. Half Land, Half Water: The Northern Lakes Natural Region

Lee A. Casebere

Above the wet and tangled swamp
White vapors gathered thick and damp,
And through their cloudy curtaining
flapped many a brown and dusky wing-
Pinions that fan the moonless dun,
But fold them at the rising sun.

—*John Greenleaf Whittier*

In pre-settlement Indiana in the Northern Lakes Natural Region, the Native Americans surely enjoyed great sustenance. Clearly this was good country. Forests, prairies, oak savannas, and myriad wetlands—lakes, streams, marshes, swamps, bogs, and fens-were all juxtaposed in a marvelous blending of one habitat into the next, creating an incredible diversity of plant and animal life.

In these various habitats ranged game animals from bear, bison, and elk to beaver, muskrats, and squirrels. Upland game birds included wild turkeys, prairie chickens, and passenger pigeons. Innumerable waterfowl—especially during migrations—included rails, cranes, plovers, geese, and ducks. The lakes, rivers, and streams were well stocked with fish, and loamy soils were easily worked for crops of maize and squash. This was good country indeed!

When the European settlers came and began to eke a livelihood from the wilderness, they were aiming to raise farm animals and plant crops close to home on a piece of their own land. The home place was often extremely wet in this region, so they plied the soggy places with drag line and tile. Over the decades, draining the wetlands, clearing the forests, and plowing the prairies has changed the Northern Lakes Region significantly from when it was wilderness.

There are no virgin forests left, only scattered woodlots. The prairies and savannas are gone, as are thousands of acres of swamps, bogs, and marshes which disappeared forever. Many large lakes became small lakes. But in spite of the methodical and persistent alteration, the Northern Lakes Region has fared better than some other Indiana natural regions. Many lakes and wetlands remain—the essence of this region survives.

This essence traces its origin to glacial times. The Northern Lakes Region contains the most diverse expression of the results of glaciation that exists in Indiana, and is covered now with a thick and complex deposit of glacial material that exceeds 450 feet in places.

During the Pleistocene Epoch, glacial ice extended into Indiana at least three times. Each of the cold periods was followed by a warmer interglacial episode, during which the glaciers melted. The total effect of these several glaciations on the landscape and resources of northern Indiana as well as all of northeastern North America was vast.

—*William J. Wayne, "Ice and Land," in* Natural Features of Indiana *(1967)*

Surface topography is also very complex, and local relief of 100 to 150 feet or more is not unusual. Glacial features include knob-and-kettle topography where till-filled knobs and kame complexes of gravel and sand are interspersed with kettles (ice block depressions),

The Northern Lakes Natural Region

Northern Indiana wetland at dawn, with mist rising.   *Photo by Richard Fields*

which are the basins for the prevalent lakes and wetlands that characterize this natural region. Meltwater channels, valley trains, outwash plains, lacustrine plains, and other associated features of various sizes and shapes complete the package of glacial expression. Not surprisingly, soil types and associations are many and complex. Given the complex nature of the soils and the abundance of water in this glacially influenced region, it follows that the original plant communities also were especially diverse.

> It has a chain of beautiful small lakes, nice oak-hickory forests on the slopes, all stages of the usual aquatic succession of plants and animals, including bogs, and dry land areas undergoing natural succession. The display of submerged aquatic vegetation is the finest we have seen in Indiana.
>
> —*Lindsey, Schmelz, and Nichols, "Wing Haven," in*
> Natural Areas in Indiana and Their Preservation
> *(1969)*

Forested communities made up the largest share of the vegetative cover in the Northern Lakes Region. Forests dominated by oaks and hickories, which thrived on the dry and dry-mesic uplands, covered approximately half of the region. The most common trees are red, white, and black oaks, along with shagbark and pignut hickories.

Mesic sites characteristically have American beech, sugar and black maples, and tuliptree as the most common species. These forests have spectacular displays of ephemeral spring wildflowers. Because of variations in slope, aspect, soil type, and soil moisture, floral diversity was great.

Forests throughout the Northern Lakes Natural Region have poorly drained areas where vernal pools, containing shallow standing water for a few weeks to perhaps four or five months, provide important breeding sites for woodland amphibians. Deeper, longer-lasting pools usually contain the shrub buttonbush. These ponds host the explosive breeding activities of wood frogs, spring peepers,

and western chorus frogs, whose loud choruses are a harbinger of spring. At the same time, large gatherings of mole salamanders go largely unnoticed because of their silent, nocturnal activities.

Floodplain forests in this natural region are typical of similar forests throughout Indiana. Sycamore, American and red elm, green ash, silver and red maple, cottonwood, hackberry, and honey locust are common elements of this community.

Extensive areas of highly saturated muck soils commonly provide the setting for swamp communities bordering lakes and wetlands or in former lake basins. Trees in these swamps typically include red and silver maples, black and green ashes, and American elm. Locally, the boreal relict yellow birch may be common. Seep springs are often associated with these swamps, so the mottled spathes of skunk cabbage share these mucky places with the golden-yellow marsh marigolds. Ferns abound, and great beds of cinnamon and royal ferns, to four feet tall, often lend a lush, tropical look to what is otherwise a boreal plant refugium.

Bogs are more numerous here than in any other natural region, but because of drainage their numbers are a mere fraction of what they were in former times. Perhaps more than any other natural community in Indiana, bogs are full of mystery, fascination, and intrigue. Their acid peats and waters are part of a nutrient-poor environment where plants with specialized adaptations for survival in harsh growing conditions are able to thrive. Even more than the swamps, these bogs contain species with boreal affinities.

Bogs commonly consist of a floating mat of sphagnum mosses and sedges which creeps out over the open waters of a lake or pond in a glacial depression. Walking out over the floating mat is often compared to walking on a water bed. These mats can be unstable and somewhat treacherous, and the thought of breaking through one of them conjures up feelings of fear or daring that usually outweigh any real dangers.

The bog community contains numerous shrubs and vines in the

Autumn aspect with full color of tamaracks across Needham Lake in early November.   *Photo by Lee Casebere*

heath family, including leatherleaf, bog rosemary, large and small cranberry, and highbush blueberry. Nestled in deep cushions of sphagnum mosses are pitcher plants and sundews, specialized plants that supplement photosynthesis in a nutrient-poor environment by assimilating insects.

> Francis Darwin continued his father's investigations, growing sundew plants in two lots, one fed with insects, the other unfed. The fed plants were more vigorous, had more and stronger flowers, and more and much heavier seeds. . . . revealing that the plants do trap insects, do digest them, do absorb nitrogen and other nutrients from their bodies, and do profit from that absorption.
> —May Theilgaard Watts, *"History Book with Flexible Cover," in* Reading the Landscape (1957)

Other components of the bog community add their own elements of interest—the fluffy white heads of cotton grasses, tall beds of Virginia chain fern, and the respect-commanding shrub poison sumac. The deciduous conifer tamarack, with its feathery tufts of needles that turn golden yellow before dropping off in November, often grows in bogs.

Among the most beautiful of all bog plants are the several species of orchids which are denizens of these mossy places, including rose pogonia and grass pink, whose brilliant pink flowers, upon close inspection, appear to be studded with a layer of tiny jewels.

Another peatland plant community in the lake region of much interest and intrigue is the fen. Unlike the still-water, nutrient-poor bogs, fens are kept wet by nutrient-rich water flowing through the peatland. Before emerging into the fen, the water picks up calcium and other minerals as it flows through glacial gravel deposits. Frequently fens are located on the edges of glacial moraines near river valleys or by lakes. Where the water flows out from the peat, minerals are often deposited on the surface to form marl flats and tufa

deposits. Marl is a kind of limy mud originating from the shells of minute aquatic animals, and tufa is a crusty limestone formation. Emerging waters often converge to form spring runs which meander through the fen.

The plant community of a fen is a combination of species from other habitats, resulting in a distinctive hybrid community of its own. Numerous prairie plants and wet sedge marsh plants grow together with a long list of species which prefer limy habitats. Here, little bluestem grass, a plant typical of dry prairies, occurs with swamp milkweed, a plant of wetlands. Some of the lime-loving plants associated with fens include shrubby cinquefoil, grass-of-parnassus, sticky tofieldia, small white lady's-slipper, and white camass. Sedges and grasses make up the dominant groundcover.

Marshes are a characteristic natural community in the Northern Lakes Natural Region, and are associated with many lakes and old lake basins in muck soils. More difficult to typify than some other natural communities, marshes have a broad range of expression. Most are dominated by marsh vegetation ranging from cattails and bulrushes to sedges. Typical associates include swamp loosestrife, white water lily, water shield, pickerelweed, pondweeds, arrow arum, hornwort, wild celery, and bladderworts.

> A dawn wind stirs on the great marsh. With almost imperceptible slowness it rolls a bank of fog across the wide morass. Like the white ghost of a glacier the mists advance, riding over phalanxes of tamarack, sliding across bog-meadows heavy with dew. A single silence hangs from horizon to horizon.
> —*Aldo Leopold, "Marshland Elegy," in* A Sand County Almanac (1949)

Prairies and savannas, characteristic communities of the Grand Prairie Natural Region, were found intermixed throughout the Northern Lakes Natural Region. These existed as small islands within the larger forest complex, quite the opposite of the true Grand Prairie, where forest groves were islands in the prairie sea. Some of these prairies, however, covered hundreds, if not thousands, of acres. Today, no high-quality examples remain, only some tiny, degraded remnants and isolated prairie plants here and there.

From these little remnants and scattered plants, and from early plant collection records, we know that these prairies were indeed rich in plant diversity. They did, however, represent pinched-off appendages of the Grand Prairie, and perhaps they are best characterized by the typical prairie species which are absent. It appears that lake-region prairies lacked prairie violets, cream wild indigo, prairie gayfeather, prairie gentian, and pale purple coneflower.

Perhaps just as interesting, numerous prairie mammals and reptiles either were absent from or barely entered the prairies, barrens, and savannas of the Northern Lakes Region. These include plains garter snake, western fox snake, prairie kingsnake, smooth green snake, Franklin's ground squirrel, and plains pocket gopher. Although now apparently extirpated, the endangered Karner blue butterfly did occur historically in the sand barrens of the Northern Lakes Region.

Although much smaller in extent, sand prairies and barrens occurring here were very similar in plant species composition to those present in the Grand Prairie Natural Region. These communities occupied sand deposits in western Marshall County and northern St. Joseph, Elkhart, and Lagrange counties.

Bur oak savannas, which occupied richer, more loamy soils than the sand barrens, were common in places and often closely associated with the prairies. The largest areas of this community were found in northwestern Steuben County, northern Lagrange County,

Showy lady's-slippers, typical of northern bogs, are among Indiana's most beautiful wildflowers.
Photo by Michael Kirk

Bog rosemary, a state-threatened wetland shrub, glistens with frost and dew on a May morning. Note urn-shaped flowers typical of the heath family.
Photo by Lee Casebere

The stocky eastern massasauga rattlesnake is capable of inflicting a very painful, though seldom fatal, bite.   *Photo by Tom Hulvershorn*

Yes, native cranberries do grow wild in northern Indiana bogs!
Photo by Lee Casebere

Grass pink brightens a grassy meadow in a wetland community of a northern Indiana nature preserve.
Photo by Perry Scott

Pitcher plants often grow alongside sundews in bogs of Indiana. Both capture and assimilate insects. Note the recurved spines, which serve to retard insect escape.
Photo by Lee Casebere

Blazing stars blooming in early August across a northern Indiana fen. *Photo by Lee Casebere*

and parts of Noble and Kosciusko counties. No examples of this community remain, although old squatty bur oaks still grow in fencerows in a few places where bur oak savannas once occupied many acres.

Several animal species are either restricted to or characteristic of the Northern Lakes Natural Region. Star-nosed moles occupy mucky soils in several types of wetland communities; four-toed salamanders prefer mossy swamp forests; massasauga rattlesnakes are found in several types of wetlands, but seem to reach their peak abundance in fens; Blanding's turtles like shallow ponds and lakes; spotted turtles usually choose sedge marshes, bogs, and fens; sandhill cranes are attracted to cattail and bulrush marshes; swamp sparrows will live in various marshy places.

The Northern Lakes Natural Region is a repository of much natural and cultural history, of scenic beauty, and of ample resources, especially of water from which springs forth an abundance of life and diversity. The wide range of glacial landforms and the many lakes and wetlands set this region apart from all others in Indiana. In spite of the many changes we have made here, this continues to be good country indeed!

Windswept dune crests and rippled moving sands are representative of blow-out areas in the Indiana dunes complex.   *Photo by Richard Fields*

26. Dunes, Swales, and Glacial Ridges:
The Northwestern Morainal Natural Region

Thomas W. Post

Tucked away in the extreme northwestern corner of the state is one of the smallest natural regions, the Northwestern Morainal, covering portions of only Lake, Porter, and LaPorte counties plus a fraction of St. Joseph County. What this region lacks in size, it more than makes up for in biological diversity, particularly in the number of rare plant species. This great diversity is due to several factors, including varied topographic relief. More than 300 feet of elevational difference occurs from the top of the Valparaiso Moraine to the shore of Lake Michigan. This difference creates many microclimates and niches, which in turn harbor a variety of plant species.

A second factor contributing to this great diversity is the biological meeting ground at the southern end of Lake Michigan. Here elements of three biomes meet: the prairie, the eastern deciduous forest, and the northern boreal forest. It is not unusual to find a prairie plant such as little bluestem grass growing with a northern jack pine, while nearby are eastern forest trees such as American basswood. The moderating effect of Lake Michigan also plays a role by keeping conditions cooler near the lake, allowing more-northern plants to live far south of their normal range.

> Where I grew up the knotted burr oaks stood, their boughs so long they arched down to the ground again. And it was under these living arches that my people came driving their wagons. They saw the green and bronze of the first prairie grasses, the wild gardens of the New World flora, aster and sunflower and great golden foxglove; they saw the black earth, and they called these spots the oak openings.
>
> —*Donald Culross Peattie,* A Prairie Grove *(1938)*

As with other natural regions in northern Indiana, the physical features of this natural region were directly produced by the last ice age. The Valparaiso Moraine wraps around the southern end of Lake Michigan, continuing from Michigan through Indiana into Illinois. This large moraine once acted as an effective dam to the waters of glacial Lake Michigan. Eventually an outlet released this water and the lake receded. The complex swell and swale topography found at the south end of the lake is an excellent marker of the slow recession to its present level. Lake Michigan itself has contributed massive amounts of sand to the dunes along the Indiana shore.

The Northwestern Morainal Region is composed of three sections: Valparaiso Moraine, Chicago Lake Plain, and Lake Michigan Border. All share certain plants and animals in common, but each has its own unique character.

VALPARAISO MORAINE SECTION

In walking the length of the Valparaiso Moraine, all major community types of northern Indiana would be encountered. The high, rolling hills of the eastern end of the moraine originally were cloaked in mesic forests of American beech, sugar maple, tuliptree, and red oak, with an abundance of characteristic spring wildflowers. Inter-

spersed among the hills were a variety of wetlands ranging from shrub swamps of buttonbush to kettle lakes with floating mats of yellow spatterdock, white water lilies, and water shield. Two of the more interesting wetland types in this section are fens and bogs, and excellent examples of both remain today.

> Pinhook bog represents that landscape feature rare in Indiana, the well-developed sphagnum bog typical of the northern lake states and Canada. At its present late stage, while still having a somewhat quaking bog mat, the latter is well covered with shrubs, especially high-bush blueberry and leatherleaf. . . . Tree-size tamaracks are abundantly distributed among the shrubs.
>
> —*Lindsey, Schmelz, and Nichols, "Pinhook Bog," in* Natural Areas in Indiana and Their Preservation *(1969)*

Some interesting amphibians and reptiles occur in these wetland and forest complexes. Among them are the red-backed, the tiger, the spotted, and the interesting Tremblay's salamanders. This latter species is a triploid complex composed entirely of females; no

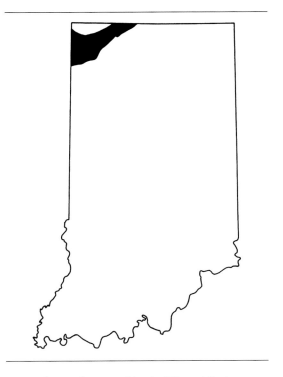

The Northwestern Morainal Natural Region

Aerial view of Pinhook Bog showing classic bog succession patterns, La Porte County. *Photo by Hank Huffman*

Black oak–dominated savanna in the Inland Marsh Unit of the Indiana Dunes National Lakeshore. *Photo by Lee Casebere*

known male populations exist. Two rare turtles that occur in these wetlands are Blanding's and spotted. In fens and open wetlands it is prudent to look for the eastern massasauga rattlesnake before putting your foot down among the hummocks.

Farther west in Porter and Lake counties, the forest thinned into oak openings dominated by bur and white oaks. The true tallgrass prairie, characterized by big bluestem grass, Indian grass, compass plant, prairie dock, leadplant, and purple prairie clover, was found in western Lake County and extending into Illinois.

CHICAGO LAKE PLAIN SECTION

Located below and northward of the Valparaiso Moraine is the bed of glacial Lake Chicago. This flat, poorly drained area is underlain by sands and mucks. As a result wetlands were numerous, especially along the Little Calumet and Grand Calumet rivers. Much of this area has become highly industrialized and urbanized, but small, high-quality remnants still remain to give us an idea of the natural history of the region.

Perhaps the most interesting feature of this section is the swell and swale topography. This mosaic of alternating east-to-west wetlands and uplands originally consisted of more than 100 ridges extending south from Lake Michigan. Wetlands varied from shrub swamps to cattail and bulrush marshes, with floating aquatics such as pondweed, pickerelweed, water lilies, and milfoils present. Sand prairie and savanna occurred on the tops and sides of the dry, sandy ridges. Prairie was composed of little bluestem, sand reed grass, blazing star, stiff aster, butterfly weed, wild strawberry, prickly pear cactus, and spiderwort, among other species. The savannas had many of the same prairie species but also included more typical species such as black oak, bracken fern, wild sarsaparilla, lupine, and goat's-rue. An outstanding example of this landscape is preserved in the Clark and Pine Nature Preserve.

In the extreme eastern portion of this section, a forest with distinct northern affinities developed on poorly drained soils. It is known today as a boreal flatwoods natural community. Standing water and tip-up mounds made by tree windfalls were common. Overstory trees included northern pin oak, black gum, red maple, tuliptree, and white pine. The ground flora was an interesting assemblage of several ground pine species, wintergreen, partridge berry, and gold thread scattered among fronds of royal and cinnamon fern.

LAKE MICHIGAN BORDER SECTION

The Lake Michigan Border Section is perhaps the most easily recognized section within this natural region. It occupies a narrow strip of land, at best a few miles wide, immediately adjacent to Lake Michigan from the eastern edge of Lake County to the Michigan state line. The most prominent physical features in this section are tall sand dunes towering in some areas more than 175 feet above the lake.

The East end of Lake Michigan is bounded by a mountain (ridge) of sand about 100 feet high. This hill has been accumulating since the foundation of the lake. . . . The wind is always changing the position of this ridge. . . . Twelve miles further is the mouth of the Great Calumet. Here the sand mountains end. Twenty miles further is the mouth of the Little Calumet. These two rivers are of the greatest consequence to the traders on the lake. They are both about twenty yards wide at the mouth, but very deep.

—*William Johnson's journal of a trip from Fort Wayne to Fort Dearborn (Chicago) in 1809*

The rare white lady's-slipper, one of Indiana's showiest orchids, is found occasionally in fens or wet prairies.
Photo by Delano Z. Arvin

Yellow-headed blackbirds, which are endangered in Indiana, occasionally nest in marsh vegetation.
Photo by Delano Z. Arvin

Karner blue butterflies, whose larvae feed on lupines, are an endangered insect species in Indiana.   *Photo by Richard Fields*

Starting at the water's edge and proceeding inland, one passes through several interesting communities beginning with the beach itself. The beach, baked by summer sun, windswept all year long, and pounded by winter storms, presents harsh conditions for plant life. Annuals such as sea rocket, bug-seed, and seaside spurge make their homes there. Just inland are the foredunes, which have become stabilized by deep-rooted grasses such as little bluestem, beach grass, and sand-reed grass. Shrubs such as red-osier dogwood, aromatic sumac, sand cherry, and prostrate juniper add color and diversity to the foredunes. The federally threatened Pitcher's thistle occasionally occurs on the foredunes. This species is found only along the shores of Lake Michigan and Lake Huron.

Scattered among the foredunes are shallow depressions created by winds scouring the dunes. These areas usually retain water all year long and are called pannes. Characteristic plants include Kalm's lobelia, fringed gentian, rose gentian, stiff aster, and bladderworts. Many of these plants also occur in fens in the uplands of the moraine.

After an exhausting climb into the high dunes, two different types of plant communities are encountered. Savannas dominated by white and black oaks with an understory of Pennsylvania sedge, bracken fern, lupine, and other sun-loving wildflowers are found on dry, sunny, south-facing slopes. Cool, north-facing slopes have species which are more mesic, such as red oak, basswood, flowering dogwood, and hepatica. Scattered through the dunes are stands of white pine and jack pine, remainders of the cooler climate typically found farther north.

Then we turned our backs on the lake, and looked steeply down the leeward slope. We continued to look, for a long time. It rested our eyes. Beneath us lay a peaceful deep hollow filled with familiar woodland. We had turned our backs on pioneers and relicts and invaders from the arid southwest. . . . We had turned our backs on the xerophytes, . . . because we had found shelter from wind and sun. We slid down among the mesophytes, the plants occupying the middle ground between wet and dry.

—May Theilgaard Watts, "Picnic in a Gritty Wind," in Reading the Landscape (1957)

The Northwest Morainal Natural Region is characterized in part by the large number of rare plant species found here. A partial list will illustrate the diversity: From the prairie are bluehearts, Hill's thistle, white lady's-slipper orchid, prairie gentian, rough white lettuce, and prairie parsley. From the northern forests are bearberry, paper birch, sweetfern, trailing arbutus, ground cedar, green adder's-mouth, and white pine. Another group of plants is more characteristic of wetlands and quite common along the Atlantic and Gulf coastal plains, but are not encountered again until they are found in the wetlands near Lake Michigan. Some are inconspicuous small, green plants that grow on the edge of wetlands. These "belly plants" are best seen by literally getting down on your stomach! Some examples are black-fruited spike rush, umbrella sedge, bald rush, and a small bladderwort.

Botanists have long come to the northwest part of Indiana to see this wide diversity of plant species growing in proximity to each other. No other region of the state has such a rich and varied flora. Fortunately, a number of outstanding natural areas are preserved by the National Park Service, the Indiana Department of Natural Resources, and The Nature Conservancy.

Sundews entrap insects with sticky tentacles, then assimilate them, apparently as a nitrogen supply, in their acidic, nutrient-poor bog habitat.
Photo by Richard Fields

Lupine, a showy legume, is a food host for Karner blue butterfly larvae.
Photo by Lee Casebere

Prickly-pear cactus, more typical of the American Southwest, occurs in xeric sandy habitats of the Indiana dunes.
Photo by Delano Z. Arvin

The beauty of paper or canoe birch is commonly seen in forests of the northern U.S., but the species is rare in Indiana.
Photo by Lee Casebere

27. The Southern Tip of the Big-Sea Waters: The Lake Michigan Natural Region

Michelle Martin Hedge

I know a lake where the cool waves break
And softly fall on the silver sand:
And no steps intrude on that solitude,
No voice, save mine, disturbs the strand.

  —*Fitz-James O'Brien,* Lock Ine

The Native Americans called it *Mikesen,* or "large lake." When early explorers first arrived, they saw a wide, blue stretch of water, the wind dancing across its surface, waves breaking against the shore. It is Indiana's most unusual natural feature—Lake Michigan. It is a cold, deep lake with clean water, except near large cities where humans have disturbed the balance of its natural biological systems.

Lake Michigan's history involves processes that occurred over millions of years, as the Great Lakes were forming. During the vast time period that followed the establishment of a bedrock foundation, the terrain was sculptured by weathering and stream erosion. The land was then uplifted and tilted by movements of the Earth. Great continental ice sheets invaded the region several times. As the last, or Wisconsinan, ice sheet receded, there emerged a series of mighty basins, scoured and molded by the retreating ice. These basins, of which Lake Michigan is the southernmost, became the world's largest reservoir of fresh water.

Because of Lake Michigan's size and character, several natural phenomena are present. Normally in a lake there will be a temperature gradient (thermocline) where warm circulating water at the surface meets the colder, calmer water in its depths. Since Lake Michigan's great mass of deep offshore water warms much more slowly than water lying over the shallows near shore, the lake tends to warm from the shore outward, forming a vertical cold water/warm water interface. This thermal bar starts near the shore and moves slowly offshore as summer progresses. This vertical rather than horizontal interface has profound effects on the life within its water, the breeding cycles of wetlands-dependent animals, and even the climates of nearby cities.

Lake Michigan's tides are, for the most part, small. Periodically, however, high winds or a rapid change in barometric pressure can cause its water to oscillate from shore to shore, like water sloshing in a giant bathtub. These motions, called wind seiches, can last anywhere from a few minutes to a few days. Infrequently, high winds combine with barometric pressure changes to form a minor tidal wave. Seiches have been known to raise the water level in Lake Michigan by as much as 13 feet in just a few minutes.

Lake Michigan is a relatively young lake. As a result, food chains in its water are relatively simple, short, and easily disrupted. Benthic drift organisms, which are microscopic life forms that are fed upon by smaller fish, are an important part of the food chain and are of relatively few types. They have adapted to the environment of Lake Michigan—to its currents, thermal bar, and wind seiches. In fact, it has been found that chlorophyll-containing species do most of their photosynthesizing during the first three hours of their exposure to sunlight, usually enabling them to complete that part of their cycle

The Lake Michigan Natural Region

Steelhead trout (shown here) and coho salmon have been introduced into Lake Michigan and now are important game fish. *Photo by Richard Fields*

Aerial view of Lake Michigan shoreline and associated dune communities. *Photo by Richard Fields*

Close view of the wave-washed shoreline at Indiana Dunes. *Photo by Marion Jackson*

Lighthouse and pier at Michigan City extend into frozen shallows of Lake Michigan. *Photo by Delano Z. Arvin*

Michigan City shoreline of Lake Michigan is a favorite birding spot. Shown here is a hooded merganser. *Photo by Delbert Rust*

before a seiche comes along and forces them below the zone of light penetration.

The composition of the fish fauna was quite different in the days of the early explorers. They found the nine-spine stickleback, long-nose dace, longnose sucker, lake herring, lake sturgeon, and Lake Michigan muskellunge, among others. The two main predators were the lake trout and the lake whitefish, which also became the most sought-after species for commercial use.

Because of overfishing, alteration of migration routes to their spawning grounds, and water quality changes, many fish species no longer occur in Lake Michigan in commercially valuable numbers. With the loss of the predators, a destabilized environment exists in the lake. Prey species populations have exploded. These conditions, and the opening of the St. Lawrence Seaway, permitted the invasion of this ecosystem by two alien species, the sea lamprey and the alewife. Also, species new to the lake, such as the coho salmon, carp, and rainbow smelt, have been deliberately introduced to replace some of the species which have disappeared. The ecosystem has been altered enough that the natural balance that controlled populations is lost. These factors, combined with inputs of soil sediments and wastewater plus the destruction of wetlands, ushered in the era of instability that persists today.

Recently, another problem species has entered Lake Michigan. The zebra mussel, a species native to the Caspian Sea, has invaded the Great Lakes. Besides being an economic nightmare, this prolific species has intensified competition for food and space with native fish larvae and with already endangered native mussels.

Lake Michigan represents millions of years of continual change. No one can look across its vast expanse without feeling a sense of awe for this natural wonder. Our Great Lake is a special natural resource that profoundly affects the natural systems surrounding it. There are continuing efforts to protect the shoreline along Lake Michigan, as well as to monitor and manage the species found within its waters. We are learning that the quality of life around the lake will determine the life in the lake and its survival for future generations.

> Reflecting on the lake, I love
> To see the stars of evening glow;
> So tranquil in the heavens above,
> So restless in the wave below.
>
> —*Reginald Heber,* On Heavenly and Earthly Hope

Morning glow over the "banks of the Wabash."   *Photo by Richard Fields*

The Riverine System

28. Waters in Motion: The Big Rivers Natural Region

Hank Huffman

The name was doubtless suggested by the river itself, as its waters were remarkable for their clearness. So that when the Indian stood upon its banks, or rowed his bark canoe over its surface, he naturally called it Ouabache, which meant in his language, white. The once small boy of the village easily recalls, how, when he went in swimming up at the sandbar, the white sand glittered through the clear water, at a depth of several feet; also how the white pebbles and mussel shells with their rainbow colors, could be plainly seen, and the delight he took in diving for them.

> —*Blackford Condit,* The History of Early Terre Haute
> from 1816–1840 *(1900)*

The Ohio River, the lower Wabash River from its mouth at the southwesternmost tip of Indiana north to Attica in Fountain County, and the lower White River from the Wabash to the confluence of its East and West forks constitute a distinct natural region known as the Big Rivers. The watersheds of these three large, wide rivers drain many thousands of square miles, resulting in average flows of 7,000 cubic feet of water per second or greater.

These rivers usually flood each spring, and occasionally in other seasons. The Ohio River has crested at more than 60 feet above its normal level, with peak flows of well over 10 times those recorded at low flow levels. With each flood these rivers rearrange themselves, eroding away vulnerable shorelines and islands, elsewhere depositing new sandbars and shoals. Sometimes they change course completely as they cut through narrow bends, leaving old channels as abandoned oxbows. In contrast, during times of summer drought these rivers may be only 1 to 3 feet deep or less in certain locations, and may be easily forded.

Interestingly, the Big Rivers Natural Region shares many characteristics with the Lake Michigan Natural Region. Whereas Lake Michigan lies along Indiana's northern border and is only a small part of the much larger Great Lakes System, the Big Rivers form the southern and part of the western borders, and are tributary extensions within the Mississippi River System—the third-largest river system in the world. Both natural regions are aquatic environments of tremendous size, each with its own distinct assemblage of aquatic organisms.

The present locations and configurations of the Big Rivers are largely a product of the glacial advances across Indiana. As the ice sheets began to retreat, great volumes of meltwater formed new patterns of drainage across the landscape, which coalesced into our rivers and streams as we know them today.

Once the present courses of the Ohio, Wabash, and White rivers were established and environmental conditions stabilized at the close of the ice ages, numerous species of animals and plants used these aquatic corridors to migrate into Indiana. Aquatic organisms spread throughout the network of smaller rivers and tributaries, while many terrestrial animals closely followed these waterways. The influence of rivers on adjacent floodplains and river bluffs also helped funnel many plant species along these corridors, thereby playing a key role in shaping the present distribution of much of the state's native flora and fauna.

More fish species reside in the Big Rivers than in any other water body in the state. More than 100 species are known from the lower Wabash River, with silvery minnows, gizzard shad, channel catfish, bluegill, freshwater drum, shortnose gar, white crappie, and longear sunfish among the most common.

> Harris, an early nineteenth century traveler, mentions black catfish ranging from six to 110 pounds; yellow catfish from six to fifty pounds; pike from eight to thirty-five pounds. Most of these fish stories come from the upper part of the Ohio River but there is no doubt that the fishing was equally good all the way to the Mississippi. . . . Early fishermen, for example were impressed by a mere sixty-pound catfish, not guessing at the size of the huge Mississippi River "cats," who seem to have sent only their smaller relatives up the Ohio as far as Pittsburgh.
>
> —*John Bakeless, "The Wild Middle West," in* The Eyes of
> Discovery *(1950)*

The steady current in the main channels and the slower, deeper pools provide a habitat for a number of fish typically not found in smaller rivers, including some of which are the largest, rarest, and most interesting species: paddlefish, lake sturgeon, shovelnose sturgeon, alligator gar, Ohio muskellunge, goldeye, mooneye, skipjack herring, and blue sucker.

Two other unusual denizens of the big rivers are the hellbender and the alligator snapping turtle. The hellbender, a giant-sized salamander reaching lengths to 18 inches, is capable of inflicting painful bites if carelessly handled. The alligator snapping turtle, the largest reptile found in the Midwest, can be more than two feet long

At the Grayville cutoff in Posey County, the Wabash turned 180° in a meander loop. River water now flows across the neck of the loop.
Photo by Richard Fields

Among the largest of river fishes, the shovelnose sturgeon is of ancient lineage, dating back to Mississippian time. *Photo by John O. Whitaker, Jr.*

and weigh up to 160 pounds. This very capable predator has powerful jaws capable of causing severe injury to a human hand or foot.

> Colonel May was much startled by "a terrible fish if such may be called. . . . It was about eighteen inches long; as big as a man's wrist; with large flat head, something like a bull-frog. He had four legs of the bigness of a gray squirrel's, and a tail five inches long, near two inches wide; and was of a sickly ash-color, and as spiteful as the devil." The colonel was getting his first glimpse of one of the giant salamanders, still common in eastern American streams, usually known as . . . "hellbenders." . . . As

they are quiet creatures, protectively colored, they stick close to the beds of streams, most people never guess that they exist.

—*Bakeless, "The Wild Middle West"*

These rivers also provide habitat for an equally important group of animals, the freshwater mussels. Mussels, or "freshwater clams," are bivalve (two-shelled) mollusks. These bottom-dwelling creatures begin their lives as microscopic larvae that attach to the gills and fins of fish, where they metamorphose into tiny juvenile forms. They then drop off and bury themselves in substrates of stable sand and gravel in riffles and shoals, where they continue to mature and grow. Living as long as 50 years, these rather sedentary creatures feed by filtering algae and microscopic organisms from the water.

Originally more than 75 species of freshwater mussels occurred in the Ohio, lower Wabash, and lower White rivers—with such colorful names as sheepnose, spectaclecase, purple warty-back, elephant ear, pig-toe, and monkey-face. Several mussel species are quite distinctive of the Big Rivers Region, including the fat pocketbook, white cat's paw, tubercled-blossom, pink mucket, and Wabash riffleshell. The fact that mussels existed in very high populations is evidenced by the large accumulations of shells occasionally found along river banks. Known as shell middens or shell mounds, they were left by prehistoric Native Americans.

> Freshwater mussels remain one of Indiana's most valuable commercial wildlife resources, as well as the most endangered group in the state. These living fossils made of mother-of-pearl can continue to quietly filter water for millennia to come if we give them room to live.

—*Robert Anderson and Robert Ball, "Musseling In," in* Outdoor Indiana *(1993)*

Confluence of the White (*center*) and Wabash rivers (*foreground*) at border between Knox (*left*) and Gibson (*right*) counties. *Photo by Richard Fields*

Two areas within the Big Rivers Region are particularly noteworthy: the Falls of the Ohio between Clarksville and Louisville and the Old Dam on the Wabash River near New Harmony. The Falls of the Ohio is an ancient fossilized coral reef of Silurian and Devonian limestone, which forms an island and rapids across that portion of the river.

It was here that multitudes of American bison crossed the river in pre-settlement times as they migrated from Illinois along the buffalo traces of southern Indiana to the salt licks of Kentucky. These rapids were an impediment, however, to the early pioneers and their flatboats, thus catalyzing the settlement of the Falls Cities—Jeffersonville, Indiana, and Louisville, Kentucky. It was from here that Meriwether Lewis joined William Clark in 1803 to set out on their famed expedition to the West. The naturalist John James Audubon resided nearby for several years and made several hundred sketches of birds in the Falls area. The Falls themselves have been the subject of numerous studies over the years, with hundreds of species of fossil corals having been first discovered and described from there.

The Old Dam near New Harmony is likewise a natural rock ledge forming a rapids across the lower Wabash River. Like the Falls of the Ohio, it also became an important site for the early study of natural history. In 1826 a small group of scientists and intellectuals from the Philadelphia Academy of Natural Sciences traveled by flatboat to take up residence in New Harmony. This "Boatload of Knowledge" included such notables as William MacClure, the "Father of American Geology"; Thomas Say, the "Father of American Zoology"; and the famous French artist and naturalist Charles LeSueur.

Land of the West, we fly to thee!
Sick of the Old World's sophistry,
Haste then across the dark blue sea.

Land of the West, we rush to thee!
Home of the brave: soil of the free
Hurrah! She rises o'er the sea.
    —*Sung by the Owenite party on the "Boatload of Knowledge"*

The Old Dam and adjacent portions of the river became a favorite collecting site. It was here that LeSueur first discovered and described for science two new fish species, the black crappie and the grass pickerel, as well as the smooth softshell, spiny softshell, false map, and red-eared turtles.

Since streams mirror the patterns of land use within their watersheds, the Big Rivers unfortunately no longer hold all the natural treasures they formerly did. As settlement of the Midwest resulted in clearing of the forest for farms and cities, along with drainage of Indiana's wetlands, water quality in the Big Rivers declined steadily. The period 1820 to 1940 saw a significant increase in sediment load, dissolved minerals, and toxic pollutants within these rivers. Locks and dams built along the length of the Ohio River altered its flow and character, with nearly two-thirds of the Falls of the Ohio destroyed by these constructions.

Today the alligator snapping turtle, the hellbender, and several of the region's distinctive fish are rarely, if ever, found prowling these large rivers. Of the 75 or more mussel species known to have occurred in the Big Rivers Natural Region, 7 are endangered in, and 14 are extirpated from, Indiana waters. And 4—the leafshell, round combshell, Tennessee riffleshell, and Wabash riffleshell—are globally extinct, now existing only as empty shells in museum collections.

But improvements are being made in water quality within Indiana's streams (see also chapter 39, "Beneath the Water's Surface").

The "old dam" across the Wabash River at New Harmony in Posey County is visible at the low water level during the drought of August 1991. The "dam" consists of natural bedrock ledges.
Photo by Richard Fields

Improved agricultural practices and better wastewater treatment have resulted in marked improvements in stream and river conditions in recent years. While they are not back to the pristine clarity of pre-settlement days, when "the white sand glittered through the clear water, at a depth of several feet," the last 30 years of environmental efforts have resulted in greatly improved riverine habitats.

> Oh the moonlight's fair to-night along the Wabash,
> From the fields their comes the breath of new-mown hay;
> Thro' the sycamores the candle lights are gleaming,
> On the banks of the Wabash far away.
>
> —*Paul Dresser, "On The Banks of the Wabash" (1913)*

The alligator snapping turtle is potentially the largest of Indiana turtles. Its current population status is not well known.
Photo by Sherman A. Minton

The largest, and likely the most endangered, Indiana salamander is the hellbender, an aquatic species that requires unpolluted streams and rivers.
Photo by Sherman A. Minton

Indiana has long been famous for its rich fauna of freshwater mussels. Some have been extirpated, and several others are currently endangered.
Photo by Richard Fields

Part 3: The Biota of Indiana

Lichen and moss species are typical of spore-producing plants that begin succession in rock outcrop ecosystems.   *Photo by Lee Casebere*

Diversity and Reproduction

29. A Diversity of Forms

Marion T. Jackson

All living things are interwoven, each with the other; the tie is sacred, and nothing, or next to nothing, is alien to ought else.

—*Marcus Aurelius*, Meditations

Attention is riveted today on threats to the biodiversity of Planet Earth. Most simply, biodiversity is the total richness of life in a given region, or worldwide. Whether biodiversity of a given area is rich or impoverished is determined by the relative mix of habitat types represented, the number of species present, and the amount of genetic variation within each species. Biodiversity is presently declining rapidly worldwide, if even the most conservative estimates of loss rates are accepted. Reductions in biodiversity occur when pristine habitats are severely modified or eliminated by natural events or human-induced changes. Such changes, in turn, cause the loss of species locally (extirpation) or globally (extinction).

The vast array of life represented on Planet Earth developed over an enormous period of time—some 3.5 billion years. Today this biota is the sum of several million (perhaps as many as 50 million) species of microbes, fungi, plants, and animals. The primary reason for the wide range in estimates of the total number of species which exist worldwide is that a majority remain unknown to science and not classified. The number of individual organisms of all species collectively is staggering, surely many trillions, perhaps quadrillions, or even more.

It is widely believed that the total richness of life (biodiversity) at the time humans became the dominant species was the greatest it has ever been throughout Earth's history. Now, largely because of our activities, it may also be the most vulnerable that it has ever been.

The most wonderful mystery of life may well be the means by which it created so much diversity from so little physical matter. The biosphere, all organisms combined, makes up only about one part in ten billion of the earth's mass. It is sparsely distributed through a kilometer-thick layer of soil, water, and air stretched over a half billion square kilometers of surface.

—*Edward O. Wilson*, The Diversity of Life *(1993)*

HABITAT DIVERSITY

The whole of nature is divided into habitats, each of which, together with the life it supports, is what ecologists term an *ecosys-*

tem. Ecosystems may be small or large. They range in scope from a lichen-covered rock, a fallen log, a pile of animal dung, or a temporary pool—to the Amazonian rainforest, African savanna, or Pacific Ocean—to the planetary ecosystem or ecosphere, which is the entire world and the totality of life (biosphere) it supports.

Habitats group broadly according to physical medium into marine, freshwater, and land systems, with obvious transitions at their margins, e.g., estuaries, wetlands, and floodplains. These global ecosystem types divide further in response to climatic differences, substrate patterns, vegetation structure, animal communities, or water characteristics into biomes or realms—deciduous forest, desert, grassland, open ocean, coral reef, tundra, or tropical rainforest.

The 36,291-square-mile portion of North America that has been delineated and named Indiana (and described fully in the "Natural Regions" chapters) originally sat astride the transition between deciduous forest and grassland biomes, with about seven-eighths formerly forested. In contrast, the much smaller area of freshwater habitat in Indiana is divided more equally between standing water (lentic) and flowing water (lotic) habitats.

Transitions (called ecotones or continua by ecologists) varied continuously within these broad categories as substrate, slope, soil, water depth or velocity, moisture availability, light intensity, or other ecological conditions changed. The cumulative effect of these environmental differences was that at no point on the original Indiana landscape could habitats be separated with complete confidence, thereby permitting even an experienced ecologist to say with certainty that "this spot is *this* habitat" or "that spot is *that* habitat."

Original Indiana, then, was not a single uniform expanse of undisturbed natural vegetation, predominantly a deciduous forest wilderness of tall trees. In reality it was a continuously varying mixture (in both space and time) of land and water, forest and prairie, or early successional and mature communities, each particular site harboring a slightly different and likely unique set of plant and animal species. There is a saying that "you can never step in the same stream twice." Doubtless you cannot step into the same forest, prairie, bog, or any other habitat twice. The only constant in nature is change.

How rapidly communities of organisms change across the landscape from Point A to Point B depends less on the distance involved than on the steepness of the environmental gradients which occur. For example, original forests occupying the relatively uniform topography (environment) typical of the Central Till Plain of Indiana likely varied less in a 100-kilometer distance than did those forests that clothed contrasting south- and north-facing slopes, and were separated by a ravine only 100 meters wide, in the southern Indiana hill country. Put simply, wrinkled landscapes house more habitats than do smooth ones.

This is not to say that no patterns exist in the structure and functioning of biotic communities in nature. Repeating combinations of similar species which do similar things do occur (and, within limits, are even predictable in their occurrence) in habitats with closely similar topography, soils, microclimates, ages, and developmental histories.

Such diversity of habitats as once occurred, even in a state as generally uniform as Indiana, created conditions favorable to the relatively large number of plant and animal species living here in pre-settlement times. Given a choice, over time nature usually selects the highest diversity a given environment will support. Simple ecosystems are the exception worldwide, diverse ones the rule. There is abundant evidence that diverse ecosystems are more stable than are simple ones which occur in similar environments. This should be a flag of caution to humans in our global rush to simplify habitats and to convert most ecosystems to monocultures.

SPECIES DIVERSITY

The fundamental unit of life is the species, a population of highly similar individuals, each potentially capable of reproducing in nature with others of their kind, but generally incapable of interbreeding with the members of other species. Each species has its own ecological life history which determines, and is determined by, the size and lifeways of its individuals; the way that they use the resources (space, food, water, cover) of their habitats; the social organization among members of that species and their interactions with other species; how they obtain nourishment, while avoiding becoming nourishment for another; how they choose mates, reproduce, and nurture offspring—in a word, their ecological niche, which is the sum of the lifeways of a given species. Each niche can permanently support but one species, and only one species can completely and permanently fill a given niche. Evolution, then, becomes in large part the process of niche emptying and niche filling as environments change over vast time periods.

The specific role played by each species is determined by the several dimensions of its particular niche. Niches can be wide or narrow, with the species filling them being generalists or specialists, respectively. Generalist species typically survive as large populations within a range of environmental conditions, frequently being widely distributed and resilient to change. Specialist species usually are more restricted in numbers, in what they can do and where they can do it, and frequently are vulnerable to habitat modification. It follows logically, then, that specialist species are often more susceptible to extinction than are generalists.

Nature's focus is on the species—the population—not the individual. Only human society emphasizes the worth and welfare of the individual. For wild populations, individuals pass across the stage of life, some having larger roles than others, but nature's continuing drama is the pageant of species, each playing out the script encoded within its genes, each having a separate role, each unique: in the succinct words of the late G. E. Hutchinson of Yale University, "the ecological theater and the evolutionary play."

GENETIC DIVERSITY

Biodiversity ultimately becomes, then, in large measure, the range of genetic material present in a given habitat—hence, the kinds of species present and the genetic variability within each. In a sense, each species is one volume in nature's library, the text of each varying according to the differences in the genetic code (language). Saving biodiversity then becomes a matter of saving the books (species) in nature's genetic library, even if they are untitled or unread.

Individual character does not matter to Nature. In the end she absorbs all individualities. She knows only races and their rise and fall.

—*Donald Culross Peattie,* A Prairie Grove *(1938)*

INDIANA'S BIODIVERSITY

The biodiversity of original Indiana was likely about average for Planet Earth, prior to recent human-induced changes. Compared with lush, wet tropical forests, or nutrient-rich, equable coral reefs, our diversity was impoverished. But in contrast to harsh, austere polar zones or open-ocean environments, life in Indiana was teeming and rich, in both numbers and kinds.

Temperate zones, by definition, have moderate climates and represent (with their seasons of nearly equal length) more closely the average conditions for life on the planet—conditions favorable also for humans, the toolmakers, to develop their civilizations. It is no happenstance that the wave of advancing civilization rolled first through the temperate zones, while only now it is marching inexorably across the tropics, and beginning to advance into polar regions.

Both the soil and biota of temperate habitats can absorb greater impact of human activity without their ecosystems collapsing than is possible in tropical or polar regions. As a consequence of this greater ecological resilience in temperate zone environments, a larger percentage of the biodiversity present in original Indiana has survived the changes of the past two centuries than could have occurred in a similar-sized area in Ecuador or Labrador. What remains of the diversity once present in natural Indiana is the subject of parts 3 and 5 of this book.

The array of living systems that greeted our first settlers took some 10,000 years after the end of the Glacial Age to assemble and sort itself out along the several environmental gradients represented in pre-settlement Indiana. With the flintlock, ax, match, ditch, plow, and cow, the pioneers took it all apart in three short human generations. The wilderness that *was* Indiana disappeared a shot, a chip, a bonfire, a scoop, a furrow, and a bite at a time. Multiplied at a hundred thousand sites, the wave rolled on relentlessly for nearly a hundred years, destroying most, dissecting the remainder into widely separated postage stamp–sized remnants of natural habitat.

But nature held on and fought back with the tenacity known only to ecological succession. Nature has a way of surviving in small natural enclaves, then reoccupying disturbed areas when conditions improve. Survivors of the settlement storm attempted to repair the damage we had wrought—at least in the unshorn fields and forests—while our attention centered on new quests. Most species persisted and "made do," as reduced populations in the wild nooks and crannies that remained in places we still had not "got around to changing," or in the scattered natural areas protected by the visionary few.

Fish Creek Fen in La Porte County. Fens have neutral to alkaline waters that flow slowly, providing habitat for both wetland and prairie species. *Photo by Richard Fields*

Indiana Dunes of Porter County. The range of successional stages on this varied landscape provides habitat for the highest diversity of species in the state. *Photo by Marion Jackson*

Merry Lea Nature Preserve in Noble County. Natural lakes and cattail marsh grade into oak-hickory forest on the glacial ridges. *Photo by Marion Jackson*

Tallgrass Prairie along railroad right-of-way in northeast Indiana. Tom Bushnell, an early Indiana soil scientist, is dwarfed by big bluestem grass. *Photo by Alton Lindsey*

The stones forming Hindostan Falls of East Fork of the White River in Martin County were once harvested for whetstones. Originally the clear waters of the White and Wabash rivers were famous for fine bass fishing.
Photo by William B. Barnes

Oak-hickory forest of Brown County is now mostly secondary forest, but this area once had magnificent hardwood timber. *Photo by Richard Fields*

Sandstone cliffs of rugged Martin County are habitat for a host of lower plant, fern, and flowering herb species. Many interesting animals also live along rock faces.
Photo by Richard Fields

High canopy of beech-maple forest in Hoot Woods, Owen County, in autumn. Huge tuliptrees are also prevalent, along with about 20 other tree species.
Photo by Marion Jackson

Cypress swamp forest in Posey County represents one of the northern extensions of this habitat type in the U.S.
Photo by Lee Casebere

Big Wyandotte Cave in Crawford County is representative of the vast, dark underground habitat of southern Indiana. Without photosynthesis, the food base for animals must originate from outside.
Photo by Richard Fields

Flatwoods on nearly level land in Ripley County. Silt loam soils of the region have a fragipan, creating ponding for several months each year due to slow internal drainage. *Photo by Lee Casebere*

Chestnut oak glade habitat in Floyd County has thin soil over shallow bedrock, creating droughty conditions much of the summer.
Photo by Perry Scott

CLASSIFICATION

Naming, organizing, sorting, storing, and interpreting information is basic to human understanding of the universe we inhabit. Collectively, such information becomes knowledge. Knowing and naming habitats and their species memberships is no exception. As mentioned previously, habitats sort out according to the environmental conditions that control their ecological characteristics and distribution patterns. Moisture availability and substrate type are the major controls in Indiana landscapes.

Habitat or community classification can be as general or specific as you wish, depending upon objectives. In Indiana the range of habitat conditions is from deep, clear glacial lakes to xeric dune sands. In between are a host of wetland types—marsh, fen, panne, bog, wet prairie, seeps, springs, shrub swamp, swamp forest, flatwoods, floodplain. Mesic (intermediate moisture) sites harbor predominantly moist deciduous forest or mesic tallgrass prairie. Dry-adapted communities of plants and animals include xeric forest, savanna, sand prairie, barrens, glades, and exposed rock outcrops. Sheltered sites with favorable microclimates (e.g., moist sandstone ravines) permit relict species typical of other locales to survive here (e.g., forests of hemlock and/or eastern white pine).

Several habitat types have been essentially eliminated (extirpated) from Indiana, although they may be reasonably well represented in other states. Probably the rarest habitat types in Indiana are bur oak savanna, black-soil prairie, sand prairie, gravel hill prairie, sand forest, acid seep, sinkhole swamp, and glacial lakes in natural condition. Most of these, except black-soil prairie and glacial lakes, were widely scattered and of limited areal extent originally. None has fared well in the face of extensive landscape alteration, pollution, and lake margin development. All of these types are now restricted to a few sites of small size and often of marginal quality.

> Indiana has often been a . . . scene of vegetational . . . advance and retreat; and . . . over half of the species of ferns and seed plants occurring in the state are, in Indiana on the borders of their present day range.
>
> —*Ray C. Friesner, "Indiana as a Critical Botanical Area,"* in Proceedings of the Indiana Academy of Science *(1936)*

Probably all states, because of their diversity of habitats and/or extensive geographic area, harbor species typical of other biogeographic regions. Indiana is no exception, and in that sense is a critical biotic area. A number of Appalachian species extend into the hill country of southeastern and south-central Indiana. Mississippi River Valley forms are found in the lower Wabash Valley. A peninsula of tallgrass prairie and associated types occupied large areas of western Indiana originally. Northern species find refuge in bogs, lakes, and dunes of the upper tiers of counties. Some habitats even harbor species typical of the Atlantic Coastal Plain. Such floral and faunal inclusions greatly enrich the diversity and interest of our native biota.

Species are classified by taxonomists into a standardized hierarchy of units that is almost universally accepted and applied by scientists worldwide. As a result there is much less confusion and misunderstanding than exists for the classification of habitats. Further, species usually have reproductive barriers to the blending of units, creating more distinct separations than is possible at the individual community level in habitat classification. Finally, members of taxonomic units are usually presumed to have common ancestry and similar developmental histories.

From large to progressively less inclusive units, the hierarchy for classifying organisms is: kingdom, phylum (or division), class, order, family, genus, species. A further subdivision, subspecies, is used to separate populations of some species. Usually several equal-ranking taxa at a given level in the hierarchy group into the next-higher unit on the scale; e.g., several families compose one order, or one genus may contain a number of species.

For example, the common crow would be classified as Kingdom Animalia, Phylum Chordata (having vertebrae), Class Aves (the birds), Order Passeriformes (perching birds), Family Corvidae (crows, jays, etc.), Genus *Corvus* (crow), Species *brachyrhynchos* (crowing or cawing). The scientific (or Latin) name for this species (kind) of bird is then *Corvus brachyrhynchos* Brehm. The latter name (species epithet) corresponds to a human "given" name, the former (generic name) to the human "family" name, e.g., Jane Doe. (The abbreviation following the species epithet is the scientist who first described the species.) Another very familiar bird, the blue jay, is closely related to the crow, and also in the family Corvidae, but in a different genus and species, *Cyanocitta cristata* (Linnaeus), or blue jay with a crest.

BIOTA OF INDIANA—THEN AND NOW

Of all the many and varied species of organisms that have lived recently in Indiana, people tend to be most familiar with vertebrate animals and vascular plants. Since the beginning of European settlement, 766 species of vertebrate animals (which are the best-known group of all organisms) have been recorded in Indiana: 201 fish, 39 amphibian, 51 reptilian, 407 avian, and 68 mammalian species. Remarkably, only 26 native vertebrate species in Indiana have become extinct or extirpated, a loss of only 3.4 percent of the recorded total. Apparently only 2 species which occurred here, the passenger pigeon and the Carolina parakeet, have become extinct globally.

This survival rate, which has occurred despite more than 99 percent of Indiana's habitat being altered from original conditions, is encouraging, but does not give reason for complacency. An additional 99 species (13 percent) presently require protection owing to human impact. Several others have rather small populations at widely scattered locations, making them potentially vulnerable.

Of all vertebrate groups, hoofed mammals were hit hardest, losing all three original species. Of course, the white-tailed deer was reintroduced about 60 years ago, and has increased until it now borders on being a nuisance. Next was mammalian carnivores, which lost 9 of the original 19 species, a loss rate of 47 percent. Amphibians currently are most vulnerable as a class, with 8 of 39 species (20.5 percent) requiring protection. More may follow as breeding sites, especially, become increasingly modified.

The most recent checklist of vascular plants included 2,265 species. Although Indiana contains only 0.5 percent of the North American land area north of Mexico, our vascular flora includes 11 percent of the species found in that same region.

Of the nearly 1,900 species of vascular plants native to Indiana, some 77 taxa have apparently been extirpated from the state, a significant total, but a loss rate of only 4 percent. However, approximately an additional 495 species (26 percent) are on the state list of those endangered, threatened, or of special concern.

A vastly greater percentage of exotic vascular plant species have become naturalized (now reproducing on their own) into the plant communities of Indiana, than is the case for vertebrate animals. Not including exotics grown ornamentally or agriculturally, an estimated *one-fourth* of all vascular plant species which now grow somewhere in Indiana are exotics.

Sourwood tree in fruit with beautiful fall color. Rare tree in far southern Indiana.
Photo by Marion Jackson

Promethea moth larva prepares to weave its pupal cocoon within a wild black cherry leaf, a part of the insect's complete metamorphosis life cycle.
Photo by Pearl M. Eslinger

Yellow-crowned night heron, once rather common, is now endangered in Indiana.
Photo by Delano Z. Arvin

Brome grass silhouetted against the rising sun symbolizes the photosynthetic pathway that supports all life.   *Photo by Lee Casebere*

The black rat snake, shown here at Big Walnut Nature Preserve, is an important predator of small birds and rodents, especially.   *Photo by Lee Casebere*

Edible, tasty sulphur mushrooms, known also as "chicken of the woods," often occur on decaying oak logs and stumps in autumn. Fungi are vital in the decay cycles that make nutrients available to other forms of life.   *Photo by Pearl M. Eslinger*

Christmas fern, so named for its persistent green fronds in winter, is shown here unrolling new "fiddleheads" in spring.
Photo by Bill N. McKnight

Maryland meadow beauty, an endangered wildflower in Indiana, is noted for its delicate beauty and elongated yellow anthers.   *Photo by Lee Casebere*

Large yellow lady's-slipper orchids are found occasionally in bogs or mesic woods. Under no circumstances should wild orchids be collected.
Photo by Perry Scott

"And Adam gave names to all cattle, and to the fowl of the air, and to every beast of the field." Genesis, II, 20.

But Adam overlooked the insects. The "sons" of Adam have given names to more than two hundred thousand species of insects since Linneaus took up the unfinished task of Adam.

—*W. J. Holland,* The Butterfly Book *(1899)*

Invertebrate animals, though vastly more numerous in total species (perhaps more than 25,000 totally in Indiana), are much less precisely known than are the vertebrates. More than half are insects, with Gene Kritsky's current inventory of 13,314 species, representing 24 orders, being the most accurate recent tally. More than 11,100 species of this total for insects are members of only 4 groups (orders): beetles (3,877 species), flies (3,072), butterflies, moths, et al. (2,200), and ants, bees, wasps, et al. (1,955 species). Seven orders are represented by a total of 10 or fewer species each, with a total of only 21. Only 1 species of termite occurs in Indiana, despite its astronomical number of individuals. Only 9 insect species are currently listed as extirpated, including the lovely Karner blue butterfly, a tallgrass prairie species.

Perhaps 10,000 species of other invertebrates occur in Indiana, the majority of which are various worms, protozoans (ca. 3,000 species), spiders, and other arthropods. Aquatic and terrestrial snails and slugs total about 200 species. Crayfish are represented by only 17 species.

Of the 76 species of freshwater mussels recorded from the state's waters, 10 have already become extirpated (4 of which are globally extinct), and no less than 22 of those that remain are listed as federally or state endangered, threatened, or of special concern. Losses in water quality, siltation, and other alteration of stream habitats are the prime causes. Because all streams mirror the land-use practice within their watersheds, these aquatic "canaries in the cage" tell us a great deal about what has gone wrong on the land, as well as within the water. When streams look like well-creamed coffee much of the year, there are serious problems with land management upstream.

If we include the non-green fungi, the number of species of non-vascular plants is also large—perhaps approaching 15,000 species—with more than two-thirds of them fungi. Only a very few species of all groups combined are known to have been extirpated, a number likely to increase as surveys of these forms become complete. Just a handful are endemic (found only) in Indiana. Algae is the largest group of lower green plants at about 1,500 species known, with a total of perhaps 2,000 eventually expected to be recorded in Indiana. Presently the lichens (350 species), mosses and liverworts (380), and ferns and their allies (80) total just over 800 species combined. When the final tally for these groups is in, they are not expected to have a combined total of more than about 1,000 species.

Overall, then, the total biota of Indiana is almost certainly less than 50,000 species—most likely around 43,000. This total represents slightly more than an average of 1 species per each of the 36,000 square miles within the state. Combined, the vertebrates and vascular plants total only about 3,000. The other 40,000 species that we pass by largely unnoticed, ignore, step on, swat, or spray with pesticides, represent the vastly more numerous lower plant and invertebrate animal species.

Just because these latter groups are generally small, inconspicuous, and usually not economically important (unless they bother us, or compete with humans or domesticated plants and animals), it does not follow that they are unnecessary, or unimportant ecologically. These species are the cogs and gears, the nuts, bolts, and rivets, that hold nature's machinery together and keep ecosystems (habitats) functioning. They complete decay cycles, form the bases of food chains, and ameliorate the impacts of pollution. If we remove or lose them one by one, it is highly likely that eventually we will render dysfunctional those ecosystemic processes that balance and maintain the structural integrity of nature.

The wild places are where we began. When they end, so do we.
—*David Brower, Former Executive Director, Sierra Club and Friends of the Earth*

An excellent climber, the opossum, our most primitive mammal, has 50 teeth, the most of any Indiana mammal. A true omnivore, it eats everything from persimmons to decayed flesh.   *Photo by Delano Z. Arvin*

The orange cave salamander has a long, whip-like tail. It is usually found in the twilight zone of caves or in damp habitats just outside.   *Photo by Sherman A. Minton*

Turkey vultures, with their keen eyesight, are important scavengers. They locate dead animal carcasses as they soar on thermal air currents above Indiana.   *Photo by Marion Jackson*

Honeybees, though an introduced species, are important pollinators of many domesticated and wild plants.
Photo by Richard Fields

A small slug examines a soapwort gentian flower at dawn in Hoosier Prairie.
Photo by Lee Casebere

The Indian paintbrush's bright color is from showy bracts, not from true petals. Though green and photosynthetic, it is also partially a root parasite.
Photo by Marion Jackson

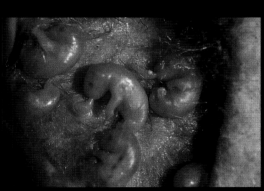

Insect-sized baby opossums nursing on teats in mother's pouch represent Indiana's only marsupial.   *Photo by Delano Z. Arvin*

One of our showiest songbirds, the seed-eating goldfinch, which is common at our bird feeders in winter, nests in late summer, often lining the nest cavity with thistledown.   *Photo by Delano Z. Arvin*

Ghost-like saprophytic Indian pipes, which obtain nourishment from decaying organic matter, lack chlorophyll but are true flowering plants.   *Photo by Delano Z. Arvin*

Sumac colonies often originate via vegetative reproduction by above-ground shoots arising from underground stems, creating one large genetically identical clone.   *Photo by Richard Fields*

30. Reproductive Strategies

Marion T. Jackson

I have called this principle, by which each slight variation, if useful, is preserved, by the term Natural Selection.

—*Charles Darwin,* The Origin of Species *(1859)*

Reproduction of its own kind is the goal of every form of life. Without perpetuating itself, that genetic lineage dies. Its ancestry has existed, but that particular inheritance is not passed to the future.

Biologists refer to the capability of a species or an individual to place offspring into the next generation as fitness. Fitness varies greatly from species to species and among individuals of a population. The potential for survival among the offspring produced is then time-tested by natural selection—nature's process of sorting inherited characteristics according to their chances for success in their natural environment.

Obviously, not all individual organisms reproduce, nor do all offspring survive. Natural selection eliminates genetic combinations with lesser long-term survival potential, while enhancing those combinations more favored by that particular environment. Stated simply, organisms better adapted to their environment survive and reproduce at higher frequencies than do those less suited. Nature is often harsh and disciplined, but is not judgmental or unfair. It is an honest and impartial, yet stern, regulator of biological success.

If an individual fails to reproduce, only one thread is removed from the genetic fabric of that species. Regional failure of all individuals of a species to reproduce forces its extirpation from that portion of its geographic range. Total reproductive failure for an entire species dooms it to global extinction, thereby erasing that genetic information from the biological chalkboard of time. This distressing fact becomes abundantly clear when one realizes that extinction is forever.

Overall biological diversity at a given site is a product of the fitness of all its component species. Environments fill with species in response to their differing abilities to evolve into, and to adapt to, the available niches: in a sense, the creation and maintenance of that environment's own "diversity of forms."

The many ways that the different groups of living organisms found in Indiana maintain their fitness and existence is the subject of Part 3 of this book. The richness of Indiana's own diversity of forms that once occurred here (and, to a large extent, still persists) is a product of the collective strategies of thousands of individual species for reproduction and for survival in that part of the world ecosystem now called Indiana.

To those who study her, Nature reveals herself as extraordinarily fertile and ingenious in devising *means*, but she has no *ends* which the human mind has been able to discover or comprehend.

—*Joseph Wood Krutch,* The Modern Temper II

Asexual reproduction may occur by fragmentation, which involves portions of the plant or animal separating from the parent, then growing independently. For other species, spores, buds, or shoots are produced on the parent organism, which later separate and germinate, or grow vegetatively. In a number of invertebrate and certain plant groups, unfertilized eggs sometimes develop into adult organisms, although these adults frequently are sterile. All of the above types of asexual reproduction are, in the broadest sense, forms of cloning, in most cases resulting in offspring that are genetically identical to the parental stock.

Non-flowering plants are characterized by two distinct life forms which alternate in successive generations of their life cycles. The conspicuous form (e.g., a cushion of moss), which contains but one set of chromosomes, produces both male and female sex cells. These sperm and eggs fuse at fertilization to form a separate plant with two sets of chromosomes (e.g., the spore capsules or sporophyte of a moss). The sporophyte, in turn, produces spores, usually in very large numbers—hence a "wealth of spores."

Flowering plants typically reproduce by a variety of "seed strategies" which ensure pollination and seed dispersal. Details of reproductive mechanisms employed by different groups of seed plants are discussed in later chapters.

The vast majority of animal species reproduce by means of fertilized eggs, with the number of offspring produced being roughly inversely proportional to the survival rate of the progeny. Even mammals, most of which produce living young, merely carry fertilized eggs during their development in the uterus, until they "hatch" at the end of gestation.

Specific life histories of this diversity of forms are discussed in the chapters which follow on the biota of Indiana.

Tall sporangium and bright fronds of cinnamon ferns at Shell Dune and Swale Nature Preserve, Lake County.
Photo by Perry Scott

The World of Plants

31. A Wealth of Spores: Non-Flowering Plants

Bill N. McKnight

Past, present, and future, we may rest assured, that the humblest individuals of the lowest of the Cryptogamia have been, and ever will be, as essential in the great unity, which we call Nature, as the loftiest forest tree, or the most odoriferous of beautiful flowers.

—*M. C. Cooke*

Most plants in Indiana do not produce seeds. Those that do not are the bacteria, fungi, lichens, algae, liverworts, mosses, ferns, and fern allies. Since the reproductive structures of these "lower plants" are not readily visible, early botanists were unsure how these plant groups reproduced. Their secretive or hidden method of reproduction is by spores instead of seeds. Although the bacteria and the fungi are often placed in separate kingdoms, and are not considered true plants, they are included here since they produce spores or spore-like structures.

Spores are small, often one-celled, reproductive structures that are typically produced in large numbers, much like the pollen in the higher plants. But, unlike pollen, spores do not need to fuse with another cell to form a new organism. Spores are similar in purpose to the seeds of flowering plants, and like seeds, spores come in a variety of sizes and shapes. Most spores are small, lightweight, and thick-walled. The low water content of spores renders them resistant to drying and temperature extremes. They thereby serve as resting organs during times when environmental conditions are unfavorable for vegetative growth.

Spore walls can be smooth or highly ornamented and thereby are useful for identifying species. They can easily become airborne and are capable of traveling thousands of miles. Spores have been found more than 10 miles above the earth's surface in the atmosphere, although exposure to ultraviolet light, which is more intense at high altitudes, can kill them. Some spores are capable of propelling themselves in water, while others stick to animals, especially insects, and are transported by them.

Spore-formers are thought to be ancestors of the flowering plants. Spores, which can be produced either sexually or asexually, are structurally simpler than seeds and therefore can be produced in greater numbers with less expenditure of energy. However, spores are not as efficient a means of regeneration. For example, seeds are able to remain dormant or viable for longer periods of time than spores, an evolutionary strategy of obvious significance to land plants. But,

while spores are individually much less complex than seeds, the fact that they are produced in vast numbers entails no less of a physiological investment. Theirs is a strategy of success with numbers, survival by means of "a wealth of spores."

There are about 2,500 species of flowering plants and gymnosperms growing outside of cultivation in Indiana. The number of species of spore-formers is at least five times as large. Although the spore-formers include many of the most frequently encountered organisms in the state, most go unnoticed even though we are affected by them. We spend millions of dollars a year trying to eradicate them from our fields (disease-causing fungi), our bodies (disease-causing bacteria and fungi), and water bodies (algal blooms). Millions more are spent to cultivate them for a myriad of uses, particularly as food or food additives (algae, mushrooms, and yeast), in horticulture (ferns), and in the production of medicines (algae, bacteria, and fungi). As primary decomposers, bacteria and fungi help prevent the buildup of dead organic materials and serve to recycle nutrients. Many mosses help stabilize soils, thereby reducing erosion, while at the same time they provide a seedbed for germination of higher plants and suitable habitat for many invertebrates.

These interesting organisms commonly occur on trees in forests and urban settings; in the soil of old fields; on rock outcrops, stone sidewalks, and walls; on old fenceposts and logs; in every pond and stream; and even on old roofs and gravestones. They are everywhere—all the places you would find flowering plants and then some. The importance, habitat preferences, and characteristics for distinguishing the various groups and species are the subject of this chapter.

BACTERIA

This was for me, among all the marvels that I have discovered in nature, the most marvelous of all; and I must say, for my part, that no more pleasant sight has ever yet come before my eyes than these many thousands of living creatures, seen all alive in a little drop of water.

—*Anton van Leeuwenhoek (1676)*

Bacteria are an ancient group of primarily microscopic organisms that closely resemble what is considered to be the general form of the earliest life on Earth. The bacteria have four different life forms: rod-shaped, spherical, spiraled, and occasionally "colonial." None has a membrane-bound nucleus, and reproduction is always asexual. As a result of these and other characteristics, bacteria are placed in their own kingdom, the Prokaryota, or more recently into several different kingdoms. Members of this group exhibit both animal and plant characteristics; in fact, some are photosynthetic.

Despite their small size (the average bacterium is less than 1/25,000th of an inch in diameter) and limited number of species (approximately 2,500 described), bacteria are likely the most abundant organisms in the world. It is estimated that the total weight of all bacteria exceeds that of all other living organisms combined. An ounce of fertile soil may contain more than 20 billion bacteria!

The members of this kingdom occur in all habitats and can survive in environmental conditions unsuited to almost all other organisms (e.g., glacial meltwaters, hot springs, and deep ocean trenches). They also are capable of amazing feats of suspended animation. Bacteria one million years old recovered from beneath 1,500 feet of ice in Antarctica immediately resumed metabolic activity when their temperature was elevated. Bacteria are capable of living in an oxygen-free or anaerobic environment; in fact, some require this condition to survive. They are excellent colonizers and, along with fungi, are primary decomposers.

This group is economically quite important, with both helpful and harmful species. Bacteria are used as a commercial source of important antibiotics and in the fermentation process of products such as cheese and yogurt. They are responsible for some of the most serious animal diseases (e.g., anthrax, diphtheria, gonorrhea, Legionnaire's disease, pneumonia, tetanus, tuberculosis) and plant pathogens (e.g., blights, galls, soft rots, wilts). *Escherichia coli,* a resident of our intestinal tract and an indicator of fecal contamination in waterways, is probably the most widely used experimental organism. So familiar is this bacterium that it is usually referred to simply as *E. coli.*

Bacteria also play an important role in the spoilage of food and other stored organic products. Most food poisoning is caused by *Staphylococcus.* Another bacterium that causes food poisoning is *Clostridium botulinum,* an anaerobe associated with spoiled canned foods and whose presence is indicated by swollen containers. It seems to be most common in canned green beans. This bacterium produces botulin, the most poisonous natural substance known; one gram is enough to kill at least 10 million people! Fortunately, this dangerous organism is seldom encountered in nature, but on occasion it does cause heavy mortality in waterfowl populations.

Cyanobacteria. Historically the cyanobacteria were treated as blue-green algae, although most biologists now consider them to be a type of bacteria which lacks a membrane-bound nucleus. They are simple

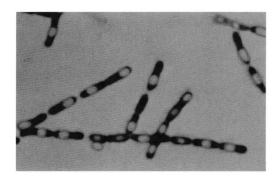

Bacterium *Bacillus anthracis* causes anthrax in cattle and sheep. Open circles are spores. This gram-positive spore former is shown at 1,000x magnification before photo enlargement.
Photo from Indiana State University Clinical Laboratory Sciences Slide Files

organisms that have chlorophyll, a red pigment, and a blue pigment called phycocyanin, hence the group name. The Red Sea gets its name and color from a "blue-green." This ancient group most likely contained the first organisms to fix energy via photosynthesis, liberating oxygen in the process. Our present atmospheric composition had its beginnings with the cyanobacteria.

Like all bacteria, the cyanobacteria are unicellular, although some can form colonies or filaments more than one foot long. The most familiar blue-green is *Nostoc,* a filamentous genus of several species found in both terrestrial and aquatic habitats. On bare soil it can form an edible, though repulsive-looking, ground covering called witch's butter. In lakes and ponds of the Midwest, *Nostoc* may occasionally form spherical masses called *Nostoc* balls which may reach a diameter of one-half inch. Another filamentous blue-green (*Aphanizomenon*) is found in water blooms, where it resembles chopped grass. It is toxic to some farm animals when ingested.

One of the easiest ways to find cyanobacteria in Indiana is to pull up a soybean plant and shake or wash the soil off the roots. The numerous small round nodules on the roots are created by the nitrogen-fixing bacterium *Rhizobium.* This process involves the incorporation of abundant but unusable atmospheric nitrogen into available nitrate nitrogen and other compounds. The role of bacteria in fixing atmospheric nitrogen into a form usable by higher plants and other organisms is of crucial ecological importance.

FUNGI

The fungi shall inherit the earth.

—*Anonymous*

What exactly is a fungus? These organisms have classically been treated as plants, but most textbooks now categorize them as a distinct kingdom, the Fungi or Myceteae. Since it is difficult to disregard my classical training, they are offered here as ancestral hemi-plants that are mostly terrestrial and multicellular. Fungi are, however, about as distinct from mosses, ferns, and flowering plants as they are from animals.

The most obvious difference between fungi and almost all other plants is that fungi lack chlorophyll. Green plants are oxygen liberators, while fungi are oxygen consumers. Green plants also pull carbon from the air and nutrients and water from the soil, thereby initiating the food chain or web of life. Fungi operate at the other end of the food chain, digesting organic compounds which are released into the atmosphere as carbon dioxide and into the soil as nutrients, especially nitrogen-containing compounds, thereby linking the food web and ecological cycles.

Unable to manufacture their own carbon compounds, fungi are relegated to being saprobes or parasites. Saprobes obtain their nourishment from dead organisms or organic matter such as decaying leaves or wood. Parasites, conversely, derive food from other living organisms, which are often harmed or sometimes killed in the process. Some fungi are capable of functioning as both parasites and saprobes.

The body of a fungus is composed of numerous threads or filaments, collectively referred to as mycelia. For most fungi, these structures go unnoticed since they are buried in the substrate on which they grow, be it soil, wood, or even flesh. Fungal threads can easily be seen in forest soils beneath leaf litter.

Fungal mycelia associated with roots of flowering plants are called mycorrhizae, literally "root fungi." This is a mutualistic relationship in which the flowering plant supplies carbohydrates to the fungus. The fungus reciprocates by providing miles of hair-like threads that, sponge-like, absorb water and nutrients which are passed on to the host plant through connections with its root system. An estimated 90 percent of tree species and about 80 percent of all land plants are at least partially dependent on mycorrhizae, some being wholly unable to grow without their fungal partners.

Although fungi are primarily terrestrial, they are ubiquitous, as demonstrated by a basic experiment used in general biology classes. If a sterile dish containing agar, a gelatin-like growth medium, is exposed briefly to the atmosphere and then covered, round colonies will appear within a few days. The individual colonies, each of which originated from at least one fungal or bacterial spore, may differ in color and texture. Similar growth occurs any time baked goods are left uncovered and unrefrigerated. Refrigeration slows the process by reducing the rate of enzymatic activity, thereby retarding spoilage.

Any statement of the economic importance of fungi must focus on their role as primary decomposers. They are equipped with an arsenal of enzymes that serve to break down organic products. Fungi attack both living and dead organisms, causing disease and decay, especially in the tropics, where warm, damp conditions are ideal for fungal growth. During World War II, less than 50 percent of the supplies sent to tropical areas arrived in usable condition. Most people would assume that the fungi damaged mainly foodstuffs, but they also attacked leather, paint, fuel, ammunition, and even the coating on optical lenses. The fungi have made a profession and a living out of recycling for millions of years.

Fungi are categorized into several classes according to their means of producing spores. Our discussion here is largely limited to the sac-forming fungi (Ascomycetes) and the gilled and pored fungi (Basidiomycetes) because they are the most familiar groups. The suffix -mycetes is from the Greek myketos, meaning fungus, which also is the base for mycology, the study of fungi. The prefix refers to the spore-producing structure characterizing the group. For example, Ascomycetes form spores in sac-like structures; Basidio- refers to the basidium or stalk or club upon which the spores are produced. Fungi also are capable of reproducing asexually by fragmentation.

It is estimated that there are at least 500,000 different species of fungi in the world, but only about 100,000 have actually been named; a thousand or more species are still being discovered and described every year. Perhaps 10,000 species inhabit Indiana, although no accurate count has ever been made.

Ascomycetes (sac fungi). The most-sought-after non-flowering plants in the Midwest are morel mushrooms. At least six different morels are found in Indiana along with a group of mimics called false morels. False morels usually appear in the spring at about the same time as true morels but should not be eaten since some of them cause illness (anemia) and even death.

All true morels are edible, with the white and yellow morels being the preferred choices. There are actually festivals celebrating these culinary delicacies. Black morels are edible, and often more common than the white or yellow, but the texture and flavor are not as fine, except when the mushrooms are dried and used for making sauces.

Harvesting morels does not harm the population in most cases, since the spores have already matured and dispersed prior to the harvest. In addition, not all of the available specimens are discovered by mushroom hunters. Moreover, the mycelium is not harvested. Soil compaction from increased foot traffic or off-road vehicles may actually affect morel populations and the general ecology of woodlands to a greater extent. As with the highly prized truffle, itself a sac fungus, we must rely on wild-collected specimens since there has been only limited success in growing morels commercially.

No one will tell you exactly where their favorite mushroom-collecting sites are located, any more than people who fish will reveal

Morel mushrooms are the most sought-after spore-forming organism in the state.   *Photo by Delano Z. Arvin*

their best fishing spots. The best time to search for morels is in April after a warm spell and rain, when the redbud and flowering dogwood are in bloom. Favored places to look include old apple orchards, woody fencerows, and hardwood forests, where morels sometimes seem to pop out of the ground overnight. Morels can occur anywhere soil organic matter accumulates, even urban lawns or pasture fields.

A few years ago, a preferred place to look for morels was near dead and dying elm trees. In most cases the elms had succumbed to Dutch elm disease, which, ironically, is caused by another kind of sac fungus, believed to have been inadvertently brought to this country from Europe on logs imported from Holland about 1930. As a consequence of the introduction of this invasive exotic pathogen, our best shade tree, the American elm, has all but disappeared from streets, parks, and woodlands throughout the eastern United States and adjacent Canada. Apparently other native and ornamental elms are more resistant. All attempts to eradicate or control the disease have been unsuccessful.

Another tragic irony is that the fungus which invaded this country has since evolved and returned to Europe as a vigorous pathogen that has killed about 90 percent of their native elms since the late 1950s. The new aggressive strain presumably originated in Illinois.

The half-inch-long, cigar-shaped, purple-black structures occasionally found on the grain of certain native grasses and cereal crops (especially rye) belong to a fungus called ergot. This insignificant-looking parasite seldom does serious damage to the crop, but the fungus contains powerful alkaloids that are capable of affecting both people and animals. It can cause hallucinations or more serious problems when ingested.

It has been suggested that bread made with flour contaminated with ergot was responsible for the famous "witches" in colonial Salem, Massachusetts. This same fungus caused the deaths of hundreds of thousands in medieval Europe. There are also records of epidemics of the disease in Ohio as recently as the early decades of this century. The symptoms of this awful malady include burning sensations in the extremities caused by constriction of blood vessels (eventually leading to gangrene, or even madness), resulting in the name St. Anthony's Fire.

In a strange but nice turn of events, ergot is now used to treat migraine headaches, as an important drug in childbirth, and in psychiatry (LSD). During the 1970s one million pounds of raw ergot were used annually in the United States. Indiana produces a portion of the grain from which ergot is obtained.

Among the many other sac fungi are the yeast used in baking bread and brewing, as well as most of the molds associated with food spoilage. Other representatives are the cup fungi, which produce spores in cup-shaped structures. The goblet fungus forms chocolate brown to black goblets up to six inches tall in association with decayed fallen timber in vernal woodlands. Moist decaying woodland logs often feature the eyelash fungus, a small, bright red disk with black marginal hairs and lemon cups, which looks just like its name. A much larger brilliant red cup fungus is the scarlet cup. Its two-to-three-inch-diameter cups, which are less red on the bottom side and lacking the black marginal hairs, can be found among leaves in woodlands throughout Indiana during the fall.

Basidiomycetes (club fungi). Basidiomycetes include the puffballs, coral fungi, earth stars, stinkhorns, shelf or bracket fungi, and mushrooms, as well as the destructive plant pathogens called smuts and rusts. The bracket fungi cause enormous destruction to living trees, while other saprobic fungi are responsible for the decay of logs and lumber. This fungal group is especially important in Indiana because the state is a major producer of hardwood lumber.

Mushrooms and toadstools are probably the most familiar club fungi. An informal distinction between the two groups is that mushrooms are considered to be edible while toadstools are thought to be poisonous. Separating fungi on the basis of such informal definitions or folklore is very dangerous. There is no foolproof method of separating poisonous and non-poisonous fungi. The best rule is simply to avoid eating any fungus you do not know to be edible. Moreover, the susceptibility to toxicity may vary from person to person, such as occurs with the reaction to false morels.

A key feature used to distinguish certain groups of club fungi is the texture of the spore-production surface. Gills are paper-thin layers of the underside of the cap upon which the spores are borne in many of the club fungi. A feature useful in determining the identity of a specimen is spore color and pattern. This is accomplished by removing the cap from the stem and placing it bottom side down on a piece of paper. Over the course of several hours, the spores will discharge and fall in piles on the paper, creating a spore print that reveals their color and the design of the spore-bearing surface.

Several of the gilled fungi are common, easy to recognize, and edible. The honey mushroom is so named because of its color. It is a parasite of oak trees and can be found from September to November. It forms clumps of individual fruiting bodies that are best eaten young and should be cooked because uncooked honey mushrooms taste peppery. Actually it is advised that all mushrooms be cooked prior to eating.

In relatively uniform habitat such as fields and lawns, fairy rings can occasionally be found. These rings are produced as the underground fungal threads expand outward, producing fruiting bodies at the margin. The inner portion of the rings is dead or inactive because of limited nutrition. The fungus which produces fairy rings found in urban lawns is usually the toxic parasol mushroom. Recently, very large fairy rings were discovered in Wisconsin that have been touted as the world's largest organism.

Mycelia of the honey mushroom which penetrate decaying wood are capable of bioluminescing (glowing in the dark), the source of foxfire, an eerie glow sometimes seen in nighttime woods. The Jack-o'-lantern fungus, a parasite of oak trees, is another that bioluminesces during autumn. Unlike the honey mushroom, this species is quite poisonous. Bioluminescence is an alternate pathway for energy production; the advantage to the fungi, if any, is not understood.

The death or destroying angel is an attractive white mushroom that is commonly found on the forest floor in the fall. Its beauty, however, belies its deadly nature. If ingested, a piece no larger than a pea is all that is necessary to cause death, and amanita poisoning is described as a slow and horrible process.

One of the largest and most visible groups of the club fungi is the polypores, which bear a series of minute pores at the open end of a long spore-producing tube. Some of the woody polypores form perennial fruiting bodies that can grow and continue to form spores year after year. The bracket or shelf fungi range from leathery to woody and persist from season to season. One of the more interesting, but uncommon, bracket fungi in Indiana is the varnished

The beauty and symmetry of the underside of gill-forming fungi. Spores are produced on the gills. *Photo by Lee Casebere*

Mushrooms and wintergreen surround decaying stump at Pigeon River, Lagrange County.   *Photo by Lee Casebere*

polypore. Its large shelf-like fruiting bodies have a shellacked, red to reddish-orange upper surface. The reason for their infrequent occurrence is the rarity of their preferred host, hemlock trees, which occur as glacial relicts in fewer than 20 native locations in Indiana.

A commonly encountered shelf fungus is the artist's fungus. Large specimens, ranging up to two feet in diameter, can be found growing from decaying logs in woodlands throughout Indiana. The lower pore surface is smooth and whitish, and the flat top of each specimen is tan or brown. When scratched or marked, the pore surface becomes brown. One of the most frequently found club fungi in the Midwest in late summer is corn smut, which when mature forms dark, dry, tumor-like masses of spores. Young corn smut is fleshy, greenish-gray, and edible. It is considered a delicacy in Mexico.

Another group of club fungi that parasitizes crops is the rusts. However, the two most familiar rusts are not found in agricultural fields. Many eastern red cedar trees are infested with cedar-apple rust, which forms hard dark red balls (cedar apples) that produce orange gelatinous tentacles several inches long in the spring. Apple trees are the alternate host essential for the completion of the life cycle of this fungus. Mayapple rust appears as large, hard-to-miss yellow-orange splotches on the leaves of its host in the late spring woodlands. A different species causes the same affliction on Jack-in-the-pulpit. Another rust, which occurs as a parasite of grass in lawns, produces numerous round clusters of spores that sometimes coat shoes, turning them orange.

A special small group of club fungi are called jelly fungi, most of which are found on logs and branches. All have a gelatinous flesh, and many are quite colorful (red, orange, yellow), occasionally colorless or white. They flourish in cool, moist weather, quickly disappearing when the environment warms and dries. One edible type, which looks like a large brown ear, is sometimes available at groceries, either fresh or dried.

Who among us has not "exploded" a puffball, thereby liberating millions of fungal spores? Puffballs are familiar club fungi which have spore production inside special structures that give these organisms their unique shape and name. Their spore chamber also contains numerous filaments that facilitate spore dispersal over a period of time, thereby ensuring successful reproduction. Puffballs which occur in colonies on decaying logs have individuals only 1 to 2 inches in diameter, but giant puffballs, which are usually found as solitary specimens in fields during late summer and fall, can attain a diameter of 20 inches and weigh several pounds. One monster specimen found in New York state measured five by four feet, stood 10 inches high, and produced a wealth of spores estimated to be at least 160 trillion! All puffballs are edible when white throughout, but they are not as flavorful as many other fungi.

The earthstars, which are apparently more common in the sandy northern counties, are peculiar in having two walls. The outer wall splits open with low humidity, creating a firm, star-shaped structure surrounding a second internal "puffball," a mechanism that ensures that the spores will be released when conditions are suitable for aerial dispersal.

Among the most curious members of this group are the bird's nest fungi. Their fruiting bodies, about the diameter of a pencil, resemble clusters of miniature bird's nests, complete with tiny flat "eggs" which are parcels of spores. The nest is shaped so that when a raindrop makes a direct hit, the eggs are splashed out of the nest for considerable distances. Raindrops also play an important role in

Colony of small puffballs decomposing wood on forest floor.
Photo by Richard Fields

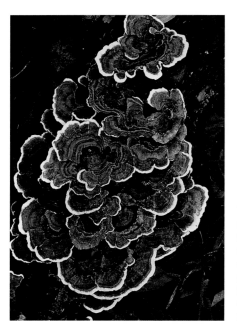

Turkey-tail fungus, so named for its fanlike shape and crescent markings, occurs on decaying wood. It is edible when newly formed, but leathery to woody later.
Photo by Delano Z. Arvin

Scarlet cup fungi are frequently found on dead wood or leaf mold in forests during moist periods.
Photo by Pearl M. Eslinger

helping to disperse spores in puffballs and many other spore formers.

Stinkhorns resemble a morel but have an unpleasant and unforgettable odor that is detectable long before the fungus itself is spotted. The odor attracts flies which then disperse the spores. Members of this group can be found near decaying wood or with the mulch in flower beds. The spore-producing forms, sometimes called devils' or witches' eggs, are often malodorous, but some people actually eat them.

Myxomycetes (slime molds). The slime molds are small and often beautiful organisms that appear to have been created by a master architect or artist. Most slime molds are encountered in warm, shady, moist places in woodlands, but a few occur in open areas. One forms bluish colonies on grass in city lawns during rainy periods; another Indiana species mimics a group of tiny puffballs, which are pinkish when immature, then brown at maturity. The common hairy slime mold is elongate and produces sooty masses of brown spores.

Oomycetes (water molds). This group of some 500 species of saprobes and parasites is separated from other fungi because, like the flowering plants, they have cellulose in their cell walls. Most fungi have chitin in their cell walls, the same material found in the exoskeleton of insects.

The oomycetes can occur on land and in water (water molds) and include some species of major economic importance. Some water molds cause disease in fish. Two terrestrial species are extremely important to humans. The downy mildew of grapes threatened the entire French wine industry in the 1870s. This pathogen, which had been inadvertently brought into France from the United States, was controlled by treatment with Bordeaux mixture, the first fungicide used to control a plant disease.

Other economically important members are a group of nearly 40 species of plant pathogens which attack many crops and are referred to as the plant destroyer fungi. The best known of these (late blight of potato) produced the great potato famines in Ireland in 1845–47. More than 1 million people died, and half of the survivors, about 4 million people, emigrated to America during the decade that followed, many settling in Indiana. The fungus prospered owing to favorable cool and damp weather.

LICHENS

> Oh; lowly plant, how oft thou'est spurned,
> Or passed unseen by common eye
> As though of thee no good was learned,
> Thine only lot to live and die!
>
> But closer look with care and thought,
> Strange are thy forms and wondrous fair;
> With grace enchanting they are wrought,
> Their coloring rich, their shading fair.
>
> —*H. A. Green*

A lichen is a unique organism, part fungus and part alga. This complex relationship, called mutualism, is a partnership which benefits both organisms and is required for the lichen to exist. The fungus provides physical support and protection, while the alga manufactures and supplies the food. The scientific name assigned to a lichen is based on the fungus since it is the primary component and the organism that reproduces sexually. Moreover, the alga is capable of independent living, but the fungus occurs most commonly in the lichen symbiosis and not as a free-living organism.

Lichens are capable of growing in a wide range of habitats and often grow where no other plants or animals can survive. For

The brilliance of a lichen-moss combination on a boulder.   *Photo by Bill N. McKnight*

example, lichens are the dominant plants in the Antarctic, where only a few flowering plants exist, and in high mountain areas.

One key to survival in such harsh environments is their ability to rapidly reduce moisture content to less than 10 percent of their dry weight. When they have dried out, photosynthesis stops and they become dormant. Most of the moisture that rehydrates and revitalizes lichens is obtained from the surrounding air and rainfall.

Lichens are some of the slowest-growing plants and may increase in size only 0.1 millimeter (1/250th of an inch) per year in some species. Moreover, with some individual lichens more than 2,000 years old, they rank among the oldest living organisms. Yet, despite their resilience and widespread occurrence, they are sensitive to atmospheric pollution. This sensitivity is a result of absorbing materials from the atmosphere which then accumulate and eventually have a damaging effect on the alga, reducing its ability to produce food. Because of this sensitivity, lichens have been used as biomonitors to determine pollution levels, and are often poorly represented in locations subject to high levels of air pollutants such as sulfur dioxide. It is a strange twist that analysis of the chemicals produced by lichens is an important taxonomic tool that is useful to separate species.

Lichens in general are prone to breakage if handled or walked on when dry. However, if water is applied, within a few minutes they become as supple as leather. Fragmentation is a common and effective means of asexual reproduction.

Lichens, mosses, and to a lesser extent algae are all important initiators of primary succession on many exposed surfaces. This is a critical ecological role that many people overlook. On bare rocks, gravestones, brick walls, tree trunks, bare soil, in birdbaths or temporary ponds, it is the spore-producing plants that arrive first with large enough populations to start changing things. However, these colonizers are usually unable to survive once the site has been altered to the point where it is suitable for seed plant invasion—which is, of course, a perfect example of succession. Estimates place the number of lichens worldwide at 25,000 species. Since the first published report in 1862, there have been 350 lichen species reported in Indiana, although at least 100 more taxa may yet be discovered.

Lichens are categorized somewhat artificially into four groups on the basis of growth form: crustose (crust-like), foliose (leaf-like), fruticose (shrub- or hair-like), and squamulose (scale-like). Variations within the cross-sectional structure of the lichen plant body are the basis for the different categories.

Crustose lichens. Crust-like lichens consist of a thin layer closely attached to the underlying surface or sometimes actually submerged in it. Two of the most common crustose lichens in the Midwest are a yellow-orange lichen (*Coloplaca*), found on almost any aged concrete and flagstone in both urban and rural areas, and an associated tiny crust with gray dots, *Lecanora dispersa*. Paint-like patches of yellow on tree bark result from another common crustose lichen called yellow bark. Bark powder also is common throughout the region. The preferred habitat for this powdery white to gray-blue lichen is bark at the base of mature trees in woodlands, and on shaded rock outcrops.

One of the more interesting crustose lichens is the script or hieroglyphic lichen, which typically grows on the smooth bark of musclewood trees throughout the state. This distinctive lichen appears as a circular, paint-like, whitish to gray-green splotch upon which are produced numerous small black spore-producing structures. These are linear and variously curved, thereby giving the appearance of Arabic writing.

A peculiar species seen on boulders in wooded ravines is the pearl button lichen, its name derived from the small, gray, circular fruiting bodies whose black margins contrast sharply with the white, paint-like lichen body. It is not uncommon to find round pearl button lichen barrens one foot in diameter on rocks that are otherwise covered with mosses. This species is so closely adherent to the substrate that it is separable only with hammer and chisel, but please do not do this as it is both dangerous and destructive.

Foliose lichens. The leaf-like lichens are probably more familiar to the layperson since, in addition to being conspicuously colored, they can exceed one foot in diameter. They are flattened and, in contrast to crustose lichens, their upper and lower surfaces differ in color and surface features.

Foliose lichens are typically divided into numerous branches called lobes; their shape is important in defining species. In the case of the abundant gray shield lichen, the central older portion looks and feels rougher than the outer margin because of the presence of numerous small finger-like structures. Another feature of this lichen is small clumps of a few algal cells surrounded by fungal threads. These clumps, which are visible with the unaided eye, occur near the margins of the shield, causing the lichen body to appear as though it has been pricked hundreds of times. In other species such clumps may be in lines, along margins, or scattered. These structures function in asexual reproduction in lichens and are key features used to separate species.

Other abundant foliose species in Indiana are bark crust, bark stars, yellow-green shield, and dog lichens. Dog lichen, which is sometimes a foot across, is the most common species in a group of 11 similar Indiana species of the genus *Peltigera*. This extremely variable species is found on soil, often intermixed with mosses. Its upper surface is light brown, with a whitish cast when dry, but turns deeper brown when wet. A distinctive characteristic of this genus is the production of root-like masses of fungal threads called rhizines.

The rock tripes are flattened like the typical leaf-like lichens, but lack lobes or branches and are attached to the substrate at one central point like an umbrella, somewhat like an umbilical cord. The most common umbilicate lichen in Indiana is the wafer lichen or cliff wafer, which is often found on glacial erratic boulders along streams.

Fruticose lichens. A third group of lichens is called fruticose because they often resemble tiny shrubs. This large and diverse group of unrelated species is distinguished by plant bodies that are round to flattened in cross section with no upper and lower surface. One of the most conspicuous and widespread shrubby lichens is the reindeer lichen, or reindeer "moss" as it is sometimes incorrectly called. The name is derived from its occurrence in the Arctic, where reindeer and caribou regularly consume it. Reindeer lichens form gray, sponge-like individual tufts that can approach one foot in diameter and up to six inches thick. These reindeer lichen flats can cover large areas atop wooded bluffs and forest openings across the state, especially in southern barrens.

Occasionally fruticose lichens can be found hanging from tree branches. Two pendent lichens, horsehair and old man's beard (*Usnea*), apparently once more common in Indiana, are now considered rare because of their extreme sensitivity to air pollutants. The well-known Spanish moss (actually a flowering plant in the pineapple family) resembles but is unrelated to these two lichens.

Squamulose lichens. The squamulose lichens are an artificial group in which the main body consists of small, lobe-like structures that lack both a lower cortex and root-like structures (rhizines). The most common lichens in this group are some of the 40 species of the most diverse Indiana genus, *Cladonia*.

British soldier (Cladina), of the squamulose group of lichens, in fruiting stage on fallen log.   *Photo by Bill N. McKnight*

Frequently these gray to gray-green flake-like masses produce hollow-stalked structures upon which are produced colored reproductive bodies. The most widely recognized species has bright red reproductive structures. The common name is British soldiers, from these "red coats." This is a species commonly found on decaying logs, on soil in old fields, and on roof shingles. Fruiting structures in other related species may not be as obvious as in the British soldiers, and colors can range from black to brown, orange, or yellow. The spores produced are fungal, not lichen spores, that must be dispersed, germinate, and become associated with the appropriate alga or perish. This harks back to the statement about the risks associated with a reliance on sexual reproduction.

The lichens of Indiana deserve more study, as suggested in 1891 by Dr. Lucien Underwood, a famous botanist formerly at DePauw University: "Mosses, hepaticae, algae, lichens and fungi form just as much a part of the flora of a county as do the seed plants and ferns and often furnish more valuable information regarding the true character of a region than can be gained from a study of the higher plants alone."

ALGAE

Grass of many waters.

—L. H. Tiffany

Nearly all members of the "algae" are photosynthetic. These plants range in size from tiny single-celled organisms, to colonial species, to marine specimens more than 200 feet long. Scientists who study algae are sometimes referred to as algologists, but the term *algae* has largely been abandoned in modern classification because the various groups are not closely related to one another.

Algae are often the aquatic forests—it is largely a matter of scale. In marine environments they assume the same ecological role as the green plants of terrestrial habitats. Both provide habitat and food sources for many other species. Worldwide and in Indiana, they have a substantial ecologic and economic impact. They may clog filters, taint the taste and odor of our drinking water, or produce toxic compounds. Such problems are usually caused by massive population growths of algae, called *blooms*.

In Indiana and at other non-marine sites, these blooms are promoted by the flushing of nutrients, especially nitrates and phosphates, into a body of water. These nutrients are found in agricultural fertilizers, which leach readily from farm fields or urban lawns. The bloom blocks sunlight, thus stopping or retarding photosynthesis, and depletes the oxygen as the dead algae decay. These processes contribute to eutrophication, often causing fish kills and producing unpleasant odors, thus seriously reducing the recreational value and usefulness of affected lakes. Shallow water depth, warm temperatures, and turbulence also contribute to make a bloom possible.

On the positive side, algae are the most important food source for aquatic invertebrates and fish. The phrase "grass of many waters" indicates that algae serve the same purpose in aquatic systems as grasses do on land. Algae are the chief source of food for many animals and an increasingly valuable source of food for humans. Algae, especially the phytoplankton, are also the main worldwide supplier of oxygen, hence the name "meadow of the sea." Moreover, they commonly serve as biomonitors since the presence of certain algae may indicate pollution problems. Similarly, the absence of an expected type of organism may also announce an environmental change.

Algae are classified according to their pigmentation, life cycle characteristics, and the type of stored food. Major groups are the greens, charophytes, browns, reds, dinoflagellates, diatoms, and euglenoids. Most are aquatic, although some species are capable of surviving considerable periods stranded. Aquatic species often possess hair-like flagellae that enable them to be motile, but many phytoplanktons simply float at the mercy of currents. Others attach to the substrate with root-like structures called holdfasts or rhizoids.

Estimates place the number of algae worldwide at 20,000 species. No one knows exactly how many algae are found in Indiana, but an estimated 2,000 species is reasonable since Faye Daily reported nearly 1,500 species from Indiana in a 1972 publication.

Green algae. The green algae or chlorophytes are common and abundant in Indiana, where they often turn pools, ditches, and ponds bright green. This is especially true in barnyards where there is a heavy nitrogen load from animal wastes. When present in large quantities, the infestation is often referred to as pond scum. Such ponds and ditches also often contain BB-sized colonies of *Volvox.* This spherical green alga is composed of a single layer of hundreds to thousands of bi-flagellated cells; the number varies from species to species. Strangely, these spheres rotate clockwise and have distinct poles.

Tree green is a single-celled green alga found coating bark and old fence rails. However, the most conspicuous greens are filamentous forms. *Spirogyra,* a slimy, thread-like species (often called frog spittle), is common in spring in ponds and lakes. Another frequently encountered green is *Cladophora,* which is abundant on stones in slow-flowing streams and attached to the sides of watering troughs. Unlike *Spirogyra, Cladophora* and a sister green are both coarse to the touch like horsehair. *Cladophora* filaments occasionally grow as spherical balls to an inch in diameter and float to the surface as the interior cells die and release gases. One of the more spectacular green algae in Indiana is water net (*Hydrodictyon*), which can grow in loose mats nearly a foot long in permanent ponds and lakes. This "hairnet of the water" is obvious to the unaided eye, and may foretell trouble in the water supply.

Not all greens are green. *Haematococus,* a single-celled alga often found in birdbaths or other basins temporarily filled with rainwater, has green and motile vegetative cells but can transform into larger, unmoving red-pigmented structures that can withstand long dry periods. Red pigments completely obscure chlorophyll, causing the algae to be red. Related forms are responsible for producing the strange phenomenon of red snow, whereby the algae grow and reproduce in suspended droplets, falling to earth only during storms.

Charophytes (stoneworts). The stoneworts are closely related to green algae, with some superficially resembling miniature horsetails. Of three Indiana genera, the most familiar are *Chara* and *Nitella,* which frequently form "aquatic meadows" at the bottom of shallow lakes and ponds (especially barrow pits and old quarries) throughout the state, often with limy deposits encrusting their stems. Stoneworts comprise only a few hundred living species, but they are well represented in the fossil record.

Red algae. The red algae (Rhodophyta, "red plants") are multicellular organisms, largely of warm marine waters. Two (dulse and nori) are consumed for human food; agar, a gelatin used as a culture medium in biological and medical research, is a product of red algae.

Only about a half-dozen genera of red algae are found in Indiana. One (*Lemanea*) contains several difficult-to-separate species that can exceed four inches. Like most of our Indiana reds, this group is usually found only in unpolluted fast-flowing water such as is found at rapids, dams, and falls. Apparently *Lemanea* is better represented in Indiana streams than in any other state, but it is distributed largely in southern areas on limestone rocks. A new species, apparently present only in extreme south-central Indiana, was recently discovered and named (*Lemanea deamii*) in honor of Indiana's most famous botanist, Charles Deam.

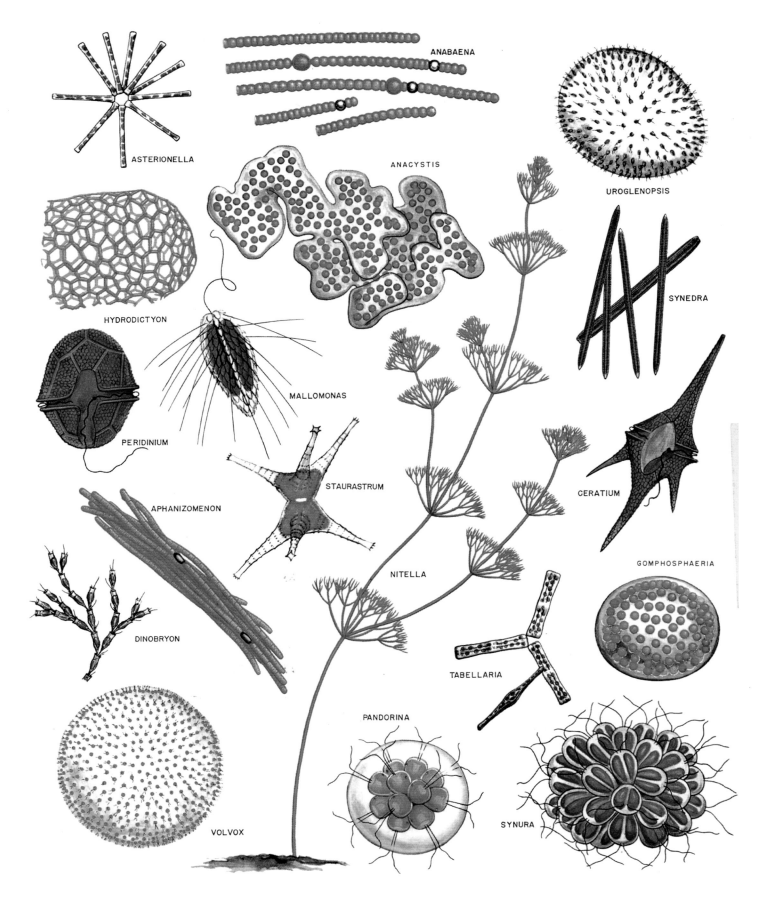

Variety of algal types, representing diverse body shapes and adaptations to habitat differences, several of which are found in Indiana waters.
Drawn by Harold J. Walter and Sharon Adams under the supervision of C. M. Palmer. Photo courtesy of William A. Dailey.

Diatoms. Diatoms make up about 40 percent of all algae species worldwide; about 250 species have been reported from Indiana, but there are undoubtedly many more unreported. These microscopic algae are abundant in fresh and salt waters and in the soil, and occasionally grow on filamentous green algae. It has been suggested that people should not live in glass houses, but the diatoms have no choice. Each of the numerous species is encased in silica shells which consist of two halves like a box. *Diatom* literally means "two parts" (di-atom). With their beautiful shapes and forms, they are the "jewels of the plant world."

Deposits of dead diatom shells from ages past, termed *diatomaceous earth,* are sometimes thick and extensive enough to mine. Minable deposits do not exist in Indiana, but we regularly use the material in scouring powders, in polishes, as an absorbent, and as a fine filter for swimming pools. These deposits can also be quarried as stone for use where a lightweight construction material is needed, such as domed roofs. On the negative side, diatoms are responsible for clogging filter systems in our water treatment plants, and decaying accumulations of diatoms cause surface waters to turn brown in summer and often produce a fishy odor. Toothpaste formerly contained diatomaceous earth, but this use was halted because it was too abrasive.

BRYOPHYTES

Behold the tiny moss, whose silken verdure clothes
The time-worn rock, and whose bright capsules rise,
Like fairy worms, on stalks of golden sheen,
Demand our admiration and praise. . . .

—*Anonymous*

Bryophytes are the mosses, hornworts, and liverworts. The completion of the life cycle of these groups involves the alteration of two generations of very different plant life forms. Most commonly observed is the low-growing "leafy" perennial stage, often found growing as cushions on rocks, soil, or logs. These plants, which initially grow from spores, produce both male and female sex cells. Following fertilization of the "egg" by a sperm transferred by a film of water, the embryo grows into a spore-producing capsule atop a leafless stalk that is attached to and nutritionally dependent upon the "parent" plant. At maturity the tiny capsules of this second generation open, releasing the spores. Following dispersal, the spores germinate and give rise to a new generation of "leafy" plants, and the cycle repeats.

Asexual reproduction is also common in these groups and occurs in several ways. In fact, some bryophytes have never been found with capsules and therefore are dependent on asexual reproduction. A common and effective method of vegetative propagation is fragmentation of the "leafy" plants. A major disadvantage of asexual reproduction is that the production of clones diminishes variability, thereby slowing evolution, which can jeopardize the bryophyte's continued existence at that location as conditions change.

It is suspected that the bryophytes and flowering plants independently evolved from green algal ancestors, but the basic appearance of mature algae and bryophytes is quite dissimilar. Any ancestral connection with flowering plants is unclear since bryophytes lack woody tissues that could easily be preserved as fossils, and because fossil spore capsules are rarely found attached. But one point is clear: the frequent assertion that mosses are primitive plants is not well supported; they may be more diverse today than in ancient times.

Although bryophytes are small, a hand lens will suffice for an interested amateur to identify all but the most troublesome species. One of the especially appealing characteristics shared by bryophytes and lichens is that with few exceptions they are available for study year-round. They are seasonal, however, in the sense that the production of spore capsules is caused by seasonal climatic changes. This perennial nature is a result of their not being able to initiate dormancy by any means other than drying.

One of the most interesting aspects of bryophyte biology is their desiccation tolerance. Many mosses and liverworts are capable of withstanding long periods, at least several months, without water, but have the ability to resume photosynthesis shortly after rehydration. It is even possible to resurrect some species that have been stored in packets in collections for long periods. Bryophytes can change leaf orientation, curling leaves and branches inward to slow water loss. Moreover, once dry they can tolerate extremely high or low temperatures, curiously with the youngest tip showing the most tolerance.

Bryophytes also grow in environments ranging widely in acid-alkaline reaction or pH. In areas with limy seepage, they play an important role in helping to form tufa, a brown, crunchy limestone formed by accumulating insoluble calcium carbonate (lime) as the water evaporates. Such deposits can become quite thick. Other bryophytes prefer acidic habitats such as those rich with decaying organic material (e.g., peat moss of bogs). Bryophytes occur in all types of habitats from wilderness to urban and from the wettest to the driest, but they are usually best developed in wet sites since they require at least a film of water to complete their life cycle, the "amphibians of the plant world."

About 25,000 bryophyte species exist in the world, but only about 370 have been reported in the literature from Indiana (270 mosses and 100 liverworts). However, based on the flora found in adjacent states, 450 is a more accurate estimate of our actual total. Curiously, there are few if any alien species found in Indiana, and apparently none occurs here that is not found elsewhere (endemic).

Hornworts. The hornworts are a small group of diminutive plants that often are regarded as a special kind of liverwort. Both differ somewhat in form from the mosses, especially in the leaves and reproductive structures. The four hornwort species occurring in Indiana are most commonly found in the fall, when they may be observed in pastures, in cultivated fields, along paths, and on moist, shaded sandstone outcrops. Spore color, which is visible to the unaided eye, is a key characteristic used to separate the species. Some hornworts and liverworts have colonies of blue-green bacteria growing embedded in their bodies, providing the host with a source of usable nitrogen.

Liverworts. The term *liverwort* is an example of the old "doctrine of signatures" concept, whereby a plant was named according to the body part that it was "created" to resemble, this being a sign of its intended use. *Wort* is the Old English word for plant. Thus the liverworts are the liver-like plants. Likewise, the Greek word for liver (*hepatikos*) was used as the base for the scientific name for this group, the Hepaticae or hepatics. Unfortunately, there is no evidence to support the ancient claim that they possess curative properties.

The liverworts are separated into ribbon-like and leafy types. The former look like small forked ribbons or rosettes and are found primarily in wet sites throughout Indiana. The most familiar are *Conocephalum* and *Marchantia*. *Conocephalum* is the original cone-head (as the name translates), although it is more commonly referred to as the scented liverwort—from the spicy, earthy fragrance emitted when the plant is crushed. The obviously pored surface also has led to its being called the alligator-skinned liverwort. The light green, inch-wide ribbons can be found covering relatively large expanses of moist, shaded sandstone and in mucky wetlands. Individual scented

Carpets of moss, such as *Trichocolor tomentella*, shown here, frequently upholster boulders and fallen logs in moist ravines.
Photo by Bill McKnight at Rocky Hollow Nature Preserve

liverworts sometimes grow nearly a foot long. Most bryophytes contain chemical substances which repel herbivores, but one caterpillar occasionally eats *Conocephalum*.

Marchantia is a large liverwort which is frequently and unnecessarily confused with *Conocephalum*. The darker green ribbons of Marchantia have a false midrib and often bear conspicuous cup-like reproductive structures. It occurs on soil or rock along streams and in recently burned sites, and is a greenhouse weed.

One of the most interesting liverworts is a true aquatic, *Ricciocarpos natans*. (Unfortunately, like so many of the spore-forming plants, even the larger unusual species have no generally used common name.) Its thick, fan-shaped body, up to an inch in diameter, floats on the surface. When it is removed from water, dark purple scales on its undersurface are obvious; they are often teeming with invertebrates which cause the scales to wiggle. *Ricciocarpos* is found in swamps and other still bodies of water, usually in association with duckweed, which it dwarfs.

Two-thirds of the liverworts in Indiana are classified as leafy liverworts or scale mosses. In this group the "leaves" are attached along either side of a "stem" and the plants are generally quite flat, being attached to a substrate on one side by root-like structures called rhizoids. The plants are often branched and possess a third row of leaves on the underside. The characteristics of underleaves are used to separate species and to help distinguish them from similar mosses. *Frullania eboracensis* is probably the most common leafy liverwort in Indiana, but few people notice it. This small bark-inhabiting species has the appearance of a dark zipper; in more exposed sites the plants are reddish to purple.

One of the smallest liverworts (*Cephaloziella rubella*) goes unnoticed on soils all over Indiana. To see it, one must kneel and search for what will appear to be a black to reddish-brown crust on bare soil. This insignificant-looking plant plays an important role in reducing erosion by binding the otherwise bare soil surface. The role of bryophytes in succession is mentioned frequently, but their role in preventing and reducing erosion has been largely overlooked.

MOSSES

The word *moss* is arguably one of the most misused of plant names. It has been applied to flowering plants (Spanish moss, moss pink, moss rose), lichens (Irish moss, reindeer moss), algal blooms (sea or pond moss), and fern allies (clubmoss, spikemoss), but these are all impostors. The true mosses are a distinct class (Musci) divided into three orders. Indiana lacks suitable habitat for one of the orders (the granite mosses), but the other two (peat mosses and true mosses) are well represented. And, while a rolling stone may not gather moss, stationary stones all across the state often do, as does soil, bark, wood, and even bodies of water.

All peat mosses belong to one large genus (*Sphagnum*) with approximately 200 species worldwide, about 20 in Indiana. The peat mosses, true to their name, are common in wet habitats (especially peatlands), where they form wide and often deep mats or mounds (hummocks) which hold water like a giant sponge. These mats can range in color depending on exposure and the species involved, but the separation of species can be quite challenging. Some individual plants are large, often a foot or more long. It is estimated that peat moss may be the most abundant plant on earth—it certainly is in Canada—and that there is more organic matter tied up in peat moss than is produced by all living plants on Earth in a single year.

Peat moss leaves have special water-absorption cells that allow the plants to retain up to 20 times their weight in water, thus making them the most economically important bryophyte. *Sphagnum* played a major role in developing the peaty soil found in northern Indiana. These deposits, which can be a renewable resource if properly managed, have been substantially reduced as a result of over-exploitation by mining of peat.

The peat mosses have enormous economic importance because of their use as a fuel source and especially as a landscaping material. Yet the most significant contribution of peat moss does not have a direct price tag. They help control water loss and erosion and serve as a seedbed for numerous vascular plants. Extensive peatlands such as those found in northern temperate regions can influence the hydrology, and even the climate, because of peat's capacity to retain large quantities of water.

Peat moss also has been used as packing material and, during World War I, as a surgical dressing, because of its antiseptic properties, thus freeing cotton for use in the manufacture of ammunition. Some individuals who work with *Sphagnum* may develop a skin condition called sphagtosis. A benefit associated with lots of walking in *Sphagnum* bogs is that the acidic water sometimes will help kill the fungus that causes athlete's foot.

Sphagnum species produce spores in capsules like other mosses, but there are no teeth around the capsule opening. Spore discharge from these spherical capsules is quite impressive. As the capsules mature and dry, they contract, causing internal pressure which ultimately blows off the capsule lid explosively, liberating the spores with an audible popping sound.

The true mosses, which comprise more than 95 percent of moss species, are divided into two major groups based on their growth form—one erect and usually cushion-forming, the other trailing and much branched, even feathery. The former group has spore capsules at the tip, the others laterally. Identifying individual plants can be confusing because mosses typically grow in mats or clumps of many plants. Capsule color and morphology also are important in distinguishing species.

The largest erect mosses in Indiana are the hair-cap mosses, named in reference to the hairy sheath which covers the developing capsules. Another common name, pigeon wheat moss, is based on the supposition that birds use the large capsules of this genus as a food source. After thousands of hours in the field, I have yet to see a bird eat or even look hungrily at a pigeon wheat moss capsule. Perhaps the name applied to usage by the formerly abundant, but now-extinct, passenger pigeon. The largest of our six species grows in wetlands, where they can grow to one foot long. Sandy soil and the edges of sandstone outcrops are the places to look for the white-tipped hair-cap, which is only about one inch tall.

> It is the moss that wholly hides
> The rotted old oak-stump.
>
> —*Samuel Taylor Coleridge*

The star mosses (genus *Mnium*) are among the most common in eastern North America, where they are found in shaded lawns, in moist forests, on decaying logs, and elsewhere. For example, the cusped-leaved star moss may be present in every township in the state. Another common weedy erect moss is the silvery bryum, found in disturbed sites, especially cracks in sidewalks and on old roofs. This species thrives in both rural and heavily polluted urban areas.

The cord moss is another weedy species. The leafy generation is often less than one-half inch tall, but the sporophyte can reach two to three inches. The capsule, which resembles a type of street lamp, is attached to the end of a slender stalk that twists or straightens based on relative humidity, thus another common name, the water-

Mix of lichens and mosses growing on rock outcrop at Portland Arch
Nature Preserve.   *Photo by Lee Casebere*

Lovely textures represented by zonation of mosses and lichen at
Bloomfield Barrens.   *Photo by Bill N. McKnight*

measuring moss. The cord moss is often found around old burn sites
where, like the cup-forming liverwort (*Marchantia*), it prospers until
the minerals released by the fire are leached away and larger vascular
plants provide too much competition.

There is a special group of tiny, weedy, soil-inhabiting mosses that
are rarely noticed. These ephemeral Lilliputians, called the pygmy
mosses or brownies, are found by getting down on hands and knees
during spring or fall and parting the vegetation in old fields, pastures, and lawns. The bryophytic equivalent of annuals, they do not
persist at a given site.

A walk through many wooded ridgetops in Indiana offers an
opportunity to confront the pin cushion moss and the common
windswept moss. The pin cushion moss forms circular cushions

several inches deep and a few inches to a foot in diameter. Occasionally it will form an extensive moss carpet that softens the footfalls of
any intruder and serves as an important seed bed for many plants.
This extensive water-holding cushion plays a critical ecological role
by serving as preferred habitat for many invertebrates. Bryophytes
are also used as nesting materials by many species of birds. A
frequent associate of the pin cushion moss is the glossy green windswept or broom moss, so named because the leaves appear to have
been swept to one side.

The Wisconsinan glacial margin serves as a general distribution
boundary for several species of bryophytes. Sword moss is considered a relict species because of its restricted range, which is along the
glacial boundary or just south of it. The sandstone canyons along
Sugar Creek in west-central Indiana are fantastic for bryophytes;
sword moss is located there. Curiously, this unusual moss has not
been found with capsules in the United States since the early years of
this century. The worm moss is found south of the glacial boundary
or, if north of it, along major rivers. This large, distinctive trailing
moss is common in southern Indiana, where it is abundant along
roadsides. It seems to thrive on clayey soil.

The trailing mosses are found in the same habitats as the erect
forms and include some of our most common moss species. I use the
common name "apron mosses" to describe members of the genus
Anomodon because they commonly form large aprons at the base of
mature trees, on stumps, and on rocks, especially limestone. *Play-
gyrium repens* is a shiny dark green creeper that forms mats on logs
and trees in dry sites. It is one of our most common and least
interesting epiphytic mosses and does little to substantiate the old
claim that "mosses grow better on the north side of trees." In many
sites they do not; it is largely a matter of exposure to light and
available moisture. Actually, since most of our winds which carry
spores are westerly, it would seem that most species would be found
on the western side of trees.

A walk through a wet forest might reveal both tree moss and fern
moss. The branched stems of fern moss resemble the foliage of a fern
or white cedar; it is found on moist soil and decaying logs throughout
Indiana. The tree moss spreads by means of an underground stem
that produces erect tree-like branches that reach to four inches high
and almost as wide. This impressive moss is easy to identify, but
when subjected to flooding, it takes on a flattened form with
irregular branching resembling the water or brook moss, a truly
aquatic genus found submerged in flowing water. Its trailing dark
green strands are often several feet long and, when stranded, blanket
large areas. It has been estimated that in 5 percent of most ecosystems, bryophytes cover 100 percent of the land surface; that figure
would be much higher in the northern United States and Canada.

FERNS AND FERN ALLIES

Nature made ferns for pure leaves to show what She could do in
that line.

—*Henry David Thoreau*

The fern allies are an old and largely artificial grouping that
includes the clubmosses, spikemosses, quillworts, horsetails, and
scouring rushes. With a few exceptions, fern allies all produce spores
which give rise to small photosynthetic heart-shaped alternate generation plants (gameophytes). (The exceptions to this are the adder's-
tongues and some clubmosses which produce non-green underground forms.) These small plants produce both gametes, eggs and
sperm, which fuse at fertilization to produce the familiar spore-
producing stage of the life cycle (sporophyte).

The groups are divided according to differences in their spore-producing structures and vegetation. They are sometimes called the vascular cryptogams because, unlike almost all other non-flowering plants, the ferns and fern allies possess true conducting or vascular tissue. Unlike other spore-formers, ferns and fern allies also possess true roots (rhizomes), stems, and leaves (fronds). The fronds range from simple and rudimentary to complex leaves up to six feet long and variously divided. About 10,000 ferns and fern allies have been described worldwide (mostly in the tropics), some 400 have been reported in the United States and Canada, and about 80 species are found in Indiana.

A discussion of Indiana ferns should include mention of Lucien Underwood, a well-known pteridologist (fern expert) who shipped specimens from Putnam County to collections all over the world. The small, now almost defunct community near the site he often frequented was named Fern, and the site itself (now a preserved natural area) was christened Fern Cliff.

FERN ALLIES

Clubmosses. Early botanists considered these to be mosses, hence the common name. Most reproduce vegetatively by horizontal stems and from spores produced in a club-like erect, often cone-shaped sporophyte.

The clubmosses of Indiana are represented by eight species in a single genus, *Lycopodium,* so named because of a presumed resemblance to a wolf paw print (although recent workers have divided this group into six or seven genera). None is common in the state, although one species (the fan clubmoss) is rapidly expanding its range and producing large populations in second-growth forests across Indiana. Some colonies cover several thousand square feet.

The shining clubmoss, an attractive but rare plant of moist woodlands and sandstone outcroppings, produces spores in kidney-shaped structures in the axils of the upper leaves. Clubmoss spores (called lycopodium powder), flammable when mixed with air, were once used for illumination during photography, and also have been used to coat pills. Because of their evergreen nature (hence "ground pines" as a common name), the clubmosses are used in Christmas decorations, a practice that should be discouraged because such gathering often destroys entire populations. Clubmosses apparently have a special mycorrhizal relationship which makes them difficult to transplant.

Spikemosses. The spikemosses, which are closely related to club-mosses, belong to a single genus (*Selaginella*). Two of the three Indiana species are delicate creepers that grow in swamps and wet meadows. The two are quite similar in form, and are often mistaken for a moss. The third species, rock spikemoss, is typically found on exposed rock ledges or in sandy fields. Most species are tropical, and none is common in Indiana.

Quillworts. This group gets its name from the fact that spores are produced in the swollen bases of quill-like leaves. Our two species are small and well camouflaged, looking like a small rush or bunch of chives. A diligent search may reveal quillworts at the edge of lakes, in periodically inundated woods, and sometimes partially submerged on wet rock ledges. But be prepared to spend some time searching, because quillworts are among the rarest and most reclusive plants in the Midwest.

Horsetails and scouring rushes. These are the most frequently encountered of all the fern allies. There are only 15 species currently living worldwide, half of which occur in Indiana. All have silica incorporated into the grooved, variously hollowed, and segmented stems. Spores are produced in a terminal cone-like structure, and the leaves, which are reduced and scale-like, encircle the conspicuously

Close view of ground pine (*Lycopodium obscurum*) showing detail of sporangia.
Photo by Lee Casebere

Spikemoss (*Selaginella rupestris*) at Portland Arch Nature Preserve.
Photo by Lee Casebere

Different species of horsetails or scouring rushes grow in a variety of habitats from railroad track ballast to old fields to wetlands.
Photo by Marion Jackson

A Wealth of Spores / 249

jointed stems. The common name of the unbranched species (scouring rushes) is descriptive of their use by pioneers to scour cooking utensils, thanks to the high silica content.

The name horsetail is taken from the heavily branched species' resemblance to the hair of an equine tail, hence the genus *Equisetum*. Evergreen scouring rush is most common of that group in Indiana, forming dense stands of erect, reed-like stems along shores and wet roadsides in every county. The common field horsetail can be found growing in cultivated fields, the only fern or fern ally found on cultivated lands except for bracken fern of northern Indiana. The field horsetail can be weedy and difficult to eradicate as it spreads by underground stems that produce separate sterile and fertile stems. Both of these common *Equisetum* species grow widely on gravelly ballast of railroad embankments. Many non-flowering plants do not have common names, but these species have too many, at least 30 for each.

Both clubmosses and horsetails are of special interest because during the Carboniferous (Coal Age) geological period they were represented by tree-sized forms. These giant ancestors produced an enormous amount of organic matter, both vegetation and spores. Their partially decayed and fossilized remains contributed to coal and oil deposits in Indiana and elsewhere. Enormous numbers of their spores sometimes accumulated in wet depressions, becoming fused over time into thin layers of highly flammable cannel coal that can be ignited by a match.

TRUE FERNS

Adder's-tongue and grape ferns. These are the most primitive members of the true ferns. Each adder's-tongue has a single, undivided leaf with obvious net-like veins and a single spore-producing spike with two rows of spore cases. Both Indiana species are inconspicuous and are more likely to be found in the southern part of the state, one on limestone ledges and the other in moist woods, on sandstone ledges, and in groves of evergreens.

Grape ferns have divided leaves and branched fertile spikes. The common name refers to the similarity of fertile spikes to a cluster of grapes (botrys), hence the genus *Botrychium*. The most common grape fern in Indiana is the rattlesnake fern, as suggested by the fertile spike. If you touch the spore-producing leaf when it is "ripe," spores will fly like yellow dust. The rarest member of this group in Indiana is the pygmy moonwort; found in northern bogs, it is about the size of a dime.

Royal ferns. These are among the largest and most handsome ferns in the Midwest, hence their common use by gardeners as ornamentals. Included in this group are the interrupted, royal, and cinnamon ferns. All three Indiana species occur in deep, swampy woods, seep springs, or bogs, where they can reach a height of five feet. The spores are produced on modified fertile leaflets that either interrupt the sterile frond or terminate it. These are spectacular ferns which have led to the statement "With fronds like these who needs anemones?"

True ferns. The remainder of the ferns discussed herein have spores borne in spore cases that are themselves clustered in "fruiting" structures called sori. The morphology of the individual sorus and its location on the frond are key to identification of all true ferns. The presence of "fruit dots" has caused much confusion from early times. Lacking as they do an obvious means of "seed production," it was once thought that ferns reproduced at night in some clandestine manner. Seeing the brownish "fruit dots" for the first time, even today it is not unusual for the uninformed to complain that their fern

Royal fern gleams in sunfleck in dark seep-spring habitat.
Photo by Bill N. McKnight

Christmas fern in late fall at McCormick's Creek State Park, Owen County. *Photo by Perry Scott*

has developed an insect infestation or a disease. These structures, of course, are the clustered spore cases (sori).

Undoubtedly the most common fern in Indiana is the short fragile fern, which in spring sometimes carpets entire woodlands. A sister species, the bulblet fern, is found growing at the base of moist rock outcrops, on talus slopes, and in northern swamps. Its deciduous fronds are tapered and can reach two feet or more, with fertile fronds tending to be longer than sterile ones. The common name is based on the presence of small, lobed, pea-sized bulblets on the undersurface of the stem. Easily dislodged, these structures are capable of reproducing more fronds asexually that will, in turn, bear bulblets.

Broad beech fern is typically found in moist, rich woodlands throughout the state. Since it is not uncommon to see plants of ginseng in close proximity, the broad beech is also known as the "sang" fern— "sang" being a colloquialism for ginseng. Mesic sites of the same woods often harbor the maidenhair fern, with its attractive fan-shaped fronds, green leaflets, and shiny dark red to black petiole. As this species uncoils in the early spring, it is delicate and pinkish. The three species of lady ferns also grow in moist, rich woodlands; all are deciduous and capable of reaching heights of at least three feet. The degree of leaf dissection is a simple means of separating the glade fern, silvery glade fern, and lady fern.

Wetlands of Indiana commonly harbor two species of true ferns: the marsh fern, common in northern Indiana, and the sensitive fern, found throughout the state. The latter has once-divided sterile leaves that wilt and discolor with frost, thus the common name. The fertile leaves produce substantial apical clusters of spore cases on both sides of a woody stalk. These spore-producing leaves persist and are often used in dried floral arrangements.

Christmas fern, so named for its evergreenness, can be found on wooded slopes throughout Indiana. It may form a dense population if an opening in the canopy should occur. The sori of this species are confined to modified terminal pinnae of certain fronds. Early settlers collected its fronds for use in Christmas decorations. Interestingly, the individual leaflet (pinna) resembles a Christmas stocking when viewed vertically, and is shaped like Santa's sleigh when horizontal.

Christmas fern transplants readily, and is sometimes moved for landscaping purposes. If the nearby forest is rocky, shield or wood ferns may be encountered. Their scaly rhizomes give way to once-divided leathery fronds that overwinter. In the spring these fronds suddenly drop around the crown, allowing new uncoiling fiddle-heads to take their place for the next year. An inspection of the surrounding ground will reveal several layers of discarded brown fronds from years past. There are several species of shield ferns in Indiana, but identification is often difficult, since hybridization is common.

Rock outcrops throughout the state support an interesting assemblage of ferns. Among these is the strange walking fern, whose species name (*rhizophyllus*) means "rooting leaf." The simple, 4-to-12-inch-long evergreen fronds taper in an exaggerated fashion to a tip that takes root as it contacts the substrate, giving rise to another leaf that takes a second step, followed by a third. Typically, only three to four generations (strides) can be found attached to one another in this fashion.

Eight spleenworts are found in Indiana, and all are evergreen. Spleenworts are so called because of the shape of their spore cases, which were thought to cure diseases of the spleen. According to Gerard, a seventeenth-century herbalist, "If the asse be oppressed with melancholy he eats of the herbe spleenwort and so eases himself of the swelling of the spleen." The ebony spleenwort is a fern commonly found in fencerows and second-growth forest. Most of the other species are confined to rock, and as with the wood ferns, hybridization is common, often creating puzzling complexes.

On rock ledges, primarily in western and southern Indiana, thick stands of the common polypody occur. Its characteristic leathery, once-divided leaves arise from a knobby and scaly rhizome. In southern Indiana the gray polypody or resurrection fern (smaller than its sister species) sometimes grows as an epiphyte on tree trunks or branches. During dry periods the leaves curl up, exposing dorsal surfaces replete with brown spore cases, then uncurling when re-moistened, hence the name resurrection fern. This species is found in Indiana only in far southern counties, where it is rare.

Some of the rarest ferns in Indiana are small rock-inhabiting species. The filmy fern grows on only a few cool, deeply shaded, moist sandstone outcrops in southern Indiana. It belongs to a family with primarily tropical members and has leaves that are only one cell layer thick, hence filmy. Wall-rue spleenwort is found on limestone rock along the Ohio River at Clifty Falls and in Clark and Harrison counties. Mountain spleenwort is known from only two populations on sandstone ledges in Crawford and Owen counties.

In ponds and standing water, especially in the southern regions along major water courses, close inspection may reveal a small floating greenish-red plant that seems to have neither stems nor leaves, and might be mistaken for the aquatic liverwort, *Ricciocarpos*. This is the mosquito fern, a member of the water fern family. As with so many of the plants discussed in this chapter, its means of reproduction is cryptic, but careful inspection reveals both microspores and megaspores. These small and large spores ultimately produce male and female gametophytes, respectively.

The production of different-sized spores is absent in other true ferns but is characteristic of the spikemosses and quillworts. The seed plants carry this dichotomy even further. In fact, some of the ancient, now extinct, relatives of our modern ferns actually did produce seeds and were called seed ferns. Fossil remnants in Carboniferous-aged rocks are the only evidence of these once-abundant seed-bearing ferns, but they now exist through the legacy of their descendants, the seed plants, which presently hold dominion over the botanical world. But the once-dominant spore producers still enrich the field experience of any naturalist who cares to look closely enough to discover the product of their "wealth of spores."

32. Wildflowers and Spring

Robert O. Petty

EACH YEAR, WITH THE RENEWED GIFT OF LONGER LIGHT, wildflowers give shape and symmetry to some old purpose of the sun. Green plants live closer to energy's prime source. Earth-tilt cues the pace of life's new year and sets the rhythm of seasons. Soon, wildflowers spread across a boulder-strewn meadow. At wood's edge their colors mottle, run quilted under a lattice of branches still leafless. Flowers flood the desert lands, rise along mountain ridges, trace the wetland borders.

It is a warm spring morning. A naturalist and a photographer beg the scene to hold that perfect slant of light, the flowers opening in dew, the pollen ripe, the insects visiting. Eyes blink, focus, stop to such measure of radiance. The camera clicks, advances. Next week, next month, the view will change. There will be different flowers, the earlier ones gone to fruit, scattering seed, enough to possess whole fields. Within one person's memory, fallow fields can vanish into forest as wave after wave of flowering plants appear over the weeks and months and years. . . .

The year moves on in mornings. Most of us awaken in our niche of civic landscape, in comfort purchased long ago by the death of trees and forest wildness, flowers, and all else to which wildness gives life. We would not trade back, unsell. Still, within the business of our busy lives, "days of accounts due," we stop beside a meadow or a woods edge, a fragment of that vast green expanse that was once America. For us, even this remnant is a sometimes strange and other world. With care we step into that world, its damp hush, its bird-pierced haze. We must leave soon, but turn, wait, look back at this still mysterious realm of waking seeds and bulbs and buds. There we imagine, as from a dream's distance, seasons that move through months like mythic gods, speaking names that take the shape of flowers.

This essay originally appeared as the Introduction to the 1983 National Geographic Society Engagement Calendar titled *Wildflowers of North America.* Reprinted by permission.

Yellow trout lilies carpet the forest floor in Monroe County on an April morning.   *Photo by Perry Scott*

Common milkweed has a most successful reproductive strategy. Exceedingly fragrant flowers attract both bumblebees and butterflies as pollinators. In fall its plumed fruits soar widely on silken parachutes, adrift on autumn winds. *Photo by Delano Z. Arvin*

33. The Seed Strategy: Higher Plants—An Introduction

Paul E. Rothrock

All the flowers of all the tomorrows are in the seeds of to-day.

—*Chinese proverb*

While I was growing up in the coal country of eastern Pennsylvania in those years before more stringent environmental laws, open scars on the land, underground mine fires, and heaps of waste culm were familiar sights. Such scenes were also common in years past in the Carboniferous-age coal fields of southwestern Indiana. During my junior high years, one old culm heap stood behind our school playground. Each day during recess or before the starting bell rang, some of us would explore the pile for curiosities. As a young teen I first became acquainted with the fragments of a 300-million-year-old plant world—a Paleozoic flora of giant horsetails, lycopods, and ferns, all preserved as fossils within the coal measures. But in spite of many hours of searching, we never found any signs of flowering plants or conifers and, of course, we never would. In that Carboniferous world, separated from us by a chasm of time, these "advanced" plants still did not exist. Most of the vascular land flora of that time reproduced by spores, not seeds.

Among Coal Age fossils, though, if searched carefully, the earliest of seed plants could be discerned. These were the seed ferns, plants with fern-like leaves bearing seeds on their surfaces. These plants, in a sense, developed a reproductive strategy that would change the entire world of plants for all time to come—the "seed strategy."

What is a flower? To our minds' eye it is pattern and beauty. To the evolving plant species it is much more, encompassing a whole strategy of adaptation which is crucial to its survival. The flower has been recognized as a sexual apparatus since . . . the late 17th Century. Seed production and dispersal are two enormously important events in the life cycle of a flowering plant, and a flower's form derives from the function to accomplish these.

—*Robert O. Petty, "Strategies," in* Wild Plants in Flower III: Deciduous Forest *(1974)*

Reproduction by seeds offered the seed ferns and their descendants several tremendous advantages over that which had gone before. Their male sperm could be delivered to the female reproductive structures in near-indestructible pollen. Even when free water, rain, and dew were lacking in the environment, seed ferns could readily fertilize their egg cells. A second improvement shown by the new seed strategy was the careful packaging of the embryo with a store of food and a protective seed coat. This permitted the seed to be ferried to new locations with the help of various vectors, including animal transport. After landing at its destination, the seed could wait in a dormant state—sometimes for decades or centuries—until conditions conducive to germination and rapid growth became available.

Since the end of the Coal Age nearly 300 million years ago, the superiority of the seed strategy among vascular land plants has been very apparent as first gymnosperms and then true flowering plants dominated the flora of the world. The ascendancy of flowering plants has been coincident with, and largely dependent upon, the co-evolution of their insect pollinators.

Without question, the greatest degree of co-evolution pertaining to flower structure relates to agents of pollination. Elaborate specializations abound. . . .

Perhaps the most common types of attraction relate to the promise of food which the pollinating insect associates with the flower's odor, form or color. Food offering varies, from deceit or no food at all to the common solutions of sugars from nectaries. Food may be offered as expendable tissue, as in the sterile stamens of primitive magnolia or tulip tree flowers. Food as excess grains of pollen is a major inducement to certain insects.

—*Petty, "Strategies"*

Today about 97 percent of vascular plants native to Indiana produce seed. We celebrated the importance of flowering plants by choosing an ancient seed plant as our state tree—the tuliptree. The next chapter, "The Life and Times of the Tuliptree," offers a view of the adaptations which have made this species and its many seed-plant relatives so successful. Although eminently successful, the evolution of seed plants is not finished. The processes of adaptation and speciation will continue as long as environmental change interacts with genetically variable populations. And, of course, the environment varies continuously, with today's rapid rate of change largely being due to human activity. Chapter 35, "The Diversity of Indiana's Flowering Plants," surveys the major groups of seed plants in Indiana and how they have adapted to specific environments.

All plants overlap in some of the things they do, but each species has adapted to a unique niche that only it can fill completely. In their ongoing adventure, each species has evolved slightly different solutions to acquiring the space, nutrients, light, moisture, and pollinators it requires. Some generalists have a fairly broad niche; other species are narrow specialists. Only time will tell which reproductive lineages have the right genetic combination to avoid extinction and to continue the process of diversifying into new species.

Humans are a relatively recent addition to the environment of seed plants. The influence of *Homo sapiens* upon plant life in Indiana measures only in the thousands of years, rather than the tens of millions of years that seed plants have been present on Earth. In fact, even the entire span of human dominion worldwide covers little more than 1 percent of the 120 million–year existence of flowering plants. Thus, our earliest ancestors found a world already richly stocked with different kinds of plant resources.

Taxonomists estimate today's count of flowering plant species to be at least 215,000 worldwide. Each species has slightly different properties, properties that we often find to be useful. Trees produce widely different kinds of wood and fiber; food plants provide a variety of tastes and nutritive values; others contain different chemicals for medicines, dyes, solvents, resins, and rubber. As a result, humans have a deep-seated relationship with plants.

Chapter 36, "What's the Use?" examines the traditional relationship that existed between both Native Americans and early settlers and the plant base that sustained them. But, as we know so well, humans are a culturally evolving species whose behaviors can change rapidly. Since the industrial revolution, we have mentally moved away from old ways where a single individual could see how a parcel of land was the source of all our needs. As much of our knowledge of plant resources has become relegated to "lore," and we feel less and less connection to the land that supports us, we struggle to understand ancient principles of stewardship.

For me as a young teenager, fossils in a coal waste heap alerted my imagination to a world beyond the hideous ruin caused by uncontrolled industry. I discovered that there can be great joy in the world of plants, whether extinct or living. We hope that the following discussions on seed plants will open you to an expanded relationship with natural Indiana, and help you reestablish your connection with the plant life of our state.

The joy of knowing is very great; the delight of picking up the threads of meaning here and there, and following them through the image of confusing facts, I know well.

—*John Burroughs*

The tuliptree, named for the shape of both its flower and its leaf outline, is one of Indiana's most loved trees.   *Photo by Ron Everhart*

34. The Life and Times of the Tuliptree

Paul E. Rothrock

The leaf [of a tuliptree] is a masterpiece of design. Because it has a squared-off summit, it suggests the primitive simplicity of Inca architecture as contrasted with the Gothic style of the maple leaf.

—*Rutherford Platt,* Discover American Trees *(1968)*

Long before citizens of Indianapolis and Fort Wayne erected towering buildings of steel and glass, Indiana boasted many fine pieces of natural architecture. These architectural wonders, made of wood and leaves, were the beeches, oaks, hickories, ashes, maples, walnuts, basswoods, and tuliptrees of our pre-settlement forests.

During the early nineteenth century, surveyors undertook the precise marking off of this great forest city into mile-square sections. Their original notes, now housed in the State Archives, included careful observations of the species and size of individual trees then occupying each block of land.

Every block was a melange of architectural designs ranging from the art deco of American beech, to the Gothic style of sugar maples, to the rococo of white oak. Among the architectural wonders of that original forest city was the Inca style of the tuliptree—arguably the most beautiful of our tree species, the future state tree of Indiana.

Mounds State Park, a short drive from my home, has a stand of deciduous trees near the Great Mound that must look very much like those of the original forest city. It has many large maples, oaks, beeches, and a few tuliptrees. Surveyor notes, as well as current forest inventories, confirm that the tuliptree or yellow-poplar is widely distributed throughout most of Indiana, and reaches great size and abundance in the southern part of our state. In the Central Till Plain region, they unfortunately are a minority in forests dominated largely by American beech and sugar maple.

However, in one area of the park, on a knoll south of the Great Mound, is a small grove of tuliptrees, each about 20 inches in diameter. And down in a nearby ravine, next to a small brook, is a "parent" poplar, some 40 inches in diameter. As is typical of many tuliptrees, the lowest 80 feet of its overall 120 feet is a straight trunk, standing like a ship's mast or a cathedral pillar. Counts of annual growth rings on trees of similar size suggest that this edifice of nature has been shaped by more than 175 seasons of growth. It was probably a young, vigorous sapling when European settlers moved into Madison County in the 1820s.

BUILDING A TREE

Don't view me with a critic's eye,
But pass my imperfections by.
Large streams from little fountains flow,
Tall oaks from little acorns grow.

—*David Everett,* Lines Written for a School Declamation *(1791)*

The secret of the tuliptree's longevity and size lies between its bark and its wood. Here a perpetually young growth layer, the vascular cambium, generates new cells. Young cells generated toward the inside of the cambium form an annual ring of xylem or wood, while young cells generated toward the outside develop into important sugar-conducting tubes of the phloem which link leaves to hungry roots, buds, and flowers. Each year the cambium repeats its cycle of growth—new wood, new food tubes—slowly adding to the girth of the natural skyscraper.

Obviously, though, a tree is not only wide but tall. Rapidly growing yellow-poplars can add two to five feet of height in a single year. This past spring I looked more carefully at the terminal buds, the source of this new length of stem. Each bud is covered by a pair of scales shaped something like a duck's bill. These are actually the stipules of the first leaf hidden within the bud. As the bud expands in spring, it soon becomes apparent that there is another pair of stipule scales covering another leaf inside the first, and yet a third set of stipules and leaf within the second. My sample of several well-formed buds consistently revealed five or six miniature leaves nested like Russian dolls. Deep within the center of each bud lies the actual growth point or apical meristem which makes the new foliage and twig.

During the long days from April to August, the apical meristem continuously fashions new leaves and adds to the length of the tuliptree twig. In August, as shortening days presage the coming of cold weather, the twig ceases growth and prepares for winter by creating dormant buds.

The combination of apical growth from buds and growth in girth from the vascular cambium has resulted in the attainment of massive dimensions by some tuliptrees. The tallest present-day individual on record (at a site near Asheville, N.C.) has a height of 200 feet and a diameter of 10 feet. Very large individuals have also been recorded in our region. In 1875, the state geologist reported of his visit to T. F. Belding's land in southern Jackson County:

I measured four [yellow] poplar trees that stood within a few feet of each other; the largest was 38 feet in circumference three feet from the ground, one hundred and twenty feet high, and about 65 feet to the first limb. The others were respectively 18 and a half, 18 and 17 feet in circumference at 3 feet from the ground.

Even today large monarchs can be found. Hemmer Woods, in the lower Wabash Valley, presently has two which tape at almost 5 feet in diameter and 150 feet tall.

While all plants have apical meristems, not all have an active, long-lived vascular cambium. For this reason, the above-ground portion of these plants tends to live but a single growth season and to be softer or more herbaceous in texture.

Among flowering plants, none of those belonging to the monocot group have a cambium. In the shade of the "parent" tuliptree are numerous examples of monocots: nodding trillium, trout lily, Hitchcock's sedge, wood rush, and twayblade orchid. The monocots are unique in other ways as well. Most have their apical meristems nestled at the ground level, below the reach of grazing teeth of most herbivores. This is one structural feature which makes grasses such

View of giant tuliptree that once stood on the farm of William L. Jennings (aged 82) near Lering in Scott County.   *Date and photographer unknown.*

valuable pasture plants and also allows us to mow them into uniform green carpets. The leaves of monocots are generally distinctive, with their long, narrow blades and veins that run parallel from the base to the tip of the leaf. This is in sharp contrast to the highly branched netted venation of a dicot leaf such as the tuliptree.

Monocots and dicots differ in reproductive structures as well as in vegetative features. Flowers, pollen, and seeds of each group have a characteristic form. In fact, it is a feature of the seed—one cotyledon versus two cotyledons—which gives the groups their familiar names of monocot and dicot. The cotyledons are the first leaves of the embryo. These seed leaves serve as food-storing or food-absorbing organs and, during seedling establishment, may carry on photosynthesis. The number of flower parts provides yet another way that monocots and dicots can be distinguished. Monocot flower parts are typically in whorls of three, while dicot flower parts usually occur in fours or fives.

PHOTOSYNTHESIS: GROWING UP PLANT-STYLE

Life is a windfall from a dying star. The sun's energy comes to us through the metabolism of green plants. Ecologically, plant and animal species are a part of a larger whole, a system which in itself is an ultimate unit of survival, for it maintains the continuous flow of energy and nutrients necessary for life.

—*Robert O. Petty, "Strategies," in* Wild Plants in Flower III: Deciduous Forest *(1974)*

When children look at the adult world, it is hard for them to conceive of mom and dad as once having been children. Likewise, a tree 120 feet tall seems worlds apart from an embryo in a seed. And yet, the persistent, indeterminate growth from a plant's apical meristem and vascular cambium does connect these extremes.

The seeds of tuliptree, in particular, germinate and survive where deep, moist, loamy soils are exposed to abundant light. Perhaps the favorable germination site arose as a gap in the tree canopy left by the fall of an old tree. Or perhaps the opening was created by a larger event such as massive windthrow or fire or clear-cutting of timber.

Under these site conditions, a tuliptree seedling often experiences accelerated growth, sometimes attaining a height of 15 to 18 feet in five years. The seedling grows a deep taproot up to 2 feet long in the first season. The root follows endogenous chemical cues emanating from the root tip. Through small changes in the concentration of calcium ions and plant hormones, the taproot grows with surety toward gravity. In contrast to the root's sensitivity to gravity, the shoot is very responsive to the availability and quality of light. Through minute changes in concentration of its auxin hormone, the stem bends toward the brightest spots of light overhead, adjusting and readjusting to maximize its position relative to the sun.

The energy to fuel this rapid growth arises from 93 million miles away. Each packet of solar energy takes eight minutes to reach Indiana. Through the miracle of photosynthesis, the energy of sunlight becomes converted into chemical energy bound in such carbohydrate molecules as glucose and fructose. Of course, these simple sugars have matter as well as energy in their structure—atoms of carbon, oxygen, and hydrogen. In order to make sugars, therefore, the tuliptree must acquire energy from the sun, carbon and oxygen atoms from carbon dioxide gas in the atmosphere, and hydrogen atoms from water absorbed from the soil.

Although it sounds impossible, the four or more tons of woody tissue in a large tree comes largely from scarce, invisible carbon dioxide gas in the air, starlight energy, and a dash of water! The remainder of the bulk of a plant consists of nutrients absorbed from soil colloids, nutrients such as nitrogen, phosphorus, potassium, iron, and calcium.

How does the tuliptree pull off this incredible biochemical feat? Its large leaves, with a silhouette reminiscent of a cat's face, serve as efficient solar collectors. Their broad, flat surface coupled with a thin cross-sectional area maximizes the light-capturing area while minimizing structural material. Within the leaf we find tightly arranged palisade cells packed with chloroplasts. Each chloroplast, a mere 0.0002 inches in diameter, is a fully self-contained energy converter.

Chloroplasts process the sun's energy in two stages. In the first stage, a green pigment, chlorophyll, absorbs packets of light. Light causes electrons of the chlorophyll to flow, almost like electricity, along membranes. The energy carried by these flowing electrons is tapped to make temporary energy-holding, phosphorus-rich compounds called ATP and NADPH. Also, as an important aside for animal life, this light-trapping stage of photosynthesis gives off oxygen gas as a "waste" product.

The photosynthetic action now moves into a second stage in the enzyme-rich fluid which surrounds the membranes. Here ATP and NADPH release their parcels of energy to forge carbon dioxide molecules into sugars such as fructose. As these sugars accumulate in excess, they either become converted and stored away as starch or enter the phloem tissue, which transports them to other organs of the plant.

The photosynthetic activity of tuliptrees and all green plants bestows on them the invaluable ecological role of primary producers. In terrestrial communities, flowering plants serve as the base of food webs that service all animal life. For example, tuliptree foliage may be directly fed upon by larvae of moths and butterflies or tulip-gall flies (*Thecodiplosis liriodendri*). Twigs can become the feeding ground for scale insects (e.g., *Toumeyella liriodendri*) or be browsed by hungry deer. Wood-boring beetles may tunnel into sapwood. Fallen leaves and twigs enter a detritus food web within the litter and

humus layers of the forest soil. The most familiar detritus feeders are earthworms and millipedes. But this web includes a long list of bacteria, fungi, mites, springtails, beetles, centipedes, and many others.

With so many potential feeders around, a plant must have some means for protecting itself. Thorns can be one answer; however, the mature forest of Indiana virtually lacks these. Instead, sharply armed hawthorns, brambles, roses, and locusts are found in old-field and young forest communities.

> Many final pathways in a plant's chemistry lead to the synthesis of substances which make plants (especially their reproductive tissues) unpalatable to insects and larger herbivores. Many "waste" products such as metabolic acids are employed as a passive defense. High concentrations of organic acid alone can make plant tissue inedible.
>
> —Petty, "Strategies"

Chemicals can provide another defensive strategy, and here yellow-poplar seems to be a master. The bark and heartwood are rich in potentially poisonous alkaloids. In addition to alkaloids, their leaves have hydrogen cyanide plus more than 40 other secondary metabolites. Extracts from these tissues demonstrate potent anti-bacterial activity against both gram-positive and gram-negative bacteria. It should come as no surprise that yellow-poplar can affect human physiology as well. In carefully controlled doses, the acrid inner bark may serve as a tonic or powerful heart stimulant.

Potent chemical cocktails, analogous to those found in tissues of yellow-poplar, are concocted by a wide range of wild seed plants. A quick survey of other common trees in Indiana, including box-elder, black cherry, buckeye, honey locust, and white oak, indicates that 80 percent of our native trees contain substances that either alter the physiological condition of animals or are outright toxic. In a world full of hungry herbivores, to complete the life cycle of the seed strategy requires avoiding becoming an easy meal.

THE CARBON DIOXIDE–WATER DILEMMA

> Though leaves are many, The root is one.
>
> —*William Butler Yeats*, The Coming of Wisdom with Time (1910)

In thinking about photosynthesis, we have focused mostly upon the flow of energy from sun to plants to animals. There remains another critical question for our consideration, the acquisition of carbon atoms. Since carbon dioxide is a scarce gas in our atmosphere at less than 0.04 percent of the total mix of gases, how can a leaf absorb adequate quantities for building all the sugar needed for starch or for the cellulose that composes most of the substance of wood?

The answer lies in the epidermis of leaves. The lower surface of tuliptree leaves, in particular, is densely peppered with microscopic pores or stomata through which carbon dioxide can readily diffuse from the surrounding air into the leaf's interior, and ultimately to the chloroplasts themselves. A square inch of leaf surface may have more than 120,000 stomata, permitting gases to easily enter or exit leaves.

Unfortunately, these pores cannot distinguish one gas molecule from another; carbon dioxide gas "looks" about the same as a molecule of water vapor. As a result, plants must make a compromise with their physical environment. To acquire carbon dioxide for sugar production, valuable moisture must be given up. And so plants transpire huge quantities of water to the atmosphere. Large trees such as the tuliptree have been estimated to transpire 100 to 200

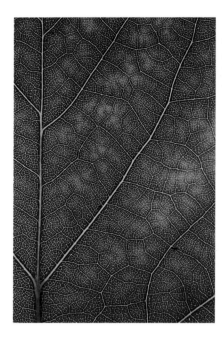

Close view of vein patterns and chlorophyll surface of tuliptree leaf.
Photo by Paul Rothrock

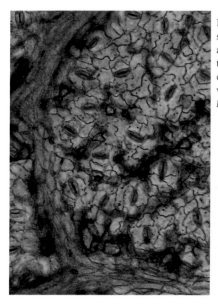

Detail of tuliptree leaf structure showing veinlets and stomata, openings through which carbon dioxide, oxygen, and water vapor molecules pass.
Photo by Paul Rothrock

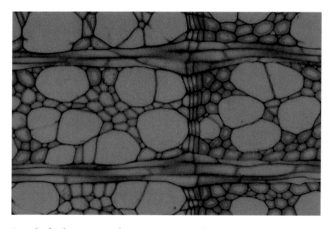

Detail of tuliptree wood in cross-section showing large open cells of spring wood and small narrow cells of summer wood.
Photo by Paul Rothrock

gallons of water per day. Even a single corn plant will transpire 50 gallons of water during a growing season.

Obviously this compromise has implications for living on land where water is not concentrated; namely, can the water lost from leaf tissue be quickly replenished? The wood or xylem of higher plants provides the needed plumbing. Microscopic pipes made of vessel and tracheid cells channel the water upward from an extensive root system. The forces needed to move the water are provided by suction at the top of the microscopically thin columns of water. Botanists have figured out a plausible mechanism, dubbed the cohesion-tension theory, to explain the necessary balance of forces for moving this sap river at a rate of 18 or more feet per hour to the top of a 150-foot-tall tuliptree.

One of the curious extravagances of nature, however, is that only a small fraction of a tuliptree's wood actually channels the sap to the leaves. This functional sapwood, lying just beneath the cambium, usually includes only that wood produced during the most recent year or two. To be sure, the rest of the wood retains its structural strength for many years and continues to support the massive weight of limbs and leaves of nature's skyscraper, but it quickly loses its water-handling ability.

Over time, the older sapwood slowly becomes remodeled into heartwood. In the change from sapwood to heartwood, the remaining living cells die, metabolism slows, and a wide variety of organic compounds—e.g., tannins, gums, and resins—are deposited. The old wood deepens in color to the warm green-brown of "yellow"-poplar lumber, and generally experiences a loss of moisture content. Commercially, of course, the heartwood is the desired wood. Its lower moisture content allows it to cure well, and the store of organic compounds yields the color we associate with fine woods—the red of cherry, the brown of walnut, the yellow of tuliptree.

THE "BIRDS AND THE BEES" OF PLANT REPRODUCTION

A flower, after all, is simply an organ, like a root or a leaf. It has none of the industry of leaves, none of the thrift of roots. . . . The whole is that organ that lives to give life away; that is born to die in the bearing of seed. It is the blind beauty, the lonely fragrance, the twisted art, the seduction without shame, that we adore, and call a flower.

—*Donald Culross Peattie,* The Flowering Earth *(1939)*

By late May the tuliptree enters its period of flowering. The forest floor has just finished its spring peak of wildflower activity. Wild ginger, baneberry, violets, spring beauty, bloodroot, may-apple, and many others either are ripening their fruits or, this essential work done, may even be going dormant.

The timing of flowering is often cued by changes in the length of days along with other subtle prompting provided by temperature and the physiological condition of the plant. Some plants flower in response to lengthening days and have been called long-day plants. Tuliptrees and many herbs which flower in mid-summer seem to fit this category. On the other hand, another large group of plants flower as days get shorter—short-day plants. Examples may be seen in the autumn woods: heart-leaf aster, zigzag goldenrod, and small-flowered leafcup.

Photoperiod is detected by a leaf pigment called phytochrome. In spite of many decades of scientific investigation, essential aspects of how phytochrome triggers flowering remain poorly understood. One early surprise in this research, however, was that the pigment actually tracks the changing length of night and not the length of day. Scientists, like other people, have their biases. Humans tend to associate activity with light, a bias against the multitude of species (both plant and animal) which prefer the darkened world.

The large flowers of a tuliptree are borne high in the forest canopy and are usually noticed only when knocked down by storms or squirrels. They have features associated with very ancient flowering plants. Their numerous male stamens and female carpels have a striking similarity to fossil *Archaeanthus* flowers which lived 95 million years ago, before the extinction of dinosaurs. Even the leaves of *Archaeanthus* have a shape reminiscent of tuliptree. Though ancient, the tuliptree ancestor was not the earliest of flowering plants. Trees similar to sycamore (*Platanus*) and extinct members of the rose family also lived at that time.

Macroscopic fossils of flowering plants as old as 120 million years and pollen to about 130 million years have been found, suggesting that this refined seed strategy developed during the Mesozoic Age, long after coal was formed from the lush vegetation of earlier spore-bearing plants.

Nonetheless, other major flowering plant groups were clearly absent when *Archaeanthus* was living. Absent were the bean, carrot, and lettuce families, to name a few obviously important dicot groups. Among monocots, there were still no grasses, lilies, or orchids.

By 65 million years ago, fossils show that the ancestors of tuliptree were part of an extensive forest community covering most of the Northern Hemisphere. This Arcto-Tertiary forest became fragmented some 60 million years ago by uplift of several mountain ranges (the Rockies, Alps, Himalayas, and Andes), and especially, during the past 1 million years, by cycles of climatic change and repeated advances of glacial ice sheets.

Today the deciduous forest biome remains as a landscape community in eastern North America, eastern Asia, and Europe. A number of genera of flowering plants co-occur in these widely disjunct areas, but few species still remain in common. The long periods of isolation have allowed speciation to occur. As a result, our tuliptree, known as *Liriodendron tulipifera,* has a sibling species, *L. chinensis,* in southeastern Asia. Likewise, may-apple, twinleaf, dogwood, and ginseng, to name a few, have sibling species in Japan or China, as do oak, beech, elm, maple, and linden in Europe. In fact, more than 60 percent of our woodland species have affinities with Asian species.

In geological time, flowering plant evolution closely parallels the evolutionary progress of the insects. . . . The chief, highly adapted, nectar-feeding pollinators such as bees, wasps and butterflies had not evolved by the time angiosperms originated in the Mesozoic. Beetle fossils are abundant from this period, however. Beetle pollinated plants, such as magnolia [and tuliptree], are considered primitive. They have many expendable parts with which to feed their voracious pollinators.

        —Petty, "Strategies"

The ancestors of the tuliptree were undoubtedly insect pollinated since they had large, showy flowers. Today's tuliptree, whose flowers are the descendants of a long, unbroken reproductive lineage, are visited by flies, beetles, honeybees, and bumblebees. Bright orange petal markings direct the movements of insects within the flower, and nectar gives them needed conditioning rewards.

Outcrossing, i.e., carrying pollen from one plant to another, by insects is very important for this species. The vigor of the seedling and the number of sound seed are correlated with the number of insect visits. Even so, only about 35 percent of its open-pollinated fruits set sound seed. Is the loss of the other 65 percent a result of insufficient numbers and varieties of pollinators? Or can a single shoot supply the energy needs of only this smaller cohort and thus ignore the rest? Hand pollination, which yields 90 percent seed set,

Flower structure of an *Archaeanthus* flower, a relative of the tuliptree that has apparently been extinct since the Cretaceous era. Flower and leaf structure reconstructed from fossil evidence by Dr. David Dilcher, formerly of Indiana University.
Drawn by Megan Rohn

The beautiful flower of tuliptree has numerous flower parts, which is typical of ancient, primitive families of flowering plants.
Photo by Delano Z. Arvin

would seem to suggest that the problem lies with an inadequate supply of pollinators!

The competition for pollinators helps us to understand why plants have such a diversity of pollination mechanisms and so many different solutions to the problems inherent within their seed strategies. Some specialize and employ the services of a particular pollen vector. Trumpet creeper vines, with orange tubular flowers, work beautifully with hummingbirds, while butterflies seek out thistles or mullein-foxglove with deep, narrow-throated flowers.

Many trees (e.g., oaks, walnut, hickories, cottonwood, and maples) and the monocot grasses and sedges rely upon wind as their pollen carriers. Since wind is a less predictable vector than a foraging animal, these plants make prodigious quantities of pollen to increase the probability that some will successfully land on a receptive female stigma. On the other hand, without the need to attract and reward an animal pollinator, these same plants need not expend valuable energy making large, showy, fragrant, nectar-rich flowers.

Some plants hedge their bets and use multiple pollination strategies. Jewel-weed is one of the most adept. Large orange or yellow flowers attract insects, while other, smaller flowers self-pollinate before they open—a method called cleistogamy or, roughly translated, "sex in a closet." Since jewel-weed lives but a single season, this self-pollination ensures the presence of some minimum seed crop.

After pollination successfully places compatible pollen on the female part of the flower, the sperm cells generated by pollen still must find and fertilize the egg and accessory cells within the immature seed. Primitive plants, such as ferns and mosses, have free-swimming sperm which move through films or droplets of water, an apparent carryover from the aquatic origins of land plants. As a wonderful adaptation to life on land, the pollen of seed plants grows a tube down to the egg within the immature seed. As a result, fertilization can be completed even in the absence of abundant environmental water.

In a very few seed plants, e.g., *Ginkgo* and cycads, the sperm still use beating hairs, like those seen on fern sperm, to move through the pollen tube. Tuliptree sperm lack these microscopic flagella and instead are gently ushered, though movements of the cytoplasm, along the pollen tube to the nuptial chamber.

It is during the period of reproductive activity that many biologically critical differences between true flowering plants and a second great group of seed plants, the gymnosperms, become evident. Gymnosperms in Indiana include native conifers such as pine, hemlock, and juniper, along with a host of ornamental and cultivated evergreens.

The word *gymnosperm* means "naked-seeded" plants; i.e., their seeds are not produced inside a fruit, such as the winged samara of tuliptree, the berry of blueberry, the drupe of dogwood, or the achene of asters. Our native gymnosperm species mostly produce their seeds on the surfaces of woody scales clustered in cones. In a few species (such as eastern red cedar) the scales that cover the seeds become fleshy and develop into blue-green juniper "berries" that smell like dry gin.

The gymnosperms have other dramatic differences from flowering plants. Conifers require two full summers to mature their seeds. A full year elapses between pollination (pollen landing on the young female cone) and actual fertilization of the egg cell inside the immature seed. Conversely, the tuliptree completes its reproductive cycle from flower to seed in a single summer. Some flowering plants have sped up their reproduction even more. In the spring beauty, the lowest branches of the inflorescence may be observed dropping seeds while a flower or two still lingers at the tip of the shoot—an elapsed time of only several weeks.

For the tuliptree, maturation of fruit is somewhat more leisurely than for spring beauty. Not until September do the winged samaras separate from the cone-like cluster and flutter to the ground. In a good year a 20-inch tree has been estimated to yield 29,000 seed that can easily be spread by wind currents to a distance four or five times the height of the tree. The majority of the seeds quickly become part of the food web—a feast for the purple finch and cardinal, red squirrel and gray squirrel, and small rodents such as chipmunk and white-footed mouse. Many which survive to germinate are choked out in the shade of larger trees or dense ground-layer plants.

Still other seeds remain viable but dormant on the forest floor for a period of four to seven years. Even those that fall on favorable sites will not germinate immediately, since winter would kill tender seedlings. As with many temperate-zone plants, at least 70 to 90 days of near-freezing temperatures are needed to overcome the internal dormancy of a tuliptree seed. Some seeds may even require two periods of cold stratification before being ready to germinate. Following that, they need the moisture and warmth that only spring can provide.

Every plant is a desert plant when it is a seed. For before the seed can germinate, there must be water. . . . Into the prison of the seed comes water, the liberator. Without water there can be no growth. . . . The seed coat drinks it up, and the vat begins to swell . . . the force which actually bursts the prison is that of the life within the grain . . . from within, the embryo shouldering against the door.

—*Peattie,* The Flowering Earth

Wind provides only one possible vehicle for moving seeds of forest plants to favorable openings. Biologists continue to study and to be surprised by the variety of vectors. It would seem obvious that squirrels disperse acorns. While that is true, blue jays apparently are equally important. Large fleshy fruits attract birds and mammals.

Recently, however, an array of small fruits or seeds with fleshy fat bodies called elaisomes have been investigated. These species, which include bloodroot, hepatica, some woodland sedges, spring beauty, trillium, and wild ginger, are irresistible to ants. Ants feed the lipid-rich elaisomes to their larvae and then deposit the seed in the loose, fertile compost of their nest. The resulting seedlings which germinate from seeds "planted" by the ants are larger and more numerous in their composted seed beds than those growing elsewhere.

In Mounds State Park, samaras of the "parent" poplar have been wafted about by wind currents decade after decade. Almost all of these experiments with life, as conducted by these millions of yellow-poplar seeds, failed. The particular combinations of genetics and environmental conditions did not harmonize.

However, during a period around the early part of this century, a few experiments did succeed, and the "parent" poplars completed the crucial task of producing at least one successful offspring to carry on future genetic experiments. Actually they succeeded in producing a small grove of even-aged trees on a knoll north of the ravine. At that time, the area must have been cleared of trees to make room for an amusement park, a popular attraction reached by Interurban Railroad in the years before the state acquired the property. After the decline of the amusement park, yellow-poplar seed fell on open, fertile ground and outgrew other potential competitors for that site. The seed strategy worked. Today the human edifices are gone; natural architecture has taken their place.

Seed "cones," which produce numerous winged wind-dispersed seeds, enable tuliptree seedlings to easily invade forest openings or open land adjacent to wooded areas. *Photo by Marion Jackson*

SURVIVING LEAN TIMES

I like trees because they seem more resigned to the way they have to live than other things do.

—*Willa Cather,* O Pioneers! *(1913)*

As summer days shorten to autumn, tuliptrees begin to prepare for their six months of winter dormancy. The superstructure of roots, trunk, branches, and twigs must be preserved as a living factory for yet another cycle of growth and seed production. Increasing concentrations of dormancy-inducing hormones such as abscisic acid initiate the formation of terminal and lateral buds. Soft summer growth, easily killed by freezing temperatures, hardens off until it can tolerate −40°F.

Then cool nights and short days stimulate the gradual shutdown and eventual disposal of the solar collectors. The tuliptree is preparing to lay off its thousands of seasonal workers from its carbohydrate factory. Stockpiles of mobile raw materials (i.e., nutrients) retreat back into the mass of the plant. Meanwhile, the energy-converting chloroplasts undergo changes that are particularly dramatic to our eyes. Their green chlorophyll pigments break down, revealing hidden accessory pigments. It is these pigments, chemically known as carotenoids, which give the tuliptree leaf its yellow coloration in September. Other hormonal changes, especially changes in the distribution of auxin in leaf versus twig, permit an abscission layer to develop at the junction between leaf stalk and twig. When the leaf hulk finally does fall, a protective corky callus has already formed over the leaf scar.

The herbaceous plants beneath the tree canopy have their own preparations for winter. Some spring ephemerals, such as trillium, toothwort, and trout lily, have already been dormant for several months. They formed underground bulbs and corms. Others, such as Solomon's-seal and may-apple, have made horizontal rhizomes with dormant buds protected by a layer of soil. Several woodland species, most notably false mermaid, jewel-weed, and blue-eyed Mary, are annual plants. Only their seeds survive the dormancy period. Each wildflower species has a different regeneration strategy as part of its own particular niche.

Adaptation to winter requires more of a tuliptree than simply a tolerance to freezing temperatures. This fact has been made especially clear by severe ice storms during recent winters. Bushels of twigs snap off large trees, and in many cases whole limbs or treetops break under the weight of ice. Intact bark provides a virtually impenetrable barrier to disease. But open wounds, like those caused by ice or windstorms or lightning, create entry points for pathogens such as bacteria, fungi, and insects. Plants, like animals, have complex healing and disease-preventive mechanisms—their own damage control.

A wound results in immediate chemical changes in the affected tissue. Slime plugs instantaneously clog the damaged ends of phloem food tubes. Bacterial invasion can stimulate increased respiration and ethylene release in less than a minute. Fungal activity can turn on phytoalexin or plant antibiotic synthesis within five minutes. Over time a wounded area becomes walled off or compartmentalized through structural and chemical changes of the sapwood. Within the wound, callus tissue proliferates, and the cambium begins to build an impenetrable wall between the site of tissue damage and any future woody growth. During the season of active growth, new wood and phloem cells are detectable by 10 days after wounding.

PLANTS AND HUMANS

The tree is no sooner down, but everyone runs for his hatchet.

—*Thomas Fuller,* Gnomologia

Until European settlers arrived in Indiana, tuliptrees had the opportunity to freely test their endurance against natural catastrophe and age. Once their life experiment ended, large fallen boles would take decades to decay. In undisturbed forests, these old monarch trees left a mound of humus long after they had rotted beyond recognition. These humus-rich sites became fertile nurseries for seedlings of future canopy trees or beds of ground-layer herbs. Today the possibility for that full-life dynamic has become largely restricted to state parks, nature preserves, or state and national forests. On the other hand, the harvest of trees has greatly enriched our human culture and shows something about the relationship and responsibility we bear toward these stately and valuable natural resources.

The tuliptree has long been a favorite timber tree because of its soft, smooth, even-grained wood. The Bronnenberg home, built in the 1840s, still stands at Mounds State Park. Its structural members, hand-hewn and still resistant to decay and termites, were shaped from giant tuliptrees. Perhaps those timbers came from the parents of the "parent" poplar in the southern end of the park. In 1831, a massive covered bridge of tulipwood was constructed across the White River near Indianapolis's Military Park. For more than 50 years it greeted tens of thousands of settlers heading westward in search of new opportunities.

Canoewood, another common name applied to tuliptrees, reveals yet one more piece of cultural history linked to this species, for both Native Americans and settlers. With the use of fire and adze, the long, straight tuliptree boles could be hollowed out to extreme thinness to make canoes. Daniel Boone made a canoe 60 feet long from a yellow-poplar log to sail from Kentucky down the Ohio to Spanish territory.

The tuliptree also had numerous more mundane uses. It was a choice wood for lining wells and early water mains since it does not impart a taste to water. Many common articles were fashioned out of tuliptrees—siding, furniture, even broom handles. Our love affair with the species continues to the present day. Among hardwood lumber, only oaks supply a greater wood volume than yellow-poplar from Indiana forests.

In the end, though, the value of the tuliptree (as well as of oak, maple, or walnut) cannot be measured by board feet alone. Nor can an enlightened mind, aware of life's remarkable economy, view trees simply as "green things that stand in the way." The natural architecture of a mature tuliptree possesses a priceless aesthetic. Landor has observed: "Old trees in their living state are the only things that money cannot command." But, despite being priceless treasures, this beauty is free to all, just as is the fine architecture of our cities. "Trees are wonderfully public property," says Hugh Johnson. "Wherever you go you are enjoying somebody's tree; and not a penny changes hands." And tuliptrees, the skyscrapers of Indiana's trees, offer much potential enjoyment to those who would visit a piece of our remaining forest city. Besides, the tuliptree is Indiana's much-loved state tree.

Despite the splendor of its dimensions, there is nothing overwhelming about the Tuliptree, but rather something joyous in its spring straightness, in the candle-like blaze of its sunlit flowers, in the fresh green of its leaves, which, being more or less pendulous on long slender stalks are forever turning and rustling in the slightest breeze; this gives the tree an air of liveliness lightening its grandeur.

—*Donald Culross Peattie,* A Natural History of Trees of Eastern and Central North America *(1949)*

The redbud, one of Indiana's best-loved trees, is a member of the legume family. *Photo by Richard Fields*

35. The Diversity of Indiana's Flowering Plants

Michael A. Homoya

Botanizing is surely interesting. You are not likely to get into jail in following such an avocation. It brings health and pleasure and grows as you get older.

—Charles C. Deam, letter to a young botanist friend

With nearly 2,000 species of native flowering plants occurring within the boundaries of our small state, it is safe to say that Indiana is botanically rich. True, though our diversity does not compare in richness to that found in the tropics, or even that of many other eastern states, we have a grand flora nonetheless. "Biological crossroads" is a description used perhaps all too often for areas having the presence of species with diverse regional affinities, but Indiana truly is a state where the eastern flora meets western, and northern meets southern.

Dr. Ray Friesner, of Butler University, stressed this uniqueness of the Indiana flora in 1936 in his presidential address before the Indiana Academy of Science, entitled "Indiana as a Critical Botanical Area." Not many states can boast of this as we can, because it is here that the eastern edge of the tallgrass prairie laps into western extensions of American beech and sugar maple forest, and bald cypress swamps and cranberry bogs reach the northern and southern limits of their ranges, respectively.

It is exceptionally difficult to address adequately such diversity in the few pages provided here. In fact, such a task may be impossible, because no botanist thoroughly knows all species of Indiana's flowering plants. Nevertheless, the following discussion provides at least a sampling of our most common floral elements, as well as describing several select groups of the interesting, rare, beautiful, and bizarre. There is also a section on "Botanical Fact or Fiction," wherein little-known facts and myths about Indiana plants are presented.

As was written earlier, there are many ways in which things can be classified or arranged. In this discussion the common plants characteristic of Indiana are divided into woody and herbaceous categories. The woody plants are further divided into trees, shrubs, and woody vines. Several, but not all, of the major plant families within each group are discussed. The herbaceous group is composed of families represented by many species, as well as special groups of plants, e.g., carnivorous and aquatic.

WOODY PLANTS

Trees. Trees, whose arboreal growths tower skyward and dominate many plant communities, are extremely important components of our flora. Indiana has approximately 110 species of trees native to the state, but only 15 to 35 tree species typically occur in most individual forest stands. The 40-acre Calvert-Porter Nature Preserve in Montgomery County, with 40 species present, has the richest known tree diversity of any forest of its size in the state. Aside from their own presence, trees modify the environment so that a host of other species can survive. Think of all of the plants and animals that depend on trees for food and shelter. Without trees, many of those species could not persist. Put simply, a forest is not a forest without the trees!

Trees are important to people because they give us shade from the sun and we get paper, pencils, furniture, lumber, and baseball bats from trees. Trees look pretty in our yards. People also use trees for firewood to heat their homes. Trees are also important to animals. Birds rest in trees and build their nests . . . squirrels live in trees and get their food from trees. Animals use trees for shade from the sun and to block the rain and wind.

—Monty Clark, age 11, Bedford, Indiana, quoted in
Outdoor Indiana, *December 1989*

Five families of trees dominate the Indiana landscape: beech, maple, walnut, elm, and olive. Together they contain 45 species of the 110 total. The beech family is clearly the largest in terms of species, and perhaps presence on the landscape. American beech and the multitude of oaks are generally the common, larger trees in most tracts of timber. American beech is easily recognized by its smooth, gray trunk, often with initials carved into the bark. American beech produces a "beechnut" enclosed in a spiny bur, whereas in the majestic oaks, acorns are the trademark.

Acorns are distinctive, and can be used to separate the many species of oaks. Just compare acorns of bur, chestnut, pin, and overcup oak and note the great differences.

Oaks occupy a range of sites from swamplands and wet woods to steep, xeric ridgetops. A sampling of the former includes swamp white, swamp chestnut, pin, overcup, and bur oak, whereas white, black, chestnut, scarlet, post, and blackjack occupy the latter. Oaks, especially those on dry sites, have a lot of character; their trunks are twisted and thick, with gnarled limbs rigid and strong, the leaves like lacquered green leather.

> A song to the oak, the brave old oak,
> who hath ruled in the greenwood long!
> Then here's to the oak, the brave old oak,
> who stands in his pride alone!
> And still flourish he, a hale green tree,
> when a hundred years are gone!
>
> *—Henry F. Chorley,* The Brave Old Oak

Another tree of this distinguished group is the American chestnut. This magnificent species once graced our southern Indiana hills, but because of the introduced Asian chestnut blight, it now exists only as sprouts from ancient root systems. The blight kills only the aboveground part of the tree by causing stem lesions which girdle the trunk, but root tissues are unaffected. Sometimes root sprouts grow large enough to reach tree size before they succumb, giving us a glimpse, albeit brief, of the grandeur of these once-common and important trees. Perhaps the best place in Indiana to see native American chestnut is in the knobs of Floyd, Clark, and Washington counties.

The walnut family, which includes both the walnuts and hickories, is another major tree group of Indiana's forests. Who does not know this impressive group, with their much-esteemed wood and

The smooth gray trunks and spreading crowns of American beech make it one of the most frequently recognized trees in the state. Beech-maple forests once covered about 50 percent of Indiana. *Photo by Perry Scott*

nuts? Black walnut and its uncommon relative, the butternut, are the only walnuts native to Indiana, while there are nine kinds of hickories here.

Probably the best-known hickory is the shagbark, identified by its noticeably shaggy bark and tasty nuts. Less palatable nuts are found on pignut hickory, while those of bitternut hickory are aptly named. Many people are surprised to learn that the pecan, that delicacy of pie connoisseurs, is actually a species of hickory. Wild pecans are native here, but not widespread, being found only in the southern part of the state in bottomlands along larger rivers. Big shellbark hickory, butternut, and black walnut bear the largest seeds of any native Indiana trees.

Members of the maple and elm families are typically found in moist sites, particularly in floodplain forests and deep ravines. There are only five species of native maples, but they represent a sizable portion of the total trees in many forest stands, partly because maples tolerate shade and can grow under the canopy of larger trees. Also, they are quick to colonize sites, as their propeller-shaped fruits are wind dispersed far from a parent tree. Perhaps the best-known is sugar maple, a tree prized for its outstanding fall foliage and sap for making maple syrup. Also valued, especially for shade trees, are red and silver maples. Silver maple, though easily broken by wind or ice, is clearly the most common landscape tree found in Indiana lawns.

Formerly American elm was the most loved and widely planted ornamental tree in the eastern United States. Colonnades of stately elms lined the residential streets of most towns and cities. But populations of American elm, both in urban environments and in the wild, have been devastated by Dutch elm disease and phloem necrosis. Small trees are still common in our forests, but large trees are becoming rare everywhere.

Another native, the red elm (also known as slippery elm because of its mucilaginous sap), has declined, but not as seriously as American elm. Large trees of red elm can still be found in moist woods. Northern hackberry and sugarberry, typical of floodplain and other moist forests, are relatives of the elms. They are easily distinguished by their smooth gray bark interspersed with corky, wart-like projections.

Many are surprised to learn that members of the olive family occur naturally in Indiana. Our "olive" trees are ash, and have winged dry fruits similar to those of maples. Indiana has five species of ash, with white and green ash being important timber trees in most Indiana forests (white ash is the prized wood for the Louisville Slugger baseball bat).

The other ash species in Indiana are not as common, but are very interesting trees nevertheless. Pumpkin ash, which usually grows in southern swamp forests, often develops a swollen trunk base similar to that of bald cypress and water tupelo. Black ash also likes wet feet, but prefers the cool seepage wetlands of northern Indiana. Blue ash, although present in moist woodlands, occurs most commonly on dry limestone cliffs. It is easily identified by its square twigs, a feature unique among Indiana ash. Pioneers obtained a blue dye from its inner bark for coloring their homespun cloth.

There are many other families of trees in Indiana, but those not to be overlooked are the magnolia and legume families and the three families of conifers. The ancient magnolia family has three interesting representatives, the tuliptree (our state tree), the rare cucumber tree, and the distinctive umbrella magnolia. The latter looks like a tropical species, having the largest simple leaves of any Indiana tree.

Most Indiana members of the legume family are herbaceous, but at least six species are trees. All have tough, durable wood, compound or twice-compound leaves except redbud, and two have armed twigs or trunks. The rare yellowwood and now-widespread black locust are noted for their showy clusters of creamy fragrant flowers. Redbud is one of the best-loved trees of the eastern forest, with its vivid splashes of pink-red flowers which appear in April before leafing. The uncommon Kentucky coffeetree, honey locust, and water locust are the remaining three.

Indiana is not known for conifer forests, but several species of gymnosperms dot our landscape. Three species of pine occur here naturally—eastern white, jack, and Virginia. All had restricted natural ranges before widespread planting occurred. Virginia pine was confined to the knobs of Clark, Floyd, Washington, and Scott counties. Jack pine occurred only in the dunes along Lake Michigan. Eastern white pine occurred naturally in west-central Indiana along Sugar, Big Pine, and Little Pine creeks, and in northwestern Indiana.

Eastern red cedar, a tree ubiquitous today in old fields, pastures, and roadsides, was probably an uncommon species before European settlement. Research indicates that it was confined to steep, rocky crags, where it was safe from the flames of wildfire, to which it is very vulnerable. With fire suppression and the creation of fields following settlement, the red cedar spread and prospered.

Eastern hemlock, with its soft, drooping foliage, prefers steep slopes and cliffs at scattered localities in southern and west-central parts of the state. Its presence gives a very northern, or Appalachian mountain, character to the landscape.

An opposite effect is created by the presence of bald cypress. Indeed, bald cypress is native to Indiana, occurring naturally as far north as Knox County, where the northernmost cypress swamp in the Midwest occurs. Only one stand in Delaware is farther north in the world. This denizen of southern swamps still occurs naturally at a few locations along the floodplains of the lower Wabash and Ohio rivers. Any trees outside this restricted geographic area have been

Virginia pine, one of a handful of conifers that are native to Indiana, is widespread in some southern counties.   *Photo by Richard Fields*

planted, or are naturalized from nearby plantings. Bald cypress, a relative of coastal redwoods, is unusual in being a deciduous conifer, i.e., losing all of its needles in the autumn. Likewise, tamarack, which inhabits Indiana bogs, is a deciduous conifer that accents northern Indiana lake borders and wetlands with a golden cast in autumn.

> If you can't be a pine on the top of the hill,
> Be a shrub in the valley—but be
> The best little shrub by the side of the rill,
> Be a bush if you can't be a tree.
>
> —*Douglas Mallock,* Be the Best of Whatever You Are

Shrubs. Shrubs are woody plants that, unlike trees, rarely grow taller than 10 feet or have a single trunk. They have multiple stems, each typically less than a couple of inches in diameter. Occasionally shade-grown shrubs attain the growth form of a very small tree. There are more than 160 species of shrubs native to Indiana (including brambles), making it a much more diverse group than the trees. Again, only the major families, and a few special others, are discussed here.

One of the largest groups of shrubs belongs to the rose family. Besides the beloved wild rose, several species of blackberries, raspberries, hawthorns, and chokecherries are widespread in Indiana. This family is difficult taxonomically, as anyone attempting to separate species of blackberries or hawthorns can attest. It is an important group, even if most of its members do have sharp prickles and thorns. Blackberries, raspberries, and dewberries are similar, related shrubs that produce edible fruit; another, the uncommon flowering raspberry, does not, but its beautiful purple flowers rival the best of ornamentals.

The hawthorns, while not producing fruit desirable to most humans, are a boon to wildlife, especially birds. Washington hawthorn is popular in ornamental and wildlife plantings. Other native shrubs of the rose family include ninebark, black chokeberry, hardhack (spirea), shrubby cinquefoil, and sand cherry. These latter species are not often encountered except in selected habitats.

Speaking of berries, the heath family, which includes blueberries, cranberries, and huckleberries, should not be overlooked. This is a large group consisting almost entirely of shrubs, sourwood being our only native tree species. Heath plants, without exception, are inhab-

itants of acid soil, whether it be wet or dry. Wet-site species, such as cranberry and highbush blueberry, grow in sphagnum bogs or on acidic sand. Because of drainage of northern Indiana wetlands, wild cranberries and blueberries are no longer common, but at one time cranberries were grown commercially here. Xeric species, such as farkleberry and deerberry, grow in dry forests and barrens.

Perhaps the showiest member of the group is mountain laurel, which is confined in Indiana to the southernmost counties between New Albany and Tell City. Growing most commonly on the upper edges of sandstone cliffs, this evergreen shrub is a delight when in full bloom. Other favored species of heaths include trailing arbutus, with its delightful floral fragrance, and wintergreen, whose crushed leaves give off a scent of teaberry.

The mostly tropical cashew family is represented in Indiana by the sumacs and poison-ivy. Of the five species of sumac occurring in Indiana, shining and smooth sumacs are most abundant, highlighting almost any roadside, old field, or forest edge with brilliant autumn foliage so appreciated by those seeking fall colors. The others can be equally colorful but are less common statewide. One to be avoided, or at least kept at a distance, is poison sumac. This tall shrub is an inhabitat of wetlands with sand, muck, or peat soils, e.g., fens, bogs, and seep springs. Most common in the northern quarter of the state, it is found sparingly as far south as Dubois County. It, like poison-ivy, can bring about a painful rash when touched.

The dogwood and willow families each contain a large number of shrubs in Indiana. Many people think of these groups as containing only trees, but most species are shrubs. Typically they prefer moisture, and thus are most common in wetlands. There are some 15 species of shrubby willows, and 8 to 10 of shrubby dogwoods. Better known are pussy, sage, sandbar, prairie, and silky willows, along with pagoda, red-osier, and gray dogwoods. Both groups can be rather difficult to identify until you become familiar with their leaf and twig characters; newcomers will also find flowers and fruits to be helpful.

The honeysuckle family is a popular group of shrubs and vines that are important for wildlife and ornamental uses. Commonly found in Indiana are honeysuckle, elderberry, coralberry, and viburnum. The viburnums are perhaps the most important horticulturally, and rightly so, as they are handsome, fragrant shrubs with great utility. Several species occur naturally in Indiana, including arrowwood, the most frequently cultivated native species. Other native species include blackhaw, maple-leaved viburnum, and nannyberry. An extremely rare viburnum is the American highbush cranberry (not a true cranberry). Similar to the closely related European variety, which is widely cultivated and naturalized in the wild, this shrub has been seen only a few times in wetlands in extreme northern Indiana.

Another rarity of this family is the fly-honeysuckle, our only native shrubby species, though not seen here in decades! The only shrubby honeysuckles seen here recently are exotic Asian species, the Tartarian and Amur honeysuckles. These aggressive, invasive species are destroying our woodlands by out-competing native plants.

Any discussion of Indiana shrubs should include those interesting or common species that do not belong to a single large family. Some obvious choices include buttonbush (a common wetland shrub), spicebush (an aromatic species found in almost every floodplain and mesic forest), witch-hazel (one of the last plants to flower in autumn), bladdernut (a tall shrub of rocky slopes, possessing attractive bell-shaped flowers and curious inflated seed capsules), and wahoo (with its distinctive fuchsia-colored fruits).

Two species of deciduous hollies occur in Indiana: possumhaw occurs in southwestern Indiana, while winterberry is mostly a

The swamp rose of northern Indiana is one of our showiest shrubby species. *Photo by Perry Scott*

northern species. Both, like the popular American holly, produce attractive red berries.

Perhaps the most unusual shrub is mistletoe, which lives on the branches of trees, root-anchored to a limb while it parasitizes the life juices within. Mistletoe is restricted in Indiana to only the southern few tiers of counties. It is less common than formerly, perhaps because it is too tempting for the romantics around Christmas time!

> It hath been writ that anye manne
> May blameless kiss what maybe he canne
> Nor anyone shall say hym "no"
> Beneath the holye mistletoe.
>
> —*Oliver Herford,* The Enchanted Oak

Woody vines. Vines need little description or introduction, as most everyone is familiar with this plant life form, whether they be pole beans, grapes, or poison-ivy. These twining, climbing plants are opportunists; unable to support their own elongated bodies, they clamber over other plants or structures by twining or anchoring themselves by tendrils or sticky pads. Many are the sprinters of the plant world, achieving phenomenal growth as they seek a place to climb or scramble. Some appear to grow as you watch!

Wild grapes are our largest woody vines, commonly growing to the tops of the tallest forest canopy trees, and sometimes with stem diameters inches thick. There are seven species of grapes native to Indiana, several of which have palatable fruits, although perhaps not as sweet as the cultivated varieties. Many cultivated grapes were derived from our wild species, especially from the fox grape, which is the parent of the Concord, Catawba, and other popular cultivated varieties.

In the wild, fox grape is found only in the northern and southeastern quarters of the state, where it prefers moist, acid soils. The smallest is catbird grape, found only in a few swamps and floodplain forests along the lower Wabash and Ohio rivers. The commonest are summer, riverbank, and frost grapes. The rarest is sand grape, which occurs only along gravelly banks of one drainage in southern Harrison County.

A member of the grape family, but not a true grape, is Virginia creeper. This non-toxic vine has five leaflets and is often unnecessarily confused with poison-ivy, which has three leaflets.

Poison-ivy has the dubious distinction of being the most unpopular vine. Many people are sensitive to the plant's toxic oils, and develop an itching, painful rash following contact. Remember the saying: "Leaflets three, let it be—berries white, take flight."

Although poison-ivy most commonly grows as a vine, it can assume many forms, including a shrub or a creeping groundcover. Its leaves are also variable, having leaflets with entire or toothed margins. Such variation, plus the fact that some vines climb high into trees, has led some people to believe that another rash-producing plant species occurs here, namely poison-oak. Despite what any pharmacist, physician, or whoever declares about the source of your rash, if it originated in Indiana, it did not come from poison-oak. (True poison-oak occurs elsewhere in the U.S., but not the Midwest.)

Such woody vines as Kentucky wisteria, crossvine, and trumpet creeper have spectacular flowers. The latter is found in a variety of habitats, but most commonly along fencerows. Wisteria and crossvine are southern plants, reaching their northern limits in our southern counties. Bittersweet is another attractive vine, although for its fruit and not for showy flowers. Its bright orange-red berries are sought during autumn by both birds for food and humans for floral arrangements.

HERBACEOUS PLANTS

Herbaceous plants in our region of the world differ from woody plants in that they rarely possess a cambium which generates persistent woody tissue in their aboveground stems. Consequently, herbs rarely grow as tall as trees (climbing herbaceous vines are exceptions), mainly because they cannot support themselves. The aboveground stems of herbs typically die back in cold weather, with annual renewal from subterranean stems and roots, or seeds.

Of Indiana's approximately 1,900 to 2,000 native plant species, about three-fourths are herbaceous. Of these, some 1,500 species are distributed among approximately 115 families, with the 12 largest families collectively containing a total of about 900 species.

Poison-ivy is an easily distinguished vine by its three leaflets with coarse notches and its white berries during autumn.   *Photo by Perry Scott*

In contrast, non-toxic Virginia creeper or woodbine is a vine with five saw-toothed leaflets.   *Photo by Richard Fields*

This discussion categorizes the herbs into two headings: special herbaceous groups and major families. Special groups have distinctive and often more interesting features, e.g., carnivorous plants. The families are "major" in that either they possess a large number of species, or their presence in great numbers of individuals make them a major component of the vegetation.

SPECIAL HERBACEOUS GROUPS

Wetland and aquatic plants. These specialized plants grow and prosper while submerged or partially submerged. Their leaves, flowers, or fruits may occur at or above the surface, but normally their roots are completely submerged. Some true submerged aquatics even flower and fruit underwater. A few classic wetland and aquatic plants are cattails, bulrushes, water lilies, pondweed (several species), coontail, water milfoil, water purslane, bladderwort, naiad, water stargrass, and eel grass.

Several plant families are represented in this ecological grouping. These plants may grow as marshes of emergent or floating-leaved aquatics or create extensive underwater "meadows" in lakes or ponds, the latter creating scenes that few have observed. The best places to observe the interesting submerged aquatics are the clear, natural lakes in the northern part of the state. Most of these species are sensitive to elevated levels of water pollutants and are easily eliminated.

Xerophytes. At the opposite environmental extreme from the aquatics are xerophytes, so named because they grow in xeric (moisture-deficient) environments. Examples of such habitats include exposed cliffs, gravel slopes, sand dunes, and areas of thin, rocky soil on south-facing hillsides. These sunlit sites are dry because of excessive drainage and/or exposure to drying heat and wind to a greater degree than most habitats.

Most natural communities with such conditions are known as barrens, and are home to several of Indiana's xerophytes. Many can withstand extremes in drought, heat, and wind, because they possess thick or waxy cuticles, succulent stems and leaves, reduced leaf area, dense hairs, and large taproots. Examples include prickly pear cactus, fame flower, hoary puccoon, pinweed, false aloe, and pagoda plant.

Parasites and saprophytes. Plants that derive much of their nutrition from living or decaying plant or animal material are termed *parasites* and *saprophytes,* respectively. The vast majority are nonvascular, e.g., fungi, but several notable vascular species exist. In a pure sense, there are no true vascular saprophytes, because there is always a fungal "liaison" between the living vascular plant and the decaying organic matter. This fungal association (termed mycorrhiza) is common in the wild, making many plants at least partial saprophytes. There are also connections via fungi between living vascular plants, thereby making the recipient at least partially parasitic.

To simplify discussion, only those plants which have been traditionally thought of as parasites and saprophytes are considered here. Perhaps the best-known parasite is mistletoe, discussed previously under "shrubs." Beechdrops is an herbaceous parasite growing only on the roots of American beech. Squawroot (which grows only on oak roots) and cancer-root (parasitic on many kinds of plants) are relatives of beechdrops found in mesic forests of Indiana. Dodder, with its yellow/orange spaghetti-like strands twining around other plants, is a very common parasitic plant of stream banks or wetlands, and sometimes in meadows or hayfields.

Prickly pear cactus occurs naturally in Indiana on sites that are like miniature deserts, that is, places that get extremely hot and dry in summer.   *Photo by Michael Homoya*

Dodder is a flowering plant that is a true parasite. It has specialized absorption structures called haustoria that embed in the host plant, siphoning water and nutrients from its vascular tissue.

Photo by Marion Jackson

Of the saprophytes, Indian pipe is probably the best-known. This ghostly plant thrives in the deep leaf mold of forests throughout the state. A lesser-known but spectacular saprophyte is the crested coral-root orchid, a true orchid which grows on dry limestone slopes in the southern part of the state.

Carnivorous plants. Few plants are as marvelous or fascinating as those that devour animals! Many people are surprised that Indiana is the home to several carnivorous plants. The largest are pitcher plants, strange-looking plants that grow in wetlands in the northern half of the state. Their vase-shaped leaves are modified to hold water, creating a cistern that serves as a drowning pool into which numerous insect victims fall prey. Commonly growing with pitcher plants is another carnivorous specialist, the sundew. This plant traps and eventually dissolves and digests any insect unfortunate enough to encounter its sticky tentacles.

The most common group of carnivores go by the name of bladderworts. These mostly aquatic plants possess bladders that "swallow" nearby swimming invertebrates. This is accomplished by a trap door that, when triggered, quickly opens and sucks water and all else with it into the bladder, including any animals. The prisoners inside are doomed, as the door swings only one way, and it is not to exit. Fortunately for human swimmers, these bladders are only a fraction of an inch!

> It is not raining rain to me,
> It's raining daffodils;
> In every dimpled drop I see
> Wildflowers on the hills;
> A health unto the happy,
> A fig for him who frets!—
> It is not raining rain to me,
> It's raining violets.
>
> —*Robert Loveman,* April Rain

Spring ephemerals. Many plants within this category are forest species which live out their short lives in the spring season. They are a special group because of their great mass and wide appeal; i.e., they typically occur in great numbers, and bloom together during the few short weeks of spring before tree canopy closure.

These wildflower displays are what draw so many people to the woods at winter's end, particularly in Indiana, as our fertile soils produce some of the finest floral displays in the country. Some classic spring ephemerals are white and yellow trout lilies, harbinger-of-spring, bluebell, Dutchman's breeches, squirrel corn, spring beauty, toothwort, rue anemone, and purple spring cress. By summer, when most other plants are fully developed and growing, little or no sign of these plants is evident. But the plants have not died. They are simply dormant, awaiting another spring to accomplish their timeless ritual of renewal.

MAJOR FAMILIES: INDIANA'S DOZEN LARGEST HERBACEOUS PLANT FAMILIES

Sedge family. With more than 200 native species, the sedge family is the largest in Indiana, and yet most people do not even know that such plants exist! The primary reasons are thus: Most sedges are rather small and without showy flowers, and therefore are overlooked, but the main reason is that people confuse these plants with grasses.

Indeed, sedges do resemble grasses, being about the same size, possessing long, narrow leaves, and lacking showy flowers. Sedges differ in a number of ways, however, especially in their stem structure and flower parts (yes, sedges and grasses do have flowers, they just do not have colorful petals). Typically, sedges have triangular stems, whereas most grasses have round stems (of course, there are exceptions). Just remember the phrase, "Sedges have edges [meaning sharp angles to their stems]; grasses and rushes are round." Sedges range the gamut in size, from some annual species being no taller than an inch or two, to bulrushes that attain heights of seven feet or more. Sedges are important components in many natural communities, especially wetlands.

> The sedge has withered from the lake,
> And no birds sing!
>
> —*Keats,* La Belle Dame sans Merci

Many of our marshes and meadows are dominated by sedges, and even forests have sedges, including some very attractive ones that rival our best greenhouse foliage plants. Most members of the sedge family are in the genus *Carex,* which is commonly known simply as "sedge," but there are many more genera, including spikerush, cotton "grass," bulrush, beakrush, flatsedge, and nutrush.

Grass family. Most people are familiar with this family, perhaps even more than they know. For example, our grain crops, such as wheat, rye, oats, and corn, are true grasses. And, of course, we mow lawns usually consisting of either Kentucky bluegrass or tall fescue (or crabgrass!), but none of these grasses are native to Indiana.

Our state has a rich diversity of grasses, with more than 150 species known. Many of these, like the sedges, blend into the landscape and are not noticed except by keen observers. Some cannot be missed, however, such as plume grass, common reed, and giant cane. These grasses commonly grow to heights of six feet or more.

Cane, which grows in our deep southern counties, is especially interesting, in that it is our only woody grass. Also known as bamboo, this grass used to grow in dense thickets called "canebrakes," but no more, as they have been cleared for agriculture (see also chapter 20, "A Taste of the South").

The prairie, home to many magnificent grasses, is also largely gone, but in a few places original Indiana prairie can be seen. Classic prairie grasses include big bluestem, Indian grass, prairie dropseed, side oats grama, switchgrass, and prairie cordgrass.

Sedges are important in both wetlands and forests. No other genus of Indiana plants approaches the number of species in *Carex*. Bur sedge, with its large fruits, is shown here.   *Photo by Lee Casebere*

Forests are home to a high diversity of grasses as well, especially to a group called panic grass, from the generic name, *Panicum*. Species of this group are often difficult to separate from one another. Other major groups of native Indiana grasses are wild rye, bluegrass (wild species), indigenous fescues, lovegrass, muhly, three-awn grass, and beardgrass.

Worldwide, the grass family is far and away the most valuable economically of all plant families. More than half of human food calories come from the grasses.

I believe a leaf of grass is no less than the journey-work of the stars.

—*Walt Whitman,* Song of Myself

Aster family. This is a conspicuous family in Indiana's landscape, possessing some of our showiest wildflowers, as well as some of the most bland. As the name states, asters are part of this family, and clearly they are showy plants. In contrast to these are the ragweeds, a nemesis of all who suffer from hay fever.

These two groups of plants, the asters and the ragweeds, illustrate how amazingly dissimilar members of this family can appear. The common denominator is that they all have a "composite" of several flowers arranged together on a single receptacle (head); hence the group is also known as the composite family. Many composites have two kinds of flowers, disk flowers and ray flowers. Each ray flower consists of one large, showy petal; together these form the "halo of petals" that encircle the smaller disk flowers. Some composites have all disk flowers, and some have all ray flowers.

Asters and sunflowers are classic examples of the family, but there are many, many different genera and species known. They occur in almost every environment, from dry woodland to marsh, but they are especially well represented in prairie, creating one of the best floral displays anywhere. The yellow flowers of sunflowers, tickseeds, rosinweeds, black-eyed Susans, and goldenrods; the pinks and purples of blazing stars, asters, coneflowers, and ironweeds; the whites from bonesets, Indian plantains, pussytoes, fleabanes, and asters combine to create some spectacular natural wildflower gardens.

> The flower-fed buffaloes of the spring
> In the days of long ago,
> Ranged where the locomotives sing
> And the prairie flowers lie low.
> —*Vachel Lindsay,* The Flower-Fed Buffaloes

Asters and goldenrods are especially well represented in Indiana, with approximately 25 species known for each. Some are weedy species, but for the most part they are rather conservative, "behaving themselves" in good-quality natural areas. Some are very rare, such as the squarrose goldenrod and the forked aster. Worldwide, the aster family is one of the largest in the plant kingdom, with more than 20,000 species.

Legume family. Whether you call it the bean, pea, or legume family, it is one and the same. With few exceptions, its members have bilateral flowers that resemble those of garden-variety peas and beans, and like them, produce elongated pods with seeds in a row. They typically have compound leaves and purple or white flowers. Although legumes occur in a variety of habitats, they are most frequently found on dry, poor soils, especially on thin-soiled hills of southern Indiana.

The largest group of legumes, with about 15 species, is called tickclover, or tick-trefoil. As anyone walking through woods and fields in autumn knows, these plants produce multitudes of diamond-shaped seeds adept at clinging to clothing and hair. They do this by means of numerous tiny, hooked hairs on the seed covering, attaching to material not unlike the way Velcro works.

Another large group of legumes is known as bushclover. These plants prefer habitats similar to those of the tickclovers. As a rule they are smaller than tickclovers and do not possess clinging seeds. They are very important as wildlife food, as their seeds are very nutritious. Other groups of important legumes include clover, milk pea, wild bean, and indigo. The bean family also has trees, as discussed previously. The large family of legumes is exceptionally valuable to humans as food and forage for domestic animals, and as fixers of atmospheric nitrogen.

Mint family. This is a plant group that, at least to the uninitiated, is recognized more by odor than by appearance. Everyone knows what mint smells like, but how many could recognize one on sight? This family consists of plants of many shapes, sizes, and colors, but most species have in common opposite leaves, square stems, bilateral flowers, and odors that are pungent or minty.

True field mint, native to Indiana, occurs in almost every county, whereas the introduced mints, e.g., spearmint and peppermint, are grown commercially, mostly on muck soils in northern Indiana. While these mints are not particularly showy, other members of the family are outstanding.

Of special note are the wild bergamots (bee balm), several of which are popular garden flowers. Also attractive are false dragonhead, pagoda plant, mountain mint, and skullcap. The latter is the largest group of the mint family in Indiana, and perhaps the most unusual. This is due to the shape of the fruiting calyx, which to some botanists resembles a tractor seat, and to others a skullcap. Additional notable mints are bugleweed, horsebalm, lyreleaf sage, stonemint, and hedge nettle. A large number of species of the mint family have been used as culinary and medicinal herbs for millennia.

Many herbs and spices were once medicines, and to obscure their pungent taste, they were sprinkled on food. This practice later became reversed, the medicine or spice "doctoring" the flavor of food.

—*Robert O. Petty, "Strategies," in* Wild Plants in Flower
III: Deciduous Forest *(1974)*

Figwort family. This family, also known as the snapdragon family, is well represented in Indiana, with 20 genera and more than 40 species known. The best-known members are the beard-tongues (also called penstemons or foxgloves). These plants are particularly attractive with their tubular flowers of white to lavender. In late spring beard-tongue is at its peak bloom and becomes conspicuous in abandoned fields, in forest edges, and along our rural roadsides. A very special foxglove, known as Deam's foxglove, occurs in a few areas in deep south-central Indiana. Amazingly, it occurs (in the wild) nowhere else in the world!

Another showy group of figworts called false foxgloves have large yellow flowers, but because they are uncommon and confined to dry woodlands, few people are familiar with them. A smaller type of false foxglove has purple flowers and is much more common. The most colorful of all figworts has to be Indian paintbrush. Brilliant scarlet bracts make the paintbrush an unmistakable and unforgettable plant!

Several species of the figwort family have become rare in our state, including plants with such interesting names as kittentails, blue hearts, American speedwell, and American cowwheat (not related to wheat, the grass). More common members, but with equally interesting names, include monkeyflower, turtlehead, blue-eyed Mary, toadflax, and lousewort.

Orchid family. Yes, there are wild orchids in Indiana, and amazing as it may seem, the family is one of the top 12 families for number of species in the state! Forty-two species of orchids occur in Indiana, with every county having at least a few. Most species are found in natural wetlands and forests, in the northern and southern portions of Indiana, respectively. Few people see orchids, mainly because they are often rare and the flowers of most species are small.

Orchids are identified by their special floral characteristics, namely three sepals, three petals (one, the lip, is typically lowermost and differs in shape and color), and a column. The column is a reproductive structure that houses the stamen and pistil.

The largest and showiest of the native orchids are the lady's-slippers—the showy lady's-slipper is the largest, and the small white is the smallest. The most "common" and widespread statewide is the yellow; the pink, also known as moccasin flower, occurs uncommonly along bog borders in northern Indiana

Less sizable, but not necessarily less showy, are rein orchids, ladies'-tresses, and coral-roots. The rein orchids include the brilliantly colored orange fringed-orchid and purple fringeless-orchid, as well as the drab small green wood orchid. The ladies'-tresses, named for their flower arrangement which resembles a braid of hair, are frequently encountered orchids. They grow in a variety of habitats, including old fields. The coral-roots are interesting in that they lack leaves and chlorophyll, and thus must acquire nutrition through a fungal host.

Our orchids may not be as large or showy as their tropical and greenhouse counterparts, but they are, in their own way, just as beautiful. Seeing one should not be missed.

A wild plant, born of a wet night, born of an hour of sunshine; sprung from wild seed, blown along the road by a wild wind. A wild plant that, when it blooms by chance within hedge of our gardens, we call it a flower; and when it blooms outside we call a weed; but, flower or weed, whose scent and color are always wild.

—*John Galsworthy,* The Man of Property

Buttercup family. Few people need an introduction to buttercups, as these favorite flowers are easily recognized by their brilliant yellow petals. However, the family includes such non-buttercup-like plants as columbine, larkspur, clematis, and anemone, all possessing enough features in common (especially reproductive) to be relatives.

But back to the true buttercups. The buttercup genus is the largest in the family within the state, with at least 10 different species occurring here. Most occur in moist habitats, yet some may grow on dry sites. They all have waxy yellow (rarely white) petals, although some are so tiny as to be practically invisible to the unaided eye, e.g., low spearwort. Another abundant, even weedy, species is appropriately named small-flowered buttercup! Meadowrue, hepatica, black cohosh, baneberry (doll's eyes), marsh marigold, and goldenseal are well-known members of the buttercup family.

Lily family. To many, the word *lily* is synonymous with *flower,* as lilies are such popular ornamentals for gardens and floral arrangements. The lilies we typically think of do not occur in Indiana, but

Few plants enthrall us as do orchids. Crested coralroot orchid may not be as large as those grown in greenhouses, but it is clearly as beautiful.
Photo by Lee Casebere

Lance-leaved coreopsis is a prairie member of the aster or sunflower family.   *Photo by Lee Casebere*

Few families have showier flowers than the lily family, with Michigan lily being no exception.
Photo by Lee Casebere

Well named for their scarlet, birdlike blooms, cardinal flowers are among our most beautiful.
Photo by Lee Casebere

our native lilies rival the best that horticulturalists have to offer. Of the four species of native lilies, Michigan and prairie lily occur mostly in northern Indiana, while American turk's-cap and Canada lily occur mainly in the hills of the southern half of the state. None is common in Indiana, with Michigan lily the most prevalent.

There is more to the lily family than lilies, however, as 20 additional genera exist in Indiana. Some, such as garlic and onion, do not seem to belong. Most do look like some version of a lily, however, at least on a small scale. Many are familiar woodland flowers such as trilliums, trout lilies, bellwort, Canada mayflower, Solomon's seal, and false Solomon's seal. One of the most spectacular, rivaling even the true lilies, is spider-lily, which reaches its northern range limit in the bottomland forests of far southwestern Indiana. Spider-lily typically blooms during the hottest, most humid days of summer, but the effort to track it down in its native haunts is well worth it!

> 'Tis the heaven of flowers you see there;
> All the wild-flowers of the forest,
> All the lilies of the prairie,
> When on earth they fade and perish,
> Blossom in that heaven above us.
>
> —*Longfellow,* Hiawatha's Childhood

Mustard family. There are almost as many introduced species in this large family as there are native. Many people are familiar with such exotic weedy species as yellow rocket and dame's rocket, which grow in crop fields and roadsides, but fewer recognize the native ones. Mustards can usually be identified by having four petals, six stamens, and a flattened seed pod divided into two halves by tissue. In addition, most of the species are spring bloomers.

Of the native species, the rockcress group is the largest, with 10 species. But rockcress individuals are usually much less numerous than toothworts. A walk through the forest in early spring will convince anyone that toothworts, in particular cutleaf toothworts, are abundant. There are four different species in Indiana, but only cutleaf is common statewide. Other native mustards, some common, some rare, include bittercress, wallflower, yellowcress, and purple rocket.

Parsley or carrot family. Although the garden carrot and parsley are not native to Indiana (nor to North America), approximately 30 species of the family are native here. Most members of the family are easily recognized by flowers arranged in characteristic flat-topped umbels, but some, such as rattlesnake master and the sanicles, have round inflorescences.

Of five species of sanicle native to the state, all are common except the southern sanicle, which is confined to three southern counties. Another, the Canadian black snakeroot, is perhaps our most common native "umbel." Other common members of this family include honewort, golden Alexanders, sweet cicely, chervil, cowbane, water hemlock, and harbinger-of-spring. The latter, also known as salt-and-pepper (from its dark anthers and white petals), is one of the very first wildflowers to bloom each year, sometimes opening in moist forests as early as February.

Several species are quite rare, normally not seen except by a diligent field botanist. These include American pennywort, prairie parsley, nondo lovage, eastern eulophus, and hemlock parsley. Perhaps the rarest is the pennywort, with only a few stems of this creeping herb known in Indiana. The pennywort requires constant soil moisture, whereas the lovage occurs in some of the driest, rockiest environments in the state.

Besides parsley and carrot, other widely used food and herb plants of this family include celery, fennel, coriander, dill, parsnip, and caraway. Another species is the deadly poison hemlock.

Rose family. Few plant families are as well known and as beloved as this one. Many are woody species, as discussed earlier, but notable herbaceous species include wild strawberry, cinquefoil, queen-of-the-prairie, avens, agrimony, and Indian physic. The common denominator for the family is the presence of five petals arising from a fleshy disk of tissue called a hypanthium.

Everyone knows what a strawberry is, but how many have eaten a wild one? Wild strawberries are much smaller than the cultivated ones, but considerably sweeter. The effort to pick them is well worth it! Queen-of-the-prairie, most commonly found in seepage wetlands, is one of Indiana's most spectacular wildflowers, and is quickly becoming a popular garden plant. Cinquefoils and agrimony occur in most old-field habitats throughout the state.

BOTANICAL FACT OR FICTION

The following is a compendium of little-known information about native Indiana vascular plants, arranged into "what is" categories. For example, what is the smallest flowering plant? The showiest? The most unusual? etcetera. Answers to some of the "what is" categories are obviously subjective responses. Perhaps you also have favorite candidates.

Smallest flowering plant. This award goes to a floating aquatic called water-meal, a pinhead-sized plant with even smaller flowers! They occur locally by the millions on the surface of calm water in some swamps and small ponds. In places they are so dense that the surface of the water is completely covered with green. Water-meal commonly grows with the larger and more widespread duckweeds.

Largest flowering plant. No consistent winner here; whatever tree happens to be the largest at the time wins. Since some of the largest trees succumb to wind and disease each year, it is difficult to pick an individual winner. Species with top contenders are sycamore, cottonwood, tuliptree, bur oak, and bald cypress. Apparently, the current state record tree is a sycamore in Harrison County that is an amazing 142 inches in diameter.

The largest flower of any Indiana plant may be that of the umbrella magnolia, with a petal spread as much as 8 to 10 inches. Perhaps equally large is the American lotus, with some flowers approaching 10 inches across.

Tallest herbaceous plant (excluding vines). Two plants that consistently get 8 to 10 feet or more in height include common reed grass and tall blue lettuce. Common reed was reported by one early observer to have attained 19 feet in height, but modern specimens rarely approach such dimensions. The blue lettuce is a relative of our garden lettuce, but very different in appearance. It is a woodland plant, while common reed is a plant of open wetlands. Under good growing conditions, other species also get quite tall, including giant ragweed, plume grass, compass plant, and bulrush.

Largest leaf. Without question, the largest true leaf of any Indiana plant belongs to devil's walking stick (also known as Hercules' club), a thorny small tree of southern Indiana. Its doubly compound leaves may be 5 feet long and 3 feet wide.

The umbrella magnolia, a rare tree in deep south-central Indiana, has unlobed simple leaves that average 2 feet long and 8 to 10 inches wide. Leaf clusters of this beautiful tree droop slightly, giving the impression of an umbrella made of leaves. The heir apparent for the largest simple leaf of an herbaceous plant is American lotus. Its round leaf centered atop a single stem commonly measures 1½ to 2 feet across.

Oldest living. Unknown, but most likely the antiquity award would go to either an eastern red cedar or a bald cypress. Some of the gnarled red cedars that grow on the south-facing limestone cliffs bordering the Ohio River may be more than 800 years old (based on ring counts from similar-sized trees elsewhere), and perhaps much older. They look remarkably like the ancient bristlecone pines of the western U.S. Bald cypress may rival the red cedar in longevity, as some bald cypresses well over 1,000 years old have been documented in the southern U.S.

> The flower that smiles to-day
> To-morrow dies;
> All that we wish to stay
> Tempts and then flies.
> —*Percy Bysshe Shelley,* Mutability I

Shortest-lived. Many annuals persist for only a short time to produce seed for successive generations. Those that grow in wetland habitats, and germinate only when enough water has evaporated to expose the muddy bottom, have perhaps the shortest lifespans. Some germinate, grow, and set seed in a matter of a few weeks. However, such plants are usually smaller than their usual size and produce fewer seeds. Various flatsedge species, and autumn sedge, are good examples. A species not dependent on water level fluctuations, with a very short life cycle, is false mermaid. This woodland plant germinates in winter and dies in late April and May (at least in southern Indiana).

Earliest-flowering. Many plants have the reputation for being the earliest to produce flowers; no single species is a clear winner here. Some top contenders are harbinger-of-spring, skunk cabbage, purple spring cress, hazelnut, and snow trillium. During early season warm-up in southern Indiana, these plants have been documented to have bloomed as early as mid-February; it is very likely that some have flowered earlier.

An early bird, skunk cabbage, named for its putrid odor, sometimes blooms in the snow, as rapid respiration raises the temperature within the spathe, thereby accelerating flower maturation.   *Photo by Perry Scott*

Latest-flowering. The most consistent late bloomers are common witch-hazel and mistletoe, which flower from late September through October. However, the witch-hazel retains its petals for long periods, commonly well into December! Occasionally species not known for late flowering will bloom when cold weather is late to arrive. Good flowering specimens of Indian tobacco were seen on a sheltered slope in southern Indiana as late as December 12.

> As aromatic plants bestow
> No spicy fragrance while they grow;
> But crush'd or trodden to the ground,
> Diffuse their balmy sweets around.
>
> —*Oliver Goldsmith,* The Captivity, An Oratorio

Most fragrant. Clearly a subjective category because what smells good to one person may not appeal to another. Fortunately, many deliciously aromatic plants occur in Indiana, not only those with fragrant flowers, but also many with fragrant foliage. In the floral category, it is hard to beat showy orchis, trailing arbutus, butterfly pea, squirrel corn, and the Great Plains ladies'-tresses. Those with pleasant-smelling foliage include sassafras, spicebush, wintergreen, aromatic sumac, smooth sweet cicely, vanilla grass, and several members of the mint family.

Most malodorous. Another subjective category. Several plants smell bad, but perhaps the marsh fleabane is the greatest offender. Negative comments are commonly made when a specimen of marsh fleabane is in the room.

> This plant emits a disagreeable odor which is noticeable several feet from the plant. . . . The nearest approach to it is the odor of the skunk, and I think it should receive a common name to suggest its vile odor.
>
> —*Charles C. Deam,* Flora of Indiana *(1940)*

Most attractive. How bold of anyone to suggest what is the showiest, most attractive plant in Indiana. There are so many top contenders that making a decision is difficult. Showy lady's-slipper may be the winner, but then again, there is spider lily, or perhaps Turk's-cap lily. And what about royal catchfly, blazing star, queen-of-the-prairie, mountain laurel, yellow coneflower, purple coneflower, wisteria, wood poppy, fragrant water lily, cardinal flower, Indian paintbrush, butterfly weed . . .

Most entertaining. Of course plants can be entertaining, and not just by way of the food, drink, and recreational products that we derive from them. Touch-me-nots (also called jewel-weed) might just be most entertaining; the pleasure of touching their seed pods is the greatest! Ripe pods explode with the slightest touch, catapulting the seeds several feet away. Such startling displays are addictive; if you touch just one of these pods, you will wind up touching a hundred! Besides, the ripe seeds are edible, and even tasty.

Most painful to touch. Ouch!! Certain pain occurs upon ramming a thorn or prickle into your flesh, but that takes some physical effort to pierce the skin. From just a simple touch, perhaps the most intense, burning pain comes from stinging nettles. Walking through a colony of nettles with shorts on brings some people to tears, as the pain is so severe. Fortunately, the pain is short-lived, but that is little solace to those just stung. Imagine the pioneers wearing clothing woven from the retted fibers of stinging nettle stems!

Most deadly to ingest. There are many native plants which are poisonous—far too many to list here. Some of the more notable ones include water hemlock, common nightshade, death camas, and white snakeroot. Snakeroot toxins are present in the milk of cows that eat the plant. Milk sickness, which results from drinking tainted milk, is the disease that killed Abraham Lincoln's mother.

Most rare. The rarest plants are those that occur with only a few individuals in a single, extant population. These plants, because of their low numbers and occurrence in only one place in the state, make them especially vulnerable to extirpation. They are the rarest of the rare. Top contenders are American barberry, long-awn hairgrass, tree-like clubmoss, shaggy false gromwell, heart-leaved plantain, bog-candles, dwarf chinquapin oak, sand grape, and large-leaf snowball.

Most common. This category is much more difficult than the one for rare species. It is impossible to determine the abundance of widespread native species, since they number in the millions, even billions, and often cover thousands of acres. Candidates for the most common are white snakeroot, spring beauty, Canada snakeroot, tall goldenrod, cut-leaf toothwort, common ragweed, horseweed, and hairy aster. Among introduced species, Kentucky bluegrass, tall fescue, corn, and soybeans must be the top four contenders.

Largest plant family. This award goes to the sedge family, with more than 200 native species. The aster and grass families each have more species if the introduced ones are included.

Smallest plant family. Several families have but one species in our state, so there is no single winner. Some co-winners are the plane-tree, pokeweed, pipewort, custard-apple, and ebony families.

Lookalikes. There are structures in some plants that resemble things other than plant parts. For example, the calyx of skullcap resembles a helmet, cap, or tractor seat. Parasitic dodder looks like strands of orange or yellow spaghetti. Seeds of nut rush appear as tiny white golf balls, dimples and all. Miterwort produces flowers that look like delicate snowflakes, and fruit like a miter, or bishop's cap. Cranefly orchid flowers look like mosquito-like crane flies.

Believe it or not. Can you believe that the large white "petals" of a flowering dogwood are not petals, but white bracts which are modified leaves? That poison-ivy climbing up an oak tree, or any tree, does not become a different species, i.e., poison-*oak*? Poison-oak does not occur in Indiana; goldenrods are not the source of problems for hay fever sufferers, because goldenrod pollen is normally too heavy to be dispersed into the atmosphere; there are far more orchids native to Indiana (42 species) than to Hawaii, which has only 3 species; grasses have flowers, albeit small and so specialized that they do not look like a "flower"; some populations of resurrection fern grow on the bark of tree branches, making it Indiana's only epiphytic vascular plant; cactus grows wild in Indiana, on dry sites such as sand dunes and rocky south-facing slopes; the "Indiana banana" is really a pawpaw.

Native plants commonly used in agriculture and horticulture. Most U.S. food crops and ornamentals originated in other countries, but several of them have "roots" here in Indiana. Blueberries, raspberries, blackberries, strawberries, cranberries, and grapes are all native to Indiana, as are pecans and black walnuts. These and other species have been bred to produce the fruits we enjoy today. Ornamentals that we use that grow wild here include hydrangea, winterberry, shrubby cinquefoil, arrow-wood, black-eyed Susan, garden phlox, purple coneflower, and blazing star.

> Our attitude toward plants is a singularly narrow one. If we see any immediate utility in a plant we foster it. If for any reason we find its presence undesirable, or merely a matter of indifference, we may condemn it to destruction forthwith.
>
> —*Rachel Carson, "Earth's Green Mantle," in* Silent Spring *(1962)*

Wild relatives of familiar domestic garden plants. These plants are not the same ones used in developing our cultivated varieties, but they are of the same genus. Similarities between the cultivars and the wild ones show their relatedness. Native to Indiana are wild yam, wild blue lettuce, wild sweet potato vine, wild plum, and wild green bean.

Derivation of interesting botanical names. Botanical names can be informative and even great fun once a person overcomes the intimidation of Latin pronunciation. Consider *Lithospermum,* the puccoon, whose white seeds are very hard (*litho* = stone, *sperma* = seed). Lizard's tail, *Saururus,* has a fruiting spike resembling a lizard's tail (*sauros* = lizard, *oura* = tail). The rhizome of bloodroot, *Sanguinaria,* contains red juice which has a remarkable resemblance to blood (*sanguinarius* = bleeding). Bugbane, *Cimicifuga,* is a plant with properties that supposedly repel insects (*cimex* = bug, *fugere* = to drive away).

Indiana's own. With one exception, all of the vascular plants that occur in Indiana are also found in other states. That one exception is Deam's foxglove. Named for Charles Deam, Indiana's foremost botanist and author of *Flora of Indiana,* this foxglove is known only from the hills in deep south-central Indiana. It has been reported from elsewhere, including other states, but such have been proved to be incorrect. Thus, nowhere else in the world can this plant be found in the wild other than in Indiana.

*   *   *

Care for These Trees

There is no such noble and protective a friend of man as the tree.
You who pass by and raises up your gun to do me harm, look at me
    closely.
I am the heat of your home during winter nights.
I am the friendly shade that protects you against the sun.
I am the post that supports the roof of your house, the tablet of
    your table, the bed in which you rest.
I am the handle of your tools.
When you are born I have wood for your crib. When you die, I
    accompany you to the depth of the earth.
I am the bread of kindness and a flower of beauty.
If you love me as I deserve, defend me against the insensitive.

> —*Anonymous. Original in Spanish, on a cement tablet*
>   *under a lone mesquite tree in a school yard in Reynosa,*
>   *Mexico. Translated by Beth Gruenewald.*

Of all the vascular plants known to occur in Indiana, Deam's foxglove (named for our preeminent pioneer botanist Charles Deam) is the only species that occurs here naturally and nowhere else in the world.
Photo by Michael Homoya

The Diversity of Indiana's Flowering Plants / 277

Serviceberry or Juneberry has ethereal white blooms in early May and fruit ready for pies by late June. *Photo by Marion Jackson*

36. What's the Use?

Marion T. Jackson

Time got his wrinkles reaping thee
Sweet herbs from all antiquity.

   —*Sidney Lanier,* The Stirrup-Cup

PLANTS FOR SURVIVAL

Immediate access to grocery, clothing, and hardware stores, lumberyards, physicians and pharmacies, vehicle dealerships, and fossil fuel energy supplies makes it almost impossible for us to comprehend that Native Americans and our pioneer ancestors were almost totally dependent upon plants for their livelihood. Food, clothing, utensils, building materials, medicines, conveyances, and fuel supplies were derived directly or indirectly from plants—some from around their doorsteps, gardens, or crop fields, but largely from those growing wild in the surrounding fields and forests. Plants met life needs from cradle to coffin.

Native Americans were closely attuned to the nature that supported them, discovering over thousands of years which plants were edible or toxic, irritating or soothing, those with preventive or curative medicinal properties, those useful or cultivable. Early settlers in Indiana learned much of this botanical lore from the Indians they rapidly displaced, or from their ancestors who had similarly discovered the uses of wild plants from earlier Native Americans when the states "back east" were settled.

Typically, an early Indiana homestead consisted of a small, ragged clearing around the log house and barn, all completely surrounded by the unending forest. Except for maize (corn), pumpkins, and squash from the Americas, their crop fields and gardens contained species brought from the Old World, along with an array of exotic weeds carried incidentally among their seeds for planting, or in the intestinal tracts, forage, or bedding of domestic animals. Plantings of culinary and medicinal herbs were common near the house site, the majority also introduced to the colonies from Europe.

> Amongst their few belongings these first settlers of America took with them were treasured seeds and roots of their favorite herbs. Many herbs quickly flourished in their new environment and became native [naturalized] plants. These included soapwort, comfrey and yarrow, chamomile and coltsfoot.
>
>   —*Arabella Boxer and Philippa Bock,* The Herb Book
>   (1980)

Fruit trees, grapevines, a peony at the doorstep, a lilac, and a couple of rosebushes in the front yard by the rail fence completed the "domesticated" flora, most of these also alien species.

Plants for all other purposes were diligently sought from the surrounding wilderness. A thorough knowledge of native plants, their uses, their cycles and seasons was essential for survival in a sea of wildness. The ability to accurately identify native plant species and their uses was an art transferred from parents to children as a part of the frontier-survival tool kit.

Wood from the largely unbroken forest provided the raw material from which settlements were forged. Indiana, with its 100-plus species, has a tree flora as rich as is present in all of continental Europe. Two dozen species of oaks and hickories alone occur in Indiana. Our impressive forests contained trees up to 10 or more feet through and towering to 150 feet. Here were trees to meet every need that generations of frontiersmen could imagine.

A TREE FOR EVERY PURPOSE

Several of the foods sustaining the pioneers came from the trees. Persimmons, nature's sugar plums (*Diospyros* means "the pear of the gods"), were eaten raw and flavored rich puddings; pawpaws (Indiana bananas) were also eaten fresh, filled pies, or flavored hand-cranked ice cream. Nuts of walnut, hickory, beech, and hazel were cracked during winter evenings on smooth flatirons, with the handle held firmly between the knees of frontier children. Bushels of chestnuts went to fatten farm animals and wild game, to stuff wild turkeys, and to roast on their hearthstones. There was also the special taste of Juneberry pie—known also as serviceberry or just "sarvis" in southern Indiana because the tree flowered at the time of the first service given by circuit rider preachers.

Wild plums, blackberries, and raspberries grew in thickets or tangles edging the clearings. Butternut, black walnut, or hickory nutmeats flavored fudge or cookies. Red haws, wild crabapples, wild cherries, and mulberries were nibbled by children, baked into sweet-smelling pastries, or fermented into robust wines. From the sugarbush, often spared from the ax for that special purpose, came maple syrup and sugar. Honey trees—basswood, sourwood, and black locust—also provided sweetnin' to supplement the supply of home-grown sorghum molasses. A passable coffee (naturally decaffeinated) was brewed from the rock-hard ground-up seeds of the Kentucky coffeetree.

At one time or another, all tree species were probably used for fuel wood to stoke the ever-hungry fireplaces in the drafty cabins. Hard maple, beech, and ash provide excellent coals and the even heat necessary for cooking and baking. Wood from ash trees—being in the olive family—contains an olive oil–like resin that permits it to burn readily even when wet or green. "Ash, even green, is wood fit for a queen," was a common frontier expression. Hickory, oak, beech, black locust, ash, hard maple, apple, and birch all yield high heat output, with hickory the premier choice. Birch bark, aspen, cedar, and pine were popular for tinder and kindling.

Trees and shrubs were the source of teas, tonics, tannins, medicines, and dyes. Sumac ade and tea from sassafras or spicewood were common beverages. Natural emollients in the bark of slippery elm soothed sore throats; weak cyanic acid extracted from wild cherry bark loosened persistent coughs and croupy chests; nature's aspirin from willow or cottonwood (their barks contain salicylic acid, hence the family name Salicaceae) eased frontier headaches or menstrual cramps. Native Americans sometimes diapered their babies with the soft inner bark of cottonwood for its absorbency; its mild aspirin content also helped to prevent rashes. Storax, for treating bronchial problems, came from sweet gum resin. Early prostheses to replace

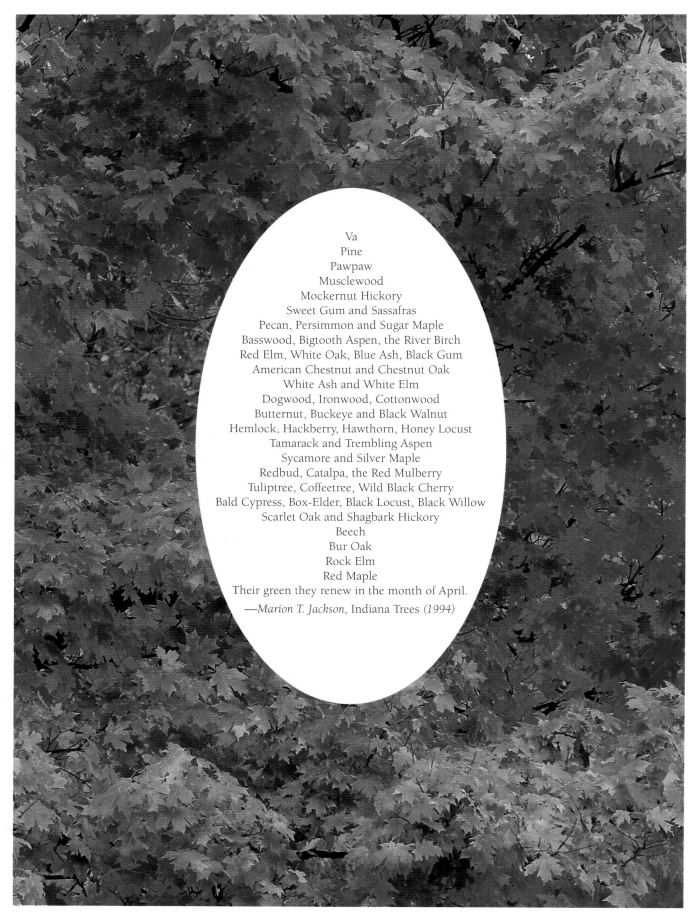

Va
Pine
Pawpaw
Musclewood
Mockernut Hickory
Sweet Gum and Sassafras
Pecan, Persimmon and Sugar Maple
Basswood, Bigtooth Aspen, the River Birch
Red Elm, White Oak, Blue Ash, Black Gum
American Chestnut and Chestnut Oak
White Ash and White Elm
Dogwood, Ironwood, Cottonwood
Butternut, Buckeye and Black Walnut
Hemlock, Hackberry, Hawthorn, Honey Locust
Tamarack and Trembling Aspen
Sycamore and Silver Maple
Redbud, Catalpa, the Red Mulberry
Tuliptree, Coffeetree, Wild Black Cherry
Bald Cypress, Box-Elder, Black Locust, Black Willow
Scarlet Oak and Shagbark Hickory
Beech
Bur Oak
Rock Elm
Red Maple
Their green they renew in the month of April.

—*Marion T. Jackson,* Indiana Trees *(1994)*

The fall coloration of sugar maple is among Indiana's finest.   *Photo by Richard Fields*

Blackberry abounds in abandoned farm fields or fencerows about five years after clearing.
Photo by Marion Jackson

Hawthorn fruits make delectable jelly or wine.
Photo by Richard Fields

Persimmons are nature's "sugar plums" if eaten when fully ripe.   *Photo by Delano Z. Arvin*

limbs lost in warfare or accidents were fashioned from supple, lightweight bolts of buckeye or black willow.

Tree barks to tan hides and leathers came from American chestnut, hemlock, or chestnut oak, all high in tannic acid. There were dyes for homespun cloth—browns from butternut or walnut hulls; blue from blue ash bark; yellow xanthophylls from the xylem of yellowwood, mulberry, or prickly ash; scarlet from the inner bark of dogwood; sienna from sumac.

> For trees, you know are friends indeed,
> They satisfy each human need;
> In summer shade, in winter fire,
> With flower and fruit meet all desire,
> And if a friend to Man you'd be,
> You must befriend him like a tree.
>
> —*Charles A. Heath*

Wood for every purpose in life came from the rich forests. Preferred for log cabin construction were durable woods that split and hewed easily and resisted decay and termites. Yellow poplar and chestnut were favored because they were lightweight and easily worked. Beech and oak, although very heavy, also enjoyed wide usage since one or the other was abundant throughout the state. Soft maple, white pine, or yellow-poplar sashed windows. Window blinds raised or lowered on basswood rollers. Later on, Venetian blind slats, of basswood, cucumbertree, or white pine, shielded people's eyes from the sun. Shingles or shakes rived from red oak, red cedar, or bald cypress covered their roofs. Closets and brides' boxes were lined with red cedar for fragrance and to repel moths. Butternut chests presumably kept silverware from tarnishing. Carefully adzed puncheons of poplar or chestnut served as floorboards or tops of trestle tables and benches. Finer furniture and cabinetry were handcrafted from the beautiful woods of black walnut, wild cherry, chestnut, ash, butternut, oak, maple, or birch.

Farms were "worm fenced" with rails from easily split trees—yellow-poplar, chestnut, or black walnut. Later on, barbed or woven wires were posted with "lasty" woods such as black locust (planted near farm buildings because the settlers thought locust trees served as "natural lightning rods"), chestnut, catalpa, mulberry, red cedar, Osage-orange, or sassafras. Posts from these trees would outlast several postholes, boasted the early farmers!

> Should farmer John require a post
> To stand and stay and serve the most,
>
> One that will last for years and years
> And be as firm as ancient piers,

> A post that saves time and expense
> And makes an everlasting fence,
>
> But few posts come within the class
> Of sound and seasoned sassafras.
>
> Search far and wide in any land,
> A post of sassafras so grand
>
> And well conditioned, without doubt,
> Will wear a dozen post holes out.
>
> —*E. A. Richardson, "Sassafras Fence Posts," in* Indiana and Other Poems *(1930)*

Charcoal from beech, oak, maple, or willow fueled the forges for smelting iron or blacksmithing, while coals of hickory smoked meats. Slack cooperage of chestnut, basswood, soft maple, or the various red oaks shipped and stored the settlers' flour, sugar, salt pork, and salted fish. White oak barreled and aged their molasses, rum, and whiskey. Buckeye, basswood, cottonwood, elm, maple, white ash, and pawpaw—woods easily carved and free of tastes or odors—were used for such housewares as dough bowls, food canisters, butter tubs, cream skimmers, potato mashers, lemon squeezers, and wooden spoons. Churns or wooden pails were typically made from red cedar or larch.

Beautiful bowls were turned on foot-powered lathes from burls of many species. Home basketry was hand-woven from black ash or white oak splints or willow withes. Fruit bushels were made from veneer strips of elm or sycamore. Ironing boards came from cottonwood, aspen, or tupelo. Clothespins were of beech; toothpicks and tongue depressors of paper birch. Matchsticks were usually white pine or aspen.

The hard, smooth woods of flowering dogwood or persimmon were used to shuttle their looms, spool their thread, sheave their pulleys, and later on, to head their golf clubs. Sycamore (the buttonwood tree) was the source of buttons for pioneer clothing and, being almost non-splittable, also butcher blocks.

Tiger-stripe or bird's-eye maple, black walnut, wild cherry, and occasionally apple or yellowwood stocked their flintlock rifles and dueling pistols. Beauty and balance, plus recoil and shock resistance, were properties sought in selecting these woods. Cabinetmakers' planes were of such hard, dense woods as sugar maple, beech, apple, or sycamore for the same reasons. Handles for shovels and pitchforks were ash, as were ballbats and snowshoe frames. Handles for axes to cut down the trees were froe-split, then hand-shaved with drawknives from shagbark, pignut, or bitternut hickory, and finally heat hardened for long use in fireplace chimneys. Sledges, hammers, and other impact tools were also handled with hickory, or sometimes

Pawpaw or "Indiana banana" is our largest edible forest fruit—it ripens in October. The soft, strong wood was carved into wooden spoons, cream skimmers, and fishing bobbers by the pioneers.   *Photo by Delano Z. Arvin*

ironwood. Froe mallets for riving shakes and shingles came from ironwood or dogwood burls, while wooden gluts (wedges) for splitting logs or rails were hewed from hornbeam.

Rulers for schoolchildren, or carpenters' folding models, were of holly, boxwood, or dogwood. Pencil leads were encased in red cedar. Applewood perfumed fireplace fires; unburned, the best pieces often cased mantle clocks in rich, warm brown tones. Hard, smoothly polished wooden cogs fashioned from blocks of apple moved the mechanisms of early grandfather clocks.

Hollow tupelos became crude "bee gums," while basswood, aspen, ash, or elm provided finished hives and honey frames. Chickens were cooped in crates of cottonwood, white pine, or big-tooth aspen. Stable and barn floors and loading platforms were planked with tough, abrasion-resistant black gum. Even sharply shod horses would scarcely dent seasoned gum planking. Silage fermented in silos of bald cypress (later, redwood was used). Plow handles were steam-bent to fit farmers' hands from white ash or red elm. Ladders usually had spruce rails and rungs of bitternut or shagbark hickory. Farm sleds and stone boats skidded on runners of sourwood or sassafras; specially selected trees had natural crooks which formed the upturned ends. Disk harrows rotated on cylindrical "boxings" (bearings) of sourwood or dogwood. Creaking gristmills ground grains with gears of musclewood or seasoned oak.

Small boats for sportsmen most commonly were of white or black spruce, white cedar, bald-cypress, or white ash construction—strong, durable, easily crafted, and bouyant. Oars and canoe paddles were spruce or white ash. Hunting decoys were carved from basswood, butternut, white pine, or white cedar for ease of shaping, paint retention, and good flotation.

Masts of sailing ships were from tall, straight, strong white pines. One of the earliest laws restricting unlimited forest cutting stipulated the selection and marking of the finest New England pines in the seventeenth century to be used as masts for the Royal Navy. Ships' knees of specially selected oak crotches secured the gunnels to the main deck, and the finest oak beams keeled their hulls. Tall, straight white oaks from flatwoods forests became the pilings driven into shoreline muds to form the docks and wharves.

Packsaddle trees were fashioned from American elm, willow, or buckeye—lightweight, strong, and easily shaped. Covered with leather, they formed modern riding saddles. Wooden stirrups were

steam-bent elm. Buggies, sleighs, and carriages contained a medley of woods, perhaps best described in these whimsical lines from Oliver Wendell Holmes's satirical poem *The Deacon's Masterpiece or The Wonderful One Hoss Shay,* which "ran 100 years to the day":

> So the Deacon inquired of the village folk
> Where he could find the strongest oak,
> That couldn't be split nor bent nor broke,—
> That was for spokes and floors and sills;
> He sent for lancewood to make the thills;
>
> The crossbars were ash, from the straightest trees,
> The panels of white-wood, that cuts like cheese,
> But lasts like iron for things like these;
> The hubs of logs from the "Settler's ellum,"—
> Last of its timber,—they couldn't sell 'em.

Later on, early automobile bodies (many made here in Indiana) were crafted from oak, ash, and sometimes yellow-poplar, while spokes for their elaborately painted wheels were usually oak. Until the mid-1930s, auto bodies were crafted by skilled woodworkers, then overlain with hand-hammered sheet metal. Our local abundance of high-quality hardwoods is a major reason why wagon and carriage works located their manufacturing plants in Indiana, later to give way to the state's early diverse automobile industry; e.g., the Studebaker Wagon Works, started in the mid-nineteenth century, later developed the Studebaker automobile.

As the "iron horse" entered the transportation picture, almost uncountable "sleepers" were needed to carry the rails. They came from a wide variety of trees, but the various oaks, beech, birch, chestnut, locust, hard maple, or tuliptree were the most commonly used woods for railroad ties.

When the wood-using days of a pioneer drew to a close, a local carpenter (often a relative or close friend) turned to the trees one last time for coffin lumber. Durable, straight-grained, pretty woods were preferred. Black walnut heartwood two to three inches thick was the prime casket wood. Squire Boone (Daniel's younger brother) was interred in such a coffin in a cave in southern Indiana, which now bears his name. The burial box was partially intact when rediscovered nearly a century after his death. Other favored woods (many still widely used today) were chestnut, oak, cypress, cherry, yellow-poplar, white pine, basswood, and mulberry. Interestingly, Nebuchadnezzar, the Babylonian king, was buried about 650 B.C. in a mulberry coffin. Apparently the ancients valued woods for the same properties as did our pioneer ancestors.

> Moons waxed and waned, the lilacs bloomed and died,
> In the broad river ebbed and flowed the tide,
> Ships went to sea, and ships came home from sea,
> And the slow years sailed by and ceased to be.
> —*Longfellow,* Lady Wentworth

HELPFUL AND HEALTHFUL HERBS

Probably at one time or another each of us, during our childhood or youth, has idly plucked a fluffy dandelion seed head from the lawn, made a wish, and blown the parachuted seeds away. Or taken a white ox-eye daisy and pulled the ray flowers off one by one, saying, "He loves me, he loves me not." Typically the number of ray flowers of the inflorescence head is uneven, thereby making the prophecy pleasing! But do we give a passing thought to how vital wild plants were to human comfort and survival in the not-too-distant past?

Certain herbs were literally "supermarket" species for Native Americans and pioneer families. A dozen or so species served as common sources of food, beverages, seasoning, tonics, medicines, veterinary treatments, pest repellents, cloth, fiber, or dyes. Before herbicides were widely broadcast on the land, many such herbs grew abundantly in lawns, garden borders, fencerows, or abandoned clearings—dandelion, heal-all, ground-ivy, pokeberry, bedstraw, violets, burdock, mullein, field sorrel, sow thistle, yarrow, milkweed, goldenrod, catnip, soapwort, or wild onion. Such species were viewed as weeds when growing in gardens or crop fields, but were tolerated or encouraged elsewhere for their many uses.

What is a weed? A plant whose virtues have not yet been discovered.

—*Emerson,* Fortune of the Republic

Abundant folklore developed around the real or presumed qualities of herbs. Since many were introduced from Europe, often the folklore is centuries old, with its origin lost in antiquity. Native Americans developed their own folk medicine from the severe trial and error of survival over millennia. The knowledge of plants and their uses that served the Indiana pioneer was an amalgam of information handed down from their ancestors and fused with plant lore of the Indians.

Friendly Indians showed the new inhabitants many plants already growing in the country that had culinary and medicinal value. The best known of these was bergamot, the leaves of which the Indians used as a tea called Oswego tea.

—*Arabella Boxer and Philippa Bock,* The Herb Book (1980)

The efficacy of treatment of medical problems with wild botanicals is often questioned, but modern ethnobotanists worldwide are diligently researching the uses of plants by primitive and rural peoples. Regardless of past usage or the purported benefits from a given plant species, *no plant should be eaten or used medicinally unless you are absolutely sure of its identification and chemical and physical properties.*

A commonly applied concept to guide the use of a particular plant in earlier times was the *Doctrine of Signatures.* Under this precept, characteristics of the plant such as shape, color, or odor (the plant's signature) were presumed to be a revelation or guide for its intended use or medicinal effect.

A well-known example is ginseng, whose name originated from the Chinese *Jin-Chen* (man-like), suggesting its value in maintaining or restoring human health or vigor. Its Latin name, *Panax,* is from the Greek *pan* (all) and *akos* (cure)—literally "cure-all." Both names derive from the resemblance of the ginseng root to the human torso. Belief in ginseng's magical powers is reflected in the extensive harvests during recent years and its present elevated price.

For example, nearly seven *tons* of wild dried ginseng root was reported as being harvested in Indiana during the 1992–93 growing season and sold to more than 60 dealers. The average harvest during the past five years was nearly five tons per year, making the collection and sale of ginseng a multi-million-dollar industry in Indiana. A license to harvest is required in Indiana to assist in monitoring ginseng population trends. Responsible gatherers harvest only in the autumn, simultaneously planting the ripening red seeds to perpetuate the population and future crop.

The history of ginseng harvest in North America is as old as settlement here. Pioneers, including Daniel Boone, searched avidly for it as a cash crop on the money-impoverished frontier.

Other Doctrine of Signatures plant correlations include the use of hepatica (liver-shaped leaf) to treat liver problems, and the yellow root of goldenseal or curly dock or celandine sap to "cure" "yaller" jaundice. The reddish color of sassafras tea signified its value as a blood purifier. Merrybells (genus *Uvularia*) was considered useful for throat ailments because of the bell-like flower's resemblance to the uvula. Similarly, heal-all and butter-and-eggs were used for mouth and throat conditions because their bilateral flowers are open-mouthed. Sow thistles with their milky sap were fed to pregnant sows and also to nursing human mothers, hopefully to increase milk supply.

Farfetched, humorous, and even ridiculous examples of the Doctrine of Signatures include eating the sticky green seed structures of burdock to help your memory (help things "stick" in your mind), eating stinging nettles with their profusion of irritating hairs to stimulate hair growth, or adding coreopsis plants to mattresses to repel bed vermin because those seeds resemble bedbugs!

Common names of many herbs suggest actual or presumed uses or properties of the plants: Joe-Pye weed reputedly is named for its use by Native Americans in treating typhoid fever (*jopi* was Indian for typhoid); orange milkweed was called pleurisy root by the pioneers; early on wild ginger was called birthwort, from its wide use to ease childbirth; orange hawkweed was lungwort; while butter-and-eggs was gallwort, from its use to cure gallstones in poultry and perhaps humans. Solomon's seal was derived from the shape of its rhizome scars, which resemble the seal of Solomon, who presumably put his "seal of approval" on the medicinal values of the plant. Feverfew, wild quinine, fleabane, bee balm, and loosestrife are largely self-explanatory.

Merrybells (genus *Uvularia*) was a classic example of the Doctrine of Signatures. It was used to treat throat problems since the flower resembles (vaguely) the human uvula. *Photo by Lee Casebere*

Many herbaceous plants had interesting specialty uses in pioneer households. Soapwort, which gives off a bubbly lather in water when its leaves are bruised, was used as a saponifier (hence *Saponaria*) for bathing and washing clothes. It was widely believed to have been sent to the Friars by God to keep them clean and healthy ("Cleanliness is next to godliness"!).

Dried seed capsules of teasels (to tease), which were used to tease or comb the nap of woolen cloth, were introduced to the U.S. by fullers for that purpose. Teasel heads were also used by pioneer women to sprinkle clothes before ironing because they held and released water in the proper amount. Now they are widely used along with cattail, goldenrod, Queen Anne's lace, curly dock, and others in dried flower arrangements.

Bedstraw was used by pioneers as a mattress filler, as it stays flexible, smells like cured hay, and presumably repels insects. Clean, dry newly fallen tree leaves (especially beech) were also used by the earliest settlers in the deep forest. Similarly, cattail seed tufts, milkweed down, and sow thistle floss were used to insulate quilts or stuff pillows. Dried may-apple fruits with their delicious aroma were used as sachets among stored clothes; in contrast, the strong-scented leaves of tansy were placed in coffins to help preserve the bodies of the deceased.

Dyes and colorings were obtained from many species. Native Americans used the red-orange sap of bloodroot for war paint, and to dye cloth or baskets. Anthocyanins from pokeweed yielded a purple dye and a passable ink. Yellow dyes were obtained from goldenseal root, dandelion flower heads, the ray flowers of wild sunflowers, or contrasting yellows from the two-colored flowers of butter-and-eggs. Green dye was extracted with acids from mullein leaves.

Pioneers of early Indiana continually had to cope with the presence of insects, spiders, snakes, and other "vermin," which invaded their homes, worried their domestic animals, and infested their bodies, bedding, and food. Any plant suspected of repelling or killing insects, especially, was used at one time or another.

Stinging nettle leaves and roots were boiled in water, as were coffeetree leaves, to produce natural insecticides. Fleas and lice were repelled (not very effectively) with daisy fleabane or powdered tansy leaves. Pussytoes flowers were added by early country people to their shampoo to rid themselves of head lice. They also "larded" their heads for that purpose, much as farmers now oil their livestock. Bloodroot juice or goldenseal root mixed with animal fat was used by Indians to repel mosquitoes and other insects. Red clover blossoms, pussytoes flowers, or red cedar shavings were packed with clothes or furs to repel moths. Solomon's seal was dried and sprinkled on the cabin floors to "rid out" spiders and snakes. Wood betony, likewise, was thought to repel snakes, as snakes were believed to lash themselves to death if caught in a bed of betony.

Farm animals were treated with home remedies concocted from herbs when lame, sick, or injured. Mullein leaves were burned in the presence of animals to relieve wheezing, pulmonary congestion, and respiratory ailments. Sow thistle (high in vitamin C) was used to treat animals for high blood pressure and heart disorders. Bloodroot rhizome was given to sick horses and mules, while falconers used bits of celandine root to cure their sick birds. Skunk cabbage was used for lockjaw, and attempts were made to treat rabies with a "mishmash" of asters. Orange hawkweed (*Hieracium*, from *hierex*, "hawk") was used for eye disorders, as it was believed that birds of prey strengthened their eyesight by sipping the juice of that plant.

Brilliant scarlet dyes were obtained from flowering dogwood.   *Photo by Delano Z. Arvin*

Bundles of loosestrife were tied to ox yokes to calm recalcitrant oxen—to cause them to "lose strife." Since the plant is a mild insect repellent, there may be some basis in fact.

Antidotes for poisoning or suspected poisoning were derived from field sorrel or, in the case of lead poisoning, the dried leaves of ground-ivy. Parsley was thought to be an antidote for oral poisoning; hence we now place a sprig on dinner plates as a token of faith that the food will be safe. Perhaps Ogden Nash's whimsical rhyme "parsley's gharstley, use it sparsely" is not always appropriate!

> Many protective plant chemicals are physiologically potent . . .
> such plants were discovered by man through trial and error and
> slowly became used as "drug plants" or as herbs and spices.
>
> —*Robert O. Petty, "Strategies," in* Wild Plants in Flower
>   III: Deciduous Forest *(1974)*

Your general health, memory, mental acuity, and longevity would presumably be improved by taking ginseng regularly, but the wizened root of ox-eye daisy was believed to stunt your growth if eaten. Rue anemone was thought to have great healing powers. Yarrow was felt to improve intelligence and to brighten your eyes. A necklace of pokeberries was believed to ward off contagious diseases, as would an asafetida bag of fennel or wild onion—likely the latter prevented anyone from getting close!

The soothing effect of Joe-Pye weed was used by Native Americans to settle their nerves. Violets were believed to calm anger (the violet's "sign" is humility) and induce sleep; hence the expression "shy as a violet." Skunk cabbage or the center red floret of Queen Anne's lace or wild carrot flowers (presumably representing a drop of blood from the pricked finger of the Queen as she tatted the lace of the flower!) was believed to relieve epilepsy and seizures. Watercress has been felt since Roman times to calm "deranged" minds. Conversely, jimson-weed fruits and seeds—perhaps a corruption of "Jamestown" weed—were used by Native Americans in carefully measured amounts to create hallucinations and visions which helped them understand the mysteries of the universe. (Presumably jimson-weed received its name when soldiers of Jamestown Colony, who ate the fruits during a food shortage, heard strange sounds and saw sights no one else could see!) The seeds should be scrupulously avoided as they are especially dangerous and can cause death, hence another common name, Devil's trumpet.

Mouth and throat disorders were relieved by heal-all (*Prunella*) tea from its spring leaves (also used to treat quinsy), cinquefoil leaf tea used as a gargle, as was powdered goldenseal root. Wild geranium root or field sorrel was boiled to treat sore throats or mouth ulcers. Trout lily tea apparently cured hiccups. Gum problems were relieved by tea from ground-ivy, curly dock, or cinquefoil leaves, or by celandine juice. Their vitamin C content may have been helpful, especially as a scurvy (which loosens teeth) preventive. Pioneers chewed yarrow to relieve toothache.

Eye inflammations were treated by Native Americans with trillium or goldenseal roots or the stem sap of Indian pipe. Phlox leaves crushed in water or the water from the leaf cupules of teasel was used to wash tired or sore eyes. Tea from butter-and-eggs leaves was used to treat conjunctivitis. Earaches or ringing of ears was putatively relieved by ground-ivy or yarrow tea.

> So, when a raging fever burns,
> We shift from side to side by turns;
> And 'tis a poor relief we gain,
> To change the place, but keep the pain.
>
> —*Issac Watts,* Hymns and Spiritual Songs

Fevers were lowered by teas of chickweed, yarrow, yellow root (for malaria), or bee balm. Native Americans relied on pipsissewa to induce sweating and break a fever, or used sliced wild onions to cover feverish parts of the body. Dizziness or headaches were relieved by Indians by applying crushed Jack-in-the-pulpit roots to their forehead, smelling bruised skunk cabbage leaves, or drinking mullein tea. Such ministrations may have caused more discomfort than the malady, thereby causing the victim to forget the problem! Violet leaf or wild onion teas were also presumed effective.

From head to toe, herbs helped maintain skin tone and healthful condition. Teas from yarrow leaves or marsh-mallow roots were used to treat dandruff, to reduce hair loss, or to improve hair and scalp. Indians used wild sunflower seed oil to dress their hair and give it a sheen. The juice of celandine, rue anemone, trout lily, or loosestrife was applied to corns, foot sores, or aching feet. Athlete's foot fungus was treated with jewel-weed juice or red clover blossoms. On the body proper, attempts were made to remove warts by applying milkweed latex, may-apple root, or celandine juice, or by washing in water from teasel or leaf-cup leaf cupules. Some victims of warts attempted to have them "charmed off" by soothsayers.

Dermatitis, itches, rashes, and skin irritations had a multitude of cures. The burning from stinging nettles was relieved by the juice of jewel-weed, curly dock, or rhubarb. Poison-ivy rashes were treated with juices from soapwort leaves, jewel-weed leaves, or flowers. The "itch," eczema, and ringworm apparently were relieved by applications of dandelion root or celandine juice. Marsh-mallow roots or ox-eye daisy flowers were boiled to soothe chapped hands. Salves from goldenseal, yarrow, marsh-mallow, or brown-eyed Susan treated skin infections or relieved breasts swollen and inflamed by breastfeeding.

Insect bites and bee stings were eased by rubbing with bee balm or marsh marigold leaves. Bedstraw or tansy tea relieved sunburn pain, but more serious burns were usually treated with jimson-weed or yarrow leaves, grated wild carrot root (carotin has healing powers), or salves made from pokeberry or jimson-weed roots and animal fat.

Acne, skin problems, and improved complexions were approached by boiling blue phlox, field sorrel, tansy, aster, or sow thistle in water and applying to face or body. Freckles were blanched or removed with celandine juice or bedstraw tea. Indian women crushed the berries of the unpalatable Indian strawberry to make a facial mask to improve their complexions.

Washing your face in water from teasel leaf cupules (Venus' basin) was believed to make you as beautiful as Venus. Quaker girls rubbed their cheeks with mullein leaves (Quaker rouge) to give a rosy complexion, since applying makeup was forbidden by their religion. Butter-and-eggs was specially cultivated in herb gardens as a source of skin lotion and salve for insect bites. Rural people believed that red clover tea improved the texture of their nails.

Poultices were once a common treatment to relieve infections, draw "poison" from wounds, help thorns to fester, ease arthritic / rheumatic pain, hasten childhood diseases to "break out," reduce swelling, or clear up bruises. Plant or sometimes animal tissue was applied on a soft cloth compress to the afflicted area for whatever time was required to relieve or cure the condition. Boiled or crushed burdock, yarrow, or ox-eye daisy leaves were such common poultices to relieve bruises that ox-eye daisy was formerly called bruise-wort. Crushed Solomon's seal root was also used by Native Americans to treat bruises. Incipient boils were frequently "brought to a head" with the leaves of field sorrel, hedge bindweed, or chickweed. Violet leaves were applied to skin ulcerations and bedsores, likely for their high vitamin A and C content. Tansy tea was drunk or used as a body wash to "bring out" measles. Dandelion served as a treatment for impetigo.

Orange milkweed or butterfly weed was called pleurisy root by the pioneers for its use in treating respiratory problems.
Photo by Richard Fields

Pipsissewa was used by Native Americans and pioneer families to treat kidney stones.
Photo by Michael Kirk

Lobelia syphilitica was so named because of its putative value in treating venereal disease.
Photo by Delano Z. Arvin

Internal problems as well were addressed via application of a wide range of herbal treatments. Overall body health and proper functioning of the system was believed to be strongly coupled to frequent elimination (to "rid the body of wastes and poisons") and "purification of the blood," the latter at least annually in the spring. "Natural" laxative "tonics" and stimulants were made from goldenseal, curly dock, or rhubarb roots. Anyone who has taken "N-R" ("Nature's Remedy") drugstore laxative tablets can vouch for their effectiveness! Native Americans relied on roots of may-apple, which contain podophyllin, as a powerful cathartic. For more gentle treatment, teas from hedge bindweed, wild geranium, blue phlox, or butter-and-eggs were used. Upset stomachs were relieved by bee balm, yarrow, or field sorrel tea.

Appetites were stimulated by a bit of fringed gentian in brandy, or by drinking Joe-Pye weed tea. In emergencies, thirsts were sometimes quenched by chewing field sorrel leaves or sipping water from teasel (*Dipsacus*, from Greek *dipsa*, "thirst") leaf cupules. If eating or drinking too much of the wrong things resulted in diarrhea, it was cured by boiling cattail root in milk or drinking tea made from Indian strawberry roots. Dysentery was treated by the Indians by chewing milkweed root or drinking wild geranium leaf tea. Vermifuges (usually extremely foul-tasting liquids) to "rid out" intestinal worms were concocted from the roots of wild carrot, fire pink, Indian pink, cardinal flower, or tansy.

In addition to sassafras tea, which was drunk in spring to thin and purify the blood, teas from red clover blossoms or burdock or ginseng roots were also used. Extracts from violets or fire pink were used (especially with sugar and/or wine) to strengthen heart muscles or soothe an "irregular" heart. Astringents to staunch blood flow or hemorrhaging were made from heal-all, yarrow, cattail, or wild geranium. Bedstraw tea was said to help blood coagulate, while a cloth soaked in nettle juice was purported to be good for nosebleed—or perhaps the resultant itching made you forget that you had one!

Bladder or kidney stones were treated by Native Americans by using pipsissewa (prince's pine). In fact, the name pipsissewa is an Indian word meaning "juice breaks down stone in bladder in small pieces." Pioneers also used this remedy. Wild onion tea was taken for gall bladder problems, while chicory, soapwort, dandelion, butter-and-eggs, and wild columbine were used for treating jaundice and a variety of liver problems.

Respiratory problems, coughs, colds, croup, pneumonia, and tuberculosis were common maladies, frequently leading to death, especially in children. Onion tea with brown sugar and honey was widely used to treat coughs and croup in pioneer children, or tea from wild ginger root for whooping cough. Indians smoked dried milkweed or jimson-weed leaves to relieve asthma. Butterfly weed (pleurisy root) and orange hawkweed (lungwort) were commonly applied treatments for respiratory problems. Cough medicines were made from red clover blossoms or ginseng. Indians used pipsissewa tea to cure consumption (tuberculosis). Desperate pioneers applied mustard plasters covered with flannel to the chests of their children, hoping to cure bronchitis or pneumonia. Sow thistle was a treatment for wheezing and shortness of breath, in both humans and horses.

Cold, drafty cabins and strenuous work in all kinds of weather likely led to immense suffering by many from the disabilities of gout, arthritis, and rheumatism, frequently perhaps at early ages. Almost any plant that even suggested relief was eagerly sought and applied. Indians steamed themselves under skin tents in which a pot of boiling herbs was placed, usually including goldenrod (*Solidago* is Latin for "to make whole").

Yet that slackened grasp doth hold
Store of pure and genuine gold;
Quick thou comest, strong and free,
Type of all the wealth to be—
            Goldenrod!

    —Elaine Goodale

Pioneers also used external applications of skunk cabbage salve or "plasters" of ground mustard seed with bread to treat rheumatism. Popular teas included ground-ivy, yarrow, mullein, tansy, dandelion, or burdock leaves boiled with honey and milk.

The love life and reproduction of early Hoosiers also received the ministrations of numerous herbal treatments. (From the size of many pioneer families, perhaps they were effective!) Ginseng has long been regarded as an aphrodisiac, being widely used in both North America and Asia for that purpose. Burdock leaves ("love leaves"), mullein leaves, and trillium roots were said to be love potions. Sleeping with yarrow wrapped in flannel under your pillow was believed to produce prophetic love dreams. Cardinal flower and sow thistle were thought to enhance desire and prolong virility in older women and men, respectively. Indian women thought their husbands would love them more if they rubbed their bodies with rattlesnake plantain.

To prevent or postpone the consequences of such amorous arousal, milkweed, wild ginger root, and leaf tea from skunk cabbage or Solomon's seal were used as contraceptives. Tansy has been used for centuries as an abortifacient. Skunk cabbage, soapwort, and lobelia (hence *Lobelia syphilitica*) were used by Native Americans and early settlers as home treatments for venereal diseases.

Pain associated with menstruation, pregnancy, and the labor of childbirth was eased by application of a number of herbal remedies. Pioneers used yarrow to regulate menstrual periodicity, tansy to promote its onset, or Indian paintbrush to cause its cessation. Tea of hedge bindweed or partridge berry was drunk to make pregnancy more comfortable.

The sex of the unborn was presumably determined by drinking tea made from cinquefoil or daisy fleabane of differing flower colors—white cinquefoil a girl, yellow a boy; white fleabane a boy, pink a girl. Pregnancy and childbirth involved greater mystery before amniocentesis!

Wild ginger was called birthwort because it was once used to ease childbirth.   *Photo by Delano Z. Arvin*

Wild ginger (birthwort), trillium (birthroot), or cattail root was given to ease the pain of childbirth. Roots of marsh-mallow, a relative of hollyhock and hibiscus, were chewed by infants as nature's pacifier and teether. Mucilage from the gelatinous mallow was released by chewing, which soothed gums and apparently calmed baby's stomach.

NATURE'S PHARMACY AND GROCERY

Obviously medicinal herbs were not waiting year-round in the fields and forests to be plucked in time of need, as one might buy a box of coughdrops or a bottle of aspirin at the grocery or pharmacy today. Instead, they were gathered in season, carefully dried, and hung with leatherwood withes or deerskin thongs from the cabin rafters or in the attic, or placed in canning jars for use throughout the year.

In addition to medicinal uses, wild herbs were also primary food sources or supplements throughout the year for Native American and pioneer families. Many were gathered, dried, jarred, pickled, or placed in gourd containers or root cellars for later use. They were also eagerly sought as fresh salad or vegetable items for their high vitamin and mineral content, especially in spring after a winter's diet of canned vegetables, dried grains, and meat, often fatty or greasy. Nothing was quite as welcomed as a meal of spring greens of curly dock, dandelion, wintercress, pokeweed, chickweed, stinging nettles, lamb's quarters, pigweed, and violet leaves, with a dash of pungent wild onion, acidic field sorrel, and peppery toothwort for seasoning. Marsh marigold (high in iron) was especially favored by those anemic.

    Violets in the holler,
    Poke greens in the dish,
    Blue bird fly up,
    Give me my wish.

      —An old pioneer song

Roots and stems of many herbs served as vegetables eaten raw as they were gathered or cooked for meals. The shoots of milkweed, pokeweed, merrybells, Solomon's seal, and cattail are remarkably tasty and as succulent as asparagus. The starchy corms or rhizomes of spring beauty, trout lily, harbinger-of-spring, cattail, and jack-in-the-pulpit are all edible, even tasty, if prepared properly. Dandelion, pumpkin, squash, or elder flowers dipped in egg batter all make fine-tasting fritters. Indian cucumber rhizome provided a nibble of wilderness pickle.

Flour or meal substitutes could be obtained from Solomon's seal or cattail root, or cattail pollen, and from curly dock or pigweed seeds. Vegetable cooking oils to supplement lard or tallow could be extracted from wild sunflower seeds.

Teas from bee balm (Oswego tea), goldenrod, ground-ivy, or red clover were summer replacements for the sassafras or spicebush beverages of early spring. A lemonade-type drink was steeped from acidic field sorrel leaves or sumac fruits. Coffee substitutes came from bedstraw seeds (in the same family as coffee) or the ground and roasted roots of dandelion or chicory (often called blue sailors). In emergencies, even the seed husks of sunflowers were roasted, ground, and used as coffee.

Alcoholic drinks were often fermented or brewed from a wide variety of native and cultivated plants. Almost any carbohydrate-containing plant part—fruit, flower, stem, or root—can be, and has been, fermented into wine, even from onions, oak leaves, and turnips! May-apple fruits make a delectable wine with a lovely bouquet. Likewise, home-brewed ale and beer were popular bever-

Sassafras tea is considered by many people to be a spring tonic and blood purifier.
Photo by Delano Z. Arvin

Red clover tea was believed to help many ailments, from respiratory problems to weak fingernails. *Photo by Paul Rothrock*

ages in frontier households and inns. Ground-ivy leaves were used to clarify and purify beer before hops were available, as were stinging nettle leaves. Soapwort was sometimes used to put a head on beer.

Wild herbs were useful in preparing a number of other foods. Bedstraw (genus *Galium,* from the Greek for "milk") has an enzyme that curdles milk; pioneers used it in cheesemaking. Red clover blossoms were used to impart a distinctive flavor to cheese. Seeds of field mustards were used in sauces and pickles, and ground as prepared mustard. Horseradish root, which grew at the garden border, was tearfully ground to make that condiment. Several wild members of the mint and parsley families, especially, were dried and used throughout the year as spices and seasoning.

Candies, syrups, and marmalades were concocted from violet flowers, wild ginger root, and may-apple fruits, as well as many wild berries. Gelatinous, sweetish root sap from the marsh-mallow was boiled, then whipped to make meringue or "marshmallows," hence the present name of that confection. Then as now, people craved sweets.

THE UPSHOT

Despite this rich history of wild plant uses as resources for human survival, food, and comfort, for the most part the *gathering or exploiting of wild species should no longer be practiced.* There are now far too many of us and too few of our wild plant neighbors. Most remaining wild populations are too small and too fragmented to sustain any kind of serious harvest. *Those that remain need to be protected in refuges for their ecological, aesthetic, and scientific purposes.*

This is not to say that none can or should be propagated and cultivated as ornamentals, food or medicine sources, or timber resources. Great future potential exists from many species for these purposes, making remaining reserves of wild genetic stock even more valuable. After all, each of our present "domesticated" plant "species" was derived from wild ancestral stock.

For example, wild columbine, Virginia bluebells, phlox, cardinal flower, Jack-in-the-pulpit, trilliums, butterfly weed, and several ferns are popular ornamentals, and could be more so if propagated for sale by nurseries. There has been a great surge of interest in prairie restoration, which has created a lively market for both seeds and vegetative materials of many prairie grasses and forbs. Bladdernut, elderberry, wahoo, native bittersweet, shrubby dogwoods, coral berry, wild roses (not the introduced multiflora!), and wild viburnums could enhance our farm field borders and dwelling landscapings. Partridgeberry, woodbine, and running euonymus are promising groundcovers for selected sites. Pawpaw, persimmon, elderberry, and may-apple could be expanded into greater cultivation as possible fruit sources. Forest geneticists have already enhanced the timber quality and growth rates of a number of tree species, including the hybrid black walnut developed at Purdue University, which has a greatly improved growth form and earlier maturity.

But let us always reserve the sites and the opportunities for all native wild plant species *to survive as wild plants* in situations as natural as can be maintained in the face of our growing human numbers. The Indiana of the present had its origin in the wildness of what Indiana *was* some 200 years ago. Let us hope that we can view wild plants from the perspective of their contribution historically, along with their present aesthetic and ecological values, as we look to their potential for the future, and not just destroy them wholesale without even knowing "what's the use?"

I went to the woods because I wished to live deliberately, to front only the essential facts of life, and see if I could not learn what it had to teach, and not when I came to die, discover that I had not lived.

— *Thoreau*, Walden II: What I Lived For

Sumac ade is sometimes used as a passable substitute for lemonade. Sumac-flavored pie is a tasty dessert, reminiscent of lemon pie.   *Photo by Marion Jackson*

Spider web with dew droplets becomes nature's jewels on a July dawn.   *Photo by Richard Fields*

The World of Animals

37. The Small and the Many: Invertebrates

P. Sears Crowell, Jr.

A distinction between vertebrates and invertebrates was first recognized by Aristotle, although he did not use these terms but divided animals into those with blood (vertebrates) and those without blood (invertebrates). Unfortunately, Aristotle's neat distinction had little to do with the facts, since many invertebrates have colorless blood, which he did not recognize as blood at all. Although Aristotle did about as well as one might expect from the limited knowledge of animal structure available in his time, it was partly because of the weight of his authority that his error was not corrected for over two thousand years.

> —*Ralph Buchsbaum,* Animals without Backbones
> (1948)

The "Small" of our title denotes that there are single-celled animals as tiny as two-thirds the size of a red blood cell, and even the largest invertebrates in Indiana, some freshwater mussels, are at best only about 10 inches long, and weigh perhaps two and a half pounds.

The "Many" has two different references. First, Indiana has about 10,000 or so species—more than 10 times as many as all the vertebrates together. Worldwide, about 95 percent of all animal species are invertebrates. Second, many forms have populations of many millions, perhaps billions. Consider the "pyramid of numbers," for example: the number of algal cells must be many times the number of little crustaceans which use them for food. The crustaceans, in turn, must be counted in the hundreds for each small fish, which in turn must be abundant enough to support the larger predators, and in the end the final carnivore, the osprey, raccoon, or fisherman.

The commonest natural death for an animal occurs when it is captured and eaten by another, often larger, animal. So as we study a particular animal, we ask what it eats and what eats it. We examine especially its means of capturing its food, and its protective devices. Much of its behavior relates to eating and avoiding being eaten. When an animal dies before being captured and eaten, its corpse will usually be consumed by scavengers or decomposed by bacteria. Bones, shells, and other hard parts may persist and even become part of the fossil record.

SINGLE CELLS: *PROTOZOA*

Wherever there is wetness we find single-celled animals, called protozoa. In Indiana the number of different species has been estimated at 3,000, not including several which occur inside the bodies of larger animals as parasites or as symbionts. The latter often aid digestion; for example, in termites and in horses and cattle, protozoa, in cooperation with bacteria, break down the cellulose of grass and woody food.

Although protozoa are too small to be seen with the naked eye, they are important to us for their role in eating bacteria and thereby aiding in control of pollution. At one of the concrete oxygenation tanks at our sewage plant, the whole inside is lined with a "fuzz" which is composed of many millions of tiny bell-shaped cells, each on a tiny contractile thread. These are *Vorticella* and its relatives.

The protozoan most often mentioned in popular writing and in cartoons is the amoeba. Seen under low magnification, it appears as a gray blob which moves about slowly as it changes its shape. Most individual cells of many-celled animals can do only a limited number of things, but an amoeba must do everything necessary for staying alive. It captures, ingests, digests, and egests food; it eliminates wastes and excess water; it responds to stimulation; it reproduces by dividing itself in half. We imagine or pretend or believe that some similar thing was the first or original animal—our grandparent many thousands of times removed.

> The genus *Plasmodium* is of very wide spread occurrence, both taxonomically and geographically. There are four species in man. . . . Malaria is probably the most important of all diseases of man.
>
> —*T. L. Jahn,* How to Know the Protozoa (1949)

The most important protozoan in the history of Indiana is the *Plasmodium,* which develops in mosquitoes. When a mosquito injects this virulent protozoan into people, it causes malaria. In early days this was a common cause of severe illness and often death. Early Hoosiers called it ague or aigger; and at one time nearly everyone had chills, fevers, and night sweats. Indianapolis, the new state capital, was such a poor choice from the public health viewpoint that it was nearly abandoned. There were 734 deaths attributed to malaria in Indiana in the five years between 1900 and 1905. With knowledge that malaria is caused by a tiny critter living in mosquitoes, and not by "bad air" (*mal aria*), we eliminated this hazard by using screens, draining swamps, spraying insecticides, and eliminating the many gristmill ponds which were suitable breeding sites for mosquitoes.

Some marine protozoa have shells of calcium carbonate. These shells, deposited on the floor of an inland sea and consolidated, compacted, and fused, produce some of our chalks and limestones. For example, the town of Oolitic in Lawrence County was named for the egg-shaped invertebrate fossils (oolites) which compose much of the Salem limestone that is quarried locally, and which has been used in many famous buildings.

SPONGES: *PORIFERA*

> Sponges, or rather the skeletons of sponges, were commonly used by the ancient Greeks for bathing, for scrubbing tables and floors, and for padding helmets and leg armor. The Romans fashioned them into paintbrushes, tied them to the ends of wooden poles for use as mops, and made them serve, on occasion, as substitutes for drinking-cups.
>
> —*Buchsbaum,* Animals without Backbones

Only one family of sponges is found in fresh water, the Spongiliidae. About 30 species have been reported for the United States. Although no survey has been made of the sponges found in Indiana, reports from Michigan, Wisconsin, Illinois, and Ohio suggest that there are about one dozen species. Some species prefer somewhat acid water, others mildly basic; some flowing streams, some lakes and ponds.

The body of a sponge is most variable even in a particular species. It may have finger-like branches which extend outward from its place of attachment, sometimes forming a mat a few millimeters thick which extends over as much as a square meter. Sponges living in good light are usually greenish because of the algae that live in their tissues and presumably provide some nutrition to the sponge. Freshwater sponges have an internal framework of needle-like spicules composed of a glass-like material which provides, along with a small amount of an organic material, the support of the body. The exact shape of the spicules can be used in identifying species.

Externally one finds many small pores and one or more larger ones; internally the body consists of many channels and chambers. Water is moved by flagellated cells so that it is drawn in through the

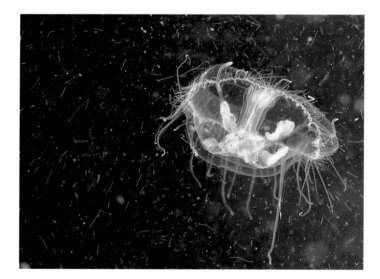

Freshwater jellyfish are exquisitely beautiful, notwithstanding that they are more than 90% water.   *Photo by Richard Fields*

many small openings and forced out through the larger. A sponge obtains nourishment by straining small particles from the water, and in turn provides shelter for many small animals. The spongilla fly is the name of one such inhabitant of freshwater sponges.

HYDRA AND JELLYFISH: *COELENTERATA* OR *CNIDARIA*

Freshwater hydras are common in Indiana. The body of a hydra is a simple tube with a mouth which is surrounded by a few tentacles at one end, and an attaching basal disk at the other. Hydras feed on small crustaceans and insect larvae, which they entrap and subdue with threads and stinging cells. Their tentacles are armed with nettle cells (which can discharge poison-containing penetrating threads) or other threads that can wrap around tiny prey.

Hydras reproduce sexually, but more often by forming buds at the side of the body. The buds are pinched off from the parent to constitute a new individual. Although a hydra will remain attached in one place much of the time, it can move by gliding and by somersaulting. In some species the disk can secrete a gas bubble, allowing the hydra to hang from the surface of the water.

The freshwater jellyfish appears sporadically in large numbers in artificial ponds and quarry holes. Often specimens are found during several summers and then no more. However, near Bloomington there is a quarry hole where jellyfish were seen each year from 1947 to 1978, and they have been in Yellowwood Lake for many years. These jellyfish are nearly an inch in diameter and swim by vigorous pulsing contractions. Often such movement will take them near the surface of the water, after which they may drop slowly down with tentacles extended.

As with most jellyfish (nearly all of which are marine), there is an asexually reproducing stage in the life cycle called a polyp, which is a small attached column similar to a hydra, but lacking tentacles. Polyps reproduce asexually by three different kinds of buds. The adult jellyfish is the sexual stage, and the four ovaries or testes are the most conspicuous structures. At any particular location all of the specimens are of the same sex; so it is believed that all are asexual offspring from polyps which descended from one ancestor, and consequently are genetically identical.

> Although many marine jellyfish are sizeable and variously colored, freshwater jellyfish measure about the size of a dime or nickel. They appear clear or translucent white, and can move up, down and sideways in an aquatic dance by expelling water through contractions of the bell-shaped body.
>
> —*Hank Huffman, "Jellyfish Alert!" in* Outdoor Indiana *(1994)*

Since its discovery in London in 1880, the freshwater jellyfish has been a biological curiosity. Its first record in the United States was 1908. Since then there have been reports from most of the United States; all reported thus far are of a single species. Lytle reported 17 locations in Indiana as of 1958, while Huffman in his report raises the number of sites known in 1994 to 25.

FLATWORMS AND ROUNDWORMS:
PLATYHELMINTHES, ASCHELMINTHES

Chandler wrote that "worm" means any elongated creeping thing not obviously something else. (Cutworms, for example, are larval insects.) Zoologists recognize about 10 different phyla of unrelated worms: some with true body cavities, some with false body cavities, some lacking body cavities; some segmented, some not, etc.

Flatworms. In fresh water we find free-living planarians mostly ½ to 1 inch long, with flattened bodies, and with cilia that enable them to creep smoothly over rocks and other surfaces. The mouth is near the middle of the underside of the body; and typically there is a tubular pharynx which is extended and draws in small bits of food from the bodies of dead animals or small living animals.

A painful irritation of the skin called "swimmers' itch" is caused by penetration into the skin of tiny larval forms of flatworms. As adults these are parasites of various birds and have an intermediate stage in freshwater snails. These blood flukes of birds are distantly related to those responsible for the serious human disease schistosomiasis (or bilharziasis), a common affliction in many warm regions of the world.

In earlier times, doctors frequently encountered patients whose thin features indicated that they were sharing their food with a guest in the form of a tapeworm. Usually the worm could be doped and made to release its hold, but Chandler reports that repeated attempts to dislodge "Horace," the name that one patient called his longtime guest, were unsuccessful. With better sanitation and better handling of beef and pork, especially freezing, cases of infection by beef and pork tapeworms are now almost unknown. However, there is a tapeworm acquired by eating raw freshwater fish which is occasionally encountered in people.

Roundworms and nematodes. Most of us do not see roundworms every day unless we try. Those that are free-living are mostly less than a quarter-inch long, while the larger ones live inside other animals, and so escape observation. Nematodes have been found from the bottom of the sea to spaces in mosses and lichens near mountaintops. Wherever there is some dampness they can be found. Cobb suggested that if everything in the universe except nematodes were swept away, our world would still be dimly recognizable. As disembodied spirits, we could identify almost everything by its film of these worms: seas, lakes, trees, plants, animals.

Some species are found under diverse conditions all over the world. Others are more specific, living, for example, on the roots of a certain plant, or as internal parasites of a particular animal or group of related animals. The free-living nematodes feed for the most part on bacteria. In the top few inches of suitable soil, there are many species in incredible numbers. One report claims that 2 to 6 billion exist in one acre of fertilized farm soil, and there are several reports of millions. Similarly, Robert W. Pennak writes in *Fresh-Water Invertebrates of the United States:* "Almost any collection of sand, mud, or vegetation from the bottom or margin of a pond, lake, brook, or river will be found to contain small roundworms, or nematodes, sometimes in great abundance."

In Indiana, soybeans are damaged by the soybean cyst worm, and seed corn by the needle nematode. Loss, in the case of the soybean crop, is estimated to be between 5 and 10 percent statewide, and occasionally as much as 50 percent at a particular location. The worm population can build up dramatically where soybeans are grown in the same field each year. Crop rotation prevents these buildups.

The best-known roundworm must be the pinworm or seat worm, which is very common in young children. The females move out of the anus and deposit their eggs in the perianal region. Diagnosis is simple. A bit of scotch tape inside out on a tongue depressor will pick off the eggs, which can then be viewed with a microscope. In the orthopedic section at Riley Children's Hospital, Indianapolis, William H. Headlee found that about one-third of the children were infected. This worm usually does no serious harm.

Hookworm infestation was once a widespread scourge in our southern states. Writing in the 1920s, Robert W. Hegner estimated that 2 million people in the United States were infested. Happily, better sanitation and education have lowered the number to almost zero.

One nematode that may kill its human host is *Trichinella.* When uncooked pork that contains cysts of this worm is eaten, the cysts hatch and the worms grow and reproduce in the small intestine. Newborn worms pass through the intestinal wall into lymph spaces and then into the bloodstream; eventually they reach muscle tissue. Here they damage the muscle and in so doing produce the poisons which may kill.

Other intestinal nematodes are rare in people, but are familiar to most of us who have been associated with dogs or cats. Of these, heartworm of dogs perhaps causes the most distress, to both the affected dog and its master. The life cycle involves three juvenile (larval) stages that develop in mosquitoes; in the third stage the parasites move into the salivary glands of the mosquito host, from which they escape into the bloodstream of a dog as it is bitten by the mosquito. After about 90 days the worms begin to settle in the right side of the heart. They grow to a length of about a foot, but are less than an eighth of an inch thick. By obstructing the flow of blood, they cause enlargement of both liver and heart, and limit the dog's ability to exercise vigorously. The veterinarian will use different drugs for the different stages of their cycle. Monthly use of a drug will often be prescribed to prevent the larvae from developing into adult heartworms in the dog. A second drug kills the adults, while a third kills the young stages released by the adult worms into the dog's blood. This latter stage is the source of infection of the next mosquito.

Looking at the brighter side, several gardeners' catalogs advertise "a biological insecticide" which, in fact, is the juvenile stage of a specific parasitic nematode. These worms live in the soil and locate soil-dwelling insects, mostly larval cutworms, beetle grubs, wireworms, etc. They develop inside the host, feeding on host tissue, and produce many offspring. Since they do not overwinter successfully, a fresh treatment is required each spring. This nematode, packaged as Biosafe Lawn and Garden Insect Control, won the "Retailer's Choice Award" at the National Hardware Show in 1990 as the product (out of 200,000) most likely to gain consumer acceptance.

Horsehair worms. These are not much thicker than horsehair but are several inches long. We most often see them where a cricket or grasshopper has fallen into water and drowned. Today this may be a toilet bowl, sink, or open rain barrel. In the days when watering troughs for horses were more common, this was usually where the worms suddenly showed up. What was more logical than to suppose that they developed spontaneously from horsehair! Actually they develop in crickets and grasshoppers, then escape to lay eggs on vegetation in water. Later, as ponds or streams dry out, the vegetation with the eggs is eaten by the host, an insect; and so the life cycle is repeated.

SEGMENTED WORMS: *ANNELIDA*

Earthworms. The largest worm found in Indiana is the night crawler (*Lumbricus terrestris*), which when extended is about eight inches long. Common smaller worms come out of the earth during heavy rain at night and often are found on pavement in the morning. A smaller reddish worm is associated with manure piles. All of these are used as bait by anglers.

Earthworms improve the topsoil that is essential for agriculture. Their burrows also permit air and water to enter the ground. Since they burrow in part by eating the soil and egest "castings" on the surface, they continually are turning over these materials.

Darwin contended that 1 acre may contain 63,000 earthworms which in a year may bring 18 tons of soil to the surface and in 20 years build a new 3 inch layer.

—*E. Laurence Palmer,* Fieldbook of Natural History (1957)

Charles Darwin, in his book *Formation of Vegetable Mould,* gave measurements of the burial of rocks and pavement as earthworms remove soil from beneath these and permit them to sink below the surface. Unfortunately, today many of our agricultural soils are almost devoid of earthworms from the repeated applications of insecticides.

Aquatic worms. There are nearly 100 species of small segmented worms which are found in ponds and streams, many of which provide food for fish.

Leeches. Our common bloodsuckers are segmented worms which feed by drawing blood from various vertebrates: fish, frogs, turtles, and some aquatic birds. Only a few species are parasitic on humans. They are occasionally encountered by people wading or swimming in Indiana ponds and streams.

A leech holds fast with a sucker at its tail end while seeking a suitable thin place in the skin. Once attached there, it makes a cut without causing pain and draws a meal of blood. If undisturbed, it may take enough blood to last several months. After the leech has departed, the incision may continue to bleed since an anticoagulant (hirudin) has been introduced into the tissues. The medicinal leech is still used sometimes to reduce the congestion of blood associated with bruises, but not for bloodletting as a remedy for diseases, a practice that was once fashionable. Legend has it that George Washington was being treated with leeches when he died; or was it King George III?

MOSS ANIMALS: *ECTOPROCTA* OR *BRYOZOA*

There are several thousand marine species of *Bryozoa,* but only a few are found in fresh water. The individual animal, called a polypide, is only about one millimeter long, but many are connected to one another to produce an easily noticed colony. The polypides have a tentacular crown which supports a row of cilia, and these collect fine particulate material for food. Most often observed near the shore of lakes is *Pectinatella,* in which several hundred polypides are on the surface of a gelatinous mass, sometimes as large as a watermelon. A totally different colonial arrangement is found in *Plumatella.* Here a branching network of tubes is attached to rocks or sticks, and the polypides project from these tubes. Bryozoa collect small particles for food and so are among the many other small invertebrates that make waters less turbid.

ANIMALS WITH JOINTED LEGS: *ARTHROPODA*

Most of the invertebrates that may be seen in daytime and out of water belong to the great Phylum Arthropoda—insects, spiders, mites, ticks, centipedes, millipedes, crustaceans, etc.—joint-legged animals with a tough outer layer (exoskeleton) that helps prevent water loss.

For a quick introduction to the land-dwelling arthropods, turn over a well-rested partly rotted log. One or two centipedes are likely to hurry off with outstretched legs and a sideways snake-like movement. They are little carnivores that can bite. Then with a slower, more dignified movement of their many legs beneath them, the millipedes also will move to a hiding place. They are vegetarians and will not bite, but sometimes they produce a protective fluid. Some of

these fluids not only have a bad odor, but are extremely irritating even to humans. Other exudates may cause blindness in chickens and other small animals foolish enough to attack the millipedes. Most kinds of centipedes, called "hundred leggers," have somewhat fewer than a hundred legs; the millipedes, or "thousand leggers," may have more than a hundred, with two pairs to each body segment.

On rare occasions, millipedes occur in immense numbers in forest environments. In October 1967, an ecology class encountered a vast population in Hoot Woods near Freedom, Indiana, that had a density of at least 100 per square meter, and ranged over several hundred square meters. The causes of such concentrations are poorly understood.

Under the log or in woodpiles we also find sowbugs and wood lice. Those species that can roll into a ball like an armadillo are called pillbugs. They are among the few kinds of crustaceans that can live out of water. (Most Crustacea—shrimps, lobsters, crabs, etc.—are found only in marine and fresh waters.) Beneath our log, or perhaps the next one, we may see an earthworm or two, snails, beetle larvae and beetles, a small spider, and ants or termites. Night and wet weather bring out other kinds of animals, and so in the early morning we find the castings of earthworms and the shiny dried mucus trails of snails and slugs.

"By their works ye shall know them" applies well to spiders. We see their fine orbs in the garden, dew-drenched webs in the grass of early morning, and, alas, dust-catching cobwebs in the house. These devices trap the spider's food—mostly insects. Wolf spiders catch their prey by pouncing on it directly. Trapdoor spiders hide in a burrow which has a hinged lid; when prey is close by, the spider can pop out and seize it. Another kind of ambush is a funnel-like hiding place from which threads may be extended; vibrations of the threads inform the predator of the presence of a potential meal. The prey are partly immobilized by injection of a poison and are wrapped in silken thread, then eaten later. Spiders' silk is so durable that it is sometimes used as cross hairs in gunsights.

The spider's touch, how exquisitely fine!
Feels at each thread, and lives along the lines.

—*Alexander Pope,* An Essay on Man I

Millipedes (*Spirobolus*) do not have 1,000 legs, as their common name suggests, but they do have two per body segment, and may total in excess of 100.   *Photo by Richard Fields*

People are sometimes bitten by spiders, most often because of unintended contact. Many bites are mild, some are painful, and there are two species of spiders found in the state whose bites are actually life-threatening, especially for children. However, these two are not often found in homes. One, which is sometimes found in outside buildings, is the "black widow," so named because the female kills the male after mating. She is shiny and has an orange or reddish hourglass figure on her underside. The other, the "brown recluse," is also called fiddleback because of a dark mark on its back resembling (not very well) the shape of a fiddle.

Take time to watch a spider build its web, and also how it handles a victim. Toss a moth or caterpillar or whatever you can catch into the web. You will be astonished by the efficiency with which the spider enshrouds its helpless victim. Also, marvel at the number and intricate beauty of their delicate orbs, especially as you walk across a dewy meadow at sunrise on a July morning.

> If in the evening you can find beads of dew on spider webs, the next day will bring good, dry haying weather.
>
> *—Retired dairy farmer in Albany, Vermont*

Spiders can claim to be the only animals which have no wings and yet travel great distances through the air, by a technique called "ballooning." Soon after hatching, some spiders spin a fine thread called gossamer, and, holding on to it, they let the wind carry them off. Some of these spiders are among the first animals to colonize newly formed islands. Darwin reported that some came aboard the *Beagle* when it was 60 miles from the nearest land.

The ticks and mites form one of the largest and most biologically diverse groups of arachnids. They occur throughout the world and rival the insects in diversity of behavior, form, and habitat. They are found in terrestrial and aquatic ecosystems, in forests and grasslands; they live in soil, in debris, in caves, on and in plants and animals including humans, and in almost any habitat where life itself exists.

As of 1950, about 30,000 species of mites had been described worldwide, but the undescribed species could easily be 20 times that number. The highest populations and diversity of mites live in the soil, where they are numerically dominant, and may account for up to 7 percent of the total weight of the invertebrate fauna. Mites may eat plants, fungi, animals, and dead organic matter; they may exist as parasites or in almost any other relationship one can envision. Those living on and in plants and animals range from live-in associates to true parasites. Many are phoretic, meaning that they use the host only for transportation.

Some of the better-known and most-disliked members of this group are the ticks (really specialized large mites) and the chiggers. Relatively little is known about these groups in Indiana, except for those parasitic on mammals which were studied by John Whitaker of Indiana State University. During his studies, 11 species of ticks, 24 of chiggers, and 151 other species of mites were found, including 47 species previously unknown to science. Many other new species of mites would be found if concentrated studies were made in other habitats in Indiana.

Most Hoosiers who enjoy the outdoors have suffered the bites of chiggers. Although 25 species occur in Indiana, only one, thankfully, infests humans. These distant relatives of spiders are six-legged young stages of harvest mites or red bugs which as adults are free-living. If you are susceptible to these creatures and prefer not to use commercially prepared chemical repellents, a dusting of "flowers of" (powdered) sulfur around your sock tops and belt line is usually an effective safeguard.

> There was a little chigger
> That wasn't any bigger
> Than the head of a very small pin.
> But if you start to scratchin'
> Then they begin to hatchin'
> And that's when the itch sets in.
>
> *—An old Hoosier country rhyme*

Sixteen species of ticks have been collected in Indiana. Two are of direct concern to people as carriers of the bacteria which cause serious diseases. In Indiana, in the 10 years through 1990, there were 65 reported cases of Rocky Mountain spotted fever transmitted by wood ticks. More recently a tiny tick has been identified as harboring the spirochete that is responsible for Lyme disease. In Indiana there were 7 reported cases in 1990, 22 in 1992.

Harvestmen or daddy longlegs are abundant on the forest floor and on and around fallen logs. They feed on soft-bodied insects but also on dead animals and fruits. Harvestmen have stink glands which are believed to discourage potential predators. In times past, farm children used to ask these leggy invertebrates, "Which way are the cows?" before going to the woods or pastures to search for the dairy herd at milking time. Presumably, the leggy critter will raise one of its long legs and point in the correct direction! The writer has not had a chance to verify this.

Looking at the array of aquatic arthropods, we find a few mites, a few spiders, many insects, and, most important, the crustaceans. There are 11 orders of Crustacea that are found in fresh water. Many are small and inconspicuous; crawdads are monsters in comparison. The list reads: fairy shrimps, tadpole shrimps, clam shrimps, water fleas, seed shrimps, copepods, fish lice, opossum shrimps, aquatic

Spiders are formidable predators for their size, and their webs are among the most effective of nature's traps.   *Photo by Lee Casebere*

After a blood meal, the dog tick increases incredibly in size, hence the crude expression in response to an offer of more food, "I couldn't eat another bite; I'm full as a tick."   *Photo by Marion Jackson*

Freshwater crustaceans such as this aquatic sowbug, *Asellus,* serve the important function of cleansing the water of detritus.
Photo by Richard Fields

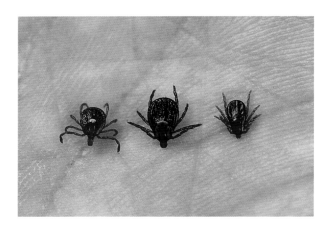

Three Indiana tick species.   *Photo by Richard Fields*

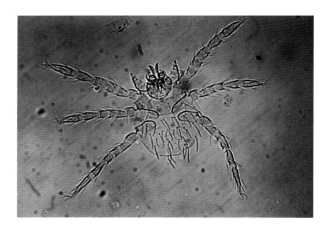

Anyone who has ever been infested with the chigger mite will never forget the episode. "Chiggers" are larval mites of the family Trombiculidae. Twenty-one species of chiggers are known from Indiana, but only the one depicted, *Eutrombicula alfreddugesi,* often attacks humans. There are probably more mite species in Indiana than vertebrate species.
Photo by John O. Whitaker, Jr.

sowbugs, scuds (sideswimmers), freshwater shrimps, and crayfish. Nearly all feed on microscopic algae and other particulate matter, which they filter from the water with an amazing array of movable legs and mouth parts furnished with hairs, bristles, etc.; in turn, they are a critical item in the food chain on which many fish depend.

Our common fairy shrimps are found in shallow temporary ponds in very early spring. By June they will have produced their hardy eggs, which will rest until winter snow and rain refill the depression. Then life is renewed. Just east of the most western overlook in Brown County State Park lies a small pool where we have found fairy shrimps (most recently February 9, 1991). The fairy shrimp is among the few animals which swim on their backs.

Among the vegetation of ponds and streams, there are many sideswimmers (amphipods, scuds) and flat aquatic relatives of equal-footed sowbugs (isopods). Indiana has one species of true shrimp, of about the size of the smallest marine shrimp that you can buy at your market.

> As a boy . . . you sat for long hours. . . .
> With deep-set eye staring at the door of the crawfish's burrow,
> Waiting for him to appear, pushing ahead,
> First his waving antennae, like straws of hay
> And soon his body, colored like soapstone,
> Gemmed with eyes of jet.
> And you wondered in a trance of thought
> What he knew, what he desired, and why he lived at all.
>
> —*Edgar Lee Masters,* Spoon River Anthology

Crayfish, crawfish, crawdads. In Indiana "crawdad" seems to be the name heard most often, but crayfish is the preferred name. Crayfish are found in streams, lakes, and ponds, even in damp, marshy places where there is no open water. Most feed during darkness and hide during daylight. Their hiding places may be under sheltering rocks or vegetation or in well-made burrows excavated by the crayfish. Some bring balls of mud to the surface in their claws and deposit them around the burrow opening so that a "chimney" several inches tall is made.

In the flat, wet soils of some areas in southeastern Indiana, these chimneys are so abundant as to have led to the term "Crawfish Flats" for that section of the state. The contribution of the crayfish in soil development seems not to have been critically studied, but we suppose that the amount of subsoil and organic material moved to the surface by hundreds, even thousands, of crayfish per acre is substantial.

Crayfish walk using their four pairs of legs, or move sideways, forward, or back. When threatened they may dart rapidly backward by flexing their abdomen and broad tail, hence the colloquial term "to crawfish" to describe someone's retreat, or a shift in version of a story being told. Crayfish are omnivorous, feeding on soft plants or meat as circumstances dictate. The pincers of the first pairs of walking legs can tear the food and pass it to the several complex mouthparts, which break it further. In addition there are grinding teeth inside the stomach.

Crayfish are excellent as human food and are harvested in large numbers in Louisiana and other southern states. They do not appear to be much used by Hoosiers, though they fall prey to raccoons and other mammals as well as some birds and fish. Of the 17 kinds of crayfish found in Indiana, 5 make burrows, 2 are restricted to caves (and are colorless), 4 are found only in running water, and the rest may be found in both lakes and streams.

Terrestrial snails are herbivores that secrete their own "house" and pave their own "highway" with mucus.   *Photo by Lee Casebere*

MOLLUSKS: *MOLLUSCA*

A huge number of mollusks of diverse form and habit, from chitons to giant squids (up to a total length of 35 feet), are represented in the world's oceans, but on land and in fresh water only by snails and slugs (univalves, gastropods) and clams and mussels (bivalves, pelecypods). Since the last comprehensive list of mollusks of Indiana was published in 1944, the tally has not changed very much in the case of the univalves. There were 6 species of shell-less snails (slugs), about 90 land snails, and more than 100 aquatic snails, including 16 limpets. Limpets have flat shells with little evidence of a spiral. To most Hoosiers, the best-known and least-loved must be the slugs that feed on some of our flowers and vegetables.

Snails and slugs creep about on a broad muscular foot which is moistened with mucus, paving their own highway as they advance. The head bears tentacles and eyes; within the mouth is a rasping device, the radula, with many tiny teeth. It can be extended to scrape and tear at food. (In some marine snails the radula is actually used as a drill and can make a neat hole in a bivalve shell.) Although most snails feed mainly on vegetation, a few are omnivorous. Above a visceral mass is a well-developed mantle, which secretes the shell. The land snails and many of the freshwater snails breathe air, and the mantle provides the cavity and surfaces which serve as a "lung."

In some families of snails the sexes are separate; in others an individual may have both ovaries and testes at the same time or in succession. Eggs are fertilized within the body of the ova-producing animal. Courtship and copulation take many strange forms. (In the edible European snail, each of the pair fires a "love dart" into the partner's flesh, and this presumably enhances sexual activity.) Eggs are laid within a gelatinous mass, where development takes place.

Freshwater bivalves nearly all fall into one of two families, which differ strikingly in size and method of reproduction. The large ones are called mussels. Females produce huge numbers of eggs, which are moved into spaces in the gills. Sperm released by male mussels are carried in the water currents to the eggs, where fertilization occurs.

Development of the eggs in the gills may take several months, with the small offspring being little more than two small shells joined by a strong closing muscle. These are released and lie at the bottom of a pond or stream until they are able to hitch a ride on a fish, where they resume development until they have the structure of adult mussels in miniature. After release, they burrow into the bottom of the stream or pond to which the fish has taken them.

Mussels lie in sand or gravel, with only a little of the shell exposed. The shell is slightly open most of the time, and one can see the incurrent and outflowing openings. The nearly continuous flow of water brings in small particles of food, as well as oxygen, and the current also carries away wastes. Mussels have a large muscular foot which is used to burrow and enables them to move slowly along. They cannot move over ledges or leap waterfalls, so their dispersion depends on that feature of their early life when they steal rides on fish as described above.

Crayfish are among the largest invertebrates in Indiana.
Photo by Richard Fields

How did these beautiful rainbow tints get into the shell of the fresh-water clam, buried in the mud at the bottom of our dark river?

—*Henry David Thoreau*

The larger mussels whose shells are lined with mother-of-pearl are harvested commercially. Formerly pearl button factories were numerous along our major streams, but now the shells are sold to Japanese and East Indian producers of cultured pearls. The shells are cut up and milled into small spheres. These are inserted into the mantle tissues of oysters, where they serve as nuclei around which the oysters secrete layers of pearl. The hearts of milady's cultured pearls may well have come from the Wabash River.

In the past, mussels were found in most of Indiana's rivers and streams. Of 77 species which were known, only 60 are still to be found, and nearly 20 of these are on the state or federal endangered or threatened list. Mussels have disappeared from many former locations—a consequence of several factors: pollution, damming of streams, overharvesting, and collecting with methods which damaged beds or killed small mussels.

A drastic depletion of mussels in 1991 led to closure of the season six weeks before its end. At least three events contributed to the overharvesting. The price had nearly doubled, as had the number of musselers. Licenses were issued to 950 musselers, compared with an average of 508 for the three previous years. Low water exposed areas for collection which earlier could not be reached, and hand picking was relatively easy.

The value of the 1991 harvest was about $3 million, which is about three times that of other recent years. Since 1991 the Division of Fish and Wildlife has been making surveys with the hope that this valuable resource can be restored.

There are many kinds of freshwater clams, rarely as much as an inch in diameter, with thin shells that lack the pearly layer. Called fingernail clams, they produce only a few young at a time (in contrast to mussels); they nurture them in spaces of the inner gills, and when released they are already little clams. They provide food for several species of bottom-feeding fish.

In addition to the larger native mussels and the tiny fingernail clams, two intruders have appeared recently. The Asiatic clam (*Corbicula*) has invaded many of our streams. It is small with a thick shell and is sometimes abundant enough to be a nuisance at water intakes.

A second, more serious pest is the zebra mussel (*Dreissena*). First recognized in 1988 in Lake St. Clair between Lakes Huron and Erie, it has spread as far south as New Orleans and as far east as the Hudson River. This rapid territorial expansion is principally due to the fact that it has a free-swimming larval stage called a veliger, which can live as long as four weeks before it settles on a hard surface. Here it becomes attached and grows into an adult mussel that can reproduce after about one year.

The zebra mussel has been found in the intakes of municipal water systems in such numbers that they block the flow. For example, in the city of Monroe, Michigan, the water supply was cut off completely for 56 hours, and restoration of service cost about $300,000.

In Indiana, zebra mussels are found in Lake Wawasee, where they attach to native mussels, interfering with the opening and closing of their shells, or by sheer mass of numbers kill them. There is serious concern that they will spread and destroy our commercial mussel fisheries. The Indiana Department of Natural Resources has published a pamphlet urging boat operators to take great care not to move water from one place to another. The veligers can travel in ballast tanks, fish tanks, fish buckets, and even in water held in engine-cooling systems. In addition, adults may cling to boat bottoms and gain a ride to a new location.

Freshwater mussels have been widely harvested for their shells, and their habitats have been destroyed by silt and other pollutants.
Photo by Richard Fields

When Louis Agassiz, the noted nineteenth-century scientist and teacher at Harvard University, was asked, "What do you regard as your greatest work?" he replied: "I have taught people to observe." Take the time as you traverse Indiana by foot or by canoe to observe the myriad forms of "the small and the many" that occur in every habitat of the state. You will find a fascinating and varied aspect of nature that you perhaps never realized was there.

In the earliest schematizations of animal evolution, the animals were usually pictured as ascending, on a vertical ladder, directly "from ameba to man," with the other animals placed on intermediate rungs according to their order of increasing complexity. Now it is realized that animals do not form a continuous series and that their relationships to one another are more correctly represented by a branching "tree." A "tree" not only fits the facts more closely than a ladder, but its many separate branches, representing independent lines of specialization, help to suggest why we find such endless variety among the animals without backbones.

—*Buchsbaum*, Animals without Backbones

The zebra mussel is an introduced species that is an efficient traveler, especially by attaching to boat hulls. It is now a serious pest in several Indiana waters.   *Photo by Richard Fields*

Male cecropia moth, one of our most spectacular moths, resting on its cocoon after emergence.   *Photo by Pearl M. Eslinger*

38. An Abundance of Insects

Gene Kritsky

Entomology extends the limits of being in new directions, so that I walk in nature with a sense of greater space and freedom. It suggests, besides, that the universe is not rough-hewn, but perfect in its details. Nature will bear the closest inspection; she invites us to lay our eye level with the smallest leaf and take an insect view of its plane.

—*Henry David Thoreau*

A SUCCESSFUL LIFE STRATEGY

Sitting outside on a warm summer night and being swarmed by hungry mosquitoes might make you think that you were living in the age of insects. In reality, it has been the age of insects for 300 million years. Insects have proved to be the most successful class of animals in Indiana, with more than 13,000 species and the number of individuals likely in the trillions! The 25 orders of insects include many that are immediately familiar to us. The largest order in Indiana, with nearly 4,000 species, is the Coleoptera, commonly called beetles. Even the second largest order in Indiana, the Diptera, or flies, includes just over 3,000 species statewide.

This evolutionary success is tied to their form and ways of life. They have a body divided into three parts: a head with appendages modified for chewing, sucking plant juices, or draining the blood from animals; the thorax, equipped with six legs and usually two pairs of wings for locomotion; plus an abdomen that contains the organs for reproduction, digestion, and respiration. The ability of insects to reproduce successfully under the variety of environmental conditions represented in Indiana has led to "an abundance of insects" in our state.

Insects' success is also closely linked to their method of development. Some insects, such as grasshoppers, have an incomplete development, with the immature insects looking like miniatures of the adults. But the vast majority of insects—nearly 85 percent of them—have a complete development.

Common examples include all of our butterflies. Their eggs hatch into young caterpillars that do not look anything like an adult butterfly. As they grow, they molt into another stage of caterpillar. The last stage before the adult butterfly is the pupa, a normal resting stage of its life cycle during which the internal organs undergo an incredible rearrangement as the insect develops wings, compound eyes, antennae, and mature reproductive organs. This complete form of development affords these insects the advantage of adapting adults and young to live in different niches, thereby reducing competition between them.

When we speculate about finding life on other planets, we often speak of life as we know it. Insects are wonderful examples of life *not* as we know it. They perceive the world differently, seeing with compound eyes with hundreds of lenses. The hairs on their bodies, which allow them to taste, smell, and detect touch, have nerves connecting with the central nervous system, allowing them to process information about their environment. And insects can do what humans dreamed of doing for centuries—fly. In fact, insects were the first animals to evolve wings, hence the ability to fly.

The insects were among the first land animals in that part of the ancient continent that was to become Indiana. During the Upper Carboniferous period of the Paleozoic era, beginning some 300 million years ago, Indiana was home to giant cockroaches, primitive grasshoppers, and some unusual insects with long sucking mouthparts which likely fed on giant trees of the Coal Age. All these insects became extinct ages ago, but it is possible to document their former existence from fossils collected in the spoil heaps of Indiana coal mines.

Over time the climate changed, and many of these early species became extinct, while others evolved into forms recognized today. The most common beetles from the age of the dinosaurs were reticulated beetles, small insects with intricate wings. This group is still represented in Indiana, providing us with an insect link to the Mesozoic.

The past million years of Indiana history were marked by the Pleistocene ice ages. As advancing sheets of ice slowly extended down the state, the insects were forced south. When the glaciers retreated, cold-adapted insects moved northward onto vacated landscapes near the ice margin. Fossil deposits from around 20,000 years ago reveal that Indiana was then populated by insect species that are now found in Canada!

Indiana's insects range from giant silkworm moths with wingspans of nearly six inches to members of the minute fungus beetle family only one millimeter long. The greatest diversity of species are evident on warm days in summer, but some are active throughout the year. The snow scorpionflies and springtails sometimes occur on snowbanks. Many insects fly or creep over surfaces, but others bore into wood, ride deer, swim in ponds, and even live between the upper and lower surfaces of leaves.

> Indiana is a small state, lacking in extreme topographic features and located within a rather similar climatic environment. Yet for all its commonness, it represents a vast laboratory for biogeographic analysis. Containing a heterogeneous assemblage of insects, the distributional patterns are not hopelessly confusing.
>
> —*Leland Chandler, "The Origin and Composition of the Insect Fauna," in* Natural Features of Indiana (1966)

INDIANA'S AQUATIC INSECTS

The ecological relationship between insects and their environment is best experienced by firsthand observation. A visit to a pond will reveal how insects have adapted to living above, on, and in the pond. As you approach the water on a warm summer day, you will likely see dragonflies patrolling the pond's perimeter. These winged carnivores are marking out territories by their flight. They are attempting to lure a mate and provide a place for her to lay eggs. While adult dragonflies are terrestrial predators, their immatures are capable aquatic carnivores that can kill and eat small fish.

Before you explore the insects in the pond, stop and take a careful look at the water surface. Indiana is home to several pond surface

301

Widely contrasting body forms and vastly different food habits permit many insect larvae to occupy different niches from those of their adult counterparts, one secret of the group's enormous success. Royal walnut moth shown here.   *Photos by Pearl M. Eslinger*

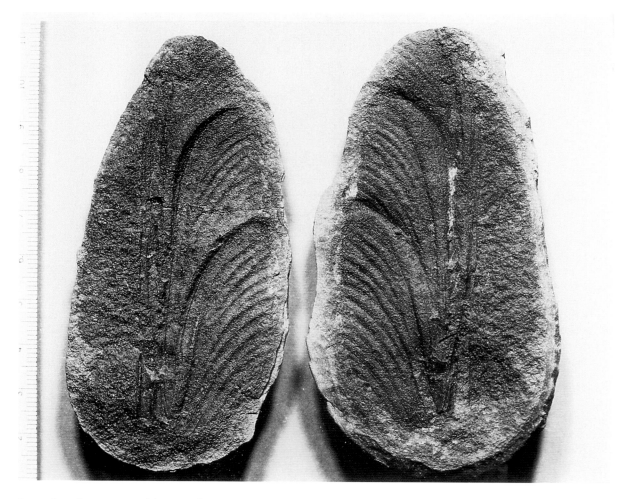

Insects have been a successful group of organisms on Earth for an incredibly long period of time, as this 300-million-year-old Indiana fossil attests.   *Photo by Gene Kritsky*

predators, such as the water striders. These true bugs are supported by the surface tension of water, where they skate about in search of food. They have an unusual method of communicating with one another—by moving their legs rapidly, they create slight ripples that warn neighboring individuals if they come too close. This helps the striders move in concert and to partition the pond's food resources.

Also swimming frequently along the surface are flat, black, shiny beetles gyrating about in clusters. These whirligig beetles have successfully adapted to life on the surface while keeping a watchful eye on life below the water. They have evolved four separate eyes, one pair that enables them to look up to see above the water while the other pair faces downward to see underwater. This separation of the eyes enables the whirligigs to see both worlds without the surface distorting their field of view. Further, these beetles have adapted to water by evolving oar-shaped legs which allow them to swim rapidly and efficiently.

Another insect world reveals itself as we move below the water surface. Fierce, biting giant water bugs can be found under rocks. These insects have adapted to a submerged life by evolving a snorkel consisting of two tail-like tubes that they periodically extend above the water. Moreover, the water bugs, like the whirligig beetles, have evolved flat oar-shaped legs to help them swim efficiently as they search for prey. These insects also have reversed parental roles, as the female lays her eggs on the back of her mate to carry until they hatch. Water bugs are fierce predators who catch prey animals and hold them with their forelegs, meanwhile forcing large piercing mouth-parts into their victim to suck out the internal fluids. Even small frogs and fish fall victim to these voracious bugs.

> There are some terrible robbers in the pond world . . . a larva of the waterbeetle Dytiscus . . . is a slim, streamlined insect, rather more than two inches long. . . . The wide, flat head bears an enormous pincer-shaped pair of jaws which are hollow and serve not only as syringes for injecting poison, but also as orifices of ingestion. . . . "Prey" for these creatures, is all that moves or that smells of "an animal" in any way. . . .
>
> In the confined spaces of an aquarium, a few large Dytiscus larvae will, within a few days, eat all living things over about a quarter of an inch long. What happens then? They will eat each other, if they have not already done so.
>
> —Konrad Z. Lorenz, "Robbery in the Aquarium," in King Solomon's Ring (1952)

Among the best-adapted of the pond inhabitants are the predaceous water beetles, which swim underwater by simultaneously flexing their oar-shaped hind legs. They breathe underwater by trapping air below their wings, essentially carrying their own aqualung, which enables them to remain submerged for extended periods.

Streams, like ponds, select for special adaptations of Indiana's insects. Caddisflies are moth-like insects commonly attracted to insect lights. They live as aquatic immatures by making unusual cases of cemented sand grains that they carry around for protection and to conceal themselves while capturing prey. Others sieve for food with silk nets of their own construction. Caddisflies are found more often in streams than ponds because flowing water provides a constant supply of food and oxygen.

Other common stream insects are the stoneflies, so named because their larvae live under and around stones, which increase the oxygenation within flowing water. As adults, stoneflies live only a few days, and many do not eat.

The insects just described are found in clean ponds and streams.

A visit to a stagnant pool or a polluted pond will reveal different insects. Indeed, combinations of insect species can be used as indicators of water quality. For example, an absence of stoneflies usually suggests low levels of oxygen as well as the presence of pollution. Sewer drains are common homes to moth flies. Discarded tires, eavestroughs, and discarded drink cans all catch rainwater and provide habitat for disease-carrying mosquito larvae.

The diversity of Indiana's aquatic insect fauna is reduced by the careless activities of humans. Pollution ushers in a different group of insects adapted to the fouled water. *Culex pipiens*, the mosquito that spreads a form of encephalitis, prefers standing dirty water as found in ditches, large trash bins, or even old tires. Such receptacles hold water long enough for mosquito eggs to hatch and produce adult mosquitoes. Adult females require a blood meal to produce eggs, which in turn are laid on the water surface of another polluted or stagnant pond. Meanwhile the herbivorous males feed by sipping nectar. Mosquitoes spread many other diseases. Prior to World War II, malaria was a major disease in America. But the development of insecticides and an understanding of how mosquitoes breed enabled us to interfere with their life cycles, permitting the successful eradication of malaria from the United States.

INDIANA'S TERRESTRIAL INSECTS

The lark is up to greet the sun,
   The bee is on the wing;
The ant its labor has begun,
   The woods with music ring.
     —Jane Taylor, The Sun Is Up

To see how insects have adapted to the diverse conditions found in wooded areas, study the insects in one of Indiana's many forests. On the forest floor, the litter of decaying leaves is home to many ground beetles, ants, and crickets. Ground beetles, as their name implies, are predators near the soil surface. These common beetles are usually black and more active at night. One of the larger and more colorful ground beetles in Indiana woods is the caterpillar killer, a large metallic green-golden form that often climbs trees in search of its favorite food—caterpillars.

Ants are very abundant on the forest floor. Scientists have estimated that one-fourth of all the animals in the world are ants. These social insects construct complex nests that house a reproductive female called the queen, numerous sterile females who function as workers and soldiers, and a few reproductive males. Ants are important ecologically because they turn over more soil than earthworms, some help decompose dead animals, many are dispersers of plant seeds, and other species help with the breakdown of fallen trees.

Rotting logs, like ponds, are special environments for insects. If possible, examine the insects living inside a rotting log. In addition to ants and other social insects, termites are often found. Indiana has only one species of termite, a subterranean form, which nests in the soil. While termites are usually thought of as pests, the ecological contribution of these wood-inhabiting insects is important for returning nutrients contained in wood to the soil. Humans did not "invent" recycling. Termites have been recycling wood for millions of years.

Two kinds of crickets are often found on the forest floor. Camel crickets are flightless and humpbacked, active at night, and usually collected under logs, stones, or in the leaf litter. The true crickets are the familiar black-winged insects with large rear legs for jumping. True crickets are also nocturnal and feed on plant materials. Unlike the camel crickets, they have evolved the ability to produce and hear chirping sounds.

Crickets make their sounds by rubbing thickened parts of their wings together. To amplify the sounds, some individuals will situate themselves in the end of a rolled leaf or a corner structure that functions as a megaphone. The sounds broadcast from this cricket home are important in attracting mates as well as in declaring their territory. Interestingly, the frequency of chirping is roughly proportional to temperature, becoming slower as autumn replaces summer. The number of chirps heard in 14 seconds added to 40 will tell you the approximate air temperature in degrees Fahrenheit.

Not all crickets live on the forest floor. Tree crickets, which live in bushes or trees, are green, permitting them to blend with their surroundings just as black ground-dwelling crickets are able to avoid detection as they scurry over dark surfaces.

Many insects in the woods are camouflaged for protection. Such butterflies as the commas have brightly colored upper wing surfaces, while their mottled gray-brown undersurfaces enable them to blend in with the bark of trees. Annual cicadas, which "sing" loudly in the dog days of summer, have green and black markings which effectively conceal these noisy insects within the forest canopy.

At first glance around the woods, it might appear that only a few insects are present. One reason for this is that the vast majority of Indiana's insects are less than a quarter-inch long. But sweeping the leaves with an insect net will reveal that the woods are teeming with small bugs, beetles, caterpillars, flies, wasps, ants, and other insect types. All are essential components of the forest ecosystem of Indiana.

Open fields provide another opportunity to observe how the insects have adapted to natural habitats in Indiana. A fall walk through a field dominated by goldenrod, asters, grasses, and other old-field plants will reveal a totally different insect fauna from that encountered in a forest or the pond. Grasshoppers, grazers of the insect world, announce your progress through the field by leaping ahead of you. Hiding among the goldenrod blooms are yellow and black soldier beetles, which eat pollen, drink nectar, and consume small insects. They seem oblivious to the small fierce yellow and black ambush bug lurking among the blooms, ever ready to pounce on prey such as butterflies, bees, or flies, and pierce them with strong sucking mouthparts. Their colorful markings and flaring abdomen help ambush bugs blend in with the flowers.

Also found on goldenrod are the locust borers, yellow and black striped beetles which, as adults, feed on goldenrod pollen. After feeding, they must return to the woods to lay their eggs on black locust trees. After hatching, the larvae bore into the black locust wood, pupate, and emerge as adults in the late summer. Hence, these insects have life stages adapted to life in both fields and woods. The assemblage of yellow and black insects and spiders living on and among the goldenrod blooms demonstrates the importance of natural selection in evolving incredibly diverse co-evolutionary complexes.

Some insects have adapted to their surroundings in ways that are repulsive to humans but are essential to ecosystem functioning. For example, the next time you find a road-killed animal, if you can tolerate the odor, stop and examine the insects that are taking advantage of this protein windfall. Several species of silphid beetles, in addition to various species of flies, have evolved as carrion feeders. They detect their food by its scent, then land and lay their eggs near the carcass. The larvae hatch in just a couple of days and feed on the kill. After consuming the carcass, they pupate in the soil and later emerge as adults during the summer months.

This insect use of what may seem an unusual food source is of critical importance in recycling dead organisms. Thus, insects play an essential role in heterotrophic succession. By feeding on dead animal remains, insects assist in recycling organic matter. Some insects, such as the dung beetles, contribute further to recycling of organic matter by processing their required nutrients and energy from cow patties or the dung of other mammals.

What were they doing there, all these feverish workers? They were making a clearance of death on behalf of life . . . transforming that horrible putrescence into a living and inoffensive product. They were working their hardest to render the carrion innocuous.

Others will soon put in their appearance, smaller creatures and more patient, who will take over the relic and exploit it ligament by ligament, bone by bone, hair by hair, until the whole has been restored to the treasury of life.

—*J. Henri Fabré, "The Burying Beetle," in* The Insect World of Henri Fabré (1912)

Other beetles have taken advantage of carrion in indirect ways. Hister beetles feed on the larvae and fly eggs laid on a carcass. These beetles are only a quarter-inch long, but have sharp jaws that they use to slice up their insect victims.

Feeding on other insects is not an unusual insect occupation. If the insects have taught us anything, it is that no ecological opportunity will be missed. Any available food source or nest site will be exploited by some species of insect.

One of the strangest of insect life cycles is that of the Strepsiptera, a small group of degenerate beetles that have evolved as parasites of other insects. One of the strepsipterans found in Indiana is a parasite of wasps. Indeed, sometimes as many as 30 percent of the wasps in a given nest are parasitized. Strepsipterans live part of their lives inside the body cavities of their wasp hosts. The adult female is essentially a bag of ovaries and never leaves the body of the wasp! The male, on the other hand, has large eyes, lobed antennae, and a body cavity filled with testes and no digestive organs. After the adult male emerges from the host wasp, he lives for only a few hours, but this is usually sufficient time to find a wasp parasitized by a female strepsipteran, with which he mates. The fertilized eggs develop inside the wasp and hatch into small, active larvae that leave the wasp to invade another host. Once inside, the larva loses its legs and feeds until it becomes an adult.

Insects have also evolved into efficient ectoparasites of mammals. Indiana has 31 species of fleas and 21 species of lice that have adapted to life on mammals. Dog or cat fleas live as adults on our pets and sometimes infest our homes. They are laterally flattened to facilitate movement between the strands of the host animal's hair, and are excellent leapers to hitchhike new rides. Lice have evolved special claws on their legs which enable them to hold firmly onto their host's hair.

The entomological diversity of Indiana's many habitats is enhanced by special natural areas that harbor unusual insect species. The Indiana Dunes region is home to a group of tiger beetles, with separate species living in each of the successional stages from the shoreline to the woods.

Light-colored sands near the Lake Michigan shoreline harbor a white tiger beetle. If you move inland, a series of plant communities and associated soil types will be traversed, with corresponding changes in the species of tiger beetles encountered. Brown soils of mid-successions have brown tiger beetles, which in turn are replaced by metallic green tiger beetles along the paths of the woods. Being strong fliers with excellent eyesight, tiger beetles are efficient preda-

Ladybird beetles are predators on aphids and other small insects.   *Photo by Richard Fields*

Walking sticks feed on forest trees and resemble the twigs on which they perch.   *Photo by Delano Z. Arvin*

Dragonflies are the "birds of prey" of the insect world.   *Photo by Richard Fields*

Predaceous praying mantids mating.
Photo by Lee Casebere

Katydids blend with the vegetation upon which they feed.   *Photo by Delano Z. Arvin*

Bald-faced hornets build paper nests in summer; only the queens overwinter in hibernacula in logs.   *Photo by Delano Z. Arvin*

Sequence of emergence of adult seventeen-year cicada from pupa case to an adult ready for mating. Note the red eye, characteristic of that species.
Photos by Richard Fields

tors of spiders and small insects. Usually they flush at your approach, land several feet in front of you, then turn and watch your progress, again taking flight as you get near.

Among the most fascinating insects of the Indiana Dunes are the digger wasps. They excavate nest chambers in the sand, in which they lay eggs. They also provision the cavities with comatose insects for their offspring. These prey insects were stung previously by the adult wasps. Organic material which is also added to their nests by these wasps aids in soil formation, which facilitates plant invasion and succession.

> With her fore-tarsi, which are armed with rows of stiff hairs and suggest at the same time a broom, a brush and a rake, she works at clearing her subterranean dwelling. The insect stands on its four hind-legs, holding the two at the back a little wide apart, while the front ones alternately scratch and sweep the shifting sand. The precision and quickness of the performance could not be greater if the circular movement of the tarsi were worked by a spring. The sand, shot backwards under the abdomen, passes through the arch of the hind legs, gushes like a fluid in a continuous stream, describes its parabola and falls to the ground some seven or eight inches away.
>
> —*Fabré, "The Bembex Wasp," in* The Insect World of J. Henri Fabré

Among the best-known of the insects found in Indiana are the periodical cicadas, incorrectly called 17-year locusts. Periodical cicadas have the longest known insect life cycle. As nymphs they live underground, feeding on plant juices from the roots of trees. They may be out of sight but are actively tunneling in soil. After 17 years, the adults emerge in such large numbers that they have been thought of as a plague.

Adults fly into the trees, where the males stridulate in great choruses to attract females. After mating, female cicadas lay their eggs within the terminal new growth of trees by piercing the outer bark with their saber-shaped ovipositor. Twigs bearing uniformly spaced eggs appear to have been stitched by a sewing machine. As the eggs hatch, the terminal leaves turn brown and the twigs break, but they hang on the tree, giving the characteristic flagged appearance typical of cicada years.

Mass emergence of periodical cicadas usually begins in late May and is completed by the end of June. Indiana has four established broods of cicadas (three 17-year broods and one 13-year brood) that have been recorded by residents of the state every 17 or 13 years since 1834. During the 1953 emergence, the shrill cacophony of their massed stridulations made it nearly impossible to hear the June commencement address at Indiana University.

> Above the arching jimson-weeds flare twos
>   And twos of sallow-yellow butterflies,
> Like blooms of torn primroses blowing loose,
>   When autumn winds arise.
>
> —*James Whitcomb Riley*

Butterflies are among the most popular of Indiana's insects, with at least 149 different species recorded for the state. Very active pollinators, especially of yellow and orange flowers, they sip nectar through flexible soda straw-like mouthparts, held coiled beneath their head like a watchspring when not in use. People love to watch them fluttering lazily among their flower beds or meadows.

Probably the best-known is the monarch butterfly, whose bright orange and black markings make it obvious as it moves about open fields. The monarch butterfly is special for two reasons. First, it is the model for a mimicry complex. This type of mimicry occurs when an edible species evolves a resemblance to a distasteful species. The monarch larvae feed on milkweed leaves, which contain chemicals that make the insects distasteful to birds and other predators. Monarchs have evolved a bright orange coloration that warns birds and their other would-be predators that they are distasteful. Viceroy butterflies are similarly marked even though they are not distasteful. Protection is gained from close resemblance to the monarch and would-be predators' general lack of ability to distinguish between

the two. Birds, upon seeing the orange and black pattern, simply avoid both the viceroy and the monarch as insurance against a beakful of sour butterfly.

The monarch is also a long-distance migrant. Like waterfowl and many other birds, monarchs fly south in autumn. Large numbers of migrating monarchs may be seen as you drive across the state, especially in September. Whereas monarchs continue southward from Indiana and other states into Mexico, other butterflies, such as some skippers, migrate into Indiana to escape the prairie winters of Illinois.

Above open fields on a bright summer morning, you might see large groups of flying insects milling in place in what looks like a tumbling mass of confusion. In most cases, you are witnessing a mating swarm of chironomids. These tiny insects look like mosquitoes but do not have mouthparts for drawing blood. Male chironomids have feathery antennae and often form swarms over a mating station, often a brightly lighted tree or shrub. Such swarms are usually seen near water and are composed almost entirely of males. As soon as a female chironomid flies into the swarm, she is immediately mated with and the pair drops out of the swarm. Chironomid swarms near Martinsville have been observed that were so large and dense that the trees appeared to be emitting smoke.

Although the natural habitats of Indiana are filled with hundreds of insect species, you need not go to the woods, fields, or lakes to encounter considerable insect diversity. You could simply turn on your porch light on a warm summer evening and allow the insects to come to you! June beetles are large brown insects that frequently come tumbling onto lighted screens. They are herbivores, feeding on the leaves of trees and shrubs in the area. The recognizable hum made during their flight even caught the attention of Shakespeare, who described this insect as "the shard-borne chafer with his drowsy hum." Fishermen prize their large, succulent gray-white larvae, the grubworms of garden soils and compost heaps, for live bait.

In mid-summer, your front yard becomes a pyrotechnic display of flashing fireflies, soft-winged beetles giving their mating signals. Careful observation will reveal different flashing patterns that represent the visual signatures of several different species. Some species have even evolved the ability to mimic the signals of others, thereby luring a deceived "mate" in closely so that it can be captured for food.

Many a night I saw the Pleiades, rising thro' the mellow shade,
Glitter like a swarm of fireflies tangled in a silver braid.

—*Alfred Lord Tennyson,* Locksley Hall

The insects' evening performance continues as moths start flying into the lights. Large hawk moths, noctuid moths, and plume moths, with their unusual habit of holding their wings in such a way as to give them a T-shaped appearance, are common players.

Being nocturnal is a wonderful adaptation to avoid being eaten by birds, many of which are active insect feeders during the day. The most capable nocturnal predators of insects, especially night-active beetles, are bats. As you sit on your porch to watch the insects that are attracted to the lights, you may see bats swooping to catch moths that are fluttering about. Bats emit high-frequency sound waves, or sonar, to detect flying insects. In response, some moth species have evolved a special organ to detect the sonar pulse, thereby permitting the moth to go into a confused flight pattern away from the bat's open jaws.

Other insect species are attracted to sweet or aromatic mixtures. A favorite method used by insect collectors for attracting sucking insects is "sugaring." Their lure is usually a mixture of brown sugar, white corn syrup, bananas, and beer. After the mixture has brewed and fermented, it is "painted" onto tree trunks, rocks, or any other surfaces. It serves as a wonderful attractant for sap-feeding insects such as moths, butterflies, wasps, and flies.

INSECTS AND HUMAN ACTIVITIES

The variety of natural habitats in Indiana has provided insects with a myriad of opportunities. But human activity has greatly modified natural Indiana, causing equally great changes in composition of the insect fauna. After visiting natural habitats such as woods, fields, and ponds, it is instructive to compare the insect diversity present in those natural sites by walking through a monoculture such as a field of corn.

Tall corn plants harbor some insects, but only a few different kinds. Wandering about the leaves are small green spotted northern corn rootworm beetles. Upper leaf surfaces may be covered with masses of aphids, along with an occasional ladybug feeding on the aphids. Unhusk an ear, and the larvae of earworms may be feeding on the kernels, leaving undigested frass in their wake. Moving deeper into the field will reveal an obvious lack of insect diversity.

The cutting of Hoosier forests to make way for agriculture and settlement had an effect similar to what is presently occurring as a result of the destruction of South American rainforests. Indeed, we have greatly altered the original plant communities and replaced them with essentially a sea of corn and soybeans which surrounds the tiny islands of native vegetation that remain. This loss of plant

Life cycle of zebra swallowtail butterfly from larva, to pupa, to emergence, to adult. Our attempts to control insect pests frequently result in the elimination of many of our most beautiful forms. *Photos by Pearl M. Eslinger*

diversity means that areas of the state that once supported hundreds of species of insects, each an integral part of food webs and serving to keep other species in balance, are now home to only a few species, but each frequently populated by huge numbers that often reach pest proportions.

Whoever destroys an elephant creates a thousand rats or a million flies.

—*R. A. Piddlington,* The Limits of Mankind

Moreover, this great food resource we have planted for our consumption has been a bonanza for insect species that are able to exploit the energy supply offered by our crop fields, thereby allowing their populations to explode to levels not usually present in diverse areas. These population explosions represent the insect pests of our crops. An example of the reproductive potential of insects may sometimes be observed when wheat is followed by corn in no-till farming. Some of these cornfields produce legions of armyworms, the immature stage of a drab moth, which can eat several acres of young corn plants a day!

Our response to uncontrolled insect populations was the search for chemical methods of insect control and the application of thousands of tons of insecticides on Indiana farms, orchards, and lawns every year. Such insecticides, while sometimes controlling the pest species in the short run, also kill most other species of beneficial insects that may inhabit the field, thereby further lowering diversity. Finally, many chemical insecticides are resistant to breakdown, remain in the environment for long periods, and run off from farm fields during heavy rains. Eventually they find their way into aquatic food chains and into humans. Some insecticides used previously on Indiana's crops have been shown to be carcinogenic.

Insects have adapted to the use of pesticides just as they adapted to the changing Indiana landscape during the past 300 million years. The increased use of pesticides has resulted in rapid evolution of genetic resistance to chemicals by many insect species. During the late 1940s, it was believed by many that DDT and associated chemical insecticides would literally wipe the housefly off the face of the earth. But the housefly is still with us even in the face of a new arsenal of pesticides. Resistance to control has forced both farmers and urban residents to use even more potent poisons in greater doses, which in turn has further increased the genetic resistance of the pests, along with reduced diversity of beneficial insects.

Fortunately, entomologists now recognize that a diversity of insect species can have a balancing effect that helps keep populations of pest species in check. New techniques of integrated pest control are being developed in Indiana and elsewhere, in which it is not necessary to destroy every insect in a field. Instead pest populations are often managed by biological control in which predacious insects eat herbivorous pest insects. Delicate green lacewings, which are voracious predators of aphids, can be reared in huge numbers and released to control aphid infestations. Ladybug beetles and certain wasps are examples of other beneficial insects that are becoming more appreciated by midwestern farmers.

The sense of death is most in apprehension,
And the poor beetle, that we tread upon,
In corporal sufferance finds a pang as great
As when a giant dies.

—*Shakespeare,* Macbeth

Not all insect pests in Indiana are the result of human modification of natural communities. Many of our most serious pests are species which have been introduced into the state. One of the more bizarre examples is a mosquito that can spread LaCrosse encephalitis. Native to the mountains of Japan and southeast Asia, this dangerous mosquito has recently been collected in Indianapolis in large piles of abandoned rubber tires!

The insect was brought to Indiana indirectly, as a consequence of American tires being made of synthetic rubber, while tires in Japan are made from natural rubber. Old tires from Japan were shipped to this country, where they were stacked into great mounds of millions of tires. Some scrap dealers believe that natural rubber will eventually become a valuable resource and have been purchasing old Japanese tires as an investment. The Asian mosquito often lays its eggs in standing water found naturally in tree holes, but now breeds in water which collects inside the stockpiled scrap tires. When the water evaporates, the eggs adhere to the inside tire wall. When temperatures are right and there is another rainfall, the eggs hatch. Unfortunately, by that time the tires had been imported to Indiana.

Not all insect species introduced in the state are detrimental. Several, in fact, have improved our lives. The honeybee is not native to America, but was introduced from Europe. Native Americans called honeybees "white man's flies." Honeybees are popular insects and have served as an inspiration for many literary works.

His labor is a chant,
    his idleness a tune;
Oh, for a bee's experience
    Of clovers and of noon!

　　　—*Emily Dickinson,* The Bee

Honeybees are enormously important economically. They are responsible for the pollination of nearly three-quarters of the food plants we consume. Without honeybees we would not have as many apples, berries, melons, and cucumbers, just to mention a few, nor would many native plants set seed.

Beekeepers are carefully watching for tracheal mites that are already in the state and are killing half of our honeybee colonies each year. Efforts to stop this destruction have not been successful on a large scale. Failure to control this problem will result in significant reductions in the yields of food crops pollinated by honeybees, as well as reducing honey production.

The large Chinese praying mantis is another introduced insect that has benefited Hoosiers. This insect can grow to nearly four inches long and is an important predator. The name praying mantis comes from the mantis's raptorial forelegs that are held like supplicating hands. In reality, it is a voracious feeder, ever ready to pounce on nearby prey when within grasp. More appropriately, it should be called the preying mantis! Because of its appetite, the Chinese mantis was introduced into the United States in 1896 and became widely protected by farmer and gardeners. Even today, many people will still proclaim that killing a mantis is an unlawful offense!

The future does not promise to correct the impact of human interference with our insect diversity. We are continually monitoring our woods for the gypsy moth that is sometimes introduced into the state by unsuspecting campers who inadvertently bring back cocoons or eggs when they return from their vacations to eastern forests. To date, state officials have been successful in eradicating this threat from Indiana forestlands, but some states are suffering serious losses of forest trees.

Given the increasing human population, the present approach to agricultural production, and the world's dependence on food grown in the United States, it is unlikely that pesticide use on crops will be decreased unless new or more effective techniques of insect control are found. The most promising avenue of attack is to use natural means of control, such as beneficial insects and insect diseases.

Simple approaches to lower pesticide use involve careful monitoring of pest populations in the field and application of chemicals only when there is a pest population large enough to damage the crop. Indiscriminate spraying on a calendar schedule, whether pests are present or not, kills most of the insects, beneficial as well as harmful, and further reduces the insect diversity in the state. Fortunately, the increasing costs of pesticides may lead farmers, foresters, and homeowners to limit pesticide use and move toward safer and more natural means of control.

The insects are the only conspicuous creatures indubitably holding their own against man. When he matches wits with any of the lower mammals they always lose. But when he matches his wit against the instinct and vitality of the insects he merely holds his own at best.

　　　—*Joseph Wood Krutch, "Insects and Man," in* The Great Chain of Life *(1956)*

Bright color of male long-eared sunfish in breeding condition. *Photo by Richard Fields*

39. Beneath the Water's Surface: The Fishes

James R. Gammon

On the banks o' Deer Crick mil'd er two from town
'Long up where the mill-race comes a-loafin' down,
Like to git up in there 'mongst the sycamores
And watch the worter at the dam, a-frothin' as she pours:

Crawl out on some old log, with my hook and line,
Where the fish is jes' so thick you kin see 'em shine
As they flicker round yer bait, coaxin' you to jerk,
Tel yer tired ketchin' of 'em, mighty nigh, as work!

> —*James Whitcomb Riley,* On the Banks o' Deer Crick
> *(1883)*

If you want to learn something about Indiana fish, just go fishing with a worm. Bait your hook with a lively crawler, drop it into a deep, shaded pool, sit down, relax—watch out for the patch of poison-ivy—and wait for a bite. The fishing purist using his favorite lure may fool a bass or trout, but has almost no chance of catching all those other fish which locate food in other ways.

For every species of "popular" fish, there are dozens of other species that can be caught. Then there are clams, water snakes, and turtles, too. With a small hook and a tiny worm, you can catch 180 different species of fish. Only about two dozen of them are considered game fish.

If you want to talk with a fish "expert," do not consult the "bass buster" with a carpeted 100-horsepower boat. Instead, drive the back roads and watch for old men or bicycles at bridges. Small boys with bikes have time and freedom to explore. So do retired people, who, remembering their earlier years and former curiosity, are again free to wander.

> The naturalist-angler is a common species. . . . Fishing takes him bird's-nesting, insect-watching, flower-gathering, into places where otherwise he would be a trespasser.
>
> —*J. C. Mottram*

Fish-watching will never rival bird-watching in popularity, but there are similarities. Species of bass, northern pike, muskellunge, walleye, sauger, salmon, and flathead catfish are like birds of prey. Small, brightly colored darters are similar to warblers or humming-birds. Scavenger crows and vultures have channel catfish and carp as counterparts. The sparrows of the aquatic world are the minnows.

A few fishes are relative newcomers to Indiana: smelt, salmon, carp, alewife, sea lamprey, white Amur, and goldfish. Most, however, have been here for thousands of years with ancestors millions of years old. Ancient indeed are sturgeon, gar, bowfin, and paddlefish, all of which are common in Indiana. But they are not well known to Hoosiers and would seem still stranger to a foreigner. Both the gar and the bowfin are even rarer and occur only in eastern North America.

STREAMS

A river is more than an amenity, it is a treasure.

> —*Oliver Wendell Holmes*

Indiana has about 36,000 miles of streams and rivers large enough to support aquatic life. The larger rivers such as the Wabash, White, and Ohio are mostly located at Indiana's edges, so it is the smaller streams which are most common within the state. The St. Joseph, Kankakee, Eel, Wildcat, Tippecanoe, Big Pine, Sugar, Blue, White-water, Driftwood, Big Blue, and their tributaries are a few of the better-known streams. Regardless of where they are located, all of these streams share some characteristics. Given Indiana's gently undulating landscape, the low-gradient streams tend to meander. Small headwaters are generally steeper than the lower courses near their mouths.

Like a string of beads, streams consist of an alternating sequence of deeper, quiet pools and shallow, faster riffles. For some unknown reason, adjacent riffles are usually spaced about five to seven stream-widths apart so that small headwaters consist mostly of riffles. Large rivers such as the Wabash and lower White consist mostly of pools. That is why small streams usually have coarse, rocky bottoms and large rivers have sandy bottoms. For many of the same reasons, their width increases much faster than their depth as streams increase in size.

These relationships are modified by bedrock and treefall. Trees on stream banks resist a stream's tendency to meander. They block summer sunlight and keep the water cool. Trees also provide the chief source of energy to streams—leaves.

> It is interesting to contemplate a tangled bank, clothed with many plants of many kinds, with birds singing on the bushes, with various insects flitting about.
>
> —*Charles Darwin*

Long ago, Indiana streams drained shallow wetlands, and the entire watershed was mostly forest. Today only about 10 percent, or 100,000 acres, of the original wetlands remain, mostly near our northern and southern borders, and even this is disappearing rapidly. Before the settlers arrived, Indiana was about 87 percent forest. Today only 17 percent is forest, with 55 percent in crops, mostly corn and soybeans.

Streams once flowed more constantly than streams of today because of the permanent perennial vegetation of the watersheds. There were floods, but not as many as today. There were droughts, but they were less severe and shorter than today. The loss of these wetlands, forests, and prairies has affected and continues to influence the biological character of the fish community simply because the physical nature of the streams changed.

The physical attributes of the streams are of great importance to fishes because species differ as to where they can live, feed, and reproduce. Brook trout, creek chub, redbellied dace, blacknose dace, redside dace, and some darters live in small permanent streams throughout their lives. Many other species migrate into the headwaters to spawn in the spring and live downstream the rest of the year.

Rivers are more diverse and harbor 30 to 40 species of fish, each preferring a distinct portion of the stream. Riffles with shallow, fast-flowing water and rocky bottoms typically contain hog suckers,

311

Creek chubs are smaller "forage fish" that are often eaten by large aquatic predators. *Photo by John O. Whitaker, Jr.*

Several species of darters, including the greenside, are found in high-quality, well-oxygenated flowing waters. *Photo by John O. Whitaker, Jr.*

suckermouth minnows, stonerollers, river chub, brindled madtom, sculpin, and various species of darters. The pool just below the riffle is the preferred habitat for shorthead redhorse or "redtail," sucker, stonecat, and smallmouth bass, if cover is present. The deepest pools contain silver redhorse, white crappie, and channel catfish.

Other species such as golden redhorse, black redhorse, quillback carpsucker, and striped shiner range widely in the pools. Black-striped topminnows and nearly transparent brook silversides slowly patrol quiet shallows, eating small morsels floating on and near the surface. Spotfin shiner, sand shiner, silverjaw minnow, rosyface shiner, redfin shiner, and bluntnose minnow occupy shallow, sandy areas. Log perch, a large, vividly marked darter, are often present. And buried up to their eyeballs in sand may be nearly translucent sand darters hiding from predators and waiting for small invertebrates to eat.

The diversity of fish may be enhanced by occasional schools of longnose gar moving slowly along the surface. Small brindled madtom search for food in gravel beds, their sharp pectoral spines fitted with multiple barbs and a poison gland, dangerous but not lethal. Larval brook lamprey like to burrow in the soft backwater mud. Unlike their parasitic sea lamprey cousin in Lake Michigan, these inoffensive little fellows mature after a few years in the muck, build a shallow nest in gravel at the heads of riffles, spawn, and then die without ever again eating. They live only in the cleanest streams and, like darters, are indicators of good water quality.

Gizzard shad graze on algae coating logs and rocks in open, quiet areas. In fact, anglers would be more likely to catch one by baiting their hook with algae than with worms. Gizzard shad and stonerollers are our only native vegetarians.

Carpsuckers, bluntnose minnows, and a few others eat small bits of organic matter called detritus and digest what they can. This unlikely food, together with dead leaves, also supports a smorgasbord of invertebrates living on the bottom. The vast array of small invertebrates occupying the bottom form the chief food of most species of fish. Small worms, clams, snails, bryozoans, planaria, protozoans, and legions of insect larvae are absolutely essential food for most.

I love any discourse of rivers, and fish and fishing.

—*Izaak Walton (1593–1683), The Compleat Angler*

Smallmouth bass and white crappie are the usual target of fishermen in small streams, except perhaps in early spring when redhorse and carpsuckers are spawning. Shorthead redhorse (redtails), golden redhorse, black redhorse, and quillback carpsuckers (sicklebacks) are virtually ignored despite their abundance. They make up 25 to 60 percent of the total weight of fish in streams.

Their popularity would be far greater were it not for the numerous small Y-bones in their flesh. There is, however, an easy way to make them good to eat. First scale and fillet the fish. Put each fillet skin side down on a board, and use a very sharp knife to slice through the muscle and bones down to the skin every eighth-inch or so from head end to tail. Cut the fillet into pieces, and roll them in beaten egg and cracker crumbs. Heat oil just below smoking, place each piece *skin side up,* and fry hard. Then turn and fry skin side down till brown. The little Y-bones cook thoroughly, and the fish tastes as good as walleye fillets.

The smallmouth bass is the undisputed king of streams and might better be called the river, bronze, or brown bass. Indiana lies in the middle of its original geographic range—the Great Lakes, the Ohio, and the upper Mississippi river systems. It has been widely stocked and now lives in most of the U.S. and southern Canada and in Europe, England, Russia, and Africa as well. In Indiana it prefers small to medium-sized streams with good gradients, but also lives in a few lakes and reservoirs in northern Indiana.

They were very abundant throughout the White and Wabash systems 150 years ago. They were even common in the lower main stems of the White, Wabash, and Ohio. David Thomas wrote in 1819: "The Wabash abounds with fish of many kinds; which, in the months of April, May, and June, may be readily caught with the hook and line. . . . The black perch or bass is excellent, and weighs from one to seven pounds."

Bottom-feeding suckers such as this redhorse help remove detritus, thereby cleansing their habitat. *Photo by Delbert Rust*

Dunn (1910) quotes George Pitts, an early resident of Indianapolis: "There was no end of fish in the streams in those days. I went up to McCormick's dam (just above the Country Club) four miles above town on the river one day and sat down at a chute that had broken out and where fish were running through. There were wagon loads of fish, and I threw out with my hand eighty-seven bass, ranging in size from one pound up to five."

Smallmouth bass were all but eliminated from these waters by 1900. David Starr Jordan, in an address to the State Fish and Game Convention on December 19, 1899, stated: "There never were such [smallmouth] bass streams as in Indiana, and that White River is the best bass stream they have ever known. I think probably nothing better could be done—if we could devise a way—than to bring the bass back."

Smallmouth bass continue to disappear from Indiana streams, largely because of agricultural impacts. When I first visited them 30 years ago, Big Raccoon Creek and Little Walnut Creek in Putnam County contained an abundance of smallmouth, sunfish, rock bass, and darters. Few of these existed here and in many other small streams in the early 1980s. The Eel River (Logansport) "lost" its smallmouth bass in 1980 and retains only a small remnant of a once-flourishing population.

Many other small streams could support smallmouth bass if the runoff of soil, nutrients, and other agricultural chemicals into streams were reduced. The rapid adoption of no-till farming of corn and soybeans in the last decade of the twentieth century may be beneficial, but there is still fall plowing, and hogs and cattle are pastured directly in streams. The band of permanent riparian vegetation (riverine wetlands) which buffers streams from tilled fields is critical to the health of streams. Its roots hold soil and reduce streambank erosion. Soil particles and nutrients from flanking fields are trapped and sucked up. Riparian trees shade streams and keep the water cooler, an essential factor, since smallmouth bass are less tolerant of heat than largemouth. The canopy shade also keeps algae mats from forming, important for maintaining a good dissolved oxygen balance.

The life cycle of smallmouth bass begins with spawning in spring, when the water temperature reaches about 60°F. The male builds a small nest in gravelly shallows and fertilizes the eggs deposited by several females. Then he guards the nest diligently, driving away other fish looking for an easy meal. The eggs develop rapidly, and the fry hatch in less than a week. They remain in the nest for a few days before scattering throughout the stream. The jet-black fry can be seen easily at this time. They feed on small invertebrates, grow rapidly, and gradually become brownish in color.

Smallmouth may spawn several times each year, a distinct advantage for fish that live in the changeable environment of a stream. Feeding mostly upon invertebrates, the juveniles become 2 to 3 inches long by fall and grow to 6 to 7 inches during the second year. Although invertebrates continue to be eaten, more and more fish and crayfish are included in their diet, and they reach 9 to 11 inches in length by the end of the third year. They may mature to spawn the next spring, but few survive long enough to become as large as the 6 pound 15 ounce fish taken in 1985 from Sugar Creek in Shelby County.

LARGE RIVERS

By shallow river, to whose falls
Melodious birds sing madrigals.

—*C. Marlowe,* The Passionate Shepherd to His Love

How big is a "large" river? That might be best discussed on a cold winter's night while sitting near a woodstove sipping wine and listening to Smetana's *The Moldau.* Like this sound portrait of a river which traces its beginning as a small stream to its final meeting with the ocean, flowing waters are open-ended ecosystems which change seasonally, and gradually along their length. A more practical definition might be that it is too big to wade and requires a boat to fish properly.

Indiana's large rivers are found in the southwestern third of the state and include the Ohio (356 miles), White (about 150 miles), and Wabash (300 miles). Other than just being larger, they are environmentally different. They generally have lower gradients, fewer riffles, finer bottom sediments, higher temperatures, and "muddier" water than small streams.

Many of the fish that make up the "large river" community are the same ones found in smaller streams or their sister species. Others are quite different. Gizzard shad are undoubtedly the most abundant kind, making up about one-third of the total fish biomass of large rivers. Large schools of bottom-feeding northern river carpsucker are also present, while shortnose gar and longnose gar often bask at the surface.

Various species of redhorse, carp, and smallmouth buffalo, freshwater drum or "white perch," shovelnose sturgeon, and blue sucker suck invertebrates from the bottom gravel. Channel catfish reach their greatest population density here, no doubt partly because taste buds on their barbels and skin enable them to locate food in the darkest water.

Fish-eaters include flathead catfish, spotted bass, white crappie, white bass, mooneye, goldeye, skipjack herring, sauger, and even an occasional American eel getting ready to return to the Caribbean to spawn after maturing.

On the white sand of the bottom . . .
Lay the sturgeon, King of Fishes . . .
There he lay in all his armor.

—*Longfellow,* The Song of Hiawatha (*1855*)

Part of the intrigue of large rivers is that the size of the fish living there matches the expanse of the water. W. S. Blatchley described with detailed clarity his encounter with a sturgeon at least 8 feet long in the Wabash River near Montezuma in 1906. In the early 1800s, travelers described 100-pound flathead catfish, 30-pound drum or "white perch," 7-pound smallmouth bass, 30-pound buffalo, and 20-pound walleye. Occasionally when electrofishing, we will stir up a 6-foot paddlefish, the toothless "shark" of the Wabash. Rarely will it be brought to net, but just knowing that there are large, mysterious denizens lurking beneath the surface is reward enough. Who knows when someday a mermaid will appear? Some smaller species are here, too: mountain madtom, slenderhead darter, emerald shiner, bullhead minnow, and silver lamprey, a smaller parasitic relative of the sea lamprey. Other small-stream fish congregate locally at the gravelly mouths of tributaries.

As a newcomer from Wisconsin, I found the turbid Wabash River less attractive than Indiana's clearer, smaller streams. I learned how deceptive superficial appearances can be after we first electrofished the river between Montezuma and Big Raccoon Creek in October of 1965. The river was low, as it usually is that time of year, and relatively clear and cool. Using a boat which was too small and a makeshift rig, we electrofished time and again through the fast-water section just above Big Raccoon Creek, catching an absolutely astounding variety of fish: blue suckers, shovelnose sturgeon, shorthead redhorse, smallmouth bass, sauger, buffalo fish, and many others.

White crappie is a common game fish sought in ponds, lakes, and higher-quality streams.   *Photo by James Gammon*

Freshwater drum are one of the great variety of fishes found in Indiana's larger streams and rivers.   *Photo by James Gammon*

We first studied the effect of electric generating stations and their introductions of heated water into the river. We found that fish had an accurate internal thermometer, and also that each individual species preferred to live in water having a certain temperature. Some fish preferred cooler temperatures and avoided the heated water (redhorse, smallmouth bass, and sauger). Others enjoyed the additional heat (flathead catfish, largemouth bass, and carp). After several years we recognized that heat was but one of many possible influences in the river, and we began to systematically study more of the river and its tributaries.

More than two decades and over 2,000 miles of electrofishing have ensued since then, and we now have a good picture of the fish community and ecology of 165 miles of the Wabash River and its tributaries. Two insights are particularly valuable: (1) the dominant organisms are not fish, but microscopic algae; and (2) the fish community of the Wabash River is very diverse, but could be even better.

For a decade in the 1970s and early 1980s, our catches of fish varied little. In 1984, however, we noticed a slight increase in a variety of desirable species from Delphi to Attica. We saw further positive changes the next year and still more in 1986. There were increases in both the numbers and biomass of fish captured, in several measures of species diversity, and in the abundance of sport fish. So great is the biotic potential of fish, among other organisms, that the poorest populations of fish found in 1983 produced the best populations by 1985–86.

The combined catch rate of sport fish (white bass, channel catfish, centrarchid bass, crappie, sauger, and walleye) averaged only slightly more than 2.0 fish per kilometer from 1974 through 1983. The catch rate doubled to 3.7/km in 1984 and then expanded further to 9.1/km in 1985 and 12.4/km in 1986. After 1987 it fluctuated between 7.5 and 3.0/km. The most improved areas were from Lafayette to Covington, but equally dramatic changes occurred between Delphi and Lafayette, in Lafayette itself, and even downriver from Terre Haute.

One desirable environmental change in the river in recent years is a significant decrease in the biochemical oxygen demand (BOD). BOD is a measure of the amount of decomposable organic matter such as sewage, leaves, etc. Lower BOD values indicate better water quality. During the 1960s, the mean annual BOD was about 4.5 to 5.0 mg/l in the river water. The BOD has steadily and dramatically decreased since 1970 to 2.5 to 3.0 from Peru to Vincennes, except, importantly, during the summer when algae is so abundant.

Part of the reason for lower BOD may be steady improvements in waste treatment at Lafayette, Kokomo, Frankfort, and other sizable communities in the upper watershed. Fertilizer use decreased sharply in the 1980s, perhaps the result of more fallow fields and economic difficulties for the agricultural community. Aided by the federally subsidized PIK program (designed to encourage removal of erodible land from crop production), there was a 25 percent reduction in acreage of corn grown and fertilizer usage in 1983.

A contributing factor was that the summers following 1983 were unusually dry, with droughts in 1988 and 1991. Low stable spring and summer flows foster good reproduction and survival of young fish in our rivers. Non-point-source agricultural pollution is reduced during dry years. All of these recent events may or may not have combined to trigger the improvement in the fish community. Whatever the causes, the improvements show that the Wabash River is capable of becoming a valuable recreational resource.

> And really, fish look bigger than they are before they're caught—
> When the pole is bent into a bow and the slender line is taut,
> When a fellow feels his heart rise up like a doughnut in his throat
> And he lunges in a frenzy up and down the leaky boat!
> Oh, you who've been a-fishing will indorse me when I say
> That it always *is* the biggest fish you catch that gets away!
>
> —*Eugene Field,* Our Biggest Fish

One undeniable barrier to increased recreational use of the Wabash is its perception as a "dirty" river. Indeed, the water is usually turbid and yellow-brown in color during the summer. However, this is caused not by silt, but by extremely high densities of small, unicellular algae called diatoms.

These diatoms have a direct and indirect influence on the fish community. They can directly affect fish at some times and in some places by reducing dissolved oxygen concentrations. For example, fish kills near Montezuma in 1977 and 1983 were caused primarily by diatoms settling out in a lake-like section of river created by the buildup of gravel at the mouth of Sugar Creek. At very low summer flows, diatoms may reach densities of 100,000 cells per milliliter. When water reaches wide, deep sections of a river, it travels more slowly, and the diatoms settle to the bottom, decompose, and use up

Indiana's rivers, streams, and reservoirs are cleaner with pollution control and improved farm tillage practices, permitting improvements of fish populations in riverine habitats.   *Photo by James Gammon*

oxygen in the water, causing the fish to die. Although diatoms "make" oxygen during the day, they must "breathe" at night. Thus, there are times when the masses of respiring diatoms can reduce oxygen concentrations, and this can negatively influence the fish community.

Furthermore, the high turbidity levels hinder predator fish in finding food. Yet spotted bass, sauger, and flathead catfish are somehow able to live more successfully in turbid water than others. Nonetheless, if water clarity were improved, perhaps there would be an increase in other desirable species such as smallmouth bass, northern pike, walleye, muskellunge, and white bass.

The primary reason why so many diatoms exist, of course, is the large amounts of nutrients entering the river. According to one study, about one-third comes from point sources, such as cities and industries, and the other two-thirds from agriculture. Since the abundance of diatoms seems to be controlled by the amount of phosphorus, anything that reduces phosphates entering the river should also reduce the diatoms.

Indiana banned phosphate detergents in 1972. A tertiary stage which helps remove phosphates and other nutrients has been added to several waste-treatment facilities in major cities. Since phophates enter streams primarily with sediment, reduced soil erosion should also help.

The role of wetlands as they relate to water quality is largely misunderstood. Reestablishing permanent riparian vegetation cover (riverine wetland, filter strips, or greenbelts) along waterways is an example of the kind of action needed to deal with this serious problem. As mentioned before, no-till agriculture should help restore our major rivers to their former productivity by reducing sediment pollution. However, society as a whole must recognize this problem before significant progress can be made.

The Ohio River is Indiana's newest large river, except to Hoosiers from Lawrenceburg to Mount Vernon, who have always regarded it as "theirs." More than 350 miles of shoreline were acquired in November 1985, and Indiana now "owns" up to half the river which makes up its southern boundary. However, it will take some time for most northerly Hoosiers to realize its full recreational potential.

Navigation dams have converted the Ohio from a free-flowing river into a series of "lakes" relatively constant in width and depth. In the Indiana segment, dams are located near Markland, New Albany, Cannelton, and Mount Vernon. Although the river water is still completely mixed from top to bottom, the reduced current and silting of the gravelly river bottom have severely reduced redhorse, sturgeon, paddlefish, and blue suckers. On the other hand, creek mouths adjacent to the main stem have been flooded to form embayments favored by the basses, sunfish, and crappie.

As in the Wabash, water quality has improved throughout the Ohio over the past 20 years. Point-source pollutants have been reduced, and water transparency is better because of sediment-trapping off-river reservoirs. As a consequence, many species of fish have increased in population density.

The water understands
Civilization well;
It wets my foot, but prettily
It chills my life, but wittily,
It is not disconcerted,
It is not broken-hearted:
Well used, it decketh joy,
Adorneth, doubleth joy:
Ill used, it will destroy,
In perfect time and measure
With a face of golden pleasure
Elegantly destroy.
          —*Ralph Waldo Emerson,* Water

Lock rotenone studies have been used since 1957 to evaluate the fish communities along the Ohio River. Boat traffic ceases for a day while the upriver gate is closed and the downriver gate stays open. Early the next day the lower gate is closed, and rotenone is mixed into the water. Rotenone prevents fish from extracting oxygen from the water, so they come to the surface, where they are captured by netters. Although these limited samples probably do not represent fish everywhere in the river, the studies do provide information about changes in fish over time.

For example, studies at Cannelton during 1978–80 indicated that carp were most common, followed by freshwater drum, smallmouth buffalo fish, channel catfish, river carpsucker, flathead catfish, and gizzard shad. Sauger, white crappie, and white bass were the most abundant sport fish. The potential for recreational fishing and boating far exceeds current use, and a rosy recreational future for the beautiful Ohio River is predicted if present trends continue.

LAKES AND RESERVOIRS

The fishes of Indiana lakes and reservoirs have undergone vast changes in the past 20 years thanks to innovative management programs of the Department of Natural Resources, Division of Fish and Wildlife. Unlike rivers and streams, lakes can be managed because they are relatively closed systems. Most of the reservoirs have been constructed within the past 25 years, and while the real value of changing stream valleys to reservoirs may be hotly debated, there is no denying their fishing benefits.

Once the exclusive domain of largemouth bass, bluegill, channel catfish, and crappie, Indiana lakes and reservoirs are now also home to white bass, walleye, northern pike, muskellunge, and "wipers" (hybrids of white bass and marine striped bass), thanks to innovative hatchery operations of the Indiana Department of Natural Resources.

Even the fish community in southern Lake Michigan has undergone a startling transformation. More than 30 years ago, a community dominated by lake trout and whitefish was decimated by the sea lamprey. Cisco or lake "herring" and yellow perch would soon be replaced by alewife. Salmon were stocked to eat the alewife, and now one can catch coho salmon, chinook salmon, brown trout, and steelhead in addition to lake trout. All of these are now stocked regularly and provide fishermen in the Great Lakes region with unparalleled fishing opportunities. The completion of fish ladders along the St. Joseph River now permits salmon and trout to travel inland.

> Ah, dainty monarch of the flood,
> How often have I cast for you,
> How often sadly seen you scud
> Where weeds and water-lilies grew!
> How often snapped my treacherous line!
> Yet here I have you on this plate,—
> You shall swim twice, and now in wine.
>
> —*Eugene Field,* The Fisherman's Feast

Smelt, yellow perch, and, of course, carp are still common today along with other small species, but it is alewife which sustains the gamefish populations of the Great Lakes. Feeding on crustacean zooplankton, the alewife makes up about 80 percent of the weight of fish in Lake Michigan. It has direct value for making cat food and fertilizer, but its indirect economic value as the primary food of salmon and trout is far greater.

Despite the abundance of game fish, there are problems which were unknown 30 years ago. Some of the many chemicals used by our society eventually end up in lakes and streams. They adsorb to sediments and concentrate in aquatic organisms. Rarely do these concentrations kill fish, but there is concern when fish are eaten by humans.

The U.S. Food and Drug Administration (FDA) recommends concentration levels in fish which are regarded as "safe." Because of aerial transport, no fish on this planet are completely free of these organic materials. A safe level depends upon a substance's toxicity and its chemical and biological properties. Some substances increase in concentration as they are passed along the aquatic food chain. Chemicals which are both persistent and fat soluble are of particular concern.

The Indiana Department of Environmental Management (IDEM) regularly monitors levels of toxic materials in fish. Fish and bottom sediment from stations scattered throughout the state have been regularly tested since 1979. Each sample consists of five individuals, made up of two species of bottom-feeding fish and one piscivorous species. The concentrations of 25 organic compounds and 6 metals in whole fish are determined. Since many of the toxic compounds concentrate in fat and the liver, the concentrations in edible fish flesh alone is generally less than in whole fish.

IDEM issues "fish advisories" whenever fish are found to contain unsafe levels of potentially harmful chemicals. Polychlorinated biphenyls (PCBs), DDT, chlordane, dieldrin, and aldrin have all been banned as general-use materials, but because of their chemical properties, they continue to persist in the sediments of lakes and streams and in the fish that inhabit them.

> It was inevitable that serious destruction of fishes would follow the widespread use of the new organic pesticides. Fishes are almost fantastically sensitive to the chlorinated hydrocarbons that make up the bulk of modern insecticides. And when millions of tons of poisonous chemicals are applied to the surface of the land, it is inevitable that some of them will find their way into the ceaseless cycle of waters moving between land and sea.
>
> —*Rachel Carson, "Rivers of Death," in* Silent Spring (1962)

Not all species of fish concentrate organic chemicals to the same extent. Pike, walleye, bass, perch, flathead catfish, and bluegill rarely contain dangerous concentrations because they have little fat. On the other hand, lake trout, salmon, carp, and channel catfish may be seriously contaminated.

Time of exposure is another important variable. Smaller, younger fish generally contain less than larger, older fish. Most low-fat fish such as smelt, perch, small bass, and northern pike may be eaten safely once each month, except by pregnant women and children, who should eat none. Larger individuals of these same species, as well as carp, large salmon, and trout, should not be eaten more often than once every two months, again except by pregnant women and children, who should avoid eating them at all.

Risks of eating fish from inland lakes and streams is generally low, except for large carp, which are both fatty and long-lived. An encouraging decline in contaminant levels has occurred since 1979 almost everywhere in Indiana. However, there are still problem waters here and there. For more detailed information, contact the Indiana State Department of Health, Environmental Epidemiology Section, P.O. Box 1964, Indianapolis, IN 46206–1964.

The risks involved in eating fish caught in suspicious waters can be minimized by proper preparation and cooking. Filleting and skinning fish and then broiling or baking the meat on a rack can significantly reduce the fat and contaminants.

Bluegill are likely the most frequently caught fish in Indiana waters by young and experienced anglers alike. *Photo by Delbert Rust*

PONDS

The 40,000 or so small impoundments and ponds which dot the Indiana landscape are almost universally inhabited by largemouth bass and bluegill, with a few channel catfish, yellow bullhead, redear sunfish, and white crappie thrown in for variety. Ponds are created for a variety of purposes in addition to fishing, so they are more subject to problems than most waters. Proper location is important. Subsoils should contain enough clay to render the pond watertight.

Since ponds depend upon surface runoff to replace evaporative and seepage losses, there should be 6 to 10 acres of drainage basin for every acre of pond. The cost of installing a device for draining the pond will be well worthwhile in the long haul. The structure of the drainage basin is also important. It should mostly be covered by permanent vegetation such as woods or brushland to minimize sediment runoff. It should not receive drainage from barnyards or tilled fields. Cattle should not have access to the pond, or at least it should be limited in order to prevent high turbidities.

The pond should have a considerable volume of water deeper than 15 feet so that the danger of winterkill is minimized, especially in the northern snow belt. Winterkill occurs in shallow lakes and ponds when snow cover prevents sunlight from penetrating into the water, thereby diminishing photosynthesis and oxygen production by algae. Decomposition continues unabated, and fish die from insufficient oxygen.

Once the pond is filled with water, it may be stocked with 10 to 30 adult bass and 500 to 1,000 bluegill fry per acre. Populations of both species should reach the carrying capacity of the pond within three years. After that it is up to the owner to maintain a balance. Ponds tend to become oversupplied with bluegills and scarce in largemouth bass because of overfishing of the latter. Pond owners should strive to maintain bluegill populations where bluegills larger than 6 inches are 40 percent to 60 percent as abundant as bluegills between 3 and 6 inches. In order to maintain good bass populations, it may be necessary to limit fish removed from the lake to a size "window" of perhaps 12 to 14 inches, returning all fish smaller and larger than this to the pond. In this strategy, there are larger fish to provide sport and for reproduction.

The addition of other species such as white crappie, channel catfish, or redear sunfish is largely a matter of preference of the owner and generally will not interfere with the other species.

In summary, we know something about the distribution and abundance of our fish species, but not nearly enough about their lifestyles, their ecological relationships, and their environmental requirements. On the environmental front, we have made some positive progress by reducing pollutional effects from industries and cities. However, we are losing ground, literally and figuratively, where agricultural effects are concerned.

No high ambition may I claim—
I angle not for lordly game
Of trout or bass, or weary bream
A black perch reaches the extreme
Of my desires, and goggle-eyes
Are not a thing that I despise;
A sunfish, or a "chub" or "cat"—
A "silverside"—yea, even that!

—*James Whitcomb Riley*

Largemouth bass are among the most sought game fish in Indiana's waters, especially in farm ponds and small lakes. *Photo by Delbert Rust*

Painted turtles are commonly seen basking on logs or stones, making them a favorite reptile for many Hoosiers.   *Photo by Delano Z. Arvin*

40. Creepers, Crawlers, and Hoppers: Amphibians and Reptiles

Sherman A. Minton, Jr.

There is no more reason why a person should boast, "I just killed a snake," than that he should boast, "I just killed a robin."

—*Henry Hill Collins,* Complete Field Guide to American Wildlife *(1959)*

Reptiles and amphibians had a bad public image in Indiana when I was growing up. Snakes were loathed and feared. Most were believed to be deadly; they ate eggs and chickens or stole milk from cows. Snapping turtles would bite and not let go 'til it thundered. Toads gave people warts. Turtles and water dogs spoiled fishing. "Red lizards" poisoned milk and water. Today public attitudes toward these creatures are changing. It is widely recognized that most snakes are non-venomous, some people think they are pretty, and a few understand their ecological roles. Frogs and turtles are seen as amusing and charming.

Many amphibians and reptiles that were common in Indiana at mid-century are now disappearing at an alarming rate. In most cases we really do not understand why, although large-scale physical and chemical modification of the environment seems to be largely responsible. Amphibians and reptiles are sensitive indicators of environmental change. Many have exacting requirements for moisture, temperature, shelter, and food during all or part of their life cycles, and are sensitive to pesticides, herbicides, and industrial wastes. Compared with birds, mammals, and insects, they have poor powers of dispersal. Most spend their entire lives—in the case of a box turtle, up to a century—within the area of a few city blocks, often within the area of an ordinary suburban lot.

Two major groups of amphibians—salamanders and frogs/toads—and three of reptiles—turtles, lizards, and snakes—occur in Indiana. The salamanders, with 20 species, are probably the least known and in some ways the most diverse. Most are small creatures less than a foot long and have an elongate body, four short legs, and a long tail. They are secretive, nocturnal, and moisture-loving; three Indiana species are wholly aquatic. Salamanders feed for the most part on small invertebrates, but the larger species may eat small vertebrates.

The typical salamander life history begins with eggs deposited in water followed by an aquatic larval or tadpole stage that becomes an adult. However, some species lay eggs in damp terrestrial sites and dispense entirely with the aquatic larval stage. About half of Indiana's salamanders belong to the family Plethodontidae, which has neither lungs nor gills in the adult stage; respiration takes place through the skin and mucous membranes of the mouth.

Indiana's 15 species of frogs and toads belong to four families, but more than half are members of the genus *Rana,* which includes the typically "frog-like" frogs. Tree frogs, family Hylidae, have toes that end in clinging pads. However, in two of the four Indiana species, the pads are barely detectable, and the frogs themselves are not climbers. Three Indiana amphibians have the stout body and dry, warty skin associated with toads. Two are true toads of the cosmopolitan genus *Bufo;* the third belongs to an entirely different family.

Frogs and toads are predators of some economic importance, for pest insects make up a significant part of the diet of some species. The larger frogs, particularly the bullfrog, will eat almost any creature they can catch and swallow. All Indiana frogs and toads deposit eggs in water and have an aquatic tadpole stage.

The Cenozoic came, and with it progressive drought, and the turtles joined the great hegira of swamp and forest animals to steppe and prairie, and watched . . . as the mammals rose to heights of evolutionary frenzy . . . and . . . they just kept on watching as *Eohippus* begat Man O' War and a mob of irresponsible and shifty-eyed little shrews swarmed down out of the trees to chip at stones, and fidget around fires, and build atom bombs.

—*Archie L. Carr,* Handbook of Turtles (1952)

Turtles are an ancient reptile group, dating back to the dawn of the age of the dinosaurs. There is great variation in size and shape among the 15 Indiana species. Most are basically aquatic but spend variable amounts of time on land. Most turtles eat both plant and animal foods. All turtles lay eggs that the female buries in moist soil. With many turtles, the temperature of incubation determines the sex of the offspring. It is widely believed that turtles grow slowly and reach a great age, but this is true of only a few species.

A faunal peculiarity of the northeastern and north-central United States is the scarcity of lizards, the most familiar reptiles in most parts of the world. Indiana has six species of lizards, belonging to four families. They feed almost exclusively on insects and spiders, and all lay eggs.

The 31 species of Indiana snakes include four venomous pit vipers. Whether the other species belong to one or several families is a matter of contention among herpetologists. In any case, they are a diverse lot that vary in length from 12 inches to 8 feet and include semi-aquatic, arboreal, and burrowing species. All snakes are predators; some are scavengers as well. Prey may be killed by venom, constriction, or being swallowed alive. Seventeen species of Indiana

Young black snakes (and black racers also) are clearly spotted, unlike the adults of these species.   *Photo by Ron Everhart*

snakes give birth to young during late summer. The others lay eggs during late spring or early summer; these hatch in late summer.

The composition and distribution of Indiana's herpetofauna reflect events since the Wisconsinan glaciation. When ice sheets covered more than half of Indiana, some species of amphibians and reptiles probably survived close to the edge of the glacier just as wood frogs, chorus frogs, and garter snakes live today in northern Canada. These species moved northward as the glacier retreated. About 10,000 years ago, coniferous forests were replaced by the hardwoods, permitting an influx of the amphibian and reptile species that dominate the state fauna today. Between 3,000 and 5,000 years ago, the climate was warmer and drier than today, and prairie species such as the bull snake spread eastward, particularly in northern Indiana. At the same time, semi-aquatic southern reptiles such as the copperbelly, cottonmouth, and red-eared turtle moved northward along rivers. Recent changes in the Indiana landscape and its herpetofauna have been brought about by humans.

AMPHIBIANS OF A FOREST POND

Woodland ponds that fill with winter rains or snow and often dry by midsummer are essential for many amphibians, and are the site of the first amphibian activity in late winter. Almost any time after the first of January that there are two or three nights with rain and temperatures above 50°F, some salamanders begin to breed. Jelly-like egg masses attached to submerged twigs or stems of water plants are laid well below the surface of the water, and will usually survive a hard late freeze. Depending on weather, it will be a week to two months before they hatch.

The first salamanders to breed in these ponds belong to the mole salamander group that live underground most of the year and are rarely seen. Jefferson's salamander and the smallmouth salamander are dark without distinct patterns, while the tiger and spotted salamander have yellow spots on a dark background. The tiger salamander, the largest terrestrial salamander in Indiana, is sometimes 12 inches long. The smaller spotted salamander often has orange head spots.

The marbled salamander is silvery to white with black crossbands. Mating occurs in autumn. The female lays her eggs on land near the border of a pond, gambling that autumn rain will flood the nest before the first hard freeze. If so, the eggs hatch in a few minutes, and the larval salamanders swim off into the pond. If not, the eggs for that year are lost, although the female usually lives to try again. The larvae grow slowly through the winter and by spring are just the right size to eat newly hatched larvae of other salamanders and frogs. They grow rapidly and leave the pond early, an advantage in a dry year.

Newts are peculiar little salamanders that inhabit woodland ponds and ditches. Adults are three to four inches long, with males having a conspicuous keel or fin on the tail. They often show small red spots on the side of the body. They are basically aquatic and, unlike most salamanders, often are active by day. Courtship is in late winter and spring, with most eggs laid in May. Following the usual aquatic larval stage is a unique land stage known as the eft, a stocky little creature whose orange to brown skin is dry and faintly rough, and has secretions toxic to many predators. Indiana newts seem to spend one season in the eft stage, after which they become aquatic adults.

Frogs also use woodland ponds for breeding and advertise their presence with their calls. In southern Indiana, calling usually begins late in February if there are mild days, but calls have been heard on Christmas. The first species to call is usually the striped chorus frog, followed by the spring peeper. Both are tiny frogs with body lengths

of about one inch. Despite their small size, hundreds calling from a favorable pond can be heard for a half-mile or so.

Amphibians were the first vertebrate group to evolve true vocalizations. The great American frog choruses of swamps and wet woods impressed early visitors to our land.

> To the stranger walking for the first time in those woods during the summer, this appears the land of enchantment, he hears a thousand voices, without being able to discern from whence or what animal they proceed, but which are, in fact . . . frogs.
>
> —W. Priest, Travels (1802)

After the danger of frost has passed, the gray treefrog calls from woodland ponds. It is twice the size of the spring peeper and has conspicuous adhesive discs on its toe tips. An expert at color change, it can go from putty white to pale green to dark gray within a few minutes. Except for the breeding season, when embracing pairs enter water to deposit eggs, these frogs spend their lives in trees or occasionally on rock faces or walls of buildings.

Spotted salamanders are distinguished from larger tiger salamanders by their separated spots, in contrast to the coalesced spots on the tiger. In mating the male deposits a conical sperm mass, called a spermatophore, which the female later clasps and admits for fertilization. Small egg masses (30 to 50) are glued to a stick in temporary ponds in spring. *Photo by John O. Whitaker, Jr.*

Tree frogs have expanded, adhesive toe pads which enable them to climb even smooth surfaces.   *Photo by Delbert Rust*

Woodland is home for one of Indiana's best-known turtles, the eastern box turtle. The hinge in the lower shell or plastron that allows the front to fold upward and protect the head distinguishes box turtles from other local species. Box turtles are most active during warm weather after rain, when many are killed by road traffic, a major factor in reducing their numbers in the Midwest. During hot, dry weather, they move to woodland ponds and pools in creeks, where they dig into the mud.

Box turtles mate in spring and fall. Females deposit eggs in early summer. Loss of newly laid eggs to raccoons, skunks, and other predators is great, but the long-lived females can lay many clutches in a lifetime. Box turtles eat a wide variety of plant and animal food and are fond of strawberries, tomatoes, and melons. Every year my mother gathered turtles from our garden and released them farther out in the hills, but replacements always moved in. Marking turtles with initials or dates cut or burned in the shell was common practice in early years of this century, and provided a way to follow individual turtles over many years. Evidence for eastern box turtles living more than a century is fairly convincing.

Snakes are uncommon deep within Indiana forests, although many species live in the forest edge. The 12-to-15-inch ringneck snake likes forest if it is hilly and rocky. It is a crevice dweller not often seen in the open. Small salamanders and earthworms are its principal food.

> Once a memorable autumn afternoon I discovered a sunning blacksnake brooding among the leaves like the very simulacrum of old night. He slid unhurriedly away, carrying his version of the secret with him in a glittering menace of scales . . . and I am sure he carried his share of the common mystery into the stones of my neighbor's wall and is sleeping endlessly on in the winter darkness with one great coil locked about that glistening head.
>
> —*Loren Eiseley,* The Immense Journey *(1946)*

The largest woodland snake is the black rat snake, which occasionally grows to more than six feet, but four to five feet is average. Only northern Indiana snakes are predominantly black; south of Indianapolis, a blotched pattern is more or less evident. These snakes are found in forest, along edges of fields, and in old buildings. They often hibernate in rocky outcrops with other snakes. Black rat snakes can climb tree trunks and vertical rock faces, where they hunt for birds, bats, and young squirrels. They also eat mice, rats, and young rabbits, and do not pass up young chickens and eggs. The young eat lizards and tree frogs. These big snakes often hunt around barns and pastures, and this led to the belief that they suck milk from cows.

Milk snakes are represented in Indiana by two subspecies: the widely distributed eastern milk snake, and the colorful red milk snake of southwestern Indiana. Average length is about three feet. Milk snakes prefer dry forest, but often live near houses and barns and are called house snakes in parts of Indiana. Adults feed largely on mice and other small mammals; the young eat small snakes and lizards.

Racers are large (circa four feet), slender snakes of open country and forest edge. The blue racer occurs in the northern half of Indiana and the black racer in the southern third; in between is a region where the two intergrade. They are alert, active snakes, but their ability to dodge and utilize cover has given them a reputation for greater speed than they have. In experimental trials, this snake has been clocked at 3.5 miles per hour, just a brisk walking pace. Racers eat a wide variety of food, including insects, small mammals, birds, snakes, lizards, and frogs. Females lay eggs in early summer, sometimes nesting communally. On August 25 in Perry County, I found 64 eggs under a large rock. Such communal nesting is known for some other midwestern snakes.

The first snake I caught was slender, bright green, and the only one found around New Albany which my father was sure was not poisonous. The 20-to-30-inch rough green snake is found in the southern part of the state. The "rough" refers to its ridged scales that are slightly rough to the touch. It is arboreal, typically found in bushes or vines at the forest edge or along streams. Plentiful near New Albany in the 1930s, it is rare today. It feeds almost entirely on insects and spiders, so increased use of pesticides has probably hurt it. Also, its tendency to "freeze" into immobility when alarmed is a shortcut to destruction on a paved road.

A 1793 account of the region bordering Lake Erie mentions "the hissing snake . . . about 18 inches long. . . . When you approach it, it flattens itself . . . and its spots become visibly brighter through rage; at the same time it blows from its mouth a subtle wind . . . if drawn in with the breath of the unwary traveler will infallably bring a decline that in a few months must prove mortal." The hognose snake, found throughout Indiana, has such local names as spreading viper, blowing viper, or puff adder. It looks and acts like everyone's idea of a dangerous snake, is extremely variable in color, and can be mistaken for a rattlesnake or copperhead. If its threatening behavior does not discourage an enemy, the hognose snake gapes, writhes, regurgitates any food in its stomach, rolls onto its back, and becomes limp. It will remain this way as long as it feels threatened, but if placed on its crawling surface will promptly roll onto its back again. Hognose snakes prefer rather dry, open terrain where the soil is loose or sandy. They lay eggs and feed principally on toads.

The only venomous snake likely to be encountered in Indiana woodland is the copperhead. It is well named. The top of its triangular head is usually coppery without conspicuous light or dark markings. At very close range, the heat-sensing pits between the eye and nostril and the vertically elliptical "cat-eye" pupil can be seen. Where copperheads are fairly plentiful, the local people usually identify them correctly; where copperheads are rare or do not occur at all, any snake with a tinge of reddish brown around its head may be identified as a "copperhead."

Their range is roughly the southern half of the state. A rocky, lightly wooded hillside is the expected habitat, but they also occur in barns, dilapidated buildings, and suburban lawns. A snake seen in a creek or pond is much more likely to be a banded watersnake than a copperhead. During the summer, copperheads are often active at night. Both spring and fall matings have been reported. Litters of up to a dozen young are born during late summer. The tail tip of the young snake is bright yellow and is used as a lure for prey such as small frogs and lizards. Copperheads take a variety of foods, including large insects, frogs, snakes, lizards, and small mammals.

There are copperhead bites in Indiana every summer, often when the snake is stepped on or disturbed during outdoor activity, or when people try to catch or kill snakes or handle captives. Copperhead bites are painful and unpleasant but rarely life-threatening.

The largest venomous snake In Indiana is the timber rattlesnake, which can reach six feet. Its bite can be fatal so one should quickly take a victim to a physician, rather than attempting first aid. Size and presence of the rattle are usually enough to identify this snake.

The original state range was probably much the same as that of the copperhead. Typical of many old accounts of rattlesnakes is this one from Adams Township, Decatur County, about 1825: "Rattlesnakes were abundant. . . . On one occasion about seventy were killed in one day near Paul's mill where they had crawled out from their den in the rocks. This was considered rather better than an ordinary day for

Blue racers appear to move faster than they actually do. A human walking briskly can usually keep pace with them. *Photo by Delano Z. Arvin*

Hog-nosed snakes are more bluff than threat when they flatten their neck and head when confronted. Toads are a major prey item.
Photo by Delano Z. Arvin

The copperhead, found most commonly along rocky slopes in southern Indiana, is one of four poisonous snake species in the state.
Photo by Sherman A. Minton

Juvenile five-lined skinks have bright blue tails. Lizards have scales and are more dry-adapted than salamanders. *Photo by Delano Z. Arvin*

snakes." A century later, there were no rattlesnakes in Decatur County, but bones found in caves attest to their presence there, and at numerous other sites where they no longer exist. Today the surviving snakes seem to be scattered and solitary, usually found in fairly open areas on the tops of ridges and perhaps hibernating in old groundhog burrows.

Timber rattlesnakes mate in late summer, and females bear young during the first half of September. Small mammals are the principal food. Even newborn snakes are large enough to eat small mice, and chipmunks are a favorite food of adults.

Forest openings, or around buildings near woodlands, are likely places to find Indiana's most widely distributed lizard, the five-lined skink. Skinks are a large family of lizards that generally have smooth, overlapping scales. The five-lined skink, like many reptiles, changes color and pattern with growth. At hatching it is coal black with a bright blue tail and five yellow stripes. As it grows, the bright colors fade. The heads of males become bright orange-red during the spring breeding season. Skinks lay eggs during early summer, favorite nesting sites being under a thin, flat rock or the loose bark of a fallen tree. They defend their nests, sometimes against even such enormous enemies as human beings. Hatching occurs about a month after the eggs are laid.

The fence lizard is a common reptile in the southern Indiana hills, particularly in open, rocky places, and is rarely seen except on bright sunny days. When rail fences were a common feature of the landscape, the lizards used them as basking sites. Males have vivid blue patches on the sides of the belly and throat; females have only faint throat patches. They eat insects, and are especially fond of catching winged forms of ants and termites when these emerge in spring. Eggs are laid in early summer, usually hatching in August.

INHABITANTS OF LAKES AND STREAMS

Indiana's largest amphibians and reptiles inhabit streams, ponds, and lakes. In 1949, an enormous turtle was reported in a pond near Churubusco, and got national news coverage for most of the spring and summer. It was never identified, much less captured, but lives on in Hoosier mythology.

A genuine giant is the alligator snapping turtle, one of the largest freshwater turtles in the world, with a record weight of 236 pounds. It looks like an exaggerated version of the common snapping turtle, with an even more massive head and three heavy ridges on its shell. It is a southern species and may not breed in Indiana, but a few strays have been found along the lower Wabash. One caught near New Harmony was exhibited at county fairs in the 1890s, walked about with a man standing on its back, and bit broom handles in half. In March of 1991, a female alligator snapper weighing about 40 pounds was caught near Martinsville.

The common snapping turtle is a big reptile in its own right, with records to 68 pounds. Indiana specimens in the 40-to-46-pound range have been reported, but any snapper above 20 pounds is exceptional. Recognized by a massive head, small lower shell, and relatively long tail, they can be found in almost any lake, pond, marsh, or stream in the state. Snappers nest almost any time during the warm months, laying 20 to 30 spherical, hard-shelled white eggs, somewhat smaller than a ping-pong ball. Eggs laid in the late spring hatch at the end of summer; those laid in late summer overwinter in the nest.

When surprised on land or taken from the water, snapping turtles defend themselves vigorously, but it is unlikely that swimmers or waders are nipped by turtles. Bites can be painful but usually do no serious damage. Snappers eat most types of animal food and some plant material. They are too slow to catch game or pan fish under ordinary conditions, but big turtles sometimes take ducklings. Snappers themselves are a good food turtle. Many small towns along Indiana rivers used to boast restaurants specializing in turtle soup or fried turtle.

Another common large turtle is the spiny softshell. Softshell turtles are a widely distributed family in which the flat, bony shell is covered by a thick, leathery disc that extends beyond the shell margin. The neck is long, and the nose projects as a sort of snorkel. Females reach a much greater size than males; the largest I have seen weighed about 13 pounds. In young turtles and adult males, the disc is marked with dark dots and circles; large females lose these markings. At the front edge of the disc are short, blunt spines that give the turtle its name.

Softshells are thoroughly aquatic but often bask on banks or logs. They prefer water with a soft mud or sand bottom in which they can bury themselves, and often lie in shallow water, occasionally poking the tips of their elongated snouts to the surface for a breath. Softshells eat mostly animal food, particularly crayfish, aquatic insects, and small fish. Their eggs resemble those of the snapping turtle, and often are buried on sandbars.

Map turtles are of medium size, with shell lengths of six to nine inches for adult females, rarely more than five inches for males. The midline ridge of the common map turtle is low and smooth; that of the false map turtle or sawback is higher and has distinct projections. Both species are fond of basking and thus are easy to observe, although they are quick to tumble into the water if alarmed. Water snails and other shellfish are favorite foods of map turtles, plus crayfish, insects, and water plants.

The red-ear turtle, first described from New Harmony in 1839 by the German naturalist Prince Maximilian zu Wied-Neuwied, is one of the best-known turtles in the world. The baby turtles' beautifully patterned green shell and red head stripes have made them universal favorites in the pet trade, although their sale in the U.S. has been stopped because they carry Salmonella bacteria. Indiana is at the northern edge of the red-ear's range; however, it has a wide distribution in the state and seems to have become more plentiful in the past 25 years, possibly owing to release of pet turtles.

Large red-ears reach a shell length of 10 inches. The colors of the head and shell darken, making big turtles hard to identify. They like quiet water with plentiful aquatic vegetation and logs for basking. Males have very long nails on the forefeet and use them to stroke the face of the female during courtship. Nesting in Indiana is during early summer, with hatching in autumn. Adult turtles feed largely on water plants; the young eat insects and crustaceans.

If the midland painted turtle is not the most plentiful turtle in Indiana, it is the one most often seen. The smooth, dark shell with red pattern around the edges identifies it. Found throughout the state, it may live in any body of water except those that are very cold, swift, or deep. Often a dozen or so may be seen sunning on logs. Painted turtles are active from March well into November and nest during May and June. Hatchlings usually emerge in fall but sometimes overwinter in the nest. Painted turtles eat plant and animal food in about equal amounts.

Indiana's three largest salamanders are aquatic. The water dog or mudpuppy is brownish with black spots, averages 10 to 12 inches long, and has conspicuous bushy gills just behind the head. Mudpuppies once were common in larger streams and in the northern lakes such as Maxinkuckee, where they were accused, without much evidence, of being detrimental to fishing. They have been decreasing in numbers since about 1940 and are now uncommon, perhaps because of water pollution. Mudpuppies feed heavily in winter on small fish, fish spawn, crayfish, and insects. Clusters of eggs are attached to the undersides of submerged objects during early summer and hatch after six to eight weeks.

The hellbender is one of the world's largest salamanders, with a record length of 29 inches, although Indiana specimens are in the 15-to-20-inch range. It is a grotesque, flabby-looking animal with a wide head, wrinkled skin, and a prominent skin fold on each side. At the turn of the century, hellbenders were common in the larger, rocky tributaries of the Ohio and apparently were found locally in the river itself. They were feared as being venomous and generally were destroyed when encountered. About 1930 they began to disappear

Hellbenders are among the largest salamanders in the world. They are endangered in the state, the only known viable population being in the Blue River of southern Indiana.   *Photo by Sherman A. Minton*

and are now endangered in Indiana. Eggs are deposited in late summer under large rocks and attended by the male; they hatch in November. The young require several years to reach sexual maturity. Crayfish are the principal food of the hellbender, but fish, frogs, and large insects are occasionally eaten. Although they are not venomous, hellbenders will bite if sufficiently annoyed.

The 12-to-15-inch lesser siren is a most peculiar creature, resembling an eel with a pair of stubby legs located behind the head and its external gills. The siren prefers warm, quiet, shallow water with a mucky bottom and much aquatic vegetation. It is characteristic of cypress swamps, but is also found in northern Indiana swamps and lakes. If its habitat dries, it can survive by burrowing into mud. Little is known of its life cycle, but apparently eggs are laid in early spring. Sirens eat a variety of bottom-dwelling invertebrates, as well as earthworms and land insects that may be washed into their habitat.

For generations of American biologists and biology students, "the frog" has been the leopard frog, of which there are at least seven species in the U.S. Two are widespread in Indiana and formerly were very plentiful. These slender, long-legged frogs with body lengths of two to three inches are typically bright green with dark spots. Leopard frogs are most numerous in marshes, wet meadows, and open ponds but also inhabit creeks and inlets of larger streams and lakes. They breed in spring, usually from late March through April. Their voice is a series of guttural, chuckling notes, not unlike the clucking of chickens. During summer they may move into damp grassland or woods. Leopard frogs have been disappearing from many parts of North America since about 1970. In Indiana, for reasons unknown, the northern leopard frog has gone from very common to moderately rare, while the southern leopard frog remains common.

The one-inch cricket frog has warty skin and often shows a bright green or rusty midline stripe. They may be active in March, and begin breeding about May first. Their call is a series of sharp clicks increasing to a rattle. In proportion to their size, cricket frogs are the champion jumpers among local species. In contrast to larger frogs, if they land in water, they often leap or swim to shore immediately.

> Old croakers, deacons of the mire,
> That lead the deep, batrachian choir.
> —*Anonymous*

The bullfrog is the largest North American frog and one of the largest frogs in the world, sometimes reaching a body length of almost eight inches and weighing more than a pound. It is so named because of its deep, hoarse voice, which, to some, vaguely resembles a bull's bellow. The resonating *"jug o'rum, more rum"* of a dozen large bullfrogs in chorus around an Indiana pond on a July night is a sound of nature not easily forgotten.

Bullfrogs are olive-brown to green, sometimes with dark mottling; males have a yellow chin and throat. Indiana bullfrogs breed in late spring and early summer in permanent water. Up to two years are spent in the tadpole stage. A most voracious predator, the bullfrog will eat almost any creature it can swallow. Baby alligators and birds as large as towhees have been eaten. My brother shot a bullfrog in Texas that had eaten a 17-inch coral snake. Bullfrogs often eat other frogs, and have seriously depleted native species in some states where they have been introduced.

The green frog resembles the bullfrog but is smaller, rarely exceeding a body length of 3 ½ inches. It also breeds in late spring and early summer. Both of these frogs lay their eggs in a film at the surface of the water.

Bullfrogs and green frogs are common throughout Indiana, and do not seem to have been affected by whatever has caused popula-

Northern copperbelly snakes have striking color contrast above and below. They are most often found in certain southern Indiana wetlands.
Photo by Sherman A. Minton

tions of leopard frogs and some other species to decline in recent years. All local frogs are edible, but only the bullfrog and green frog are plentiful enough and have enough meat to make them worth hunting.

Several Indiana snakes live in or close to water. A traveler writing of the region near Vincennes about 1850 said: "I have seen on a very warm and bright day such numbers of water vipers twined round the limbs and trunks which margin the pond that it would be almost impossible to wade a yard without being in reach of one of them. They certainly have all the appearance of being venomous; the inhabitants say, however, they are harmless."

The banded watersnake is one of the most widely distributed and abundant Indiana reptiles, being found in almost all aquatic habitats. It is often called "water moccasin," and is frequently confused with the copperhead. It is a snake of moderate build, usually 25 to 40 inches long. Adults have dark brown to reddish crossbands on a paler background; the belly is cream to reddish with dark markings. Young are pale gray with blackish crossbands. These snakes tend to congregate where there are rocky ledges, old stone dams or bridge piers, stumps, and piles of drift; here the larger snakes often bask. Young are found under rocks or rubbish at the water's edge. Mating usually takes place during May, with litters of up to 50 young born in August or early September. Fish are their main food; frogs, toads, and salamanders are also taken. Large prey often is dragged out of the water before being swallowed. When cornered, banded watersnakes will flatten their bodies, strike, and bite.

The northern copperbelly is the largest Indiana watersnake, averaging 35 to 50 inches. Adults are dull black above and red to orange clouded with black below. Young resemble small banded watersnakes. This is a snake of swamps, sloughs, and shallow ponds, rarely found in streams or larger lakes. It has a curious distribution, being found in the southwestern tip of the state, the Muscatatuck lowlands, and a few localities in extreme northern Indiana. Copperbellies feed largely on frogs and salamanders, with fish eaten less frequently.

The venomous cottonmouth or water moccasin was not recorded in Indiana until 1983, although its presence in the southern part of the state had been suspected for more than a century. It is known only from a swamp in Dubois County, and an area near the junction of the Blue River with the Ohio. Typical habitat for the cottonmouth in the northwestern part of its range is a swamp or sluggish stream near a rocky bluff or hillside where the snakes hibernate. They eat a wide variety of small vertebrates. Small litters of young are born in late summer.

In the field, it is not easy to distinguish the cottonmouth from non-venomous watersnakes. Color of the inside of the mouth is pale in both venomous and non-venomous species, and is not diagnostic. When a cottonmouth is cornered, it does open its mouth in a threat gesture, something non-venomous snakes rarely do. The head of the cottonmouth is heavier and more strongly triangular than that of non-venomous snakes; at very close range the facial pits and elliptical pupils can be seen. Young cottonmouths are bronzy with darker crossbands, which become indistinct as the snakes darken with age. Adults are 35 to 55 inches long.

WOODLAND SALAMANDERS, GARDEN TOADS, AND VACANT-LOT SNAKES

Woods containing small rocky streams are typical habitat for the plethodont or lungless salamanders. The two-lined salamander is about 3 1/2 inches long and yellowish with a broad dark stripe on each side of its body. It is usually found under a rock or other object at the edge of water, and quickly wriggles away when disturbed. In the spring, the female attaches a disc-like mass of eggs to the underside of a stone resting in water. The stream must have at least a trickle of water throughout the year, for the larvae, which can be mistaken for tiny minnows, take up to two years to mature.

The cave salamander is orange with black dots and slender with a long tail. Adults live in the twilight zone near mouths of caves and often cling to the walls or roof. They may also be found in streams and wet places near caves. Eggs are attached to rocks in underground streams, and larvae may be found in pools deep within caves. In times when spring houses served as refrigerators for many southern Indiana families, these "red lizards" were often found on the walls and even in containers of food.

Although living in damp woods, five Indiana salamanders have divorced themselves from water. The best-known is the redbacked salamander, which can be found in woodlots throughout the state. It is about 3 1/2 inches long with a slender body and short legs. As its name suggests, many individuals have a broad red to orange stripe, but also common is a dark gray to brown phase with scattered flecking. These salamanders are rarely seen aboveground but may be numerous under rocks or logs. They mate in late autumn, and females lay their eggs the following summer, usually in a cavity within a decaying log or under a stone. Females remain with their eggs until they hatch in late summer or autumn. The little salamanders resemble adults and remain with their mother for a few days before they disperse.

The slimy salamander, typical of southern Indiana hills, is considerably larger (to 7 inches) and more robust than the other woodland salamanders. It is shiny black with a variable amount of white speckling and mottling. This salamander richly deserves its name, for if it is handled, it exudes a sticky, non-toxic secretion that is difficult to wash off. Eggs are laid in rotten wood or damp soil under rocks during early summer and hatch in the fall.

Toads are easily recognized by their stocky build and dry, warty skin. On the shoulder region are a pair of glands that secrete a creamy fluid containing powerful toxins that affect the heart and nervous system. Exuded only when the toad is badly stressed or injured, it is no threat to humans, but most warm-blooded predators, including cats and dogs, are effectively deterred. However, many species of snakes eat toads.

There are two species of toads in Indiana, both with nearly statewide distribution. They are quite similar, and young specimens may be almost impossible to identify. Moreover, they hybridize. However, typical specimens of the American toad have dark dorsal spots that enclose only one or two large warts and a mottled belly, while typical Fowler's toads have larger spots enclosing several smaller warts, and a white belly usually with a dark breast spot. Both species live in a wide variety of habitats and breed in collections of quiet water ranging from wheel ruts to edges of lakes. American toads begin calling about the end of March and have a prolonged, rather melodious trill; Fowler's toads begin about a month later and have a short, harsh trill. Both deposit long strands of eggs that hatch quickly. Tadpoles complete development in a month or two, emerging as little toads about the size of a housefly.

The spadefoot toad looks like a toad but belongs to a family of burrowing frogs found mainly in western North America. Its prominent eyes have vertical elliptical pupils. Spadefoots are known from only about a half-dozen localities in southern Indiana, but it is not known if this indicates genuine rarity, or the difficulty in finding these subterranean creatures that emerge only briefly at night to feed. Breeding is triggered by torrential rain during late spring and early summer; then the toads appear in large numbers to mate and lay their eggs in temporary pools. They have a loud call somewhat like the cawing of crows. If there is not suitable rain, the colony may skip breeding for a year, a pattern common among frogs of desert and semi-desert regions, but unusual for Indiana species.

Garter snake is a name often used for any small, nondescript snake, particularly one found near a house or garden. Of five Indiana species, the eastern or common is most widely distributed, plentiful, and variable. Typically it is dark brown with three light stripes. The midline stripe may be indistinct, and some southeastern Indiana specimens have no stripes, but are checkered. Adults average 22 to 30 inches; a very big female may slightly exceed 3 feet. Eastern garter snakes may be found almost anywhere, including urban vacant lots, but their favorite habitats are damp, open meadows and sparse forest bordering streams or lakes. They are unusually tolerant of cold, and sometimes may be seen sunning on mild winter days.

Garter snakes mate in both spring and fall, usually near their hibernaculum. Sometimes six or eight males may simultaneously court one female. Litters of 15 to 50 or so young are born in late July and early August. Eastern garter snakes eat a variety of small creatures, but frogs, toads, and earthworms make up most of their diet. Garter snakes often bite when picked up, and their teeth can draw blood. In rare cases there may be pain, swelling, and discoloration around the bitten area.

Two small relatives of garter snakes often are found in urban situations. A trash-strewn vacant lot bordering a small creek or pond is a much better place to look for Kirtland's snake than any unspoiled natural environment. Its range centers in Ohio, Indiana, and Illinois, and it is best known from populations in urban areas. Before there were vacant lots, it probably lived in wet meadows and margins of swamps, where it may occasionally be found today. Because its urban colonies are vulnerable, it is listed as threatened in Indiana and most other states where it occurs. Kirtland's snake is reddish brown with a red belly bordered by rows of black dots, and rarely is more than 18 inches long. It feeds almost entirely on earthworms.

Another little 11-to-15-inch snake of vacant lots and trash piles is the Midland brown snake, although it can be found in many other situations. It is grayish to reddish brown with dark markings that may form a "ladder-back" pattern. Most often seen on cool, sunny days, it eats slugs, snails, and earthworms.

STRAYS, ORPHANS, AND RARITIES

Every fauna has species that exist in small, scattered enclaves. Often they are holdovers from an era when landscape, climate, and vegetation were different. Sometimes they are the advance party of an invasion. Today they often reflect selective destruction of habitats by humans. Several reptiles, rare or unknown in other parts of the state, live in northwestern Indiana, which was largely prairie at the time of settlement.

The bull snake is the largest Indiana snake, sometimes reaching eight feet in the western part of its range. Bull snakes are yellow with a bold pattern of black and brown blotches. Their sharply pointed noses are an adaptation for tunneling through soft soil. In Indiana they are strongly restricted to sand prairie and spend much of their time underground. When cornered, they hiss loudly and do not hesitate to bite.

The fox snake resembles the bull snake, but has a rounded rather than pointed nose, and reaches a respectable five-foot length. The top of its head is often reddish, causing it to be confused with the copperhead. Fox snakes survive better than most snakes in intensively cultivated land. Both the fox snake and bull snake feed largely on small rodents and are of economic value, although they also eat ground-nesting birds and their eggs. Both species lay eggs.

A narrow fellow in the grass
Occasionally rides
You may have met him—did you not?
His notice sudden is,
The grass divides as with a comb,
A spotted shaft is seen;
And then it closes at your feet
And opens further on . . .
But I never met this fellow,
Attended or alone,
Without a tighter breathing
And zero at the bone.

—*Emily Dickinson, "A Narrow Fellow in the Grass"*

Fox snakes are beautifully marked and reach a large size but are no threat to humans. *Photo by Sherman A. Minton*

Two lizards are largely confined to the northwestern counties. The six-lined racerunner is a slender, long-tailed lizard with six yellow stripes on a dark background. Its minute granular dorsal scales distinguish it from skinks, which have larger, overlapping scales. Since it is the sole eastern representative of a large lizard genus characteristic of deserts of the western U.S. and Mexico, it is not surprising to find it in the desert-like environment of the Indiana dunes and sand prairies. It lives entirely on the ground and is active only in hot, sunny weather. It is very alert and a fast runner.

A lizard ran out on a rock and looked up, listening
no doubt to the sounding of the spheres.
And what a dandy fellow! the right toss of a chin for
you and swirl of a tail!
If men were as much men as lizards are lizards
they'd be worth looking at.

—*D. H. Lawrence, "Lizard"*

One of Indiana's oddest reptiles, the western ophisaur or glass lizard is a limbless, snake-like creature usually 20 to 30 inches long and light brown with darker stripes. However, it lacks the large belly scutes seen in all midwestern snakes and has external ear openings and movable eyelids, features never seen in snakes. Its tail, which makes up about two-thirds of its total length, breaks readily if the animal is restrained or injured. The broken pieces flip about, and often sufficiently distract a potential predator to allow the lizard to escape. The lizard then grows a new tail, not as long as the original. The ophisaur is an uncommon grassland reptile that is most active when temperatures are moderate to cool.

The crawfish or gopher frog is an unusual prairie species formerly found from Benton County south to Evansville. It is about the size of the green frog but heavier, and is light gray to yellowish with dark circular spots. It lives in burrows of the large chimney-building crayfish, which it rarely leaves except during a brief breeding season in late March and early April, when the frogs assemble in large, shallow ponds in open country. The loud, snoring call is distinctive. Common until about 1960, these frogs have decreased steadily and are listed as threatened in Indiana.

A few reptiles are characteristic of the wetlands that covered much of northern Indiana at the time of its settlement. Because this environment has largely been destroyed by drainage and agriculture, all of these species are threatened in the state. The spotted turtle is a typical example. At one time it was locally common throughout the lake plains, with disjunct populations found as far south as Indianapolis. A small turtle, it has an upper shell of deep brown to black with scattered yellow spots, and bright yellow to orange markings on the head. Spotted turtles prefer bogs and marshes but sometimes are found in ditches and sluggish streams. They spend a fair amount of time on land and often mate there during April or early May. Eggs are laid in June and presumably hatch in early fall.

Blanding's turtle is larger, with shell lengths of 6 1/2 to 9 inches. The upper shell is black to dark brown with small pale yellow dots. The long neck and bright yellow throat are distinctive. This turtle inhabits prairie ponds and marshes and the shallow margins of lakes. It often wanders about on land and frequently is killed on roads. Mating may occur in spring or fall, and eggs are laid in June. Young Blanding's and spotted turtles are very hard to find. This makes it difficult to know if these species are reproducing in localities where only an occasional adult is seen.

The massasauga is a small rattlesnake characteristic of prairie and wetlands and once found south at least to Hendricks County. It is a stocky snake usually 20 to 30 inches long, although exceptional individuals may reach 3 feet. Snakes of northwestern Indiana are

Spotted turtles are sometimes found in northern Indiana, but are listed as threatened in the state.   *Photo by Sherman A. Minton*

distinctly blotched; in northeastern Indiana, some adults become completely black, except for a white stripe on the side of the head. Massasaugas usually are found in wet places during spring and fall, and in drier habitats such as pastures and woods during summer. Limited evidence indicates a spring mating season, with litters of 5 to 14 young born in late August and early September. Meadow mice and other small rodents are the chief food of adult snakes; young eat frogs and small snakes. Massasaugas are as quick to strike as other rattlesnakes, and their venom is quite toxic. Fatal bites have been reported from Indiana in times past.

Two small snakes are known in Indiana only from the knobs near New Albany, where they are found in the open, rocky glades characteristic of this region. Disappearance of this habitat from natural forest succession and modification by human agency is reason to list these species as threatened in the state. Both are widely distributed in the Southeast.

The scarlet snake has a wedge-shaped head with pointed snout, wide red saddles on a pale background, and an unmarked white belly. It is a very secretive nocturnal snake, usually less than two feet long. A major part of its diet is reptile eggs. If an egg is too large to swallow, the snake slits the shell with its teeth, inserts its head, and eats the embryo and egg fluids.

The small crowned snake or blackheaded snake (to 12 inches) is slender and pale brown with a black head and black collar. It is a very secretive snake usually found under rocks. It feeds on centipedes and insect larvae. The crowned snake has minute fangs and may have venom but is far too small to inflict injury to a human.

The knobs country also is home for two salamanders typical of the Appalachians. The northern red salamander is known only from near New Albany. It resembles the cave salamander in color, and also lives in clear, cold streams near cave entrances, but is much stockier with a shorter tail. Eggs are laid in water, and there is an aquatic larval stage lasting about three years. The green salamander was not recorded from the state until 1993, when a population was discovered in Crawford County. This small, bright green salamander with darker mottling lives in moist rock crevices, where its eggs are laid in grape-like clusters which are attended by the female.

As mentioned often in this account, many of Indiana's amphibians and reptiles are now decreasing in numbers for reasons not well understood. Deliberate killing has almost eradicated rattlesnakes in Indiana; today both native species are protected. The larger non-venomous snakes still are sometimes killed on sight, but habitat

destruction, the use of pesticides, and roadkills have been more important in the decline of some snake populations. Many turtles are also killed by road traffic, and others are taken for food and for the pet trade.

A decline in amphibian populations of apparently global scope has been a concern to biologists in recent years. In some cases, this has involved populations remote from human contact or on protected land. Populations at high altitudes have particularly been affected, leading to a hypothesis that increased ultraviolet radiation associated with a decrease in the ozone layer may be involved. However, habitat destruction, acid rain, other environmental contaminants, disease, and introduction of non-native predators have probably played more important roles.

Indiana species most conspicuously involved have been the crawfish frog and northern leopard frog. The striped chorus frog in central and southern Indiana suffered a drastic loss in numbers in the early 1980s, but now (1995) seems to be staging a strong comeback. It is not always easy among amphibians and reptiles to distinguish natural population fluctuation from environmental catastrophe. These creatures are part of a web of life that has existed for millions of years and endured much attrition. Nevertheless, humankind would do well to avoid gratuitously unraveling the fabric.

Natures Poem

Oh Natures intersting I know
With animals frisking to and fro

A frog on a old roten log
Will eat plants in the bog
Thump, thup tump
Oh you scared him now hill jump

Snaky snaky swishy shine
Yol race in a crooked line
Swch swich swich
Go in that mudy dich

Turtle turtle with a hard shell
Don't fall in that deep deep well
Crawl crawl crawl
O turtle now you fell

Toad toad nice and browned
Catch the flys up on the ground
But try your best
Not to go in that birds nest

Lizard lizard with hard scales
There arn't all girls and there arn't all males
Toses you lay eggs just once a year
The yong ones you don't have to fear
Tere won't be all girls and there won't be all sons
There won't be just one and there won't be tons

Salamander salamander slimy and gay
Eat water plants and not thereshed hay
Thoo you may live not even a year
Enyemys you don't have to fear

O Natures intersting I know
With animals frisking to and fro.
    —*Brooks Rutherford Minton (age 8), November 1953*

The great horned owl is our most capable nocturnal bird of prey.   *Photo by Russell Mumford*

41. Wings across the Sky: Birds of Indiana

Russell E. Mumford

Look at this beautiful world, and read the truth
  In her fair page, see every season brings
New change to her of everlasting youth—
  Still the green soil, with joyous living things
Swarms—the wide air is full of joyous wings.

—*William Cullen Bryant*

Approximately 411 species of birds have been recorded from Indiana, and about 170 nest here. More than half of the state's total vertebrate species are birds. Many people will be surprised to learn that so many species have occurred in our small state. Some are very widespread and common; some were found once; a few are extinct; others no longer visit our area.

Nineteen of the 27 orders of birds (Class Aves) found worldwide are represented in the state list. By far the most important (with regard to numbers per order) is the Passeriformes, the perching bird group often called "songbirds," with some 169 species known from Indiana. There are 77 members of the order Charadriiformes (gulls, terns, shorebirds, etc.), 40 Anseriformes (ducks, geese, swans), and 22 Falconiformes (hawks, eagles, osprey, vultures, etc.). From 1 to 15 species are known here from each of the remaining orders.

Most of the common birds that people enjoy, feed, and see about their homes are passeriforms, of which about 100 species nest in Indiana. Among these familiar birds are the American robin, northern cardinal, blue jay, American goldfinch, gray catbird, house wren, eastern bluebird, chickadees, tufted titmouse, sparrows, warblers, red-winged blackbird, Baltimore oriole, and many more. The group provides much pleasure to birdwatchers and contains some of the most beautiful species in the United States. Most of the important game birds are in the orders Galliformes (quail, grouse, pheasant, turkey, etc.) and Anseriformes (the waterfowl).

The conditions under which organisms live in a particular area are continually changing; thus we can expect changes in their populations. This is true of Indiana birds. Numerous species have first appeared in the state since Amos W. Butler wrote *Birds of Indiana* in 1898; others have since disappeared. The way that humans use the land is the key to most recent (and future) changes in bird life. To maintain the greatest diversity of birds, we must preserve the greatest diversity and quality of habitats that support them.

Take the first step in ornithology and you are ticketed for the whole voyage. The thrill of delight that accompanies it, and the feeling of fresh, eager inquiry that follows, can hardly be awakened by any other pursuit.

—*John Burroughs*, Wake Robin (*1871*)

ACCOUNTS OF THE ORDERS OF INDIANA BIRDS

The loon order is represented by three species, of which the common loon is by far the most abundant. Loons are heavy-bodied water birds known for their diving and swimming ability underwater and their wild, ringing calls. They are considered to be among the most ancient of modern bird groups. Records indicate that the common loon last nested here in 1893. Loons are primarily fish-eating birds. During migration, large numbers have been observed about the southern end of Lake Michigan.

Five species of grebes occur; the pied-billed is the most common and the only one that nests here. Grebes also subsist mainly on fishes, and are commonly called "helldivers" by laypersons. Nests of the pied-billed are placed at the water's surface in emergent vegetation of marshes, ponds, and lake borders. In late fall and early winter, as many as 500 horned grebes have been seen in counties bordering Lake Michigan, and more than 200 pied-billed grebes have been seen in a single flock.

A band-rumped storm-petrel found at Martinsville in 1902 constitutes the only Indiana record for its order, Procellariiformes.

Pelicans, cormorants, gannets, and their allies are in the order Pelecaniformes. All are mainly fish-eating birds inhabiting water areas. The double-crested cormorant nested in Indiana until about 1953, but has since declined drastically in numbers. The last regular nesting site was in the cypress trees about the border of Hovey Lake (Posey County). Of the two pelicans that occur, the American white is by far the most regular and abundant; the brown can be considered an accidental wanderer to our state.

The order Ciconiiformes contains numerous interesting species, many of them tall, leggy waders, including herons, ibises, bitterns, flamingos, egrets, spoonbills, and storks. The most easily observed and largest heron in Indiana is the great blue, often called a "blue crane" in this region. It congregates to nest in colonies (rookeries) which may remain occupied for many years, often with numerous nests present in a single large tree. Among the species of the order that are mostly white are the great egret, little blue heron (immatures), cattle egret, and snowy egret. The cattle egret was first recorded in the state in 1964 and will probably eventually be found nesting here. In its native Africa, it associates with both domestic and wild animals (including elephants). It has been found with cattle and sheep in our state, accompanying the animals (even perching on their backs) to gather insects.

Another common heron is the green heron, a small bluish-green species often called "shitepoke" or "fly-up-the-crick," as it frequents streams and ditches. It may nest in a thicket some distance from water, but obtains most of its food near or in water. It is much more likely to be seen than two of its relatives, the American bittern and least bittern. Bitterns live in dense emergent vegetation (often cattails) about marshes and lake borders, where they nest. They are quite secretive and silent except in the courtship season. The strange sounds made by the male American bittern when courting are said to resemble those made by an old-fashioned wooden pump.

And, now and then, a wild bird flies
From hidden haunts among the reeds;
Or, faintly heard, a bittern cries
Across the tasseled water weeds;

Or, floating upward from the green
Young willow wands, with sunny sheen

The little blue heron is white when immature. Its diagnostic yellow feet do not show here.   *Photo by Michael Ray Brown*

Or pearly breast, and wings outspread,
A white crane journeys overhead.

    —*Evaleen Steen, "The Marshes," in* Indiana Poetry and
    Poets

Wood storks formerly visited Indiana, and one report exists of a roseate spoonbill. The black-crowned night-heron once nested in many rookeries scattered about central Indiana. It has decreased alarmingly, and no active rookeries are now known in the state. Its close relative the yellow-crowned night-heron frequents sloughs and streams, usually nesting in trees overhanging the water. One of its favorite foods is crayfish. As their names imply, both night-herons tend to be more nocturnal than other herons.

Most Hoosiers thrill at the sight of honking flocks of Canada geese passing over during spring and fall migrations. Waterfowl and their movements have always fascinated humans, who also expend much time and energy hunting them for sport. The order is thus the favorite group of birds for many, including birdwatchers. The common mallard is the wild ancestor of the various forms of domestic ducks now raised around the world. It is probably also the best-known of native waterfowl, along with the Canada goose. There are 32 species of ducks, 3 of swans, and 5 of geese known to have occurred in Indiana.

The large trumpeter swan, which once nested in the Kankakee River Valley, has been extirpated, but the tundra swan remains a fairly regular migrant. The mute swan, an exotic from Europe, has long been kept on private estates, in parks and zoos, and in other places.

The beautiful wood duck is a common nesting bird along Indiana streams and in other wooded areas. Nests are in tree cavities and may be a mile from water. The ducklings jump from the nest (at times more than 30 feet above the ground) after hatching and flutter to the ground. The female leads them to water, where they remain until able to fly. The overland journey from a dry-land nest site to available water renders the brood vulnerable to predators, accidents, automobiles, and other hazards.

Other ducks that regularly nest in the state are the mallard, blue-winged teal, and hooded merganser. The teal and mallard are much more abundant than the others. Hooded mergansers also nest in tree cavities or in nest boxes erected for them and the wood duck.

Several species of waterfowl have declined in numbers to alarming lows in recent years. Some of the deep-water ducks (canvasback, redhead) have been given protection from hunting from time to time. However, these fine ducks have been unable to reach their former abundance. Large flocks of canvasbacks are now seen in our state all too infrequently. The creation of reservoirs and lakes associated with power plants has aided diving ducks and other species. Shortly after the Gibson power plant was in operation, wintering canvasbacks gathered there to feed on small gizzard shad, a fish plentiful in the lake.

The Canada goose was a rare nesting bird in Indiana by the 1930s. When the Jasper-Pulaski Fish and Wildlife Area was created during that period, a small captive flock of these geese began nesting there. Other groups of nesting geese are now established throughout the state. Thus, the Canada goose has been successful and has increased its numbers to unexpected levels. Under some conditions it has even become a messy nuisance, and "problem" birds have been transported to wilder areas.

The regular migratory movements of large numbers of waterfowl are among the thrills of birdwatching, hunting, or casual observations in nature. Such a spectacle can easily be witnessed at the Jasper-Pulaski area in spring and fall. A viewing blind has been provided for visitors who come primarily to watch the greater sandhill cranes, but often large flocks of geese and ducks can be found there as well. Some of the rarer species of ducks appear most regularly along the southern end of Lake Michigan. In late fall and early winter, the old-squaw, king eider, harlequin duck, or all three species of scoters may be found. The Michigan City harbor is a popular birding spot that has provided many people with the opportunity to see rare and unusual water birds during the past 40 years. Although the day may be past when 3,000 old-squaws could be seen there in a day, there are still sufficient birds to make the site a must for birders.

Vultures and hawks have sometimes been looked upon unfavorably by the public. Poultry raisers formerly complained of losses of their birds to hawks. Hunters have blamed hawks (with no foundation in fact) for shortages of bobwhites, cottontails, etc. Eagles have even been considered a threat to small children. And the sight of vultures feeding on dead animals is repulsive to many persons. In short, birds of prey (order Falconiformes) did not have a good press in earlier years. In light of more research and the dissemination of knowledge to the public, our view of these interesting birds has changed, and most people do not now consider them "bad" or dangerous to our interests. The persecution of hawks, eagles, and owls was long-standing. In the 1940s and 1950s, it was not uncommon to find dead birds of these groups hanging on fences or barn walls throughout the state. Their killers displayed such "trophies" and considered themselves justified in shooting or trapping any bird of prey they saw. Today these birds are all protected (some by federal laws).

The bald eagle's huge stick nests, used year after year, were sometimes familiar landmarks. From 1897 until 1990, no successful nests were known for Indiana. The Department of Natural Resources program aimed at reestablishing the bald eagle as a nesting species

The wood duck, which nests in Indiana in tree cavities near water, is likely our most-loved waterfowl.
Photo by Lee Casebere

resulted in a successful nest in 1991. In general, our national bird has had tough times but now appears to be showing signs of increasing its low populations, which were brought about by DDT poisoning and illegal shooting. The major food of this spectacular bird is fish, but it also eats other animals (both live and dead) and frequents water areas that attract numbers of water birds and provide fishes. Golden eagles also visit Indiana.

Our most common large hawk is the red-tailed, usually seen perched in a tree at the border of a wooded area, on a utility pole, or in an isolated (often dead) tree in a field. Here it watches for potential prey, then glides down to capture food first detected by its remarkable eyesight. A wide variety of food is eaten, including mice, voles, birds, rabbits, snakes, other animals, and carrion.

> The Red-tailed Hawk's shrill *Kee-er-r-r* attracts our attention to its circling flight over . . . its favorite haunts. It is a slow-moving species. Frequently it is seen perched on a tree look-out where it watches for the small quadrupeds, especially mice, which form its principal food.
>
> —*T. Gilbert Pearson, ed.,* Birds of America *(1917)*

A small, colorful hawk may sometimes be seen perched along roadsides on telephone wires or posts. This is the American kestrel (once called the sparrow hawk), a small falcon. In summer it eats many large insects and earthworms, but also takes mice, voles, smaller birds, and other animal material. It is widely distributed throughout the state and may be locally common in winter in parts of southwestern Indiana. It nests in tree cavities (or nest boxes) and may even inhabit vacant lots and waste areas within the city limits of large towns. One method of hunting is to hover over a likely spot before diving down to grasp an unwary vole or shrew.

Some hawk migrations, especially in the fall, can be quite spectacular. At certain places around the state, hawks regularly pass in some numbers when conditions are right. Broad-winged hawks travel in flocks, which pass over in fall, circling, milling, but drifting southward. Other species migrate as individuals, although dozens may pass a given point in a day. Rough-legged hawks arrive in the fall, stay for the winter, and depart in spring. These big birds may be found in open areas, foraging over fallow fields and other habitats harboring mice and voles. From time to time a hunting bird may hover in the air, a behavior not usually seen in other large hawks.

The magnificent peregrine falcon, formerly called the duck hawk, is a powerful flier and can easily overtake and capture any prey it chooses. Most of its food consists of birds taken on the wing; some of the captures are fascinating to watch, and one must marvel at the speed and grace of the hawk as it plucks a duck from the sky. The peregrine has gone through numerous years of low populations, but hopefully will be able to recover somewhat in the near future. It was another of those unfortunate species that felt the effects of DDT poisoning, which caused lowered reproduction in the birds. Birders do not forget the day they see their first peregrine falcon, and each subsequent observation is another thrill. The Department of Natural Resources has been releasing birds to establish a breeding population. Successful nesting was reported in 1989.

The chicken-like birds have not fared too well in Indiana. Originally there were the wild turkey, ruffed grouse, greater prairie-chicken, and northern bobwhite. All were hunted for food and sport. The turkey and grouse were forest-inhabiting species, once widespread throughout the timbered regions. But humans eliminated the turkey around 1900. Its size and desirability as a food item caused it to be a common target for the pioneer settler and hunter. Pioneers

The peregrine falcon, with prey at the Indiana Dunes, is listed as state endangered, but breeding pairs have been successfully reintroduced on tall buildings in major Indiana cities. *Photo by Delano Z. Arvin*

could sometimes stand in the doors of their cabins and shoot wild turkeys. As the vast forested areas of Indiana were cleared, much habitat was destroyed. Further encroachment by humans finally wiped out this fine fowl. The ruffed grouse nearly met the same fate but was able to persist in isolated areas in the south-central hill region, where it was quite rare by about 1930.

Several attempts were made to reintroduce turkeys, but all failed until the late 1950s. Perhaps by then the habitat was more suitable for the bird, or the introduced stock more adaptable to Indiana conditions. Today, turkey are common in many areas, are still being restocked in new sites, and have been hunted legally since 1970. Ruffed grouse were also restocked in a few counties in southern Indiana about 1951. The ultimate fate of these released birds is obscure, but later the grouse did enjoy a tremendous increase in numbers (again, possibly the result of favorable habitat development). Grouse are now doing well and have been hunted since 1965, after a closed season in force nearly 30 years.

Two foreign birds, released throughout the state beginning in 1899, were the gray (Hungarian) partridge and the ring-necked pheasant. It was found that the pheasant was particularly well suited to northwestern farmlands and the partridge to eastern and central Indiana. The partridge population decreased greatly by 1960, and the species has evidently not been reported from the state since about 1977. Thus, the cycle of establishment to extirpation was about 80 years. It is generally felt that changing land use was the key to the fate of the partridge. The pheasant has undergone highs and lows in population size. Various releases were made and several genetic varieties of pheasants were introduced in hopes of finding one more adaptable to Indiana conditions. An estimated 2 million pheasants were released statewide from 1899 to 1962. The severe winters of the late 1970s killed many of the birds in northwestern Indiana, along with the northern bobwhites there.

There were an estimated 1,000 greater prairie-chickens in Indiana in 1941. Legal hunting had ceased in 1937. But the pressures of cash grain farming and other intensive land uses detrimental to the species caused a rather steady decline until the last was seen in 1972. This grand bird of the prairies required fairly large expanses of native grasses. As the Indiana prairies were plowed, the prairie-chicken could no longer survive here.

The sights and sounds of 75 courting male prairie-chickens on a booming ground at dawn in April was a spectacular experience enjoyed by few people. I was fortunate enough to be one of those persons while conducting research on the prairie-chicken for five years. Many mornings were spent in a blind, usually entered well before daylight. The cold, cramped quarters and blustery wind sweeping across the prairie were soon forgotten as the males began assembling to court. Some walked onto the area; others flew in and alighted directly upon the courting arena.

> On frosty spring mornings, as the sun rises over the prairies, one may at times hear a singular, resonant, booming note *boom-ah-b-o-o-m, boom-ah-b-o-o-m*. It is the love-song of the Prairie Hen. He may be near at hand or possibly two miles away, so far does this sound, unobstructed by tree or hill, carry in the clear air.
>
> —*Frank M. Chapman, "The Love-making of the Prairie Chicken," in Pearson,* Birds of America

Booming grounds were usually established where the grasses were rather short, and frequently the site was on top of a slight rise (or knoll) in the prairie. Each male displayed in, and protected from other males, a small portion of the grounds; this was his territory, into which he attempted to entice females for mating. As each male took his place and began courting in earnest, the resulting calls, dancing, wing flapping, jumping, chasing, foot stomping, etc., resulted in an exhibition difficult to describe adequately, but a show worth the effort, cold fingers and toes, and loss of sleep to witness time after time. When a female appeared on the booming ground, each male courted more diligently. If a male tried to follow the female into the territory of another male, he was immediately met by the latter and usually forced to return to his own site.

A foraging northern harrier would cause the birds to cease their display and crouch lower to the ground. If the hawk happened to fly over the booming ground, some of the prairie chickens might flush and fly long distances. One mid-April morning a flock of 50 golden-plover flew in and lit among the courting prairie chickens—a memorable sight seen only once. On the edge of one of the booming grounds in Newton County, a small iron bridge spanned a drainage ditch. A colony of barn swallows built their nests on the steel I-beams supporting the bridge floor. An inspection of the nests revealed that most of the birds had used prairie-chicken feathers in the nest linings.

The Gruiiformes are represented in Indiana by the sandhill crane, common moorhen (formerly the Florida gallinule), purple gallinule, American coot, and several species of rails (king, Virginia, sora, yellow, black). In earlier years, the whooping crane visited the state on a regular basis. By far the most visible and noisy member of the above group is the sandhill crane. It is a stately bird with a wild, loud trumpet-like call and can be seen in large numbers each fall and spring at the Jasper-Pulaski Fish and Wildlife Area near Medaryville, a staging area for migrants between their summer and winter areas. Only a few cranes now nest in the state; from 1939 to 1982 we had no verified nesting record.

The American coot is probably known to more persons than any other species of the group. It is distributed throughout the state, sometimes in large numbers on some lakes. Many know it by the vernacular name "mud hen." Huge flocks once gathered during spring and fall migrations on larger lakes such as Manitou, Maxinkuckee, and Wolf, where hunters came each year and harvested tremendous numbers.

> If there is a more amusing bird anywhere, I should like to see it . . . their odd ways make one laugh, and I recommend the funny Coot as an antidote for the "blues."
>
> —Herbert J. Job

Rails and gallinules are secretive marsh inhabitants that most persons hear but do not see. It took many years for ornithologists to sort out and identify the numerous calls of the various species. These unidentified and mysterious sounds coming from a marsh at dusk were challenging as to their origin. Rails are especially adapted for living in rather dense vegetation where visibility is often poor. Their bodies are flattened laterally, giving them a narrow shape that allows them to move about more easily between emerging plant stems. This type of body has led to the expression "thin as a rail." In the marsh, they stealthily forage for food in the shallow water and soft mud, coming out to the edges of plant cover mostly at dawn and dusk—the best times to see rails.

By far the most common and easiest to observe is the sora, whose numbers appear large at times during migration. But these numbers are usually implied by the calls, rather than by direct sightings. The presence of soras in a marsh in spring can be easily determined by some type of loud, sharp noise—such as clapping the hands, slam-ming a car door, striking a canoe paddle on the water, or throwing a stone into the marsh. Birds within hearing distance will frequently call; this call, in turn, is taken up by birds farther away and relayed across the marsh.

Rails, coots, moorhens, and gallinules can still be hunted, but only coots are harvested in large numbers by Hoosier hunters. Coots are more easily found, tend to form large flocks on open waters, are easier to hunt, and are large enough to furnish some meat for the table.

The numerous gulls, terns, sandpipers, and other members of the order Charadriiformes are interesting species. Some (American woodcock, common snipe) are game birds. Many other sandpipers and plovers were hunted before game regulations gave them needed protection. The lesser golden-plover was once abundant on the prairies of northwestern Indiana, and today, flocks totaling several thousand may still be seen on an April day during spring migration. Flocks sometimes follow farmers when they are plowing, and for some years after the birds were taken from the game-bird list, a few farmers carried a shotgun on the tractor with them during spring plowing operations. A nice mess of fat plovers was frequently shot this way.

In the late 1800s, the wet prairies around Chalmers (White County) attracted hordes of waterbirds. Hunters came from Chicago, Cincinnati, and other places to hunt there in the spring. Birds and other game shot were often salted and packed in barrels, then shipped by train to markets in Chicago. Many such shipments were sent from Francesville. Among the now-rare shorebirds shot were the Eskimo curlew (thought to be extinct today), marbled godwit, and long-billed curlew. An Eskimo curlew was shot by a Cincinnati hunter near Chalmers on 15 March 1879. Another specimen was reportedly taken there 19 April 1880.

> The Eskimos once waited for the soft, tremulous, far-carrying chatter of the Eskimo curlew flocks and the promise of tender flesh that chatter brought to the Arctic land. But the great flocks no longer come. Even the memory of them is gone and only the legends remain. For the Eskimo curlew, originally one of the continent's most abundant game birds, flew a gantlet of shot each spring and fall, and, flying it, learned too slowly the fear of

A prairie nester, the upland sandpiper (plover), is endangered in Indiana.
Photo by Delbert Rust

the hunter's gun that was essential of survival. Now the species lingers on precariously at extinction's lip.

—*Fred Bodsworth,* Last of the Curlews *(1954)*

The most familiar shorebird species in Indiana today is the killdeer, which frequents pastures, crop fields, roadsides, airports, pond, marsh, or lake borders, and streams. Nests are on the ground, usually on a gravel, pebble, or cinder surface. There is one report of a recent nest on the flat-topped, graveled roof of a building.

To see a variety of gulls, terns, and other charadriiforms, one should visit the southern end of Lake Michigan at various times of the year. The ring-billed gull and herring gull are by far the most common species of gulls found there throughout the year. But numerous rare and unusual gulls have also been recorded in the area. Large tern concentrations are also present at some seasons. Jaegers appear mostly in the fall, and are more likely to be found there than any other place in Indiana. Among the interesting shorebirds of the region are the purple sandpiper, red phalarope, American avocet, and marbled godwit.

Indiana has few native species of pigeons and doves. The mourning dove, a relative of the now-extinct passenger pigeon, is a common bird that has adapted to nearly all habitats. It is a familiar roadside species and also nests about human habitations and frequents bird feeding stations. Doves have a long breeding season (February to November), with some pairs raising four or five broods of young a season. Large flocks congregate in the fall, and many doves migrate to states bordering the Gulf of Mexico in fall. Waste grain, bird feeders, livestock feedlots, and other sources of food allow many doves to remain all winter.

The state once had its share of passenger pigeons. The birds gathered on migration at various sites, such as French Lick, New Harmony, and others. On 5 June 1817, William Corbett visited the former locality and wrote that a large wooded area appeared dead, for the leaves were all brown and branches were broken from recent use by multitudes of pigeons. When the last captive, a female named Martha, died in 1914 in the Cincinnati Zoo, the chapter was closed on a species whose numbers were once calculated to be in the billions.

The little common ground dove and the band-tailed pigeon are accidental visitors. Our other resident pigeon, the barnyard or domestic pigeon (properly called a rock dove), has obviously been very successful since its introduction from Europe. It has become a persistent pest in many places, namely in cities and around human dwellings, but some of the birds now nest in wild areas such as beneath bridges, on cliffs, and around abandoned stone quarries. Numerous overpasses along Indiana interstate highways now support one or more pairs of resident pigeons.

The history of the order of parrots in Indiana is of interest. Formerly we had the Carolina parakeet, a colorful wild parrot found mostly in the southern part of the state until about 1859. The species is now extinct throughout its range. The birds were gregarious and noisy, according to early travelers who observed them in our state. They were said to be fond of eating cocklebur seeds. In 1969, the exotic monk parakeet (an escape from captivity) appeared in Indiana. Several nests were reported, but no one appears to have a record of success in raising young from them.

The yellow-billed and black-billed cuckoos are members of the order Cuculiformes. Cuckoos are slender, brownish birds with secretive habits and low-pitched (sometimes rather guttural) calls. They are among the few birds which seem to relish eating hairy tent caterpillars, whose unsightly webs ("tents") are often found on black walnut or wild black cherry trees. Some persons call the cuckoos "rain crows" because of an old belief that their mournful songs predicted rain. Shiny, blackish relatives of the cuckoos, called anis, have been observed at least three times in Indiana.

Of the 11 species of owls reported from Indiana, 8 are regular residents or migrants. The other 3 (hawk-owl, burrowing owl, great gray owl) are quite rare, and only the burrowing owl can now be reasonably expected to occur here. The snowy owl is a winter visitor. The remaining species that nest in the state are the barn-, screech-, barred, great horned, long-eared, short-eared, and saw-whet. The snowy is the largest, and the saw-whet the smallest.

Barred owls are often called "hoot owls" or "eight hooters" because of their noisy hooting during spring courtship, and at other times of the year to a lesser degree. One is not likely to soon forget the barred owl's call—a series of notes in a cadence that resembles the words *"who cooks for you; who cooks for you all."* This species is most at home in the bottomland woods and swamps, but may be found in drier, wooded habitats. In the dim crepuscular light of dusk, it may be seen perched along roadways that pass through timberlands; its soft color, dark eyes, and rounded head are then best seen to advantage.

The other common large owl in the state is the great horned owl, a powerful predator capable of killing a turkey. Its call is a series of about five low notes and is rather monotonous compared to the barred owl's call. Great horned are also owls of the forest, but may be found in towns and small, isolated upland woodlots. The conspicuous ear tufts give the species its name. It is an early nester, sometimes laying eggs in January. It does not construct its own nest, but uses old nests of hawks or crows or cavities in hollow trees. Where trees are scarce, as in more western states, it may nest in the banks of deep erosion gullies or in rocky outcrops. Great horned owls have been known to take over bald eagle nests for their own. Some of the larger owls, including the great horned, may kill and eat smaller owls.

When he heard the owls at midnight,
Hooting, laughing in the forest,

Saw-whet owls are our tiniest species of owl and one of the most approachable.   *Photo by Delano Z. Arvin*

"What is that?" he cried in terror
"What is that," he said, "Nokomis?"
And the good Nokomis answered:
"That is but the owl and owlet,
Talking in their native language,
Talking, scolding at each other.
—*Longfellow, "Hiawatha's Childhood," in* The Song of
Hiawatha *(1855)*

Owls have always been sort of mystery birds of the night. There is considerable folklore regarding them, and (as with some other nocturnal creatures—the bats especially) numerous misconceptions have arisen about these interesting birds. However, some of the true characteristics of owls are as astounding as those of fancy. Owls have a generally silent flight, an adaptation for aiding their capture of alert rodents and other prey in the dark. The leading edges of their wings have feathers with a roughened edge of barbules, which muffles the sound of air passing over the front wing surface. This enables owls to fly more silently than most other birds. Some owls can catch living mice in essentially total darkness.

Owls' ears are large and asymmetrical in position on the sides of the head. Sounds are received unevenly by the two ears, thus allowing the owl to determine the direction of its prey. The outer edge of the ruff surrounding the owl's eye covers the large, internal ear openings. By changing the position of the ruff, the owl can regulate how sound is received by the ears. This allows the bird to determine the direction of a sound; mammals must move their external ears about to do the same.

Another fascinating owl characteristic is the casting (regurgitating) of pellets composed of bones, fur, feathers, etc., ingested when feeding. These materials are not digestible, but are compacted in the stomach, then "coughed up" by the owls to eliminate them from the digestive tract. Owls are not the only birds that cast up pellets; some hawks, gulls, swifts, grouse, and goatsuckers (whip-poor-will relatives) also have this ability. To enable scientists to determine what owls eat, pellets can be collected beneath roosting sites and analyzed to determine what prey items are in them. Much of the food of owls is made up of mice and voles, whose skeletal remains from pellets can be identified to species.

The barn-owl is found throughout the world and has numerous vernacular names. It is sometimes called the "monkey-faced owl" because of its peculiar heart-shaped face and dark eyes. In past years, many barn-owls in Indiana lived in barns and other buildings. But old barns, silos, abandoned buildings, and hollow trees (all nesting sites) are now much less abundant. The barn-owl has declined drastically in the state, and nesting boxes are now being furnished for them.

The most abundant owl in the state is the little eastern screech-owl, found in urban, suburban, and wild areas, wherever it can find nesting and roosting sites. It lives mostly in tree cavities, but also uses buildings and nesting boxes. The quavering, whistling call (not a screech) may be heard nearly any time of the year. Surprising numbers of screech-owls may live in towns where there is an abundance of old shade trees with natural cavities. Some Indiana screech-owls are mainly reddish in color; others are mostly grayish. These color phases may occur in the same brood, and in some localities reddish ones may be more common, with the reverse true in other areas.

The owl as an art object can be traced to antiquity. Owl motifs are present among Egyptian tomb paintings, on early Greek coins, and on early Chinese pottery.

Two members of the order Caprimulgiformes, the whip-poor-will and chuck-will's-widow, repeat their names persistently when singing on warm spring and summer evenings. They are nocturnal and feed on insects taken on the wing. During courtship, a male whip-poor-will may repeat his call hundreds of times, with little pause between calls, much to the consternation of campers in wooded regions.

Where the deep and misty shadows float
In forest's depths is heard thy note.
Like a lost spirit, earthborn still,
Art thou, mysterious whip-poor-will.
—*Marie Le Baron*

A third member of the group is the common nighthawk, sometimes called a bull-bat. Nighthawks nest today mostly on the flat gravel-topped roofs of buildings (rarely on the ground). Most Indiana towns probably support at least one pair in summer. The birds forage over city streets for insects attracted to street lights. Nighthawks are more diurnal than whip-poor-wills or chuck-will's-widows, and large numbers may be seen in migration during any part of the day, at times just ahead of approaching storms.

The order Apodiformes, translated to mean "without feet," contains the hummingbirds and chimney swift. These birds have feet, of course, but they are of limited use and very small. The ruby-throated hummingbird is the species normally found in Indiana. The small size of the hummingbird, and the fact that it is a warm-blooded organism, makes it necessary for the bird to feed throughout most of the daylight hours to enable it to obtain sufficient food to maintain its body temperature. In fact, during cooler weather, and at night, the birds may go into a type of torpor, to decrease their energy demands until daylight. Yellow, orange, or red flowers appear most attractive to the hummingbird, which feeds by hovering at the flowers and inserting its long tongue into the corolla to extract nectar. In early September, groups of hummers gather to feed on the flowers of jewel-weed. Some birds cross the Gulf of Mexico to reach their winter homes—a remarkable feat for such a small bird.

The chimney swift is well named, for it nests and roosts mainly in chimneys. In pre-settlement times, it probably nested in hollow trees and possibly on cliff faces. We know of only a few cases of its nesting in hollow trees in Indiana during the past hundred years. The nest is constructed of dead twigs fastened together (and to the nest supports) with a sticky saliva secreted by the swifts. Suitable twigs are gathered by the birds as they fly about the crown of a dead tree breaking off twigs with their beak.

Hundreds of swifts congregate in the fall for migration, roosting each evening in suitable chimneys. Stiffened tail feathers help support the birds as they cling to the inside of chimneys with their feet.

The belted kingfisher is the only member of the order Coraciiformes in the state. It is a striking bird, with a large, shaggy crest, rattling call, and fish-catching habits. A resident throughout the year, it can usually be found along streams, about lakes or ponds, and along ditches—wherever it can find small fish to eat. Foraging birds perch above the water and dive into it to catch fish in their beaks, or hover in flight, then dive after prey. Nests are built in tunnels dug by the birds into vertical banks and may be some distance from water.

Nine species of woodpeckers have been found in Indiana. They range in size from the common little downy to the extinct ivory-billed, a large black and white species probably never found here in numbers. Male woodpeckers have some red on the head; females may or may not have such markings. Both sexes of the familiar red-headed woodpecker have completely red heads, but immatures have dusky heads.

Woodpeckers spend much time gleaning food from the bark of trees and are adapted for climbing on tree trunks and branches by

The chuck-will's-widow. Camouflaged adult on nest, eggs, and chicks.
Photos by Delano Z. Arvin

feeding on them. During flicker migrations, usually in April and October, dozens of the birds may gather in pastures and other grassy areas.

> The woodpecker pecked out a little round hole
> And made him a house in the telephone pole
> One day when I watched he poked out his head
> And he had on a hood and a collar of red.
>
> And when the streams of rain pour out of the sky,
> And the sparkles of lightning go flashing by,
> And the big, big wheels of thunder roll,
> He can snuggle back in the telephone pole.

> —*Elizabeth Madox Roberts, "The Woodpecker," in*
> Treasury of Life and Literature (1930)

All woodpeckers excavate nesting and roosting holes in trees, stumps, posts, and telephone poles. At times they peck holes in house siding. One lady reported a downy woodpecker pecking holes in her house, then storing sunflower seeds in the holes. In some parts of the country, the large pileated woodpecker damages utility poles by its persistent boring of holes in them. Part of the spring courtship behavior of male woodpeckers is a fast pecking (drumming) on hollow tree limbs or metal objects, such as transformers or rain guttering. Homeowners are frequently awakened by the clatter at dawn on spring mornings when a northern flicker chooses to use a downspot to attract a mate. The red-headed woodpecker is highly migratory in some years, when winter food is in short supply. In years of a good mast (nuts, seeds, acorns, berries) crop, more of the birds remain and may be locally common. They are often attracted to supplies of beechnuts or pecans.

The pileated woodpecker has staged a remarkable comeback from several decades ago, when it was thought to be on the verge of extirpation from Indiana. It seems to be particularly common in parts of Brown County, where a friend observed 14 at the same time from his window.

Most of the woodpeckers can be attracted to feeders in winter by suet. The many holes constructed by various woodpeckers are important for other wildlife species. Among birds that use such cavities are the American kestrel, screech-owl, crested flycatcher, tree swallow, both species of nuthatches, both chickadees, titmouse, house wren, house sparrow, European starling, bluebird, and prothonotary warbler. Squirrels, mice, bats, snakes, frogs, lizards, and insects also find homes in abandoned woodpecker holes.

The remainder of the birds found in Indiana belong to the order of songbirds, Passeriformes. This is a quite diverse assemblage and contains the following groups, among others: flycatchers, larks, swallows, jays and crows, chickadees and titmice, nuthatches, creepers, wrens, mimic thrushes (mockingbirds, etc.), thrushes, gnatcatcher, pipits, waxwings, shrikes, starling, vireos, warblers, weaver finches, blackbirds and orioles, tanagers, finches, and grosbeaks.

One of the tragedies of modern bird conservation is the lack of knowledge concerning the cause of declines of certain species. Why are some birds virtually gone from an area which appears to still have suitable habitat? A case in point is the Bewick's wren. In the later 1940s and early 1950s, this wren was common in southern Indiana. It frequented the vicinity of houses and could be heard singing in numerous towns (Brazil, Corydon, Freetown, Brownstown, Houston, Stone Head). The appearance of a Bewick's wren today is nearly a thing of the past.

Another songbird that was formerly not uncommon along roadsides is the loggerhead shrike. A predatory species, it eats insects, small mammals, small birds, snakes, and other prey. We used to

having strong feet and tail feathers with stiffened tips. Another important adaptation is a strong, chisel-like beak for pecking holes in both living and dead trees. Much of the food of woodpeckers consists of insects, but berries, seeds, fruits, nuts, and other items are eaten by the various species. The yellow-bellied sapsucker drills hundreds of shallow holes in the bark and phloem layers of trees. As tree sap wells up and fills these depressions, the birds drink the sap (and capture insects attracted to it). The sap wells of this sapsucker can be seen on Scotch pine, tuliptree, apple, river birch, and other species of trees. The northern flicker, often called the "yellow hammer," is fond of ants and spends considerable time on the ground

Blue-gray gnatcatcher in its lichen-covered nest, which resembles the ruby-throated hummingbird's.
Photo by Delano Z. Arvin

The ruby-throated hummingbird is our smallest bird species.
Photo by Delano Z. Arvin

The yellow-throated warbler is beautiful in its spring plumage.
Photo by Delbert Rust

Woodpeckers (hairy shown here) have two toes fore and two aft for clinging, and stiff tail feather barbs for support.
Photo by Delano Z. Arvin

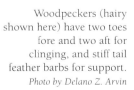

watch for its appearance in the prairie regions of the state about the first week of April. Most birds were seen on utility wires or fences, and nests were built in shrubby bushes along a fence, or in an Osage-orange fencerow. Old or unkept pastures or fields grown up to scattered clumps of hawthorn trees and other shrubs were also good places to find this shrike. Its presence around trees with thorns and about barbed wire fences is utilitarian. It impales its prey on thorns or other sharp objects. Today it is difficult to find except in the southern one-third of the state.

One of the indications of how land use has affected bird life throughout the countryside is the change in species composition of birds one observes along roadsides. The eastern meadowlark was formerly quite numerous in the open farmland of Indiana. For example, the number counted between Greencastle and Lafayette on trips on 13, 20, and 27 May 1946 was 39, 54, and 39, respectively. This same route driven many times within the past 20 years reveals that fewer than 10 are now seen. Changes in land use appear to be one of the major reasons for the decline of this field bird. There are now fewer pastures, hayfields, and fallow fields.

The common summer roadside bird today is the red-winged blackbird, which was seldom encountered in 1946. In fact, away from the more forested areas of Indiana, the red-winged blackbird is the most common bird now seen along roads except in winter. It has adapted to a life in drier habitats than formerly, when it was largely confined to cattail marshes, wet areas along ditches, lake borders, etc. The changing habits of this blackbird has enabled it to enjoy a tremendous increase in numbers and to even become a widespread pest.

> Again the blackbirds sing; the streams
> Wake, laughing from their winter dreams,
> And tremble in the April showers
> The tassles of the maple flowers.
>
> —*John Greenleaf Whittier*

Another familiar bird of the roadsides is the indigo bunting. Males are conspicuous, sing from about 1 May to about 1 October, and are usually most abundant around the borders of fallow fields or along roads paralleled by a fence with brambles, woody sprouts, and weeds growing alongside.

The dickcissel may be a common bird some summers and nearly absent in others. Males like to sing from utility wires, and this sparrow-sized bird, which looks like a diminutive meadowlark, is sometimes easily observed from a motor vehicle. But there are years when the birds fail to return to a particular area; this type of population fluctuation has been noted for many years.

Great numbers of European starlings are often seen today along Indiana highways and roadsides, where they feed on spilled grain and other seeds. Starlings may be observed all year; flocks of youngsters able to fly begin forming in June. Throughout the late summer, fall, and winter, large flocks may be seen; some of these gatherings roost in places where their noise and droppings are a nuisance.

The adaptable starling will likely be with us for a long time. Its aggressive nature enables it to compete successfully for nesting sites with many hole-nesting native birds—even flickers. This objectionable habit has caused many birdwatchers much concern and has led to the shooting of starlings by persons wishing to have more desirable birds nesting near their homes. All in all, bringing the starling to North America was a huge mistake. It has become the most commonly observed roadside bird in winter.

The American crow is a survivor and has adapted today to much different conditions from those around 1900. Some roosts at that time were estimated to contain 300,000 birds. The crow was considered a pest; crow shoots were common, and bounties were paid for dead birds. Although these activities appear to have had little effect on crow populations, the destruction of nesting and roosting habitats caused a drastic decline. Woody fencerows, woodlots, and riverine trees were prime nesting sites. The species was placed on the game bird list in Indiana to give it protection. During the past decade or two, crows have moved into cities, parks, cemeteries, and other urban areas. This is a departure from earlier years when the birds were really more at home in the countryside.

Perhaps nearly every Hoosier knows the cardinal ("redbird"), for it has been our state bird since 1933. It is found in many habitats and especially near human dwellings. Winter flocks gather in weedy, brushy areas along streams and other places where food is abundant. Delano Z. Arvin once counted 45 cardinals at his feeder near Buck Creek. The cardinal was a rare species in much of northern Indiana (especially northwest) around 1900, and is still most numerous in the southern half. The male feeds the female during courtship. With its bright plumage, loud and pleasing song, and affinity for living near humans, it will always be one of Indiana's favorite songbirds. Before laws prohibited it, cardinals sold in the state for two dollars a pair and were kept as cage birds.

> Swept lightly by the south wind
> The elm leaves softly stirred,
> And in their pale green clusters
> There straightway bloomed a bird!
>
> His glossy feathers glistened
> With dyes as richly red
> As any tulips blooming
> From out the garden bed.
>
> But ah, unlike the tulips,
> In joyous strain, ere long,
> This redbird flower unfolded
> A heart of golden song!
>
> —*Evaleen Stein, "The Redbird," in* Indiana Arbor and Bird Day Annual for the Schools of Indiana *(1902)*

The eastern bluebird has long been a favorite of many people because of its bright colors and pleasing song. But numbers fluctuate greatly, and in years when populations are small, many think the bluebird is becoming rare. Actually, from time to time large numbers are killed by severe winter or unusually cold spring weather. Such events happened in 1894–95, 1959–60, and 1976–77, 1977–78, and 1978–79. In intervening years the population increases. Early settlers saw bluebirds nesting in their orchards or in the numerous rotting stumps left from the clearing of the forest. Amos W. Butler called the bluebird "one of the most domestic of birds" in 1898. Many bluebirds sometimes winter throughout southern Indiana, fewer in the north.

The Baltimore oriole is a colorful summer resident. Its hanging nests are often placed high in large trees. The American elm, with its large, spreading crown and drooping branches, was a favorite nesting tree. But most of the elms are gone. Orioles now utilize sycamore, oak, maple, and other tall species, often building their nests over a road. Orioles are fond of riverine habitats. On 10 May 1950, we saw 33 males along the Salamonie River from Montpelier to Warren (15 miles). Nests are woven of grasses, string, strands of plant fibers, hairs, and other materials. Jane L. Hine reported a nest made entirely of black horsehair except for one piece of black string.

There is much concern recently about apparent declines in the populations of a number of summer resident passerine bird species,

especially those nesting in the interior of older-growth forests. Many of these species are migrants to Central and South America, where they often overwinter in tropical forests. Forest destruction in the tropics, further fragmentation of Indiana woodlands, and increased nest parasitism by brown-headed cowbirds have all been postulated as possible causes of songbird decline. Probably all of these, and likely several other factors, are partly responsible. Research is currently under way on the Hoosier National Forest and elsewhere to document the status of summer breeding bird populations.

Most likely, no other pursuit of nature study has given as much pleasure and satisfaction to so many as has birding, feeding birds, and the unofficial study of birds. Let us do everything we can to ensure that no future "silent spring" occurs when, in the words of Keats, "no birds sing."

> Ornithology cannot be learned satisfactorily from books. The satisfaction is in learning it from nature. . . . The books are only the guide, the invitation. . . . Bought knowledge is dear at any price. The most precious things have no commercial value.
> —*Burroughs*, Wake Robin

Bluebird populations seem to cycle in response to the severity of the winters. They are a favorite avian neighbor all year long.
Photo by Delano Z. Arvin

Bluebird eggs in nest box.
Photo by Delano Z. Arvin

Female cowbird is a nest parasite.
Photo by Delano Z. Arvin

Deer fawns achieve protection from predators by being extremely difficult to see when immobile, and being largely devoid of odor.   *Photo by Lee Casebere*

42. Our Native Mammals

Russell E. Mumford

Animals are such agreeable friends—they ask no questions, they pass no criticisms.

—*George Eliot, "Scenes of Clerical Life," in* Mr. Gilfills Love Story

LARGELY UNSEEN ANIMAL NEIGHBORS

There are currently 57 species of wild mammals known to be living in Indiana. Seven orders are represented, with the numbers in each as follows: Marsupialia (opossum), 1; Insectivora (shrews, moles), 8; Chiroptera (bats), 12; Lagomorpha (rabbits), 2; Rodentia (mice, squirrels, muskrat, etc.), 22; Carnivora (foxes, raccoon, weasels, etc.), 11; Artiodactyla (deer), 1.

Although many species are distributed throughout the state, some have restricted ranges. Some occur as large populations over a huge area, but others are sparsely scattered and likely to be rare everywhere. Certain bats are abundant seasonally, being common in summer and absent to rare in winter. Other species may be cyclic, enjoying times of large populations interspersed with periods of low populations. During a long term of years, we may see wide fluctuations in numbers of some species, but fairly stable populations of others. Taking these variations into account, it is evident that much more needs to be learned about our native mammals. This may be especially true for important game species, major pests, or threatened and endangered forms.

To obtain population data for any species normally requires a long-term research program, so that seasonal or annual fluctuations may be detected and evaluated. We seldom have the luxury of being able to obtain this type of information; studies are more apt to be of short duration and may or may not correctly reflect the true picture. In addition, land use practices are constantly altering habitats, thus having substantial effects on both species composition and numbers of mammals.

It has become increasingly difficult to locate a research area where long-term studies under "natural" conditions can be carried out for the necessary number of years to acquire good statistical data on populations. Such studies must take into account the complex ecological relationships of mammals to other animals, vegetation, parasites, diseases, climate, and human activities—to name a handful. In a state so densely populated with humans as Indiana, we can nearly forget "natural" conditions and attempt to determine how mammals (and other organisms) operate where they are forced to coexist with humans.

All animals are equal, but some animals are more equal than others.

—*George Orwell,* Animal Farm

Mammals are not as popular as birds with the average person. Birds are more easily observed, have loud and musical songs, are more approachable, possess brighter colors, present a multitude of different species, and generally pose no threat to people. Mammal watching is much lower on the scale of outdoor activities than birdwatching. Some of the more observable mammals include the opossum, eastern cottontail (rabbit), gray squirrel, fox squirrel, red squirrel, woodchuck, eastern chipmunk, 13-lined ground squirrel, muskrat, red fox, gray fox, raccoon, striped skunk, and white-tailed deer.

The remaining 42 species are less well known because of small size, habits, or difficulty of identification. Even though we may see little of this latter group when conducting our ordinary activities, we may see clues to their presence. These clues (or "sign") include beaver dams and lodges, mounds of earth piled up by moles and pocket gophers, tracks, droppings, trails, remains of foods eaten, burrows constructed in the ground, articles that have been chewed (wood, bone, antlers, etc.), and odors (besides the skunk, deer, and foxes, shrews, moles, mice, bats, and badger).

We may see mice, voles, and shrews scurrying across roads, flying squirrels coming to a bird feeder at night, a big brown bat flying in a building, and Norway rats or house mice about our homes. An occasional mink, weasel, or Franklin's ground squirrel is seen dead along a roadway. The family dog or cat may bring moles and shrews (and also mice and voles) to the doorstep and leave them there. But many of the small, interesting native mammals will not be seen in their natural settings by most of us during our lifetime.

The professor finally straightened up, his eyes snapping. Normally of a quiet, retiring nature, he now became highly garrulous [after drinking too much persimmon beer], proceeding to deliver us a grandiloquent lecture on the 'possum, and in his best classroom manner. He descanted at length on its idiosyncrasies, its love life, its intimate family affairs, with numerous references to "nocturnal and arboreal habits," "prehensile tail," and what not. He wound up or rather unwound with: "It is the only native marsupial in this country. . . ."

—*Havilah Babcock, "'Possum up de Simmon Tree," in* Hunting Trails *(1961)*

The Virginia opossum is related to kangaroos, the koala, and many other Australian mammals. The order name is derived from the word *marsupium* (pouch). In most species of marsupials, the female has a well-formed and conspicuous pouch to carry and nourish the young for various periods of time during their development. The Virginia opossum is an ancient type of mammal, whose ancestry can be traced by fossils back 130 million years to the beginning of the Cretaceous geologic time period, when dinosaurs were still dominant.

One might think it poorly adapted with a small brain, low level of "intelligence," passive response to danger (feigning death, or "playing 'possum"), and conspicuousness. Obviously, looks are deceiving; it has the ability to survive considerable physical damage (broken bones, etc.) and to eat almost anything, and has been able to adapt to numerous environmental changes. It has served as a food item and a fur product. If the numbers of opossums observed dead on Indiana roads are an indicator, the species is thriving.

Female opossum with young clinging to fur.　*Photo by Delano Z. Arvin*

NOT-SO-TAME SHREWS AND MOLES

The six species of Indiana shrews are poorly known by the average person. They tend to burrow in leaf litter and may be found in moist areas. They have poor eyesight but an acute sense of smell, which enables them to find food and mates, and otherwise carry on their lives. The short-tailed shrew (the largest species in Indiana) has venom glands from which poison flowing down the teeth is injected with the saliva into prey bitten by the shrew. Such prey usually includes earthworms, slugs, snails, and other invertebrate animals.

This shrew in captivity will kill and eat mice (or other shrews) if caged with them. Similar predation may occur occasionally in the wild, and the venom may assist in subduing small mammals. The strong-smelling, musky secretion from specialized scent glands of the short-tailed shrew (and moles) at times renders them unpalatable to foxes, dogs, and cats. These mammals may kill, but not eat, the shrews and moles frequently found discarded along trails used by foxes, etc.

Some vocalizations of shrews are ultrasonic and used in echolocation (as in bats). The significance of these calls requires more research. Sonar (echolocation) may be useful in obstacle avoidance or communication between individuals.

Shrews may be quite abundant locally and more numerous in some years than others. This seems especially true of the short-tailed shrew, for which we have the best data. Abundance is sometimes detected in an interesting way. For example, James B. Cope once examined a dead rough-legged hawk that contained 47 least shrews in its digestive tract. Obviously this hawk had found a site where this normally uncommon shrew was plentiful.

Food habits studies of the various Indiana shrews have been conducted by John O. Whitaker, Jr., and his students at Indiana State University. Although shrews are in the order Insectivora, foods they consume are not restricted to insects. Plant material is eaten, as is some carrion, but to a considerable extent shrews tend to be carnivorous.

Because of their small size and the fact that they are warm-blooded, the smaller Indiana species (among the smallest living mammals in the world) must consume great quantities of food to maintain their normal metabolic rate. Pygmy shrews normally weigh about the same as a dime (2.5 grams). However, pygmy shrews from Indiana are the smallest known of this group, averaging only 2.0

grams. This puts them in competition with the bumblebee bat for the title of "world's smallest mammmal." Heat loss from the body of such a small mammal is extremely rapid because of the wide ratio of body mass to surface area. Thus, shrews are forced to forage for food much of their short lifespan.

The geographic distribution of shrews is variable. The short-tailed and least are found statewide, while the smoky and pygmy are confined to unglaciated regions of south-central Indiana. The southeastern occurs over most of southern Indiana, and the masked occurs throughout most of the state except for the unglaciated area where the pygmy and smoky are found.

Shrews normally do not leave much indication of their presence. They tend to move about in the same areas repeatedly (such as along the edge of a fallen log), but paths or "runs" they create are usually inconspicuous. On my lawn, however, short-tailed shrews create easily seen trails through the bluegrass. The trails are less than an inch wide and radiate out from the vegetation about the foundation of the house, across the open lawn to other clumps of vegetation or a hedgerow. Shrews have poor vision and frequently tumble into window wells, postholes, swimming pools, and other excavations. One effective way of collecting shrews for study is to bury containers with their rims at ground level in places where shrews are suspected to be.

Shrews are mostly nocturnal. At bird feeding stations, they may become unwary enough to leave their burrows under the leaves and grass and emerge into the open (usually rapidly and for a short distance) to grab a portion of food by day. Hunters sitting quietly in wooded areas during daylight hours have reported observing shrews "playing" about them in the leaves on the ground. At such times they may be quite active and even utter audible squeaking sounds.

At times they enter houses and outbuildings. We once kept a caged short-tailed shrew about six months. We cut a piece of sod about five inches thick the size of the inside of an old aquarium. When the shrew was placed in this cage, it constructed burrows throughout the sod, established certain spots where it urinated or defecated, and made a nest. When we wanted to place food in the cage, we would tap lightly on the glass at the mouth of one of the burrows. The shrew soon began to appear at this spot and accept the food offered it whenever we tapped the glass.

The two moles (eastern and star-nosed) have similar habits. They are fossorial (burrowing) animals, and when foraging they form ridges along the surface of the ground. Both also bring up soil while digging their burrows and deposit it as "molehills" or small mounds. Much of their food consists of earthworms and other invertebrates. Moles are adapted for digging, with strong claws on the front feet and powerful front legs to supply power for pushing through soil. The larger eastern mole is much stronger and capable of moving through dense soil, while the star-nosed lives in damp areas, where it is easier to dig. Star-nosed moles have smaller feet, are somewhat aquatic, and readily swim underwater; they may use burrows that are partially flooded.

Both make use of an acute sense of smell. The naked snout is both a probe and a sense organ. The nose of the star-nosed is surrounded by 22 fleshly tentacles that form the "star," thus the name. The nostrils are near the tip of the snout and are equipped with valves to permit their closure so that soil and water cannot enter. Star-nosed moles have longer and hairier tails and store fat seasonally in the base of the tail.

The eastern is found throughout Indiana except in rather dry habitats. It occurs in woods, fields, pastures, on lawns and golf courses, in cemeteries, along roadsides, and about moist borders of lakes, marshes, or streams. Star-nosed moles are restricted mainly to the northeastern corner of the state, primarily in moist to wet habitats. They were once more widespread but have suffered from the drainage of wetlands. They may be fairly common locally in good habitats. Most of the damage to lawns, golf courses, and other mowed areas is done by the eastern mole. In the yard of a house north of Terre Haute where dozens of unsightly molehills were visible one spring, the homeowner had erected a sign reading "Moles for Sale."

BATS: BENEFICIAL, NOT HARMFUL

Bats are among our most maligned and misunderstood native mammals. The 12 species in Indiana are all insect eaters, with different species of bats feeding on different groups of insects, primarily beetles. For example, big brown and evening bats eat mainly beetles and true bugs; hoary and big-eared bats feed heavily on moths; and the myotis consumes flies and small moths. That bats eat hordes of mosquitoes apparently is folklore, as food habits analysis does not indicate that any Indiana species eats more than a few mosquitoes.

Big brown bats are particularly valuable feeders on agricultural pests, with the spotted cucumber beetle totaling a third of their food. The larva of this beetle is the corn rootworm. An average colony of 150 big brown bats could eat enough cucumber beetles to prevent the production of 16 million corn rootworms. All Indiana farmers should want a colony of big brown bats on their property.

Identification of bats is difficult for the inexperienced because all species are relatively small, and many tend to be brownish and look quite similar. The red bat is a showy species, with each sex colored differently, an uncommon occurrence in mammals. The uncommon hoary bat is the largest, with distinctive gray-brown hair frosted at the tips.

The big brown bat is the only species in Indiana that winters in buildings, but other species, especially the little brown bat, sometimes roost or form maternity colonies in buildings. The smallest is the eastern pipistrelle, found in caves in winter and mostly in tree foliage in summer. The silver-haired bat migrates north through Indiana in spring to breed, but is not a summer resident here. A few winter in Indiana caves.

Five species of bats are so rare that they have been classified as endangered on state or federal lists. These include the Indiana, evening, gray, southeastern, and big-eared. The latter two are probably extirpated. The Indiana bat was described to science in 1928, from specimens taken in Big Wyandotte Cave, Crawford County. Big Wyandotte Cave once supported great numbers of wintering bats, most presumed to have been Indiana bats. We have read about clusters on the ceiling as large as a piano. Since about 300 Indiana bats may occupy a square foot in such winter congregations, one can visualize former numbers. In 1989–90, about 10,000 Indiana bats wintered in Big Wyandotte Cave, but much larger numbers of Indiana bats still winter in a few other caves.

The eastern big-eared bat, probably never common in Indiana, is known from a scant dozen reports in the past century. The first published record was December 1894; the latest known report was December 1962. It is an interesting species, with ears about two inches long. When the bat is in deep sleep, its ears are usually folded along the sides of its head (much like the coiled horns of a bighorn sheep). As the bat awakens, the curled ears slowly straighten, transforming its appearance.

Bats are largely beneficial consumers of insects, but eat few mosquitoes, contrary to popular opinion. Unfortunately they have received much undeserved bad press.   *Photo by Richard Fields*

The gray myotis (gray bat) was considered rare in the state until a single maternity colony was found in Clark County in 1982. Since the gray bat is easily disturbed, barring humans from entering caves when it is present may be imperative for its eventual survival.

Eight bat species bear young in Indiana. The red and hoary are solitary, having their offspring among plant foliage. The six social species form maternity colonies: big brown, little brown, and evening in buildings; the pipistrelle and northern myotis usually in tree hollows or under bark; only the gray bat reproduces in caves in Indiana.

Another seemingly rare species is the chocolate-brown evening bat. Eleven maternity colonies (all in buildings) were known from the late 1950s to the mid-1960s, but all are now gone. There appears to have been a remarkable decrease in this bat. Only two colonies are presently known in Indiana, one each in Vigo and Clay counties. It is the only Indiana species that has not been found here in a cave.

RABBITS AND RODENTS

Our two native rabbits are the eastern cottontail and the larger, less-known swamp rabbit. The familiar cottontail is known simply as "rabbit" to most Hoosiers. It is common and widespread and has long been the most important game mammal in the state. Most young hunters began by hunting cottontails. From about 1940 to 1959, more than 2 million were harvested annually by Indiana hunters. In 1941 they took an estimated 3 million. But since 1960 the numbers have decreased, and the estimated kill during the 1986–87 season was 470,000.

The cottontail is an important part of the ecosystems of waste areas, fallow fields, brushy fields, cultivated areas interspersed with the above habitats, and open, brushy woodlots. When Indiana was first settled, there were probably relatively few cottontails throughout most of the state, which was forested. But as the timber was cut and more openings and farms were created, no doubt rabbit populations underwent a tremendous increase, quickly spreading from the prairie and other open areas into habitats previously forested.

The cottontail is important as food not only for humans but for foxes, coyotes, some hawks and owls, and other animals. Crows are fond of nestlings and rob rabbit nests of their young. Domestic cats and dogs catch quantities of young and adult cottontails, and a large number are killed each year by motor vehicles. Surprisingly, many rabbits now survive in cities and towns, despite the several hazards of such habitats.

The swamp rabbit was a secretive inhabitant of the state until the first museum specimens were preserved in 1930 from Posey County. Its presence was suspected in Knox County by 1895. Subsequent research has resulted in records of the swamper from Gibson, Knox, Posey, Spencer, Vanderburgh, and Warrick counties. These big rabbits live in the region of swampland forests, sloughs, and floodplain wooded areas, and riparian habitats in extreme southwestern Indiana.

It is not easy to distinguish between cottontails and swamp rabbits in the field when both species occur together. Large swampers reach a weight of six pounds, but average between four and five pounds. In contrast, the largest cottontails weigh about three and one-half pounds; most average about two and three-quarters pounds. Hunters may shoot a swamper and remark about its large size, sometimes not being aware that it is a different species from the cottontail. But

Cottontail rabbits are still widely hunted, but are now much less common than formerly.   *Photo by Marion Jackson*

some hunters learned years ago about the big swamp rabbits in Gibson and Knox counties and sought them for sport hunting, often with beagle hounds.

The removal of floodplain forests and other land use has now greatly diminished the numbers of this species. It may be the next native mammal extirpated from our state. To save it, suitable habitats need to be preserved and the remaining small numbers spared from hunting. The estimated population in 1996 was 53; we hope that more are present. The real threat to their survival in Indiana today is humans.

And a mouse is miracle enough to stagger sextillions of infidels.

—*Walt Whitman, "Song of Myself," in* Leaves of Grass

The rodents, or gnawing mammals, are represented by species which range in size from the tiny harvest mouse (about 11 grams) to the beaver (60 pounds or more). Rodents are characterized by their strong, large incisor teeth, with which they eat insects, larvae, seeds, fruits, grasses, bark, and other foods, and chew down trees.

The various mice and voles are major components in the food chains of numerous animals, and are thus of considerable importance to the ecosystem. The coyote, red fox, gray fox, mink, least weasel, long-tailed weasel, badger, striped skunk, and bobcat all eat different amounts of mice and voles. A coyote killed near West Point, Indiana, had 14 prairie voles and two white-footed mice in its stomach. Food habits studies of both foxes reveal that voles and mice are taken in considerable numbers.

Hawks and owls consume large numbers of these prey animals. Voles make up much of the food of the long-eared, barn-, short-eared, and great horned owls. Screech-owls feed extensively on white-footed mice. The northern harrier and red-tailed hawk are important vole eaters, as are the snowy owl and rough-legged hawk during their winter visits to Indiana. Other avian predators of mice and voles include the American kestrel, saw-whet owl, barred owl, great blue heron, and two species of shrikes. Some of the larger snakes and a few species of fishes (basses, pike) also consume mice.

Mice and voles (except for the hibernating jumping mouse) are active throughout the year and represent a reliable and continuous food supply. Two or more species inhabit nearly every habitat in the state—from urban to rural. Most have a high reproductive rate, and thus are capable of creating and maintaining large populations. Furthermore, this abundance can sometimes act as a buffer that may help protect other prey, such as rabbits, songbirds, game birds, furbearers, poultry, and other farm animals, from predation by foxes, coyotes, and other species.

The natural productivity of living things is almost beyond belief. . . . Our populations of small animals operate under a one-year plan of decimation and replacement; and nature habitually maintains a wide margin of overreproduction.

—*Durward L. Allen, "The One-Year Plan," in* Our Wildlife Legacy *(1962)*

Among the less well known Indiana rodents are the plains pocket gopher, eastern woodrat, Franklin's ground squirrel, and western harvest mouse.

The pocket gopher has fur-lined external cheek pouches ("pockets") on the sides of its head, hence its name. It is rarely seen aboveground, and its underground burrow system is complex. The uppermost burrows are used when foraging near the ground surface, and as it digs it encounters plant roots and stems, which are chewed off and eaten. Loose soil from burrows is brought to the top of the ground and deposited in mounds that look similar to those pushed up by moles, perhaps confusing many people as to their origin.

The pocket gopher has a limited distribution in Indiana in the area surrounded by the Kankakee, Wabash, and Tippecanoe rivers. It is mostly found in loam or silt-loam soils, where burrowing can be accomplished with ease. Rocky soils or soils permeated with large tree roots and other obstructions limit gopher activity. Local gopher populations in good habitat may be quite large. The gopher has relatively few natural predators owing to its secretive behavior below ground. At night, gophers come to the surface on the ground and feed on vegetation around the burrow entrance.

The eastern woodrat is now limited to rocky escarpments in Crawford and Harrison counties. While it was first collected in Indiana in 1930, its presence in Big Wyandotte Cave was suspected as early as 1872. Recent research by Ronald L. Richards has shown that it once enjoyed a much larger Indiana range, for its remains have been found as far north as Shelby County. The woodrat is often associated with caves, where the animals store food and construct nests. Woodrats are gentle and trusting in these sites; we have touched them without their showing fear.

Nests examined were constructed almost entirely of shredded bark of red cedar, with some grasses; they were round, with a hollow center and an opening on one side. Scattered about one nest were bits of nuts, pieces of bone, sticks, and numerous green sprigs of red cedar twigs. Some foods were cached inside the cave, or in fissures in rocky escarpments. Woodrats at one site had stored the fruit heads of pokeberry and bunches of wild grapes.

Non-food materials of all descriptions are gathered by the rats and stacked in large piles in their retreats. Such a "midden" heaped on top of a large, flat boulder on the cave floor at Tobacco Landing on 19 March 1954 contained the following: the seeds or fruits of 13 plant species, leaves, twigs, bark, and bits of charcoal. Miscellaneous items included bones, shell, bits of glass, foil, metal, paper, cardboard, cellophane, a cigarette butt, a rubber band, feathers, a mammal dropping, plastic, cloth, and a grasshopper head. In a midden in Sullivan's Cave (Lawrence County) were bones of the porcupine, spotted skunk, and elk (all now extinct in Indiana), and eight other species of mammals. The bones were possibly a hundred to several hundred years old.

Franklin's ground squirrel is a relatively rare species in northwestern Indiana. It somewhat resembles a gray squirrel but has a smaller, less bushy tail and shorter ears and legs. Today's populations are found mainly along railroad rights-of-way, overgrown ditch banks, roadsides, brushy waste areas, and similar habitats. Although its smaller relative, the 13-lined ground squirrel (often called the "striped gopher"), frequents open areas supporting mowed or short grasses, Franklin's ground squirrel is much less visible and prefers more dense cover of weeds and woody sprouts. In 1936, Franklin's was found mainly in the area bordered roughly by Lake, St. Joseph, Carroll, Tippecanoe, and Warren counties. There appears to have been little range extension within the past 50 years. Ground squirrels hibernate, and Franklin's is usually seen aboveground only from about late April to late October.

Two tree squirrels, the fox and the gray, have long been important game animals in Indiana. Since nearly nine-tenths of the state was originally covered with hardwood forest, the habitat for these species was extensive and abundant. When early settlers came to Indiana, cleared a patch of timber, built a cabin, and planted crops, they found squirrels a major nuisance. It was necessary to protect gardens and cornfields by shooting the squirrels, whose numbers seemed astronomical in some areas.

Organized hunts, known as "burgoos," were conducted in south-

Nocturnal flying squirrels are rarely seen, but residents in wooded areas may hear them glide onto their roofs at night.　*Photo by Delbert Rust*

ern Indiana. Around the spring of 1843, one man killed 200 squirrels on one farm by 10 A.M. A hunt in the Vevay area of Switzerland County around 1823–24 resulted in the shooting of 13,006; 28 of the men got 1,007, and another group bagged 3,166.

Some settlers resorted to utilizing the entire family to go through the crop fields making noise. As the squirrels retreated to the woods, other family members shot them about the edges of the fields. The above accounts do not differentiate between gray squirrels and fox squirrels, but it is assumed that gray squirrels probably outnumbered fox squirrels during that period.

Huge movements of thousands of squirrels were reported in earlier years. In 1819, John J. Audubon, traveling down the Ohio River between Indiana and Kentucky by boat, saw large numbers of gray squirrels swimming across the river. Many drowned or were killed by hunters, according to Audubon's detailed description of the event. Other migrations (or emigrations) have been reported from Franklin, Knox, and Wabash counties, but none has occurred in recent years.

Hoosiers have always hunted squirrels, and if you have ever eaten fried squirrel, with squirrel gravy and hot biscuits, you can easily understand this fact. As of about 1969, hunters harvested roughly 300,000 gray squirrels each season in the state. In 1986 the kill was about half that number.

Major logging operations in the late 1800s depleted much of the timberland in Indiana, and the gray squirrel probably decreased dramatically as a result of this habitat loss. After most of the forest was cut, the fox squirrel became more abundant statewide than the gray squirrel. The fox squirrel was better able to survive in small woodlots, city parks, residential areas, and other habitats providing small amounts of wooded habitat. Thus, more than 1 million fox squirrels were taken annually by hunters from 1943 to 1948 and from 1963 to 1965.

Strangely enough, in some cities gray squirrels became so well established that they caused the elimination of the fox squirrel. On the Purdue University campus and in the surrounding West Lafayette area, gray squirrels now abound; fox squirrels are absent. In the spring of 1986, I trapped and removed 22 gray squirrels from my backyard in West Lafayette in one month. There are certain other Indiana cities where gray squirrels either have been restocked or have appeared on their own and are doing quite well. So, even though we have usually associated the gray squirrel with extensive woodlands where there is less disturbance from humans, it can adapt to city living.

The black squirrels were common—forming about one-third of the total number of squirrels in southeastern Indiana at the period of first settlement. Now they have completely disappeared.

　　—*Rufus Haymond,* Mammals Found in Franklin
　　　　County, Indiana *(1869)*

When Indiana was first settled, "black" squirrels (melanistic grays) were widely scattered throughout the state, but evidently were most numerous in the northern part. These black animals, once reported as fairly common along the Kankakee River, were eliminated earlier than the gray ones. Reintroductions of the black color phase of the gray squirrel have been made in several places; one successful establishment has been in the Goshen (Waterford Mills) area of Elkhart County.

The familiar woodchuck (groundhog) has long been shot and otherwise persecuted by man. The numerous burrows it constructs in the ground are used by a variety of insects, other invertebrates, amphibians, reptiles, and mammals. Even bobwhite quail and ring-necked pheasants may use the burrows in severe winter weather or when injured by hunters. The benefits of such burrows to other wildlife are important, and the presence of woodchucks should be encouraged unless they are causing significant damage by feeding or burrowing. The woodchuck hibernates for three to four months in winter. When alarmed, it may give a whistle, thus earning it the name "whistle-pig."

The porcupine once lived in Indiana, but is known only from skeletal remains. A live one was present in northeastern Indiana some years ago; someone even mailed me several quills removed from a dog's nose. Another was found dead on the road in Newton County. Both had evidently been brought to Indiana from elsewhere.

Muskrats thrive in shallow water areas with an abundance of emergent vegetation, such as cattail, which is eaten, is used to construct houses, and provides protective cover. Nearly any water area, including drainage ditches and small ponds, may be inhabited by this common and prolific rodent. The muskrat has been an important furbearing species for many years. About 75 percent of those trapped come from northern Indiana.

It must have been present in incredibly high numbers in some of the larger Indiana marshes prior to 1900. The Grand Marsh of the Kankakee River formerly covered about 500,000 acres and was evidently prime habitat. It was said that muskrat houses were so closely spaced that a man could open three or four at a time from an anchored boat. One trapper reportedly caught 10,000 muskrats in one year about 1811. In 1871, L. N. Lamb caught more than 80 per night in 100 traps. Roy Granger told me in 1952 that he and his father caught more than 300 in one night in the early 1900s. He also related how he speared 72 through the ice in a single day. When new, clear ice strong enough to support a man's weight formed on the marsh in the fall, one could walk about and kick the houses. This caused the occupants to dive out of the house into the water, then surface beneath the clear ice. An iron rod sharpened to a point on one end was used to spear them.

Most of the larger marshes have long been drained, and muskrats, though widely distributed throughout the state, are much depleted in numbers. During the 1931–32 season, an estimated 586,000 were killed. The average annual catch from 1952 to 1958 was nearly 200,000.

The beaver once prospered in what is now Indiana, but activities of the early fur trappers and subsequent settlement evidently eliminated it by about 1830 to 1840. In the 1930s, beavers appeared in northern Indiana, and more were brought from other states and released. The species increased sufficiently to allow a legal trapping season in 1951. Beavers occur in many counties today.

Hardly another mammal has played so romantic a part in our history. Demand for its beautiful and useful pelt first lured trappers into the North American wilderness. . . . Excessive trapping extirpated the species over wide areas. Now it is being restocked and is creating ponds and wetlands of great value.

—*Henry Hill Collins, "Beaver," in* Complete Field Guide to American Wildlife *(1959)*

THE FLESH FEEDERS

All living things are destined to die and be recycled as a part of the flow of energy through the life community. Which is to say, a creature must feed, and sooner or later it will be fed upon.

—*Durward L. Allen,* Wolves of Minong *(1979)*

The carnivores have large canine teeth for holding and ripping apart their prey. They are not strictly carnivorous, for most feed also on vegetable matter and carrion. Species now living in Indiana are the coyote, gray fox, red fox, raccoon, least weasel, long-tailed weasel, mink, badger, striped skunk, bobcat, and river otter. The least weasel weighs a scant 20 to 65 grams and is the smallest carnivore in the world. Larger carnivores that have been extirpated include the black bear, wolverine (if present), mountain lion, red wolf, and gray wolf. Although a wolverine was reported in 1852, there is no physical evidence to support its former presence in the state.

There was probably depredation on livestock by the black bear, mountain lion, and wolves, but their supposed danger to humans has been greatly exaggerated. The red wolf was undoubtedly quite rare in the state and insignificant with regard to its potential damage. We do not know exactly when the red wolf or the gray wolf disappeared, for the coyote was also here and was hopelessly confused with wolves. Early settlers engaged in numerous, well-organized wolf hunts, and also caught wolves by luring them into deep pits.

Although the wolves were eliminated, the coyote (or "brush wolf") adapted well to changing conditions and prospers today. In the farmlands of central Indiana, it spends much of the day in cornfields, which provide excellent and abundant cover for many months. Originally the coyote was probably confined mainly to the prairies, but it now lives throughout the state. In recent years, it has become more abundant on the lands formerly surface-mined for coal.

It is possible that black bears and mountain lions were once present throughout the forested regions. Neither species was common, as far as can be determined, and the bear was no doubt more numerous than the lion since various Indiana county histories and other early published accounts refer to the black bear. Most were eliminated by 1850, but one was reported about 1888. Between 1804 and 1811, from a fur-trading post at Fort Wayne (Allen County), 448 bearskins were shipped to other markets. The moun-

Hunting red fox makes a successful kill.   *Photos by Richard Fields*

tain lion was last reported in 1851, from Marion and Morgan counties. It seems unlikely that it was abundant, and its numbers could have been determined in part by the number of white-tailed deer, a favorite food. The deer was evidently extirpated from the state by 1900, and there were marked declines in numbers as early as the 1830s.

Among the remaining carnivores, the raccoon is of greatest importance. Its population was quite low in the mid-1940s, but it has since become abundant. It has also shown a remarkable ability to survive in many habitats, including cities. Long an important furbearing animal, the raccoon has been harvested in large numbers in the state for many years.

Raccoon hunting has long been a popular Hoosier sport and still has its avid followers. One has to admit that there is pleasure in being outdoors on a cold, crisp November night and hearing the hounds hot on the trail of a 'coon. Excitement mounts as the dogs finally bark "treed" and you make your way cross country to reach the site where the dogs have forced their quarry to cease running.

Frequently the raccoon takes refuge in a den tree, with cavities in which the animal can hide and remain secure; at other times it chooses a tree free of cavities. A hunter shines the beam of a flashlight among the branches, searching for the telltale eyeshine of the animal as it looks at the light. All the time, the dogs are barking, milling about the base of the tree, and even trying to jump up the trunk as far as possible. The hunt usually is ended by a shot from a .22 rifle, and the dead raccoon falls to the ground to be harassed by the dogs, until they realize that their prey is dead.

> There was a young man from the city,
> Who saw what he thought was a kitty.
> Saying, "nice little cat,"
> He gave it a pat . . .
> They buried his clothes out of pity.
>
> —*Anonymous*

The striped skunk, though well known, has never been seen alive in the wild by many persons. More often, they see the dead animals along the roadways, for the motor vehicle is the way many skunks meet their demise today. Probably nearly everyone is familiar with the odor of skunk; it is a persistent scent that lingers about an animal killed by a car or is carried for some distance through the air on damp

Skunks feed primarily on insects, eggs, and small vertebrates.
Photo by Delano Z. Arvin

nights. Many persons have had to banish the family dog from the house until the effects of its encounter with a skunk have finally faded away. Ladies' coats made of skunk pelts may even give off a faint odor when wet.

Fossil evidence indicates that at one time the spotted skunk occurred in Indiana, and there are reports of this animal's presence until after 1900. Fur buyers often called it a "civet cat," and fur dealers in Mt. Vernon are said to have bought four or five in the early 1900s.

The current status of the bobcat is an intriguing puzzle to biologists. For years there have been reports of bobcats (mostly from the south-central portion), but most could not be confirmed. Despite its size, the bobcat is a secretive and silent animal; thus, it may be present without calling attention to itself. From about 1920 to 1960, only occasionally was one shot or trapped. More recently, there are a few verifiable reports. A fine road-killed specimen was recovered from Interstate 64 in 1990. This recent evidence may indicate an increase in numbers, but the bobcat is still considered rare.

The badger is another interesting species, with regard to its occurrence. From the earliest report (1833) to about 1936, most were found in the northern one-third of Indiana, south to Vermillion County in the west and Grant County in the east. An isolated area was occupied in Franklin County. This big member of the weasel family inhabits open country and is a powerful burrower. During the past 50 years, it has greatly expanded its range southward to Vanderburgh, Crawford, and Dearborn counties. Thus, today it may appear in suitable habitat anywhere in the state. The increase in range and numbers has made more Hoosiers aware of this unique mammal; many people are still surprised, however, to learn that badgers occur here.

The varied diet of the carnivores allows them to subsist under present-day conditions. For example, foxes may prefer cottontail rabbits, but they also eat a considerable number of mice, shrews, and voles, as well as birds, snakes, frogs, seeds, nuts, fruit, insects, and carrion. The gray fox at times consumes a considerable amount of corn; individuals may gorge themselves on grasshoppers.

Weasels appear to eat mostly small mammals and birds, but the long-tailed weasel is capable of killing a cottontail. Weasels do attack poultry and other caged birds. Least weasels are frequently found about buildings, where they may be attracted to mice. The mink, a close weasel relative, feeds also on small mammals and birds (including poultry). Since it is more aquatic than the weasels, it also takes fishes, frogs, and snails. Locally, its main summer foods have been reported to be crayfish and bullheads (catfish).

LARGE HERBIVORES

Most of the hoofed mammals once found in Indiana are now extirpated or extinct. Although there has been much written about the American bison (featured on the state seal), there is little evidence that large numbers were present. The famous Buffalo Trace across southwestern Indiana marks the migration route of bison from near Vincennes to near Louisville. Early European visitors who traveled in this region in the late 1700s observed bison. When LaSalle and his men came down the Kankakee River in 1679, they observed bison, attesting to the former presence of these large prairie-inhabiting mammals in northwestern Indiana. Bison were possibly still here until about 1830.

> In common with the forests, the bison herds seemed endless.
> But a tide of humanity drove westward, multiplying as it came.
> It was a characteristic biological force similar to those we
> habitually misjudge because of their small beginnings. If un-

checked, they can take over the world while our backs are turned.

—*Durward L. Allen,* Our Wildlife Legacy *(1962)*

The elk, or American wapiti, appears to have been eliminated about the same time as the bison. Antlers of this large member of the deer family have been dredged from the Kankakee River and found in other parts of the state.

The white-tailed deer was probably locally common in pre-settlement times. Numerous county histories contain descriptions of deer hunts and provide some data on numbers killed from time to time. But by the 1880s, deer were being seen only occasionally in the Kankakee River Valley. The latest record for one in the Indiana dunes is for the early 1870s. The decrease in numbers was quite rapid after the mid-1800s, and the deer were evidently gone by 1900.

But the deer came back. Those reported in Harrison County in 1934 evidently arrived on their own, possibly by crossing the Ohio River. The Indiana Division of Fish and Game began restocking deer in 1934 and by 1955 had released more than 400 obtained from Michigan, North Carolina, Pennsylvania, and Wisconsin. It was thought that the deer population in 1944 was about 1,200, distributed over 35 counties. The population had quadrupled by 1951, and in November of that year hunters were allowed to legally hunt this game species in Indiana for the first time since 1900. By 1966 deer were probably present in each of the 92 counties. The white-tail has continued to prosper, peaking in herd size at over 300,000 statewide in 1991. Since many landowners are now complaining about damage to crops, orchards, etc., and many deer are being struck each year by motor vehicles, an effort is under way to reduce the population to a more sustainable number.

WILD ANIMAL VALUES

Our native mammals have always been an important resource, providing food, hunting, and enjoyment to outdoor enthusiasts. Visitors to our parks, wildlife areas, forests, zoos, and other facilities spend considerable time watching and photographing mammals.

Indiana ranks high in the annual production of furs. Forts (Miami,

A common, friendly rodent species known to most people is the pert chipmunk.   *Photo by Delano Z. Arvin*

Albino mammals are relatively rare and, being highly visible, likely do not survive as well as those individuals that have the typical color patterns.
Photo by Richard Fields

Ouiatenon, Vincennes) were built between 1715 and 1732 to protect the lucrative fur trade (mostly in beaver skins). It is estimated that in the late 1700s, about $25,000 worth of furs was shipped each year from Fort Vincennes and some $40,000 from Fort Ouiatenon. Those operations evidently ended around 1846 to 1848; the beaver was possibly extirpated by 1830. With no beaver left, the muskrat, raccoon, skunk, and opossum became important. Other species contributing to the harvest were the deer, mountain lion, wolf, otter, bobcat, red fox, gray fox, black bear, elk, marten, fisher, mink, coyote, badger, and weasels.

Fur prices fluctuate from time to time. In 1900, a muskrat pelt was worth about 10 cents, a mink or red fox one dollar. During the 1919–20 trapping season, Indiana red fox pelts brought 35 cents and muskrats five dollars. The estimated value of furs sold in Indiana in 1924 and 1931 was half to three-quarters of a million dollars. Muskrats, skunks, and opossums probably made up most of the total. The average annual income from 1953–57 was around one-half million dollars; from 1963–67, it was about $400,000.

During the 1970s, there was a great demand for long-haired fur (coyote, fox, raccoon). The raccoon became more important than the muskrat for the first time since the mid-1800s. The 1979–80 Indiana fur season resulted in a market value of $12.2 million. At that time, Indiana ranked fifth in the production of gray fox, seventh for raccoon, muskrat, and opossum, and ninth for red fox and mink.

Synthetic furs and pelts from commercially grown mammals have helped drive down values of wild-caught animals. Also, there is a strong anti-trapping sentiment in the country. Fewer persons are buying and wearing fur apparel.

Regardless of their economic value or their importance as game species, we can still enjoy our Indiana mammals in many ways. Their ecological and aesthetic value, plus just knowing that they are still "out there," justifies their continued existence and protection.

There is in every animal's eye a dim image and gleam of humanity, a flash of strange light through which their life looks out and up to our great mystery of command over them and claims the fellowship of the creature if not of the soul.

—*John Ruskin (1819–1900)*

Ground pine amid fallen leaves at Clubmoss Woods, La Porte County.   *Photo by Lee Casebere*

43. Biogeography: Of Organisms, Habitats, and Time

Russell E. Mumford and Marion T. Jackson

Each species inhabits only a part of the earth's surface, occurs only in some habitats, and varies in abundance over its geographic range. These ranges change dynamically, usually starting small, experiencing increases and decreases in size, and finally decreasing to extinction. Contemporary forms will eventually become extinct as well, leaving future species in their places.

—*James H. Brown and Arthur C. Gibson,* Biogeography (1983)

BIOGEOGRAPHIC CONTROLS

The flora and fauna of an area are almost never static, but are constantly changing as climate, vegetation, land use, and other factors exert their influences on the distribution patterns of populations of plants and animals, and on habitat use by individual organisms. The documentation of these changes, historical and earlier, for many species is incomplete, but there are fairly good data for some. Most of the historical writings and observations by naturalists, hunters, travelers, and others who might have made comments on the natural history of our state, date from after 1800. Information from earlier periods is dependent on the sketchy fossil record or other paleoecological evidence.

The flora and fauna of Indiana are composed mostly of species widely distributed throughout the eastern United States. Since our state was originally primarily heavily wooded with deciduous forests, as was much of the country eastward to the Atlantic Ocean, it is not surprising that these eastern affinities are evident in species found here today. A few species with more western associations, formerly present on the prairie areas, have extended their ranges eastward or have invaded from the west as the forests were cut away and the state became largely farmland and open country. A small group of plants and animals is restricted to the southern part of Indiana, where they are near, or at, one of the northern limits of their geographic distribution. In addition, a few species of more northern origin and affinities remain, some perhaps as relicts from the glacial age.

In general, most plants, invertebrates, amphibians and reptiles, and mammals (with the possible exception of bats) tend to be more sedentary and to have less extensive ranges than do winged insects, stream fishes, and birds. Flight enables winged insects and birds to more easily find and exploit new habitats and to move into them, and allows species to surmount barriers that make it impossible for small terrestrial, non-flying forms to expand their ranges. Streams, being largely continuous, open-ended habitats, allow fishes to move rather freely over long distances, hence to disperse widely. Such mobility allows individuals to live in one area in summer and another in winter; thus the birds that migrate annually. Many species of birds leave Indiana in the fall to winter in South America. A few bats may also carry out rather extensive seasonal migrations, as do some insects.

But a small shrew or meadow vole may spend its entire life in an area of less than one acre. Even animals as large as cottontail rabbits are quite sedentary if all their habitat needs are met locally. A given species can be confined to a certain small geographic area by necessity; its demands for life may be met there, but not in adjacent areas. It must have space, food, water, shelter, a place to reproduce, and perhaps other needs; the absence of any of these required resources will render that habitat untenable. Under those conditions, the animal must find an alternate, suitable habitat or perish.

Just what makes a habitat livable for a particular species is not always apparent to the human eye. We may look at two areas which appear about the same to us. Yet, if we sample the plant or animal life in these locations, we may find certain species present in one, but not the other.

Our inability to recognize and quantify habitat characteristics necessary to sustain some species frequently makes our job of protecting and managing wild species quite difficult. No doubt research will continue in this area for a long time. We do know that many of the differences may be subtle and complex. The interdependence of organisms may be so intricate and so delicately balanced that some slight, apparently insignificant, change in conditions may destroy the entire system. Unfortunately, humans are changing local environments almost daily and at such a rapid rate that we can rarely obtain vitally needed research data at the same pace.

One of the major features of habitats is the amount and type of vegetation. It is quite obvious that certain birds and mammals live in grassy and weedy fields, and different species live in forests. Indiana originally offered animals roughly three major habitats—deciduous forests, prairie grasslands, and aquatic areas (lakes, marshes, rivers, etc.).

These prevailing habitats were the results of the glacial, climatic, geologic, and other historic events that operated for thousands of years to exert their effects on plant and animal life. The last glacial ice sheet retreated from the state some 10,000 years ago, so what we see today is the result of changes since that time. The south-central hill region that was not under the influence of glaciation exhibits a much different topography from that of the remainder of Indiana. And even though there are no mountain ranges in Indiana and elevations statewide do not differ greatly, numerous plant and animal species do not occur throughout the state. Indeed, some are quite restricted in their geographic ranges.

FAUNAL DISTRIBUTIONS

The amount of moisture available is obviously important to most plants and may be important to some shrews. Woodrats are usually associated with limestone escarpments or caves; caves also provide ideal wintering habitat for several species of bats. Nesting short-eared owls prefer rather extensive grasslands (which resemble the prairies these owls find to their liking). The greater sandhill crane prefers to avoid humans as much as possible during the nesting season and frequents somewhat isolated marshy sites. Only small numbers of both of these birds now nest in Indiana, mainly because of the lack of suitable habitat and (perhaps) because of human disturbance.

Cattle egrets originally were native to Africa, but have successfully colonized the Western Hemisphere, including Indiana, where they are fairly regularly seen. *Photo by Michael Ray Brown*

I am earth's native;
No rearranging it!

—*Robert Browning*

There is tremendous variation in the ability of species to adapt to environmental changes. Some simply seem incapable of such adaptations, and thus have been extirpated from the state. A good example is the greater prairie-chicken; through the destruction of the prairie areas needed by the birds, human land use eliminated the species. In the 1930s, scarcely anyone thought the pileated woodpecker would survive for long. The sighting of one of these great birds in the wooded counties of southern Indiana at that time was a real treat. But it made a remarkable comeback and is still moving back into areas where it had been absent for more than 75 years.

We do not know by what mechanism some species are able to adapt to change; for those that cannot, extinction may be their final fate. The coyote was a resident of Indiana (though probably mostly restricted to the original prairie region) for hundreds of years. When the forests were removed, the coyote was able to take advantage of this large amount of open habitat formerly not suitable for it. The extermination of the wolf throughout most of the eastern U.S. may also have allowed the coyote to partially exploit the niche formerly occupied by timber wolves. Also, wolves possibly took coyotes as prey during times of food shortages. Coyotes are now found throughout the state and to the eastern coast of the United States. They adapted not only to major habitat changes, but to living successfully with humans. In this way, the coyote is similar to the red fox and gray fox. All three canid species have been persecuted by man for decades, yet each has survived and is doing well.

Coexisting with humans has become a prerequisite for the survival of several species. Most nesting chimney swifts in Indiana now construct their nests in chimneys. Before European settlement, the birds probably nested in hollow trees (a few still do), which are less common in today's forests. The mourning dove has readily accepted

people and their surroundings, frequently nesting around human habitations. Crows have also adapted well to human presence, now common residents and nesters in cities, suburbs, and urban parks. Road-killed animals provide a ready protein source for crows and opossums. We hardly need to mention the house sparrow, European starling, and domestic pigeon, all imported aliens that not only find human haunts to be congenial places to live, but also have become serious pests.

Native species of birds that live in urban-residential areas include the American robin, northern cardinal, chipping sparrow, song sparrow, Baltimore oriole, chickadees, tufted titmouse, woodpeckers, blue jay, common grackle, and many others. In recent years, a newcomer, the house finch, has appeared on the scene. It is a western species that was originally absent east of the Mississippi River. It became established on Long Island (and probably other places), from which it moved westward to invade Indiana and other states.

In some areas, there may be about as many raccoons and cottontails living in cities as there are in the surrounding intensively cultivated farmlands. White-tailed deer, squirrels, cottontails, raccoons, opossums, mice, rats, shrews, bats, and sometimes even foxes or mink all associate with humans in urban situations.

The prime enemy working against wildlife in urban environments is not so much the crowded human community itself as it is the monoculture created by humans.

—*William L. Robinson and Eric G. Bolen*, Wildlife Ecology and Management *(1991)*

As the human population continues to increase and habitats are altered, we will find other species adapting, and some failing to do so. Fragmentation of habitats, more roads, and increased vehicular traffic all combine to pose a serious threat to many animal species, owing to road kills and lack of habitat units of suitable size. Box turtles and snakes which bask on warm macadam roads at night are especially vulnerable to road kill. Mammals seem most prone to road kill during the fall and spring "shuffles." During the former, young of

Our largest woodpecker, the pileated, is much more common now than it was several decades ago. Apparently regrowth of second-growth forests has favored its increase. *Photo by Delano Z. Arvin*

The pretty green salamander was discovered within the past decade in Crawford County, for a new state record. They are more prevalent from Kentucky eastward into the Appalachians, and may be a recent addition to Indiana's vertebrate fauna.   *Photo by Richard Fields*

the year move about searching for home ranges in which to spend the winter; in spring, males and females range more widely seeking mates, hence they likely are less cautious.

Among the mammals found in Indiana that typically have a more northern distribution are the red squirrel, masked shrew, star-nosed mole, and least weasel. Some of the nesting birds in this category are the veery, long-eared owl, short-eared owl, least flycatcher, chestnut-sided warbler, Canada warbler, rose-breasted grosbeak, and swamp sparrow. Of the northern mammals, the star-nosed mole is most restricted in range in Indiana. Most of the known populations are in the northeastern corner, where the mucky soils and swampy/marshy habitats suitable to the moles are found.

The only Canada warbler nest found in Indiana was also in this region, but the bird has been noted in other northern sites during the breeding season. Similarly, the only verified record of magnolia warblers breeding here occurred in 1995 in northern relict habitat at Shades State Park. The short-eared owl presents an interesting case. The few nesting records for the state were in northern Indiana prior to 1940. When coal companies created prairie-like habitats by reclaiming large acreages of surface-mined lands in southwestern Indiana, this owl began nesting there. To our knowledge, the species had never before nested in this region.

Southern birds that more or less reach one of the northern limits of their total nesting range in Indiana include the black vulture, worm-eating warbler, summer tanager, and Bachman's sparrow. Similar mammals are the eastern woodrat, swamp rabbit, southeastern shrew, gray myotis, southeastern myotis, and eastern big-eared bat. Amphibians and reptiles with southern affinities include the green salamander (recently found as a new state record in Crawford County), alligator snapping turtle, crowned snake, scarlet snake, cottonmouth moccasin (known here for only about a decade), and ravine salamander (which occurs primarily in southeastern Indiana).

Although there are no recent records for the big-eared bat, its habitat (caves) appears unchanged from earlier years. Its exact status at this time is conjectural. The swamp rabbit presently seems to be the most threatened species owing to habitat destruction; its range has decreased considerably within the past 30 years. We could witness its extirpation in the next decade, although its small population of about 53 individuals appears to be holding steady during the last two years. Bachman's sparrow has virtually disappeared since around 1950, when it was widely scattered and nesting throughout much of southern Indiana. We have no idea what caused its decline, but habitat changes were possibly the reason.

Some birds have invaded from the west and now nest in Indiana, but did not at the turn of the last century. Again, this expansion eastward was in response to the opening up of land originally forested, and altering habitats to more prairie-like or open field conditions. Relatively new arrivals include the western meadowlark, Brewer's blackbird, and Bell's vireo. Although only one nest of the western meadowlark has been found in Indiana, the species has been present at least since the late 1930s. The first reported nesting of Bell's vireo was in 1945, but there are sight records for the species as early as 1922. Brewer's blackbird was reported from Lake County in 1949, and the first nest was found there in 1952.

With the exception of the western harvest mouse, there have been no new mammal immigrants from the west. But the 13-lined ground squirrel, badger, and coyote (all characteristic of prairie-like habitats) have enjoyed eastward range expansions in Indiana following wide-scale land clearing. It is quite likely that the prairie vole and eastern cottontail also followed this pattern of distribution change in times past. The spadefoot toad, western ophisaur or glass lizard, and crayfish frog are primarily western species, but apparently not recent to Indiana. The appearance of the house finch represents the only significant invasion of a bird or mammal into Indiana from the east in recent times.

SOME FLORISTIC CHANGES

The vegetation and individual plant species of pre-settlement Indiana were still adjusting to climatic changes and soil development following the glacial retreat when clearing and other land-use changes began. Plant species, as well as animals, are continually on the move, adjusting their distribution ranges as landscapes and their associated environments change. If conditions become suitable and propagules are available for dispersal, they will arrive.

Sometimes in a fragmented landscape such as Indiana now is, it may be necessary that a habitat island be relatively large in order for an invading plant species to "find" it—much as a larger target is easier to hit. For example, some species that are rare or unique in the state apparently have arrived at the 65,000-acre Jefferson Proving Ground (JPG) in southeastern Indiana since it was acquired by the federal government in 1939. Just recently, the rare climbing fern (*Lygodium palmatum*) was discovered in JPG as a new floral addition to the state. Other species that have extended their ranges into Indiana at other locations by dispersal of airborne seeds or spores include spring ladies'-tresses orchid, the netted chain-fern (*Woodwardia areolata*), and three new species of Eupatorium, a genus which also includes the more common Joe-Pye weed, white snakeroot, and boneset. All of these floral additions were unknown in Indiana prior to 1975.

Additional new species such as primrose willow and Virginia buttonweed apparently arrived from the south by entering Indiana along the Ohio River. Some species of primarily western distribution have used highways, roads, and railroads as artificial migration corridors to extend their ranges eastward into Indiana. Foxtail-barley, which thrives on saline soils, now waves its glistening, long-awned, grassy flower heads along many highway and road margins of the state in midsummer and autumn. Similarly, sea blite, stinking marigold, and freeway-sedge (*Carex praegracilis*) are western species now occurring here.

During and following the Great Depression, the abandonment of once-cultivated fields created habitats that permitted the increase

THE GYPSY MOTH

EGG MASS

LARVA
(CATERPILLAR)

PUPA

ADULT MALE

ADULT FEMALE

Although the gypsy moth has not become epidemic in Indiana, it has elsewhere in forested areas of the eastern United States, and could become a pest here and greatly influence the survival of a number of forest tree species.   *Photo by Richard Fields*

One of the largest blocks of essentially unbroken forestland in Indiana is Jefferson Proving Ground (JPG), shown here amid surrounding Ripley County farmland. Large habitat islands provide much more likely "targets" for the seeds or spores of invading plant species.
Photo by Richard Fields

and spread of such old-field and prairie species as prairie three-awn and little bluestem grasses, hairy-sheathed sedge (*Carex hirsutella*), and two lovely wildflower species, little ladies'-tresses orchid and plains blazing star. Similarly, native species in Indiana that were once rare but are now relatively common and expanding their ranges (perhaps because of genetic adaptations to disturbance) include oval ladies'-tresses orchid and southern ground-cedar (*Lycopodium digitatum*).

But some of our best-loved plant species (including favorite trees) have declined drastically in recent times. American chestnut was lost as a forest species in Indiana (as elsewhere in the eastern U.S.) as the result of an introduced fungal pathogen whose cankers girdle and kill adult trees. Occasional root sprouts from chestnut stumps are still found in southern Indiana, but fruiting trees are exceedingly rare. Our most prized shade and street tree, the American elm, has been essentially eliminated from both urban sites and natural forests as mature trees. The introduced Dutch elm fungus in tandem with phloem necrosis, a stem disease, has devastated both American and slippery elm populations, but the former has been hardest hit. More recently, all ten species of dogwoods native to Indiana, including the beautiful flowering dogwood, have become infested internally by a fungal blight (*Discula destructiva*) that appears to be increasing mortality rates among dogwoods in Indiana and elsewhere in the eastern U.S. Hopefully, these and other declining species can hold on as native populations until we can find ways to help restore them to their former importance.

Frequently it is quite difficult to determine if a species is expanding its geographic area, or if its range is contracting. One clue to changing distributions is the residence of outlier populations disjunct from the geographic range the species occupies generally. A common geographic principle, though by no means universally true, is that population *advances* across a landscape are characterized by a more uniform range margin, whereas *retreats* typically have outlier populations along the trailing edge. For example, northern relict species such as eastern hemlock, Canada yew, and eastern white pine lag behind as scattered stands in the cool microclimates of refugia along the Sugar Creek Valley on the deglaciated landscape of Montgomery and Parke counties, and most likely represent holdovers of retreating species.

Species ranges and the distribution patterns of individual animals are continually varying as the populations fine-tune their adjustments to the constantly changing environment. When tolerance limits are exceeded for any length of time, populations dwindle to zero, at least locally. Our hope is that continued human manipulation of remaining habitats will not create conditions whereby additional species are extirpated from Indiana. Perhaps long-existing trends in habitat destruction and environmental change can be reversed, thereby allowing threatened species to recover through the efforts of restoration ecology. Perhaps surveillance by our capable staff of the Indiana Natural Heritage Program will permit us to respond favorably to any future threats to our plant and animal neighbors.

To do science is to search for repeated patterns, not simply to accumulate facts, and to do the science of geographical ecology is to search for patterns of plant and animal life that can be put on a map. The person best equipped to do this is the naturalist who loves to note changes.

—*Robert H. MacArthur,* Geographical Ecology Patterns in the Distribution of Species *(1972)*

Part 4: The Changing Landscape

44. Change: The Essence of Nature

Marion T. Jackson

> It is sufficiently clear that all things are changed and nothing really perishes, and that the sum of matter remains absolutely the same.
>
> —*Francis Bacon,* Cogitations de Natura Rerum *(1653)*

Throughout recorded history, many of the world's foremost philosophers, scientists, and educators have contemplated the nature of a changing nature. Realization that the Earth, and the universe in which it is embedded, is in constant change must have come independently to many thoughtful persons very early in the human sojourn. Perhaps the only constant *is* change. Or in the words of the Greek philosopher Heraclitus (540–475 B.C.), "Nothing endures but change."

Contributing authors of several essays in this book have stressed the dynamic nature of Planet Earth, with particular reference to those changes the Indiana landscape and its inhabitants have experienced throughout the state's geologic and human history. Part 4, more than any other, focuses on the sweeping changes that have rolled across Indiana, especially as human populations have occupied the land during the roughly 10,000 years (some 400 human generations) that have elapsed since the massive ice sheets receded northward.

The rate of change continues to accelerate, as does the capacity of human activity to alter the land, the water, the air, the biology, and even the human species itself. Formerly only major forces of planetary dynamics wrought massive changes to the landscape. Volcanism, crustal tectonics, continental glaciation, meteorite impacts, and major climatic changes have repeatedly altered the nature of Earth's nature throughout the planet's history and continue to do so today.

Now, for perhaps the first time in the Earth's history, a single species has the capacity to effect changes of equal or even greater magnitude. Humankind has become a geological force as awesome as any of the forces of nature in its power to change this little planetary spaceship that is our only home. We need to draw on all the wisdom we can muster to guide the changes we will generate in the centuries to come. Otherwise, in time, we will totally change the nature of nature, including the last vestiges of the Garden whence we came.

> In wildness is the preservation of the world.
>
> —*Henry David Thoreau*

Humans have become a geological force, equivalent to volcanic activity or glaciation in scope and impact.   *Photo by Marion Jackson*

359

PREHISTORIC CHRONOLOGY

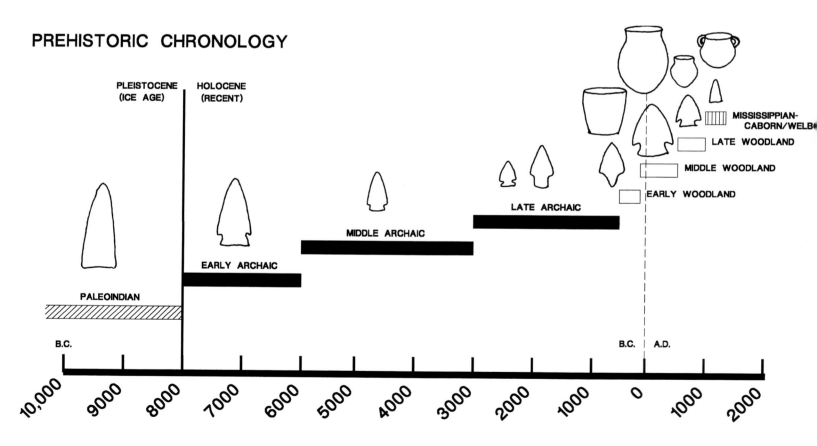

PLEISTOCENE
(ICE AGE)

HOLOCENE
(RECENT)

MISSISSIPPIAN-
CABORN/WELB●

LATE WOODLAND

MIDDLE WOODLAND

EARLY WOODLAND

LATE ARCHAIC

MIDDLE ARCHAIC

EARLY ARCHAIC

PALEOINDIAN

B.C.

B.C. | A.D.

10,000   9000   8000   7000   6000   5000   4000   3000   2000   1000   0   1000   2000

Prehistoric chronology from 10,000 B.C. to the present showing projectile points and pottery shapes for the respective periods.

45. Prehistoric Peoples of Indiana

C. Russell Stafford

For men may come and men may go, But I [nature] go on forever.

> —*Alfred, Lord Tennyson*, The Brook

As Europeans explored and began settling Indiana in the seventeenth century and later, they encountered Algonquin-speaking Miami and Potawatomi as well as other Native American tribes. These aboriginal groups were recent arrivals in what is now Indiana, having been displaced by other native peoples responding to European settlement along the eastern seaboard. These historically known groups are not directly related to the prehistoric cultures identified by archaeologists. Archaeological research during the past six or more decades has yielded a wealth of information on the varied and changing lifeways of Native Americans over the last 12,000 years. Unfortunately, much of the record of the past is vanishing through vandalism and urban development, though federal and recent landmark state legislation provide some protection.

Archaeologists base their reconstructions of the past on the widely scattered material remnants and residues left by early inhabitants found in cornfields and woodlots across the state. From these fragmentary but informative remains, four major prehistoric traditions have been defined: Paleoindian, Archaic, Woodland, and Mississippian. Most of these have in turn been divided into periods of varying length, largely based on the subtle changes in artifact styles, technology, and subsistence patterns. What follows is a sketch of prehistoric culture change over the past 12,000 years in Indiana.

PALEOINDIAN HUNTERS

The great chief Michikinikwa, or Little Turtle, one of Indiana's most illustrious sons, when told of the theory that America was originally populated by Asiatics migrating across the Bering Strait, immediately asked, like a loyal son of Indiana, why Asia and the rest of the world could not have been populated by Americans!

> —*Eli Lilly*, Prehistoric Antiquities of Indiana, *Indiana Historical Society, Indianapolis* (1937)

It has been established for some time that Native Americans crossed the Bering Land Bridge between Asia and Alaska by 10,000 B.C., perhaps earlier. The evidence for Paleoindian occupations in Indiana is meager, based primarily on the distribution of spear and dart points now in private and museum collections. These points typically have been collected from the surface of plowed fields as isolated finds, although occasionally artifact scatters or sites have yielded multiple examples from a single location. As of yet, no intact occupations have been discovered which might tell us in detail about the patterns of settlement and subsistence during this period.

Paleoindians (10,000–8000 B.C.) lived in Ice Age climates south of the massive continental glaciers which at their maximum covered much of the northern latitudes of the North American continent. As the glaciers began to retreat, spruce-dominated forests were gradually replaced by mixed conifer–northern hardwood forests in north-ern Indiana and deciduous forests in the south by 8000 B.C. These forests were inhabited by large herbivores, including mammoth and mastodon, some of which were probably preyed upon by Paleo-indians. Although the remains of mammoth and other now-extinct Ice Age mammals have been discovered in various localities in Indiana, to date no prehistoric artifacts have been found in association. (The nearest association of Paleoindian artifacts with mastodon is in eastern Missouri.)

Paleoindians possessed a distinctive and sophisticated stone tool technology, characterized by a lanceolate concave-base shaped point with a flute. The flute is a narrow channel-like depression that originates from the base of the point and facilitates attachment of a wooden shaft. Workmanship was excellent, and high-quality stone material (chert) was typically used. Many Paleoindian points found in Indiana were manufactured from Wyandotte chert, a blue-gray high-quality stone found in the exposed bedrock formations of Harrison County in southern Indiana. Some fluted points have been discovered more than 150 miles from the chert's source location.

A statewide study of fluted point locations has documented their occurrence in 55 Indiana counties, but most are from those border-ing the Ohio River. Judging by the distribution of points, Paleo-indians preferred riparian environments or nearby more elevated overlooks. Especially favored locations were marshes, major stream confluences, sinkhole ponds, kettle lakes, and springs. Paleoindians probably lived in small groups, traveling prodigious distances over the course of a seasonal cycle. Although the evidence for precise subsistence patterns is lacking, hunting was probably the focus of food-getting activities.

ARCHAIC HUNTERS AND GATHERERS

With great acuteness Indians sometimes speak of the deer as their sheep, though, outside of the bison country, the deer meant more to the ancient North Americans than did sheep to most peoples of the old World. . . . It was the main source of animal food and the principal source of raw material for clothing.

> —*John R. Swanton*, Indians of the Southeastern United States, *Bureau of American Ethnology, Bulletin 137* (1946)

The retreat of the continental glaciers and the accompanying climatic warming which marked the beginning of the most recent geological epoch (Holocene) saw dramatic changes in the composi-tion of forests and animal populations. This warming trend peaked about 5000 B.C., after which temperatures cooled to present-day conditions. This thermal peak was accompanied by an expansion of the Prairie Peninsula into northwestern Indiana. By 4000 B.C., the oak-hickory and beech-maple forests found by Euroamerican set-tlers had been established across much of Indiana. Major rivers, including the Wabash, Ohio, and White, were also undergoing significant adjustments in response to the waning influence of glacial

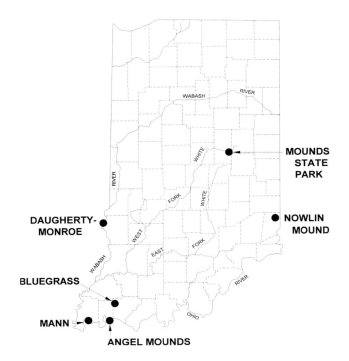

Location of important archaeological sites involving prehistoric peoples.

Projectile points of successive Paleoindian and Archaic periods during prehistory. *Photo by Russell Stafford*

meltwaters. These changes in the environment and available food resources ultimately led to dramatic changes in the way of life of Archaic peoples, especially in contrast to the previous Paleoindian period.

Early Archaic (8000–6000 B.C.) peoples largely continued the nomadic lifeway found in the preceding Paleoindian period, though it was no longer based on the hunting of large Ice Age mammals. Compared with the later Archaic, the hunting of animals such as white-tailed deer and smaller mammals was probably more important than gathering plant foods. Spear and dart points from this period, with a characteristic diagonal or corner notch at the base, are commonly made of high-quality cherts such as Wyandotte. These stone tools were an important part of the hunting tool kit and were maintained for protracted intervals by their makers through re-sharpening and repair.

Like the Paleoindian, the Early Archaic is an elusive period. Points are commonly found in upland areas in most parts of the state, but isolated or widely separated finds are typical. There is good evidence, however, that Early Archaic peoples also lived in major river valleys such as the Ohio. Largely undisturbed occupations, sometimes buried more than 10 feet below the current surface of the Ohio River floodplain, have been found in Harrison, Dearborn, and Switzerland counties. The Ohio River has been actively building its floodplain both laterally and vertically over the last 10,000 years. As a result, the ground surfaces that were present about 8,000 years ago are now buried under many feet of river sediments.

By at least 3000 B.C., a more settled way of life was emerging in southern Indiana. During the later part of the Middle Archaic (6000–2500 B.C.) and the Late Archaic (2500–500 B.C.), camps were occupied over multiple seasons rather than a matter of weeks as in the Early Archaic. Further, many settlements were located near rivers, where aquatic resources such as fish and shellfish were available. In fact, at least by the Late Archaic, some occupations along the Ohio, the Wabash, and forks of the White are characterized by vast concentrations of mussel shell called shell middens or mounds, representing locations where inhabitants repeatedly ate and disposed of shellfish gathered from rivers.

The Bluegrass site, located in Warrick County near Evansville, is a well-documented example of Middle to Late Archaic occupations typical of southern Indiana. Radiocarbon dated to between about 3250 and 3000 B.C., Bluegrass overlooks a valley containing a former Ice Age lake bed, which was probably a wooded wetland for at least part of the year. A deciduous forest with productive nut-bearing hickory and oak trees would have been found in the adjacent rugged uplands.

Extensive excavations at the site revealed evidence of an intensive occupation, as shown by a thick, organic-rich deposit or midden filled with fire-cracked rock, animal bone, and carbonized plant remains. More than 100 pits, some very large, had been excavated by the inhabitants for various purposes. Food processing associated with hickory nutmeat extraction probably accounts for at least some of the pit construction, cracked rock, and abundant hickory nutshell found at the site. Experiments by archaeologists suggest that hickory nutmeats can be efficiently extracted by a stone-boiling technique. Rocks are heated in a fire and then placed in a skin-lined pit filled with water. As the rocks cool, they are removed and replaced by other heated rocks. As this process is repeated, the liquid can be brought to a boil. Hickory nuts collected from the nearby forest were pulverized and then placed in the boiling liquid, where the heavier nutshell sank to the bottom, but the nutmeat and nut oil floated to the top, to be skimmed off and placed in containers for later use. Ethnohistoric accounts of tribes in eastern U.S. indicate that hickory milk, as it was called, was a prized commodity, commanding a high price among traders on the early frontier.

> They pound them to pieces, and then cast them into boiling water, which after passing through fine strainers, preserves the most oily part of the liquid; this they call hiccory milk. It is as sweet and rich as fresh cream.
>
> —*Bartram's description of Creek Indians' use of hickory nuts in the 1770s, as cited in* American Anthropologist *(1922): 177*

The village at Bluegrass was not only the locus of domestic activities but also a place where the dead were interred. Evidence of 80 or more human skeletons was found buried in the village midden. At this time it was generally not customary to bury the dead in a separate cemetery or mound. Male and female adults, adolescents, and infants were all found interred at the site. Individuals were placed in shallowly dug pits or at times in pits originally used for other purposes. Some were buried in an extended position on their backs, as practiced today; others were on their sides with the knees drawn partially up toward the chest, and some were tightly flexed with the knees against the chest.

Artifacts were found buried with some individuals, presumably to accompany them in their afterlife, but also as a sign of their status in the community before death. Skilled hunters were likely to attain the highest position of status. Grave goods are personal items such as a favorite stone tool or piece of jewelry. Stone spear points and drills, mussel shell, perforated dog canines, woodchuck mandibles, shell beads, bone pins, and a turtle shell rattle were all found with burials. The bone pins, which were probably used as fasteners on clothing, are engraved with intricate designs including crosshatched, zigzag, and concentric "S" line patterns.

At death, domestic dogs were also given special treatment. With one exception, however, dogs were buried on the lower slopes of the hill, away from the main occupation area. Dog burials were common during the Middle Archaic in the Midwest. These light-limbed terrier-sized dogs probably assisted in hunting.

WOODLAND GARDENERS AND TRADERS

> Three feet below the ashes, we came upon a pipe, a copper needle, pieces of pottery, and two adult skeletons, one of which was nearly entire, lying upon what must have been a log of wood. . . . The fact that both the earthen vessels were full of black mould, and that one of them also contained numerous pieces of tortoise shell, may indicate that they were filled when buried with food for the departed.
>
> —*J. W. Foster, Dr. T. Higday's 1870 account of early excavations at the Middle Woodland Goodall mounds in La Porte County, Indiana, in* Prehistoric Races of the United States of America *(1878)*

Archaic cultures used baskets or possibly skin bags as containers, but the making of ceramic pots after 500 B.C. signifies the beginning of the Woodland tradition in Indiana. The addition of the pottery to an essentially Archaic foraging lifestyle did not lead to any immediate or dramatic changes, although Woodland cultures of considerable complexity would emerge shortly thereafter. The first ceramic vessels were thick-walled (about 0.5 inches) flowerpot-shaped containers, associated with the Early Woodland period (500–100 B.C.). The clay contained large fragments of rock or temper, which, along with low firing temperatures, resulted in crude, heavy vessels. This early pottery, named Marion-thick (based on its initial description from a site in Marion County), is found widely at sites across the Midwest, but rarely in large numbers.

Perhaps the most recognizable change associated with the later Early Woodland (called Adena) and especially the following Middle Woodland (100 B.C.–A.D. 500) period was the construction of elaborate earthworks and burial mounds at regional centers. The Nowlin Mound in Dearborn County near the Whitewater River was an elliptically shaped Adena mound 165 feet across and 15 feet high. Built in several stages, it contained seven tombs or crypts constructed with logs, each holding a burial and grave goods. Burial of high-status people in specially constructed mounds was common during the Middle Woodland period as well. The prominent earthen mounds used for human burial during this period symbolize the importance of mortuary customs in Middle Woodland cultures. These practices are especially well documented in central Ohio and the Illinois River Valley, but are also represented in eastern and southwestern Indiana. Apparently, mounds with central tombs were not usually built for the interment of a single person, but were reused over time. The dead were placed in the burial crypt but were later removed once the body had decomposed; the disarticulated remains were bundled together and reburied in other parts of the mound.

Unlike burials at the Archaic Bluegrass site, some Middle Woodland interments were accompanied by exotic or well-crafted artifacts possibly representing symbols of high rank or status in the society.

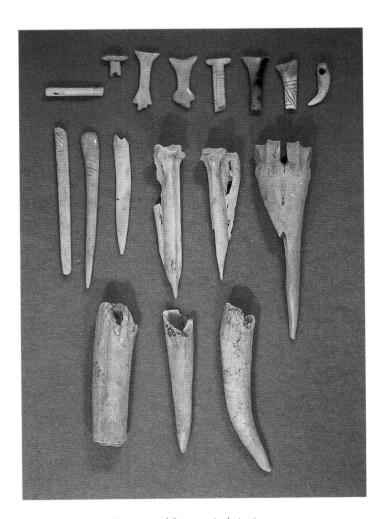

Bone and antler tools recovered from an Archaic site.
Photo by Russell Stafford

Earthenware pot of late Middle Woodland age.   *Photo by Russell Stafford*

Exotic raw materials and other items from distant sources were widely exchanged throughout much of the eastern U.S. during this period in what is called the Hopewell Interaction Sphere. Items include obsidian from the Rocky Mountains, sheet mica from the Appalachians, galena (a lead crystal used as a pigment) from the Upper Mississippi River ore district, cold-hammered native copper from the Great Lakes region, and marine shell from the Gulf Coast. These artifacts, along with finely made Hopewell pottery, distinctive from the everyday utilitarian vessels, are found in a mortuary context as well as in village refuse. In addition, high-quality stone materials were exchanged across considerable distances, including Flint Ridge chert from east-central Ohio, Burlington chert from west-central Illinois, and Wyandotte chert from Harrison County. Exchange probably involved village-to-village trading among prominent headmen in which their prestige among followers was enhanced and alliances with neighboring Middle Woodland groups were established and maintained.

Large geometric earthworks, a prominent feature of the Hopewell heartland in central Ohio, are also found in eastern Indiana. A well-known example is the Anderson earthwork complex in Mounds State Park, situated on a bluff overlooking the White River. The most imposing structure among these earthworks is the "Great Mound," a circular enclosure 384 feet across. Fill from the circular ditch was thrown on the outside perimeter, forming an embankment more than 9 feet high. The southern end was left open to form a gateway that allowed access to a low mound in the center. Excavation of this mound revealed burned platforms, an elevated rectangular structure, and an adjacent subfloor log tomb containing a redeposited cremation, a bundle burial, and grave goods. A screen or fence may have surrounded the small mound, perhaps shielding ceremonial activities from outside viewers. The complete complex at Anderson, as at other earthwork sites, was probably built over many generations spanning several centuries. These locations likely functioned as gathering places for regional populations of Middle Woodland peoples for periodic ceremonies associated with burial of the dead.

Although not as well documented, the Mann site in Posey County near the Ohio River also has series of burial mounds and earthen enclosures covering a minimum of 430 acres. Unlike the Anderson complex, Mann has an associated Middle Woodland village. Hopewellian artifacts have been recovered from both mound and village contexts and include freshwater pearls, platform pips, clay figurines, obsidian, clear quartz crystals, copper awls, shark teeth, drilled bear canines, and galena. The quantity of exotic artifacts and the strategic location of the Mann site on a major waterway have suggested to some that it functioned as a major exchange center in the Hopewell Interaction Sphere.

Accompanying these widespread contacts among prehistoric peoples in the eastern U.S. were changes in subsistence practices.

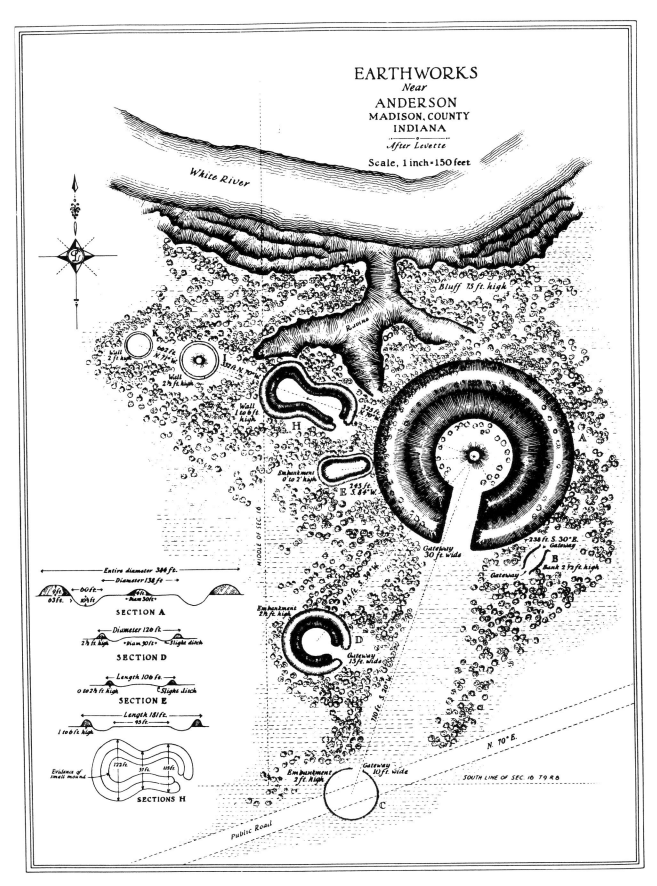

Site map of earthworks at Mounds State Park near Anderson, Indiana.

Although hunting and gathering, particularly of aquatic resources such as fish and shellfish, continued to be vital, cultivation of native oily and starchy seed crops assumed a meaningful role in the diet of Middle Woodland peoples. Oily seeds consisted of sunflower and sumpweed, while archaeologically more abundant starchy seeded plants include goosefoot, knotweed, and maygrass. The latter plants are weedy annuals that pioneer disturbed ground locations such as today's roadsides. These starchy plant foods have been found at the Middle Woodland–period Mann and Daugherty-Monroe sites in southwestern Indiana. Squash rinds and/or seeds have also been recovered from these sites. The growing of corn, a crop of Meso-american origin, was probably of little or no consequence during this period. Indigenous plants were likely grown in small garden plots near widely dispersed villages. Once harvested in the spring, seeds were prepared by boiling in conical jars over a fire. Prolonged cooking broke the seeds down into a gelatinous liquid that was possibly augmented with other foods to make a porridge-like meal.

The Daugherty-Monroe site in Sullivan County near the Wabash River represents a small village typical of the Middle Woodland period. Of particular interest are the remnants of seven house structures exposed by extensive excavations at the site. Patterns of holes that represent the locations of support posts for the walls of structures indicate roughly circular houses ranging from 7 to 24 feet in diameter. Those houses with double walls, sunken floors, and protected entrances appear to reflect cold-season conditions. Other houses, perhaps used in warm weather, have only single-wall construction, with entries simply indicated by breaks in the wall. Both within and surrounding these structures were pits that served a variety of functions, including storage and food preparation. Though estimates of village size are inherently difficult to make, as many as 100 people may have lived at the site at once.

The following Late Woodland period (A.D. 600–1000) is marked by an absence of widespread exchange, geometric earthworks, and large, elaborate mounds associated with the Middle Woodland period. The reason for the collapse of Hopewell remains elusive, but may involve population growth and the increased importance of corn agriculture. Corn (maize), which was of little or no consequence during the Middle Woodland, emerges as an essential food during the Late Woodland, but not without affecting health. Dental observations on skeletal populations have shown that cavities occur earlier in Late Woodland in contrast to Middle Woodland groups as a result of increased carbohydrate intake. The bow and arrow also generally replaced the spear and spear thrower (or atlatl) in hunting during the Late Woodland period. Arrow shafts were tipped with small triangular stone points.

MISSISSIPPIAN FARMERS

They have temples where they preserve the bones of their dead chiefs, and what is noteworthy is that the chiefs have much more power and authority than among all of our savages [to the northward]. They command and are obeyed.

—J. R. Swarton, Father Zenobe Membre describing the late-seventeenth-century Taensa of the lower Mississippi Valley, in Indians of the Southeastern United States (1946)

Archaeological dig showing layout, methods, and tools used.   *Photo by Marion Jackson*

Out of a Late Woodland culture in southwestern Indiana called Yankeetown (A.D. 850–1000) emerged the Mississippian culture (A.D. 1000–1450). When Hernando de Soto and other Europeans explored the southeastern U.S. in the sixteenth century and later, they encountered tribes such as the Natchez and Taensa, who had planned and fortified towns and temples and practiced intensive agriculture and warfare. Mississippian sites distributed throughout the lower Ohio Valley appear to reflect this historically observed pattern. Corn, beans, and squash became the mainstays of the diet. Fields were cleared by cutting and burning trees, but after a period the land was left fallow as soil fertility fell and new fields were cleared. This shifting cultivation supported large permanent communities with a ruling elite. Judging from the fortifications at these sites, warfare was chronic.

The Angel site on the outskirts of Evansville along the Ohio River is by far the largest Mississippian site in Indiana, covering more than 100 acres. The town was protected by a bastioned wall more than 6,000 feet long, constructed of an estimated 4,500 logs. A terraced flat-topped mound (Mound A) standing 44 feet high and 650 feet long is in the approximate center of the town. A large plaza is located to the west of the mound. Excavation of Mound F by Glenn Black of Indiana University in the early 1940s found evidence of a 4-foot-high primary mound on top of which was built a large rectangular structure (90 x 45 feet) likely representing a temple. Burials in intrusive pits on the east slope of the mound facing the plaza are believed to be associated with mortuary rites conducted in the temple as described for some southeastern tribes. A fluorite figurine discovered in an intrusive pit, carved in the likeness of a seated adult male, may represent an idol connected with the temple.

A residential area was also found at the site, as indicated by wall trenches containing postholes arranged in a rectangular pattern. Walls of dwellings were constructed with a cane mat plastered with clay. Complicated overlapping of wall trenches and post patterns shows that houses were periodically rebuilt in the same location within the town. Black estimated that perhaps as many as 1,000 people lived at the Angel site.

Angel was the largest of a series of related communities. Smaller villages or hamlets as well as farmsteads representing individual families existed in the surrounding region. Reasons for the demise of Mississippian culture remain mostly speculative, but may entail warfare, climatic change, and soil exhaustion. Although Mississippian culture per se ceased to exist in the lower Ohio and Middle Mississippi valleys, similar lifeways clearly continued in the southeastern U.S. In Indiana, the dispersed and unfortified settlement pattern of the immediately following Caborn-Welborn period (after A.D. 1450) suggests a significant change in settlement, and maybe subsistence strategies, just as Europeans arrived in the New World. The recovery of brass, an early European trade good probably obtained from neighboring peoples to the east, shows that these sites were occupied into the early historic period.

> We followed an Indian trail . . . in the center of which stands a trunk of a tree, no vestige of greenness or vegetation about it, but stands naked. . . . As I gazed at the tree, the thought passed through my mind that it was an emblem of the Pattawattamie nation. Its strength, greatness, and glory had passed away, but was now a weak and fast receding unglorified thing.
>
> —*George Winter, August 19, 1837, from* The Journals and Indian Paintings of George Winter *(1948)*

Contact with European explorers, traders, and settlers beginning 500 years ago had a devastating effect on indigenous cultures of eastern North America. Intertribal political and economic relationships initiated by the fur trade, co-opting of land by Europeans, and the introduction of Old World diseases, to which native peoples had little resistance, all affected the cultural and demographic viability of indigenous peoples. The historic period then is one of massive movements of cultures from their original homelands in response to pressures from other tribes and Europeans. The Miami, for example, moved into Indiana in the late seventeenth century from southeastern Wisconsin and Illinois. The Potawatomi came from the Lake Huron area, and the Delaware arrived from the east in the middle of the eighteenth century. Unfortunately, by the time anthropology was established, even as a fledgling discipline, the opportunity to study these peoples firsthand had largely been lost. We know them only from sketchy and often ethnocentric historical accounts of European travelers.

* * *

From this brief outline of Indiana prehistory, it is evident that Native American culture was not static during the last 12,000 years, but underwent a dynamic series of transformations which archaeologists have only begun to document and understand. Considerable work is yet to be done.

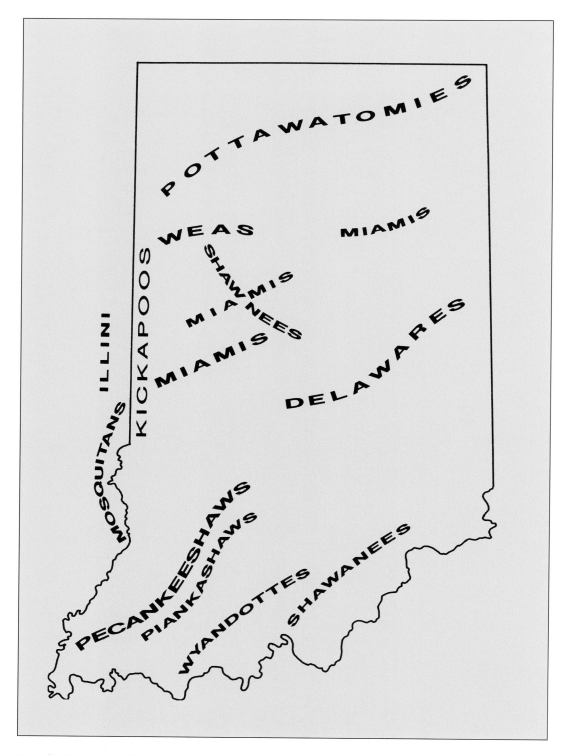

Map of Indiana showing location of Indian tribal lands.   *Modified slightly from early map by Daniel Hough*

46. The Wave of Settlement

George R. Parker

INDIANA: LAND OF INDIANS

The Great Spirit above has appointed this place for us, on which to light our fires and here we will remain. As to boundaries, the Great Spirit knows no boundaries, nor will his children acknowledge any.

—*Tecumseh, Chief of the Shawnee*

Evidence is accumulating that Native American populations were much larger in the Americas at the beginning of the historic period than once believed, but diseases brought by the Europeans resulted in rapid decline of their populations from the 1400s to the 1700s. The impact of these Native American inhabitants on the Indiana landscape was probably extensive during the period of peak population size and was still evident in the 1700s, when their population had been greatly diminished. Their occupation over several thousand years undoubtedly changed the character of natural communities as areas were occupied, disturbed, and abandoned through time. However, natural processes would have maintained a landscape dominated by forest, prairie, and wetlands.

These natural communities of the Great Lakes region supported large numbers of furbearing animals which were to become the driving force in early European occupation of the region. Fur trade with the French enriched the lives of Indian tribes and also changed their culture as they became dependent on French products in their daily lives.

The fur trade was carried on by means of an exchange of raw furs and merchandise. The trading convoys usually left Montreal in May, reached Detroit in July, and from there fanned out to the different posts. After disposing of their goods to the savages and to French hunters and trappers, they returned home loaded with peltries. The return trip was scheduled to reach Montreal before bad weather began in November. . . . Articles suitable for trade were those used by the savages and by the French woodsmen in their primitive life of hunting, trapping, and warfare. . . . The furs chiefly in demand were skins of the beaver, bear, raccoon, otter, red fox, mink, fisher, wolf, and deer. Beaver was the most desirable.

In 1715 the French government granted permission to reestablish the conge system (a licensing system allocating certain posts and trade routes to private traders), which had been discontinued in 1696. One of the reasons given was that the officials hoped to conciliate the Ottawa, Miami, and Illinois who were all middlemen in the fur trade with the more distant tribes. Along with this change in policy, the governor of New France was given authority to found and garrison as many posts in the interior as he thought necessary. Rumors which reported Englishmen among the Illinois and Miami Indians prompted this need for a military force to protect French claims.

—*John D. Barnhart and Dorothy L. Riker,* Indiana to 1816: The Colonial Period

Written accounts of Indian occupation date from these early French fur traders in the mid-1600s. Miami, Potawatomi, and Delaware had the greatest populations, with smaller groups of Wea, Shawnee, Wyandot, Kickapoo, Piankashaw, and Chickasaw also occurring in various areas of the state. These tribes were late arrivals to the state, driven through conflict with other tribes over the fur trade with the French, from the north and east during the late seventeenth to middle eighteenth centuries.

Indians of this period were well adapted to their life in the wilderness as R. David Edmunds described in *The Potawatomis, Keepers of the Fire:*

Potawatomi life followed the rhythm of the seasons. During the summer the Indians formed large villages, usually along streams or rivers, where Potawatomi women planted small fields of beans, peas, squashes, pumpkins, melons, and tobacco. They also raised an abundance of corn, which was traded to the French or to more northern tribes such as the Ottawas or Chippewas. Crops from their fields were supplemented by a variety of products which the Indians gleaned from the nearby lakes and forests. Wild rice was harvested when it was available, as were many types of nuts, roots, and berries. In the spring the Potawatomies collected maple sugar, which they used extensively as a condiment.

During the winter the Potawatomies dispersed into smaller family related villages or hunting camps and scattered throughout their territory. Although the Indians continued to catch a few fish through the ice, in the cold months they depended more heavily upon hunting, tracking animals, especially deer, through the snow. They also relied upon food stored from the summer and upon migratory waterfowl which had been killed and preserved during the autumn.

Houses or wigwams were constructed from poles bound together with basswood or skin strips and covered with the bark of elm trees or mats woven from cattails. Canoes were made from the bark of elm or linden by cutting through the bark at two places on the tree about 12 feet apart, then joining these two cuts longitudinally and removing the bark in one piece. The bark was then reversed so that the inner surface became the outside of the canoe. The two ends were then sealed, and the middle was opened using stick braces.

Native Americans practiced extensive agriculture in Indiana in pre-settlement days. Indian villages with cornfields covering several hundred acres were destroyed during early military expeditions in northern areas of the state. Corn was planted in rows or hills and kept free of weeds through hoeing by Indian women and children.

Crops were grown in natural clearings or in openings created in the forest. Stone axes were used to kill trees by bruising the bark, and fire was used to clear the underbrush. Crops were then planted between the large, standing dead trees. Since fertilizer was not used, openings declined in productivity after a few years of cropping and were abandoned for newly cleared areas. This practice of clearing, burning, cropping, abandonment, and forest regrowth must have strongly influenced forest structure over localized areas of Indiana. Indians also influenced plant and animal communities through gathering of wild plants, collection of maple sap, and trapping animals for food and fur. Wounds caused by gashing maple trees (and probably other species) to collect sap likely killed many trees within a few years and changed the structure of forests.

In addition to the use of fire in clearing land for crop fields, it was also used to burn grasslands to attract or drive game animals such as deer, buffalo, and elk, particularly in northwestern Indiana. During unusually dry seasons, these fires would have continued into the understories of woodlands. Fires maintained the prairies and grassy savannas and undoubtedly changed the structure of forests over large areas of Indiana. Many of the current old-growth forests with overstories of oak and understories of sugar maple probably resulted from Native Americans' use of fire and their cultivation activities.

Localized concentrations of such large animals as bison, elk, and deer also altered the structure of plant communities through browsing and trampling. For example, early written accounts describe salt licks covering several acres, with the surrounding forest being devoid of undergrowth for miles around.

Early travelers provide good descriptions of the Indiana landscape and activities of Indian tribes. William Johnston described the land around an Indian villiage near the Elkhart River in 1809.

> Eighteen miles further you come to the Elkshart river, a branch of the St. Josephs of Michigan. For eight miles before you come to this river you come to a thicket of young hickories and oaks, about as thick as a mans thumb, and growing so close together that it is impossible to penetrate it at any other place than by the road. This land is as rich as any in Kentucky, and there is no doubt but it would be as fruitable if cultivated.

> Immediately on crossing the river, which is about fifty yards wide, a most delightful prospect is presented to view. There is scarcely a tree in an acre of ground for three miles. Here is an Indian village of about twenty houses. . . . The village is beautifully situated on the edge of a fine prairie containing about three thousand acres. About a mile west of this prairie the road comes to the bank of the river, at a good spring of water (a thing that is scarce in this country). Here the timber is tall and thick on the ground principally white oak—the soil is a white clay.

The following account of Father Louis Hennepin, a Recollect friar, described the Kankakee River and the use of fire in December of 1679:

> The river Seignelay is navigable for canoes to within a hundred paces of its source, and it increases to such an extent in a short time, that it is almost as broad and deeper than the Marne. It takes its course through vast marshes, where it winds about so, though its current is pretty strong, that after sailing on it for a whole day, we sometimes found that we had not advanced more than two leagues in a straight line. As far as the eye could reach nothing was to be seen but marshes full of flags and alders.

> For more than forty leagues of the way, we could not have found a camping ground, except for some hummocks of frozen earth on which we slept and lit our fire. Our provisions ran out and we could find no game after passing these marshes, as we hoped to do, because there was only great open plains, where nothing grows except tall grass, which is dry at this season, and which the Miamis had burned while hunting buffalo, and with all the address we employed to kill some deer, our hunters took nothing; for more than sixty leagues journey, they killed only a lean stag, a small deer, some swans, and two wild geese for the subsistence of thirty two men. If our canoe men had found a chance, they would infallibly have all abandoned us, to strike inland and join the Indians whom we discerned by flames of the prairies to which they had set fire in order to kill the buffalo more easily.

The early pioneers found Indian villages, camping places, dancing floors, burial grounds, gardens, and large cornfields particularly in the northern half of Indiana. Indians also had extensive trail systems throughout the state. Many would later become the travel routes for European settlement. The Wabash Trail, extending from Lake Michigan, near Chicago, to the Wabash River in Carroll County, was one of the most important Indian trails in the state. It was also used by the French, and later became an important road for the early settlers of the Wabash Valley to haul their products to Chicago and Michigan City.

While Native Americans were important in disturbing plant and animal communities in Indiana, the yearly extent of their farming activities would have been small. It is probable that less than 100,000 acres of land would have been under cultivation with the estimated 20,000 Indians living in Indiana in the late 1700s. Recent estimates of Native American populations indicate that there may have been as many as 200,000 living in the state in the fifteenth century. If this larger estimate is true, their impact on the Indiana landscape would have been much greater at that time.

While their use of shifting cultivation and fire may have disturbed large areas of the landscape during their several hundred years of occupation, most of the Indiana territory was still in natural vegetation at the beginning of active European settlement around 1800. It is estimated that approximately 20 million acres of forest, 2 million acres of prairie, 1.5 million acres of wetlands, and slightly more than 1 million acres of glades, barrens, swamps, and savannas were present at that time.

THE PIONEERING ERA

> Man is everywhere a disturbing agent. Wherever he plants his foot, the harmonies of nature are turned to discord.
> —*George Perkins Marsh*

The French were the first active white settlers in Indiana, starting in the early 1700s. Trading posts were established near the Indian villages of Kekionga (Fort Wayne), Ouiatenon (near Lafayette), and Chippecoke (Vincennes), primarily for fur trading with the Indians.

Vincennes became the first settlement of white families (primarily French-Canadians) in Indiana territory. These families kept large numbers of cattle and hogs in confined pastures and grew wheat, corn, rice, cotton, and tobacco on land close to the fort. Manure was solid waste to the French and usually was placed on the winter ice of local streams to disappear with the spring thaw. The French were responsible for introducing a large number of exotic plants to the territory, including Kentucky bluegrass and white clover. Many of these species spread across the landscape as new areas were settled.

The taming of the Indiana wilderness began in earnest following the American Revolution, moving north from the Ohio River in the southeastern corner of the territory. Eighteen counties of southern Indiana were organized between 1795 and 1817. The white population of the state increased by 500 percent (24,520 to 147,178) from 1810 to 1820. Settlement proceeded north in the territory as Indian lands were ceded to the United States government. By 1820, 51 counties had been organized.

The late 1700s to the 1840s was a period of conflict between two

The present Fort Ouiatenon was built in 1930 along the Wabash River some four miles southwest of West Lafayette as a replica of the original 1717 French fort. The historical park now hosts the annual Feast of the Hunter's Moon, which re-creates the eighteenth-century gathering of French fur traders and Native Americans. *Photo by Richard Fields*

cultures, with the Indians defending their land and way of life and the pioneers seeking new lands for farming and development. An unresolvable difference centered on the concept of land ownership. Native Americans viewed themselves as belonging to the land, which their tribe owned collectively through successive generations of inhabitants. The settlers, having European ancestry, believed in the right of individual ownership of land.

The Native Americans' lifestyle changed rapidly as they adopted white man's technology. The following narrative from *The Potawatomis, Keepers of the Fire* describes changes which had occurred in Indian culture as a result of their association with French traders and early settlers:

By the 1820's the Potawatomis had accepted many of the physical trappings of white culture. Deerskin hunting shirts and dresses had been discarded for garments of brightly colored calico or flannel, and although some men still wore buckskin leggings, many others preferred cloth trousers similar to their white neighbors'. Both sexes continued to wear moccasins, but their winter dress now included a trade blanket instead of a buffalo robe or a bearskin. Potawatomi men no longer shaved their heads in the traditional manner of warriors, choosing instead to wrap their hair in a cloth turban modeled after those of the Shawnees. They were wholly dependent upon

the traders for the many necessities of life and purchased much the same hardware and dry goods as did white settlers. An inventory of merchandise at the Indian factory in Chicago resembles that of a typical frontier general store. . . . Many of the more affluent Indians, especially the mixed-bloods, constructed log cabins, although the majority of the tribe continued to live in the more traditional wigwams.

But if the Potawatomis accepted the products of American technology, they rejected the American ideal of becoming small yeoman farmers. The repeated attempts by both government and religious leaders to transform the tribe into a nation of small, self sustaining farmers met with little success. . . . Most of the tribe continued to plant their gardens, raising small crops of corn, beans, and pumpkins, but they remained horticulturists, not agriculturists. . . .

To the Potawatomis, the French trader, not the Anglo farmer, represented a goal of acculturation. The trader was a man of wealth and enjoyed economic and political influence, yet was not tied down to a farm and the back-breaking labor required to maintain it. Moreover, compared to American farmers, traders represented a more accessible goal, for many of the creoles also had acculturated toward the Potawatomis, marrying Indian women and adopting certain facets of Potawatomi culture.

Monument at Battleground, Indiana, which commemorates the battle between the Native Americans and the army of General William Henry Harrison on November 11, 1811. This battle broke the back of the Indian resistance in Indiana, opening the territory to settlement and statehood.
Photo by Marion Jackson

home of their childhood, that contained not only the graves of their revered ancestors, but many endearing scenes to which their memories would ever recur as sunny spots along their pathway through the wilderness. They felt that they were bidding farewell to the hills, valleys and streams of their infancy; the more exciting hunting grounds of their advanced youth; as well as the stern and bloody battle fields, where they had contended in riper manhood. . . . All these they were leaving behind them to be desecrated by the plowshare of the white man. As they cast mournful glances back toward these loved scenes that were rapidly fading in the distance, tears fell from the cheek of the downcast warrior, old men trembled, matrons wept, the swarthy maiden's cheek turned pale, and sighs and half-suppressed sobs escaped from the motley groups as they passed along, some on foot, some on horseback, and others in wagons—sad as a funeral procession. I saw several of the aged warriors casting glances toward the sky, as if they were imploring aid from the spirits of their departed heroes, who were looking down upon them from the clouds, or from the Great Spirit, who would ultimately redress the wrongs of the red man, whose broken bow had fallen from his hand, and whose sad heart was bleeding within him. . . .

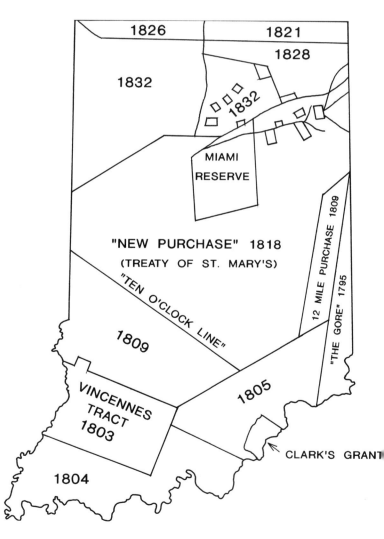

Transfer of Native American land that is now Indiana by a succession of treaties.

Native Americans were finally overwhelmed by the surge of settlement through treaties, starvation, and forced removal to western lands. One of the more tragic examples of their evacuation occurred in September 1838 with the deportation of the Potawatomis from their reservation lands in Marshall County, as was so eloquently described by Sanford Cox in *Recollections of the Early Settlement of the Wabash Valley,* in 1859:

The regular emigration of the Pottawatomies took place under Col. Pepper and Gen. Tipton, in the summer of 1838. Hearing that this large migration; which consisted of about one thousand of all ages and sexes, would pass within eight or nine miles west of Lafayette, a few of us procured horses and rode over to see the retiring band, as they reluctantly wended their way toward the setting sun. It was a sad and mournful spectacle to witness these children of the forest slowly retiring from the

Several years after the removal of the Pottawatomies, the Miami nation was removed to their western home, by coercive means, under the escort of United States troops.

The first wave of settlers were transients on the land. They "squatted" on unsold lands, built cabins, cleared a few acres for corn and vegetables, and subsisted largely on wild animals. As the country became settled, these frontiersmen would sell out to the next wave of settlers and move farther out into the wilderness. The first settlements were along the forested river valleys, where transportation was easiest. Forests were considered to be the best lands for farming since wetlands were not easily drained, and prairies, not being covered by trees, were thought to be inferior cropland. Farms expanded away from the stream valleys as the population increased and road systems improved. The following description of roads in 1830 by S. A. O'Ferrall (from *Travel Accounts of Indiana*) was typical of conditions.

From Versailles, we took the track to Vernon, through a rugged and swampy road, it having rained the night before. The country is hilly, and interspersed with runs, which are crossed with some difficulty, the descents and ascents being very considerable. The stumps, "corduroys" (rails laid horizontally across the road where the ground is marshy), swamps, and "republicans" (projecting roots of trees, so called from the stubborn tenacity with which they adhere to the ground, it being almost impossible to grub them up), rendered the difficulty of traversing this forest so great, that notwithstanding our utmost exertions we were unable to make more than sixteen miles from sunrise to sunset, when both the horse and our-selves being completely exhausted, we halted until morning. I was awoke at sunrise by a "white-billed woodpecker," which was making the woods ring by the rattling of its bill against a tree.

The clearing of forests followed the pattern used by the Native Americans. In the first year, tracts of two to nine acres were cleared by cutting the smaller trees and piling them around the larger trees for burning. These fires killed the larger trees, which were left standing. Corn was planted on the plowed land between the stumps and standing dead trees. Cultivation to remove sprouts and numerous forest herbs was done with a hoe. A small area of land was completely cleared the first year and planted to fruit trees.

After the first year, clearings were made by girdling trees with an axe during the summer or by burning brush piles around the large trees. Dead trees would fall or be cut over a three- to four-year period and were then burned. Ten to 20 acres of deadened trees were usually maintained so that a new area was always dry enough for felling and burning each year.

While some timber was used for farm buildings, split rail fences, and rafts of logs to be floated down river to New Orleans, most of the trees felled were rolled into piles and burned prior to 1860. Hundreds of fires covered the state as massive tree trunks burned for weeks on end. This clearing and burning must have resembled the current clearing of tropical forests in South America and elsewhere. Richard Lee Masgrave described the extent of fall burning on his trip to Vincennes from New Albany in November 1819: "No water, no food fit to eat, dusty roads and constantly enveloped in cloud of smoke, owing to the woods and prairies being on fire for 100 miles."

One-room schools provided the "backbone" of pioneer education, especially in rural areas and in small settlements.   *Photo by Richard Fields*

Cleared land, rail fence, and girdled sweet gum tree near Wheatland, Knox County, Indiana. Photographed about 1885, presumably by Robert Ridgway. Using the man's height as scale, the tree was determined to be 135 to 140 feet in total height.

Continuous cropping and lack of fertilizer led to decreased yields from these cleared areas within a few years, and fields were then abandoned for freshly cleared land. Cultivation did not completely remove native species, so root sprouts and new seedlings rapidly returned abandoned fields to native forest. With an expanding population, as much as 10 million acres of forestland may have been disturbed in this manner by 1860.

Early settlers generally had poor-quality livestock and did not have much use for genetically improved animals, as their semi-wild livestock were allowed to roam the forest throughout the year. Individual owners "branded" their animals by cutting their own distinctive set of notches in each animal's ear to establish ownership, hence the term "earmarked," which is still in usage today.

Hogs in particular quickly adapted and rapidly multiplied in their new surroundings, surviving on the mast of forest trees and other foods as could be found in the wild. The U.S. Census Report indicated that 1.6 million hogs were roaming the Indiana landscape in 1840. These "wild hogs," called "elmpeelers" because of their habit of feeding on slippery elm bark during winter periods, were eliminated from many parts of the state during the long, severe winter of 1843. Feeding and trampling by these introduced animals further added to the rapidly expanding disturbance of Indiana's natural communities.

Changes in the landscape also resulted in other, less dramatic shifts in plant and animal populations. Many of the oak-dominated forests existing in Indiana today are the result of disturbances that occurred during settlement. Heavy disturbance reduced competition with other tree species, allowing oak seedlings to grow and develop into the forests of today.

Wild game was abundant in the state and commonly was used for food, clothing, and trade by the settlers. Squirrel, turkey, grouse, raccoon, bear, and deer provided the major subsistence to settlers until enough land was cleared for crops and livestock. Skins from beaver, otter, raccoon, deer, and bear were traded for essentials such as salt and ammunition. Fur trade also continued with the Native Americans in northern Indiana until the 1830s, when most of them had been forced from the state.

Many of the larger animal species characteristic of the eastern wilderness (such as black bear, cougar, wolf, elk, and bison) declined during the wave of settlement as the result of unlimited harvest, and as the extensive forests were broken for agriculture. Others such as the white-tailed deer temporarily increased as disturbance habitats expanded.

William Newnham Blane, traveling from below the Falls on the Ohio to Vincennes during autumn 1822, described the hunting and selling of wild animals (from *Travel Accounts of Indiana*):

Lane to log cabin surrounded by split rail fence to keep livestock out of crops and gardens.   *Photo by Marion Jackson*

> Before arriving at Hindostan, a small villiage on the East Fork of White River, the country becomes very hilly; and being on that account thinly settled, abounds with game of all descriptions. Some idea may be formed of the abundance of it, from the price of venison at this place, and in the neighbourhood. A haunch will bring only 20 cents (about *1s. 9d* sterling), or the value of 25 cents, if the hunter will take powder, lead or goods. The shopkeepers who buy the haunches, the only parts of the deer thought worth selling, cure and dry them much in the same manner as the Scotch do their mutton hams, and then send them to Louisville or New Orleans. These dried venison hams, as they are called, are very good eating.
>
> The two young men who ferried me over the river, had just returned from a hunting excursion. They had only been out two days; and not to mention a great number of turkeys, had killed sixteen deer and two bears, beside wounding several others. The bear is much more esteemed than the deer, first, because the flesh sells at a higher price; and secondly, because his skin, if a fine large black one, is worth two or three dollars.

The once-unbroken forest canopies supported gray and black squirrels, with fox squirrels surviving on forest and prairie edges. Fox squirrels gradually spread throughout the central region of the state as the forests were reduced to scattered fragments surrounded by crop fields. This pattern is still evident today: fox squirrels occur in scattered woodlands, and gray squirrels are common in the more extensive woodlands of southern Indiana or forests along streams and urban areas. Black squirrels (a color phase of the gray squirrel), once common throughout the state, are now found mostly in far northern Indiana.

Drives were commonly used for decreasing wild animal numbers to reduce damage to crops and livestock. These were conducted by placing men and boys around the perimeter of a large land area and men with rifles on elevated platforms near the center. Animals, mostly deer and wolves, were killed as they neared the platforms in front of the ever-tightening human circle. This same practice was used to kill gray and black squirrels in smaller wooded areas.

Snakes, including rattlesnakes, were also common throughout much of Indiana in the early 1800s, but the settlers persistently reduced their number through killing, trapping, and digging them from dens where they wintered. Since hogs eat snakes and are not very susceptible to their venom, they quickly reduced the snake populations where they ranged freely.

Streams and rivers were used to move produce to markets in New Orleans after 1810. Flatboats were built on the upper reaches of small streams, to be launched and loaded during high flows each spring. Three hundred or so flatboats left the Wabash each year, loaded with products such as flour, beef, pork, hides, lard, tallow,

The forest supplied most of the early settlers' needs, including wood for all needs. Cabin logs and fence rails were among the first necessities for taming the wilderness.   *Photo by Marion Jackson*

whiskey, and livestock. Most boatmen returned on foot, often via the Natchez Trace, from New Orleans to their farms. A few with sufficient funds returned by steamboat after 1816.

Many streams throughout the state were used to power water wheels to drive gristmills and slash sawmills. By 1840 there were 846 active gristmills and 1,248 operating sawmills, with the average slash sawmill producing 800 to 1,000 board feet of lumber per day.

By 1860 the entire state had been surveyed and opened to settlement, all 92 counties had been established, roads, railroads, and canals had been constructed, and telegraph lines spread over the state. Railroads expanded tenfold, from 220 to 2,200 miles, between 1850 and 1860. The state's population had now increased to 1,350,428. In just 60 years the wave of settlement had nearly tamed a 23 million–acre wilderness.

Large mammal species such as the buffalo, elk, cougar, fisher, and wolverine (if present originally) had been eliminated from the state, and many others were rare. Bobcat, turkey, and deer were no longer common. In 1859 Sanford Cox described his feelings about changes in the natural landscape of central Indiana in the late 1820s:

Gristmills powered by water were central to frontier existence, as they provided meal and flour for the "staff of life," and often ran sawmills as well. *Photo by Richard Fields*

Early on, covered bridges, which replaced creek fords or ferries, improved frontier travel. *Photo by Marion Jackson*

Ferries were essential at deeper river crossings. One of the last in operation in Indiana crossed the Wabash just north of its confluence with the White. *Photo by Marion Jackson*

Canals flourished before railroads proved more efficient and cheaper. A portion of the filled-in canal bed and towpath still exists at Wasselman Park Nature Preserve, Vanderburgh County. *Photo by Marion Jackson*

I can well recollect when we used to wonder if the youngest of us would ever live to see the day when the whole Wea plain would be purchased and cultivated; and our neighbors on the Shawnee, Wild Cat, and Nine Mile prairies were as short sighted as we were, for they talked of everlasting range they would have for their cattle and horses on those prairies—of the wild game and fish that would be sufficient for them, and their sons, and their sons' sons. But those prairies, for more than fifteen years past, have been like so many cultivated gardens, and as for venison, wild turkeys and fish, they are now mostly brought in from the Kankakee and the lakes.

Dry prairies, such as the Wea plain, were scattered throughout the state and were rapidly occupied for pasture or plowed for crop production. Many of these grasslands were relatively small, 3 by 12 miles or so, providing ideal environments for settlement. Settlers built their cabins on the prairie-forest edge, taking advantage of the grassland for livestock forage and the forest for building materials.

All public lands had been transferred to private ownership by 1855, but large areas, particularly in the northwestern prairie-wetland region of Indiana, remained undeveloped. This area was suspected of being infertile, had little forest for fuel and shelter, was wet much of the year, was difficult to traverse, and was subject to annual wildfires. Absentee land speculators bought large tracts of land, which further inhibited settlement, to provide extensive grazing lands for sheep and cattle until better drainage could be developed. Cornfields which did exist there were generally small and located on higher ground along the sandy ridges.

NATURE IN RETREAT

The indifferent state of agriculture among us does not proceed from want of knowledge merely: it is from our having such quantities of land to waste as we please.

—*Thomas Jefferson*

While the period from 1800 to 1860 can be characterized as one of widespread disturbance and exploitation, the period from 1860 to 1900 was one of subjection of the natural landscape to human domination. This was a period of conversion of forest to permanent cropland, forest exploitation through selective harvest, drainage of

Agricultural practices of yesterday. Shocked oats, shocked corn, and small crop-field patches are largely gone from the Indiana landscape.
Photos by Marion Jackson, Delano Z. Arvin, and Richard Fields, respectively

wetlands, plowing of the prairie, development of towns and cities, and the extirpation of wild animal species.

The lumber industry expanded rapidly with the development of steam-powered sawmills and the expansion of railroads. This hastened the exploitation of the remaining uncut forests. Lumber production reached 656 million board feet by 1869, increasing to 918 million board feet in 1879, then 1,036,999,000 board feet in 1899, when Indiana led the nation. However, much of the cut timber was simply burned to expand the agricultural land area owing to the difficulty of transporting large-diameter logs unless they were near streams or roads. Only 7 million acres of uncut forest were estimated to remain in 1870, which had declined to slightly more than 4 million in 1880, then to 1.5 million by 1900. (Actual forest acreage always remained greater than the 1.5 million acres of 1900 as a result of regrowth of forests following harvest.) While forest acreage continued to decline until the 1930s, human domination of this magnificent part of Indiana's natural landscape was essentially complete by 1900.

About 14 million acres of Indiana's landscape was in farms by 1880, and the number peaked at 17 million acres in 1910. Most of the increase in farmland resulted from drainage of swamps, lakes, and wet prairies, and the permanent clearing of forests. The advent of steam power was a major factor in the rapid domination of the natural landscape during this period.

Farm size and practices were considerably different in the late 1800s than they had been earlier in the century. Horse power had replaced oxen, and farm size had increased from 100 to 160 acres. Some commercial fertilizer (often the pulverized bones of the vanished bison) was used as well as livestock manure to maintain soil fertility. Crop rotation with legumes became a common practice after 1870. Tillage practices were cleaner with better equipment, which also reduced the amount of human labor required to produce crops. Improved livestock still grazed the woodlands, but they were generally confined to the individual farmer's own land. However, these changes were minor compared with what was to come in the 1900s.

The last major portion of Indiana to be dominated by humans was described by Elmore Barce in 1925 in the *Annals of Benton County:*

> All that portion of Indiana lying north and west of the Wabash, is essentially a part of "The Grand Prairie." Of the twenty-seven counties in Indiana, lying wholly or partially west and north of the Wabash, twelve are prairie, seven are mixed prairie, barrens

The largest log ever hauled in Dubois County was moved by Henry Fitch in 1900 and measured 1,800 board feet volume.
Photo courtesy of Roy C. Brundage

and timber, the barrens and prairie predominating. In five, the barrens, with the prairies, are nearly equal to the timber, while only three of the counties can be characterized as heavily timbered. And wherever timber does occur in these twenty-seven counties, it is found in localities favorable to its protection against the ravages of fire, by the proximity of intervening lakes, marshes or watercourses. On the Indiana side, the most pronounced of the tracts of prairie occur in western Warren, Benton, southern and central Newton, southern Jasper, and western White and Tippecanoe. Benton was originally covered with a great pampas of blue-stem, as high as a horse's head, interspersed here and there with swamps of willows and bull grass, while only narrow fringes of timber along the creeks, and some five or six groves of timber and woodland, widely scattered, served as landmarks to the early traveler.

Those who early observed and explored the grassy savannas of Indiana and Illinois, always maintained that they were kept denuded of trees and forests by the action of the great prairie fires.

While limited plowing and drainage of the prairies and wetlands of northwestern Indiana was under way in the 1840s and 1850s, the

Pastured woodland in Blackford County showing almost total removal of understory shrubs and herbs.   *Photographed by Charles C. Deam, April 1922.*

most extensive activity did not begin until the 1870s. Oxen were used to pull a large plow through the wetlands, cutting a V-shaped ditch two to three feet deep. These early ditches were quickly followed by tile drainage systems to further dry the land. By 1882 there were 30,000 miles of tile drain in the state, changing thousands of acres of wetlands into some of the most productive farmland in the world. Drainage became more efficient and complete with the advent of the steam dredge boat in 1884.

A ledge of limestone rock, located on the Kankakee River about seven miles below the state line in Illinois, prevented complete drainage of the Great Kankakee Swamp, so the Indiana legislature paid $60,000 to have it removed in 1893. By 1917 the 240-mile-long river had been reduced to a 90-mile-long ditch.

Improvement of transportation systems and occupation of the land by tenant farmers quickly followed drainage of the wetlands. Overgrazing by domestic livestock and cultivation of this vast grassland area led to the elimination of fire as a controlling factor. Annual fires set by Indians to move game animals had long controlled the distribution of plant species across the landscape. With control of both fire and water, humans had succeeded in dominating the last major natural region of Indiana.

Clearing of forests and prairies and drainage of wetlands led to declining stream quality and destruction of habitat for aquatic species. Several written accounts from the early 1800s describe the clarity of the water in streams such as the Wabash and White rivers. A description by Caleb Lownes in his *Travel Accounts of Indiana in 1815* is particularly graphic:

> The Wabash rises in a level Country, consequently is not subject to those sudden floods and rapid streams, so prevalent on the Western Waters. Its rising is slow and regular, taking several Weeks to get to full beds—and as long & slow in falling—in common times it does not run more then 1 & 1/2 Miles [per] hour and seldom if ever exceeds 2 1/2. . . . It is a beautiful and valuable stream—the water generally perfectly clear & transparent—exhibiting a clean gravelly bottom—It abounds with Fish of various kinds—Bass Pickerel, Pike, Perch, Catfish.

Soil erosion from the unprotected lands had changed this by the late 1800s. There was also concern over flooding by this time. By the turn of the twentieth century, riverbank forests had been essentially eliminated. According to the *Eighth Annual Report of the State Board of Forestry* (1908):

> The amount of timber now standing along stream banks, together with its character and quality, is hardly worthy of consideration. Throughout the entire distance of three hundred and fifty miles traveled along the Wabash, but few first-class wood lots were found. The prevailing scene is open pasture, cultivated fields and bare river banks.

> Only where the persistent willow, cottonwood, and sycamore could gain a foothold is there any evidence of a forest covering or a protection for the river banks. A few elm, linden, maple, ash and hackberry, also find a poor existence possible until the undermining force of the water loosens their less retentive roots and they are swept away to form choking drifts and troublesome snags in the channel below.

In 100 years of American occupation, the natural landscape of Indiana had been severely disturbed and reduced to scattered remnants. The white man's plow had replaced the Indian's torch; the elk and the bison became the white man's domestic cow. Twenty-two animal species had been extirpated from the state, and many more were endangered. There was a developing concern over the fate of some wild creatures by the late 1800s, which translated into a few laws for protection and the authorization for appointment of a commissioner of fisheries and game, but little was done to slow the loss of habitat until after 1900.

CONSERVATION AND MANAGEMENT

Conservation is a state of harmony between men [humans] and land. By land is meant all of the things on, over or in the earth. . . . The land is one organism. Its parts, like our own parts, compete with each other and co-operate with each other.

    —*Aldo Leopold,* The Round River *(1953)*

While loss and abuse of the natural character of the Indiana landscape continues even today, the period since 1900 has generally been one of increasing awareness, protection, and management. This has been a period of healing for much of the Indiana landscape, with badly abused lands being abandoned and reforested with native or planted trees. Much of this land, particularly in southern Indiana, has been transferred from private to public ownership for parks, forests, wildlife, and recreation, beginning with the purchase of 2,000 acres in Clark County to create the first state forest reservation, now known as the Clark State Forest. Public ownership of land, including state and federal, had expanded to about 700,000 acres by 1989, with 70 percent located in the southern third of the state. These lands include 19 state parks, 13 state forests, 16 state fish and wildlife areas, 17 state historic sites, 21 state nature preserves, 9 reservoir areas, 3 national park areas, 1 national fish and wildlife refuge, and 1 national forest.

Farm practices began to improve after 1900, with better crops, improved livestock, and tidy, well-kept farms. The practices of liming soil to reduce acidity, terracing hillsides, and installing better drainage systems and erosion check dams began in the early 1900s.

The farm tractor was introduced in 1928 and gradually began to replace the horse.

Farming practices began to change rapidly after 1940 with the introduction of inorganic fertilizer (particularly nitrogen), pesticides, and better equipment. Farms changed from diversified operations with livestock and multiple crops to more specialized systems. Farms and fields increased in size as large modern equipment replaced draft animals and chemical fertilizers and pesticides reduced the need for crop rotation and animal manure.

The earth is given as a common stock for man to labor and live on. . . . The small landowners are the most precious part of a state.

    —*Thomas Jefferson, "Letter to James Madison" (1785)*

Modern farming methods greatly increased productivity and reduced the need for areas poorly suited to crop production, but also increased our ability to farm remaining natural environments in good farming areas. Farmers could cultivate larger areas with bigger equipment and began to rent land to expand their operations. Thus the level areas in the central, southeastern, and southwestern regions of the state have become the primary farming areas, with the landscape dominated by cropland intermixed with fragments and ribbons of natural communities. Currently, 13.5 million acres are cultivated in Indiana each year, with corn and soybeans covering more than one-half of the state in any given crop year.

Wetlands continued to decline as more land was tiled and streams were channelized to increase farmland and provide for urban development; now only about 10 percent of the original natural wetlands currently remain. Building of numerous farm ponds and reservoirs has partially replaced these losses. For example, nine large publicly owned reservoirs now cover 36,000 acres in the state.

Wetlands are important as water filters and storage sites, to reduce flood peaks on rivers, and as habitats for plants and animals. Efforts

Intensive agricultural systems and no-till cropping practices have revolutionized the way we grow our food, and have vastly changed the rural landscape of Indiana's grain belt.
Photo by Richard Fields

Industrialization and production of waste have created additional impact on the air, water, and land, creating the need for pollution control and recycling.   *Photos by Richard Fields*

to protect remaining wetlands and to reestablish drained areas have increased since the 1970s, with private landowners receiving government subsidies to restore wetlands throughout the state. Wetlands are being restored between setback levees along the Kankakee River to serve as natural flood-retention areas. Wetlands are also being constructed to provide treatment for municipal and agricultural waste products.

Forest clearing and abuse peaked in the 1930s and then began a long recovery, with removal of livestock and fire and reforestation of abandoned croplands. There are about 4.5 million acres of forestland in Indiana currently, with about 90 percent in private ownership, mostly in small farm woodlots. Private forestlands provide habitat for many native plant and animal species, since they usually are not intensively managed, but suffer from their small size and isolation as long-term habitats for these species. Indiana's forests also provide about 170 million board feet of lumber per year.

Management varies in intensity for forests in public ownership, depending on their designated use. State and federal forests are managed for multiple uses such as timber, wildlife, and recreation, whereas state and federal parks are managed as non-consumptive outdoor recreation areas.

Much public forestland is still recovering from the abuses of the 1800s and early 1900s. For example, the 13,000-acre Charles C. Deam Wilderness in Brown County had 81 small subsistence farms within its boundaries until the early 1900s.

The 2 million acres of prairie in pre-settlement Indiana has been reduced to small remnants along railroad tracks, in cemeteries, and in other odd corners of the landscape. Prairies, unlike forests, did not contain a commodity that could be sold (no longer the case, with high demand for prairie grass seed and plants for restoration), and were mostly found on level land easily converted to other uses. Species that dominated these grasslands, such as big bluestem grass, can still be found along roadsides waiting for their chance once again to cover the landscape.

Savannas are as rare as prairies, mostly because of fire control which allowed the development of closed understories of woody species. Glades and barrens (mostly in southern Indiana) have also

suffered from lack of fire. There are programs currently under way to restore small pieces of each of these communities through the use of prescribed fire. The best examples include the 300-acre Hoosier Prairie Nature Preserve in northwestern Indiana and barrens restoration in the southern part of the Hoosier National Forest.

Since the 1980s, private and public programs to reforest highly erosive farmlands and stream corridors are restoring some of the natural character to Indiana's landscape. These programs are also important in reducing water pollution and providing habitats for plants and animals.

The use of Indiana's landscape for highways, railroads, airports, and transmission lines continues to expand, currently encompassing more than 700,000 acres. While most of these are necessary to a modern society, they have also greatly intruded on the state's natural environment, further fragmenting communities and natural populations. In some instances they are important as habitat for native species such as the prairie communities found along railroad rights-of-way. Programs to restore highway rights-of-way to native species should be expanded to reduce maintenance costs, add scenic quality, and provide habitat. Transmission line rights-of-way can also be managed for more native habitats.

The population of Indiana has continued to expand, reaching 5,554,228 in 1990. About 14,000 Native Americans are believed to reside in the state today; many have maintained portions of their original culture. There has been a continual shift of people from the rural areas to urban centers since the early 1900s. Rapid growth in some urban areas is overwhelming natural features, increasing the need for comprehensive planning to protect open space around cities for people and for wild organisms. Industrial development has also had a heavy impact on natural communities, particularly near the Lake Michigan shoreline.

Improvement in habitat quality and better management since 1900 has allowed the reintroduction of some animal species eliminated during the 1800s. The white-tailed deer, extirpated in 1893 and reintroduced during the 1930s and 1940s, is now common enough to be hunted throughout the state and is becoming a pest in some areas. Thirty-five eastern wild turkeys were trapped in Missouri and released in southern Indiana in 1964. This release program has continued so that huntable populations of wild turkey again occur in many counties. The bald eagle is nesting again in southern Indiana for the first time since 1898.

Unfortunately, not all wildlife species have returned to the state, and additional ones have been lost. The prairie-chicken continued to decline from about a thousand birds in 1941 to none by the late 1970s. The passenger pigeon, present in the millions in the early 1800s, is now extinct, along with the Carolina parakeet. It is doubtful that wild populations of wolf, black bear, or mountain lion will ever again roam the Indiana landscape because of their need for extensive areas of habitat with few people. Many other native plant and animal species are currently in danger of being lost from the state.

There is a need to rapidly expand public lands across the Indiana landscape to ensure long-term survival of some of its once-magnificent wildness. New public lands should be located such that they provide corridors for movement of native species between large public wild areas and so that large natural areas are restored in the highly fragmented regions of the state. Corridors of restored habitat along streams would provide travel lanes for both wild animals and people and also improve water quality. Restoration of a large prairie and savanna (several thousand acres) on the black soils of northwestern Indiana should be a high priority. All lands, both public and private, will need better management to balance natural values with human needs.

As we move toward the close of the second century of American occupation of the Indiana landscape, there are positive signs that protection and restoration of the natural environment will continue. The Department of Natural Resources, federal agencies, and private organizations such as The Nature Conservancy continue to purchase lands for protection of natural resources. Government programs are slowing the loss of wetlands and reestablishing forest and grassland on highly erodible areas and along stream corridors on private lands. Overall, the natural elements are in better condition today than in 1900, but there is still much to do if we are to maintain and continue the recovery of wildness across the Indiana landscape.

Nature is not governed except by obeying her.
—*Francis Bacon,* Proficience and Advancement of Learning *(1605)*

Can nature survive in a progressively modified and often contaminated landscape?
Photo by Marion Jackson

The restored pioneer village at Spring Mill State Park, including the impressive three-story stone water-powered gristmill, is the showpiece of the Indiana state park system. Springtime color accents the quiet beauty of this frontier settlement. The large red-cedar tree on the left is the state record for that species.
Photo by Richard Fields

47. History of Public Conservation in Indiana

Louis D. Hasenstab, Sr.

NATURAL RESOURCE VALUES

Formerly resources belonged to everyone and therefore to no one. The new "conservation ethic" demands that they belong to everyone and therefore each of us.

—*Durward L. Allen,* Our Wildlife Legacy *(1956)*

The value of our natural resources is determined by our perceptions and our sense of values. To cite an example, a frequent visitor to Turkey Run State Park remarked that it was very relaxing and comforting to walk among the huge black walnuts and other tree species and appreciate the natural beauty of the woodland. To do so was an escape and respite from his daily work responsibilities. His listeners were even more impressed with his sense of appreciation of nature when he revealed that he owned and operated a lumberyard. He was able to appreciate the beauty of the trees in the park without having to think in terms of board feet and profits.

Another measure of the value of Indiana's public lands is the cost to duplicate a Department of Natural Resources (DNR) property such as a state park with an inn, a campground, and other major recreational facilities. As a conservative estimate, considering today's land values and costs of construction, it would take $3 to 4 million to purchase 2,500 acres for a state park, and from $12 to 15 million additional to construct an 80-room inn, 400-site campground, swimming pool, family cabins, service buildings, roads, other infrastructures, tools, and equipment to operate and maintain the tract. The economic value of our public forests, fish and wildlife areas, parks, nature preserves, state museum, historical sites, and reservoir recreation areas is very impressive. All 117 or so DNR properties collectively have an estimated replacement cost of at least $500 million.

Aside from the monetary value of the DNR properties, there are intrinsic values essential to our well-being—such as the realization of how dependent we are upon natural resources for our daily existence, and the understanding that we are part of the whole scheme of nature. We cannot measure the value of renewals to the human spirit when people find relaxation and a feeling of exhilaration while enjoying a meaningful outdoor experience.

AGENCY-PEOPLE PARTNERSHIP

Without love of the land, conservation lacks meaning or purpose.

—*Sigurd F. Olson,* Reflections from the North Country *(1976)*

The landholding divisions of the Department of Natural Resources, which manage Indiana's fish and wildlife areas, forests, parks, reservoirs, recreation areas, nature preserves, and historic sites, can rightly be called the state's showcases of conservation. The mention of one of these public properties generally brings to mind visions of attractive natural landscapes, sites of historic interest, recreational activities, and places to relax and renew one's spirit. Many of these areas would not have come into being had it not been for the cooperation of the public with government officials to preserve and protect the natural areas and to provide facilities for a wide variety of outdoor recreational activities.

The acquisition of acreage for the DNR properties was not a unilateral effort on the part of one or two individuals, but a result of the dreams and actions of civic leaders with the support of enthusiastic citizens and a cooperative legislature, which enacted the necessary statutes and made the appropriations. But it was the direct involvement of individuals, business groups, newspaper officials, and schoolchildren that provided the momentum for the acquisition of public lands.

The DNR is a people-oriented agency which maintains a close relationship with the public, one that promotes the best interests of the people and works tirelessly to improve the quality of stewardship of natural resources.

One example of this interaction was the formation in 1933 of the State Conservation Advisory Committee. The SCAC was composed of individuals who were members of the approximately 900 conservation clubs, which had a total active membership of nearly 400,000 in Indiana. Each club had representation on the advisory committee through a county council which, in turn, sent a member to a district meeting, thence to the quarterly meetings of the SCAC.

Another is the one-day Buffalo Riders Conference, held annually since 1973 at one of the state park inns. This conference, which takes its name from the American bison that is displayed prominently on the state seal of Indiana, provides an opportunity for DNR officials to meet with sportsmen, environmentalists, journalists with outdoor interests, and others interested in natural resources to discuss issues and listen to the people's recommendations.

The Park Patch Program, established in 1974 and sponsored by the state park naturalist service, involves park visitors directly by helping them to understand and appreciate their natural resources and the need to protect the fragile environment. It is basically a nature-study activity adapted for various age groups, including five-to-seven-year-olds (Smokey's Friends) and people eight years of age and up (Junior Naturalist), and for those who complete the Junior Naturalist program, the Hoosier Ecologist program is made available. To qualify for certificates and cloth emblems (patches), visitors are required to complete up to three hours of service in the park, attend a certain number of naturalist-led activities, and correctly answer nature questions on a standard list.

In 1981, the Division of State Parks initiated the VIP (Volunteer in Parks) program to provide additional services to the public. Volunteers may perform a variety of routine chores around campgrounds and nature centers, helping the park naturalist handle visitors, thereby allowing more time for scheduled nature programs. Participants in the VIP program receive, in turn, a campsite at no cost.

PROTECTING PUBLIC LANDS

When the original Indiana Department of Conservation (IDC) was created by the legislature in 1919, it had 5 divisions. That number has since grown to 25. The need to regulate the use of resources, the advent of technology, additional knowledge about the scientific

Conservation officers are highly trained individuals who are in charge of enforcing natural resource laws, in addition to many other duties.
Photo by Richard Fields

aspects of resource management, and the steady growth of population and increased demand for more and better recreational facilities all influenced the growth of the DNR. Of the 25 current divisions, 11 are regarded as "front-line" or "showcase" divisions.

Notis!
Trusspassers will B percecuted to the full extent of 2 mungerl dogs which neve was over sochible to strangers & 1 dubble brl shot gun which ain't loded with sofa pillers. Dam if I aint getten tired of the hell raisin on my place.

—*"No Trespassing" sign observed in southern Indiana hill country (1967)*

Division of Enforcement. When we think of law enforcement, we think in terms of individuals charged with the protection of life and property. This division is responsible for ensuring that conservation laws, especially those pertaining to hunting and fishing, are enforced uniformly throughout the state—both on DNR properties and on private land. Conservation officers must meet stringent educational and age requirements and pass security and character checks. They are required to complete intensive training in areas such as law, judicial procedure, substance abuse, firefighting, and public relations. The job of conservation officers today is far more complex than that of earlier "game wardens," whose duties were limited to apprehending violators of fishing and hunting laws.

Officers conduct education programs which stress safety in the use of firearms, snowmobile and motor boat operation, and trapping. In addition, the job includes searching for drowning victims, detection of forest fires, training people to fight forest fires, directing traffic on DNR properties, searching for lost people, investigating violations of hunting and fishing laws, and promoting the message of conservation of natural resources. Conservation officers are an important, visible link between the DNR and the public.

Some insects feed on rose buds
  And others feed on carrion
Between them they devour the earth
  Bugs are totalitarian.

—*Ogden Nash*

Division of Entomology. The Division of Entomology was an original division of the Department of Conservation. Although not as visible to the public as the DNR's landholding divisions, it has important functions as a regulatory agency dealing with insect and plant pests, honey production and apiary inspection, plus inspecting nurseries which grow trees and other planting stock. Its personnel are also responsible for ensuring compliance with USDA regulations on quarantines brought on by insect pests and diseases of plants.

A significant interest in the study of insects and other aspects of the natural resources existed during the nineteenth century when Willis S. Blatchley wrote an exhaustive report on the butterflies in Indiana. Blatchley, who served as state geologist for 16 years beginning in 1894, and his staff produced an impressive volume of scientific reports. Today we are indebted to Blatchley and others for their early research, which started in 1837, on the natural resources in Indiana. The importance of insects and the damage that can be caused to the welfare of the people prompted the governor to establish the Office of Entomology as a separate agency in 1907. Later, the authority to inspect plant nurseries and apiaries was given to the division.

Today, few people give much thought to the problems that diseases and undesirable insects can cause until damage occurs to their farm crops, lawns, gardens, or domestic animals. Homeowners and farmers throughout the state benefit directly and indirectly from the surveillance activity of the Division of Entomology.

Habitat improvement consists in bringing into useful association those conditions needed by a species for reproduction and survival. The wildlife technician is concerned constantly with the arrangement of things. With no change in the total acreage of various cover types, he may be able to shuffle them around and double or triple the number of animals a given area will support.

—*Allen,* Our Wildlife Legacy

Division of Fish and Wildlife. A major reason for the migration of settlers to lands west of the Allegheny Mountains during the early 1800s was that, in many areas of the Atlantic coastal region, human population increases and habitat destruction were causing the supply of fish and game to dwindle. For many years following initial settlement, hunting and fishing conditions were good in Indiana. But as early as a few years before the Civil War, some restrictions began to be imposed concerning the protection of deer and some game birds, and for controlling certain fishing practices within the state.

The Division of Fish and Wildlife (formerly Division of Fish and Game), which presently oversees wildlife management in Indiana, officially started in 1881 when the Office of Commissioner of Fisheries was established. In the 1880s, the legislature enacted fish and game laws which established closed seasons on woodcocks and wild ducks, prohibited the trapping or sale of live quail, and forbade the killing of wild pigeons. Even pollution of the Ohio River was recognized as a serious problem back then.

Early in this century, efforts to improve hunting conditions emphasized the establishment of game farms for raising quail, pheasants, wild turkeys, and even red foxes. The pen-reared animals were released in selected areas for their reported benefit to hunting, without much thought being given to the food and habitat needs of animals. Part of what is now Brown County State Park, and the western portion of Pine Hills Nature Preserve in Shades State Park were sites where game farms were operated and experiments on game breeding were conducted.

Today, it is generally agreed that "put and take" methods of providing game for hunters were not an answer to improving the

Hunting has been a necessary part of our lives historically, and is still an important activity of many people today.

Photo courtesy of the Indiana Department of Natural Resources

quality and quantity of small game production in Indiana. Not every person accepted the practice of raising game in captivity even then. When game farms were first established, some forward-thinking individuals recognized the futility of releasing pen-reared game by noting that a relatively small percentage of game animals raised in captivity was actually taken by hunters.

What the Federal Aid in Wildlife Restoration Act of 1937 did to provide funding for research and management of game animals, the Federal Aid in Fish Restoration Act of 1951 did for the benefit of fish and fishing conditions. The former was referred to informally as the Pittman-Robertson Act, and the latter as the Dingell-Johnson Act, for the legislators who authored those laws. This legislation generated funds for acquiring and improving fish and wildlife habitats by instituting an excise tax on arms, ammunition, and fishing equipment.

In 1940, Indiana launched a program which emphasized adopting practices of game and fish management which were based on scientific studies. The program was interrupted by World War II, but it resumed soon thereafter. The wildlife research program, which was staffed by trained wildlife and fisheries biologists, was supervised by William B. Barnes, who in the minds of many is the consummate conservationist. Barnes coordinated the two federal aid programs, then served with distinction as assistant director, Division of Fish and Wildlife, and as the first director of the Division of Natural Preserves from 1967 until his retirement in 1977.

Today, biologists who implement the federal aid programs, and who work closely with wildlife specialists at Purdue University, are largely responsible for the greatly improved habitat conditions which sportsmen find in the public hunting areas and lakes and streams on DNR properties. Private landowners have also benefited from research conducted by professional wildlife and fisheries biologists.

As of June 1994, the Division of Fish and Wildlife managed 108 properties encompassing 89,418 acres, plus 220 public fishing sites which provide access to lakes and larger streams. The division manages fish hatcheries and fish ladders, wildlife and game-bird habitats, wetlands, ponds, marshes, and accesses to dams and water control stations. In addition, sites for picnicking and camping are maintained for the enjoyment of the public.

A forest is more than an area covered by trees. In many ways, it is like a city—nature's city—constructed and peopled with trees, birds, insects, shrubs, mammals, herbs, snails, ferns, spiders, fungi, mosses, mites, bacteria, and a myriad of other living forms.

—*Jack McCormick,* The Living Forest *(1959)*

Division of Forestry. Before our country was settled by Western Europeans, almost all land between the Atlantic coast and the Mississippi River was heavily forested. In the early 1800s, about 20 million acres of Indiana's 36,291 square miles were covered by forests. By mid-century widespread clearing and intensive farming were depleting the remaining forests at an accelerating rate.

Late in the nineteenth century, conservationists saw the need to protect the remaining forests. In 1901, the state legislature created a five-member State Board of Forestry, which began coordinating the forestry movement in Indiana. Its first acquisition was Clark State Forest, by State Forester Charles C. Deam in 1903. The Division of Forestry (DF), an original division of the Indiana Department of Conservation in 1919, has grown significantly through the years—not only in the number of forest properties, but in size, responsibility, and service to the public.

The primary purpose of the Division of Forestry is to produce timber and demonstrate proper woodland management. In addition, DF promotes farm forestry, operates nurseries, and offers basic recreational facilities such as camping, hunting, fishing, conducted cave trips, picnicking, swimming, boating (electric motors only), and back-country hiking, giving residents of Indiana a wide variety of outdoor recreational facilities in beautiful, natural settings. Despite increased demand, forest managers intend to keep recreational developments in state forests to a minimum so as to preserve their naturalness and integrity.

The division manages 17 different administrative units in 13 state forests. The 145,347 acres in the state forests, plus approximately 190,000 acres in the Hoosier National Forest (administered by the U.S. Forest Service), represent a combined total of nearly 10 percent of the forested land in Indiana. Citizens in counties containing state forests share in the income derived from the sale of timber from those properties.

Division of Forestry staff have a long record of cooperating with the public to protect and improve forest conditions on private lands. In 1921, State Forester Charles C. Deam authored and urged passage of the Indiana Forest Tax Classification Act, the first such state legislation in the nation. This "Classified Forest Act" offers a major property tax reduction to forest landowners who register their forestland, protect it from livestock and fire, and harvest the timber properly. This act has been responsible for protecting and properly managing thousands of acres of farm woodlots, several of which contain some of our finest remaining old-growth forests.

Hardwood and conifer seedlings, grown in state forest nurseries, may be purchased by farmers and owners of large tracts of land for controlling soil erosion, for providing windbreaks, and for timber production, but forest nursery stock is not available to the individual homeowner for landscaping purposes. Division personnel also promote programs which train people to control forest fires—not only on state land, but also on private land and U.S. Forest Service properties.

Treasure is best protected by those who understand its value.

—*Paul B. Sears,* The Living Landscape *(1962)*

Division of Museums. The Division of Museums is responsible for overseeing the preservation and presentation of the natural, cultural,

Timber Stand Improvement (TSI) is a forest-management practice aimed at maintaining proper stocking densities and species composition.   *Photo by Richard Fields*

and industrial history of Indiana through the state museum and state memorials.

The first effort to start a state museum was a display of rocks, minerals, fossils, and curiosities put together by the state librarian in 1862. In 1869, legislation directed the state geologist to collect and preserve examples of Indiana's plant and animal life as well as specimens of rocks and minerals. In addition, a variety of war trophies, cultural artifacts, and oddities were included. In 1888, the state museum and collections were moved to the third floor of the statehouse, the specimens were labled, and the natural history collection was put in scientific order. Since that time, this state collection has grown into a museum that Indiana's citizens can point to with pride.

After being moved a number of times over the years, in 1963 the museum finally settled into its permanent home in the old Indianapolis city hall at Alabama and Ohio streets. With the appropriation of more funds, the addition of trained museum specialists, and volunteer help from members of the Indiana Museum Society, the state museum gradually has developed into a first-class facility that is now fully accredited by the American Association of Museums.

> To see the world in a grain of sand,
> And a heaven in a wild flower;
> Hold infinity in the palm of your hand
> And eternity in an hour.
>
> —*William Blake, "Auguries of Innocence"*

Division of Nature Preserves. For many years the landholding divisions, which managed state forests, fish and wildlife areas, parks,

and recreation areas, acquired and developed areas which, in most cases, contained hundreds or thousands of acres. During this time, knowledgeable DNR administrators recognized the existence of small tracts ranging in size from one to a few hundred acres which contained rare or unusual biological and physical features. These valuable tracts were not acquired, primarily because their limited size did not permit development into forests, parks, and hunting areas. Acquisition of widely scattered tracts would also present protection and management problems. However, it may be just as important to preserve a unique 5-acre tract as one containing 10,000 acres, depending on the relative natural qualities of each site.

The need for preserving Indiana's natural areas and the site locations of rare plants and animals had long been recognized by the Indiana Academy of Science and The Nature Conservancy (see also Part 5, "Protecting What Remains"). Through leadership by those groups, and with the help of committed citizens and members of the legislature, the Nature Preserves Act was passed in 1967 and established this division. The Division of Nature Preserves acquires, preserves, and manages tracts of land that contain rare or unusual examples of the state's elements of natural diversity. Their staff also assists other divisions by making exhaustive studies of the flora and fauna in areas being considered as potential state parks, forests, wildlife refuges, and recreational areas.

Although relatively new to land-resource management, the division has acquired and protected many of Indiana's best natural areas; its impact is much greater than the relatively small total number or acreage of nature preserves would indicate. While much has been accomplished, many deserving tracts remain to be protected. Hopefully, all of Indiana's remaining natural lands can be protected in perpetuity.

> Someday, Americans are going to wake up to the fact that they need more than beer and television for recreation.
>
> *—Supreme Court Justice William O. Douglas (1964)*

Division of Outdoor Recreation. During the 1950s, recreation specialists on the Indiana State Board of Health (SBH) organized a one-day meeting called the Governor's Conference on Recreation, which included directors of city park and recreation departments, physical therapists, and recreation directors from hospitals and health-care centers in Indiana. The SBH had long been interested in promoting recreation as an important ingredient of good health. Summary recommendations forwarded to the governor following the conference resulted in the appointment of the state's first director of recreation in 1961, who was charged with creating an Indiana Recreation Council (IRC) within the SBH.

In 1965, the Indiana Recreation Council evolved into the Division of Outdoor Recreation of the newly established DNR. The division is responsible for conducting studies and formulating statewide plans for recreational development in cities and towns and on DNR properties. In accordance with the federal Land and Water Conservation Act (LWCA) of 1965, funds are allotted annually to each state for the development of parks. Since 1965, the Division of Outdoor Recreation has distributed more than $89 million in Indiana for outdoor recreation.

The division is required to conduct studies every five years to determine the state's recreational needs on a regional basis. Additional responsibilities include coordinating environmental reviews, implementing the state's Natural, Scenic, and Recreational Rivers program, and developing long-distance hiking trails. The division also initiated the Indiana Natural Heritage Program, which is a unique inventory and classification program developed by The Nature Conservancy to assist in the inventory and protection of rare plants, animals, and other important natural features. This program subsequently was transferred to the Division of Nature Preserves, since it fit more appropriately into that division's mission.

The Division of Outdoor Recreation functions as a research arm of the DNR. Whenever a topic needing study is outside the scope of the resource-based divisions, or crosses their lines of authority, Outdoor Recreation is assigned to complete it.

> Many reservoirs store water for several purposes. Monroe Reservoir on Salt Creek, . . . which is the largest single body of water within the state, can store . . . flood waters and reduce floods downstream. . . . The lake behind the huge dam furnishes relaxation and recreation for thousands of people each year.
>
> *—Malcolm D. Hale, "Lakes and Streams," in* Natural Features of Indiana *(1966)*

Division of Reservoir Management. There was no need for flood-control reservoirs when the Native Americans occupied what is now Indiana. Being primarily hunters and gatherers, they cleared only small tracts of land near their villages, which were usually built on second terraces above flood level. Not so with settlers who cleared the forests, drained the wetlands, farmed both watersheds and floodplains, and built cities and towns on river banks to have convenient access to river transportation. Such land-use changes caused increased frequency, height, and duration of flooding along major watercourses.

To protect developments along major streams, and to reduce the flood damage to agricultural fields, appeals went out for action to control floods. As the problem of flood control crossed state lines and political jurisdictions, the public looked to federal agencies for leadership in reducing the tremendous cost of damages caused by floods.

Cagles Mill, constructed in Putnam and Owen counties in 1952 as part of the Army Corps of Engineers federal program, was the first flood-control reservoir built in Indiana. The primary purpose of such reservoirs was to reduce flooding and to limit the damage caused by high waters. They also became popular sites for recreational activities such as boating, fishing, and swimming, as well as camping on adjacent land areas. The economic benefits to nearby communities became an important justification for constructing reservoirs, as local businesses catered to the area visitors.

The Division of Reservoir Management was established in 1968 to take over the management of the state's reservoir recreation areas from the Division of State Parks. At that time there were three such units—Lieber State Recreation Area on Cataract, Raccoon SRA on Mansfield, and two major areas on Lake Monroe. The new division was able to concentrate on such administrative problems associated with the reservoirs as multi-purpose use, waterfowl hunting, motor-boating, wildlife management, and coordinating relationships with adjacent private landowners.

Later, Mississinewa, Salamonie, Huntington, Brookville, and Patoka reservoirs joined the division to provide Hoosiers with a selection of sites for pursuing their favorite water sports. Hardy Lake, constructed by the Soil Conservation Service in 1971, is the only reservoir of nine which is owned entirely by the state. Indiana is the only state which exercises complete control over the recreational facilities on and around its reservoirs. The Corps of Engineers retains the responsibility for controlling water levels of reservoirs and matters pertaining to flood control.

On February 1, 1996, as the result of a resolution by the members of the Natural Resource Commission, the Division of Reservoir Management and State Parks were combined into one administrative unit.

> I do not own an inch of land,
> But all I see is mine.
>
> *—Lucy Larcom, "A Strip of Blue"*

Outdoor recreation activities range from summer picnicking to family cross-country skiing.   *Photo courtesy of the Indiana Division of State Parks*

Reservoirs are managed as multiple-purpose resources, including providing sites and opportunities for water-based recreation.
Photo courtesy of the Indiana Department of Natural Resources

Division of State Parks. In ancient times, kings and emperors provided hunting preserves and areas for rest and relaxation for the privileged few, but such lands were seldom accessible to the general public. The citizens of Indiana are fortunate in having Richard Lieber as the founder and first director of the Indiana State Parks (see also Part 5, "Protecting What Remains"). Emma Rappaport Lieber reported in her biography of her husband, Richard, that during a visit to Brown County in 1910, he gazed upon part of what was then the Brown County Game Preserve and remarked: "This whole county ought to be bought up by the State and made into a state park so that all of the people in Indiana could enjoy this beauty spot."

Lieber's basic philosophy of state-park management was to acquire natural areas, make minimum developments, and provide safe and adequate facilities. To increase visitor enjoyment, Lieber advocated the construction of inns with modest accommodations. He felt that the price of admission and the cost of camping or staying at the inns should be kept at a reasonable level to permit families of moderate means to enjoy the parks. He also felt that users of the facilities should pay a fair share of park operations—a policy still in force today.

In accordance with Indiana's constitution, the state cannot go into debt. Therefore funds must be appropriated for a new state park before purchase of land or developments may begin. Indiana's pay-as-you-go policy is one of the most financially successful methods of operating state parks in the nation. From the late 1940s through the early 1970s, the Indiana park system took in more revenue from inns, concessions, entrance and camping fees, and other revenue-producing activities than was spent for operation and maintenance.

Of Indiana's 23 state parks, the earlier ones—McCormick's Creek, Turkey Run, Clifty Falls, Muscatatuck, Spring Mill, and Indiana Dunes—were selected largely because of their outstanding natural features. Of course, the remnants of the old mill and village at Spring Mill added to the value of that park. Mounds was acquired because of the archeological significance of the earthen structures built by early Native Americans, whereas Lincoln State Park was included because of the historical importance of the Lincoln family and its proximity to the Lincoln Boyhood National Memorial, which is administered by the National Park Service. Chain o' Lakes and Whitewater Memorial state parks were created with the support of local citizens who formed joint county park boards and levied mill taxes to purchase land to be developed into a state park.

Minimum developments include hiking trails, bridle trails, access roads, picnicking facilities, family cabins, and campgrounds. Whenever possible, native stone and lumber are used in construction, and first-offender correction inmates are utilized as laborers. The state transportation's department constructs major roads in the parks. Initially, in 1919, a system of modest fees and charges—originally 10 cents per vehicle, 10 cents per person, and 25 cents per night for camping—was initiated, a policy which continues today, thereby permitting users to help pay for park operations.

Residents of Indiana are fortunate to have a number of outstanding parks ranging in size from 2,000 to more than 20,000 acres. Ample opportunities are available for visitors to pursue their choice of picnicking, camping, hiking, birding, nature study, swimming, boating, horseback riding, bicycling, or just relaxing in beautiful

The Indiana Division of State Parks is one of the finest such units in the United States. Turkey Run Inn has provided year-round lodging for decades. *Photo by Richard Fields of painting by D. Omer "Salty" Seamon*

surroundings. In an effort to provide a bridge between the natural world and the visiting public, an interpretive service was initiated in 1923, with Luci Pitzschler as the first "impromptu guide." Now all state parks have naturalists on duty year-round, or at least during the summer months. Visitor centers are available in the larger parks and provide exhibits on the natural and physical history of the park.

> The stream is brightest at its spring.
>
> —*John Greenleaf Whittier,* The Countess

Division of Water. Although the Division of Water is not as well known to the public as are most of the landholding divisions, it has statewide responsibilities affecting all Indiana residents. It oversees the planning and implementation of water-resource programs involving the supply, distribution, and purity of water, the control of floods, and the development of long-range plans for an adequate supply of water in the future.

When the DNR was established in 1965, the Indiana Flood Control and Water Resources Commission was combined with the IDC's Division of Water to create the comprehensive Division of Water of today. Its authority for action, like that of other state agencies, stems from acts of the legislature. Through the years, laws pertaining to flood control, stream pollution, lake levels, water supplies, sewage disposal, and water-related matters have been enacted.

The division administers water sales from state-owned reservoirs, controls the levels of certain lakes, oversees the alteration of lake shorelines and the withdrawal of water from navigable streams, and regulates the withdrawal of groundwater in areas of the state in danger of exceeding natural replenishment. In addition, it plans flood-control programs, delineates floodways of streams and rivers, directs the construction of flood-control works, and cooperates with local units of government and conservancy districts in planning flood prevention. As part of its regulatory responsibilities, the division cooperates with cities and towns in flood-control districts, sanitary districts, water and sewer systems, drainage boards, and planning commissions, and maintains close contact with state universities, the State Board of Health, and several federal agencies directly involved in water management.

Although the Division of Water does not have direct land-management responsibilities, and is a "behind-the-scenes" kind of operation, it serves as a most important planner and regulator of our basic natural resource—water. Imagine the confusion, duplication, and threat to public health and safety if Indiana did not have an effective agency to coordinate matters pertaining to the management of water resources.

> Nothing is so firmly believed as what is least known.
>
> —*Montaigne*

Division of Public Information and Education. The Division of Public Information and Education serves as a prominent contact with the public. It does so mainly through frequent news releases, publications describing DNR services and facilities, and the department's official organ, the bimonthly magazine *Outdoor Indiana.* From its humble beginnings in 1934 as a mimeographed newsletter, this magazine has grown into a slick four-color publication which features interesting and informative articles of general interest on conservation and natural resource subjects. Its current circulation is more than 20,000. The articles are written by DNR employees and by contributing writers from the general public. The magazine is of particular interest to people attracted to the outdoors and is well adapted as a source of factual information on natural resources for teachers and school children.

> Nothing in my opinion, would contribute more to the welfare of the States than the proper management of the lands.
>
> —*George Washington*

Apprehending lawbreakers such as those who poach deer by "jacklighting" sometimes requires the use of lifelike decoys. An informed public is also a major deterrent to crime and vandalism on state-owned properties.
Photo by Richard Fields

Support divisions of the DNR. Enormous changes have occurred since the old Indiana Department of Conservation was established in 1919 and charged with managing the state's natural resources. This steady growth of responsibilities is in response to the passage of necessary legislation, the need to regulate the use of replaceable and non-replaceable resources, the advent of technology, and increased knowledge of the scientific aspects of resource management. A growing population and an increased demand for more and better recreational facilities has also influenced the growth of the DNR.

In addition to the 11 so-called showcase divisions just described, 14 other divisions/sections work behind the scenes to provide a wide variety of services. They include Engineering, Controller, Accounting, Internal Audit, Budget, Management Information Systems, Administrative Support Services, Human Resources, Historic Preservation, Oil and Gas, Land Acquisition, Reclamation, Safety and Training, and Soil Conservation. The Division of Geological Survey, which had been a vital part of the DNR for 156 years, was transferred to Indiana University in 1993 by the state legislature. In 1921, engineering matters were transferred to IDC, and the Division of Engineering was established, with the head of Purdue's School of Engineering in charge.

The DNR has a significant impact on the economy of the state. During the summer months, the department has approximately 3,100 employees on the payroll, 1,600 of whom are full-time, year-round, salaried employees. The expenses for the year 1995–96 amounted to more than $83 million, a figure that does not include the millions of dollars spent on capital-improvement projects, major rehabilitation, and repair work, virtually all of which are done by outside private contractors and companies.

LANDHOLDINGS OF THE INDIANA DNR

You and I own two kinds of property: that to which we have title as individuals, and that which we hold in community. Our tenure in both cases is acknowledged to be temporary.

—*Allen,* Our Wildlife Legacy

The amount of public land managed by the Department of Natural Resources has grown steadily since 1903, when the first 3,000 acres were purchased and designated as Clark State Forest. After the establishment of the Department of Conservation, public landhold-ings increased rapidly by acquisition of fish and game areas, state forests, nature preserves, recreation areas on flood-control reservoirs, state parks, and historic sites. As of this writing, the DNR has responsibilities for the operation and protection of 414,597 acres in 232 properties.

While impressive, this total is equivalent to only 1.8 percent of the state's 36,291-square-mile area. Even including the approximately 190,000 acres in the U.S. Forest Service's Hoosier National Forest, only 2.6 percent of the state's land is available for public use for outdoor pursuits. These publicly owned properties represent the greatest proportion of what remains of natural and semi-natural land in Indiana. This is our legacy that has survived the "civilizing processes" which have altered our "changing landscape." By no stretch of the imagination will the approximately 604,597 total acres of state and federally owned public land be adequate to provide people with good-quality outdoor experiences, considering the expected demands of an increased population during the next century.

Encouraging steps have been taken in recent years to launch a far-reaching program of land acquisition and development. In 1990, legislation was enacted to create the Indiana Natural Resources Foundation, the primary function of which is to acquire real and personal property for the DNR. On a broader scale, in 1992, with the strong support of the Indiana Chapter of The Nature Conservancy, the General Assembly established the Indiana Heritage Trust.

Designed to expand the DNR's public land, this program is being funded through a combination of legislative appropriations and income from the sale of distinctive environmental license plates. As of the end of January 1997, 257,614 of these special plates had been purchased by Hoosier motorists, enabling the department to purchase more than 7,000 acres. An additional 14,000 acres are in various stages of acquisition.

These programs are a major encouragement toward meeting the needs for natural lands in the twenty-first century and beyond. Such publicly owned properties are the legacy of quasi-natural land that will be handed down to succeeding generations so that those who follow can experience, in some measure, "the Indiana that was."

Everybody needs beauty as well as bread, places to play in where nature may heal and cheer and give strength to body and soul alike.

—*John Muir*

I N D I A N A
DNR STATE PROPERTIES

STATE PARKS
- 1. Bass Lake
- 2. Brown County
- 3. Chain O' Lakes
- 4. Charlestown
- 5. Clifty Falls
- 6. Falls of the Ohio
- 7. Fort Harrison
- 8. Harmonie
- 9. Indiana Dunes
- 10. Lincoln
- 11. McCormick's Creek
- 12. Mounds
- 13. Ouabache
- 14. Pokagon
- 15. Potato Creek
- 16. Shades
- 17. Shakamak
- 18. Spring Mill
- 19. Summit Lake
- 20. Tippecanoe River
- 21. Turkey Run
- 22. Versailles
- 23. Whitewater Memorial

RESERVOIRS
- 24. Brookville Lake
- 25. Hardy Lake
- 26. Huntington Lake
- 27. Cagles Mill Lake
- 28. Mississinewa Lake
- 29. Monroe Lake
- 30. Patoka Lake
- 31. Cecil M. Harden Lake
- 32. Salamonie Lake
  Salamonie River

FISH AND WILDLIFE PROPERTIES
- 33. Atterbury FWA
- 34. Boone's Pond PFA
- 35. Brownstown PFA
- 36. Brush Creek PFA
- 37. Chinook PFA
- 38. Crosley FWA
- 39. Cypress Lake PFA
- 40. Elk Creek PFA
- 41. Glendale FWA
- 42. Greensburg PFA
- 43. Green Valley PFA
- 44. Grouse Ridge PFA
- 45. Hindostan Falls PFA
- 46. Hovey Lake FWA
- 47. Jasper-Pulaski FWA
- 48. Kankakee FWA
- 49. Kingsbury FWA
- 50. Knop Lake PFA
- 51. LaSalle FWA
- 52. Martindale PFA
- 53. Menominee PFA
- 54. Minnehaha FWA
- 55. Mishawaka Fish Ladder
- 56. Pigeon River FWA
- 57. Pike
- 58. Scott Mill Pond PFA
- 59. South Bend Fish Ladder
- 60. Sugar Ridge FWA
- 61. Tri-County FWA
- 62. Wawasee PFA
- 63. White Oak PFA
- 64. Williams Dam PFA
- 65. Willow Slough FWA
- 66. Winamac FWA
- 67. Wilbur Wright FWA
- 68. Avoca FH
- 69. Bass Lake FH
- 70. Cikana FH
- 71. Curtis Creek FH

STATE FORESTS
- 77. Clark—Deam Lake
- 78. Ferdinand
- 79. Greene-Sullivan
- 80. Harrison/Wyandotte Complex
  Wyandotte Cave
  Wyandotte Woods
- 81. Jackson-Washington
  Starve Hollow Beach
  Vallonia Nursery
- 82. Jasper-Pulaski Nursery
- 83. Martin
- 84. Morgan-Monroe
- 85. Owen-Putnam
- 86. Selmier
- 87. Yellowwood

NATURE PRESERVES
- 88. Berns-Meyer
- 89. Crooked Lake
- 90. Eunice H. Bryan
- 91. Hemlock Bluff
- 92. Hemmer Woods
- 93. Hoosier Prairie
- 94. Laketon Bog
- 95. Olin Lake
- 96. Oscar & Ruth Hall Woods
- 97. Portland Arch
- 98. Shrader-Weaver
- 99. Twin Swamps

MUSEUMS AND HISTORIC SITES
- 100. Angel Mounds
- 101. Colonel William Jones
- 102. Corydon Old State Capitol
- 103. Culbertson Mansion
- 104. Ernie Pyle Birthplace
- 105. Gene Stratton-Porter
- 106. Grissom AFB
- 107. Indiana State Museum
- 108. James F. D. Lanier
- 109. Levi Coffin House
- 110. Limberlost
- 111. Mansfield Roller Mill
- 112. New Harmony Opera House
- 113. Pigeon Roost
- 114. T. C. Steele
- 115. Vincennes
  Indiana Territorial Capitol
  Old State Bank
- 116. Whitewater Canal

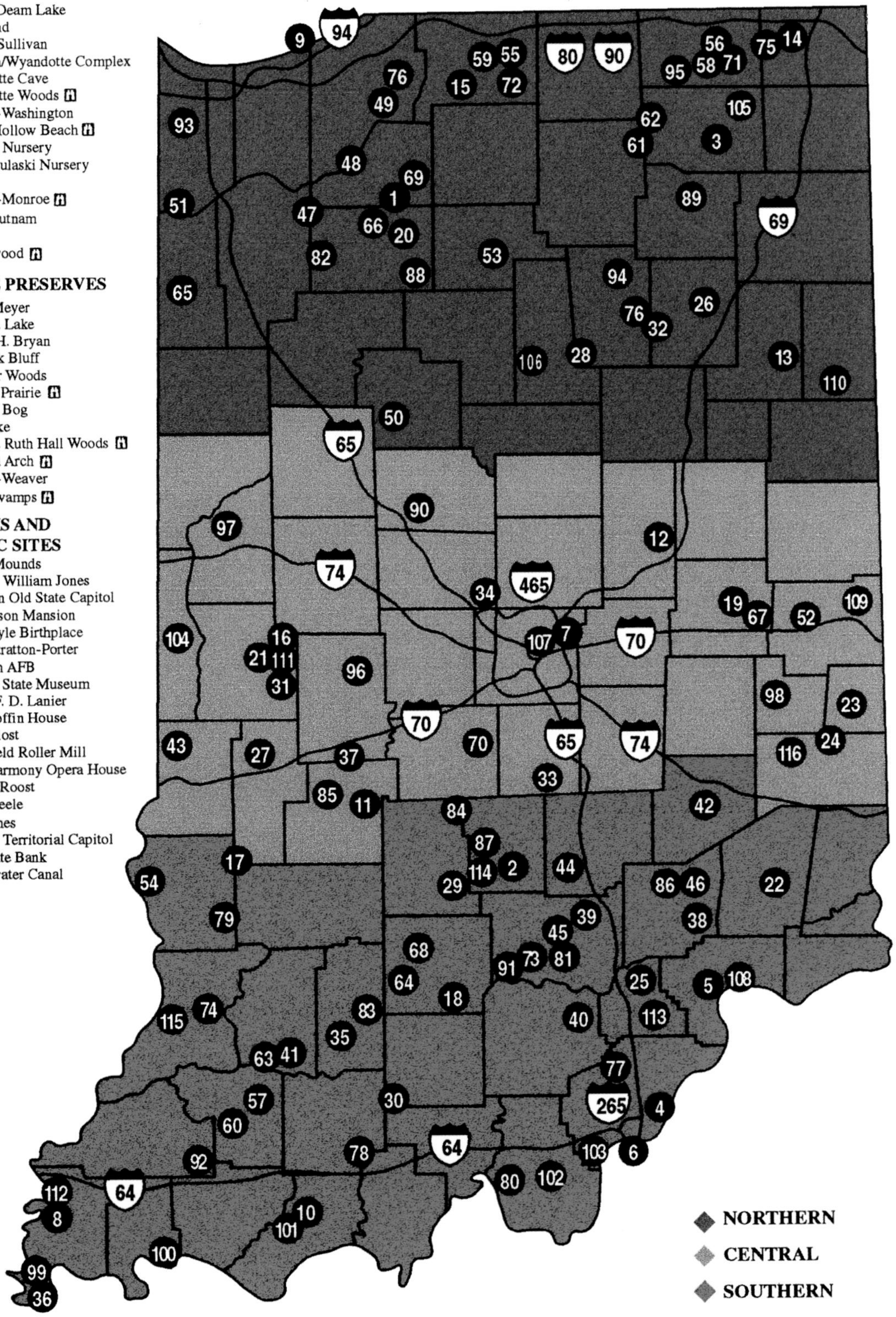

◆ NORTHERN

◆ CENTRAL

◆ SOUTHERN

Land ownership Acreage of the Department of Natural Resources

Migratory species such as sandhill cranes routinely find their way seasonally for thousands of miles without maps or place names to guide them.
Photo by Delano Z. Arvin

48. Names on the Land

Marion T. Jackson

Bee to the blossom, moth to the flame; Each to his passion; what's in a name?

—*Helen Hunt Jackson,* Vanity of Vanities

In many respects, this chronicle of the wave of human settlement that swept across the Indiana landscape is best reflected in our place names. When the origins and meanings of names we etched upon the landscape are understood, we may then begin to understand our human history, and perhaps even our human destiny as well.

As far as we know, only people find it necessary to name the features and locations on the landscape they inhabit. Assigning names to identify their surroundings is a part of the organization and classification of information which seems to be essential to human culture. Further, we have a strong need to delimit features of note on scale-model representations of our landscape, which we term *maps*.

The animals we share our state with rely on a different set of "maps" to guide their movements and to recognize destinations. The vast majority, especially those nocturnal, find their way by chemical trails laid across the surface, tiny pulses of pheromones unique to each species, which are emitted by special glands into the air downwind. These diffuse spoor pathways are sufficient to direct their movements.

Animals live in an olfactory world that we, with our dulled sense of smell, can only vaguely imagine. Wild animals read the literature of the landscape from its odors, and by their presence and passage leave their messages there, perhaps as important in endless time as these words placed by humans on perishable paper. For us to attempt to sort through the labyrinth of odors prevailing in every field or forest would be akin to an illiterate person trying to decipher the messages present in a large library. Our sensory strengths are auditory-visual. To find our way, we usually rely on place names and maps.

Land contours, watercourses, substrate features, vegetation changes, moisture differences, wind currents, temperature gradients, snow depths, solar positions, star patterns, magnetic fields, sound waves, echolocations, carbon dioxide concentrations, and light variations are among the other "roadmaps" animals use to find shelter, to find each other, to find water and food, to avoid becoming food, and to find their way daily or seasonally. Place names are not necessary for animal recognition of woodland trails, food patches, or concentrations of conspecifics—their streets, restaurants, and home towns. Only people need names on the land to find their way and where they are.

Native Americans were the first to leave names on the Indiana landscape—the land of Indians. Nature supplied the sites to be named and also the names. Mimesis of nature, the process of mimicking or imitating the sights, sounds, smells, or behaviors of the plants they gathered or the animals they captured for food, was a vital part of Indian culture and religion. Perceptive recognition of the visual-aural-oral matrix of the landscape they inhabited was autonomically woven into their names for their animal brethren and the prominent features of their Earth Mother. Myths, songs, and poems incorporated this mimetic, resonant mode of knowing intimately

their total surroundings. Such oneness with nature evolved linguistically into their alliterative or onomatopoetic names for all they encountered. Nomenclature, lifeways, and religion became inseparable parts of a living and life-giving oneness.

Ye say that all have passed away—
    That noble race and brave . . .
But their name is on your waters—
    Ye may not wash it out. . . .
Your mountains build their monument,
    Though ye destroy their dust.

—*Lydia Huntley Sigourney,* Indian Names

Settlers quickly fragmented this pristine unity, replacing nature's diversity, randomness, and wildness with the simplicity, order, and domesticity of "organized" settlements. Most political and cultural places that now fill the Indiana landscape were created after Native Americans had been largely forced from the state. For the most part the counties, cities, towns, and villages created by the settlers do not have Indian names or names based on natural features. Instead most were named for their founders, for familiar places in states or nations from which the settlers came, or for important historical personages. Still, something in us derives comfort from the names of natural features, even though the nature that once was everywhere present has been almost totally replaced by the crystallized landscapes of today.

Witness the popularity of tree names for city streets. Similarly, wild animals are popular choices for mascots of Indiana high schools and their sports teams, especially if the critter in question is noted for its real or presumed ferocity, strength, endurance, or intelligence. Native Americans have been likewise "honored" by teams called Indians, Redskins, Braves, Archers, or Warriors. For the most part, Indiana schools of more recent origin have largely moved away from wild animal or Native American names, favoring instead such monikers as Patriots, Raiders, Mounties, Vikings, or Devils of several hues.

Of the 92 counties, only Miami and Delaware bear Indian tribal names, as do the settlements of Muncie and Wyandotte (people of one speech). Other counties named for Indian words or their derivations are Ohio, Wabash, and Tippecanoe—names originally applied to nearby rivers.

The Indian had much more influence on the names of Hoosier streams and lakes than on counties and settlements, . . . translated Indian names constitute the largest class of Indian names. Descriptive stream names like Cedar Creek, Clifty Creek, Driftwood River, Eel River, Flat Rock River, Sand Creek, Sugar Creek, White River, and Yellow River are all translations from Indian languages.

—*Ronald Baker and Marvin Carmony,* Indiana Place Names (1975)

Indiana features such as streams, lakes, and landscapes are well represented by names of Indian origin. Several are descriptive of original natural conditions, animals, or plants present: Wabash

River, *Wah-bak-shik-ki,* for "white and shining"—derived from the limestone beds which were visible under the once-clear upper Wabash; Tippecanoe River, *Ke-tap-e-kon-nong,* for the buffalo fish in its waters; Kankakee River, *Tian-kakeek,* for "low, swampy land"; Muscatatuck River, *Mosch-ach-hit-tuk,* "the clear river"; Mississinewa River, *Na-mah-chis-sin-wi,* from a Miami word for "much fall in waters," from its rapid flow; Salamonie, *On-sah-la-mo-nee,* Miami for "yellow paint," a dye made from the bloodroot growing profusely nearby.

Other streams bear the names of Indian tribes: the Iroquois, Maumee, *Me-ah-me* (hence Miami), and Patoka rivers; the Wea, Kickapoo, and Big Shawnee (*Sha-wa-nee,* "southerner") creeks. Wea is an abbreviation of *Wah-we-ah-tun-ong,* the name of a Miami tribe and a French trading post (Ouiatenon) on the Wabash. The Elkhart River (and later the city of the same name) is from a Potawatomi name, derived from an island near the mouth of the stream which the Indians felt resembled an elk's heart. The Ohio River is from an Iroquois word meaning beautiful. Sugar Creek, the famed canoe stream of west-central Indiana, is from the Indian word *Pun-go-se-co-me,* the water of many sugar trees.

> Where can you match the mighty music of their names?—The Monongahela, the Kennebec, the Rappahannock, the Delaware, the Penobscot, the Wabash, the Chesapeake . . . the Susquehanna, the Tombigbee, the Nantahala, the Chattahoochee . . . —these are a few of their princely names, these are a few of their great, proud, glittering names, fit for the immense and lonely land they inhabit.
>
> —*Thomas Wolfe,* Of Time and the River, *Book VII*

Indian words were also given to Indiana's natural lakes: Muskelonge, *Mas-ki-non-ge,* "the great pike"; Shipshewana, *Cup-ci-wa-no,* "Vision of a Lion," a Potawatomi Indian; Wawasee, the largest natural lake in Indiana, for a Potawatomi chief, *Wak-we-as-see,* "full moon" or "the round one"; Winona, *Wi-no-nah,* a Sioux name for "firstborn daughter" (also Longfellow's Wenonah in "Hiawatha"); Shakamak, *Shack-a-mak,* Delaware for "slippery fish" for the nearby Eel River; and Lake Michigan, *Mik-e-sen.*

For a people who occupied Indiana for many centuries and figured so importantly in the state's history and settlement patterns, the rich and varied Indian languages left relatively few cultural "names on the land." Baker and Carmony stated in their book *Indiana Place Names* that less than 2 percent of the settlement names "are Indian or pseudo-Indian—that is, Indian names applied or garbled by people other than Native Americans."

Settlements which do trace the origin of their names to Indian words or phrases include Anoka, Sioux for "on both sides"; Cayuga, Iroquois *Gw-u-geh*—"place of taking out," or portage beginning; Coesse, Miami chief *Ko-wa-zi*—"old man"; Kewanna, Potawatomi chief *Ki-wa-na*—"Prairie-Chicken"; Mishawaka, Potawatomi *M'seh-wah-kee-ki*—"country of dead trees" or deadening; Mongo, short for Potawatomi *Mon-go-quin-ong*—"Big Squaw"; Monon, a Potawatomi word meaning "to tote or carry"—hence the Monon Railroad, "to carry" passengers and freight; Nappanee, an Indian word for flour; Oswego, Iroquois for "flowing out," outlet of Lake Tippecanoe; Wanatah, Indian chief "He who charges his enemies"; Wawaka, Indian for "big heron"; and Winamac, for the Potawatomi chief *Wi-na-mak*—"Catfish." Some anglicized names of towns are derivatives from Indian words; e.g., Anderson is named for William Anderson, a Delaware chief—*Wa-pi-mims-kink,* "chestnut tree place"; and Thorntown is from the Indian word *Ka-wi-a-ki-un-gi,* "place of thorns."

Other towns and villages reflect encounters with Indians or use of

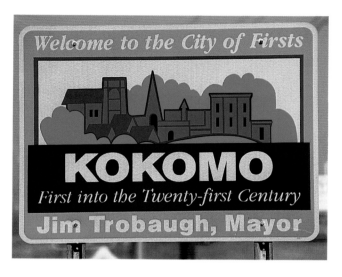

Kokomo is one of the many Indiana place names that are of Native American origin, so named in 1844 for a Miami Indian from Thorntown, *Ko-ka-ma,* "The Diver." *Photo by Richard Fields*

the landscape by Indians: Treaty in Wabash County is the site of an 1826 treaty; Battle Ground, the location of the famous Indian engagement on November 7, 1811, is named for the Battle of Tippecanoe; Greentown is named after Miami chief Green; Armiesburg in Parke County is the site of General William Henry Harrison's encampment on the way to the Battle of Tippecanoe; Indian Springs (Martin Co.) is so called after a mineral spring used by the Indians; and Indian Village (St. Joseph Co.) is named for an Indian encampment. No fewer than 10 counties were named for officers and soldiers who fought at the Battle of Tippecanoe.

A large majority of Indiana settlements were named for people directly, often the family name of the earliest settlers, prominent early members of the community, or important figures in American or Indiana history, e.g., Crawfordsville, Beck's Mill, and Madison. Many others were transferred names from states settled earlier, from Old World places, or from names used in literary works, e.g., Yorktown, Hessen-Cassel, or Cicero.

Place names originating from natural features of the state are largely descriptive of trees or other plants, animals (uncommonly), vegetation characteristics, land or water quality or characteristics, soil or climatic conditions, mineral sources, physiographic interest, landscape aesthetics, or, on occasion, natural catastrophes.

The only county bearing a name descriptive of a landscape feature is La Porte (from French for "the door"), apparently for a natural opening in the forest there, through which trade between northern and southern Indiana passed.

As would be expected, in a state as heavily forested as Indiana once was, settlers would be impressed by the dense woods, the beautiful groves, or the huge size, great variety, or rarity of tree species present in the state. No fewer than 58 place names trace their source to the trees or forests occurring nearby. The list is long: Ash Grove, Ashland, Beech Grove, Beechwood, Burr Oak, Cedar, Cedar Grove, Cedar Lake, Cypress, Edgewood, Forest, Forest City, Forest Hill, Glenwood, Green Oak, Greenwood, Groveland, Hemlock, Inwood, Lake-of-the-Woods, Linden, Linn Grove, Linwood, Locust Point, Lonetree, Magnolia (for the rare umbrella magnolia occurring nearby), Maple Valley, Maplewood, Millgrove, Mulberry, Oak, Oakford, Oak Forest, Oakland City, Oaklandon, Oaktown, Oakville, Pine, Pine Village, Plum Tree, Poplar Grove, St. Mary-of-the-Woods, Sassafras,

Sycamore (site of the largest tree ever recorded in Indiana and probably east of the Mississippi River), Tanglewood, Town of Pines (for the jack pines of Indiana Dunes, the southernmost location for the species), Tulip, Underwood, Walnut, Walnut Grove, Westwood, Willow Branch, Willow Valley, and Woodland.

Lesser plants and wildflowers also served as sources of place names, but much less commonly than tree names. Among the more conspicuous are Aroma (for the fragrance of flowering plants), Bloomingdale, Blooming Grove, Bloomington (possibly for wildflower displays in early days), Bracken (for the fern by that name), Cloverdale, Cloverland, Daisy Hill, Ferndale, Greenbriar, Phlox,

Rosebud, Rosedale, Roseland, Spiceland (for the abundant spicebush in the area), and White Rose.

Animal names were especially favored for aquatic features, e.g., Wildcat, Otter, Raccoon, Deer, and Beaver creeks; Turkey Run; the Eel and Pigeon rivers; or Bass, Duck, Goose, Wolf, and Bear lakes. Stream character, water quality, or channel characteristics in earlier times are evident in the Whitewater, Blue, White, Lost, and Flatrock rivers. Likewise for Sand, Rock, Mud, Clear, and Driftwood creeks.

Occasionally the streams themselves were salt. The water, when boiled in enormous flat kettles made for the purpose, yielded a

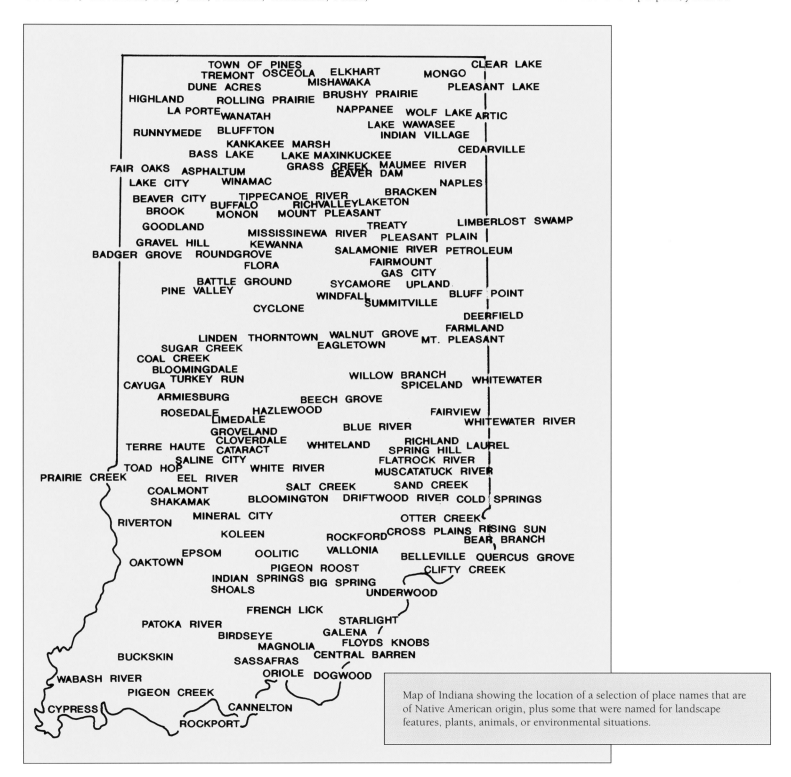

Map of Indiana showing the location of a selection of place names that are of Native American origin, plus some that were named for landscape features, plants, animals, or environmental situations.

fairly good table salt. When first boiled out the salt had a blue color, giving a bluish sediment to salt creeks and springs. In some streams and ponds even the water was blue—hence the name of the famous Blue Licks in Kentucky, or the Blue River in Indiana, which kept its clear blue color until it emptied into the Ohio.

—*John Bakeless, "The Wild Middle West," in* The Eyes of
Discovery *(1950)*

Settlements, except when they were located on watercourses previously named for animals, less commonly received animal names, but several occur across the state: Badger Grove, Bass Lake, Bear Branch, Beaver City, Beaver Dam, Buck Creek, Buckskin (for the trading post which frequently had deerskins hanging outside), Buffaloville, Deer Creek, Deerfield, Eagletown, Eagle Village, Gar Creek, Oriole, Phenix, Swan, Wolf Creek, Wolf Lake, Wolf Run (a great rendezvous for wolves in the first decade of the nineteenth century).

Descriptions and characteristics of vegetation or habitats appear in such names as Bluegrass, Brook, Brushy Prairie, Central Barren (for a prairie-like forest opening), Dune Acres, Grass Creek, Laketon, Lakeville, Marshtown, Prairie City, Prairie Creek, Prairieton, Riverside, Riverton, Rolling Prairie, Roundgrove (for the oak savanna nearby), Runnymede (which means meadow), Summit Grove (again for a local oak savanna).

Physiographic features noteworthy in the wilderness were commonly applied to local settlements: Alta (for a high elevation), Big Springs, Blue Ridge, Bluff Creek, Bluffton, Cataract, Clifty Creek, Cross Plains (for nearby cruciform flat uplands), Flat Rock, Floyds Knobs, Gravel Hill, Green Hill, Mt. Summit, Pilot Knob, Plainsville, Range Line (for an early surveyor's boundary), Ridgeville, Rockfield, Rockford, Rock Hill, Rockland, Rockport, Rockville, Sandcut Farms, Sandford, Sandytown, Shoals (for the bedrock shallows in the East Fork of the White River), State Line City, Stone Bluff, Summit, Summit Grove, Summitville, Terre Haute (built on a high terrace which never floods), Trail Creek, Tremont (named for three large sand dunes nearby—"Three Mountains"), Upland (highest point between Union City and Logansport on the railroad), Valley City, Valley Mills, Vallonia (within a valley), Waterford, West Fork (of the White River).

Places named for the presence of, or source of, mineral resources include Asphaltum, Blue Lick Creek, Cannelburg and Cannelton (for cannel coal), Carbon, Carbondale, Coal Bluff, Coal City, Coal Creek, Coalmont, Epsom, Flint, Flint Creek, French Lick (for a salt spring used by animals), Galena (source of lead), Gas City and Gaston (for abundant local sources of natural gas), Koleen (for kaolin clay found there), Limedale (limestone quarry and lime kiln), Mineral City, Oolitic (for oolites—egg-shaped fossilized invertebrates in the local limestone), Petroleum, Saline City (for a salt lick there in pioneer days), Sulphur, and Sulphur Springs.

Meteorological conditions and events occasionally were sources of place names: Artic [*sic*], Cyclone (for a cyclone which occurred in 1880), Rising Sun (the first town to see the sunrise over the Ohio River), Snow Hill (for a snowy mound in winter), Starlight, White Cloud (for mist hanging over a valley between two hills), Windfall (named for a blowdown of virgin timber by a tornado before settlement days).

Land quality or conditions reflecting the great productivity of Indiana's virgin soils are found in such names as Farmland (for rich farmland), Garden City, Goodland, Greenfield, Northfield, Oatsville, Plainfield, Richland, Richland Creek, Rich Valley, Wheatfield, or Wheatland.

Aquatic features, wetland habitats, or water quality were the sources of Blue Lake, Blue River, Clear Creek, Clear Lake, Clear Spring, Deep River, Organ Spring, Silver Creek, Silver Lake, Springboro, Springfield, Springhill, Spring Lake, Springport, Springville, Trinity Springs (for three mineral springs there), Twin Lakes, White River, Whitewater River (from the Indian *Wapi-ne-pay,* "white clear water," for its bed of white sand, gravel, and limestone).

In many cases the natural features which were the basis for these and other names on the Indiana landscape have been severely modified and are now evident only by careful inspection, or have long since disappeared entirely. Without doubt, if most of these places were being named today, they would be named for important townspeople or their constructions or accomplishments, not for the natural features found by the first settlers. Sadly for many others, even the local residents now living there either have forgotten or no longer care why their place on the map of Indiana originally received its name. Then, too, the name given to a place is often the only hint of the natural feature that inspired some unremembered settler or early resident to select its present-day name in the first place.

But we now appear to have come full circle in our application of names to the Hoosier landscape. Interestingly, now that most residents of Indiana—as elsewhere in America—have become isolated and insulated from nature in the fastness of our homes, vehicles, and workplaces, we turn again to nature when naming new residential developments, especially. After work or shopping, we head for the Quail Run, Turtle Creek, Prairie Meadows, Raccoon Ridge, Willow Brook, Maple Grove, Russet Oaks, Otter Village, or Deerfield apartments, condominiums, or subdivision.

Little does it matter that bulldozers and blacktop have long since replaced any habitat that might once have harbored quail, turtles, or otters. Or that the prairie grasses, willows, maples, or oaks once present have now been reduced to scraggly, unhealthy remnants, all too often with misshapen isolated crowns, scarred trunks, and dying tops. Still it represents "home" for a few months or years, and the return address looks prestigious on our envelopes. But then the whitetails and raccoons, being almost ineradicable, just might wander through at dusk, nipping at exotic yews or rummaging through the garbage pails. Meanwhile we glory in the marvels of wilderness excursions held elsewhere on the planet via nature programs on television. That oneness with the totality of the natural world, and the "sense of place" it conferred on the Native Americans and the early pioneers who followed them, has all but disappeared from the Indiana of today.

Regardless of their origin or reason for application to a given site or feature on the Indiana landscape, or whether they are now appropriate, we will most likely retain the names on our land for all time. Perhaps they never needed to be named at all, because in one sense, place names and maps exist only in the human mind.

In the same way that Indian names remain on the land, some of the Indian's reverence for the earth has become a part of us— some of us. I don't think it is an exaggeration to say that our health and even our survival as a civilization depend ultimately on how many of us learn that lesson.

—*Wallace Steiger,* The Gift of Wilderness

Part 5: Protecting What Remains

Memorial to General George Rogers Clark at Vincennes commemorates the soldier-scientist-statesman who was instrumental in opening the Indiana wilderness during the Revolutionary War era.   *Photo by Marion Jackson*

49. Search and Study

Alton A. Lindsey

EARLY TRAVELS AND OBSERVATIONS

We traveled as the voyageurs did by canoe, paddled the same lakes, ran the same rapids, and packed over their ancient portages. We knew the winds and storms, saw the same sky lines, and felt the awe and wonderment that was theirs at the enormous expanses and grandeur of a land that was at once as strange and challenging to them as to us.

—*Sigurd F. Olson,* The Lonely Land *(1961)*

Probably it is much easier for the average modern Hoosier to visualize himself or herself traveling around Mars than to accurately imagine how it was for missionary Father Louis Hennepin when he accompanied La Salle in 1680 into our howling, magnificent wilderness, then known as Louisiana. Fortunately, he was as literate as he was courageous, and he recorded interesting observations. But the white trappers of beaver who followed him, and the hickory-muscled *coureurs de bois,* who certainly knew the country, contributed as little to descriptions of it as they did to its permanent settlement.

Since the Indians they encountered were intimately dependent upon outdoor resources, the men and boys as hunters, the women and girls as gatherers and cultivators, and the shaman class as herb doctors, they knew infinitely more about at least practical aspects of nature than any individual living today. Most natural lore from their culture was lost for lack of written languages in the tribes, and of humble curiosity in the whites. However, as Indian culture was slipping away, the Potawatomi chief Simon Pokagon became the full-blooded American native best educated in the European way, at Notre Dame and Oberlin. Though distinguishing himself as an orator and author, he chose to live in a wigwam in his ancestral fashion. Among his writings is an excellent account of the life of the passenger pigeon in Indiana.

General George Rogers Clark is considered "the first man of science or of known scientific interests in Indiana," starting in 1778. He was the first to correctly explain the origin of Indian mounds, and Audubon sought him out as the authority on the birds of "the West." A splendid memorial building in Vincennes is well known, especially for the striking murals, including one of the winter military expedition which took the fort at Vincennes from the British early in 1779. His youngest brother was William Clark of the famed Lewis and Clark expedition.

Among descriptions of early Indiana, the most systematic, detailed, and complete was the federal survey by the General Land Office, following directions laid down by Thomas Jefferson. The deputy surveyors who conducted the field work were woodsmen and true frontier heroes, living off the country during their arduous rectilinear travels. The land survey started in 1799 and ended in the north about 1835. It recorded and platted rather cursory observations on soils, forests, prairies, Indian occupancy, Indian quarry sites, streams, lakes, ponds, marshes, land grants, settlements, windthrown timber, and salt licks. Because witness trees were noted as to species, diameter, and compass bearing and distance to the "corner" (to make the latter relocatable), modern forest ecologists are able to tell a great deal about our original vegetation cover. A map of the entire state on this basis appeared in *Natural Features of Indiana,* the state sesquicentennial volume by the Indiana Academy of Science in 1966.

General P. B. Porter made himself an expert on water routes in our Northwest Territory, including Indiana, and reported to Congress in 1810 on conditions and locations of portages. In times before agricultural drainage, half the land of Indiana north of the Wabash was covered with surface water during at least six months of a year of normal precipitation. Hence, the rivers long continued to provide the chief avenues of travel. The vast areas of lands too wet for farming were termed "the lost lands"; today they are our best agricultural soils.

Substantial observations were recorded in 1816, when English botanist David Thomas took a leisurely horseback trip from Rising Sun at Indiana's southeast corner to the Wabash Valley north of Terre Haute. His observations of everything natural were acutely made and minutely recorded. Thomas came within a hairsbreadth of recognizing landscape features of northwest Indiana as the result of a continental ice sheet, writing that a "preternatural flood" must have overridden the highest lands.

The scholarly Reverend Timothy Flint "wandered Indiana" and adjoining areas, and with supplements from earlier writings, described it with surprising thoroughness. In 1828 and again in 1832, this geographer's books contained valuable information.

THE NATURAL HISTORY ERA, 1824–1884

To the eyes of a man of imagination, Nature is imagination itself.

—*William Blake*

The period of original natural history work in Indiana began with Robert Owen's purchase of New Harmony (then Harmonie) from the Rappites in 1824, and lasted 60 years. Among the sons of that British idealist, two succumbed to the fascination of geology as exemplified by limestone fossils in the bed of the Wabash. David Dale Owen founded the U.S. Geological Survey and headed it at New Harmony for 17 years. Richard Owen, long an Indiana University professor, became in 1872 the first Purdue president. One of his distinctions was serving without salary; another was dying, at home in New Harmony 11 years after retirement, from a draught of embalming fluid served by an undertaker friend in the belief that it was "medicated water."

Half of the 10 nationally famed naturalists who lived, or at least worked, in Indiana about 1825 were living in New Harmony. Among them, English geologist and educational experimenter William Maclure was the leader among those Owenites who actually lived there. He saw to the collection of many important fossil specimens. Thomas Say achieved fame as a pioneer American entomologist and mollusk expert. He and painter-ichthyologist C. A. Lesueur often collected fish and shellfish in waters about New Harmony. Say's gravestone is the most imposing one in the village cemetery.

A Prussian prince, Maximilian of Wied (not the Mexican emperor of tragic history), studied the mammals and birds, with a taxidermist and an artist, during his five-month stay in New Harmony, beginning in October of 1832. William Wilson states in his 1964 book that "Audubon was in and out." Audubon incorporated some Indiana material into both his bird and mammal books. Much natural history was reported along with geology in early surveys by federal, state, and even county workers. The land was yielding its secrets at an accelerating pace.

MODERN SCIENTIFIC STUDIES, 1885 ONWARD

The purpose of science is not to conquer the land, but to understand the mechanisms of ecosystems and to fit man into the resources he has available on the planet on which he has evolved.

—*Joseph J. Hickey,* Wildlife Society Bulletin *(1974)*

Under this topic we shall not include ultramodern superscience. Even so, the breadth and depth of our proliferating outdoor sciences since the 1885 founding of the Indiana Academy of Science makes it impossible to more than briefly mention a few of the leading individuals, mostly early in the period. Among the 71 charter members of the academy were many nationally renowned scientists. The state academy from this start has played as effective a role in education and in stimulating and publishing research as any such group in the nation.

The key person in founding the Indiana Academy of Science was Amos W. Butler, who wrote the original constitution. Born in 1860, Butler explored the state for warm-blooded animals, and in 1898 published his book *Birds of Indiana.* The first substantial annotated list of Indiana birds was offered by Russell E. Mumford and others in 1975, and in 1984 a beautiful and definitive volume, *Birds of Indiana,* came from Indiana University Press, with the text by Mumford and Charles E. Keller, and paintings reproduced from original work by Nashville-based artist William Zimmerman.

The same Amos Butler coauthored the first list of Indiana mammals. Walter L. Hahn's 1909 book on the same subject was based on his work at Indiana University and elsewhere. In recent years Charles M. Kirkpatrick and Durward L. Allen at Purdue, James B. Cope at Earlham, and John O. Whitaker, Jr., at Indiana State have mobilized research on mammals at their schools. In 1969, the academy began its Monograph Series with Mumford's *Distribution of the Mammals of Indiana.* This was followed by a more comprehensive coverage entitled *Mammals of Indiana,* published by Mumford and Whitaker in 1982.

The first definite inventory and description of the reptiles and amphibians of the state was compiled by physician-herpetologist Sherman A. Minton and published as Indiana Academy of Science Monograph no. 3, *Amphibians and Reptiles of Indiana,* in 1972. Minton's earlier work was followed in 1997 by an updated book, *Reptiles and Amphibians of Indiana,* also published by the Indiana Academy of Science.

Two charter academy members interested in fishes were Willis S. Blatchley (1859–1940) and David Starr Jordan (1851–1931). Blatchley was brought up on a farm in or near the present outstanding Big Walnut Nature Preserve. During boyhood he often fished Big Walnut Creek, and when in maturity he was preparing his 1938 book *The Fishes of Indiana,* his seine captured 43 species there. (By 1945, when Shelby Gerking worked the same stretch, there were only 22.) Blatchley worked as state geologist in 1894–1911. That he is known as the "dean of Indiana entomologists" bears witness to his versatility.

Jordan taught at Shortridge High School in Indianapolis, received the only Ph.D. degree ever given by Butler University, and became the most eminent Indiana biologist up through his time. Many of the 50 books he wrote were on ichthyology. His published autobiography comes to 1,672 pages in two volumes. He states therein: "For half a century the writer . . . has been a very busy man, living meanwhile three more or less independent lives: first . . . that of a naturalist and explorer; second . . . that of a teacher; and third, from a sense of duty, that of a minor prophet of Democracy." Jordan served as president of Indiana University and later as chancellor at Stanford.

Carl Eigenmann, another charter member and Bloomington ichthyologist, was an authority on blind fishes such as those found in the limestone caverns of southern Indiana. He became the dean of the graduate school at his university.

Two Coulter brothers, born of missionary parents in China, were charter members and notable botanists. John M. Coulter (1851–1928) taught at Hanover and Wabash, and was the Indiana University president for three years. John achieved eminence as a plant classifier and morphologist, a prolific botanical writer, and a vital force in Indiana science for a score of years.

Stanley Coulter (1853–1943) was biology department head and science dean at Purdue, where a building on the original mall bears his name. He attained much influence in education, botany, and conservation, and founded Purdue's Department of Forestry. Among his many publications was the 1899 *Catalogue of Plants of Indiana.* His death marked the passing of the charter group of the Indiana Academy of Science.

Charles C. Deam (1865–1953), the preeminent botanical explorer of this state and the most honored of our taxonomic botanists, dropped out of college, considering it "a waste of time," but later received three honorary degrees. A pharmacist and drug-store operator by trade, he began his "hobby" of studying plants in 1896 and continued this activity for 52 years, culminating in his fourth book, *The Flora of Indiana* (1940), and a herbarium of 78,000 specimen sheets, now at Indiana University. In 1915 Deam bought a Model-T Ford, changed the body into a bizarre but practical "weed-wagon" and camper, and traveled with his wife throughout Indiana for the work of collecting and recording. This, and the state forester position discussed later, was his real lifework.

Their home in Bluffton not only was a splendid botanical library and herbarium, but also was surrounded by his 3.5-acre arboretum and garden for native species. Among Deam's many memorials, the outstanding one is the 13,000-acre Deam Wilderness, which the U.S. Department of Agriculture set apart in 1982. A biography titled *Plain Ol' Charlie Deam,* written by journalist Robert C. Kriebel and published by Purdue University Press, provides the best coverage of Deam's life, work, and colorful personality.

The smallest "state forest" is the half-acre that preserves the living Deam Oak along County Road 250N, off State Road 116 north of Bluffton. This uncommon hybrid between two common oak species was found by horticultural friends, then Deam bought the property and gave it to the state. An Illinois botanist named the tree *Quercus deamii.* This lone, independent, "self-owned" individual stands out from its neighbors as did the beloved "curmudgeon" Charlie Deam himself.

Ray C. Friesner (1894–1952) was botany head and dean of science at Butler University, and a thorough master of the state flora with special interest in the large group of goldenrods. He edited the *Butler University Botanical Studies* for decades, and worked with his colleague Dr. Potzger in research on Indiana forest ecology.

John F. Potzger (1886–1955) was an Indianapolis music teacher for 24 years before he became fascinated with botany by taking a

Charles C. Deam became Indiana's best-known botanist, although he made his living as a druggist. The Deams traveled in this modified Model T Ford to collect plants throughout Indiana.   *Photo by Mrs. C. C. Deam*

course with Friesner. As an unusually dynamic teacher of plant ecology, Potzger was an untiring field man and prolific technical writer. He succeeded Friesner as head of the Butler Botany Department. His special interest was analysis of fossil pollen grains in bogs, ponds, and lakes, in order to learn the history of vegetation on the surrounding lands. Together the two Butler botanists discovered and studied Cabin Creek Raised Bog (actually a fen), a unique alkaline wetland in Randolph County, fed by artesian springs in the very deep layer of peat.

The most honored woman in outdoor science in our state was Winona H. Welch (1896–1990). Through a long career at DePauw University, Dr. Welch was a world authority on mosses and liverwort classification, and an influential teacher. In 1948 she became the first woman president of the Indiana Academy of Science. Her 1957 book *Mosses of Indiana* joined Charles Deam's books in making Indiana one of the best-known states floristically.

Many researchers have contributed valuable information on Indiana's most important natural resource besides its climate—the soils. The most concise expression of such data appears as a map of our general soil regions resulting from Purdue's soil survey running from 1902 to the present. This Agronomy Department unit also printed detailed color maps of each of our 92 counties, based on aerial photos and ground studies. These are now being collected in one atlas.

The findings of our outdoor scientists are summarized in the semi-popular but fairly detailed book *Natural Features of Indiana*, presented to the public by the Indiana Academy of Science in 1966 to mark the state's sesquicentennial.

50. Spreading the Word

Alton A. Lindsey

THE BIRTH OF THE GREENS

Every lover of nature, every man who appreciates the majesty and beauty of the wilderness and of wild life, should strike hands with the far-sighted men who wish to preserve our material resources, in the efforts to keep our forests, and our game beasts, and game birds, and game fish—indeed, all the living creatures of prairie and woodland, and seashore—from wanton destruction.

> —*Theodore Roosevelt,* Outdoor Pastimes of an
> American Hunter *(1905)*

The first significant environmental crusade in America, from the 1850s, was protecting and artificially propagating game fish and commercial species. Angler, statesman, and pioneer ecologist George Perkins Marsh studied this issue officially for Vermont in 1856. In 1871 popular demand resulted in the United States Fish Commission, the first federal agency to address the conservation of a specific natural resource.

Sportsmen's magazines and organizations surged upward in numbers, quality, and influence in the early 1870s, promoting the traditional "waste-not" ethical code of upper-class European sportsmen, urging upon themselves bag limits and closed seasons, and opposing commercialization of game species and others for fashion, food, or hides.

George Bird Grinnell, Yale Ph.D. in zoology, explorer and hunter in the Old West, Indian authority, writer, and editor, used his *Forest and Stream* magazine to popularize this code and its practical applications among sportsmen, a group which made up a much larger proportion of the population than it does today. In 1886 he founded the first Audubon Society, the charter members being almost exclusively sportsmen-scientists. He saved the bison from extinction, and fathered our Glacier National Park. Grinnell was the most effective source of conservation ideas in American history; and his friend (and fellow Boone and Crockett Club member) Theodore Roosevelt began turning them into public policy as soon as TR's term as New York State governor started.

Whereas the first federal game refuge did not come until the first Roosevelt administration, sportsmen's clubs were establishing them privately in numbers thirty years earlier, and stimulating the states to do so officially.

Another outdoorsman of the patrician class who aided conservation early was avid duck hunter President Benjamin Harrison, a grandson of "Old Tippecanoe," President William Henry Harrison. Brought up on a farm near Cincinnati, Benjamin made Indianapolis his home from age 21 until his death in 1901. During his presidency, American industry revived and the public debt was reduced! In March of 1891, he signed into law the first federal forest reserve, of 13 million acres, resulting from the work of the first (and among the best) national forestry chief, the German professional forester and amateur hunter Bernhard Fernow.

Historian John Reiger has thoroughly documented (1986) the formerly unrecognized importance of sportsmen and sportsmen-naturalists of the eastern states in originating American conservation. He found that "hunting or fishing for pleasure was almost universal among early environmentalists; men like John Muir . . . are clearly the exception. For most, the pursuit of wildlife provided that crucial first contact with the natural world that spawned a commitment to its perpetuation."

INDIANA'S LITERARY NATURALISTS

Scientific writings may be divided into three groups: technical works intended for scientific men, popular compilations for general use, and works which contribute to literature and science at the same time. Of the first two there is no lack, but our third division is so poorly represented as to have led to the saying that those who can write on scientific subjects, have no original ideas, while those who have ideas cannot write.

> —*Foreword to Gene Stratton-Porter's* Moths of the
> Limberlost *(1912)*

Long before the excellent nature programs now being shown on television, literary naturalists were the essential middlemen of the emerging conservation-preservation movement. Gene Stratton-Porter, a self-made literary and artistic naturalist and novelist, developed a worldwide audience for nature as she found it in a small area of northeastern Indiana. Three places in the state officially memorialize this preeminent writing naturalist.

Hopewell Church, at the southern edge of the family farm of 240 acres where Geneva Stratton was born, was served by her preacher-farmer-outdoorsman father. For many years it has been the site of public meetings and exhibits by local people on the Sunday afternoon nearest Gene's birthdate, August 17. The church stands at the intersection of 500-E and 300-N, two miles north of Rt. 24 in Lagro.

Geneva was the youngest of 12 children and grew up at the end of our pioneer period. Imprinted early on outdoor things, she led the free outdoor life described for the character Little Sister in her most autobiographical novel, *Laddie*. Limberlost Swamp was not a part of her girlhood, but many of her outdoor experiences and farm neighbors were woven into her books.

The present Limberlost State Memorial in Geneva, Indiana, is a 14-room log house which she and her husband built at the very edge of the Limberlost, a swamp now long lost through drainage and lumbering. The Porters occupied this home from 1895 to 1913, when the swamp destruction was complete. Of her eventual 21 books, 5 (of her 7) straight nature books and 6 novels, which she also considered nature books, were written here. Her main outdoor interests were birds, wildflowers, and woody plants, but her most original and intellectually satisfying work proved to be *Moths of the Limberlost*. This contained her own remarkable, accurately unposed watercolors of the live, freshly emerged insects. *Girl of the Limberlost* and *Freckles* made the name of this swamp a household word the world over, since her books had 50 million readers in eight languages. Several are now offered in reprint form at the two Porter memorial houses and the state museum.

The Gene Stratton-Porter Memorial on Sylvan Lake near Rome City features the 18-room "log-cabin," which she also designed and had built of white cedar trunks from Wisconsin swampland. The 13 acres which remain, of the original 150, include an 8-acre strip of roadside woods left relatively undisturbed since she used her land in a serious and expensive effort, through a five-person transplantation crew, to preserve native wildflowers that were rapidly disappearing from destruction of their habitats, as in Limberlost Swamp. After Stratton-Porter had moved to California to advise in making movies of her novels, she was killed in an automobile accident in 1924.

Before the 1960s, when another woman nature writer, Rachel Carson, initiated the second great environmental movement, there were by my count 33 notable American literary naturalists. Nine categories among these writers may be recognized, based on the major emphases in their works. I think Mrs. Stratton-Porter represents three of these types—familiar or close-to-home nature, outdoor adventures, and the "human side" of nature. Another famed Hoosier nature writer, Edwin Way Teale, dealt with personal adventures in nature, both familiar and distant unfamiliar.

Stratton-Porter embellished nature with a romantic aura more successfully than any author among her contemporaries. Ernest Thompson Seton was read mainly by teenagers, especially boys. Thornton Burgess delighted the very young with his humanized animals in the "bedtime stories." From somewhat older children on up the age scale, Stratton-Porter's simple, unpretentious writings enjoyed phenomenal popularity. The limited extent to which they are read today does not prevent their being collectors' items. Her books and those of Seton seem more dated than those of other nature writers of their time. Hers are too sentimental and moralistic for modern taste, but young readers too unsophisticated to know this enjoy them immensely. In their own times, she and Seton led many young readers into careers in outdoor biology and conservation. In this way their influence was compounded far into the future.

Even more important, her works joined those of Muir and Burroughs, especially, in painlessly educating the general public to see the value of wild nature and the folly of the prevalent ruthless exploitation and waste of natural landscapes and vital resources. This change in the mental eye formed the groundwork for the first environmental movement, led by a professional (though part-time) literary naturalist, President Theodore Roosevelt. To play this crucial historic role, whether she was conscious of it or not, was surely Gene Stratton-Porter's finest achievement. It is high time that she receives the credit for this which she deserves.

* * *

Edwin Way Teale is best known for his four books on the seasons, which entailed travel by the Teales through 76,000 miles of America. He spent his boyhood summers on his grandparents' farm in the Indiana Dunes, and his 1943 book *Dune Boy* is a classic reminiscence of rural midwestern life in the first quarter of this century.

Young Edwin was a star debater and president of his class of 1922 at Earlham College. He married his college sweetheart, Nellie, the companion of all his travels, in 1923. "I was forty-two," he wrote, "before I really began doing what I wanted to do all the time." This was to make his living as a freelance nature writer and photographer. He wrote 26 books and was printed in more than a hundred periodicals. He built up a file of 30,000 negatives on nature subjects, many on insects. As a writer, he was the modern equivalent of John Burroughs, sensitive and poetic. Another literary naturalist, Donald Culross Peattie, who also got his start in the Indiana dunes country, wrote of Teale, "He can narrate so that we turn the page as fast as our hands can move to find out what happens next."

Gene Stratton-Porter was a preeminent literary naturalist and the author of 21 books. She wrote the 11 considered to be nature books while living in Indiana.   *Photo courtesy of the Indiana Department of Natural Resources*

John Muir was born in Scotland in 1838 and had an unusual and difficult boyhood there and in Wisconsin, where he received only two months of schooling between ages 11 and 22. An undoubted mechanical genius, young Muir worked two years in an Indianapolis machine shop. A tool slipped and struck one eye, the other went blind in sympathy, and he spent a sightless month. He decided to abandon mechanics and study instead "the inventions of God." One of those rare humans who can scarcely look upon the natural world with an even pulse, John became the bearded prophet "crying for the wilderness" of the American West. His renowned books of the unfamiliar nature and aesthetic inspirational types, his friendship with President Theodore Roosevelt, and lobbying of the Congress, made him instrumental in the push Roosevelt initiated for new national parks and forests. In 1892 Muir founded the Sierra Club, but earlier, about 1864, it appears that he originated the idea of setting aside small ecosystems as nature preserves, and tried to buy two intact ones himself, for that purpose. An amazing man, Muir was a prose-poet, scientist, mystic, farmer, explorer, pantheist, nature lover, and political activist.

SCIENCE AND EARLY PRESERVATION

One of the penalties of an ecological education is that one lives alone in a world of wounds. Much of the damage inflicted on land is quite invisible to laymen. An ecologist must either harden his shell and make believe that the consequences of science are none of his business, or he must be the doctor who sees the marks of death in a community that believes itself well and does not want to be told otherwise.

—*Aldo Leopold,* The Round River *(1953)*

Edwin Way Teale, who spent his boyhood summers in the Indiana Dunes, was a literary naturalist who wrote 21 books and rose to international prominence as an author. *Source unknown*

set aside a 51-acre portion as a nature preserve, Davis Woods, for non-consumptive forest research, which is still going forward. In 1926, each tree greater than four inches in diameter was numbered, tagged, described in detail, and located on a large-scale map of the best 21-acre section of old-growth forest within Davis Woods. Tree-by-tree comparisons of survival, growth, and death within the stand have now been made periodically for 70 years—a detailed record of ecological change that is the longest-running in Indiana, and of inestimable value.

The Ross Biological Reserve, another Purdue property, lies along the Wabash only eight miles from the main campus. Two ecology professors recognized its potential and started to use it in 1947, and it was soon turned over to the biology department for management as an outdoor classroom and laboratory. Now including 69 acres, the Ross Reserve has a striking diversity of habitats, hence of life, ranging from the Wabash waters up through wind-deposited sands, seeps, streams, and ravine-dissected oak-hickory slopes, to much flat land on the glacier-built upland above.

A detailed platting of the vegetation was soon completed, and was repeated every decade for many years. A series of M.S. theses dealt with soil types, microclimates, successional changes, and the 381 species of higher plants, 6 of which are orchids. Next, the ecological life histories of certain common plants, and physiological ecology of vertebrate and invertebrate animals were researched. Many problems requiring the natural climatic regime could not have been studied in greenhouses or animal-care quarters.

Following an expansion of the ecology staff at Purdue, and a $200,000 grant in 1977 to develop field facilities, seven ecology professors and their graduate students have given the place continuous intensive use. Since 1978, eight Ph.D. theses, three undergraduate honors theses, and 30 scientific publications have resulted, and several more studies are in progress. For use in general education, the reserve is a natural mecca for regular field trips and outdoor experiments.

The Allee Memorial Woods of Wabash College was a 1957 donation by the heirs of Dr. Warder C. Allee. He was brought up on the family farm adjoining Sugar Creek near Annapolis, in Parke County, Indiana. Between the fields and creek is an extensive forest, some of it of splendid old-growth beech and sugar maple, never used except formerly as a sugarbush. After completing a science curriculum at Earlham College, Allee soon became an ecology professor at the University of Chicago, an expert on animal social behavior. Over time he bought, near the farm, several wooded tracts which had remained largely undisturbed, improving them over the years as an expression of ecological principles.

At Chicago, Allee served as the major professor of young Willis Johnson. When Allee died, Dr. Johnson was head of zoology at Wabash College in Crawfordsville, and with him and botanist Richard Laubengayer the Allee heirs arranged to donate the forest of 180 acres, outright, for preservation by the college as a valuable teaching and research facility. In 1958 the college received a four-year grant from the Atomic Energy Commission for tracing radioisotopes through three distinct ecosystems there. This was done by Dr. Robert Owen Petty, and another Purdue doctorate was earned by Dr. Marion T. Jackson by research on effects of microclimate on flowering plant species. Located only 30 miles from the college, the tract has proved especially useful for Wabash's chief mission, undergraduate teaching, and a number of master's degree projects, including ones at Duke and Indiana State universities, have focused on Allee Woods. The combination of an exceptionally high-quality large tract with long-term, well-conceived utilization fulfills most happily Warder Allee's dream for his cherished forest.

Ecological scientists, by definition, have always been involved with natural areas. In 1926 the Ecological Society of America sponsored a 761-page book entitled *Naturalists Guide to the Americas* which described the best of them. However, any political activity in their behalf was beyond the province of a scientific society. Hence, in 1945 many of the same people organized an action group to work and lobby for preservation, The Ecologists' Union. Its name was changed later to The Nature Conservancy. Although it was then based in Washington, its new policy was to avoid political action, but to privately buy or accept, and manage or ensure suitable management of, natural lands. Over the years, nature-loving citizens from all walks of life have supplanted scientists as the predominant membership, state chapters have been set up, and the mission has caught the fancy of the general public.

Likewise in Indiana, the preservation movement was initiated largely by scientists and academicians. Needing undisturbed areas for teaching and research, they protected many tracts under college ownership. Before 1960, this was the most prevalent category of nature preserves in the state. Because time is one of the ecological factors, each new decade has increased their value exponentially.

In 1916 Purdue University acquired the Davis Forestry Farm and

Pine Hills, in the lovely Sugar Creek Valley of Montgomery County, is still one of Indiana's finest nature preserves. *Photo by Hank Huffman*

*   *   *

Pine Hills stands preeminent in its interesting geological, biological, and human history and its scenic quality, most unusual for Indiana. Its recent story is closely tied to that of the preservation movement in the state.

The deep-cut loops of Clifty Creek and of Indian Creek, just off Sugar Creek, produced six hogsback ridges or "backbones," four of which are conspicuous. Mill Cut Backbone shows substantial change by human agency, dating back to 1868, when a wide notch 20 feet deep was cut down through the sandstone and a crude dam built below it, leading water through the gap by a flume to a new woolen mill on the floodplain off the east end of Turkey Backbone. The mill was used eight months of each year until 1873, when it was moved to Pine Bluff, where the old covered bridge is located. The Mill Cut mill, with its overshot waterwheel, was reached by a wagon road through the cove south of the west end of Turkey Backbone. The tract contains five miles of clear streams.

The present Nature Preserve comprises 470 acres. At its northwest corner, the Pine Bluff or Deer Mill area (for Joel G. Deer) was a popular vacation resort for some time after 1911, by which time the Hasselman brothers, Frank and Lawrence, had bought 600 acres. A trail led upstream to Devil's Backbone, the much-visited centerpiece of the Hasselmans' "Pine Hills Nature Study Park." The super-heroic-

sized line carvings of passenger pigeons on its flat, narrow caprock were probably incised there while the birds still swept in flocks over Pine Hills. The last Indiana record for this species was in 1902. Someone carved the devil's face on this backbone in 1910; it is still clearly visible.

A Purdue dean, botanist Stanley Coulter, had proposed in 1927 that Pine Hills be made a state park. This failed because the state had never spent its own funds on such acquisition until the federal Land and Water Development Act in the early 1960s.

In 1953, the Indiana Academy of Science set up a committee on natural area preservation, chaired by Dr. A. A. Lindsey. Its first project was Pine Hills. A member in the real estate business collected the abstracts for the 17 parcels which the Hasselman family had in 1911 combined, going back to old metes and bounds surveys. Committee members visited the Hasselmans in Indianapolis many times, changing their attitude from indifference to enthusiasm, and the price from $40,000 to $15,000. The committee also guided officials of the Washington office of TNC through Pine Hills, enlisting their strong interest. The state TNC chapter, led by Dr. Lynton K. Caldwell of the Government Department of Indiana University, was chartered in 1959 specifically for the fundraising effort spearheaded by the late Dr. Jack McCormick, a consulting ecologist of Philadelphia. (The academy was not deemed an appropriate group for running fund drives or holding land.) The tract was purchased by

TNC in 1960 and donated to the state in 1961. In the section on the Indiana Nature Preserves Act, we shall see how the effort to save Pine Hills resulted also in the highly effective natural areas preservation agency of our state government.

In 1962 the Corps of Army Engineers was planning, along with 25 similar impoundments in Indiana, a reservoir on Sugar Creek to run through two state parks and up all three streams in Pine Hills to cover with 30 feet of water the trunk base of a cluster of giant white pines, the largest of their species in the state. Opposition by the state government and public ensured that this plan was liquidated.

Pine Hills was honored in 1970 as a National Natural Landmark, the 107th one in the nation. The 20 acres at its northwest corner, containing the ruin of old Hemlock Lodge, were donated in 1974 by Wabash College at the urging of Professor Robert Owen Petty, to complete the Pine Hills tract, unsurpassed among the official and other nature preserves in the state.

*   *   *

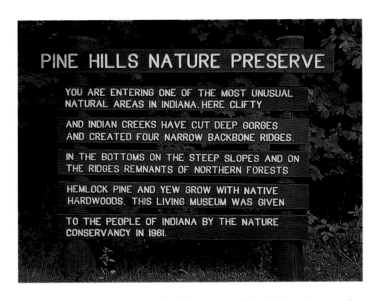

Pine Hills Nature Preserve was the first project of the Indiana chapter of The Nature Conservancy. The Indiana Academy of Science was also instrumental in protection of the tract.   *Photo by Marion Jackson*

Lord of the earth,
>We ask your blessing as we rededicate
>Pine Hills Nature Preserve:

>Its rugged hills and deep ravines,
>Its narrow backbones and twisting creeks,
>Its scattered stands of hemlock, pine, and hardwoods,
>Its yew, clubmoss, and ferns,
>Its snow trillium and wintergreen,
>Its squirrels and warblers.

Awesome forces shaped the landscape:

>Oceans laid down the grains of sand—
>>finally buried deep, pressed into stone.
>Glaciers scraped and scoured the surface.
>Icy meltwaters cut their beds of flow.
>Winds and summer heat and winter cold
>>slowly chipped away the rocks
>>through thousands of seasons.

Miami Indians roamed and hunted here.
Homesteaders came, cut the largest trees,
>and harnessed Clifty Creek to power a mill.

Some came to recognize
>the special beauty and unique richness
>of the glacial relict, values far beyond
>all practical use.

The Hasselmans gathered together the several
>parcels into one.

Friesner, Potzger, and Smith researched and reported.
The Fells of The Nature Conservancy and the Lindseys of
>the Indiana Academy began the move to preserve
>the area, accomplished by the work of McCormick.

Now thousands thank you, Lord of all creation,
>for this hallowed place.

As we rededicate Pine Hills today,
We also rededicate ourselves
>as sensitive and responsible stewards of our
>earth and all it holds.
May all who come here to walk and look and listen
>know your presence and feel your peace.

Amen.
>—*Rev. Damian Schmelz, Invocation at the rededication of*
>*Pine Hills Nature Preserve (April 23, 1990)*

51. Protection Beginnings

Alton A. Lindsey

EARLY VISIONARIES

It is the land on which we all depend in the last essence. It is the land and the very soil, the trees and waters, the dales and glens which we love. Without vision a land will die. Without inspiration we remain disconnected from the immortal order of all things.

> —*Richard Lieber, founder of the Indiana Department of Conservation*

When botanist Charles Deam was asked in 1908 to become the state forester, he replied that he didn't know anything about forestry. Stanley Coulter assured him that no one else did either. This was almost true. The first forest policy in Indiana had been to fell the timber and roll the logs into ravines for burning. Cornell University's B. E. Fernow had brought forestry from Germany and led the U.S. movement in the 1880s. Deam accepted the job partly to get around the state and collect plants.

In 1903 the state forestry board had bought 2,000 acres near Henryville, partly within the old land grant to George Rogers Clark and his veterans. Deam applied the scientific method to forestry practices, using Clark State Forest as his experimental area. His findings led to the policy of planting conifers on worn-out hardwood land, leading to the extensive evergreen plantings we still see. Deam laid the groundwork, and after he resigned in 1928, the next 11 years saw 7 state forests added. The system now boasts 12, totaling 144,600 acres. Within these largely production-oriented units, the Division of Forestry has wisely dedicated 11 nature preserves aggregating 1,648 acres.

These state forests, with their many lakes, trails, and campgrounds, provide excellent recreational opportunities, in addition to timber and wildlife, watershed protection, etc. There are no true wilderness areas managed by the state, since the land was all cut over prior to acquisition. Like the state parks, the forests still have many facilities built by the young men of Franklin D. Roosevelt's famed Civilian Conservation Corps. Although black walnut trees constitute only one-half of 1 percent of the timber harvest, their extreme value makes this commercially important. Other hardwood species furnish most of the harvest.

On the federal level, the U.S. Forest Service gives increased importance to "non-commodity values" in its 1989 plan. Besides its responsibility for the Deam Wilderness (Indiana's only designated wilderness), another 21,000 acres (of the Hoosier National Forest's 188,000-acre total) is classed as non-harvested "back country" and left to natural processes.

Deam wrote four books on Indiana plant life. *Trees of Indiana* had a lifespan which ran through most of the author's career. The writing started in 1909; at age 87 he read proof for the final 1953 edition, but he did not live to see it off the press. Available a decade before Illick's respected *Trees of Pennsylvania*, Deam's was the first good tree book for any of our states. It did not frighten non-botanists as did his scholarly *Flora of Indiana*. Even though the 1953 edition has been out of print since the 1970s, it remains in actual public use today. Robert

C. Kriebel stressed how important Deam's books were to residents of Indiana in his book *Plain Ol' Charlie Deam* (1987):

> In March 1912, ten thousand copies of the Indiana Board of Forestry's annual report for 1911 rolled off the presses. . . . The first eighty-five pages contained dry annual report minutiae. . . . *Trees of Indiana* began on page 86 and ended on page 372. . . . It was a book that the scientist could use, rich in accurate technical detail, filled with Latin names and botanical terminology. At the same time, it was a useful and understandable manual for the amateur. . . . *Trees of Indiana* proved to be one of the most remarkable books of its type ever published. . . . The state exhausted 10,000 free copies of *Trees of Indiana* in three years.

* * *

Those entering an Indiana bank or store in 1947 were likely to be confronted with a coin can, wrapped in a photograph of gigantic trees, with the plea "SAVE THE SHADES." Schoolchildren throughout the state contributed nickels and dimes to the cause. State funds from taxes were not used to buy our state parks until the early sixties; hence, most of them, including the best ones, were donated to the government by the people directly. They are the people's parks in origin, as well as intended use.

Richard Lieber, the "father of Indiana's state parks," was an archetype of the creative, hard-working conservationist in the amateur tradition. Having come over from Germany in 1891, young Lieber became a newspaper art critic and city editor in Indianapolis, but soon went into business. He became a strong conservationist in 1910 when he was entertained by outdoorsy friends in pristine Brown County, and was amazed that such naturalness existed so close to the capital city. He soon bought a family vacation place there.

In 1915 Lieber and a few others began raising funds to acquire the scenic Turkey Run tract in order to donate it to the state. Difficulties with lumber companies slowed the effort, so that both McCormick's Creek and Turkey Run parks were established by the State Park Commission in 1916.

America was good to this businessman, and he reciprocated with idealistic public service. As the first director of the Indiana Department of Conservation, he served from 1919 to 1933, presiding over 10 state parks and 4 state memorials. These included Indiana Dunes along three miles of Lake Michigan shore (1925) and his beloved Brown County State Park from 1929 on.

> State parks are meant to be the show windows of a state but more than that state parks are a dedication to the soul of the land.
>
> —*Richard Lieber, first director of Indiana State Parks*

A welcome initiative in state park policy came a quarter-century ago—the designation of certain more primeval portions as nature preserves within the existing state parks to remain in park division administration, but to be forever withheld from disturbing develop-

Colonel Richard Lieber, as the first Director of Indiana State Parks, was a visionary thinker who implemented many of the policies and practices that yet today make our State Parks program what it is.
Photo courtesy of the Indiana Department of Natural Resources

ments. Trails, footbridges, etc., are provided, but the aim of essential naturalness which Lieber and other old-timers held paramount is held to within these "miniature near-wildernesses."

There are differences in the policies governing the state parks and related lands, with distinct emphases as to kinds of uses. Three superb state areas lying close together along Sugar Creek illustrate a spectrum of uses which appeal to users of different preferences. Turkey Run, the farthest downstream of these, has been rather fully developed for a generality of visitors, offering a large swimming pool, horseback riding, an inn and conference center, cottages, a pioneer church, and a touching woodland memorial site honoring Colonel Lieber, in addition to the usual camping and picnicking facilities. It also has miles of invigorating trails, especially in the Nature Preserve portion north of the Suspension Bridge. Overall, this park is highly developed and appeals to a broad range of visitor interests. The excellent museum and active naturalist service, together with the Nature Preserve and other wild portions, serve perceptive recreation.

However, the two units of state land upstream from Turkey Run Park shift the general balance toward more naturalness, less artificiality. Shades State Park in former years had a rambling wooden hotel remaining from its pre-park days, and a dance hall nearby. Both are long gone, and the huge, ancient white oaks stand out without such interference today. It is a real asset to the state park system to have the Shades appear as pristine as it does, thus helping to balance off some of the newer state parks, which are recreational lands with little naturalness. The Shades has camping and picnicking, but no public buildings of consequence.

Adjacent to the Shades eastward, the State Parks Division (as owner) and the Nature Preserves Division (as manager) oversee the superlative Pine Hills preserve, left natural except for trails, signs,

and a few stairs and safety rails. Thus, Pine Hills has changed little since the first entry by a few settlers in 1850. The unwary hiker, bemused by the writhing courses of three streams, can easily become lost. With the Shades and Turkey Run so near, Pine Hills has no need of further artificial developments. The three units together form a splendid outdoor complex, serving a wide spectrum of tastes and interests.

Richard Lieber died in 1944 during a visit to one of his first two parks, McCormick's Creek. In the other, Turkey Run, his remains rest, in a peace-filled old-growth oak forest, beneath the deeply touching Lieber Memorial near the original log church of pioneer days. Also, overlooking Sugar Creek elsewhere in Turkey Run Park is an antique tuliptree cabin with a fine exhibit about Lieber and the state park idea. The recent Lieber State Recreation Area on Cataract Lake also helps perpetuate his name and undying service to Indiana's future.

There could be very few far-seeing, seminal conservationists like Lieber and Deam, and they could have accomplished little without a multitude of little-known co-workers and support troops. Each who advances the essential work may think of himself or herself as one link in a single shining chain that stretches unbroken through time, generation after generation. Though one nameless individual may not seem to loom large in preservation annals, without that link the great chain would have been incomplete and powerless.

COMMITTED CITIZENS

Keep a green bough in your heart and a singing bird will come.
—Motto above the door of Artist Helen Swenson, at Wing Haven Nature Preserve in Steuben County

It is time for a roll call to honor the First Families of Indiana conservation. Each owned an original forest or other natural landscape, and so loved its beauty and interest that, in a culture which most admired those who cleared land for planting crops, they stood out as peculiar mavericks. In the fortunate cases in which this attitude (and the trees or natural features) continued through generations of the family, the outcome is a group of the finest preserves we have.

In southern Indiana were the Hemmers, who bought their cherished woods in 1870; the Hougland sisters, who protected their majestic Kramer woods; the Hoot family near Freedom; the Officers, the Tribbetts, the Lubbes, and the Coxes. On the extensive Tipton Till Plain across central Indiana, our honorees are the Calverts, Hultzes (Big Walnut area), Manloves, Meltzers, Weavers, and the Holidays, who protected Cabin Creek Raised Fen. And of special note is Jesse Caster, whose beloved forest was ravaged by timber thieves in the night. North of the Wabash, a fine stand held by one family since 1838 was leveled following estate settlement, which was not an unusual situation, but, thanks to the Jackmans, Pinhook Bog survived.

The magnificent Cox Woods was all that was found of value when the estate of Joseph Cox was settled in 1941. It had been zealously protected by the family and last survivor, Joseph, since his grandfather obtained it from the public domain in 1818. Joseph had refused many offers from timber firms, despite his extreme poverty and ill health. Receipts from just one of the gigantic walnut trunks in his moist cove, "Walnut Cathedral," would have sustained him comfortably for years.

This courageous example of grassroots conservation, begun by the Coxes, was continued by private citizens of nearby Paoli. No one opposed a plan to save the forest; it boiled down simply to raising,

Among the private citizens who protected natural areas in their ownership at great personal sacrifice, Ralph and Eileen Hultz stand near the head of the list. Anne M. Petty (widow of Dr. Robert O. Petty) stands next to the stone house (built 1831) in which Ralph Hultz was born near Big Walnut Nature Preserve in Putnam County. *Photo by Alton Lindsey*

within a limited time, the reasonable amount that the new owner, a veneer company, was asking in return for selling it back. The drive benefited from a rousing article in a 1942 issue of the *Saturday Evening Post*. A new name, Pioneer Mothers Memorial Forest, was given in recognition of substantial support from a women's historical association. The U.S. Forest Service helped greatly, and agreed to protect the tract after acquisition. The Meridian Club of Paoli spearheaded the campaign. Excitement built to a crescendo, and the total $24,300 price was met with only a day to spare. Foresters estimate that the trees range in age up to 600 years. As the title of the *Post* article put it, "Joe Cox's Trees Live On."

> We who live softly in luxurious days—
>   What know we of the grim heroic life
>   In the deep forest of the settler's wife,
> Who followed him she loved thro' weary ways,
> Haunted by beast and savage, and alone
>   In hardship and in danger strove to rear
>   Her little brood, stifling her woman's fear,
> And kept the cabin that they made their own?
> Her hands were hard with toil, yet all the more
>   Honor to her who lost her youthful grace
>   And let the lines grow deep upon her face,
> While stalwart offspring to the state she bore.
>   Pray God her children be as pure and true,
>   As brave to dare, as quick and strong to do!
>
> —*William Dudley Foulke, "The Pioneer Mother," in* The
>   Memorial to the Pioneer Mother of Indiana *(1916)*

*   *   *

The push for an Indiana Dunes National Lakeshore resulted in the most protracted and bitter conservation cliffhanger in Indiana history, at least. Although Stephen T. Mather, first director of the National Park Service, had proposed a national park there in 1916, renewed effort toward it began in 1952, when a small local group, mostly women who did not accept the conventional wisdom on behalf of procrastination while the duneland was being nibbled and gulped away, formed the Save the Dunes Council (SDC). Committed as they were, they soon found that the opposition, equally so, had far greater resources. In fact, nearly everyone, weighing the odds, concluded that the SDC was backing an obviously lost cause. Only in 1966, after a struggle unlikely to be seen again on a conservation issue, was the Lakeshore authorized by the necessary legislation.

That the "whole truth" cannot be told here is suggested by the fact that the chief collection of papers on the controversy, in the Calumet Regional Archives of Indiana University Northwest at Gary, occupies 71.5 feet of shelf length. The complexity of the sequence of events discourages a facile summarization, and it may still be too soon for any historian to state that the Dunes sandstorm of the sixties (but not stirred up by militant youth of that period) changed the way the public and press regarded environmentalists, as well as the degree of confidence felt by the latter.

The turning point in the campaign came when an engineering writer and advertising executive from Fort Wayne, Thomas E. Dustin, accepted the arduous but unpaid responsibility for the SDC's public relations. This group at its peak had only about 3,500 members. Dustin was active in the powerful Indiana Izaak Walton League; he brought it in as another chief proponent. Other conservation groups rallied round. The Indiana Academy of Science lent active support and obtained the moral support of the Ecological Society of America; neither group had ever before endorsed any political cause publicly.

Among the many individuals who brought us the Lakeshore must be mentioned Tom and Jane Dustin, the Herbert Reads, the Edward Osanns, SDC presidents Dorothy Buell and Sylvia Troy, and U.S. Senator Paul Douglas of Illinois. They felt that if controversy is an evil, it is sometimes a necessary one. Conservation historian Stephen Fox pointed out that professionals keep the movement organized, and amateurs keep it honest. The Dunes campaign proved to be a conspicuous triumph of the amateur tradition. The citizen effort succeeded, in that a substantial area of the dunes was saved. But the opposition succeeded in that another substantial portion was turned over to industry and the Burns Ditch Port.

For a state to go through such a wringer without learning anything of permanent value would be most unfortunate. What was learned is probably even more important than the Lakeshore itself. At the very time when Rachel Carson's *Silent Spring* was initiating our second great environmental movement, the media discovered that the architects of this sociopolitical change were to be taken seriously. The environmentalists learned that they could be as militant as was necessary to get a fair hearing. To be protected against the abuse of deception, we have to depend not on any "authorized version," but on the journalistic game of "cops and robbers."

The thinking public came to understand that certain crucial values cannot be expressed in an engineer-economist type of benefit/cost ratio. Outdoor scientists relearned the old lesson that unspecialized citizen activists can be their best allies in preservation, and vice versa. All who followed the campaign learned the then-surprising fact that a federal bureaucratic agency loaded with know-how but short on know-whether can be successfully contradicted by "bird watchers." And the nature lovers found that politics can be bent to their purposes.

> Lord of sand and water and wind,
>   Everyday you visit this landscape with your
>   creative power,
>   Resculpturing its form,
>   Bringing forth new plants and animals,
>   As some struggle, die, and are buried,
>   and ancient pine skeletons
>   resurface in blowouts.
>
> A lobe of glacial ice built a morainal dam
>   and gouged a basin from shaly bedrock.
> Meltwater collected to form an ancient lake;
>   successive levels left behind their beaches.
> Pounding waves and whistling winds

The Indiana Dunes were targeted for preservation at least as early as 1917. Now two significant parcels of dune landscape have been protected as the Indiana Dunes State Park and the Indiana Dunes National Lakeshore.   *Photo by Alton Lindsey*

have built and rebuilt the dunes and saddles
and coves a hundred thousand times.

Henry Cowles unraveled your plan
For the barren beach to bring forth life:
the shifting sand.
Then, sand cherry, juniper, and cottonwood;
Black oak, blueberry, and bracken fern.
Finally, majestic ash and elm, maple and beech.
A mosaic of niches for beetles, bugs,
and butterflies,
Yellowthroats, green herons, and the snowy owl
from the north,
Raccoons, red squirrels, and beaver.

Nomadic Miami and Potawatomi hunted
and gathered food through here.
Joseph Bailly was but one who trapped and traded
for furs.

The Swedish Chellberg family farmed land nearby.
For over a century our cities and factories have
paved and polluted the shores.

The Park and Lakeshore remain
as remnants of refuge for plants and animals
but just as much for people.
Here the bright sun and endless waves and singing
sands restore our bodies and souls
as we swim and play and hike the trails.
But our mere presence abuses this fragile world
and counters your creating.
We have to learn its secret in order to love the Dunes.
This Nature Center and its Naturalists are our
guides for coming to understand the complexity
and to appreciate the beauty.

Bless this building and its exhibits.
Bless those who labored to build it,
those who have gathered to dedicate it,
those who will work within it.

May all who pass through these doors
be enabled to recognize your creative hand,
be enabled to respect your continuing presence.

Amen.

—*Rev. Damian V. Schmelz, Invocation at the dedication of
Indiana Dunes State Park Nature Center (May 31,
1990)*

* * *

In contrast to the confrontation over the dunes, since 1960 the quiet, low-key, but hard-working and highly successful group ACRES, Inc., in and around Fort Wayne, had acted privately to purchase deserving tracts in northeast Indiana. Jane Dustin has been its leading spirit for three decades. By the time our Nature Preserves Act of 1967 had changed the Hoosier conservation climate, ACRES had already acquired 6 areas, and today owns 28, totaling 1,625 acres. A delightful quarterly journal is produced, frequent outings are held, and meetings, lectures, and banquets are sponsored. Every major Indiana city would benefit from having such a group, like a miniature Nature Conservancy in its ideals and methods. Recently, Carolyn McNagny accepted the professional position of its first executive director.

The origin of Merry Lea Environmental Learning Center goes back to 1938, when Lee A. Rieth, recently graduated from Purdue University in civil engineering, was employed by the state to conduct geological surveys. As he studied the area southwest of Wolf Lake village in Noble County, he was much impressed by the varied scenery, flora, and fauna he found. In 1963 he and his wife Mary Jane Rieth bought 80 acres on Bear Lake as the initial parcel for a non-profit nature center which they envisioned. This they founded in 1967, and through dedicated effort they have since brought it up to 1,150 acres of forest, lakeshores of Bear and High lakes, glacial eskers, oldfields, ponds, marshlands, and limy prairie. Nothing to match it could be assembled in Indiana today.

A volunteer board has worked actively with and advised the founding couple, and planned and supervised construction of the education building. One full-time director or another has been employed since 1967; the present is Dr. Lawrence Yoder, a member of the Goshen College faculty. In 1980 an arrangement was reached with Goshen College and The Nature Conservancy which ensures perpetuation of its natural character and of its educational and scientific uses. The most natural 290-acre portion of the property is now the Merry Lea State Nature Preserve. A groundskeeper and others live on the place.

NATURAL AREA VALUES

A thing is right when it tends to preserve the integrity, stability and beauty of the biotic community. It is wrong when it tends otherwise.

—*Aldo Leopold, A Sand County Almanac (1949)*

Two sets of human values are inherent in natural areas—the old and the new. Among the oldest is that a natural area is a place made by Him, not by us, for "the groves were God's first temples." In a world of ever-accelerating dominance by ourselves and our artifacts and wastes, we need increasingly to touch and to know what came before and lies beyond. There is much hope in the fact that this ancient value is seen more clearly by each successive generation.

A more prosaic definition holds that a natural area is any outdoor site which contains an unusual biological, geological, or scenic feature, or else illustrates common principles of ecology uncommonly well. The general values we now find in those features and ideas are among the older ones, long recognized for even very small outstanding examples of the natural world. These places project the past through the present and into the future in many ways related to our science, education, overall culture, and simple personal enjoyment.

The key idea related to the typically small natural area is *perception*. The chief reason for preserving them is to promote perceptive thought and feeling. Almost anyone can see, if willing, but the mind must be well stocked before it can perceive. Most nature preserves have trails open to the public gratis, but intended more for re-creation than mere recreation. No one is invited in to kill the "natives," nor to frighten the air or tear up land and life with off-road vehicles. The popular idea that merely getting more people out on the land promotes conservation is a fallacy. Some say that nature preserves are for "passive recreation," but these places lend themselves to active mental, spiritual, and aesthetic experiences. They are too rare and special for ordinary mass recreation (often as destructive as it is ordinary), which may, however, be suitable in the many large, commonplace outdoor recreation areas elsewhere.

Joseph Wood Krutch wrote, "When someone destroys a work of art he is called a vandal; when someone destroys a work of Nature he

Phillip Meltzer (*shown*) and his family continue to own and protect Meltzer Woods in Shelby County, one of the finest old-growth forests in the state, as they have since Phillip's grandfather homesteaded the farm in the 1860s. This large tree was formerly the national champion Shumard's red oak.
Photo by Marion Jackson

is called a developer." Fortunately, the early seventies brought a new emphasis on quality of total environment, as distinct from supplies of raw materials. This reorientation led to a better appreciation of natural area values. It also convinced many that we can no longer afford to have economics always settle questions involving the quality of life. Having a good life is at least as important as making a good living.

The "multiple use" concept pushed by utilitarian conservationists of the Gifford Pinchot school is often misused. Properly understood, it does not mean that every area should be subjected to every use. In our homes, we apply multiple use to the house as a whole; we do not use every room for every purpose. A nature preserve, devoted to a complex of higher uses than ordinary commercial or outdoor recreational lands can provide, is comparable to a music room or library in a home, and to non-profit cultural assets in a city. Inappropriate use of the few really natural remnants, for some use other than their best use, is not use but abuse.

Specific practical reasons for preserving outstanding lands and waters have long been heard. Many actual and potential uses of nature-based products are found in pharmacognosy and industrial chemistry. Also, such places help us to maintain the diversity of habitats and life forms that makes our lives more interesting, and

tend to counter species extinctions. They sustain a pool of genes, often of unknown but great potential.

Thus, preserved areas throughout our planet ensure continuity to biological inheritance and to natural processes of soil development and enrichment, geological changes, and long-standing cultural relationships with nature. We need many more such reserves than we have.

THE INDIANA NATURE PRESERVES ACT OF 1967

It is essential to the people of the State of Indiana that they retain the opportunities to maintain close contact with such living communities and environmental systems of the earth and to benefit from the scientific, aesthetic, cultural and spiritual values they possess.

—*Attorney James M. Barrett III, author of the* Indiana Nature Preserves Act *(1967)*

Beginning in 1953, a natural areas committee of the Indiana Academy of Science was working with the national office of The Nature Conservancy, since the state TNC chapter was not set up until 1959. The academy did everything to save Pine Hills except the most difficult and essential job—raising the funds—and outside scientist

Jack McCormick accomplished that. These funds were used by TNC in 1960 to buy the tract as its first nature preserve in Indiana, and the next year it donated Pine Hills to the government's State Park Division. The adjacent Shades State Park was assigned to manage this tract.

Among Indiana Academy members, this specific case was considered workable, but one member considered the policy inadequate for future nature preserves distant from a state park. Therefore, he brought up the matter in a letter to Tom Dustin (who by that time had come to represent the most active meristem in Hoosier citizen conservation action) suggesting a new, official governmental body in Indianapolis with responsibility only for state-owned and -managed nature preserves. In a momentous letter of June 10, 1964, Dustin definitely approved the idea, agreeing that he was in a position to start the ball rolling in that direction, and would do so.

In 1965 the Indiana Izaak Walton League elected Dustin its president, and he wrote the league's policy resolution advocating a state Nature Preserves System, which the group adopted in May. The next year, he enlisted Fort Wayne attorney and amateur naturalist James M. Barrett III to serve as chairman of the league's Wilderness and Natural Areas Committee. About this time, Dustin began his long-term tenure as editor of the *Hoosier Waltonian* journal, and rounded up other Indiana conservation groups and key political figures. Barrett studied the laws of the few other states that had already taken a similar course, introduced new ideas appropriate to Indiana, and wrote our Nature Preserves Act, which passed the General Assembly on March 11, 1967. It is *"An Act creating a division of nature preserves, providing for their acquisition, control, use, management, and protection."* This document (see Appendix of the book *Natural Areas in Indiana and Their Preservation* by Lindsey, Schmelz, and Nichols for full text) has since become a model followed by other states, and the foundation undergirding Indiana's outstanding success in the field. No existing preserve has yet come under challenge for other, conflicting uses. It is believed and hoped that the bill (as strong as was politically possible) has the teeth needed to meet the threats likely to arise with continued increase in population.

William B. Barnes, who had been educated as a forester in Pennsylvania, moved from the deputy post in the Fish and Wildlife Division to head the new division. He was enthusiastic about its potential, and proved the perfect choice. Mild-mannered but resolute, he served very effectively until retirement (except perhaps the first year on the payroll, when the legislature made no appropriation for his work). Dustin said of Barnes, "We knew we had a person with the courage to stand up for principle no matter what the consequences."

John A. Bacone succeeded to the directorship of the Division of Nature Preserves in 1979, and has presided brilliantly over the maturing of policy and practice and the building up of an outstanding staff of dedicated and talented people. He continues at present leading this division.

* * *

In 1959 The Nature Conservancy's Indiana Chapter had as its 39 charter members those Hoosiers who had joined the national group earlier. Except for Mrs. Eli Lilly, almost all were academic persons. Two of the Purdue professor members, Durward L. Allen and Helmut Kohnke, were to become very active on their own in general conservation. Allen is not only one of the pioneers in wildlife management in North America, but also a modern philospher of conservation policy. The first chapter chairman was Lynton K. Caldwell, professor of government at Indiana University, who much later was to initiate, and write for U.S. senator Henry Jackson, the national legislation setting up the Environmental Protection Agency, the requirement for environmental impact statements and related provisions.

The state chapter of TNC depended strictly on member volunteers until attorney Dennis Wolkoff accepted full-time employment in 1974. This marked the beginning of the highly successful modern course of the Indiana Nature Conservancy, which was continued by director William W. Weeks. When Weeks became director of operations at The Nature Conservancy's national office, he was succeeded by Dennis McGrath. Under its three able state directors, the Indiana Chapter of TNC has made Indiana a leading state in the area of nature preservation.

> But how can man be persuaded to cherish any other idea unless he can learn to take some interest and some delight in the beauty and variety of the world for its own sake, unless he can see a "value" in a flower blooming or an animal at play, unless he can see some "use" in things not useful?
>
> —*Joseph Wood Krutch, "Conservation Is Not Enough," in* American Scholar

Bog-candles is well named for its tall, showy, white flowering spikes. A very rare species and seldom seen in flower.   *Photo by Perry Scott*

52. Inventory and Preservation

John A. Bacone

INDIANA'S DIMINISHING NATURAL DIVERSITY

Primitive Nature is the most interesting to me. I take infinite pains to know all the phenomena of the spring, for instance, thinking that I have here the entire poem, and then, to my chagrin, I hear that it is but an imperfect copy that I possess and have read, that my ancestors have torn out many of the first leaves and grandest passages, and mutilated it in many places.

—*Henry David Thoreau,* The Journal

Prior to European settlement, Indiana was one large natural area. Human habitation was sparse, and aggressive weeds and alien animals from the "Old World" flora and fauna had not yet arrived. Periodic floods, fires, tornadoes, and other natural disturbances, along with clearings by the indigenous peoples for villages and agriculture, occurred across Indiana. Large herds of bison and other ungulates roamed the land. All of these disturbances were followed by stages of revegetation and repopulation by native plant and animal species. Indiana was then a large, intact complex of ecosystems with random patches of disturbance that are so necessary to a healthy but dynamic ecological "steady state."

Our entire biota was composed of native species at that time. It is not possible to calculate how many species could have called Indiana "home" hundreds of years ago, but based on numerous post-settlement surveys and studies, there were almost 1,900 vascular plant, more than 20,000 insect, and almost 700 native vertebrate species. This biota had existed within the natural landscape for thousands of years following the last glaciation.

Within a short time after the arrival of the settlers, the landscape was quickly and radically altered. Forests were cut down and converted to agricultural fields and village sites. Market hunting pressure reduced game populations. Wetlands were drained, and prairies were plowed.

We can never know precisely how many species were extirpated as wild Indiana was tamed. Some of the larger vertebrates disappeared almost immediately. The last bison and elk were seen in 1830, the last Canada lynx and red wolf in 1832. The black bear, mountain lion, wolverine, fisher, and ivory-billed woodpecker were extirpated in the 1850s, the common loon and trumpeter swan in the 1890s. As more of Indiana was converted to agriculture and cities, more species disappeared. The last whooping crane was seen in 1907, the last passenger pigeon in 1902, the last timber wolf in 1908. Porcupines were gone by 1918, the spotted skunk by 1920, the river otter by 1942. We lost the prairie-chicken in the early 1970s.

The beauty and genius of a work of art may be reconceived, though first material expression be destroyed; a vanished harmony may yet again inspire the composer; but when the last individual of a race of living beings breathes no more, another heaven and another earth must pass before such a one can be again.

—*C. William Beebe,* The Bird: Its Form and Function
(1906)

There have been wholesale conversions of ecosystems, so that little, if any, remains of some natural community types—sand forests, sand prairies, sinkhole swamps, and flatwoods are represented today by very few, relatively small, examples. Wet prairies, dry prairies, bur oak savannas, and undeveloped lakes, once common community types, are, for the most part, a memory. Even the once-extensive upland forests have been dramatically changed by land use practices such as clearing, grazing, high-grading, and fragmentation.

Indiana's natural diversity does remain in relatively small pockets scattered across the state. However, it is safe to say that many of our native plants and animals are under great pressure, and are struggling to survive. There are competitive forces at work all across the landscape which are more significant than any that these species have ever had to deal with since the retreat of the last glaciers.

For example, fires once burned annually across much of Indiana. They had a profound effect on many natural communities and the life cycles of many plants and animals. Today, fires have been removed from the natural order of things. The state's waters have been dramatically altered, and water tables appear to have dropped significantly in the recent past. Our topsoil has been seriously depleted and continues to erode at the rate of 120 million tons per year. Clearing of forests and even fencerows, drainage and filling of wetlands, urban sprawl, air and water pollution, and other environmental pressures continue to accelerate.

Aggressive exotic plants and animals such as purple loosestrife, gypsy moth, zebra mussel, and many others compete against many of our native species. In fact, many of these weedy species thrive over most of Indiana on disturbances proliferated by humankind, where they often replace the native biota. More than 400 species of plants not native to Indiana have become established members of our flora. As the integrity and stability of our natural systems ebbed, these opportunistic species for the most part supplanted our native species. And this continues even today.

While it is true that species do eventually become extinct naturally, they do so at a much slower rate than is occurring today. The extinction rate in the natural world prior to human advancement has been estimated at one species per 1,000 years. By 1950, the rate had increased to one species per 10 years. The present rate worldwide is significantly more than one species per year. Some scientists believe that we are losing species at the rate of one per day, possibly even much faster than that.

Natural extinction is the process by which species unable to adapt to natural changes are culled. Humans have so drastically altered the landscape that today species go extinct because they cannot adapt to habitat changes brought on by our numbers and our technology. Many surviving native species are restricted to small natural refuges, or forced to exist in disturbed habitats.

Whereas some species adapt well and thrive, others vanish as their habitat is altered or vanishes. In many cases, these are the species which have narrow, specialized niches. Because they have fidelity to very special conditions, slight changes can result in their demise. Of the approximately 1,900 vascular plant species native to Indiana, almost 500 (26 percent) are considered endangered, threatened, rare, or of special concern. Of the almost 700 native vertebrates, 125

(18 percent) are similarly rare. Species are rare and/or vulnerable because of a number of individual factors or combinations of factors. Included are small population size, low site tenacity, shrinking habitat due to land modification, relictual habitat conditions, and narrow food preferences.

Many rare and vulnerable species have become endangered, and may ultimately be extirpated. Their habitat is currently a very small percentage of Indiana's total land mass, and in many cases occurs only as "islands" in a sea of non-natural landscape. If a species disappears from one of these "islands," immigration from another area is unlikely in a highly fragmented landscape.

> Every living thing also affects man's own evolutionary progress. When any kind of creature disappears, its influence on man goes too. The direction of his development surely changes slightly. . . . By obliterating other kinds of life, man may be destroying himself as well.
>
> —*Lorus J. and Margery Milne,* The Balance of Nature *(1961)*

Because of increasing concern over diminishing habitat and natural diversity, scientists and resource managers have been monitoring our rarest species and devising protection strategies to prevent further loss of native species from Indiana. Biologists from the Department of Natural Resources, the Heritage Data Center, and the Nongame Program, working in close cooperation with scientists and conservation organizations, have compiled lists of our rarest species.

Species are considered "endangered" if their prospects for survival in Indiana are in immediate jeopardy and they are in danger of disappearing from the state. Endangered animals include the swamp rabbit, yellow-crowned night heron, and northern cavefish. Plants are considered endangered if they are known from five or fewer sites. Endangered plants include the yellow-fringed orchid, prairie parsley, and Canada burnet.

An animal likely to become endangered in the forseeable future is considered "threatened." Included are the Franklin's ground squirrel, sedge wren, crowned snake, and four-toed salamander. Plants are considered threatened if they are known to occur at 6 to 10 locations. Some of Indiana's threatened plants are bog rosemary, Hill's thistle, and bald cypress.

Species are considered "rare" or of "special concern" if they are of limited abundance or distribution in Indiana, and if another problem is suspected, thus requiring close monitoring. Included in this category are the star-nosed mole, mudpuppy, cisco, salamander mussel, regal fritillary butterfly, and bog bluegrass.

"Extirpated" species are those which formerly occurred in Indiana, such as the bison, common raven, or twinflower. In general, the assumption is that once a species is lost, it is lost forever. This is certainly true in the case of species that go "extinct," because extinct species have been lost from the entire world. Fortunately, sometimes extirpated species can be reintroduced into Indiana, since they still exist elsewhere.

Several recent success stories provide hope for the future. In 1991, the bald eagle successfully nested in Indiana for the first time this century, culminating joint efforts by the Nongame Program, the U.S. Fish and Wildlife Service, and many private cooperators to bring this species back. A similar project is under way to reintroduce peregrine falcons. Ospreys have recently nested in Indiana, apparently as a result of reintroduction in nearby states. And on January 18, 1995, 25 river otters from Louisiana were released on the Muscatatuck National Wildlife Refuge in Jennings County. This is the first time in more than a half-century that wild river otters have been known to occur in Indiana.

Similar efforts are planned for several extirpated plants. For example, seedlings of Mead's milkweed that were grown in a greenhouse at the Morton Arboretum in Lisle, Illinois, have been reintroduced into a Lake County prairie, and the Tennessee vetch has been successfully reestablished on a hill prairie in central Indiana.

Accelerated land-protection efforts, combined with increasing attention to habitat restoration, may yet turn the tide on the forces which continually diminish natural diversity. While the "progress" that has resulted in so many negative changes to the Indiana landscape for so many years often appears insurmountable, an increasingly concerned and informed army of citizens and professionals are doing all they can to retain our natural heritage. Who knows, perhaps one day we will view "progress" as saving species, not destroying them.

A CONTINUING INVENTORY

> A rational first step toward preservation is such a detailed inventory as Dr. Lindsey and his colleagues have carried out for Indiana.
>
> —*Gordon Harrison, The Ford Foundation, in* Natural Areas in Indiana and Their Preservation *(1969)*

Begun in 1967 with a $35,000, two-year grant from the Ford Foundation, the inventory by Alton A. Lindsey and his associates was the first attempt nationwide to comprehensively inventory and assemble information on natural areas on a statewide basis. The objectives of this pioneer effort were to locate, describe, and evaluate all areas already in use as nature preserves, and also for all other known natural areas worthy of preservation.

Lindsey and his colleagues Dr. Damian V. Schmelz and Stanley Nichols learned of the natural areas they included in their inventory from previous inventory efforts, academic colleagues, scientific publications, Soil Conservation Service offices, farmers, foresters, professional extension workers, and land managers, and through their own field work. Areas were classified according to habitat type, overall quality, use, and potential (e.g., geological, terrestrial-biological). Species were catalogued, the vegetation was sampled, and priority ratings for protection were assigned. Their inventory, which consisted of an amazing amount of work accomplished in an extremely short period of time on a modest budget, became the bible for future protection of natural diversity.

In the years since its publication, a high percentage of the areas included in their inventory have been protected. An even more impressive statistic is how few areas that were inventoried have been destroyed. Incredibly, of the 155 areas included in their inventory, only 11 have been destroyed or significantly degraded during the past 25 years. This illustrates another benefit derived from the efforts of Lindsey, Schmelz, and Nichols. By reviewing the value of their lands with the owners of natural areas during their field survey, they ensured that the majority of areas in private ownership would not be destroyed inadvertently. This principle is well understood today, as landowner contact or "registry" efforts are now an important part of the protection programs of many states.

Subsequent inventory efforts to locate natural areas in Indiana have been driven by principles that spring from the pilot study of Lindsey et al. First and foremost, unknown areas must be located, so they are not lost unawares. The areas must then be evaluated and protection priorities assigned, so that preservation resources can first be focused on those of highest quality. Finally, landowners and their heirs must be apprised of the special values represented by the lands in their ownership and entrusted to their care.

The gray bat is one of the rarest mammals in the state, being known from only one locality in far southern Indiana. The colony is increasing and now has a sizable population.
Photo courtesy of the Indiana Division of Nature Preserves

Franklin's ground squirrel is a prairie species of northwestern Indiana.
Photo by Ron Panzer

Royal catchfly is a very showy wildflower that is encountered only rarely in prairie remnants and is presently threatened in Indiana.
Photo by Ron Everhart

Marestail (*Hippuris vulgaris*) once ranged from northern Indiana north to coastal Alaska. This species formerly fringed wetlands on saturated soils, but apparently is now gone from Indiana.   *Photo by Marion Jackson*

The natural areas inventory pioneered by Lindsey and his colleagues was only a beginning. Given the narrow time and money constraints, by necessity their inventory focused primarily on information already known to scientists and biologists working in natural resources fields. Since their work was published, inventory efforts have continued.

At first, special areas were located through serendipitous efforts, as they were periodically discovered during field trips, or occasionally reported by concerned citizens. In the late 1970s an effort was made to conduct a systematic, county-by-county inventory of natural areas similar to that completed recently in Illinois.

To accomplish this, first a natural community classification was developed for the Indiana landscape. Then inventory efforts focused on finding high-quality examples of all communities listed in the classification. This type of inventory combined careful analysis of aerial photography with topographic, soil, and geologic maps, plus information gleaned from the literature, original land surveys, files, and contracts.

The Carolina Parakeet (*Conuropsis carolinensis*), more accurately a conure, was a regular resident of Indiana and the southeastern U.S. in pioneer days. The species is now extinct globally. The birds were pests of fruit and grain crops on frontier farms, resulting in their relentless persecution.
Photo from Joseph M. Forshaw and William T. Cooper, Parrots of the World *(Garden City, N.Y.: Doubleday, 1973)*

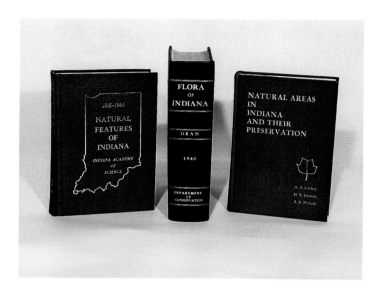

Deam's *Flora of Indiana*, published in 1940, was the most comprehensive inventory of vascular plants for any state up to that time. Studies of the natural features (1966) and natural areas (1969) of Indiana by Dr. Alton Lindsey and his colleagues were the first such inventories for any state in the nation. *Photo by Tony Brentlinger, Indiana State University*

This analysis progressed by eliminating the most obviously disturbed areas first, then scrutinizing the remainder more carefully. For example, agricultural fields were easily eliminated, whereas forested lands and wetlands were examined further. Potential old-growth forests were selected on the basis of larger crown diameters, while forests with narrow crowns and dense canopies were eliminated from further consideration. Areas with peaty soils were selected as potential bogs. Sandy soils were carefully screened for their potential to harbor prairies.

Following the selection of potential natural areas, all sites under consideration were checked from the air. This allowed a more detailed and updated view than that provided by maps and photos. Disturbances such as recent ditching, logging, pasturing, clearing, house construction, etc., usually eliminated 90 percent of the sites previously selected. Remaining sites which survived aerial reconnaissance were ground checked in the growing season, at which time other disturbances (such as exotic flora, evidence of past grazing) could be evaluated. As a general rule, for every 100 areas selected during aerial surveys that seemed to have potential, fewer than 25 proved to be of sufficient quality to merit protection efforts.

Unlike the Illinois inventory, which was funded by a $700,000 line item from the general assembly for a statewide three-year effort, the Indiana inventory did not receive special state funding. Instead, our inventory was pieced together from a variety of efforts, and funded by a number of sources. The Coastal Zone Management Program paid for an intensive inventory of Indiana's Lake Michigan watershed, which yielded a number of very special sites. The Office of Surface Mining funded inventory efforts in several counties in southwest Indiana. Special experts assisted in a number of counties, but most of the work done during the past 12 years was done by the small staff of the Division of Nature Preserves.

Some exceptional natural areas were located during the inventory, including high-quality bogs, gravel hill prairies, fens, glades, old-growth forests, savannas, and seeps—all previously unknown. There were also some major disappointments.

For example, possibly the largest and best old-growth forest in Indiana was located in Jackson County. Consisting of several hundred acres, it appeared on the aerial photos to be of higher quality than most known old-growth forests. The ground check confirmed that it *had been* the most spectacular forest in Indiana. Numerous stumps more than five feet in diameter, and tops left after very long logs had been taken, were all that remained. Unfortunately, timber thieves had cut and stolen literally hundreds of trees during the relatively short period between the time the aerial photo was taken and the ground check. Division of Forestry staff documented the woods that had been there only a few years earlier, a sad example of "postmortem" ecology.

Other disappointments, confirmed during the inventory, were the documentation that virtually nothing remained of a number of natural community types that once covered major portions of Indiana. Such unfortunate losses include black soil prairie and bur oak savanna.

In 1979, while the above-mentioned systematic surveys were just getting started, another important tool was introduced to aid the inventory efforts. In that year, the Indiana Natural Heritage Program was started. The Heritage Program, a concept developed by The Nature Conservancy, includes a systematically compiled data base and field effort to accumulate information concerning Indiana's rarest plants, animals, and natural communities, geologic features, and other natural features—these units designated as the *elements of natural diversity.*

Following consultation with experts, lists of the rarest species were compiled. Information about these "elements," such as habitat, location, and associated species, was then collected from all herbaria and museums containing Indiana species. This information was noted on a permanent set of topographic maps, and also stored in a computerized data base and companion set of manual files. Since its inception, information has been collected on thousands of locations of Indiana's rarest elements.

When combined, the Heritage Program and the systematic natural areas inventory proved to be an extremely effective and productive way not only to locate sites of rare species occurrence, but also to locate natural areas. A number of bogs, fens, savannas, and other natural community types were discovered by seeking out potential sites based on habitat information and associated species listed on herbarium labels.

Perhaps more important, the Heritage data base provides a continuously updated system by which many occurrences of the same community type or species can be compared. This is a valuable tool in assigning protection priorities on a continuing basis, even when biological information is so dynamic.

Field efforts to locate rare species have resulted in hundreds of important finds. A number of species, such as running buffalo clover and American burnet, that had not been seen in many years were relocated. Field work also has turned up new "state records," previously unknown in Indiana. These include Virginia willow, Forbe's saxifrage, and snowbell. Sadly, intensive field efforts have also documented species that no longer occur here, probably because their habitat has been destroyed. Some of these include Mead's milkweed, Hooker's orchid, and buffalo-berry.

Special inventories are sometimes needed to locate certain types of areas. For example, it has long been realized that the only "black soil" prairies left in many midwestern states are in old pioneer cemeteries and along railroad rights-of-way. Dr. Robert Betz, a professor at Northeastern Illinois University, developed a method for examining cemeteries in the prairie region and detecting prairie vegetation (if present) even in carefully manicured cemetery lawns. He looked at

the Indiana Heritage Program

The Indiana Natural Heritage Program is a statewide effort to locate and protect all of the elements of biodiversity, including rare or sensitive species, natural communities or ecosystems, and special natural features. *Photos courtesy of the Indiana Division of Nature Preserves*

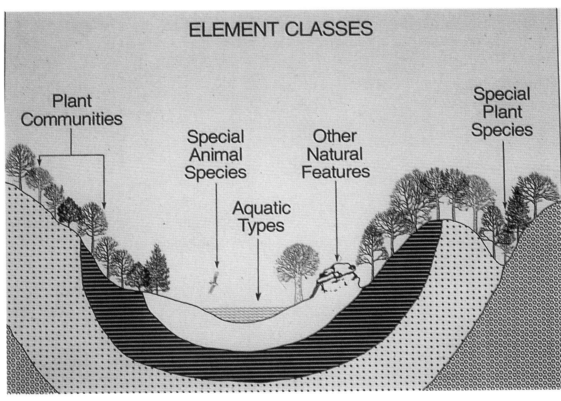

hundreds of cemeteries in northwest Indiana, and DNP field ecologists have looked at hundreds more. Only a handful of cemeteries were found to contain some remnant prairie. The few of these cemeteries that are currently managed to enhance prairie vegetation contain just about all the protected black soil prairie that we have left, so indeed they are important!

Another rapid technique for locating prairies is to fly above railroad rights-of-way in the fall, when the prairie grasses have acquired their beautiful orange-red-brown hue. Prairie remnants are easily distinguished from the white and green colors of the ubiqui-

tous fescue and Kentucky bluegrass that occupy most of these rights-of-way and surrounding fields. Fortunately, miles of railroad rights-of-way in northwest Indiana still harbor prairie vegetation today, although only a few stretches are being managed to perpetuate the prairie community.

Other special inventories have proven useful in locating pristine rock cliff communities, flatwoods, sinkhole ponds, and other areas. As more is learned about certain community types, special methodology is sometimes developed to enhance inventory efforts. These methods usually involve interpreting clues from historical writings,

Remnants of prairie communities are found occasionally in pioneer cemeteries such as this example in Sullivan County. With periodic controlled burning, native prairie species usually increase, while invading woody species are reduced.
Photo by John A. Bacone

aerial photos, soil maps, topographic maps, and aerial reconnaissance.

All inventory efforts are of necessity limited in scope because of constraints related to money and staff time. With unlimited money and time, more natural areas or rare species sites can certainly be discovered. Cases in point are detailed inventories undertaken on large federal landholdings, such as the Hoosier National Forest or Department of Defense–owned lands. Under contract with those agencies, DNP staff have been able to carefully search for rare species and natural areas. Such efforts have been most fruitful. For example, a number of barrens and cliff communities, as well as hundreds of sites of rare plants, were recently located in the Hoosier National Forest. Glades and high-quality forests have been found at several military reservations. Inventories are presently under way on a number of state parks and state forests.

This careful scrutiny for natural areas is certainly an important project, as almost all of "original Indiana" is gone. For example, it is estimated that Indiana originally had approximately 2 million acres of prairie. Today barely 1,000 acres remain. Of more than 5.6 million acres of wetlands in pre-settlement times, only 800,000 acres remain, and many remaining tracts have been heavily disturbed. Careful study of the small portion of Indiana that still resembles the original landscape is necessary in order to find the remaining high-quality natural areas, as well as to locate disturbed areas that are restorable.

The natural areas inventory in Indiana is a dynamic and continuing effort. More time and effort will presumably yield more sites worth protecting. As new sites are found, priorities continually need to be reassessed. Development pressures also continue to modify the landscape. As more land is taken for development, natural area and element location losses are certain to continue. The more complete the inventory efforts are, the more accurate our knowledge will be. Accurate information is essential to set priorities and permit wise

land-use decisions to be made, decisions that hopefully will ensure that Indiana's natural areas will continue to exist into the future.

PROTECTION STRATEGIES

The last word in ignorance is the man who says of an animal or plant: "What good is it?" If the land mechanism as a whole is good, then every part is good, whether we understand it or not. If the biota, in the course of aeons, has built something we like but do not understand, then who but a fool would discard seemingly useless parts. To keep every cog and wheel is the first precaution of intelligent tinkering.

—*Aldo Leopold,* The Round River *(1953)*

Finding, and evaluating the quality of, natural areas is only the first, and in some cases the easiest, step. Designing protection strategies for remaining natural areas can be vexing indeed. Protection priorities must be established, often forcing difficult choices in allocating limited funds and staff resources. Priorities must take into consideration the types of features present, their size and quality, the degree of protection of such features elsewhere, plus immediate and potential threats to the defensibility of the site. Funds and energy available must first be expended on the most crucial areas.

Indiana is fortunate indeed that the General Assembly had the foresight to set up a mechanism to provide permanent protection for its dwindling number of natural areas. In 1967, the Nature Preserves Act was passed, declaring the policy of the state to preserve its outstanding natural areas, both publicly and privately. It established a new Division of Nature Preserves in the Department of Natural Resources, which was charged with inventorying and establishing a system of nature preserves. The legislature was apprised that most of the "original Indiana" was gone forever; they then recognized the importance of preserving at least some of what was left, as it is an important part of our heritage.

The Nature Preserves Act set up the strongest mechanism possible to guarantee protection—that of dedication as a state nature preserve. Dedication can take place regardless of ownership, and consists of the State of Indiana accepting a permanent conservation easement whereby the current owners, while retaining ownership and appropriate use, give up their rights, and the rights of future owners, to destroy or change the area being dedicated. Each area that is dedicated has legal documents—articles of dedication and a master plan—that are drawn up to describe the boundaries and list the allowable uses. These documents are approved by the Natural Resources Commission, the attorney general, and the governor, and finally recorded on the deed in the office of the recorder of the county in which the property is located.

The law prevents the taking of a nature preserve for any other purpose except another public use, and only after a finding by the commission "of the existence of an imperative and unavoidable public necessity," and only with the approval of the governor. Before such a finding, the Natural Resources Commission must first hold a public hearing. These stipulations are believed to give as much protection as is legally possible, and to date, no nature preserve has been taken for another use.

As of the date of this book, more than 150 areas, encompassing more than 20,000 acres, have been dedicated as state nature preserves. They are in a variety of ownerships, including city and county park departments, private conservation organizations, colleges and universities, and state government (DNR's Divisions of State Parks, Forestry, Fish and Wildlife, Museums, and Nature Preserves). Existing nature preserves protect an array of natural communities, rare species habitats, and geologic features.

The first important step in an area's protection is landowner contact—making the owners aware that there are special natural features on their land. The Nature Preserves Act charges the Division of Nature Preserves with maintaining a registry of important natural areas in Indiana. The registry is also used to protect natural lands which contain features not significant enough to be dedicated. The "registry" concept was formalized in a cooperative program between the Division of Nature Preserves and The Nature Conservancy. Using a seed grant from the Lilly Endowment, TNC hired registry director Paul Carmony, who ably served in that capacity from the inception of the program until his retirement in 1992.

As natural areas are nominated by the Division of Nature Preserves, the registry director's job is to contact all natural area owners, informing them of the natural area they own, what ecological values it contains, and why the area is important. Owners who agree voluntarily to register their land receive a plaque, honoring them for their efforts. The plaques are constructed of wood from a tuliptree, Indiana's state tree, and in the shape of the state silhouette. The owners in turn agree to notify DNR or TNC if they perceive threats to the tract or if they intend to sell their natural area. Paul was the ideal choice for the job. A personable, highly competent naturalist, he gently convinced almost all private owners of natural land that he contacted of the wisdom of protecting their property.

Through the years, the registry director has maintained a relationship with these owners, periodically visiting them and sending them newsletters. In this way, many natural areas have been kept in a "holding pattern," and a number have been acquired once the owners decided to sell. It is even more important that, of the more than 500 areas that have been registered since this program began, only a handful have been destroyed. A primary factor in this success is that the registry program emphasizes the positive feelings most

Formal dedication as State Nature Preserves prevents preemption of areas so protected, unless rescinded by the Natural Resources Commission and approved by the governor. Former Indiana Governor Robert P. Orr and former TNC State Director W. William Weeks preside at dedication ceremony. *Photo by Richard Fields*

people have toward significant natural lands, as well as the pride in owning special places.

Another important protection program administered by DNR is the Indiana Rivers Preservation Act. Established by the General Assembly in 1973, the act parallels the Indiana Nature Preserves Act, and provides protection for the character of designated rivers. Rivers that qualify can be designated as natural, scenic, or recreational by the Natural Resources Commission. The Streams and Trails Section of the Division of Outdoor Recreation is responsible for administering the system. Included thus far are segments of the Blue River (Harrison, Crawford, and Washington counties), Cedar Creek (Allen and Dekalb counties), and Wildcat Creek (Tippecanoe and Carroll counties). Other streams have been recommended for study and might be included in the future.

In the years since the Nature Preserves Act was established, there have been continuing attempts to acquire areas for nature preserves. The Division of Nature Preserves is charged with acquisition as funds allow, and hence periodically requests acquisition funds as part of its budget. Division efforts have traditionally been bolstered by The Nature Conservancy, which has had considerable success in raising funds for natural area acquisition. Throughout the 1970s, a number of nature preserves were acquired through this joint effort. A number of these acquisitions resulted from the herculean efforts of William B. Barnes, first director of the Division of Nature Preserves, and Dennis Wolkoff, first state director of TNC in Indiana.

In some cases, when purchase negotiations hung in the balance, extraordinary assistance from Indiana citizens made the difference. A classic case was at Hoosier Prairie Nature Preserve, where very effective preservation efforts were spearheaded by Irene Herlocker, a local amateur naturalist and tireless preservationist. A number of other special preserves were acquired after long efforts by citizens and organizations, including Big Walnut, Crooked Lake, Gibson Woods, Manitou Island Wetlands, Olin Lake, and Portland Arch. And as pointed out earlier by Alton Lindsey, the special protection afforded by certain families down through the generations was the only reason certain areas, especially old-growth forests, remained intact to protect. This is certainly the case at Shrader-Weaver Woods, Kramer Woods, Meltzer Woods, Cabin Creek Bog, Pinhook Bog, Hemmer Woods, Hoot Woods, Officer's Woods, and a number of others.

As welcome and needed as acquisition funds were during the late 1970s, there certainly was never enough money available to do the job. Areas were disappearing much more rapidly than they could be acquired. In many cases, no funds were available at critical times, and as a result, some areas were lost. Because of this situation, W. William Weeks, then TNC state director, proposed a public-private partnership to acquire the remaining natural areas in an ambitious program entitled the Indiana Natural Heritage Protection Campaign. The program, which mutually challenged both the state government and the citizens of Indiana to match money for acquisition of nature preserves, was overwhelmingly approved in 1984 by the General Assembly. The Nature Conservancy spearheaded the private-side fundraising, successfully reaching its half of the total in a few years. The legislature has appropriated matching funds in each successive biennium, enabling the program to fund the acquisition thus far of 73 areas, totaling more than 7,500 acres. It is envisioned that this campaign will be completed by the late 1990s.

Down through the years, other important partners in acquisition efforts have included conservation organizations such as ACRES, Inc., the Izaak Walton League, and the Shirley Heinze Fund. City and county park departments have also acquired a number of significant natural areas.

Another important protection tool came with the passage of the Nongame Check-off option. Using their tax form, would-be recipients of Indiana state income tax refunds can designate any portion of the refunded amount to the Nongame Program, a branch within DNR's Fish and Wildlife Division. Funds from the tax check-off have been used to acquire habitat for some of Indiana's rarest animals.

> Whatever we tax, we tend to get less of; whatever we subsidize, we tend to get more of. . . . Diverting income tax dollars to fund wildlife programs can alleviate tax burdens, meanwhile improving the welfare of wildlife.
>
> —*Will Nixon,* Environment *magazine, vol. 4*

The Indiana Heritage Trust, established in 1992, is a major inspiration for land acquisition. The state now offers an environmental license plate, with the proceeds going to the Heritage Trust. Funds raised through this program are used to acquire land for parks, forestry, wildlife, historic, recreation, and nature preserve purposes. Proponents are optimistic that this program will significantly enhance Indiana's public land base for years to come.

A number of wetlands have been acquired and incorporated into the Division of Fish and Wildlife's Wetland Conservation Program in recent years. DNR anticipates acquiring many more wetlands in the future. The DNR Foundation, recently established by the legislature, and several new land trusts are welcome additions to the Indiana land-acquisition team.

There are a number of federally owned natural areas that for one reason or another cannot be dedicated under state law. Fortunately, most federal agencies have protection programs that speak to this need. For example, within the Hoosier National Forest (HNF), the most important natural areas can be designated as Research Natural Areas. This designation must be approved at the national level by the chief forester of the U.S. Forest Service, ensuring that it is a recognition not to be taken lightly. The intent is for such areas to fill gaps in terms of protection of forest types nationally, and to recognize the ecological values of other truly significant natural areas. Natural areas of lesser significance are designated special interest areas and are protected at the individual national forest level.

A number of such areas representing both categories have been proposed by the HNF staff, who are strongly committed to the protection of significant sites. The best-known of these is Pioneer Mothers Memorial Forest (Cox Woods), designated a Research Natural Area.

The Department of Defense and the U.S. Fish and Wildlife Service also have similar designations. Research Natural Areas have been established at the Muscatatuck National Wildlife Refuge, and several are proposed at military reservations.

National park and wilderness designations most closely resemble state nature preserves in terms of protection. The Indiana Dunes National Lakeshore protects 14,970 acres along the Lake Michigan shoreline. The Lakeshore is truly a world-class natural area. Protected within its boundaries are significant beach and dune complex, prairie, savanna, bog, and wetland communities, collectively harboring many of the state's rarest species.

The Charles C. Deam Wilderness Area was established in 1982 in the Hoosier National Forest to protect 12,953 acres of upland forest in the Brown County Hills Section of the Highland Rim Natural Region. Both the Deam Wilderness and the Dunes National Lakeshore contain areas much larger than typical nature preserves, thereby protecting viably functioning landscape ecosystems, as well as safeguarding critical habitats.

The National Park Service also is responsible for a program analogous to the Indiana Natural Areas Registry. Through its National Natural Landmarks Program, the federal government gives recognition, prestige, and moral support to owners of natural land for preserving the few most outstanding natural tracts. Its mission is to help protect nationally significant natural areas that are too small to be designated national parks or national monuments. It too is a voluntary program. After an area is evaluated and found to qualify, owners are asked if they wish to register their areas. Each site is marked, if the owner approves, by a stone cairn bearing a bronze plaque in honor of their commitment. Landmarks are monitored annually, with threatened landmarks reported to Congress, in the hopes that they can receive continued protection. Participation in the program is not mandatory, nor is protection guaranteed, but in general it has been successful in defending areas not protected otherwise.

The first natural landmark in Indiana, Cowles Bog near Dune Acres, was so designated in 1965. Pine Hills and the Big Walnut areas, both elected national landmarks in March of 1968, were only the 107th and 108th in the nation. Privately owned Meltzer Woods near Shelbyville was designated in 1973. The 29 landmarks in Indiana as of 1989 total 5,980 acres.

Another extremely important protection tool for natural areas is the "environmental review" process. Review of natural values and possible environmental impacts is required by several federally legislated programs prior to the initiation of development. Before projects such as highways can be constructed, the plans are routed to state and federal agencies (e.g., the DNR and the U.S. Fish and Wildlife Service, respectively) for review. This gives the DNR, using information in the Heritage Program data base and field reviews by its staff, the opportunity to provide suggestions and recommend alternatives that avoid sensitive sites. A number of state laws, such as the Lakes Protection Act, also provide for review opportunity and serve to minimize environmental impact.

Several state programs provide other means of encouraging natural area protection even though ownership remains private and some

The Charles C. Deam Wilderness Area within the Hoosier National Forest protects nearly 13,000 acres of forestland, largely in Brown County, one of the largest non-fragmented natural areas in the state.   *Photo by Richard Fields*

resources use is permitted. These include the Classified Wildlife Habitat and Classified Forest programs, which afford a property tax break to owners who participate. Other statutory tools, such as conservation easements and rights of first refusal when sale of natural land is imminent, can be important in some situations.

Regulatory programs administered by federal agencies (e.g., the EPA, U.S. Army Corps of Engineers, and U.S. Fish and Wildlife Service), as complemented by programs administered at the state level by the Department of Environmental Management and the DNR, also play an important role in protection. The EPA and the Corps regulate wetlands, which cannot be filled without a permit, hence affording protection to many special areas. DNR's Lake Enhancement Program is helping to protect and improve many lakes. The Soil Conservation Service is working to minimize soil erosion. Both the federal and state endangered species programs provide additional protection. Many professionals in the fields of forestry, wildlife management, fisheries, ecology, and other fields all play increasingly important roles in protecting our natural heritage.

With the use of all the "protection tools" we have, the future looks bright. Areas can be acquired and protected through dedication. The environment around them can be improved and degradation

Some of our finest tracts of national significance, such as Cowles Bog in Porter County, are designated as National Natural Landmarks by the National Park Service.   *Photo courtesy of the Indiana Division of Nature Preserves*

Inventory and Preservation / 423

avoided. Proper environmental review ensures that development occurs at appropriate locations and avoids the most sensitive areas housing high biodiversity. All of these factors combined should ensure that our present natural heritage will continue to be the heritage of future generations.

To live healthily and successfully on the land, we must also live with it. We must be part not only of the human community, but of the whole community . . . the natural as well as the man-made community. . . . It is not a sentimental but a grimly literal fact that unless we share this terrestrial globe with creatures other than ourselves, we shall not be able to live on it for long.

—*Joseph Wood Krutch, "Conservation Is Not Enough," in* American Scholar

Timber theft from nature preserves occurs rather infrequently, but its consequences are serious. A walnut tree in Meltzer Woods was partially cut with a hand crosscut saw, literally by "thieves in the night," who abandoned their effort before finishing. The tree had to be salvage logged.
Photo by Marion Jackson

53. Stewards of Nature

John A. Bacone

We are obligated, as was Noah, to round up representatives of all living things, and see them safely through the flood—the onrushing flood of civilization.

—*The Nature Conservancy, news release (1950s)*

A nature preserve is a place permitted to develop or continue its own patterns of distribution of life, and to maintain those processes which create interconnectedness among living organisms, and between life and environment. The phrase "nature preserve" implies an area to be set aside and left to function on its own. From one perspective this is true, since nature preserves are to be protected from outside disturbances, and are not to be radically altered through consumptive manipulations or development. Instead they are to be left as areas in which nature can function as it always has. This view of nature preserves sounds ideal, and might actually be true in very large wilderness areas that remain in places such as Alaska, where ecosystems can function much as they always have, since all parts of the ecosystem are still intact.

However, in Indiana and throughout much of the Midwest and the eastern United States, natural areas are a very tiny part of the landscape. They are much like "islands" in a "sea" of human-dominated landscape. Gone are the extensive prairies that once covered much of northwest Indiana. Gone are the wildfires that used to sweep annually across the prairies. Gone are the vast wetland/lake complexes that covered so much of northern Indiana. Gone are the large vertebrates, the herbivores whose browsing was an important factor in the development and maintenance of the vegetation. And gone are many of the predators that kept the populations of herbivores in check.

The extensive forests are now represented primarily by "postage-stamp-sized" woodlots (of 20, 40, or 80 acres), usually surrounded by extensive agricultural fields. Interior forest conditions are gone from such areas; sunlight now penetrates into their centers, and weedy species on the borders can permeate the entire forest. Sometimes even the trees themselves are under threat from vandals or thieves.

The sea of prairie has long since been converted to fields of soybeans and corn; the remnants of prairie, nearly obliterated, can be found only occasionally in narrow railroad rights-of-way or pioneer cemeteries. Most of the wetlands have been drained, the lakes lowered so that they are much diminished from their former sizes or fringed with cottages, eutrophic from human effluent and sediment. Water tables have been lowered on a regional basis, while tiling of farm fields causes surface water to leave the landscape more quickly.

This radical alteration of the landscape, which occurred primarily in the last 200 years, was accompanied by a number of other changes as well. The immigrants to the new world brought more than just livestock and farm implements with them from the "old world." They also brought the old world biota with them—exotic species of plants and animals. These introduced species quickly exploited the newly disturbed habitats laid open as the virgin prairie and forest soils were plowed. These alien plants and animals quickly colonized much of the new world, and their colonization was as quick and effective as that of the settlers.

Today, almost 95 percent of the Indiana landscape has been converted to exotic species. Almost every plant we see in our everyday surroundings is one that is not a native species, and most of the native species, such as oak or maple trees, are in a setting of exotic species such as the ubiquitous bluegrass lawns. Our native flora of approximately 2,000 species has been nearly displaced by an exotic flora of only a few hundred species!

It may have begun with Noah, but, wherever it started, the whole idea of rearranging the earth's wild creatures still seems irresistible. Man, the supreme meddler, has never been quite satisfied with the world as he found it.

—*George Laycock,* The Alien Animals *(1966)*

In a similar fashion, exotic animals have made great inroads as well. Introduced species such as the starling and house sparrow have aggressively expanded at the expense of native songbirds. And native animals that could tolerate some disturbance—"edge species" that do not need large tracts of undisturbed habitat—have expanded at the expense of their conservative wilderness counterparts.

Finally, the pressures of civilization continue to exert great influence on the natural areas that remain. Various types of pollution produce a major impact. For example, air pollution is believed to have caused the disappearance or decline of a number of plant species and genotypes of other plants in northwest Indiana. During the early 1900s especially, sulfur dioxide emissions eliminated "races" of white pine and also extirpated entire species of mosses and lichens.

Water pollution has eliminated many invertebrates, destroyed mussel beds, and choked a number of species of game and non-game fish from many lakes, creeks, and rivers. Toxic waste dumps, landfills, trash disposal, and other people-caused disturbances provide continuing pressure and encroachment.

All of these changes since pre-settlement times are important to keep in mind as we try to understand and care for the nature preserves that remain today. All of these factors combine to create seemingly insurmountable management problems, but management is a job that cannot be avoided. Careful stewardship is mandatory if we hope to maintain and preserve natural areas for future generations. Acquisition and protection merely begin the preservation responsibility.

The current system of dedicated state nature preserves numbers more than 150, and is growing rapidly. As recently as 1981, there were only 50. Present preserves vary in size from a 1-acre black soil prairie to a tract of more than 1,600 acres within Turkey Run State Park.

A number of organizations and agencies are responsible for the stewardship of these preserves. City and county park and recreation departments are good examples of the diversity of ownership. Such local ownership usually provides a professional staff to care for,

Nature centers are maintained at certain large preserves for providing environmental education to the public. Shown here is Wesselman Park Nature Center at Evansville.   *Photo by Marion Jackson*

Bat populations that roost or winter in caves require protection from cave visitors or vandals who deface caves. In such cases research results may justify protecting a cave from unauthorized entrance.
Photo by Richard Fields

protect, and interpret areas within their charge. Areas locally owned and managed can result in increased local use and greater appreciation of nature by nearby residents. For example, visits from hundreds of schoolchildren on field trips to these areas can result in a continuing environmental ethic being passed down through the generations. This understanding, acceptance, and "local adoption" is likely to result in better care for these preserves in the long run, especially in terms of avoiding "people problems."

Spicer Lake Nature Preserve is a fine example of a preserve owned and managed by city/county governments. An excellent boardwalk and interpretive center has been established by the St. Joseph County Park Department. Nature preserves are also owned and managed by park departments in Allen, Harrison, Lake, Marion, and Vigo counties, and by the cities of Evansville, Fort Wayne, and Terre Haute.

Colleges and universities are another excellent and most-needed cooperating group. Nature preserves are "living museums." They provide a great opportunity to measure the response of the natural world to all sorts of changes—whether induced by pollution, natural disturbance, climatic change, or humans themselves. Natural areas

also afford an excellent opportunity to observe and measure recovery from disturbance.

College and university faculty bring in the scientific and research resources needed to find solutions to the different problems of caring for nature preserves. Permanent study plots have been installed within many of these areas, affording excellent opportunities for researchers to measure ecological changes through time. Natural areas have been used as sites for graduate and professorial research projects for many years. For example, Little Bluestem Prairie Nature Preserve, owned by Indiana State University, has been the location of a number of graduate research projects in botany, ecology, zoology, and soils and ecosystem management.

ACRES, Inc., a non-profit conservation group located in northeast Indiana, has been involved with stewardship of nature preserves for more than a quarter-century. This all-volunteer organization presently serves as guardian for more than 28 nature preserves. They are cared for through work days, donations from sponsors, and careful scrutiny by volunteer "caretakers." ACRES' experience has shown that the hard work begins after an area is saved. This dedicated organization has proved that a group of committed citizens can make a major difference. In fact, the "ACRES idea" may be the best solution for preserve stewardship—a regional conservation group capable of both protecting and managing land.

The Nature Conservancy (TNC) is recognized as the largest holder of private preserves in the United States. The Indiana Chapter also owns more nature preserves within the state than does any other private agency. TNC's system of stewardship was originally very similar to that of ACRES, with a "local steward" being assigned to each area they acquired, and volunteer work days being held periodically to cover larger projects. As TNC grew and became more successful, both on the national level and in Indiana, it became apparent that a more systematic approach was needed for stewardship. The Indiana Chapter has hired a "stewardship director," a professional staff person whose job it is to set priorities and coordinate the necessary stewardship. The stewardship director coordinates volunteer work days and the rest of the volunteer steward system that has been successful in the past, and is so essential for future care of the preserves.

When the Nature Preserves Act was passed in 1967, the Division of Nature Preserves was created and charged with the acquisition, protection, and management of nature preserves. As the nature preserve system has expanded, so has the amount of stewardship required. A number of professional "natural area ecologists," who work for the DNR, are charged not only with oversight of preserves owned and managed by other agencies and organizations, but also with management of the large number of state-owned nature preserves, within their region of the state. The many preserves require much time and work, with the regional ecologists frequently assisting preserve owners with management and monitoring of many activities, an assignment that becomes quite involved. However, the stewardship of state-owned preserves remains their primary responsibility.

When a preserve is acquired, the critical first step is to protect it properly. We begin by marking the corners and boundaries, securing the area from encroachment, and removing trash and internal fences. Decisions need to be made as to what type of use the area can sustain. "People management" requires effort, and often a sensitivity in public relations. Fences may be needed to keep out cattle and off-road vehicles. Self-guiding trail systems and brochures are sometimes installed. Continual monitoring is needed to ensure that overuse does not destroy what the area was acquired to protect.

"Natural area management," or the effort needed to maintain and/or restore ecological functions, is the most important need facing many nature preserves today. Natural area management requires a "new breed" of conservationists who not only must be knowledge-able about the total biota and ecosystem functioning, but also must be capable of dealing with a town or park board or the county commissioner, and be capable as well of supervising vegetation management such as prescribed burns.

Natural systems in general are at the same time both somewhat stable and also ecologically resilient—i.e., able to recover from certain types of perturbations and somewhat resistant to invasion by exotic species. But as more knowledge is gained in the relatively new science of natural area ecology, the changes that are taking place in natural areas, as a result of changes in the modified landscape that surrounds them, are becoming more apparent. Some of these changes are obvious and have occurred quickly, as is the case with prairies.

Fire was an extremely important and necessary part of the natural ecology of prairie and several other natural communities. As the settlers arrived and developed roads and farm fields, the incidence of fires decreased. With the intentional suppression of fire, woody encroachment into the prairies occurred quickly. Large prairies became thickets almost overnight. Recently, prescribed burning has become an important stewardship tool for natural area managers.

> Within a decade or two of settlement, the remnant oak openings that escaped the ax and plow suddenly began to develop into dense, closed-canopy forests. In large part, this rapid increase in number of trees was due to previously suppressed "grubs" or oak brush which had been repeatedly killed to the ground by fire and which had persisted through production of adventitious buds from underground rootstocks.
>
> —*John T. Curtis, "The Modification of Mid-latitude Grasslands and Forests by Man," in* Man's Role in Changing the Face of the Earth *(1956)*

The amount of work that can be involved in a prescribed burn is best illustrated by the experience at Hoosier Prairie. Its urban setting in northwestern Indiana, surrounded by residences, industry, oil tank farms, railroads, and highways, requires extreme caution and strict attention to environmental conditions.

A "burn plan" is prepared annually, and fire lanes are installed. Only part of the prairie can be burned annually, so that some wildlife habitat is always left unburned. Burning takes place only on days when environmental conditions allow for quick dissipation of smoke. The vegetation is monitored annually, so that the effects of burning on the prairie and on the rare species it contains can be determined. After 15 years of monitoring, it has become very clear that fire is essential at Hoosier Prairie. For example, the populations of rare species continue to increase, and overall species richness has improved steadily.

Another major part of the natural area manager's job is the control of exotic species. Without intervention, some natural areas would be overrun and severely degraded. A case in point is with purple loosestrife. It is a Eurasian species that "immigrated" to North America and became well established in areas of the northeastern United States by the early 1800s, and has been spreading across the country ever since. As recently as 1940, it rarely occurred in Indiana. Today it is found in most Indiana counties, with mass infestations in a number of wetlands. Purple loosestrife is generally an opportunist, populating wetlands following a disturbance such as the lowering of a water table due to drainage. However, it will also invade undisturbed, high-quality wetlands.

Natural area managers attempt to locate and remove purple loosestrife from wetlands before it takes over completely. This method is feasible only with small infestations, and is accomplished by pulling or by use of "spot spraying" with a herbicide approved for

Public access must be controlled in sensitive preserves by limiting visitors to boardwalks or hard-surfaced trails. A few preserves are closed to the public because of their small size and/or extreme vulnerability. Boardwalk at Twin Swamps Nature Preserve, Posey County.   *Photo by Richard Fields*

Sensitive prairie remnants and other wildflower areas must be protected from undesired mowing or herbicide application, but they often require prescribed burning as part of their management. *Photo by Richard Fields*

Garlic mustard is an introduced plant species that is aggressively invading many forested areas of Indiana, including some of our finest nature preserves. To keep it from outcompeting and replacing native wildflowers, vigorous control programs are being used. *Photo by Lee Casebere*

application in wetlands. This technique can be used to hold the line on an impending infestation, but it requires continual vigilance.

In cases where wetlands are heavily infested, our hopes for containment lie with biological controls. These techniques are being initiated in several areas around the United States, including Indiana. Two leaf-eating beetles (*Galerucella pusilla* and *G. calmariensis*) and a root-boring weevil (*Hylobius transversevittatus*) are now being introduced in this country. Later introductions will include insects which attack the flower and seed heads as well as others which attack the stems. Caution always needs to be exercised before applying biological control of pest species. In a number of cases worldwide, the "control" organism has proved to be more of a problem than was the "disease."

In the case of biological control of purple loosestrife, the insects were carefully studied under controlled greenhouse conditions. Only after it was ascertained that these insects fed only on purple loosestrife were they approved for use. Although purple loosestrife is a pest, its showy flowers make it an attractive plant for landscaping, and it has been sold widely by nurseries for that purpose. It often finds its way into wetlands from such use. In an attempt to slow the spread of purple loosestrife by this method, the Indiana General Assembly has prohibited its sale and distribution.

A number of other exotic species are presenting increasing problems in natural areas, including teasel, glossy buckthorn, garlic mustard, black locust, and Japanese honeysuckle. The control of such species varies from pulling, to cutting, to herbiciding, to

prescribed burning, or sometimes a combination of some or all of these methods. We know that we can never get rid of most exotic species; we can hope only to control their spread.

> One must remember that an exotic population released into the wild is no longer an experiment. It is a fact accomplished, no longer under complete control. Whereas one might hope to hit the target, an unconfirmed exotic population is not unlike a bullet—once fired, it cannot be called back. A misplaced shot may have wide-reaching implications.
>
> —*William L. Robinson and Eric G. Bolen,* Wildlife Ecology and Management *(1989)*

A number of other types of natural areas, in addition to prairies and wetlands, require management. Monitoring, based on permanent plots and detailed maps, permits us to see if management is needed and, once applied, if it is working properly. Monitoring can also tell us if rare species populations are stable or are declining, or if there are changes taking place in the natural community.

For example, Donaldson's Woods, an old-growth forest in Spring Mill State Park, has had a complete woody plant census each decade for the past 40 years. Comparisons of data from decade to decade show that the old-growth oak trees in the overstory are probably not going to be replaced by other oak trees, since the understory seems to be composed primarily of sugar maple and other species more tolerant of shade. This is an ecological trend that is common throughout the Midwest. Apparently the character of old-growth forests may be changing more than ecologists previously thought. It is not yet known whether this is good or bad news, nor is it known whether it is desirable to try to prevent such change. But it does illustrate one of the dilemmas facing natural area managers.

Stewards of nature preserves are increasingly more involved with reintroduction of extirpated species into their native habitats. For example, the U.S. Fish and Wildlife Service is studying the reintroduction of Mead's milkweed, last seen in Indiana in 1890, into its prairie habitat. In all instances, before a reintroduction is undertaken, careful study and consideration is always a prerequisite, and this type of work is not to be taken lightly.

Stewards are also concerned with restoration of native communities as buffers surrounding existing preserves, or for recovery of disturbed areas within preserves. Significant progress is being made toward rebuilding prairies, bottomland forests, wetlands, upland forests, and savannas. This type of work is needed to provide additional land around the highest-quality natural areas, making them more viable in the long term. Such efforts are time-consuming and very labor-intensive.

Care must be taken so that these reconstructions are done wisely, native seed sources are used, and the success of such work is carefully documented. As in all other efforts by natural area managers, care must be taken to avoid overmanipulation. All stewards should continue to be guided by the goal of trying to maintain or restore natural conditions.

In the future, nature preserve stewardship efforts will need to increase in scope and sophistication. As human-induced development increases, the landscape setting of many preserves will change from rural to urban. Local species extinctions and increasing encroachment are likely. Therefore, nature preserves will be well served if we can make them as large as possible to ensure viability, buffer them properly, connect them with each other, and restore them to as stable a condition as possible.

It is heartening to know that there is a network of dedicated, knowledgeable, well-trained, energetic people, including both professionals and volunteers, who are fighting the battle. Years ago things did not look nearly as promising as they do today. It is clear that as people learn more about natural areas and the threats to them, they will become part of the "stewards of nature" team.

Who would not rise to meet the expectations of the land?

—Henry David Thoreau

Fragmentation of preserves and development at their perimeters is one of the gravest threats to long-term protection. Wesselman Woods Nature Preserve in Vanderburgh County, which is completely surrounded by Evansville, is a classic case. *Photo courtesy of the Agricultural Stabilization and Conservation Service*

Part 6: Prospectives

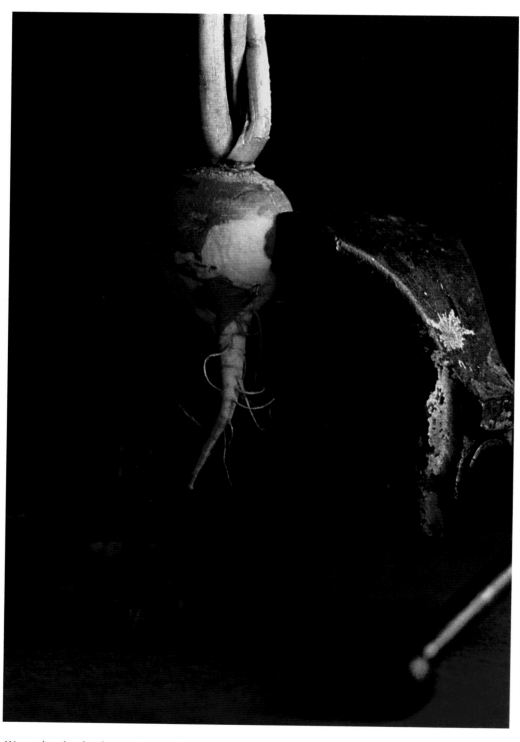

We need to decide what worldview, lifestyle, and ethical standard will permit a human well-being–sustainable Earth balance. Do we need to continually attempt to see how much blood we can extract from the "earthly turnip"? *Photo courtesy of the Indiana State University Audio-Visual Center*

54. Whence and Whither: A Question of Priorities and Values

Marion T. Jackson

> I should not only receive these things from my ancestors, but also transmit them to my descendents.
>
> —*Marcus Julius Cicero*

Our generation is but a sojourn on the human odyssey. As proprietors of the Indiana of today, we are both descendants and ancestors. What we have in our care was inherited from those who came before us; what we pass on to posterity is the estate we leave our descendants. We can only guess at what is likely to remain after probate.

In "Perspective: The Indiana That Was" we described the newly minted land that greeted the wave of settlement of the late eighteenth and early nineteenth centuries. Those who came first had the opportunity to cut the big timber, plow the prairies, and drain the wetlands. We are a part of their posterity. What is left of natural Indiana is the remnants that our ancestors did not get around to changing, or in rare instances had the foresight to protect, or what nature has recovered while human attention was focused on other pursuits.

As was pointed out by L. Keith Caldwell in the foreword to this book, the changes that our forebears made to the Indiana landscape were influenced strongly by the ethical and economic attitudes which prevailed during their lifetimes. Had we lived in that time and social setting, it is highly likely that we would have done likewise. Be that as it may, the natural estate that our generation inherited could have been vastly different had our ancestors been less destructive and wasteful—had they taken only the usufruct, but kept the natural landscape and its biota more intact. The remaining tropical forests are a present-day opportunity to practice such an approach, but limited-harvest, sustainable resource use requires that human numbers be kept perpetually below carrying capacity levels.

We Are Spending Our Children's Inheritance states the bumper sticker on a huge, expensive motor home. Although intended to be humorous, the quip strikes too close to a pervasive attitude to be funny. Far too many not only are spending their income before they receive it, but also are using up the resources that our descendants rightfully expect to receive. Such prodigality raises serious questions concerning earth proprietorship; it polarizes public attitudes and leads to conflicts over resource entitlement.

Who does own the resources, and who does have the *right* to exploit them? Is accessibility to life-support resources a *right* or a *privilege?* Do present-day inhabitants of the planetary ecosystem have the right to expend the Earth's capital for their own sufficiency, comfort, and pleasure? Was the Earth "designed and set spinning so that those living today could take a joyride," to paraphrase H. L. Mencken? Should we have access to whatever the Earth's resources can provide as part of an American birthright, even if it means depriving less fortunate individuals or nations? Do we have a responsibility to leave a resource inheritance to those residents of Indiana who follow? Admittedly, the future could be a rather long time, and, after all, what has posterity ever done for us?

That there are now more of us globally than the world can permanently sustain at even the present level of needs and wants is becoming less moot by the minute, and each day brings a *net* increase of a quarter-million to the planetary breakfast table. That the stockpiles of such potentially renewable resources as soil, wood, water, and wild species are inexorably diminishing worldwide is the subject of daily news headlines. That our now-global industrial metabolism is infusing the land, water, and atmosphere with accumulating trash, damaging pollutants, and toxic substances is now obvious to even most of the non-observant. Each annual issue of the Worldwatch Institute's *State of the World* report presents gloomier statistics concerning the global environment and its use by a perpetually expanding human population. Fairfield Osborn voiced similar concerns nearly 50 years ago in his book *Our Plundered Planet,* wherein he wrote, "The tide of the earth's population is rising, the reservoir of the earth's living resources is falling."

To move in the direction of a sustainable world economy populated by balanced human numbers, we must come to understand that our global storehouse of resources cannot continue to fuel our present overheated world economy. The future is even more frightening, for human want is a bottomless pit. It is becoming increasingly doubtful that even the most clever and optimistic economists and technologists can devise a way to permanently outrun the human exponential. Leastwise no nation ever has for any extended period of time.

That Indiana is becoming crowded as well is evidenced by each trip down an interstate highway, or each tour of new residential, shopping, or industrial developments being built on land once farmed. What we have done and continue to do in Indiana *does* affect the global ecosystem. Indiana once had a clean and productive environment, and it still is not as threatened as it will become. Can we demand and ensure that it (and the world) be kept from getting worse, perhaps even be restored? In the final analysis it is a matter of ethics.

Some of the world's best minds—scientists, statesmen, philosophers, prophets, poets—have wrestled with how humans *should* relate to the Earth, how to redirect human priorities, how to produce a new ethic. It is a curious irony that throughout history the earliest warnings of environments gone awry frequently have been voiced by prophets, philosophers, and poets, rather than by the scientists who study nature's intricacies, or the engineers or technologists who make the changes. Perhaps their perceptivity enables them to see connections and the way ahead more clearly than most. Study the writings of Isaiah, Ezekiel, Jeremiah, Plato, Pliny, Bacon, Huxley, Thoreau, Emerson, George Perkins Marsh, John Muir, Robert Frost, Albert Schweitzer, E. B. White, and many others to note the common thread.

Scientists and technologists need to be humbled by coming to understand that anything they study and begin to comprehend will turn out to be a part of something else which is larger, more complex. That is the nature of ecology, especially. Knowledge and wisdom are not the same thing. Knowing *how* to do something and having the tools available to do it is not enough, we must also know *whether* we should do it. At the policy level we need to know when and whether to do something and why (if) it was necessary in the first place.

As Buckminster Fuller once observed, "Planet Earth did not come with an instruction book." We now know a number of things about managing ecosystems, but being able to manage something does not guarantee that the results of that management will move the overall system toward the desired or proper end. When in doubt concerning a proposed change, we should do nothing. If we act without understanding, the situation may worsen. And if we wait, nature may correct the problem without human intervention.

Furthermore, there is no doubt that more will be known about the Earth and its management in the future. Delay may allow future generations who possess greater wisdom to make crucial decisions about the long-term welfare of the planet and its inhabitants. A good case in point is saving species. We need to save gene pools, if for no other more ethical and compelling reason than that they may come in handy someday.

Many also follow the misguided assumption that if our actions do cause environmental degradation, we can always correct any damage by applying more technology, especially if it is supported by a large appropriation of public funds. But more and more we learn the bitter lesson that when we destroy environments, what we are destroying are ecological humpty-dumpties. All too often all the king's horses and all the king's men, and even all the king's money, cannot restore the original ecological conditions once serious damage has occurred.

A growing number of people are beginning to realize that most of what we have done to the world environment throughout human history has been wrong—wrong because our collective actions have seriously degraded or destroyed the majority of Earth's ecosystems, have caused irreparable losses of much of the world's topsoil, have exterminated multitudes of plant and animal species, have reduced the quality of the living experience for the majority of all species that remain, have inflicted incredible suffering on large segments of humanity, and have kept many fellow humans in economic, ecological, and spiritual bondage. The destinies of millions of fellow species in the great web of life on Earth have been altered by the progressive elimination of their populations or the disruption of their habitats.

Ethics is nothing else than reverence for life. Reverence for life affords me my fundamental principle of morality, namely, that good consists in maintaining, assisting, and enhancing life, and that to destroy, to harm, or to hinder life is evil.

—*Albert Schweitzer,* The Teaching of Reverence for Life (1965)

Lack of reverence for life is the ultimate immorality—unbalancing the world ecosystem (as Aldo Leopold observed) the ultimate wrong—transgressions against Gaia (named for the Greek goddess of the Earth). According to the Garden myth, we destroyed Eden and were banished from our pristine paradise, to which we awakened as king (the paragon of nature), and were committed forever to toil, as we attempt to manage the planet.

Once we stepped on the treadmill of agriculture, there was no turning back. As food supplies increased, continual human population growth forever catalyzed our future. We could only work harder, faster, and more intrusively to keep nature at bay—to attempt to conquer the Earth. We had no choice except to cut more forest, plow more prairie, drain more wetlands, and till more soil. As William Wells phrased it in his admonition to "Mad Anthony" Wayne after the Battle of Fallen Timbers, "You whites are not at war with the Indian, you are at war with the Earth."

If we are to survive permanently on this planet, we must wave the white flag of truce—sign a peace treaty with the Earth, the terms of which are dictated by nature's laws, not human statutes. Only by coming to terms with the Earth's limits can the planet, its humanity, its precious cargo of life, and Indiana endure.

We hear repeatedly discussed the concern as to whether this or that economic decision is the correct one, if the economic system is healthy and working well. We do not know with certainty if human economic systems work at all, or have ever worked. At best, human economic systems function only temporarily by *using up* the resource base, locally or distantly. The *economy of nature* is the only time-tested system—having been in place for 4.6 billion years. Even so, the normal equilibrium of the global ecosystem has been upset violently at times during its long history, considering the number and severity of past species extinctions throughout geologic time. But in the long run, nature probably does know best; in any event, as the bumper sticker reminds us, *Nature Bats Last.* Indeed, we do need to forge a just and lasting peace between economics and ecology.

It should be obvious to any thinking person that neither the world nor Indiana can continue indefinitely along the path we have been following. We must change the way we view, relate to, and use our resource base if our descendants are to have any real hope for a high-quality living experience. Not to consider the welfare of those who follow would be to commit the ultimate act of selfishness.

Perhaps there is yet time to turn the human enterprise from its destructive path, from what sometimes seems an inevitable rendezvous with an untimely destiny. Perhaps we still may humanize our technology so that we do not "become the tools of our tools," to use Thoreau's words. Perhaps there is still time to redirect the human mission to a global goal of balanced human numbers, and a worldwide objective that all uses of renewable resources be sustainable. But the path to those ends is rocky and fraught with obstacles, not the least of which is the supreme reluctance of humans to voluntarily limit their own numbers and appetites, and to leave anything natural in its natural state.

Such lofty aims as a stable human population managing a sustainable global economy are still barely within reach, but time to achieve them grows ever shorter. Perhaps this urgency is best exemplified by an anecdote about an old Amish couple who, while asleep in their farmhouse, were awakened in the early hours of morning by the mantel clock striking 15 times. "What on earth time is it, John?" the good wife Martha asked her sleepy husband. "I don't rightly know for sure," he replied, "but it's obviously later than it's ever been before."

* * *

We do not inherit the environment from our ancestors, but we borrow it for a brief time from our children.

—*Jay D. Hair, President, National Wildlife Federation, in* National Wildlife (1987)

Do we want the sun to set on natural Indiana, or on the possibility of a quality lifestyle worldwide?   *Photo by Marion Jackson*

55. Connections: The Humans-Landscape Linkage

Marion T. Jackson

Life is a unity; the biosphere is a complex network of interrelationships among all the host of living things. Man, in gaining the godlike quality of awareness, has also acquired a godlike responsibility.

—*Marston Bates,* The Forest and the Sea (1960)

In past years when Indiana was primarily a rural society, most people grew up with a basic understanding of the natural world around them. They knew many of the wild plant and animal species, at least by their local common names, and had a pretty good idea of how they fit together into forest, meadow, and wetland habitats—a kind of experience-based environmental literacy.

During more than 30 years of teaching ecology, taxonomy, environmental science, and natural history at the university level, I have witnessed a steady and alarming erosion of the overall natural literacy of college-age youth. This is not to imply that students of today are less capable or have inferior academic preparation. They simply have a different orientation, background, and set of experiences than their predecessors. To be sure, they are more advanced in "book learning," computer expertise, and awareness of what is happening in distant regions of the world. Thanks to nature shows and videos on television, young people likely know more about the African savannas, tropical rainforests, or oceanic ecosystems than they do about what lives in their own backyards. We should be disturbed that our youth (and most adults) know the most about the Earth's creatures that they probably never will see, while those nearby largely remain as mysterious and unknown as the planet Saturn. Stated baldly, most citizens today know very little about what lives outside their air-conditioned existence, or how Indiana's environment and resources (or those of the world) are related to their own survival and comfort.

Considering the lifestyle of Americans today, it is hardly the fault of the young that they have so little direct contact with the natural environment. Children of recent generations have had little opportunity, time, or inclination to study nature firsthand. Relatively few have the chance to wile away carefree summer days exploring meadows, forests, or creeks on foot or bicycle. How many have spent an afternoon sprawled on a grassy hilltop watching "cloud pictures" change in a July sky? Who catches sunfish today with a willow pole, bobber, and hook baited with earthworms dug from one's own garden? Who takes the time to investigate beetles' paths through the "forest" of grass blades of their lawn, or has the patience to wait out the hatching of a praying mantis egg case? What boy or girl of today has ever spent a spring morning in a treetop watching wood warblers migrate through the forest? In short, we have largely lost our connections with nature—and gone also is the understanding and appreciation of nature's vital role in our lives.

This was not always the case. In the past, when a majority of Indiana's population derived much of their livelihood directly from the land, often by necessity, people lived closer to nature. Our grandparents knew less about DNA sequencing or the workings of laboratory science, but they knew a great deal about what lived where in nature, and why it occurred there. True, their knowledge was somewhat rough-hewn, and often imprecise. For example, they seldom knew such niceties as the scientific names of organisms, or even what a species is; moreover, their information was often colored by absurdities such as "hoop" snakes' taking their tails in their mouths and rolling downhill to catch prey or to elude enemies, or by such misconceptions as that all hawks, owls, and foxes are "bad" and "need to be destroyed." But they knew a great deal about their immediate world, such as the medicinal or healing properties of wild plants, or that the absence of morning dew and the presence of "mares' tails" in the afternoon sky likely foretold rain on the way, hence a poor time to cut hay or to plan a picnic. Such natural literacy, which was once common understanding to most people, was acquired generation by generation from their parents, plus by direct observation and lifelong experience.

Some of today's youth take environmental education courses which teach them to correctly identify tree leaves from a field guide, bird songs from recordings, or principles related to ecosystem functioning from classroom aquaria. Any field experience is coincidental and a rarity. Students can state ecological concepts about the balance of nature, the hazards of pollution, or the desirability of recycling, but their knowledge is frequently shallow, and few have any meaningful, direct contact with the natural environment from which such understandings have been developed. Today's students have gained the knowledge, but lost the link to the natural world. The human-landscape connection has been severed.

I suspect that such loss of environmental literacy has been (or is being) occurring worldwide, and not just in developed nations. If so, the loss of this knowledge will have an impact on everyone. For example, ethnobotanists are frantically combing the reasonably intact tropical forests with shamans and elders of local native peoples to find plants with pharmaceutical values before both the plants and the indigenous peoples disappear. In a very few decades, the drug companies will have to prospect blindly, because most of the natural lore, kept intact for millennia, will have disappeared. In the chapter "What's the Use?" many examples were given to illustrate how Indiana plants served our ancestors just a few generations ago. Few today either know or care about such early importance of nature in human survival.

With understanding of how nature is structured and how it functions, we gain appreciation and love for what is untrammeled by human activity. With love and appreciation comes protection. And with protection comes the opportunity for effective stewardship of our natural treasures. To reconnect to *our* environment is the challenge of the future education of our youth, as administered by both parents and the public and private school systems.

This education, by necessity, must begin in and around our dwellings. Almost everyone can raise a garden (even if it is in pots at the doorstep or on the windowsill), convert a portion of lawn to a haven for wild plants and animals, start a workable system for composting and recycling household and lawn wastes, or develop ways to involve the entire family in meaningful study of birds, insects, weather patterns, or the stars.

We do not have to visit the redwoods, the Alaska tundra, or a coral

Perhaps we should adopt the long-time motto of artist Helen Swenson, who lived at beautiful Wing Haven Nature Preserve in Steuben County: We need to reconnect to nature. *Photo by Marion Jackson*

reef to learn the lessons about how wild plants and wild animals live, and how humans are connected to the Earth. After all, the basics of ecology can be learned just as well, and far more easily, by studying the meadow next door, or even weed and insect populations in cracks in the sidewalk, if we are willing to take the time to observe carefully and systematically. Perception is the key. We must develop the quality of the mental eye if we are to see and understand our connections to nature.

As stated in the dedication of this book, "Sight is a faculty, but seeing is truly an art." If this book, as intended, enables the citizens of Indiana to reconnect in a more meaningful way to what remains natural in their landscape, then its primary objective will have been fulfilled.

> In nature all things are beautiful . . . if one realizes what has gone into their evolution. The mysteries of how plants live and gain their sustenance, their adaptations to environment, the infinite interdependencies between all living things make each one a miracle in itself.
>
> —*Sigurd F. Olson, "Reflections," in* Living Wilderness *(1976)*

Unwise clearing of forests in an attempt to convert steep slopes to cropland resulted in serious erosion problems and devastated rural lands, especially in southern Indiana, in the early decades of the twentieth century. Fortunately most of these lands are on their way to restoration.   *Photo by Marion Jackson*

56. The Indiana of Today: Its Background and Challenge

Marion T. Jackson

We believe that this country will not be a permanently good place for any of us to live in unless we make it a reasonably good place for all of us to live in. . . . Our cause is the cause of justice for all in the interest of all.

—*Theodore Roosevelt, White House Conference of Governors (1908)*

It is not possible to summarize the nature of natural Indiana today in the limited space available here. The range of situations is too vast and the approaches to management of our natural resources are too varied to hope to explore more than a sampling of the total. But developing an understanding of how today's management strategy came to be will help us to determine the rightness of what we are presently doing, and should guide us in designing our future course of action.

During the 1930s, both the quantity and the general health of Indiana's natural resources (and also its economy) reached their nadir. As a result of record high temperatures and record droughts, crops withered and the soil became airborne throughout much of the Midwest. One Indiana farmer remarked to his neighbor in 1936, "You have been wishing for years that you had a rich prairie farm. Well, another year or two of this drought and the wind will deliver one to your doorstep!" Rural life became so desperate that farmers in the prairie counties in northwest Indiana burned ear corn for fuel to heat their houses, because a wagonload of corn would not buy a ton of coal.

Our original forests were long since gone, and picking the bones of the second-growth stands had reduced the size of the state's woodpile to an all-time low. Loss of forestland, widespread erosion of soils and stream siltation, general destruction of habitat, shrinking wetlands, and flagrant abuse of hunting regulations had all but destroyed the dwindling wildlife resource. In the late 1930s, raccoons, presently at near-nuisance levels, were so scarce that locals would bet a coonskin as the ultimate wager.

Worldwide, as in Indiana, the Great Depression stalked the land, keeping both the spirits and the economy at their lowest ebb in two centuries. Poor people do desperate things that make the land even poorer. Battered landscapes and abandoned, eroding farms were a too-common scene in much of the state in the late 1930s. Indiana's resource base had suffered mightily by the eve of World War II.

It was against this backdrop that the Second Wave of Conservation swept across Indiana, as it did elsewhere in the United States—the first wave having occurred during the Theodore Roosevelt administration early in the twentieth century. This was the time when the alphabetical agencies came to the forefront of American conservation: the Soil Erosion Service (SES) initiated erosion control, then with county-based offices, overall land capability classification, and farm landscape planning, the agency matured into the Soil Conservation Service (SCS); the Agricultural Adjustment Act (AAA) attempted to establish a balance between farm production and market demand; the Civilian Conservation Corps (CCC) refurbished our state parks, state forests, and recreational areas; wildlife and fisheries research and habitat dollars filtered down from Pittman-Robinson

(P-R) and Dingell-Johnson (D-J) funds. Later on, the Indiana Department of Conservation (DOC) became the Department of Natural Resources (DNR). At long last the fortunes of the state's resources were climbing upward, an end to the long downward spiral that had lasted one and three-quarters centuries. The era of agency-based management of the Indiana's natural resources was now under way.

For resource management to be effective, it needs to be based on the latest and best information available. Determining ownership is often the initial step in land management. Today it is relatively easy to obtain information about the nature of our natural resources, who owns a tract of land, or how one of Indiana's more than 3 million parcels of real estate is used and managed. Remotely sensed data obtained electronically by satellite not only give a wide-scale picture of the patterns on the Indiana landscape, but also allow us to determine the exact location of any specific point via the Geographic Positioning System (GPS). Statistics are compiled routinely about land use, enabling quick access to the relative amounts of land held privately versus publicly, or that devoted to natural vegetation, forestry, agricultural production, industrial sites, or civic landscapes.

It took only 50 years to transfer essentially all of Indiana from a common ownership by Native Americans to public state ownership to private ownership. The vast majority of Indiana remains in private ownership today. Landownership grants a wide range of choices as to how that land is used. As such, any landowner pretty much chooses the destiny of a given parcel of real estate. But do we *own* the land, either individually or jointly, in the real sense of the word, or do we merely have access to certain benefits and privileges during our temporary occupancy? How we answer these questions weighs heavily on the future of natural lands in Indiana, and elsewhere. As Robert Frost wrote, "The land was ours, before we were the land's."

In less than two centuries we changed the Indiana landscape from 7/8 to 1/6 forestland. More important, the timbered portion went from one large block of essentially unbroken primeval forest to tens of thousands of wooded tracts, the majority of which are now less than 40 acres in size. Prairieland was reduced from about 1 acre in 10 originally to fewer than 1,000 total acres today. Wetlands were reduced from as much as 5.6 million acres during wet seasons to less than 800,000 acres today. Meanwhile developed land covered with civic landscapes and transportation corridors increased to some 4 million acres, or 1 acre in 6, and is still increasing rapidly. Travel routes changed from a few Indian trails originally to more than 92,000 miles of roads and highways today (1992 data). In contrast, we have only 45,000 miles of rivers and streams.

During this same two-century period, agricultural land increased from essentially none to nearly two-thirds of Indiana's more than 23 million acres. During the 1990s, in any given year, more than 1 acre in 4 of Indiana's land is planted to corn, while soybeans cover at least 1 acre in 5. Our state is predominantly agricultural, and will continue to be so during the foreseeable future. The preponderance of Indiana's crop production occurs on highly mechanized cash grain farms, which progressively decrease in number and increase in acreage.

Yields of agricultural crops have increased steadily in recent decades to today's all-time highs, but I fear that more of these gains have come from improvements in the nutrient and water pumps (the plants), rather than in the well (soil fertility levels). Despite modern fertilization practices, we cannot help but wonder how protein content, vitamin level, and mineral presence in our farm grains have fared during recent decades, as many of our soils have likely become depleted of the micronutrients which are crucial to plant nutrition, hence animal and human health.

But agricultural practices are changing rapidly as farmers discover that yearly tillage turns the soil "wrong side up," as a Native American told the midwestern pioneer farmer a century and a half ago. Limited tillage and no-till cropping systems favor earthworms and wildlife, save fuel costs, and reduce soil erosion.

"We saved 520,000 tons of soil last year in Clay County," proclaims a Soil Conservation Service-sponsored billboard along I–70 near the Vigo-Clay county line. Such an amount of soil is equivalent to an eight-inch-deep furrow slice covering more than 500 acres of land. "T" by 2000 (i.e., reducing soil losses to formation rates by the turn of the century) may yet become a reality. Every county in the state now has a comprehensive "Soil Survey Report" with detailed soils maps along with excellent information on erosion control, land management, and overall land-use capabilities. Obviously, keeping soil in place means cleaner waters, greater fish diversity, fewer threatened mussel populations, higher-quality recreational experiences, plus saving millions of dollars' worth of precious topsoil.

Farmers now eagerly discuss the merits of ecologically sound land management, organic farming, and alternative agricultural crops. Sensitivity to problems associated with excessive chemical use is growing, as is an interest in Amish farming practices and lifestyles. We have much to learn from the Amish and their gentler, more sensitive approach to working with the land. For example, Amish farmland is one of the few places loggerhead shrikes are holding their own in Indiana. Perhaps these birds of prey serve as land-use equivalents of "canaries in the coal mine." One day we may even go back to rotation farming as, knowingly, the Amish have always farmed.

Should rotation farming return, we may witness a resurgence of such farm wildlife as cottontails and bobwhites as their food and cover improve. If this happens, we can stop complaining that hawks, foxes, and coyotes have caused the long downward population spirals of farm game species, instead of blaming the real culprits, the bare fields. Throughout Indiana's grain belt, during the past 40 years, a rabbit would have had to carry its lunch and a tent to have any chance of survival on most grain farms.

Marginal croplands—those too steep for sustained intensive cropping without excessive soil loss—are being retired from grain production. Such subsidy-based encouragement as the decade-long Cropland Reserve Program (CRP) has returned some 2 million acres to permanent vegetation. In many places the greensward now covers the rolling hills of Indiana like a benediction. Where there is hope, there is life.

Given the will and the incentive, and with careful stewardship, land will revert quickly to a more natural environment. In many cases it is a matter of economics. As we find that long-term, sustainable land use pays and is socially preferable, better management will follow suit. We have come a long way from the time when the hardscrabble farmer stated, "You can't tell me nothin' 'bout farmin' as I've already wore out two farms, and now I'm workin' on my third." And there is little doubt that we already know how to farm a lot better than we are now doing. Certainly we know that we should farm in more environmentally sensitive ways.

Much marginal farmland, especially in southern Indiana, has reverted to forest, in many cases following farm failures and land abandonment during the Great Depression of the 1930s. A majority of this land on steeper slopes should never have been cleared and cultivated in the first place, and frequently suffered severe erosion while it was farmed. Despite the land degradation that often occurred, some of these tracts now contain excellent second-growth hardwoods, and such forest wildlife as ruffed grouse are doing well therein. A case in point is the Deam Wilderness of Brown County. Although it fails to qualify as true wilderness, still it is one of the largest essentially unbroken forest tracts in the state presently, practically all of which was previously cut over or completely cleared.

Even today, there is still far too much highgrading of the state's finest hardwood species—black walnut, white, red, and black oaks, ash, and wild black cherry. High timber prices have encouraged excessive harvest of top-quality walnut and oak, especially, causing them to be cut heavily, and often prematurely, to meet domestic demand for veneer and solid lumber, and to supply foreign markets. The extent of total forestland in Indiana has nearly stabilized, with regrowth acreage approximately equaling that lost to development and cleared to create additional farmland. But erosion of the quality of many privately owned stands continues when only the less desirable species and individual trees are left as seed sources. Our local hardwood industries, especially those producing high-quality furniture, continue to have problems with supply of first-rate lumber and veneer.

In many localities, wooded tracts are avidly sought for real-estate development and as private home sites. Seeing potential hardwood timber deficiencies looming, many shrewd investors, domestic and foreign, are purchasing Indiana forestland to manage long-term.

Timber stand improvement (TSI) has expanded in scope and techniques, with some progress being made in improving the quality of hardwood stands statewide. Cost-share funding for TSI has given incentive to many forest landowners, but growth and regeneration of hardwood species often takes a longer time than we are willing to wait, or longer than we feel we have available. Then, too, TSI work often removes hollow beeches and other "low-value" species, including some mast-producing trees, which have a high wildlife value. Forest management plans now consider wildlife and recreation values in addition to timber production. Old-growth stands, including their snags, den trees, and mast trees, are being protected for both hunted and non-game species of wildlife which require mature forest habitat.

The Classified Forest Program, in place in Indiana since the 1920s, has been a strong incentive to owners of private forestland to protect and manage their timber holdings according to recommended forestry practices. Property tax reductions on Classified Forest lands, which typically yield low economic return to their owners, encourage forestland holders to participate. Some of our best remaining natural areas have been protected as Classified Forests since the 1920s or 1930s (see also chapter 52, "Inventory and Preservation").

Public scrutiny of clearcutting practices in the Hoosier National Forest and elsewhere has resulted in clearcuts being diminished in individual size and overall extent. Currently new data are being sought to support different forest management objectives and techniques. We are beginning to look more seriously at forests as fully functioning ecosystems which provide homes to a range of species from trees to warblers to wildflowers, instead of just as sites for growing timber, or only for human recreation, or as habitat for hunting. As populations of summer resident birds that winter in neotropical forests continue to decline, we are searching for answers to how forests in Indiana and South America are linked. Saving ecosystems is prerequisite to saving species.

How many clear-cuts are permissible, and how large can they safely be?
Photo by Richard Fields

Wildlife managers have improved their art and craft by basing their management practices on sound ecological principles of habitat manipulation and careful analysis of population dynamics. Witness the successful harvests of species once extirpated or nearly lost from Indiana—whitetail deer (now almost too successful), wild turkey, beaver, and ruffed grouse. Through environmental education, wildlife management programs and practices are now understood by both hunters and anglers, and the public at large. From this has come a groundswell of support for wildlife-related activities and a general understanding that managing species successfully first requires the proper management of ecosystems.

Eagles and peregrine falcons are being successfully reintroduced after decades of no Indiana nests. And river otter have been returned to the wild coverts along the major streams and lakes of Muscatatuck National Wildlife Refuge and the Tippecanoe River drainage in northern Indiana. Bobcats are sighted occasionally or found as roadkills, confirming their presence here. It is sometimes tempting to believe the reports of cougar sightings by southern Indiana locals, but so far definite proof of their existence is lacking. Some of us even dream of tiny wild populations of black bear and elk being reintroduced in the largest contiguous tracts of natural cover such as the Jefferson Proving Ground in southeastern Indiana.

As mentioned earlier in more detail by John Bacone, non-game species have gained enormously in stature and financial support. Witness the surging popularity of the check-off option for those qualifying for Indiana state income tax refunds, and also the demand for environmental license plates. The Classified Wildlife Habitat Program (a companion to the Classified Forest Program) has the objective of encouraging landowners to protect lands for wildlife enhancement, with similar tax incentives available to participants.

And note the interest in everything connected with saving wildlife and wild plants—from jewelry to sweatshirts to the exquisite prints and paintings by Nashville-based wildlife artist Bill Zimmerman. There is no question concerning public interest in protecting wild plants and animals or the will to do it, we need only the space in which to accomplish it, and the additional funding necessary to make it work.

How much farmland can we afford to lose to development and urban sprawl? *Photo by Marion Jackson*

The foregoing obviously does not mean to imply that all is well with what remains of Indiana's natural vegetation cover and the fauna it harbors. Without sensitive stewardship, we can no longer assume that our remaining natural heritage can survive the changes that inevitably will come to the Indiana landscape. But what Indiana *is,* and what it can *become,* in the way of natural landscapes, is a predominant challenge as we enter the twenty-first century. Despite the enormous gains made in resource management since World War II, we must guard against being lulled into a complacency that the future has been secured.

Our generation of ecologists and land managers, like each generation that preceded us, has conviction that we have most of the answers; that we know for sure how the global ecology is arranged and works; that our approach to saving whatever is left of the biosphere in a somewhat natural state is the proper one. That is an understandable posture because more is known today, and the practice of information gathering, storage, retrieval, and manipulation relies on a more sophisticated technology which daily grows both more complex and capable.

But we also need to realize that those who follow us will be better informed than we are about how the natural world works and what must be done to protect it. Rather than set all of our present-day management practices into concrete, we need to defer changes, whenever uncertainty exists, to those who will continue our cause.

The natural heritage that will continue into the future is the choice of our generation. Let us hope that our actions as custodians of the Indiana landscape of today do not cause history to judge us harshly.

All of us are somewhere on a long arc between ecological ignorance and environmental responsibility. What freedom means is freedom to choose. What civilization means is some sense of how to choose, and among what options. If we choose badly or selfishly, we have, not always intentionally, violated the contract.

—*Wallace Stegner,* The Gift of Wilderness

We need to save and rebuild the "big pieces" of naturalness (such as this 1,000-acre woods in Daviess County), or acquire and restore tracts in areas where naturalness is essentially gone.   *Photo by Richard Fields*

57. The Future of Natural Indiana: Can We Imagine It? Guide It?

Marion T. Jackson

I would feel more optimistic about a bright future for man if he spent less time proving that he can outwit nature and more time tasting her sweetness and respecting her seniority.

—E. B. White

Making predictions is somewhat like running in the dark, with the outcome often being much the same. It is indeed difficult to see far enough ahead to avoid some very obvious obstacles. If prognostication were an exact science, most people would be far wealthier and much more successful than they usually are. Predicting the future of natural Indiana will prove equally as uncertain.

We have tried in the preceding essays to describe the Indiana of two centuries ago, the ways that it has been changed, followed by an evaluation of what remains of natural Indiana, and the efforts under way to save our natural heritage. Can we present a picture of what the portion of Indiana that remains in a natural or quasi-natural state is likely to become during the two centuries to follow, and even beyond that time? Is it possible to determine what natural Indiana *should* become? Can we guide our state's future in ways that will protect and enhance native species and their habitats?

In designing Indiana's future, we must look forward not just to the twenty-first century, which looms only a few years away. Instead, we must attempt to see 200 years ahead to A.D. 2200 to guide our planning. The next 200 years will unfold even more quickly than have the past 200, which encompassed almost all of Indiana's history. And the changes to the Indiana landscape will likely be almost as dramatic as those described in the preceding pages, which document the past 200. Furthermore, any landscapes to be restored to natural conditions will require sufficient time for the slow process of successional recovery to be guided toward the desired end. A forest, prairie, or wetland cannot be rebuilt in an afternoon, although many were destroyed in that short time period.

Do we have the vision to imagine the changes to be, or the wisdom to guide them? Can we design Indiana's future landscape in such a way that the nature that now remains, or that that nature can restore with our guidance, will be conveyed safely to those present at the turn of the twenty-third century? That is our challenge. This essay represents an evaluation of some possible eventualities, and the most promising approaches to achieve those ends.

We now know where most wild places and wild creatures are located in Indiana. Those habitats most resembling their original conditions have been mapped, photographed, and catalogued, and the information has been stored away in file cabinets, in sleeves of slides, on topographic maps, encoded on computer memories, and etched into the minds of natural heritage staff members. This wealth of information is available at the slide of a file drawer, the push of a button, or the response to a verbal query, to those interested in studying or stewarding natural areas. All species of wild creatures deemed to be of sufficient rarity or interest to justify continued monitoring are likewise being located and documented. Such is the efficiency of the Indiana Natural Heritage Data Center (see also chapter 52, "Inventory and Preservation").

That such a well-oiled, smoothly functioning system of information gathering and data management is in place is most reassuring, but in another sense it is also disconcerting. It is comforting to those of us who have been involved with natural area inventory and preservation long enough to have witnessed the loss of a prime area because it was previously unknown, or because we lacked the organizational and financial resources to save a favorite field-trip location or unspoiled habitat. It wrenches the very soul of an ecologist to be forced to "bite one's lip" and watch another patch being torn from the remaining wild fabric of Indiana, to learn of the extirpation of yet another species from Indiana's soil or waters.

But now that essentially all of Indiana is known, what does that knowing do to our sense of discovery? To the imagination of the young would-be naturalists and ecologists growing up here? Wildness, especially unknown wildness, may be necessary to the proper development of the human mind, and the human spirit. Both Thoreau and Leopold certainly thought so: "In wildness is the preservation of the world"; "I would not want to be young again without wild places to be young in." And Edith Cobb, in her thoughtful essay *The Ecology of Imagination in Childhood*, made a compelling case for the value of contact with wild nature in attitude formation by children.

But where do we turn to find the wild places in a state such as Indiana to meet such present and projected needs for open space and wild critters? This need-space equation, which becomes more unbalanced daily, will become critical during the twenty-first century. This is where the points raised earlier in chapter 55, "Connections: The Humans-Landscape Linkage," come into play. By necessity, serious, in-depth nature study should begin by parents' and schools' leading the exploration of the natural world around their doorstep.

Even if we know where many of the *elements of natural diversity* are, that is still just a beginning. To an inquiring mind, an inventory list presents far more questions than answers. Ecosystems are not only more complex than we think, they may be more complex than we *can* think. Each answer often raises several more questions. In the future, our quest for knowing must center on unraveling the mysteries of how the state's ecosystems function, not just their description. Such activity promises equally exciting discoveries, and should occupy inquisitive minds for at least a couple more centuries.

Additionally, nature at all levels is composed of fractals—units that can be subdivided further, apparently without limit. Each of these subdivisions, in turn, is a microcosm, an ecosystem in miniature. Each succeedingly smaller level provides habitat for still smaller creatures until, of course, the minimum functional niche limit is reached. As we progress down the ecosystem size scale, population densities of the "wee beasties" that live there increase proportionally. Likely, diversity does also. As David Cavagnaro pointed out, "The closer we look, the farther we see," or at least the *more* we see.

Our future challenge, therefore, is to look more closely at the nuts, bolts, and rivets of nature's machinery so that we come to understand how the larger systems are structured and why they function. For example, healthy natural soil is a medium whose billions of organisms per gram have the marvelous ability to turn everything once living into more soil and, in the process, release the raw materials

We must protect rare habitats such as this beautiful seep spring in Martin County, and species endangered in Indiana such as the bobcat and loggerhead shrike. *Photos by Lee Casebere, Marion Jackson, and Delano Z. Arvin*

necessary to build more life. Yet no one professes to begin to understand the ecology of soil. If we come to know the roles of its myriad microbes and how they affect soil fertility, hence plant health and herbivore nutrition, perhaps we can begin to arrive at why carnivorous animals succeed or fail in a given landscape. It is imperative that we preserve representative, uncontaminated, unmodified soil systems so that future scientists have the opportunity to unravel the soil's mysteries.

Just as study of fine genetic structure is enabling scientists to finally sort out the intricacies of organism health, inheritance, and evolution, so can close looks at nature permit us to resolve similar questions as to landscape health, history, and destiny. But as Alton Lindsey wrote more than three decades ago, "Analysis is sterile, unless followed by synthesis." This is where saving intact portions of wild nature comes into play. Healthily functioning ecosystems in their natural state represent nature's synthesis, the end products of the long processes of ecological succession and organic evolution. Remaining old-growth forests, virgin prairies, and natural wetlands are rare reference ecosystems that have great value as ecological controls which we can use to compare the managed landscapes that cover most of Indiana. It is to nature that we must turn for many of our answers. That is the basis of the Thoreauvian dictum "In wildness is the preservation of the world."

One of the most serious problems of the past and the greatest challenges of the future in Indiana (as elsewhere) is the rending of the wild fabric of nature, the repeated fragmentation and separation of natural habitats by human intervention. A basic problem is a human viewpoint gone askew. We attempt to homogenize nature by, in Keith Caldwell's words, "making every place the same place." In our development zeal, we continually "fractionate" and isolate the remnants of the natural landscape into smaller and smaller habitat "islands" within larger and larger "seas" of agriculture and development, creating in the process huge expanses of monocultures, residential developments, or industrial complexes. In both cases, diversity is decreased. Small wonder that the human attention span has shriveled and boredom is rampant.

In less than 200 years, we have to a large extent homogenized the landscape of our small state, which extends but 4° in north-south latitude and slightly less than 3 ½° in east-west longitude—a state formerly wild with the enormous diversity described earlier. Perhaps living in such a homogenized landscape will move us into homogenized thinking, which could lead to a "collective mind," the ultimate enemy of individual, creative thought.

Somehow, we must come to understand that most intrusions into natural landscapes destroy their integrity, rendering them unlivable to many, if not most, wild species, and possibly for ourselves. The first to go are large carnivores as the habitat islands are diminished below their home range size, or will no longer support adequately their food-base prey species. Also, frequently lost early on are the "keystone species" which serve to bind many other species together, and whose loss may trigger population collapses in many of their associated species. Lesser species then follow suit down the food chain as fractionation becomes complete. Finally, as the lowest common denominator is reached, "nature" is distilled down to largely alien species such as "weeds" in our lawns or in the cracks of sidewalks, nuisance introduced birds perched on the window ledges of our high-rise buildings, or cockroaches hiding in the crevices of our kitchens. Reduction of natural diversity is then complete.

Conversely, the more civic landscapes are fractionated, the more livable they become for humans. If we break up dreary urban expanses into smaller communities, even villages, their diversity increases dramatically and they become progressively more appealing and nurturing to human residents. Urban diversity may also help promote a sense of identity, the sense of place that Keith Caldwell discussed in the Foreword.

A case history is appropriate to illustrate the problems relating to island biogeography as outlined above. For many years, Terre Haute has been a medium-sized, somewhat sleepy Indiana city located at the state's western border. It boasts a very fine city park system, its most natural unit being Dobbs Park located near the city's far eastern edge. Originally this park was a 105-acre farm, which was donated to the city of Terre Haute in 1944 by the John G. Dobbs family to be used as a city forest. Included was a fine old-growth, mixed deciduous forest of about 15 acres.

Bill Barnes, then director of the Indiana Division of Nature Preserves, was sufficiently impressed by the old-growth woods that he succeeded in further protecting 25 acres (including some secondary forest buffer land) as a dedicated state nature preserve in 1975. At that time approximately four and a half of the six sides of the L-shaped Dobbs Park perimeter remained as open land, largely agricultural. We had hoped to protect adjacent lands to buffer the sensitive old-growth stand, and to increase the park size to something approaching a viable ecological unit. But developers got there first and surrounded the natural area with expensive residential housing, some of which borders the old-growth forest directly. At this writing, five of six sides are now, or are in the process of being, developed, with the eastern margin, bordered by busy Indiana Rt. 46, the only remaining "open" side.

In 1973–74, Ronald Helms, then a graduate student in ecology at Indiana State University, did a taxonomic and ecological inventory of the entire 105-acre tract for his master's thesis. In addition to recognizing 14 community types, he also recorded 320 species of vascular plants representing 76 families, and 189 species of vertebrate fauna (including 25 mammals, 127 birds, 14 reptiles, 11 amphibians, and 12 bony fishes) which lived in the tract or used it daily or seasonally. These lists have since been augmented substantially. Dobbs Park has exceptional diversity for an urban-edge environment with little topographic variation, harboring at one time or another about 12 to 15 percent of the plant species and 25 percent of the vertebrate animal species that have been recorded for Indiana. When the 25-year re-survey of the tract scheduled for later this decade is completed, it will be interesting to see if this high diversity changes now that this natural land is entrapped in an urban embrace. We hope that the follow-up study will not show marked diversity declines and become another example of "epitaph ecology."

This rather lengthy discourse on what has happened at Dobbs Park is given to illustrate what is happening throughout Indiana. Present development is but today's tidal bore of the settlement wave begun 200 years ago. Until the past decade, Terre Haute was far behind the pace being set almost everywhere else in the state, but now development is galloping across open lands at the city's margin. Surrounding almost every village, town, and city in Indiana, and spilling out into rural areas, the encroachment of residential and urban development into agricultural and natural land is accelerating. Perhaps we cannot stop this process; it may be doubtful that we can even slow it. But can we guide it? Here are some suggestions.

• First, we must continue and augment the momentum under way to protect the "ark of habitat," a series of "lifelands" essential to the survival of what remains of wild nature in Indiana. Since John Bacone described many of the details in Part 5, those ideas will not be repeated here, but certain points do need expansion.

We must come to realize that we cannot save biodiversity one species at a time, but we can successfully assist individual species, such as the bald eagle, in their recovery. As pointed out more than 30

Efforts to reestablish extirpated species must be continued and expanded. A bald eagle, and the hacking tower used in its reintroduction.
Photos courtesy of the Indiana Department of Natural Resources

years ago by the eminent ecologist Eugene Odum of the University of Georgia, conservation of ecosystems is the approach we should use; we should not just attempt to save this or that species. Instead of dismantling the Endangered Species Act as has been proposed recently by certain legislators, we need to broaden its provisions to protect endangered ecosystems.

As a beginning, ideally, we need to adopt a policy of "no net loss of *natural* lands," similar to the "no net loss of wetlands" policy currently in place. When the "big picture" and the distant future are taken into consideration, Indiana simply cannot afford to lose one additional acre of natural land, or of farmland either, for that matter. Some estimates state that nationally we are losing open land to development at the rate of 3 acres per minute. Whatever the loss rate in Indiana or elsewhere, in the long run it is non-supportable—a cancer destroying the very foundation of the state's ecological and economic health. New developments should occur on sites of previous development; preferably those most in decay should be the first to be razed and built again.

To protect natural diversity, we must save the finest remaining small natural areas as described earlier, but such tracts, if unconnected to surrounding natural land, may, over time, suffer the same fate as described for Dobbs Park. Protection efforts now center on larger units which represent more intact ecosystems. An example is the program targeting the "last best places" for protection by The Nature Conservancy. One of these is a 1,418-acre tract recently purchased near the confluence of the Wabash and Ohio rivers for $1.43 million. It is TNC-Indiana's largest and most expensive acquisition to date. This purchase was an addition to existing adjacent natural areas, bringing the total of protected land in that vicinity to nearly four and a half square miles—truly approaching a viable size of preserved ecosystem. A number of projects being conducted throughout the state by The Nature Conservancy will protect other ecosystem-sized segments of our best streams, wetlands, and uplands.

We also need to determine if voids exist in our preservation "ark." This is being approached by the Indiana Gap Analysis Project, which is an effort involving the use of remotely sensed and other data about the Indiana landscape to evaluate the completeness of our protection approach. Any "gaps" (unprotected habitats or species) will be identified by this methodology, and "lifeboats" will be constructed to save the elements of biodiversity which are at peril.

Corollary to preserving high-quality natural areas, we also need to expand the capabilities of local land trusts, which now collectively encompass the entire state. Perhaps this approach could be patterned after that of the Acres Land Trust of Fort Wayne. Such protection units could assist private citizens with protecting their natural land that is of great ecological value, but which may not be of nature preserve quality. Sometimes such lands, though protected from development and excessive disturbance, can be used for harvesting timber, wildlife, or other "crops" on a sustained-yield basis, yet essentially retain their natural character.

• Second, we need to develop an "ecological internet" of land corridors, greenways, stream borders, fencerows, buffer strips, road margins, highway tunnels and bridges, or other connecting links that will allow both plants and animals to move more freely among remaining natural lands. Such migration channels not only provide travel lanes for vagile organisms such as birds, flying insects, and mammals, they also permit a revolving gene exchange throughout their length by vectors which move pollen progressively over a season or a decade, and by sequential mate selection by animals along continuous interbreeding populations. Outcrossing, which is essential to most healthy, evolving species, declines or ceases to occur as populations become progressively more isolated into smaller, more distant habitat islands. The more we connect the natural habitat that remains, and the healthier we keep the large land matrix that surrounds it, the greater is the survival potential of the species in residence there. Once in place, these ecological corridors need intensive scientific study to document their effectiveness, or lack of it, and then they can be expanded if necessary.

• Third, there is an increasing interest in restoration ecology, both globally and in Indiana. The recently formed professional Society for Restoration Ecology is now rapidly increasing its membership. A growing series of examples of restoration projects throughout the world supports the idea that "if we could take it apart originally, we can go a long way toward putting it back together." While, to my knowledge, no one has ever created even one acre of true wilderness, we can successfully guide successional processes toward repair of damaged ecosystems, provided that alternation of natural conditions and human developments were not excessively destructive. As nature heals damaged landscapes with human assistance, some "scar tissue," such as old fence lines, drainage ditches, and gullied fields, may long be in evidence, but recovering communities are far preferable to "open wounds."

In Indiana, major restoration should first center on acquiring sizable contiguous tracts within each major vegetation and landscape type that formerly occurred in the state. Ideally these projects would require the purchase of about 4 square miles (1,000 hectares) in each of some 12 to 20 natural regions (units) of the state, if such habitat does not already exist on public lands. All such large tracts selected for restoration should be as free of roads and developments as possible; if such exist, they should be removed.

The highest priority for acquisition are lands in natural regions most altered from original conditions, i.e., the Central Till Plain forest and the tallgrass prairie of northwest Indiana. If sites are carefully chosen, remnant inclusions of original vegetation will serve as invasion nuclei to accelerate successional advance. Initially, alien species will need to be controlled, but once established, "climax" native vegetation will maintain its own existence, and exclude most "weedy" invaders. There is little need to reintroduce most animal species—if you build suitable habitat, they will come. Animal species tend to persist in wild enclaves, then, being highly mobile, expand their range into new habitat as it becomes available.

Except for the largest predators, intact, fully functioning ecosystems can be maintained, even including a small bison herd on the restored prairie. Large wetland-upland mosaics need restoration also. In some cases, lowlands can be reflooded merely by breaking tile lines or filling drainage ditches, thereby setting the stage for aquatic succession. If water is restored to the land, you will witness the magic of nature returning in just a few months.

It is mandatory that these sizable restoration projects be initiated immediately, because it takes from decades to centuries to rebuild prairies, and especially forests, that took only weeks to destroy originally. No need for farmers, foresters, or other citizens to lament the loss of the private land that such tracts would encompass. Research data from these sites would be far more valuable in guiding land management throughout the state than any loss of crop or timber production. Furthermore, even if a four-square-mile tract were restored in each of Indiana's 92 counties, only 368 square miles would be involved totally, barely 1 percent of our 36,291-square-mile area.

As a case study of how a large-scale ecological restoration project could be implemented, let us consider the following:

All cities in the history of cities have been built by destroying (usually totally) the natural ecosystems in their vicinity. Terre Haute, as its name suggests, is situated on a high terrace above the Wabash River, and overlooks the lower floodplain. This lucky physiographic happenstance has enabled much of the river valley that is subject to flooding to remain as undeveloped land throughout the past 200 years. Recent discussions involving landscape artists, ecologists, legislators, and industrial and civic leaders have centered on the feasibility and desirability of a cooperative venture to restore the former floodplain forests adjacent to Terre Haute to something approaching their former grandeur, a project that would require a dozen or more decades for completion. Should this come to pass, Terre Haute would be unique in all the world in retrofitting itself into its original ecological setting, returning, as it were, to whence it came.

One of the most compelling practical arguments for doing this project is that the rebuilt forest would take an enormous volume of carbon dioxide (CO_2) from the atmosphere to fuel its own photosynthesis. A major concern in recent decades is CO_2 buildup in the atmosphere, primarily a result of burning the carbon stored in the fossil fuels that we use to power our industry, vehicles, and homes. The developing forest along the Wabash would help offset CO_2 buildup locally by sequestering (storing) carbon in its tissues. Since the electrical generating plant nearby is the major user of fossil fuels (hence CO_2 producer) in the Terre Haute area, it could obtain its carbon credits (current jargon for permission to pollute the air) from helping to restore the proposed floodplain forest. If this project were completed, it would be a classic example of large-scale restoration ecology which could benefit everyone.

• Fourth, we need to enlist the services of a loosely organized but highly effective statewide cadre of observers and local naturalists to search, study, and catalogue natural species, features, and events on a local basis. With proper guidance they could also carry out necessary management of natural areas. Irrespective of age or outdoor persuasion, this ecological army could keep tabs on everything from confirming the presence of rare or interesting species, to building continuing records of population changes, to recording phenological events (i.e., repeating periodic phenomena of nature), to serving as land stewards and preserve watchdogs. Dr. Dan Janzen, a recipient of the MacArthur Medal, the highest ecological award globally, has had good success in training alert, interested local citizens to aid in RAP, a rapid assessment program for inventorying threatened species, in Costa Rica and elsewhere in the tropics. Indiana could profitably follow Janzen's example by enlisting the services of local para-ecologists and para-taxonomists. To those sufficiently interested, limited intensive training could be quickly given so that they could soon identify species and record valuable data on their own. When on their own turf, informed and committed amateurs often can outperform even the professional, for the reason that they are always nearby and are highly familiar with the local situation.

Such activities would allow a significant number of committed Indiana residents to reconnect with their natural world in ways described previously in chapter 55, "Connections." The more we reestablish contact with the Earth, the more zealously we will protect it.

> The less of our landscape there is to save, the better our chances of saving it. It is a shame we have to lose so much land to learn the lesson, but desecration does seem a prerequisite for action. People have to be outraged.
>
> —*William H. Whyte*, The Last Landscape (*1968*)

Similarly we should start an adopt-an-acre program, whereby citizens can assume responsibility for the integrity of a tract of nearby open land, public or private, their own or belonging to others. We have adopt-a-whale, adopt-a-stream, adopt-a-mile-of-highway, and adopt-a-homeless-pet programs—why not adopt natural land? About 27 of Indiana's counties presently have no dedicated nature preserves, but all have open lands worth watching. Acre observers-adopters could identify tracts worth protecting (even if they are not nature preserve quality), do species inventories and other studies thereon, and serve as an early warning system if "their" land becomes threatened.

• Fifth, perhaps our only hope for permanent protection of the biodiversity of Indiana (and worldwide) is for all interested citizens to form a coalition to protect "our" environment. It is not "the" environment—not something separated from humans and their busy lifestyles. Our environment is not just a medium from which the resources necessary to support our "things-centered" existence are extracted. Nor is it something that we pay attention to, or attempt to clean up, only if it becomes health- or life-threatening, locally or globally. "Our" environment is "our" little planetary ecosystem that is the only known habitat for life. Indiana is a small, but vital, part of our spaceship, whose long-term fate is in our hands. As the Sierra Club's motto states, "One Earth, One Chance."

Those who take the short view concerning what they feel Indiana must produce for its residents have always outnumbered, and out-financed, those who take a long view toward a goal of sustainable human enterprise and a quality lifestyle for everyone. Additionally, most citizens have not come to realize that land ownership (and its resources access) not only provides benefits, it also confers responsibility—responsibility not only to us and our contemporaries, but also to those who come after us.

For this long view to become a reality, we must form an active, informed, determined, cohesive coalition that has the ability to influence the action. One of our problems to date is that we have permitted environmental protection efforts to become as fragmented as the landscape we inhabit, rather than presenting a unified front. Protecting remaining open lands must be our goal, because as long as land remains open (i.e., not developed into crystallized uses or urban centers or transportation corridors), our options remain open. Open land must be protected, be it agricultural, managed natural land, or preserved natural land.

If only farmers, natural resource managers, hunters, anglers, outdoor recreationists, and preservationists would stop arguing among themselves and taking potshots at one another, and form an open-land alliance, we would be an invincible force for the protection of all open lands. As Lord Halifax once observed, "The angry buzz of a multitude is the bloodiest noise in the world." Rather than being divided by our separate strengths and ideological differences, we need to become united by our common purpose—maintaining an open, healthy Indiana landscape that supports the greatest possible cultural and biological diversity, now and in the future.

If enough ordinary people with extraordinary courage, and with the conviction that they are right, speak in unison of their love of the land, and with a vision of protecting the rights of the yet-to-be-born, they will be able to influence future actions. Perhaps we should consider adopting the Seventh Generation Amendment proposed by the Anishinabeg Native Americans for protecting their lands in northern Wisconsin: "Every deliberation we make must be in consideration of the impact on the seventh generation from now."

• Finally, let's rethink our notions of what is optimum land use and also of landscape esthetics. Two land-use trends have been in motion since the close of World War II that have progressively and rapidly diminished the amount of natural land available to support wild plants and animals, and also that available for agricultural crops. Together they have largely crystallized at least 10 percent of the Indiana landscape within the past 40 years.

The first and most serious is land development in which "construction" activity creates roads, highways, industrial sites, and residential areas, all of which cause "destruction" of open land, likely for all time. Environmentalists have to "save" a tract of land every time it is threatened, but developers have to "win" only once, and the area is gone forever. Jefferson voiced this concern two centuries ago when he wrote, "In the environment every victory is temporary, every defeat is permanent." Necessary developments should be shunted away from our most valuable and sensitive natural lands and crop lands.

The other land-use change is not so permanent, but is likely more pervasive—i.e., mowing landscapes with lawn mowers or "bush hogs." Unnecessary mowing is a manifestation of both our compulsion for landscape tidiness and a personal assurance that we indeed are conquerors of nature. Although the exact acreage mowed regularly is unknown, it surely must exceed a million acres in Indiana, more than 5 percent of our total land area. Nationally, in summer, we mow weekly an area the size of Pennsylvania. And these mowed acreages grow yearly. The only redeeming feature of mowed-scapes is that they will return to something more natural via biotic succession if we stop mowing for only one or two growth seasons.

Americans have a fixation with large landed estates surrounded by expanses of manicured lawn, always mowed golf-course short. Our compulsion for landscape tidiness has now extended beyond traditional lawns to almost all forest borders, roadsides, crop field margins, former meadows, and non-developed lands. Such transitions or edges between vegetation types, if left natural, have long been recognized by ecologists to be habitats which support a high diversity of plants and animals. Considering the hundreds of thousands of mowers now operating in Indiana (many clipping two acres per hour), the weekly impact on our landscape is almost beyond imagining. On these mowed-scapes nothing other than grass stands a chance, either plant or animal.

As pointed out by F. H. Bormann et al. in their classic book *Redesigning the American Lawn,* lawns are ecological disaster areas. In addition to being monocultures, they are usually chemically laden, they receive water and energy subsidies, and they require vast amounts of time-consuming and expensive maintenance. Mowers also are dangerous, noisy generators of pollution. In return, lawns yield no useful product other than visual enhancement. And other than concrete or asphalt, or possibly a cornfield, it is doubtful that any land surface in Indiana has a lower biodiversity than a lawn. Perhaps lawns and their required maintenance are God's curse for destroying our Eden!

Why not return at least one-half of the surface area mowed routinely with lawn mowers and "bush hogs" to some form of more productive cultivated or (preferably) native vegetation? Residences

in Europe and Britain typically have the space in front of the dwelling planted to flowers, with the land to the rear devoted to vegetables and herbs.

Significant portions of mowed lands could easily be returned to natural vegetation via ecological succession. Old fields and meadows are wonderful habitats for beneficial insects, small game animals, nesting birds, bats, and hosts of butterflies, all indicators of land health. Alternatively, the development of small prairies, beds of showy perennial native (wild) flowers, butterfly gardens, small ponds, or shrubby cover would favor many wild species of pollinators, small herbivores, toads, and box turtles, to say nothing of providing opportunities close at hand for our children to study nature. The return of one-half of all mowed acreages to natural cover would represent a total greater than all publicly owned land presently in Indiana. But perhaps the greatest benefits derived from such lightly managed, semi-natural lands would be the increased appreciation and perception of nature and its processes that their owner-managers would acquire.

In the final analysis it all comes down to a question of land ethics and our viewpoint about our relationship with Planet Earth. We can continue to see ourselves as the owners and conquerors of nature, and view anything natural as an adversary to be subdued or developed, or we can enter into a willing partnership with the Indiana that nurtures us. It is our choice, and the future depends on our call. Should we eventually find a way to divest ourselves of the mayhem of our present lifestyle by seeking the silence of nature and learning to read its messages, we not only will learn more about ourselves, we may discover the pathway to peace as well.

Had I really solved the riddle? . . . Would anyone find a Genesis Tree alive again? Perhaps if I searched the woods of people's lives I would find one. I promised myself to try.

My riddle was really answered long ago by the old town crier when he stood beneath the first Genesis Tree at New Harmony, Indiana, and cried out the hour of midnight:

"Again a day is passed and a step made nearer the end. Our time runs away, and the joys of heaven are our reward."

But it is not midnight here. Here it is morning.

—Lynne Doyle (age 18), "The Riddle of Genesis County" (1958)

This cloverleaf interchange was once virgin forest, as was five-sixths of Indiana.
Photo by Richard Fields

(overleaf)
In the future, may the "earthrise" continue to be seen by anyone who happens to visit the moon!
Photo courtesy of NASA

Overview

The gathering raindrops flow
To fill the seas.

Each night knows when to end
So day can break.

A single bud will burst
To start the spring.

A love will find its own;
A child come true.

Mankind will learn at last
And life go on.

—*A. A. Lindsey*

Supplementary Materials

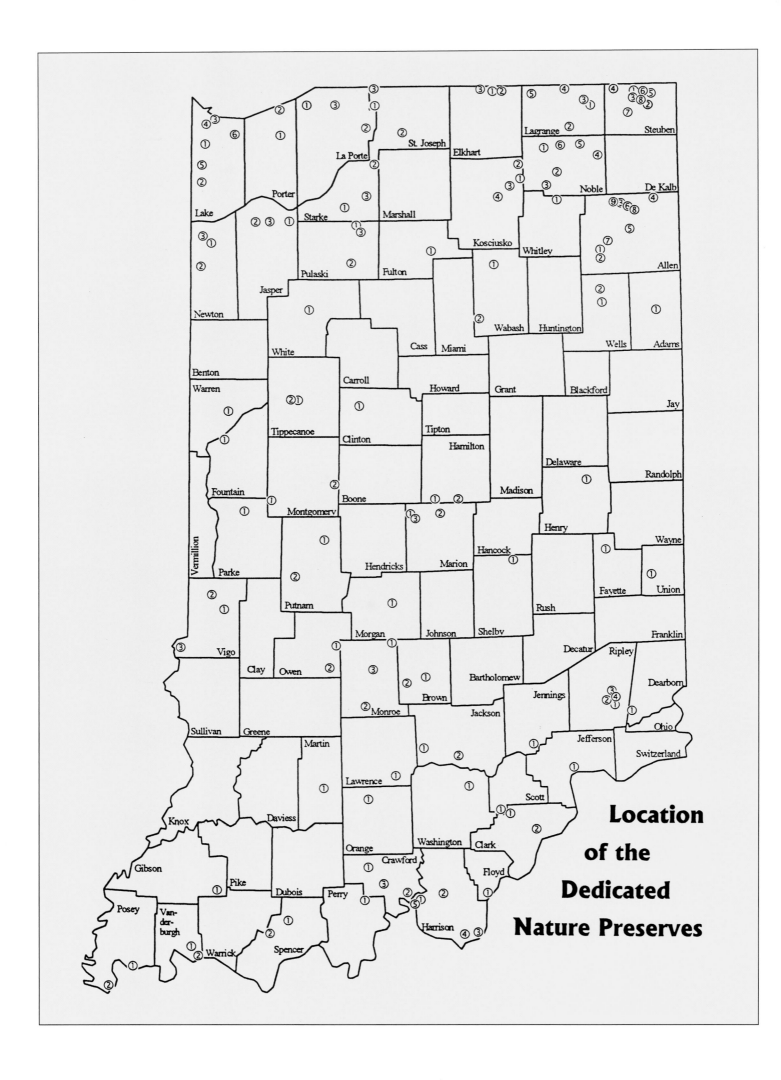

**Location
of the
Dedicated
Nature Preserves**

A. Public Lands in Indiana

Marion T. Jackson

As compared to western states, Indiana has a relatively small percentage of publicly owned land, but our total holdings are likely about average for states which are primarily agricultural. Not including city or county parks or developed public lands (e.g., school sites, state offices, etc.), Indiana has about 625,000 acres of natural and quasi-natural land in federal and state ownership (other than U.S. Department of Defense lands). This represents only 2.8 percent of the 23,226,240-acre total.

The largest landowner is the Department of Natural Resources (DNR), with a total of approximately 415,000 acres, followed by the United States Forest Service with approximately 190,000 acres in the Hoosier National Forest. Smaller acreages are administered by the National Park Service, the U.S. Fish and Wildlife Service, and other agencies.

Much of the least disturbed natural land remaining in Indiana occurs in the 133 dedicated state nature preserves (as of 1995) which are administered by the Division of Nature Preserves (DNP), totaling just slightly less than 20,000 acres. A number of nature preserves are inclusions within state parks, state forests, state fish and wildlife areas, or other DNR-owned lands. Dedication gives these preserves double protection. Additionally, land held by the Acres Land Trust, The Nature Conservancy, academic institutions, city and county parks, and some in private ownership has been dedicated. Presently the total dedicated acreage is approximately 20,000.

Thirty-five counties presently do not have a dedicated nature preserve. More than half of those counties with no preserves are located in the Central Till Plain. Only 21 counties have 3 or more preserves each, with a total of 86.

PRESERVE BY NAME

#	Name	County
1	Acres Along the Wabash	Wells
2	Asherwood	Wabash
2	Ashumbala	Vanderburgh
3	Ball Wetlands	Kosciusko
1	Baltzell-Lenhart Woods	Adams
1	Barker Woods	LaPorte
2	Barnes, Bill	Newton
1	Beaver Lake	Newton
1	Beechwood	Steuben
2	Bender, Lloyd W.	Noble
1	Bendix Woods	St. Joseph
2	Berns-Meyer	Pulaski
1	Bicentennial Woods	Allen
5	Biesecker Prairie	Lake
4	Big & Little Chapman Lakes	Kosciusko
2	Big Spring	Washington
1	Bitternut Woods	Hamilton
2	Bloomfield Barrens	Spencer
1	Blue Bluff	Morgan
1	Brock-Sampson	Floyd
1	Bryan Memorial, Eunice H.	Clinton
2	Calvert & Porter Woods	Montgomery
3	Carnes Mill	Crawford
2	Cedar Bluffs	Monroe
2	Ciurus Park, Thomas	Jasper
3	Clark & Pine	Lake
1	Clifty Canyon	Jefferson
3	Conrad Savanna	Newton
1	Crooked Lake	Whitley
5	Deam, Charles C.	Harrison
1	Dobbs, John G.	Vigo
1	Dogwood	Ripley
1	Donaldson Cave & Woods	Lawrence
2	Dunes	Porter
2	Eagle's Crest Woods	Marion
2	Eby Prairie	Elkhart
3	Elkhart Bog	Elkhart
1	Fall Creek Gorge	Warren
3	Falling Timber	Ripley
4	Fawn River Fen	LaGrange
2	Fern Cliff	Putnam
2	Fish Creek Fen	LaPorte
3	Flesher Memorial Woods, Kermit R.	Vigo
2	Fogwell Forest	Allen
1	Fox Island	Allen
2	German Methodist Cemetery Prairie	Lake
4	Gibson Woods	Lake
1	Goose Pond Cypress Slough	Posey
2	Green's Bluff	Owen
1	Greider's Woods	Kosciusko

PRESERVE BY COUNTY

County	#	Name
Adams	1	Baltzell-Lenhart Woods
Allen	1	Fox Island
Allen	2	Fogwell Forest
Allen	3	Rodenbeck
Allen	4	McNabb-Walter
Allen	5	Mengerson
Allen	6	Vandolah
Allen	7	Lindenwood
Allen	8	Meno-Aki
Allen	9	Bicentennial Woods
Brown	1	Ogle Hollow
Brown	2	Steele, Selma
Clark	1	White Oak
Clark	2	Nine Penny Branch
Clinton	1	Bryan Memorial, Eunice H.
Crawford	1	Yellow Birch Ravine
Crawford	2	Leavenworth Barrens
Crawford	3	Carnes Mill
Dearborn	1	Lubbe Woods, Gilbert & Alma Nentrup
Elkhart	1	Pipewort Pond (Lieber Memorial)
Elkhart	2	Eby Prairie
Elkhart	3	Elkhart Bog
Fayette	1	Shrader-Weaver
Floyd	1	Brock-Sampson
Fountain	1	Portland Arch
Fulton	1	Manitou Islands
Gibson	1	Hemmer Woods
Hamilton	1	Bitternut Woods
Hamilton	2	Ritchey Woods
Harrison	1	Post Oak–Cedar
Harrison	2	Hayswood
Harrison	3	Teeple Glade
Harrison	4	Mosquito Creek
Harrison	5	Deam, Charles C.
Henry	1	Zeigler Woods
Jackson	1	Hemlock Bluff
Jackson	2	Knobstone Glades
Jasper	1	Tefft Savanna
Jasper	2	Ciurus Park, Thomas
Jasper	3	Stoutsburg Savanna
Jefferson	1	Clifty Canyon
Jennings	1	Well's Woods
Kosciusko	1	Greider's Woods
Kosciusko	2	Wawasee Wetlands
Kosciusko	3	Ball Wetlands
Kosciusko	4	Big, Little Chapman Lakes
LaGrange	1	Tamarack Bog
LaGrange	2	Olin Lake
LaGrange	3	Mongoquinong
LaGrange	4	Fawn River Fen

B. Species Extirpated from Indiana

Marion T. Jackson

Extirpated species are those that formerly occurred in an area but are no longer present. An animal species is considered to be extirpated from Indiana if it has been absent from the state as a breeding population for more than 15 years. Extirpated plant species are those believed to be originally native to Indiana but without any currently known populations within the state. Extirpated species of plants and animals do exist outside Indiana as wild populations. Not included in this list are species that formerly were present here but are now globally extinct, e.g., the passenger pigeon and Carolina parakeet.

According to present records, 70 vascular plant, 18 invertebrate, and 29 vertebrate species have been lost from Indiana, largely as a consequence of human activities and landscape changes. These 117 species obviously do not represent the total of all species extirpated. Many of the non-vascular plant and invertebrate animal groups are poorly known, and their early collection was woefully incomplete. There is no way to know what species were represented here originally for many of those groups. Also not included in this listing are species once extirpated but now successfully reintroduced, e.g., whitetail deer.

Birds listed herein refer to species not known to nest here presently, but which did formerly. A few bird species listed as extirpated still visit Indiana and are sighted in the state occasionally, some frequently.

Vascular Plants
FERNS ET AL.

Asplenium bradleyi, Bradley's spleenwort
Botrychium multifidum var. *intermedium*, leathery grape fern
Dryopteris clintoniana, Clinton woodfern
Pteridium aquilinum var. *pseudocaudatum*, bracken fern

TREES

Betula populifolia, gray birch
Populus balsamifera, balsam poplar
Sorbus decora, northern mountain-ash

SHRUBS, BRAMBLES, WOODY VINES

Lonicera canadensis, American fly-honeysuckle
Rubus alumnus, a bramble
Rubus deamii, Deam dewberry
Rubus depavitus, a bramble
Rubus impar, a bramble
Shepherdia canadensis, Canada buffalo-berry

HERBACEOUS

Adlumia fungosa, climbing fumitory
Anemone caroliniana, Carolina anemone
Arethusa bulbosa, swamp-pink
Asclepias meadii, Mead's milkweed
Astragalus tennesseensis, Tennessee milk-vetch
Aureolaria grandiflora var. *pulchra*, large-flower false-foxglove
Cabomba caroliniana, Carolina fanwort
Callirhoe triangulata, clustered poppy-mallow
Ceanothus herbaceus, prairie redroot
Circaea alpina, small enchanter's nightshade
Conyza canadensis var. *pusilla*, fleabane
Corallorrhiza trifida var. *verna*, early coralroot
Cuscuta cuspidata, cusp dodder
Echinodorus cordifolius, upright burhead
Eriophorum spissum, dense cotton-grass
Euphorbia obtusata, bluntleaf spurge
Euphorbia serpens, matted broomspurge
Fragaria vesca var. *americana*, woodland strawberry
Glyceria grandis, American manna-grass
Gnaphalium macounii, winged cudweed
Gymnopogon ambiguus, broadleaf beardgrass
Hemicarpha micrantha var. *aristulata*, Drummond hemicarpha
Hippuris vulgaris, common mare's-tail
Hypericum frondosum, golden St. John's-wort
Juncus militaris, bayonet rush
Lactuca ludoviciana, western lettuce
Lechea stricta, upright pinweed
Lemna perpusilla, minute duckweed
Lemna valdiviana, pale duckweed
Lespedeza stuevei, tall bush-clover
Linnaea borealis, twinflower
Melothria pendula, creeping cucumber
Oenothera triloba, stemless evening-primrose
Oryzopsis pungens, slender mountain-ricegrass
Panicum longifolium, long-leaved panic-grass
Panicum mattamuskeetense, a panic-grass
Panicum subvillosum, a panic-grass
Penstemon tubaeflorus, tube penstemon
Platanthera hookeri, Hooker orchis
Platanthera leucophaea, prairie white-fringed orchid
Platanthera orbiculata, large roundleaf orchid
Poa cuspidata, bluegrass
Potamogeton bicupulatus, snail-seed pondweed
Proboscidea louisianica, Louisiana unicorn-plant
Psilocarya nitens, short-beaked bald-rush
Psoralea stipulata, a scurf-pea
Psoralea tenuiflora, few-flowered scurf-pea
Pyrola secunda, one-sided wintergreen
Pyrola virens, greenish-flowered wintergreen
Sabatia campanulata, slender marsh pink
Stachys clingmanii, Clingman hedge-nettle
Stipa comata, sewing needlegrass
Trautvetteria caroliniensis, Carolina tassel-rue
Utricularia resupinata, northeastern bladderwort
Veronica americana, American speedwell
Viola hirsutula, southern wood violet
Wolffiella floridana, sword bogmat

Invertebrate Animals
MOLLUSKS

Cumberlandia monodonta, spectaclecase
Epioblasma flexuosa, leafshell
Epioblasma obliquata obliquata, purple catspaw
Epioblasma personata, round combshell
Epioblasma propinqua, Tennessee riffleshell
Epioblasma sampsonii, Wabash riffleshell
Hemistena lata, cracking pearlymussel
Leptodea leptodon, scaleshell
Obovaria retusa, ring pink
Quadrula fragosa, winged mapleleaf

INSECTS

Enodia creola, Creole pearly eye
Lycaena epixanthe, bog copper
Nicrophorus americanus, American burying beetle
Oarisma poweshiek, Poweshiek skipper
Papaipema eryngii, rattlesnake-master borer moth
Pentagenia robusta, robust Pentagenia burrowing mayfly
Polystoechotes punctatus, a giant lacewing
Somatochlora hineana, Ohio emerald dragonfly

Vertebrate Animals
FISHES

Alosa alabamae, Alabama shad
Coregonus nigripinnis, blackfin cisco
Coregonus reighardi, shortnose cisco
Crystallaria asprella, crystal darter
Esox masquinongy ohioensis, Ohio River muskellunge
Lagochila lacera, harelip sucker
Lepomis symmetricus, bantam sunfish
Percina uranidea, stargazing darter

AMPHIBIANS—NONE

REPTILES

Farancia abacura reinwardtii, Western mud snake

BIRDS

Corvus corax, common raven
Euphagus cyanocephalus, Brewer's blackbird
Gavia immer, common loon
Phalacrocorax auritus, double-crested cormorant
Phalaropus tricolor, Wilson's phalarope
Sterna forsteri, Forster's tern
Sterna hirundo, common tern
Tympanuchus cupido, greater prairie-chicken

MAMMALS

Bos bison, American bison
Canis lupus, gray wolf
Canis rufus, red wolf
Cervus elaphus, wapiti or elk
Erethizon dorsatum, common porcupine
Felis concolor, mountain lion
Gulo gulo, wolverine
Lynx lynx, lynx
Martes pennanti, fisher
Rattus rattus, black rat
Spilogale putorius, eastern spotted skunk
Ursus americanus, black bear

Both the American bittern and the least bittern are now endangered in Indiana. When startled, the slender-bodied bitterns stand rigidly still and point their beaks upward, apparently attempting to protectively resemble the marsh plants where they dwell. Young least bitterns shown here. *Photo by Delano Z. Arvin*

C. Species Endangered in Indiana

Marion T. Jackson

Endangered plant species in Indiana are those which are known to occur at five or fewer locations; endangered animal species are those whose prospects for survival or recruitment are in immediate jeopardy and which are in danger of disappearing from the state.

Supplements B and C are not complete lists because floras and faunas are dynamic units, and hence ever-changing. Species presently categorized as endangered may become more secure in Indiana and be upgraded to threatened status. Conversely, they may also slide toward extirpation. Vulnerability classifications obviously change as environmental conditions change, and as populations wax or wane in response.

At present 194 species of vascular plants, 48 species of vertebrate animals, and 75 invertebrate species are considered endangered in Indiana. The site locations for invertebrate species are less well known, but endangered status for species within these groups may well increase as distribution patterns and population numbers are more accurately catalogued.

These species lists were prepared by the Indiana Natural Heritage Data Center, Indiana Department of Natural Resources, Division of Nature Preserves.

Vascular Plants

FERNS ET AL.

Asplenium montanum, mountain spleenwort
Asplenium resiliens, black-stem spleenwort
Botrychium simplex, least grape-fern
Equisetum variegatum, variegated horsetail
Isoetes englemannii, Appalachian quillwort
Isoetes melanopoda, blackfoot quillwort
Lycopodiella inundata, northern bog clubmoss
Lycopodiella subappressa, northern appressed bog clubmoss
Lycopodium dendroideum, treelike clubmoss
Lygodium palmatum, climbing fern
Selaginella apoda, meadow spikemoss
Trichomanes boschianum, filmy fern

TREES

Carya texana, black hickory
Crataegus arborea, a hawthorn
Crataegus biltmoreana, Biltmore hawthorn
Crataegus chrysocarpa, fineberry hawthorn
Crataegus grandis, grand hawthorn
Crataegus kelloggii, Kellogg hawthorn
Crataegus prona, Illinois hawthorn
Gleditsia aquatica, water-locust
Magnolia acuminata, cucumber magnolia
Magnolia tripetala, umbrella magnolia
Thuja occidentalis, northern white cedar

SHRUBS, BRAMBLES, WOODY VINES

Amelanchier humilis, running serviceberry
Berberis canadensis, American barberry
Cornus amomum ssp. *amomum*, silky dogwood
Cornus canadensis, bunchberry
Itea virginica, Virginia willow
Quercus prinoides, dwarf chinquapin oak
Rubus centralis, Illinois blackberry
Rubus enslenii, southern dewberry
Styrax grandifolius, large-leaf snowbell
Vaccinium myrtilloides, velvetleaf blueberry
Viburnum cassinoides, northern wild-raisin
Viburnum opulus var. *americanum*, highbush-cranberry
Vitis rupestris, sand grape

HERBACEOUS

Aconitum uncinatum, blue monkshood
Agalinis auriculata, earleaf foxglove
Agalinis skinneriana, pale false foxglove
Arabis drummondii, Drummond rockcress
Arabis missouriensis var. *deamii*, Missouri rockcress
Arabis patens, spreading rockcress
Aralia hispida, bristly sarsaparilla
Arenaria patula, Pitcher's stitchwort
Armoracia aquatica, lake cress
Bacopa rotundifolia, roundleaf water-hyssop
Besseya bullii, kitten tails
Bidens beckii, Beck water-marigold
Buchnera americana, bluehearts
Calla palustris, wild calla
Camassia angusta, wild hyacinth
Carex alopecoidea, foxtail sedge
Carex arctata, black sedge
Carex atherodes, awned sedge
Carex atlantica ssp. *capillacea*, Howe sedge
Carex brunnescens, brownish sedge
Carex bushii, Bush's sedge
Carex chordorrhiza, creeping sedge
Carex conoidea, field sedge
Carex cumulata, clustered sedge
Carex disperma, softleaf sedge
Carex echinata, little prickly sedge
Carex gigantea, large sedge
Carex gravida, heavy sedge
Carex leptonervia, finely-nerved sedge
Carex limosa, mud sedge
Carex pseudocyperus, cyperus-like sedge
Carex retrorsa, retrorse sedge
Carex richardsonii, Richardson sedge
Carex scabrata, rough sedge
Chaerophyllum procumbens var. *shortii*, wild chervil
Chamaelirium luteum, devil's-bit
Cimicifuga rubifolia, Appalachian bugbane
Cirsium hillii, Hill's thistle
Clintonia borealis, Clinton lily
Conioselinum chinense, hemlock parsley
Corydalis sempervirens, pale corydalis
Crotonopsis elliptica, elliptical rushfoil
Cyperus dentatus, toothed sedge
Cypripedium X andrewsii, Andrew's lady's-slipper
Dentaria multifida, divided toothwort
Dicliptera brachiata, wild mudwort
Echinodorus parvulus, little bus-head
Eleocharis equisetoides, horsetail spike-rush
Eleocharis microcarpa, small-fruited spike-rush
Epilobium angustifolium, fireweed
Epilobium ciliatum, hairy willow-herb
Eriocaulon septangulare, pipewort
Eupatorium album, white thoroughwort
Festuca paradoxa, cluster fescue
Fimbristylis puberula, chestnut sedge

Gentiana villosa, striped gentian
Geranium bicknellii, Bicknell northern cranesbill
Geum rivale, purple avens
Glyceria acutiflora, sharp-scaled manna-grass
Glyceria borealis, small floating manna-grass
Hibiscus lasiocarpus, hairy-fruited hibiscus
Hydrocotyle americana, American water-pennywort
Hymenopappus scabiosaeus, Carolina woollywhite
Hypericum adpressum, creeping St. John's-wort
Hypericum gymnanthum, clasping St. John's-wort
Hypericum pyramidatum, great St. John's-wort
Iliamna remota, Kankakee globe-mallow
Juncus articulatus, jointed rush
Juncus secundus, secund rush
Lathyrus maritimus var. *glaber*, beach peavine
Leavenworthia uniflora, Michaux's leavenworthia
Lechea racemulosa, Illinois pinweed
Lemna minima, least duckweed
Leptochloa panicoides, Amazon sprangle-top
Lesquerella globosa, Lesquereux's mustard
Ligusticum canadense, nondo lovage
Linum intercursum, sandplain flax
Lithospermum incisum, narrow-leaved puccoon
Ludwigia sphaerocarpa, globe-fruited false-loosestrife
Luzula acuminata, hairy woodrush
Lycopus amplectens, sessile-leaved bugleweed
Malaxis unifolia, green adder's-mouth
Melanthium virginicum, Virginia bunchflower
Mikania scandens, climbing hempweed
Monarda bradburiana, eastern bee-balm
Muhlenbergia capillaris, long-awn hairgrass
Muhlenbergia cuspidata, plains muhlenbergia
Myosotis laxa, smaller forget-me-not
Myriophyllum pinnatum, cutleaf water-milfoil
Najas gracillima, thread-like naiad
Onosmodium hispidissimum, shaggy false gromwell
Orobanche fasciculata, clustered broomrape
Oryzopsis asperifolia, white-grained mountain-ricegrass
Pachysandra procumbens, Allegheny spurge
Panicum annulum, a panic-grass
Panicum bicknellii, a panic-grass
Panicum scoparium, broom panic-grass
Perideridia americana, eastern eulophus
Phacelia ranunculacea, blue scorpion-weed
Phlox bifida ssp. *stellaria*, cleft phlox
Plantago cordata, heart-leaved plantain
Platanthera ciliaris, yellow-fringe orchis
Platanthera dilatata, leafy white orchis
Platanthera flava var. *flava*, southern rein orchid
Polygala incarnata, pink milkwort
Polygala paucifolia, gay-wing milkwort
Polygonum cilinode, fringed black bindweed
Polygonum hydropiperoides var. *setaceum*, swamp smartweed
Polytaenia nuttallii, prairie parsley
Potamogeton epihydrus, Nuttall pondweed
Potamogeton friesii, Fries' pondweed
Potamogeton oakesianus, Oakes pondweed
Potamogeton praelongus, white-stem pondweed
Potamogeton pulcher, spotted pondweed
Potamogeton strictifolius, straight-leaf pondweed
Potamogeton vaseyi, Vasey's pondweed

Pyrola asarifolia, pink wintergreen
Ranunculus harveyi, Harvey's buttercup
Ranunculus laxicaulis, Mississippi buttercup
Ranunculus pusillus, Pursh buttercup
Rhexia mariana var. *mariana*, Maryland meadow beauty
Rhynchospora globularis var. *recognita*, globe beaked-rush
Rubus setosus, small bristleberry
Rudbeckia fulgida var. *umbrosa*, coneflower
Sanguisorba canadensis, Canada burnet
Satureja glabella var. *angustifolia*, calamint
Satureja vulgaris var. *neogaea*, dogmint
Saxifraga forbesii, Forbes saxifrage
Scheuchzeria palustris ssp. *americana*, American scheuchzeria
Schizachne purpurascens, purple oat
Scirpus expansus, bulrush
Scirpus hallii, Hall's bulrush
Scirpus purshianus, weakstalk bulrush
Scirpus smithii, Smith's bulrush
Scirpus torreyi, Torrey's bulrush
Scutellaria saxatilis, rock skullcap
Setaria geniculata, bristly foxtail
Sida hermaphrodita, Virginia mallow
Sisyrinchium montanum, strict blue-eyed-grass
Solidago squarrosa, stout-ragged goldenrod
Spigelia marilandica, woodland pinkroot
Spiranthes magnicamporum, Great Plains ladies'-tresses
Spiranthes romanzoffiana, hooded ladies'-tresses
Stenanthium gramineum, eastern featherbells
Trifolium reflexum var. *glabrum*, buffalo clover
Trifolium stoloniferum, running buffalo clover
Trillium cernuum var. *macranthum*, nodding trillium
Utricularia geminiscapa, hidden-fruited bladderwort
Utricularia minor, lesser bladderwort
Utricularia radiata, small swollen bladderwort
Uvularia perfoliata, bellwort
Valeriana edulis, hairy valerian
Valeriana uliginosa, marsh valerian
Valerianella chenopodiifolia, goose-foot corn-salad
Viola egglestonii, Eggleston's violet
Zannichellia palustris, horned pondweed

Invertebrate Animals
MUSSELS

Cyprogenia stegaria, eastern fanshell pearlymussel
Epioblasma obliquata peroblique, white cat's paw pearlymussel
Epioblasma torulosa rangiana, northern riffleshell
Epioblasma torulosa torulosa, tubercled-blossom
Epioblasma triquetra, snuffbox
Fusconaia subrotunda, long-solid
Lampsilis abrupta, pink mucket
Plethobasus cicatricosus, white wartyback
Plethobasus cooperianus, orange-foot pimpleback
Plethobasus cyphyus, sheepnose
Pleurobema clava, clubshell
Pleurobema plenum, rough pigtoe
Pleurobema pyramidatum, pyramid pigtoe
Potamilus capax, fat pocketbook
Quadrula cylindrica cylindrica, rabbitsfoot

CRUSTACEANS

Bryocamptus morrisoni morrisoni, Morrison's cave copepod
Caecidotea jordani, Jordan Cave isopod
Caecidotea rotunda, northeastern cave isopod
Caecidotea teresae, groundwater isopod
Diacyclops jeanneli, Jeannel's Cave copepod
Gammarus bousfieldi, spring amphipod
Megacyclops donnaldsoni, Donaldson's Cave copepod
Pseudocandona jeanneli, Jeannel's Cave ostracod
Pseudocandona marengoensis, Marengo Cave ostracod
Stygobromus mackini, southwestern Virginia cave amphipod
Stygobromus sp 2, undescribed amphipod

GASTROPODS

Fontigens cryptica, Hidden Springs snail
Triodopsis obstricta, sharp wedge

INSECTS
Lepidoptera

Artogeia napi oleracea, veined white
Erynnis persius, Persian duskywing
Glaucopsyche lygdamus couperi, silvery blue
Hesperia ottoe, Ottoe skipper
Lycaeides melissa samuelis, Karner blue
Neonympha mitchelli mitchelii, Mitchell's marsh satyr
Satyrodes appalachia appalachia, Appalachian eyed brown
Schinia gloriosa, glorious flower moth
Speyeria diana, diana

Coleoptera

Batrisodes krekeleri, cave beetle
Cicindela marginipennis, cobblestone tiger beetle
Lissobiops serpentinus, a rove beetle
Pseudanophthalmus barri, cave beetle
Pseudanophthalmus chthonius, cave beetle
Pseudanophthalmus emersoni, cave beetle
Pseudanophthalmus eremita, cave beetle
Pseudanophthalmus jeanneli, cave beetle
Pseudanophthalmus leonae, cave beetle
Pseudanophthalmus shilohensis, cave beetle
Pseudanophthalmus shilohensis boonensis, cave beetle
Pseudanophthalmus shilohensis mayfieldensis, cave beetle
Pseudanophthalmus tenuis blatchleyi, cave beetle
Pseudanophthalmus tenuis morrisoni, cave beetle
Pseudanophthalmus youngi, cave beetle
Pseudanophthalmus youngi donaldsoni, cave beetle

Ephemeroptera

Anepeorus simplex, a flat-headed mayfly
Epeorus namatus, a mayfly
Ephemerella argo, Argo ephemerellan mayfly
Homoeoneuria ammophila, a sand-filtering mayfly
Pseudiron centralis, a mayfly
Raptoheptagenia cruentata, a flat-headed mayfly
Siphloplecton basale, a sand minnow mayfly
Spinadis wallacei, Wallace's deepwater mayfly

Trichoptera-Mecoptera

Goera stylata, a northern casemaker caddisfly
Homoplectra doringa, a homoplectran caddisfly
Pycnopsyche rossi, a northern casemaker caddisfly
Setodes oligius, a caddisfly
Merope tuber, earwig scorpionfly

OTHER INVERTEBRATE GROUPS

Apocthonius indianensis, cave pseudoscorpion
Arrhopalites bimus, springtail
Chthonius virginicus, pseudoscorpion
Hesperochernes mirabilis, cave pseudoscorpion
Porhomma cavernicola, cave spider
Pseudopolydesmus collinus, millipede
Pseudotremia nefanda, cave millipede
Sinella alata, springtail
Sphalloplana chandleri, Chandler's Cave flatworm

Vertebrate Animals
FISHES

Acipenser fulvescens, lake sturgeon
Amblyopsis spelaea, northern cavefish
Clinostomus elongatus, redside dace
Etheostoma camurum, bluebreast darter
Etheostoma histrio, harlequin darter
Etheostoma maculatum, spotted darter
Etheostoma squamiceps, spottail darter
Etheostoma tippecanoe, Tippecanoe darter
Etheostoma variatum, variegate darter
Notropis ariommus, popeye shiner
Percina evides, gilt darter
Typhlichthys subterraneus, southern cavefish

AMPHIBIANS

Aneides aneus, green salamander
Cryptobranchus alleganiensis, hellbender
Pseudotriton ruber, northern red salamander

REPTILES

Emydoidea blandingii, Blanding's turtle
Macroclemys temminckii, alligator snapping turtle
Pseudemys concinna hieroglyphica, hieroglyphic turtle

BIRDS

Aimophila aestivalis, Bachman's sparrow
Ardea albus, great egret
Asio flammeus, short-eared owl
Bartramia longicauda, upland sandpiper
Botaurus lentiginosus, American bittern
Charadrius melodus, piping plover
Chlidonias niger, black tern
Circus cyaneus, northern harrier
Cistothorus palustris, marsh wren
Cygnus buccinator, trumpeter swan
Dendroica kirtlandii, Kirtland's warbler
Falco peregrinus, peregrine falcon
Grus canadensis, sandhill crane
Haliaeetus leucocephalus, bald eagle
Ixobrychus exilis, least bittern
Lanius ludovicianus, loggerhead shrike
Nyctanassa violaceus, yellow-crowned night-heron
Nycticorax nycticorax, black-crowned night-heron
Pandion haliaetus, osprey
Rallus elegans, king rail
Sterna antillarum, interior least tern
Thryomanes bewickii, Bewick's wren
Tyto alba, barn owl
Vermivora chrysoptera, golden-winged warbler
Xanthocephalus xanthocephalus, yellow-headed blackbird

MAMMALS

Lutra canadensis, northern river otter
Lynx rufus, bobcat
Myotis austroriparius, southeastern myotis
Myotis grisescens, gray myotis
Myotis sodalis, Indiana or social myotis
Nycticeius humeralis, evening bat
Sylvilagus aquaticus, swamp rabbit

D. Glossary

ABSCISIC ACID. A plant hormone which, among other effects, brings about dormancy in buds.

ABSCISSION LAYER. A specialized zone at the base of a leaf stalk which permits a leaf to drop off with minimal damage to the stem.

ACROCARPUS. An erect, cushion-forming growth form typical of certain moss species.

AGAR. Substance derived from red algae used to make gel-like growth medium for microorganisms.

ALGAE (SG. ALGA). Usually aquatic unicellular or multicellular plants.

ALKALOID. A class of complex nitrogen-containing molecules produced by plants; they alter the physiological state of animals, often have bitter taste, and in some cases are very poisonous. Familiar examples include caffeine, morphine, and nicotine.

ALLUVIUM. Material deposited by a stream in relatively recent time.

ANAEROBE. An organism occurring in or living in conditions without free oxygen.

ANGIOSPERMS. Flowering plants that reproduce by bearing fruits with seeds enclosed by an ovary wall.

ANNUAL. A plant that completes its life cycle in one year.

APICAL MERISTEM. A growth point located at the tip of a shoot or a root which, through active cell division, allows these organs to grow in length.

APOTHECIUM (PL. -IA). Colored reproductive structures typical of certain lichen and sac fungi species.

AQUIFER. A body of rock, sand, or gravel located below the Earth's surface that contains sufficient saturated, permeable material to conduct groundwater to wells and springs.

ARAGONITE. A crystalline form of calcite that has a greater density and hardness, and may have a fibrous appearance. SEE CALCITE.

ARBOREAL. Of or pertaining to trees or tree-like; of animals that live in or spend time in trees.

ARBORETUM. A tract of land where woody plants are grown for scientific or educational purposes.

ARCHAEOLOGICAL SITE. A concentration of artifacts and/or features such as pits, mounds, or houses or other residue of earlier human activity.

ARTIFACT. An article made by humans for their use.

ATP. Adenosine triphosphate, a nucleotide molecule that can temporarily store energy.

AUXIN. A category of plant hormone which, among other responses, regulates cell elongation.

BACKSLOPE. The linear, steepest part of a hillslope profile of a landscape.

BARRENS. A small area of prairie vegetation surrounded by forest.

BASIDIUM. Specialized cells upon which spores are formed in the club fungi.

BEDROCK AQUIFER. Saturated consolidated or bedrock formations which yield water in sufficient quantity to be of consequence as a source of supply.

BEVEL. A large land surface that slopes downward from a plain.

BIENNIAL. A plant that lives for two years, producing only leaves the first year and flowers and seeds the second.

BIODIVERSITY. A basic environmental value dependent on the number and variety of living forms present.

BIOLUMINESCENCE. The emission of light by certain living organisms.

BIOME. A major ecological community type of landscape size, with a similar life form of vegetation throughout and having a distinctive type of climate, soil, and fauna.

BIOMONITOR. An organism or group of organisms whose condition or growth is used to assay the environmental conditions where they are living or planted.

BOG. A wetland occupying a depressional area, typically with acid, peaty soils, often with a floating mat of peat moss and low heath shrubs. Typically a stage in the successional changes which result in the filling in of a pond or small lake.

BOREAL FOREST. Coniferous forest dominated by spruce and fir, circumpolar at high latitudes in Canada, Alaska, Russia, and Scandinavia.

BRACHIOPOD. One of a class of fossil bivalve invertebrates with tentacles. They characterize much of the Paleozoic era.

BRYOLOGY. The branch of botany that deals with mosses, liverworts, and related species.

BRYOZOANS. Aquatic "moss-like" animals (mostly marine) which usually occur in colonies and reproduce primarily asexually by budding.

CADDISFLIES. Moth-like insects belonging to the order Trichoptera, usually with aquatic larval forms in stream habitats.

CALCIPHILE. An organism, usually a plant, that grows best in soils or waters that are rich in calcium, hence at neutral or slightly basic pH levels.

CALCITE. The principal constituent of limestone ($CaCO_3$ or calcium carbonate). It is usually white or colorless and dissolves in dilute acid.

CAMBRIAN. The earliest geological period of the Paleozoic era, beginning some 570 million years ago and continuing for some 70 million years. Abundant, conspicuous fossils present.

CANAL. An artificial waterway for transportation or navigation, or for draining or irrigating land.

CAPSULE. Spore-producing structure in mosses, liverworts, and hornworts.

CARNIVORE. An animal that nourishes itself by feeding on other animals.

CAROTENOID. A group of yellow to orange plant pigments.

CARPEL. The female organ of a flower which contains immature seeds and develops into a fruit. An individual section of a compound ovary of a plant.

CATENA. A sequence of soils that differ in relief and drainage but are otherwise similar.

CELLULOSE. A complex carbohydrate found in plant cell walls.

CENOZOIC. The most recent era of the geological time scale, beginning some 65 million years ago and continuing through the present.

CHERT. A crystalline form of quartz common in limestone bedrock formations used by primitive humans to make chipped stone tools (sometimes referred to as flint).

CHIRONOMIDS. Winged insects (midges, gnats) belonging to the order Diptera and the family Chironomidae.

CHITIN. Material forming the walls of most fungi and a main component of arthropod exoskeletons.

CHLOROPHYLL. The green pigment of plant cells which absorbs light energy in photosynthesis.

CHLOROPLAST. A plant cellular organelle which houses the biochemical machinery of photosynthesis.

CLASSIFICATION. Placing organisms into a taxonomic hierarchy according to their natural relationships.

CLASSIFIED FOREST ACT. Legislation passed in Indiana which gives landowners the option of classifying their forested tracts of 10 acres or more. In return, their property tax assessed valuation on the classified land may be reduced to $1 per acre per year.

CLASSIFIED WILDLIFE HABITAT. Tracts of land of more than 10 acres in size which are designated for wildlife species in Indiana. Owners receive a property tax reduction to $1 assessed evaluation per acre per year.

CLAY. Weathered rock fragments that are less than 0.02 mm in diameter. The major mineral constituent of clay and clay-loam soils.

CLEISTOGAMY. The process of self-pollination within an unopened flower.

CLIMATE. The average weather conditions of an area.

CLIMAX. The relatively stable association (community) of plants and animals that represents the final stage of succession under existing conditions of soil and climate.

CLOVIS POINT. A rather finely detailed stone projectile point produced by early Native Americans. First recovered near Clovis, New Mexico.

COMMENSALISM. A species interaction in which one member is helped and the other neither gains nor suffers.

COMMUNITY. All the plants and animals in a given habitat considered as an ecological unit.

CONDUIT. An underground passage that is completely filled with water.

CONIDIUM (PL. -IA). An asexual spore produced by certain fungi.

CONIFER FORESTS. Needle-leaved evergreen forests whose trees usually reproduce by bearing uncovered seeds on cones with woody scales.

CONSERVATION. Policy and action toward sustainability of natural resources (if renewable), or the most prudent long-range management (if non-renewable); the best management, whether through single or multiple "highest use," or else permanent preservation against destructive and inappropriate types of use.

CONTINUUM (PL. -UA). A gradient of change in species composition as related to habitat differences.

CONTOUR MAP (TOPOGRAPHIC). Map on which points of equal elevation above sea level are connected by contour lines. The contour interval is the vertical distance between contour lines.

COPPICE. A thicket or dense grove of small trees.

COTYLEDON. A seed leaf.

CRETACEOUS. The last period of the Mesozoic era, beginning some 135 million years ago and continuing some 70 million years until the beginning of the Cenozoic, when massive extinctions occurred.

CRUSTOSE LICHEN. Type of lichen that forms a thin, flat crust strongly attached to the surface on which it is growing.

CRYPTOGAM. Any non-flowering plant; spore producers.

CULEX PIPIENS. The species of mosquito which spreads a variety of encephalitis.

DECIDUOUS FOREST. A forest of predominantly broad-leaved trees which shed their leaves during a season unfavorable to growth, usually a cold or dry season.

DECOMPOSER (DETRITIVORE). An organism that lives on decaying organic matter.

DEPARTMENT OF CONSERVATION. The precursor of Indiana's present Department of Natural Resources. Its several branches are termed divisions, e.g., the Division of State Parks, Forestry, or Nature Preserves.

DEVELOPMENT. The opposite of preservation, development replaces natural scenes and features with artificial works.

DEVONIAN. Period of the Paleozoic era of the geological time scale which is between the Silurian and the Mississippian periods, spanning some 50 million years and beginning ca. 400 million years before the present.

DICOT (DICOTYLEDON). Common name for one of the two major classes of flowering plants characterized by, among other things, the presence of two cotyledons in the embryo.

DISCONFORMITY. A situation in which geological strata do not occupy the expected time sequence or pattern, e.g., older rocks overlying younger rocks.

DISJUNCT. Disconnected from the main body or structure, especially a small segment of a population separated at some distance from its main geographic range.

DRIFT. SEE GLACIAL DRIFT.

DUNE. Hill, mound, or ridge of wind-deposited sand. Dunes in Indiana take many forms, from the large parabolic dunes along the shore of Lake Michigan to the small crescentic forms that dot the sand plain south of the Kankakee River or parts of southwestern Indiana.

ECOLOGY. A biological science (not a sociopolitical movement) which deals with the structures and functions of nature.

ECOSYSTEM. A natural unit, ranging in size from microscopic to planetary units, comprising non-living and living parts functioning through interrelationships. Ecosystems are the basic units of ecological study.

ELECTROFISHING. A fish sampling and collecting technique that stuns fish by sending an electric current through the water surrounding a specially equipped boat.

END MORAINE. Ridge-like accumulation of till and gravel that marks the maximum of a glacial advance or a position of stillstand of the glacier margin.

ENDANGERED. A species vulnerable to elimination from the area in question. In Indiana, rare species present at five or fewer locations.

ENDEMIC. Native or confined naturally to a particular and usually restricted geographical area or region.

ENVIRONMENT. All external conditions affecting a living organism.

ENVIRONMENTALISM. The attitude and practice of respectful collaboration with the natural world for the benefit of both humans and nature.

EOCENE. An epoch of the Cenozoic era of geologic time, beginning some 55 million years ago and continuing for some 16 million years.

EOLIAN SAND. Wind-blown sand.

EPHEMERAL. Short-lived.

EPIPHYTE. A plant that grows upon another plant.

EPSOM SALTS. A chemical (hydrated magnesium sulfate) that occurs as a bitter, crystalline salt with cathartic properties.

EQUABLE CLIMATE. A rather stable period of Earth's history during which the climate is relatively unchanging.

ERRATIC (GLACIAL). A large boulder transported by glacial ice far south of its point of origin.

ESCARPMENT. Steep face or topographic rise that marks the edge or boundary of a plateau or upland, and that separates the upland from an adjacent topographically lower area.

ESTUARY. A coastal area of the sea where salt and fresh water mix.

EUTROPHICATION. Natural aging and death of a lake or pond; may be speeded up by pollution input.

EXOTIC. Non-native, introduced from a foreign country or area.

EXTINCT. Refers to species of organisms which have been eliminated as living entities from the global environment, but which may remain as fossils or other preserved forms.

EXTIRPATED. Refers to a species removed from a portion of its natural distribution range, but still occurring elsewhere. Black bear are extirpated from Indiana.

FAUNA. The animal life of an area of habitat considered collectively.

FEN. A sloping wetland usually associated with neutral to calcareous soils, characterized by flowing groundwater and vegetated largely by herbaceous species.

FILAMENTOUS. Occurring in long thread-like strands. Descriptive of certain algal species.

FITNESS. The ability of an organism to place copies of its genome into the next generation; the capability of reproducing offspring into a later generation.

FLATWOODS. Relatively level forested areas that have water tables at or above the ground surface for part or all of the year.

FLOODPLAIN. A nearly level alluvial plain that borders a river and is subject to flooding.

FLORA. A taxonomic listing of the plant species that occur in a given area.

FOLIOSE. A flattened (leaf-like) growth form of an alga or lichen which is loosely or sparingly attached to substrate.

FOOTSLOPE. The concave lower part of a hillslope profile.

FORB. A broad-leafed herbaceous plant, i.e., not a grass, sedge, or rush.

FOSSILS. Impressions, traces, or actual preserved plant or animal remains contained within layers of the Earth's crust.

FOSSORIAL. Burrowing underground or fitted for digging, e.g., a mole or badger.

FRAGIPAN. A weakly cemented subsoil horizon (frequently high in clay) that retards water movement and root growth.

FRAGMENTATION. Form of asexual reproduction in which a part of an organism breaks off and grows into a new organism.

FROND. Fern leaf.

FRONT (WEATHER). The forward boundary of a moving weather system, e.g., a warm front.

FRUTICOSE LICHEN. A lichen with a branched and usually upright shrubby growth form.

FUNGUS (PL. FUNGI). Spore producer that obtains its food from other organisms, as either a decomposer or a parasite.

GAMETE. Sex cell; sperm or egg.

GAMETOPHYTE. In the alternation of generations in plants, the generation (plant structure) that bears sex organs, hence the gametes or sex cells for reproduction.

GENUS (PL. GENERA). Taxonomic classification unit into which similar species are grouped; e.g., *Quercus* is the genus containing several oak species.

GEODE. A stone nodule usually with a cavity lined with crystals or minerals.

GEOMORPHOLOGY. Study of the genesis and evolution of landforms. Geomorphology stresses the processes by which landforms are created. CF. PHYSIOGRAPHY.

GEOPHYSICAL STUDIES. The sciences treating the agencies that cause alteration of the Earth's crust over geologic time.

GLACIAL DRIFT. A composite term for all glacial materials collectively. Glacial till and outwash combined.

GLACIATION. The occurrence and impact of glacial ice masses on the Earth's surface or surrounding waters.

GLACIER. A large mass of ice formed, at least in part, on land by the compaction and crystallization of snow, moving slowly downslope or outward in all directions as a result of the stress of its own weight, and surviving from year to year.

GLADE. An open area in a forest, vegetated by herbaceous plants, usually having thin soils over rocky substrates.

GONDWANALAND. The enormous combined landmass of the Southern Hemisphere prior to continental breakup and the resultant shifts in continental positions.

GRANITE. Hard, crystalline rock of igneous origin, high in quartz content.

GRAVEL. Loose rounded rock fragments of pebble size, usually shaped and deposited by glacial ice or flowing water.

GROUND MORAINE. An extensive undulating plain underlain by till (similar to till plain).

GROUNDWATER. Water in the ground that is in the zone of saturation, from which wells, springs, and groundwater runoff are supplied.

GYMNOSPERMS. A group of plants, largely coniferous trees, that reproduce by having naked seeds, i.e., not enclosed in an ovary wall.

HABITAT. The natural location, home, or haunt of a plant or animal where it carries out its life functions.

HERBACEOUS. A condition of plants that have a soft, rather than woody, stem.

HERBARIUM. A collection of dried plants preserved for educational purposes and scientific study; also the building where the plants are kept.

HERPETOFAUNA. The amphibians and reptiles found in a given geographic or ecologic area.

HERPETOLOGIST. A biologist specializing in the study of amphibians and reptiles.

HIBERNACULUM (PL. -ULA). A protected hiding place in which an organism (or a group of organisms) rests during hibernation.

HUMIC ACID. Acidic, organic matter extracted from soils and decayed plant substances.

HYBRIDIZATION. The process of crossing individuals with different genetic makeup.

HYDROLOGIC CYCLE. The constant circulation of water from the sea, through the atmosphere, to the land and its eventual return to the atmosphere or to the sea by way of evapotranspiration from plants, sea and land surfaces, or by runoff from the land surfaces.

HYDROPHYTE. A plant that grows in water or in saturated soil.

HYPANTHIUM. An expanded fleshy disk surrounding the carpels in certain plant families, e.g., the rose family.

HYPHA (PL. -AE). Growth form of a fungus that is thread-like.

ICE AGE. A time of glaciation, especially during the Pleistocene epoch of the past 2 to 3 million years.

ICE-BLOCK DEPRESSION. Closed or semi-closed depression in glacial terrane formed by the incorporation of a large block of ice in till or outwash deposits. Subsequent melting of that ice results in a lake of glacial origin.

IDENTIFICATION. Determining the name (identity) of a kind of organism, usually by using taxonomic keys to species.

ILLINOIAN GLACIATION. The period of the Pleistocene prior to the Wisconsinan glacial advances and retreats, during which time ice masses extended to the present Ohio River Valley. From about 110,000 to 220,000 years before the present.

INDIANA ACADEMY OF SCIENCE. A society founded in 1885 for the encouragement, study, and dissemination of scientific information in and about Indiana. Not to be confused with the Indiana Academy, which is not a scientific organization.

INTERGLACIAL PERIOD. A warm period between stages of glacial advance during which glacial recession and revegetation of glaciated landscapes occur.

INVERTEBRATES. A collective term for all of the animal groups which do not possess a vertebral column as a central structural support feature.

ISLAND HILL. Isolated bedrock-cored hill that is surrounded by flat areas underlain by outwash or lake deposits. Named for the town of Island, Kentucky.

JOINT. A fracture or parting of rock in which the rock shows no displacement or movement.

KAME. Isolated hill of gravel, sand, and till-like sediment formed where a meltwater stream plunged from the surface of a glacier. The sand and gravel, deposited in fan-like form against the face of the ice, are left in relief as the ice melts.

KARST. Landscape characterized by features such as caves, sinkholes, and sinking streams formed by solution of limestone bedrock. Named for a region in Slovenia where such features are prominent.

KETTLE LAKE. Lake of glacial origin, usually somewhat circular and formed as an ice block within the glacial till melts and fills the depression.

LACUSTRINE DEPOSIT. Fine-textured material deposited by slowly moving or still water.

LAKE PLAIN. A nearly level surface formed by filling in a lake with fine-textured material.

LAMELLAE. Thin subsoil horizons, or bands, in which clay has accumulated, usually in sandy soils.

LENTIC HABITATS. Standing bodies of water in nature, e.g., ponds and lakes.

LIMESTONE. A sedimentary rock consisting mainly of calcium carbonate (lime).

LITERARY NATURALISTS. Writers whose work is not to discover new principles and facts, but to popularize already known outdoor science for the reading public.

LITTLE ICE AGE. A colder period of weather in the late sixteenth and early seventeenth centuries during which mountain glaciers advanced and winters were much more severe than in previous decades.

LOESS. Wind-blown deposits consisting mainly of silt-size grains.

LOTIC HABITATS. Bodies of flowing water in nature, e.g., streams and rivers.

MARL. A limy mud deposited in certain lakes or seas that is chiefly clay mixed with calcium carbonate, often from shells of minute marine animals.

MARSH. A usually shallow wetland dominated by herbaceous plants such as cattails, sedges, reeds, and rushes.

MEANDER. Periodic or regular loop-like bend in the course of a river. Named for a river in western Turkey.

MEGASPORE. In seed plants, the cell that forms the stage that produces the female gametes.

MELTWATER. Outflow water from thawing glacial ice.

MESIC. A condition of intermediate moisture; used in describing habitats or species characteristic of such conditions.

MESOZOIC ERA. The geologic time period spanning some 160 million years from about 225 to 65 million years ago. Characterized by a large reptilian fauna.

MICROCLIMATE. Local climates, usually near the surfaces of landscape or vegetation, that are either less extreme or more extreme than the surrounding macroclimate.

MICROSPORE. In seed plants, the cell that is transformed into the pollen grain.

MIMESIS. The imitation of sights, sounds, or conditions of nature.

MIOCENE. An epoch of the Cenozoic era of geologic time, beginning some 25 million years ago and continuing for about 20 million years.

MISSISSIPPIAN. Period of the Paleozoic era of the geologic time scale which lies between the Devonian and Pennsylvanian periods. Characterized by warm, wet climates conducive to the growth of Coal Age forests.

MONOCOT (MONOCOTYLEDON). Common name for one of the two major classes of flowering plants characterized, among other things, by the presence of a single cotyledon in the embryo.

MORAINE. Material deposited by a glacier near its margin and composed of sand, gravel, or loam type soils.

MORPHOLOGY. The study of structure and form.

MUCK. Highly decomposed organic soil material in which the original plant parts are not recognizable.

MUTUALISM. An interaction between two species from which both derive benefit.

MYCELIUM (PL. -IA). The mass of thread-like filaments that make up the vegetative portion of the body of a fungus.

MYCORRHIZA (PL. -AE). The symbiotic association of the mycelium of a fungus and vascular plant roots, important in water and nutrient uptake by the plant.

NATIONAL NATURAL LANDMARK. A tract of land, usually privately owned, which the National Park Service officially recognizes in its landmark program as having exceptional natural quality, and thus national significance.

NATURAL AREA. An outdoor site, regardless of ownership, which contains an unusual biological, geological, or scenic feature, or else illustrates common ecological principles uncommonly well.

NATURAL AREAS REGISTRY. A listing of natural areas, including ecological and ownership information for use in tracking the security of non-protected sites, usually in private ownership.

NATURE PRESERVE. A natural area which is formally or officially designated as permanently protected by a private, institutional, or (usually) governmental owner.

NEW HARMONY. An exceptionally historic Wabash River town near Harmonie State Park.

NEWT. Small semi-aquatic salamander. Males often have conspicuous tail fins. The group is best represented in Europe; there is one Indiana species.

NICHE. The total ecological role played by a species of organism in its environment: its habitat (where it lives) and profession (what it does).

NITROGEN FIXATION. The conversion of atmospheric nitrogen to forms (ammonium and nitrate) usable in biological processes.

OLD FIELD. Farm land, once cultivated, that is now abandoned and permitted to undergo natural succession.

OLIGOCENE EPOCH. An epoch of the Cenozoic era of geologic time, beginning about 38 million years ago and continuing for about 12 million years.

OMNIVOROUS. Eating both plant and animal food.

ORDOVICIAN. Period of the Paleozoic era of the geologic time scale between the Cambrian and Silurian periods. It began about 500 million years ago and continued for some 70 million years.

OUTWASH. Stratified material washed out from a glacier by meltwater and deposited beyond the margin of glacial ice.

OUTWASH PLAIN. A large, mostly nearly level area not confined in a river valley and composed of glacial outwash.

OXBOW LAKE. Crescent-shaped lake formed when a river cuts off part of a meander (which see) and abandons a part of its channel.

PALEOECOLOGY. The scientific study of the interactions of organisms and environments in the geologic past.

PALEOZOIC ERA. The earliest geologic time period whose rocks are characterized by abundant, conspicuous fossils. It began some 570 million years ago and continued nearly 350 million years, until the Mesozoic era.

PALUSTRINE. Of environments adjacent to or influenced by swamps and their immediate surroundings.

PALYNOLOGY. The science of reconstructing past natural communities and their associated environments by analysis of fossil pollens taken from bog or other sediments.

PANNE. A shallow interdunal pond closely associated with the Great Lakes.

PARASITISM. An interaction between species in which one species lives in or on another, from which it derives benefit, to the harm but usually not the immediate death of the other.

PCBs. Polychlorinated biphenyls, chemicals used as insulators in electrical transmission and other industrial uses. Serious contaminants of soils and waters.

PEAT. Slightly decayed plant material that accumulated in water.

PENNSYLVANIAN. Period of the Paleozoic era of the geologic time scale between the Mississippian and Permian periods. Characterized by a warm, wet climate conducive to forming coal deposits. Ended some 280 million years ago.

PERENNIAL. A plant that lives and produces flowers and seeds year after year.

PERMIAN. The most recent of the geologic periods of the Paleozoic era, beginning about 280 million years ago and continuing for some 55 million years to the beginning of the Mesozoic.

PHLOEM. The tissue responsible for sugar translocation in vascular plants.

PHOTOPERIOD. The cycle of light versus darkness, often used by organisms to time life-cycle events such as reproduction.

PHOTOSYNTHESIS. Production of carbohydrates by green plants from carbon dioxide and water in the presence of sunlight energy.

PHYSIOGRAPHY. Descriptive study of landforms. Physiography stresses the classification and physical shape of landforms. CF. GEOMORPHOLOGY.

PHYTOALEXIN. A toxic compound synthesized by plant cells in response to infection or injury.

PHYTOPLANKTON. Passively floating plants, largely algae, in bodies of water.

PINNACLE ROCK. A usually tall or spire-shaped rock remnant isolated from the main body of rock by erosion.

PISCIVOROUS. Of organisms that prey and feed upon fish.

PIT VIPERS. A major group of venomous snakes characterized by a pair of heat-sensing pits on the side of the head between the eye and nostril. Rattlesnakes are the best-known members of the group. This group includes all Indiana venomous snakes.

PLANOSOL. A soil, usually on rather flat topography, that has a clay layer below the surface which impedes normal internal drainage. CF. FRAGIPAN.

PLATE, NORTH AMERICAN. A crustal unit of the Earth's surface that contains most of the North American continent, and which is subject to tectonic movements.

PLEISTOCENE EPOCH. A geologic time period beginning some 2 to 3 million years ago. Its climate was characterized by lowered temperatures and elevated precipitation, culminating in several continental glacial advances.

PLETHODONT SALAMANDERS (PLETHODONTIDAE). Members of a salamander family whose most unusual feature is the absence of lungs and gills in the adult animal. Respiration takes place through the skin and mucous membranes of the mouth. These salamanders are largely restricted to North and Central America; there are several species in Indiana.

PLEUROCARPOUS. Of a trailing, much-branched, feathery growth form typical of certain moss species.

PLIOCENE EPOCH. A geological period just prior to the Pleistocene (which see), beginning some 7 to 8 million years ago and lasting for about 5 million years.

POLLEN PROFILE. A diagram showing the relative pollen composition of bog or lake sediments, arranged by depth, hence age.

POLYPLOID. An organism having more than the usual two sets of chromosomes in the nucleus of each cell.

PRAIRIE. An open, usually treeless area with its vegetation composed primarily of grasses and wildflowers.

PRECAMBRIAN. The whole of geological time prior to the Cambrian period, which began some 570 million years ago. Characterized by only primitive life and the general absence of fossils.

PREDATOR. An animal that eats other organisms to obtain nourishment.

PROTHALLUS. Small, heart-shaped gamete-forming stage of ferns.

PTERIDOLOGY. The science or study of ferns and their allies.

RADIOCARBON DATING. A dating technique based on the amount of radioactive carbon (C^{14}) left in organic materials such as charcoal or plant remains.

RARE. Said of a species of organism that occurs in a few widely separated clumps or singly as a thin scatter.

REEF. A chain of bedrock deposits formed in marine environments. May be the result of growth of corals and other marine animals, or sediments becoming cemented into solid rock.

RELICT. A population or community of organisms that persists in favorable microclimates long after the preferred regional climate has changed.

RESERVOIR. An artificial lake where water is impounded by a constructed levee and kept in quantity for use.

RETICULATED BEETLES. Primitive beetles belonging to the family Cupedidae.

RHIZOIDS. In ferns and bryophytes, the root-like filaments that anchor the plant and also provide absorption.

RHIZOME. A horizontal underground stem of a plant.

RIPARIAN. Pertaining to or occupying riverbanks, especially vegetation.

RIVERINE. Of habitats adjacent to or influenced by a larger stream and its immediate surroundings.

ROSETTE. A cluster of leaves growing at the surface of the soil.

RUST. Type of club fungi that are often serious pathogens of crops; they have a complex life cycle often involving alternate hosts.

SALEM LIMESTONE. Limestone prevalent in Mississippian-age rock strata of southern Indiana, having excellent qualities for building construction.

SALMONELLA. A group of bacteria widespread in nature. Typically they inhabit the intestinal tracts of many kinds of animals, including reptiles. In humans they commonly cause food poisoning, and occasionally more serious infections such as typhoid fever.

SALTPETER. A chemical (potassium nitrate) that can be found in unconsolidated cave deposits. It is used for preserving meat and in the manufacture of gunpowder.

SAMARA. A type of winged dry fruit.

SAND. Weathered rock fragments usually in the size range of 0.2 to 2 mm in diameter. Typically worked and deposited by moving water and wind.

SANDSTONE. Sedimentary rock containing mainly sand-size particles.

SAPROPHYTE (SAPROBE). Any organism that derives nourishment from dead or decaying organisms.

SAPWOOD. The outer wood layers of a tree trunk in which active water transport occurs.

SAVANNA. An area of predominantly prairie mixed with scattered individual trees or groves of trees. Vegetation is transitional in type between grassland and forest.

SCHISTOSOMIASIS. A waterborne disease caused by trematodes (certain flatworms) infesting the liver and the digestive and urinary tracts.

SCORPIONFLIES. Insects belonging to the order Mecoptera.

SEED POOL. A reservoir of dormant seeds stored in soil. Also frequently called a seed bank.

SEICHE. An oscillation of the surface of a lake or landlocked sea, varying in periodicity from a few minutes to a few hours.

SHALE. Sedimentary rock containing mainly clay-size particles.

SHOULDER. The convex part of a hillslope profile of a landscape; it occurs between the summit and the backslope.

SHRUB. A low (usually less than 3m tall) woody plant, usually several-stemmed; a bush.

SILT. Weathered rock fragments usually in the size range of 0.02 to 0.2 mm in diameter. Frequently becomes wind-blown and deposited as loess (which see).

SILTSTONE. Sedimentary rock containing mainly silt-size particles.

SILURIAN. Period of the Paleozoic era of the geologic time scale between the Ordovician and Devonian periods. Began about 430 million years ago and continued for about 35 million years.

SINKHOLE. In limestone terrain, a somewhat circular depression in the ground formed by subsidence of soil as the soil collapses into solution-formed openings in the underlying bedrock. The depression may hold water, either perennially or seasonally.

SLACKWATER LAKE. Lake formed in a valley tributary to a major outwash-carrying stream. The lake level rises slowly as coarse sediment builds up in the main valley. Fine-grained sediments are deposited in the lake.

SLIME MOLD. A fungus of the myxomycete group, some of which are capable of movement.

SMUT. Type of club fungi that can be serious plant pathogens; has a relatively simple life cycle.

SOIL HORIZON. A layer of soil with distinctive properties.

SOIL PARENT MATERIAL. The material from which a soil forms, usually mineral material but also organic material (peat and muck).

SOLUTION. A process of chemical weathering of rock in which a rock material is dissolved.

SORUS (PL. -I). In ferns, a small cluster of spore-containing structures (sporangia) variously situated on the fronds (leaves), or in terminal clusters.

SPECIES. A population of similar individual organisms that are usually capable of gene exchange (reproduction) among component members, but which usually do not reproduce with other such populations. The evolutionary unit in nature.

SPECIES EPITHET. The scientific name of an organism; a binomial composed of genus and species names.

SPORE. A one-celled reproductive structure (or resistant resting cells) produced by non-flowering plants, fungi, and certain protozoans.

SPOROPHYTE. In plants with alternation of generations, the individual or generation that bears asexual spores.

SPRINGTAILS. Hexapods belonging to the Order Collembola. These arthropods are usually considered insects even though technically they are not. They possess an abdominal appendage which enables them to "hop."

SQUAMULOSE. Of a lichen growth form that is similar to foliose but with numerous small scales (squamules).

STAMEN. The male, pollen-producing organ of a flower.

STEWARDSHIP. The care, protection, and management of natural lands to afford the best long-term preservation possible.

STIGMA. In a flower, the pollen-receptive surface of a carpel.

STIPULES. Small, often leaf-like appendages at the base of the leaf stalk in many kinds of flowering plants.

STOMATA. Gas-exchange pores in the epidermis of leaves and young stems.

STONEFLIES. Insects belonging to the order Plecoptera.

STRATIGRAPHY. The arrangement of layers of geological materials. The area of geology that studies layering, its processes, and effects on landforms.

STRIDULATE. To make a noise by rubbing two structures together.

SUCCESSION. A natural sequence of change in which one community of plant and animal life gradually replaces another, often trending toward a more stable natural order and greater diversity.

SUMMIT. The highest part of a hillslope profile of a landscape.

SURFACE WATER. All waters on the surface of the Earth, including fresh and salt water, ice, and snow.

SUSTAINABILITY. The quality of management or protection of natural resources which enables them to maintain long-term existence and usefulness without deterioration.

SWALE. A slight depression in the midst of generally level land.

SWAMP. A shallow wetland dominated by trees rather than by marsh or bog herbs and shrubs. Indiana examples are tamarack swamps in the north and bald cypress swamps in the south.

SWELL. A slight rise in the midst of generally level land.

SWELL AND SWALE TOPOGRAPHY. An area composed of alternating linear wetlands and uplands, typically found at the southern end of Lake Michigan or across the Central Till Plain.

SYMBIOSIS. An ecological relationship between organisms of two different species that live together in direct contact.

TAXONOMY. The science of classification of plants and animals according to their natural relationships.

TECTONICS. The area of geology concerned with large-scale movements of the Earth's crust.

TERRACE. A step-like surface in a valley, usually composed of outwash.

TERRESTRIAL. Of the land; growing on land.

TERTIARY PERIOD. Geological period which comprises most of the Cenozoic era. The Tertiary began some 65 million years ago and continued for more than 60 million years.

THALLUS (PL. -I). The entire body of a plant that lacks roots, stems, and leaves.

THERMOCLINE. A zone of rapid temperature change in a body of standing water.

THREATENED. Said of species that occur at few locations (10 or fewer in Indiana) or are declining in numbers. Often moving toward endangered status.

TILL. Non-sorted, non-stratified sediment deposited by a glacier.

TILL PLAIN. Broad, relatively flat to undulating land surface formed by glacial deposition of till (which see). The flat till deposit itself sometimes is called ground moraine.

TOESLOPE. The lowest part of a hillslope profile, on alluvial fill.

TOPOGRAPHY. The shape or configuration of a landscape including its relief, location of streams, valleys, landforms, lakes, and other features.

TRILOBITE. Any of several of the extinct groups of segmented fossil arthropods of the Paleozoic era.

TRIPLOID (POLYPLOID). An organism having three sets of chromosomes in the nucleus of its cells, instead of the usual two. Polyploids may have more than three sets.

TUFA. A crusty, porous limestone rock, usually formed as a deposit from springs or streams flowing from limy soils or substrates.

TUNDRA. Relatively level plains north of the tree line, or alpine areas above the timberline. Characterized by low-growing, largely herbaceous vegetation, cold, damp climates, and very short growth seasons.

TUNNEL VALLEY. Topographic valley formed by a meltwater stream that flowed beneath the ice or in an ice-walled open channel near the margin of a glacier. Within and alongside the valley are complex deposits of outwash and till-like sediment deposited by the wasting glacier and its meltwater.

UNCONSOLIDATED AQUIFER. Sediment that is loosely arranged or unstratified, whose particles are not cemented together, which yields water in sufficient quantity to be of consequence as a source of supply.

VALLEY TRAIN. Sorted glacial outwash materials deposited in a valley and often extending for some distance.

VASCULAR CAMBIUM. The growth layer in the stem of a tree that produces new wood and inner bark.

VEGETATION. The display that the plant life of an area makes collectively.

VERTEBRATES. Animals characterized by having a spinal column (backbone) as their central internal structural feature.

WETLAND. Land area where the soil is saturated or inundated for a significant part of the year.

WHIRLIGIG BEETLES. Insects belonging to the family Gyrinidae.

WILDERNESS. A large land (usually) or water area, relatively remote from developments and other human disturbance, and supporting large plant-eating animals together with some species of their large natural predators.

WISCONSINAN GLACIATION. The most recent series of glacial advances and retreats that affected Indiana and the Midwest. Generally believed to have occurred within the past 110,000 years, last evacuating Indiana about 10,000 years before the present.

XEROPHYTES. Plants typical of dry habitats, or plants having characteristics which retard water loss or desiccation.

XEROTHERMIC. A warm, dry interglacial period between 6,000 and 3,000 years ago, during which time the tallgrass prairie likely migrated eastward into western Indiana.

XYLEM. The water and mineral conducting tissue of a vascular plant.

ZOOPLANKTON. Passively floating or weakly swimming small animals living in water.

E. Suggested Readings

GENERAL REFERENCE

Blatchley, W. S. 1912. Woodland Idylls. Indianapolis: The Nature Publishing Co. 242 pp.

Carson, Rachel. 1962. Silent Spring. Boston: Houghton Mifflin. 368 pp.

Doyle, Lynne. 1958. The Riddle of Genesis County. Boston: Houghton Mifflin. 171 pp.

Leopold, Aldo. 1949. A Sand County Almanac. New York: Oxford University Press. 295 pp.

Lindsey, A. A., ed. 1966. Natural Features of Indiana. Indianapolis: Indiana Academy of Science. 629 pp.

Lindsey, Alton A.; Damian V. Schmelz; and Stanley A. Nichols. 1970. Natural Areas in Indiana and Their Preservation. Indiana Natural Areas Survey, Department of Biological Sciences, Purdue University, Lafayette, IN. 594 pp.

Muir, John. 1965 (reprint). The Story of My Boyhood and Youth. Madison: University of Wisconsin Press. 246 pp.

Stratton-Porter, Gene. 1909. Girl of the Limberlost. Reprint, Bloomington: Indiana University Press.

Teale, Edwin Way. 1943. Dune Boy: The Early Years of a Naturalist. Reprint, Bloomington: Indiana University Press. 263 pp.

Watts, May Theilgaard. 1957. Reading the Landscape: An Adventure in Ecology. New York: Macmillan. 240 pp.

CONSERVATION—MANAGEMENT

Allen, Durward L. 1962. Our Wildlife Legacy. 2nd ed. New York: Funk and Wagnalls. 422 pp.

Barnes, William B. 1966. A Brief History of Fish and Game in Indiana. Indianapolis: Department of Natural Resources. 27 pp.

Brown, Lester R. 1996. State of the World: 1996. Washington, D.C.: Worldwatch Institute.

Favinger, John A. 1983–84. A History of Conservation in Indiana. Series in four issues of Outdoor Indiana:

Title	Vol. Number	Date	Pages
A Look Back	48	10 Dec. 1983	28–35
Resourceful Gain	49	1 Feb. 1984	26–33
A Time of Progress	49	2 Mar. 1984	28–36
Environmental Era	49	3 Apr. 1984	24–33

Latta, W. C. 1938. Outline History of Indiana Agriculture. West Lafayette: Alpha Lambda Chapter of Epsilon Sigma Phi and Purdue University. 372 pp.

Martin, Alexander C., et al. 1951. American Wildlife and Plants: A Guide to Wildlife Food Habits. New York: McGraw-Hill. Reprint, New York: Dover, 1961. 500 pp.

McReynolds, H. E., ed. 1976. Fish and Wildlife in Indiana, 1776–1976. Proceedings of the joint meeting of the American Fisheries Society and the Wildlife Society. Hoopeston, Ill.: Mills Publications. 87 pp.

Reiger, John F. 1986. American Sportsmen and the Origins of Conservation. Norman and London: University of Oklahoma Press. 316 pp.

ECOLOGY—INVASIONS

Elton, C. S. 1958. The Ecology of Invasion by Plants and Animals. New York: John Wiley and Sons. 181 pp.

McKnight, B. N. 1993. Biological Pollution: The Control and Impact of Invasive Exotic Species. Indianapolis: Indiana Academy of Science. 261 pp.

Nalepa, T. F., and D. W. Schloesser, eds. 1992. Zebra Mussels: Biology, Impacts, and Controls. Ann Arbor: Lewis Publishers.

GEOLOGY—SOILS

Burger, A. M.; C. B. Rexroad; A. F. Schneider; and R. H. Shaver. 1966. Excursions in Indiana Geology. Indiana Geological Survey Guidebook 12, Bloomington. 71 pp.

Bushnell, T. M. 1944. The Story of Indiana Soils. Purdue University Agricultural Experiment Station Special Circular. 52 pp.

Chamberlin, T. C. 1883. Preliminary Paper on the Terminal Moraine of the Second Glacial Epoch. U.S. Geological Survey Annual Report 3, pp. 291–402.

Franzmeier, D. P.; J. E. Yahner; G. C. Steinhardt; and D. G. Schulze. 1989. Understanding and Judging Indiana Soils. Purdue University Cooperative Extension Service, ID–72. 71 pp.

Hillel, Daniel. 1991. Out of the Earth. Berkeley: University of California Press. 321 pp.

Jenny, Hans. 1941. Factors of Soil Formation. New York: McGraw-Hill. 281 pp.

Kohnke, Helmut, and D. P. Franzmeier. 1995. Soil Science Simplified. Prospect Heights, Ill.: Waveland Press. 162 pp.

Leverett, Frank, and F. B. Taylor. 1915. The Pleistocene of Indiana and Michigan and the History of the Great Lakes. U.S. Geological Survey Monograph 53. 529 pp.

Malott, C. A. 1922. Handbook of Indiana Geology, Part II: Physiography of Indiana. Indiana Department of Conservation Publication 21, pp. 61–256.

Melhorn, W. N., and J. P. Kempton, eds. 1991. Geology and Hydrogeology of the Teays-Mahomet Bedrock Valley System. Geological Society of America Special Paper 258. 128 pp.

Mohr, Charles E., and Thomas L. Poulson. 1966. The Life of the Cave. New York: McGraw-Hill.

Owen, D. D. 1987. A Geological Reconnaissance and Survey of the State of Indiana in 1837 and 1838, with Introduction and Commentary by Henry H. Gray. Indiana Department of Natural Resources, Geological Survey, Bulletin 61. 121 pp.

Powell, Richard L. 1961. Caves of Indiana. Bloomington: Indiana Geological Survey.

ICE AGES

Hay, O. P. 1912. The Pleistocene Period and Its Vertebrata. Indiana Department of Geology and Natural Resources, 36th Annual Report, 1911, pp. 541–782.

Kurten, Bjorn. 1988. Before the Indians. New York: Columbia University Press. 158 pp.

Kurten, Bjorn, and Elaine Anderson. 1980. Pleistocene Mammals of North America. New York: Columbia University Press. 443 pp.

Martin, P. S., and R. G. Klein. 1985. Quaternary Extinctions: A Prehistoric Revolution. Tucson: University of Arizona Press.

Martin, P. S., and H. E. Wright, Jr. 1967. Pleistocene Extinctions: The Search for a Cause. New Haven: Yale University Press.

Richards, R. L. 1984. The Pleistocene Vertebrate Collection of the Indiana State Museum, with a List of the Extinct and Extralocal Pleistocene Vertebrates of Indiana. Proceedings of the Indiana Academy of Science 93: 483–504.

Shaver, Robert H. 1979. Geologic Story of the Lower Wabash Valley with

Emphasis on the New Harmony Area. Bloomington: Indiana Department of Natural Resources Geological Survey Occasional Paper no. 27. 14 pp.

Wayne, W. J. 1966. Ice and Land. In A. A. Lindsey, ed., Natural Features of Indiana, pp. 21–39. Indianapolis: Indiana Academy of Science. 600 pp.

Webb, T., III; E. J. Cushing; and H. E. Wright, Jr. 1983. Holocene Changes in the Vegetation of the Midwest. In H. E. Wright, Jr., ed., Late-Quaternary Environments of the United States, vol. 2: The Holocene, pp. 142–165. Minneapolis: University of Minnesota Press.

Whitehead, D. R.; S. T. Jackson; M. C. Sheehan; and B. W. Leyden. 1982. Late-Glacial Vegetation Associated with Caribou and Mastodon in Central Indiana. Quaternary Research 17: 241–257.

Williams, A. S. 1974. Late-Glacial–Postglacial Vegetational History of the Pretty Lake Region, Northeastern Indiana. Geological Survey Professional Paper 686-B.

INDIANA HISTORY

Baker, Ronald L., and Marvin Carmony. 1975. Indiana Place Names. Bloomington: Indiana University Press. 196 pp.

Barnhart, John D., and Dorothy L. Riker. 1971. Indiana to 1816: The Colonial Period. Indianapolis: Indiana Historical Bureau and Indiana Historical Society. 520 pp.

Buley, R. Carlyle. 1950. The Old Northwest: Pioneer Period, 1815–1840. Vols. 1 and 2. Bloomington: Indiana University Press.

Esarey, Logan. 1922. History of Indiana. New York: Harcourt, Brace and Co. 362 pp.

Flint, Timothy. 1828. A Condensed Geography and History of the Western States, or the Mississippi Valley. Vols. 1 and 2. Cincinnati: E. H. Flint.

———. 1832. The History and Geography of the Mississippi Valley. Vol. 1. 2nd ed. Cincinnati.

Gray, Ralph D., ed. 1989. The Hoosier State: Indiana Prehistory to the Civil War. Bloomington: Indiana University Press. 390 pp.

McCord, Shirley S. 1970. Travel Accounts of Indiana, 1679–1961. Indiana Historical Bureau. 331 pp.

Wilson, William E. 1964. The Angel and the Serpent: The Story of New Harmony. Bloomington: Indiana University Press. 256 pp.

INDIANA SCIENTISTS

Daily, William A., and Fay K. Daily. 1984. History of the Indiana Academy of Science, 1885–1984. Indianapolis: Indiana Academy of Science. 254 pp.

Jordan, David Starr. 1922. The Days of a Man. Vols. 1 and 2. Yonkers-on-Hudson: World Book. 1,672 pp.

Kriebel, Robert C. 1987. Plain Ol' Charlie Deam, Pioneer Hoosier Botanist. West Lafayette: Purdue University Press. 193 pp.

Visher, Stephen S. 1951. Indiana Scientists: A Biological Director and an Analysis. Indianapolis: Indiana Academy of Science. 294 pp.

INVERTEBRATES—INSECTS

Borror, D. J., and R. E. White. 1970. A Field Guide to the Insects. Boston: Houghton Mifflin Co.

Chandler, A. C. 1949. Introduction to Parasitology. 8th ed. New York: Wiley.

Cummings, K. S., et al. 1987. Survey of the Freshwater Mussels (Mollusca: Unionidae) of the Wabash River Drainage. Phase 1: Lower Wabash and Tippecanoe Rivers. Section of Faunistic Surveys and Insect Identification, Technical Report 1987 (5), Illinois Natural History Survey.

Evans, H. E. 1985. The Pleasures of Entomology. Washington, D.C.: Smithsonian Press.

Goodrich, C., and H. Vander Schalie. 1944. A Revision of the Mollusca of Indiana. American Midland Naturalist 32: 257–326.

Marquart, W. C., and Demaree, R. S. 1985. Parasitology. New York: Macmillan.

Meglitsch, P. A. 1972. Invertebrate Zoology. 2nd ed. New York: Oxford University Press.

Milne, Lorus, and Margery Milne. 1988. The Audubon Society Field Guide to North American Insects and Spiders. New York: Knopf.

Pennak, R. W. 1953. Fresh-water Invertebrates of the United States. St. Louis: Ronald.

Stratton-Porter, Gene. 1924. Moths of the Limberlost. New York: Doubleday Page & Co.

NATIVE AMERICANS

Black, Glenn A. 1967. Angel Site: An Archaeological, Historical, and Ethnological Study. Indianapolis: Indiana Historical Society.

Edmunds, R. David. 1978. The Potawatomis: Keepers of the Fire. The Civilization of American Indian Series. Norman: University of Oklahoma Press. 362 pp.

Hicks, Ronald, ed. 1992. Native American Cultures of Indiana: Proceedings of the First Minnetrista Council for Great Lakes Native American Studies. Muncie: Minnetrista Cultural Center and Ball State University.

Keller, James H. 1983. An Introduction to the Prehistory of Indiana. Indianapolis: Indiana Historical Society.

Lilly, Eli. 1937. Prehistoric Antiquities of Indiana. Indianapolis: Indiana Historical Society.

NATURAL REGIONS

Homoya, M. A.; D. B. Abrell; J. R. Aldrich; and T. W. Post. 1985. The Natural Regions of Indiana. Proceedings of the Indiana Academy of Science 94: 235–268.

PLANTS

Crum, H. A. 1983. Mosses of the Great Lakes Forest. 3rd ed. Ann Arbor: University of Michigan Herbarium.

———. 1991. Liverworts and Hornworts of Southern Michigan. Ann Arbor: University of Michigan Herbarium.

Deam, Charles C. 1929. Grasses of Indiana. Indianapolis: Indiana Department of Conservation. 356 pp.

———. 1932. Shrubs of Indiana. Indianapolis: Indiana Department of Conservation. 380 pp.

———. 1940. Flora of Indiana. Indianapolis: Indiana Department of Conservation. 1,236 pp.

Deam, Charles C., and Thomas E. Shaw. 1953. Trees of Indiana. 3rd ed. Indianapolis: Indiana Department of Conservation. 330 pp.

Galston, A. W. 1994. Life Processes of Plants. New York: Scientific American Library. 245 pp.

Grout, A. J. 1924. Mosses with a Hand-lens. 3rd ed. with Hepatics. New York: published by the author.

Homoya, Michael A. 1993. Orchids of Indiana. Bloomington: Indiana University Press. 276 pp.

Johnson, Hugh. 1973. The International Book of Trees. New York: Simon and Schuster. 288 pp.

Lellinger, D. B. 1985. A Field Manual of the Ferns and Fern-Allies of the United States and Canada. Washington, D.C.: Smithsonian Institution Press.

Pepoon, H. S. 1927. An Annotated Flora of the Chicago Area. Chicago: Chicago Academy of Sciences.

Prescott, G. W. 1964. How to Know the Freshwater Algae. 3rd ed. Dubuque, Iowa: Wm. C. Brown Co.

Radosevich, S. R., and J. S. Holt. 1984. Weed Ecology: Implications for Vegetation Management. New York: John Wiley and Sons. 265 pp.

Raven, P. H.; R. F. Evert; and S. E. Eichhorn. 1992. Biology of Plants. 5th ed. New York: Worth Publishers. 791 pp.

Swink, Floyd, and Gerould Wilhelm. 1994. Plants of the Chicago Region. Indianapolis: Indiana Academy of Science. 921 pp.

Welch, W. H. 1957. Mosses of Indiana. Indianapolis: Indiana Department of Conservation.

PROTECTION—PRESERVATION

Frederick, Robert A. 1960. Colonel Richard Lieber, Conservationist and Park Builder: The Indiana Years. Bloomington: Indiana University Press. 430 pp.

Lieber, Emma Rapport. 1947. Richard Lieber. Chicago: The Norman Press. 170 pp.

Michaud, Howard H. 1966. State Parks. In A. A. Lindsey, ed., Natural

Features of Indiana, pp. 561–581. Indianapolis: Indiana Academy of Science. 629 pp.

Shelford, Victor, ed. 1926. Naturalists' Guide to the Americas. Baltimore: Williams and Wilkins Co. 761 pp.

Whitaker, J. O., Jr., and J. R. Gammon. 1988. Endangered and Threatened Vertebrate Animals of Indiana: Their Distribution and Abundance. Indiana Academy of Science Monograph no. 5. Indianapolis. 122 pp.

VEGETATION—PLANT COMMUNITIES

Braun, E. L. 1950. Deciduous Forests of Eastern North America. New York: Hafner Publishing Co.

Lindsey, A. A.; W. B. Crankshaw; and S. A. Qadir. 1965. Soil Relations and Distribution Map of the Vegetation of Presettlement Indiana. Botanical Gazette 126: 155–163.

Madison, J. 1985. Where the Sky Began: Land of the Tallgrass Prairie. San Francisco: Sierra Club Books.

McCormick, Jack. 1959. The Living Forest. New York: Harper and Brothers. 127 pp.

Petty, R. O., and M. T. Jackson. 1966. Plant Communities. In A. A. Lindsey, ed., Natural Features of Indiana, pp. 264–296. Indianapolis: Indiana Academy of Science. 629 pp.

Petty, R. O., and T. Korling. 1974. Wild Plants in Flower: Deciduous Forest. Evanston, Ill.: Torkel Korling. 96 pp.

Transeau, E. N. 1935. The Prairie Peninsula. Ecology 16: 423–437.

Weaver, J. E. 1954. North America Prairie. Lincoln, Nebr.: Johnsen Publishing Company.

Wilhelm, G. 1990. Special Vegetation of the Indiana Dunes National Lakeshore. Midwest Region, National Park Service, Omaha, Nebraska.

VERTEBRATES

American Ornithologists' Union. 1983. Check-list of North American Birds. 6th ed. Washington, D.C.: American Ornithological Union.

Capula, M. 1989. Guide to Reptiles and Amphibians of the World. New York: Simon and Schuster.

Conant, R., and Collins, J. T. 1991. A Field Guide to Reptiles and Amphibians of Eastern and Central North America. Boston: Houghton Mifflin.

Freshwater Fishes. Peterson Field Guide Series.

Gerking, S. D. 1945. Distribution of Fishes in Indiana. Indiana Lakes and Streams 3(1): 1–137.

Halliday, T. R., and Adler, K., eds. 1986. The Encyclopedia of Reptiles and Amphibians. New York: Facts on File, Inc.

Jones, J. Knox, et al. 1986. Revised Checklist of North American Mammals North of Mexico, 1986. Occasional Papers, The Museum, Texas Tech University, no. 107. 22 pp.

Minton, S. A. Jr. 1972. Amphibians and Reptiles of Indiana. Indianapolis: Indiana Academy of Science Monograph no. 3. 346 pp.

Minton, S. A. Jr. 1996. Amphibians and Reptiles of Indiana. Indianapolis: Indiana Academy of Science. 346 pp.

Moyle, P. B. 1993. Fish: An Enthusiast's Guide. Berkeley: University of California Press.

Mumford, R. E., and J. O. Whitaker, Jr. 1982. The Mammals of Indiana. Bloomington: Indiana University Press. 537 pp.

Mumford, Russell E. 1969. Distribution of the Mammals of Indiana. Monograph no. 1. Indianapolis: Indiana Academy of Science. 121 pp.

Mumford, Russell E., and Charles E. Keller (illus. William Zimmerman). 1984. The Birds of Indiana. Bloomington: Indiana University Press. 394 pp.

WATERS—WETLANDS

Gammon, J. R. 1994. The Wabash River Ecosystem. A Report for PSI-Energy, Plainfield, Indiana, and Eli Lilly and Company, Indianapolis, Indiana.

Hynes, H. B. N. 1970. The Ecology of Running Waters. Toronto: University of Toronto Press.

Mitsch, W. J., and L. A. Meserve, eds. 1989. The Ohio River: Its History and Environment. Ohio Journal of Science 89(5).

Simons, Richard S. 1985. The Rivers of Indiana. Bloomington: Indiana University Press.

WILDERNESS

Bakeless, John. 1950. The Eyes of Discovery. J. B. Lippincott. Reprint, New York: Dover Publications. 439 pp.

Denevan, William M. 1992. The Pristine Myth: The Landscape of the Americas in 1492. Annals of the Association of American Geographers 82(3): 369–385.

Fox, Stephen. 1981. John Muir and His Legacy. Boston: Little, Brown. 448 pp.

Johnson, Howard. 1978. A Home in the Woods. Bloomington: Indiana University Press. 133 pp.

Thomas, David. 1819. Travels through the Western Country in the Summer of 1816, Including Notes of the Natural History. . . . Auburn, N.Y.: Printed by David Rumsey.

WILDLIFE MANAGEMENT

Allen, Durward L. 1962. Our Wildlife Legacy. New York: Funk and Wagnalls. 422 pp.

Leopold, Aldo. 1933. Game Management. New York: Charles Scribner and Sons. 481 pp.

Contributors

D. Brian Abrell has a B.S. in Biology from Milligan College (Tenn.) and an M.S. in Ecology from Indiana State University. Following two years with the Peace Corps surveying the biota of the Chaco in Paraguay, since 1985 he has been with the Division of Nature Preserves, DNR, and now serves as Regional Ecologist in southwest Indiana.

John A. Bacone has been Assistant Director, Division of Nature Preserves, Indiana DNR, then Director, DNP, since 1980. Prior experience includes three years as Natural Areas Ecologist with the Illinois Natural Areas Inventory and Permanent Naturalist at Turkey Run State Park. A native of Chicago, John received a B.S. in Botany and Zoology from Eastern Illinois University, Charleston, and an M.S. in Forest Ecology from the University of Illinois, Champaign-Urbana.

Lynton K. Caldwell is Professor Emeritus of Political Science and Professor of Public and Environmental Affairs at Indiana University. He holds graduate degrees from Harvard University and the University of Chicago, and has served on the faculties of the University of Chicago, Syracuse University, the University of California, and Indiana University, with engagements in more than 75 additional institutions of higher education and research in 32 different countries. His publications include 12 books and 250 major articles with translations into 20 different languages. He has a long record of public service, for example, with the United Nations, UNESCO, the U.S. National Research Council, and numerous governmental and scientific advisory bodies. He is noted especially for his role in drafting the National Environmental Policy Act of 1969, and for his concept of an environmental impact statement.

The late Ronald K. Campbell was born in Evansville and reared in southwestern Indiana. He graduated from New Harmony High School (1959), then completed a B.S. in Zoology at Indiana University. After serving in the air force and working in biomedical research, he joined the Division of Nature Preserves, Indiana DNR, in 1975. He retired in 1993 for health reasons, and died in 1995.

Lee A. Casebere, a native of northwestern Ohio, has worked for DNR's Division of Nature Preserves since 1980, where he is the Assistant Director. He has a B.S. in Biology from St. Francis College in Fort Wayne. His main interests include natural communities, botany, herptiles, and especially birds. He is an outstanding nature photographer, and enjoys landscaping at home using native plants.

P. Sears Crowell, Jr., is Professor Emeritus of Biology, Indiana University, where from 1948 until retirement in 1979 he taught Invertebrate Zoology. For years he spent summers at the Marine Biological Laboratory (MBL) in Woods Hole, where he researched the life cycles and growth of sea anemones and hydroids (attached early stages of some jellyfish) and taught in the famed zoology course of the MBL. Activities at MBL included 16 years as trustee and two terms on its Executive Committee, plus hosting Emperor Hirohito, an authority on hydroids. Crowell was Program Officer of the American Society of Zoologists and served five years as editor of its *American Zoologist*. He has been active in the Indiana Academy of Science for many years.

Richard Dunbar completed a B.S. in Biology from Principia College and an M.A. in Zoology from Southern Illinois University. A field biologist for the Division of Nature Preserves, Indiana DNR, since 1981, he has been Regional Ecologist in northeastern Indiana since 1983, where, among other projects, he has searched for remnants of the Black Swamp community.

Donald P. Franzmeier, a native of Wisconsin, has been Professor of Agronomy at Purdue University since 1967, where he teaches Soil Classification and Soil Genesis and Survey, as well as conducting research and publishing widely in the areas of soil formation and soil landscape relationships. Franzmeier received B.S. and M.S. degrees in Soil Science from the University of Minnesota, and the Ph.D., also in Soil Science, from Michigan State University. He has traveled worldwide to study soils, including field research in Brazil, Portugal, Hungary, and the eastern U.S.

James R. Gammon is Professor Emeritus of Zoology, Department of Biological Sciences, DePauw University. He has conducted research and published extensively on river and stream ecology for more than three decades. Gammon has a B.S. from Wisconsin State, Whitewater (1956), and an M.S. and Ph.D. from the University of Wisconsin, Madison (1957, 1961). Activity in professional organizations includes the American Fisheries Society, the Society of Environmental Toxicology and Chemistry, the Natural Areas Association, and the Indiana Academy of Science (Fellow, Past Secretary, President—1996). His many honors and awards include Sagamore of the Wabash, Danforth Fellow, Most Distinguished Professor and Tucker Career Achievement Awards (DePauw), and Distinguished Alumnus (UWW).

Henry H. Gray is a native of Indiana who received his formal education at Haverford College, the University of Michigan, Pennsylvania State University, and The Ohio State University. Interspersed with these sessions were a brief but varied career with the U.S. Geological Survey and four years as a faculty member at Kent State University. He worked for the Indiana Geological Survey, as Coal Geologist, Map Editor, and Head Stratigrapher, from 1954 until his retirement in 1987. He has about 120 publications under his name, including many geologic maps and studies especially of southern Indiana.

Louis D. Hasenstab, Sr., was employed by the Indiana DNR in several capacities for more than 35 years, including 27 years as Director, Division of State Parks, prior to his retirement in 1984. He has B.S. and M.S. degrees from Butler University. Hasenstab has held offices in several outdoor organizations, including The Nature Conservancy, and has received a number of awards for his service.

Michelle Martin Hedge was formerly the Information Manager for the Indiana Natural Heritage Data Center of the Division of Nature Preserves, Indiana DNR. She worked with the DNP for 10 years after graduation as a Life Science major from Indiana State University in 1985.

Roger L. Hedge is a field ecologist for the Indiana Natural Heritage Data Center, Division of Nature Preserves, Indiana DNR. He has been with the department since 1978. His current work includes natural areas and rare species inventories and preserve management. Hedge holds a B.S. in Natural Resources and Biology from Ball State University. His interests are natural communities, botany, birds, and travel.

Michael A. Homoya has been a botanist and plant ecologist for the Division of Nature Preserves, Indiana DNR, since 1982. Rare species and floristic inventory, natural area inventory and assessment, and nature preserve management are some of his duties. He has published numerous scientific and popular articles on Indiana's native flora and natural landscape, including *Orchids of Indiana*, a book on the wild orchids of the state. A native of Carterville, Illinois, Homoya completed the B.S. and M.S. in Botany at Southern Illinois University–Carbondale.

Robert C. Howe is Professor of Geology at Indiana State University. He has a B.S. in Geology from Louisiana State University (1961) and M.S. and Ph.D. degrees in Geology from the University of Wisconsin–Madison (1962, 1965). His research interests include microfossils, remote sensing, terrestrial plant volcanism, and meteoritic impacts. A former director of ISU's Remote Sensing Laboratory, Howe became Director of the Hook Observatory in 1986.

A sixth-generation Hoosier, Hank Huffman received a B.A. in Individualized Studies at Indiana University (1984) and is currently employed as a field biologist for the Division of Nature Preserves, Indiana DNR. Huffman is co-author of the book *Indiana from the Air* and of several popular articles. He resides with his wife Ellen in Monroe County and enjoys gardening, caving, kayaking, and stargazing.

MARION T. JACKSON has a B.S. in Conservation of Natural Resources and the Ph.D. in Plant Ecology from Purdue University (1961, 1964). For 33 years he has served as Professor of Ecology at Indiana State University. His research on plant communities and natural areas has yielded some 70 technical and popular articles and book chapters. He served six years as chairman of the Indiana Chapter, The Nature Conservancy, and five years as editor of *Proceedings of the Indiana Academy of Science.* His honors and awards include the National Defense Education Act Fellowship, the Oak Leaf Award from The Nature Conservancy, the James Mason Environmental Services Award, the Caleb Miller Outstanding Teaching Award from Indiana State University, and Fellow of the Indiana Academy of Science. *The Natural Heritage of Indiana* is his first full-length edited book.

JAMES H. KEITH was Assistant Director, then Director of the Division of Nature Preserves (1975–1979), Indiana DNR. He received the Ph.D. from Indiana University, and has authored about 20 scientific and popular articles on caves, cave biology, and natural areas. He conducted site evaluations and a theme study for the National Park Service National Natural Landmarks Program. He presently manages environmental projects, including karst studies for highway projects, wetland delineations, hazardous waste sitings, and investigations of real-estate transactions. In addition to caving, he enjoys gardening, photography, and fly fishing.

GENE KRITSKY is Professor and Chair of Biology at the College of Mount St. Joseph (Ohio) and Adjunct Curator of Entomology at the Cincinnati Museum of Natural History. He received an A.B. in Biology from Indiana University and the M.S. and Ph.D. in Entomology from the University of Illinois. A former Fulbright Scholar to Egypt, Kritsky specializes in insect evolution and systematics. Recent studies involve the evolution of periodical cicada broods in Indiana. He was President of the Indiana Academy of Science in 1995.

ALTON A. LINDSEY, born in Pittsburgh, Pennsylvania, in 1907, was educated at Allegheny College (B.S., 1929) and Cornell University (Ph.D., 1937), and taught Ecology, at Purdue mainly, until he became Emeritus in 1973. His research was in the Arctic and Antarctic, southwestern deserts, the north woods, midwestern, alpine, and tropical forests, and included a five-year study of the floodplain environments of the Wabash and Tippecanoe rivers. His research on the lava bed near Grants, New Mexico, initiated the establishment of El Malpais National Monument there. His studies resulted in 9 books and 90 articles, technical and popular, including *Natural Features of Indiana* and *Natural Areas in Indiana and Their Preservation.* He also served as editor of four scientific journals.

Dr. Lindsey was naturalist and vertebrate zoologist on the Byrd Expedition to the Bay of Whales, Antarctica (1933–35), and was honored in 1960 by having a group of 12 islands in antarctic waters named the Lindsey Islands. Other awards and honors include Eminent Ecologist, Ecological Society of America; the George B. Fell Award, the Natural Areas Association; President of the Indiana Academy of Science (1966); and honorary Doctor of Science degrees from Allegheny College and Purdue University. In 1996 he received the Distinguished Scientist Award of the Indiana Academy of Science.

BILL N. MCKNIGHT, born in Flora, Illinois, received an M.S. in Botany on ferns at Eastern Illinois University, Charleston. He presently teaches Biology at Park Tudor High School, Indianapolis. He is the author of about 20 articles (mostly dealing with sporeformers) and the editor of *Biological Pollution: The Control and Impact of Invasive Exotic Species,* in addition to chairing the Publications Committee, Indiana Academy of Science.

WILTON N. MELHORN, Professor Emeritus, Purdue University, taught and did research in the Department of Geosciences from 1954 until his retirement in June 1991. Research interests include archaeological geology, engineering geology, geomorphology, and Pleistocene geology of the Midwest. He completed his B.S. Degree at Michigan State University, his M.S. at New York University, and his Ph.D. at the University of Michigan. Activities with the Indiana Academy of Science include Fellow, President, and former Executive Director. Melhorn has published 75 papers and books.

SHERMAN A. MINTON spent his professional career at the Department of Microbiology and Immunology at the Indiana University School of Medicine, where he was Professor for 36 years before retiring in 1984. But his lifelong avocation is herpetology; he has served as research associate (Department of Herpetology) at the American Museum of Natural History since 1957. His world travels lecturing and doing research on herpetology (especially venomous snakes) have taken him to Pakistan, Iran, Australia, China, Switzerland, Japan, Brazil, and Mexico. Minton has authored more than 100 technical papers, including a monograph and the book *Amphibians and Reptiles of Indiana.* A graduate of the Indiana University School of Medicine with an M.D. degree in 1942, Minton has served in many professional societies and has received a number of awards.

RUSSELL E. MUMFORD received the B.S., M.S., and Ph.D. degrees in Forestry and Wildlife Ecology from Purdue University, then served as Professor in Purdue's Department of Forestry and Natural Resources, where he did research and taught Ornithology and Mammalogy for 30 years before retiring in 1988. Mumford is author of more than 200 technical and popular articles, including wildlife bulletins, monographs, and book chapters. He is co-author of the beautiful book *Birds of Indiana,* and also of *Mammals of Indiana.* His research studies have involved many bird and mammal species, including flycatchers, prairie-chicken, ruffed grouse, several waterfowl, bats, and shrews. He

enjoys fishing, birding, collecting antiques, woodcarving, and travel.

ERIC MYERS is Director, Office of Planning and Quality Development, Indiana DNR. Prior to January 1995 he was Director of the Division of Outdoor Recreation. Employed by the State of Indiana since 1975, he has served as Grants Coordinator, IDNR, and as Environmental Scientist, Indiana Department of Transportation. At the federal level, Myers worked for the Fish and Wildlife Service and the National Park Service. His education includes B.S. and M.S. degrees from Indiana University's School of Public and Environmental Affairs and a Directorate from Indiana University's School of Health, Physical Education and Recreation.

JAMES E. NEWMAN, Professor Emeritus, Purdue University, spent a 38-year career teaching (Biometeorology and Climatology) and researching the weather and climate of Indiana and the Midwest. He authored more than 100 scientific articles and chapters in textbooks. Much of his research dealt with seasonal weather and climate impacts on the midwest "Corn Belt." He has B.S. and M.S. degrees from The Ohio State University and completed graduate and post-graduate study at Purdue and the University of Wisconsin. His honors include Fellows in the American Association for the Advancement of Science, American Society of Agronomy, and Indiana Academy of Science, plus the American Meteorological Society Award for contributions in biometeorology and climatology.

GEORGE R. PARKER received a B.S. in Forestry and an M.S. in Plant Ecology from Oklahoma State (1964, 1967), and the Ph.D. in Forest Ecology from Michigan State (1970). He has been Professor of Forestry and Natural Resources at Purdue since 1970. Parker received the "Sagamore of the Wabash" (1988) for his service as gubernatorial appointee to the Indiana Pesticide Review Board (1980–1990) and the Indiana Watershed Task Force (1991). Sabbaticals were with the Institute of Ecology, the University of Georgia, and The Nature Conservancy. Activities with the Ecological Society of America include Vegetation Section Chairman and Certified Senior Ecologist. Other professional societies include the Society of American Foresters, the International Association of Landscape Ecology, the Indiana Academy of Science (past Program Chairman), and The Nature Conservancy (Board of Trustees).

ROBERT O. PETTY was equally gifted as an ecologist and writer, publishing widely as a scientist, literary naturalist, and poet. He received a B.S. in Botany from Butler University, and the M.S. and Ph.D. degrees in Plant Ecology from Purdue University. For 30 years he was Professor of Biology at Wabash College, inspiring a number of undergraduates to pursue professional careers in ecology. During his last decade he wrote extensively for the National Geographic Society, in addition to crafting the text for *Wild Plants in Flower III: Deciduous Forest.* Those who knew him miss his inspiring words, wise counsel, and unwavering friendship. His family collected the poetry he wrote throughout his life (nearly 90 poems) in a tribute volume titled *Splitting the Witness Tree* in 1991.

THOMAS W. POST is currently a Regional Ecologist with the Division of Nature Preserves, Indiana DNR. He has been with DNR for 15 years, following work on natural area inventories in Illinois and Indiana. He holds a B.A. from Trinity Christian College and an M.S. in Biology from Northeastern Illinois University. His research interests include prairie and savanna ecology as well as rare flora associated with these communities.

RICHARD L. POWELL received B.A. and M.A. degrees from Indiana University and the Ph.D. from Purdue in 1976. He was a geologist with the Indiana Geological Survey, Coal Section for 15 years. As a consulting geologist since 1975 (with Geosciences Research Associates, Inc., and WW Engineering & Science), he examines the geology and hydrology of landfill and hazardous waste sites, and evaluates minable industrial minerals and coal deposits. He has conducted theme studies for the National Park Service National Natural Landmarks Program. Powell, a Fellow of the Indiana Academy of Science and the National Speleological Society, has written more than two dozen papers about caves and karst features in Indiana, as well as the book *Caves of Indiana* (1961).

RONALD L. RICHARDS is Curator of Paleobiology and Chief Curator of Natural History at the Indiana State Museum. He has researched Quaternary-aged Indiana cave faunas and Pleistocene and Holocene animal communities since 1964, resulting in more than 30 technical papers and popular articles on those subjects. He has recovered several species new to the state, and is compiling records of all extinct and extirpated Quaternary vertebrates of Indiana. Richards received an A.B. in Zoology at Indiana University.

PAUL E. ROTHROCK, Professor of Biology at Taylor University, Upland, Indiana, since 1981, received his M.S. and Ph.D. degrees in Botany from Pennsylvania State University. Research interests include taxonomic studies of the genus *Carex,* plant life histories, flora of Indiana, and the Flora of North America project. Indiana Academy of Science activities include the Plant Taxonomy Section and Biological Survey Committee, and associate editor of the *Proceedings.*

JOHN N. SIMPSON received a B.S. in Civil Engineering from Rose Polytechnic Institute and has been with the Division of Water (DNR) since 1960, serving as Director of the division since 1983. He also worked with the Illinois Division of Waterways and the Illinois Division of Highways. He holds Professional Engineer and Registered Land Surveyor certificates.

EDWIN R. SQUIERS is a terrestrial plant ecologist with advanced degrees from Rutgers University (M.S., 1973) and Ohio University (Ph.D., 1976). He is the author of numerous scientific papers, and his research interests include the dynamics of ecosystems, the use of geographic techniques in environmental problem solving, and the application of environmental ethics to questions of lifestyle and worldview. He has taught Ecology and Environmental Science at Taylor University, Upland, Indiana, for 19 years, where he now serves as Chairman, Environmental Science Department.

Raised in Southern California, C. RUSSELL STAFFORD received master's (1976) and doctoral (1981) degrees in Anthropology (Archaeology) from Arizona State University. His dissertation research focused on the Mogollon culture of east-central Arizona. For many years he has conducted research in west-central Illinois and Indiana, in geoarchaeology and Archaic hunter-gatherers. From 1980 to 1987 he was Research Archaeologist at the Center for American Archaeology in Kampsville, Illinois. Currently he is Associate Professor of Anthropology and Director of the Anthropology Laboratory at Indiana State University.

JOHN O. WHITAKER, JR., has been Professor of Life Sciences at Indiana State University for 35 years. He received the B.S. and Ph.D. degrees in Vertebrate Zoology from Cornell University (1957, 1962). His research interest in Vertebrate Zoology, especially Mammalogy and studies of food habits and ectoparasites of mammals, has produced more than 250 scientific publications, including 6 books and monographs, plus several book chapters. Whitaker received the first Indiana State University Research Award, the H. H. T. Jackson Award from the American Society of Mammalogists for service to mammalogy and to the society, and the College of Arts and Sciences Distinguished Professor Award at ISU.

DONALD R. WHITEHEAD is Professor of Biology at Indiana University, where he has been on the faculty since 1967. Educated at Harvard University (A.B., 1954; A.M., 1955; Ph.D., 1958), he was a Fulbright Scholar in Denmark in 1959. He taught at Williams College and was Visiting Professor at the University of Bergen, Norway, Washington State University, and the University of Maine. His ecosystem research includes the effects of climate change, acid precipitation, and developmental history on watershed-lake ecosystems; of Ice Age climates on forests; and of landscape patterns on reproductive success of neotropical land birds in southern Indiana.

Index / 473

Index / 475

Index / 477

Index / 479